THE CAMBRIDGE COMPANION TO

ARABIC PHILOSOPHY

Philosophy written in Arabic and in the Islamic world represents one of the great traditions of Western philosophy. Inspired by Greek philosophical works and the indigenous ideas of Islamic theology, Arabic philosophers from the ninth century onwards put forward ideas of great philosophical and historical importance. This collection of essays, by some of the leading scholars in Arabic philosophy, provides an introduction to the field by way of chapters devoted to individual thinkers (such as al-Fārābī, Avicenna, and Averroes) or groups, especially during the 'classical' period from the ninth to the twelfth centuries. It also includes chapters on areas of philosophical inquiry across the tradition, such as ethics and metaphysics. Finally, it includes chapters on later Islamic thought, and on the connections between Arabic philosophy and Greek, Jewish, and Latin philosophy. The volume also includes a useful bibliography and a chronology of the most important Arabic thinkers.

OTHER VOLUMES IN THE SERIES OF CAMBRIDGE COMPANIONS

ABELARD *Edited by* JEFFREY E. BROWER *and* KEVIN GUILFOY
ADORNO *Edited by* THOMAS HUHN
AQUINAS *Edited by* NORMAN KRETZMANN *and* ELEONORE STUMP
HANNAH ARENDT *Edited by* DANA VILLA
ARISTOTLE *Edited by* JONATHAN BARNES
AUGUSTINE *Edited by* ELEONORE STUMP *and* NORMAN KRETZMANN
BACON *Edited by* MARKKU PELTONEN
SIMONE DE BEAUVOIR *Edited by* CLAUDIA CARD
BRENTANO *Edited by* DALE JACQUETTE
CRITICAL THEORY *Edited by* FRED RUSH
DARWIN *Edited by* JONATHAN HODGE *and* GREGORY RADICK
DESCARTES *Edited by* JOHN COTTINGHAM
DUNS SCOTUS *Edited by* THOMAS WILLIAMS
EARLY GREEK PHILOSOPHY *Edited by* A. A. LONG
FEMINISM IN PHILOSOPHY *Edited by* MIRANDA FRICKER *and* JENNIFER HORNSBY
FOUCAULT *Edited by* GARY GUTTING
FREUD *Edited by* JEROME NEU
GADAMER *Edited by* ROBERT J. DOSTAL
GALILEO *Edited by* PETER MACHAMER
GERMAN IDEALISM *Edited by* KARL AMERIKS
GREEK AND ROMAN PHILOSOPHY *Edited by* DAVID SEDLEY
HABERMAS *Edited by* STEPHEN K. WHITE
HEGEL *Edited by* FREDERICK BEISER
HEIDEGGER *Edited by* CHARLES GUIGNON
HOBBES *Edited by* TOM SORELL
HUME *Edited by* DAVID FATE NORTON
HUSSERL *Edited by* BARRY SMITH *and* DAVID WOODRUFF SMITH
WILLIAM JAMES *Edited by* RUTH ANNA PUTNAM
KANT *Edited by* PAUL GUYER
KIERKEGAARD *Edited by* ALASTAIR HANNAY *and* GORDON MARINO
LEIBNIZ *Edited by* NICHOLAS JOLLEY

LEVINAS *Edited by* SIMON CRITCHLEY *and* ROBERT BERNASCONI
LOCKE *Edited by* VERE CHAPPELL
MALEBRANCHE *Edited by* STEVEN NADLER
MARX *Edited by* TERRELL CARVER
MEDIEVAL PHILOSOPHY *Edited by* A. S. MCGRADE
MEDIEVAL JEWISH PHILOSOPHY *Edited by* DANIEL H. FRANK *and* OLIVER LEAMAN
MERLEAU-PONTY *Edited by* TAYLOR CARMAN *and* MARK HANSEN
MILL *Edited by* JOHN SKORUPSKI
NEWTON *Edited by* I. BERNARD COHEN *and* GEORGE E. SMITH
NIETZSCHE *Edited by* BERND MAGNUS *and* KATHLEEN HIGGINS
OCKHAM *Edited by* PAUL VINCENT SPADE
PASCAL *Edited by* NICHOLAS HAMMOND
PEIRCE *Edited by* CHERYL MISAK
PLATO *Edited by* RICHARD KRAUT
PLOTINUS *Edited by* LLOYD P. GERSON
RAWLS *Edited by* SAMUEL FREEMAN
QUINE *Edited by* ROGER F. GIBSON
THOMAS REID *Edited by* TERENCE CUNEO *and* RENE VAN WOUDENBERG
ROUSSEAU *Edited by* PATRICK RILEY
BERTRAND RUSSELL *Edited by* NICHOLAS GRIFFIN
SARTRE *Edited by* CHRISTINA HOWELLS
SCHOPENHAUER *Edited by* CHRISTOPHER JANAWAY
THE SCOTTISH ENLIGHTENMENT *Edited by* ALEXANDER BROADIE
SPINOZA *Edited by* DON GARRETT
THE STOICS *Edited by* BRAD INWOOD
WITTGENSTEIN *Edited by* HANS SLUGA *and* DAVID STERN

The Cambridge Companion to ARABIC PHILOSOPHY

Edited by

Peter Adamson
King's College London

Richard C. Taylor
Marquette University

CAMBRIDGE
UNIVERSITY PRESS

CAMBRIDGE UNIVERSITY PRESS
Cambridge, New York, Melbourne, Madrid, Cape Town, Singapore, São Paulo, Delhi, Dubai, Tokyo, Mexico City

Cambridge University Press
The Edinburgh Building, Cambridge, CB2 8RU, UK

Published in the United States of America by Cambridge University Press, New York

www.cambridge.org
Information on this title: www.cambridge.org/9780521520690

First published 2005
7th printing 2011

Printed in the United Kingdom at the University Press, Cambridge

A catalogue record for this publication is available from the British Library

Library of Congress Cataloguing in Publication data
The Cambridge companion to Arabic philosophy / edited by Peter Adamson and Richard C. Taylor.
p. cm. – (Cambridge companions to philosophy)
Includes bibliographical references (p.) and index.
ISBN 0 521 81743 9 – ISBN 0 521 52069 X (pb.)
1. Philosophy, Arab. I. Adamson, Peter, 1972– II. Taylor, Richard C., 1950– III. Series.
B741.C36 2004
181′.92 – dc22 2004049660

ISBN 978-0-521-81743-1 Hardback
ISBN 978-0-521-52069-0 Paperback

CONTENTS

NOTES ON CONTRIBUTORS

PETER ADAMSON is a Lecturer in Philosophy at King's College London. He has published several articles on the circle of al-Kindī and is the author of *The Arabic Plotinus: A Philosophical Study of the "Theology of Aristotle"* (2002).

DEBORAH L. BLACK is Professor of Philosophy and Medieval Studies at the University of Toronto. She is the author of *Logic and Aristotle's "Rhetoric" and "Poetics" in Medieval Arabic Philosophy* (1990), and of several articles on medieval Arabic and Latin philosophy, focusing on issues in epistemology, cognitive psychology, and metaphysics.

CHARLES BURNETT is Professor in the History of Arabic/Islamic Influence in Europe at the Warburg Institute, University of London. He has written extensively on the transmission of Arabic learning to the West and has edited several Latin translations of Arabic texts.

CHARLES E. BUTTERWORTH is Professor of Government and Politics at the University of Maryland, College Park. His publications include critical editions of most of the Middle Commentaries written by Averroes on Aristotle's logic; translations of books and treatises by Averroes, al-Fārābī, and al-Rāzī, as well as Maimonides; and studies of different aspects of the political teaching of these and other thinkers in the ancient, medieval, and modern tradition of philosophy. In addition, he has written monograph analyses of the political thought of Frantz Fanon and Jean-Jacques Rousseau and has also written extensively on contemporary Islamic political thought. He is a member of several learned organizations.

CRISTINA D'ANCONA is research assistant in the Department of Philosophy of the Università degli Studi di Pisa. Her research focuses on Greek and Arabic Neoplatonism. The author of *Recherches sur le "Liber de Causis"* (1995) and numerous articles about the transmission of Greek thought into Arabic, she is currently writing a commentary on and translation of the Graeco-Arabic Plotinus.

THÉRÈSE-ANNE DRUART is Professor of Philosophy and Director of the Center for Medieval and Byzantine Studies at The Catholic University of America. Her recent publications include "Philosophy in Islam" for *The Cambridge Companion to Medieval Philosophy*. She publishes regular bibliographies in Islamic philosophy and theology and is preparing a book on al-Fārābī's metaphysics.

STEVEN HARVEY, Professor of Philosophy at Bar-Ilan University, Israel, is the author of *Falaquera's Epistle of the Debate: An Introduction to Jewish Philosophy* (1987) and the editor of *The Medieval Hebrew Encyclopedias of Science and Philosophy* (2000). He has written numerous articles on the medieval Jewish and Islamic philosophers, with special focus on Averroes' commentaries on Aristotle and on the influence of the Islamic philosophers on Jewish thought.

MICHAEL E. MARMURA is Professor Emeritus at the University of Toronto and a Fellow of the Royal Society of Canada. His area of research is Islamic thought, and his publications in this area have included numerous articles on Avicenna and al-Ghazālī. They also include editions and translations, including a facing-page translation of al-Ghazālī's *Incoherence of the Philosophers* (1997) and Avicenna's *Metaphysics* from *al-Shifā'* (forthcoming).

JOSEF PUIG MONTADA is Professor of Arabic and Islamic Studies at Universidad Complutense of Madrid. He has edited and translated texts of Avempace and Averroes, on whom he has published an introductory monograph, *Averroes: juez, médico y filósofo andalusí* (1998). He has also published articles on a number of Arab thinkers and on various subjects of Islamic philosophy and theology.

MARWAN RASHED is research fellow at the CNRS in Paris. His area of research includes ancient and medieval philosophy. He has published *Die Überlieferungsgeschichte der aristotelischen Schrift*

"De Generatione et Corruptione" (2001), and his edition of the *De Generatione et Corruptione* will appear in the Budé series in 2004. He is currently working on the edition of the fragments of Alexander of Aphrodisias' commentary on Aristotle's *Physics*.

DAVID C. REISMAN is Assistant Professor of Arabic-Islamic Thought at the University of Illinois, Chicago. He is author of *The Making of the Avicennan Tradition* (2002) and editor of *Before and After Avicenna* (2003).

SAJJAD H. RIZVI is Research Associate in Islamic Philosophy at the University of Bristol. A specialist on later Islamic philosophy and hermeneutics, he is the author of the forthcoming *Understanding the Word of God* and *Mulla Sadra: A Philosopher for Mystics?*

TONY STREET is the Hartwell Assistant Director of Research in Islamic Studies at the Faculty of Divinity at the University of Cambridge. He has published a number of articles on Arabic logic.

RICHARD C. TAYLOR, of the Philosophy Department at Marquette University, works in Arabic philosophy, its Greek sources, and its Latin influences. He has written on the *Liber de Causis*, Averroes, and other related topics. He has a complete English translation of Averroes' *Long Commentary on the "De Anima"* of Aristotle forthcoming.

JOHN WALBRIDGE is Professor of Near Eastern Languages and Adjunct Professor of Philosophy and of History and Philosophy of Science at Indiana University, Bloomington. He is the author or co-author of four books on Suhrawardī and his school. He is currently working on two books on the role of rationalism in Islamic civilization.

PAUL E. WALKER is a research associate in Near Eastern Languages at the University of Chicago. He is the author of *Early Philosophical Shiism* (1993), *Hāmīd al-Dīn al-Kirmānī* (1999), and *Exploring an Islamic Empire: Fatimid History and Its Sources* (2002), along with several editions and translations of important Islamic texts including *A Guide to Conclusive Proofs for the Principles of Belief: Kitāb al-irshād ilā qawāṭi' al-adilla fī uṣūl al-i'tiqād* by al-Juwaynī (2000) and numerous articles on aspects of Ismā'īlī history and thought.

ROBERT WISNOVSKY is Associate Professor in the Institute of Islamic Studies at McGill University. He is the editor of *Aspects of Avicenna* (2001) and the author of *Avicenna's Metaphysics in Context* (2003) as well as of a number of articles on Arabic and Islamic philosophy and theology.

HOSSEIN ZIAI is Professor of Islamic and Iranian Studies at UCLA. He has published many articles and several books on the Arabic and Persian Illuminationist system of philosophy. He has published several text-editions and translations of Arabic and Persian Illuminationist texts including Suhrawardī's *Philosophy of Illumination*, Shahrazūrī's *Commentary on the Philosophy of Illumination*, and Ibn Kammūna's *Commentary on Suhrawardī's Intimations*.

NOTE ON THE TEXT

Please note that all names in this volume are given in full transliteration (e.g., al-Fārābī, not Alfarabi or al-Farabi), except for Ibn Sīnā and Ibn Rushd, where we defer to tradition and use the familiar Latinized names Avicenna and Averroes. The same goes for all Arabic terms; thus we write Ismāʿīlī rather than Ismaili, Qur'ān rather than Koran, etc. We have generally followed the transliteration system used in the *International Journal of Middle Eastern Studies*, but used the simplest transliteration conventions possible: the feminine ending *tā' marbūṭa* is always written *–a*, and the definite article is always written *al-*.

There is a numbered bibliography at the end of this book. Chapter authors refer both to items in this bibliography and to unnumbered works specific to their chapters.

CHRONOLOGY OF MAJOR PHILOSOPHERS IN THE ARABIC TRADITION

The following is a list of the dates of the major philosophers and other authors in the Arabic tradition who are mentioned in this volume, in approximate chronological order according to the date of their death. The main sources used in compiling this set of dates are *The Encyclopaedia of Islam* [16], Nasr and Leaman [34], and C. Brockelmann, *Geschichte der arabischen Literatur*, 5 vols. (Leiden: 1937–49). (Note that the dating of the *Epistles* of Ikhwān al-Ṣafā' is disputed. For a discussion see *Encyclopaedia of Islam* [16], vol. II, 1072–3). Dates are given in A.H. (the Muslim calendar) followed by C.E. Jewish authors' dates are given in C.E. only. Dates elsewhere in this volume are generally given in C.E. only. For conversion tables between the two calendars, see G. S. P. Freeman-Grenville, *The Muslim and Christian Calendars*, 2nd edn. (London: 1977). Figures from the twentieth century are not included here; for these thinkers see chapter 19. The editors thank David Reisman for corrections and suggestions.

Sergius of Resh'aynā (d. 536 C.E.)
Ibn al-Muqaffa' (d. 139/757)
Al-Muqammaṣ, Dāwūd (early 9th c.)
Māshā'allāh (d. ca. 200/815)
Ibn al-Biṭrīq (fl. ca. 200/815)
Abū al-Hudhayl (d. ca. 226/840)
Al-Naẓẓām (d. between 220/835 and 230/845)
Al-Ḥimṣī, Ibn Nā'ima (fl. ca. 215/830)
Al-Kindī (d. after 256/870)
Ibn Isḥāq, Ḥunayn (d. ca. 260/873)
Al-Balkhī, Abū Ma'shar (d. 272/886)

Ibn Qurra, Thābit (d. 288/901)
Ibn Ḥaylān, Yuḥannā (d. 297/910)
Ibn Ḥunayn, Isḥāq (d. 298/910–11)
Ibn Lūqā, Qusṭā (ca. 205/820–300/912)
Al-Jubbā'ī, Abū 'Alī (d. 303/915–16)
Al-Dimashqī, Abū 'Uthmān (d. early 4th/10th c.)
Al-Rāzī, Abū Bakr (d. 313/925)
Abū Tammām (4th/10th c.)
Al-Balkhī, Abū al-Qāsim (d. 319/931)
Al-Jubbā'ī, Abū Hāshim (d. 321/933)
Al-Rāzī, Abū Ḥātim (d. 322/934)
Al-Balkhī, Abū Zayd (d. 322/934)
Al-Ash'arī, Abū al-Ḥasan (d. 324/935–6)
Ibn Yūnus, Abū Bishr Mattā (d. 328/940)
Gaon, Saadia (882–942)
Al-Nasafī, Muḥammad (d. 332/943)
Al-Fārābī (d. 339/950–1)
Israeli, Isaac (d. 955)
Ikhwān al-Ṣafā' (The Brethren of Purity) (4th/10th c.)
Al-Sijistānī, Abū Ya'qūb (d. ca. 361/971)
Ibn 'Adī, Yaḥyā (d. 363/974)
Al-Sīrāfī, Abū Sa'īd (d. 369/979)
Al-Sijistānī (al-Manṭiqī), Abū Sulaymān (d. ca. 375/985)
Al-Andalūsī, Ibn Juljul (d. after 377/987)
Al-'Āmirī (d. 381/991)
Ibn al-Nadīm (d. either 385/995 or 388/998)
Ibn Zur'ā, Abū 'Alī 'Īsā (d. 398/1008)
Al-Kirmānī, Ḥamīd al-Dīn (d. ca. 412/1021)
'Abd al-Jabbār (d. 415/1024–5)
Ibn Miskawayh (d. 421/1030)
Avicenna (Ibn Sīnā) (370/980–428/1037)
Ibn al-Haytham (Alhazen) (d. ca. 432/1040)
Ibn al-Ṭayyib, Abū al-Faraj (d. 434/1043)
Al-Bīrūnī (d. 440/1048)
Ibn Gabirol, Solomon (Avicebron) (1021–58 or 1070)
Ibn Ḥazm (d. 456/1064)
Ibn Marzubān, Bahmanyār (d. 459/1066)
Ibn Ṣā'id al-Andalūsī, Abū al-Qāsim Ṣā'id (d. 462/1070)
Ibn Mattawayh (d. 469/1076–7)

Nāṣir-i Khusraw (d. ca. 470/1077)
Al-Shīrāzī, al-Mu'ayyad fī al-Dīn (d. 470/1077)
Al-Juwaynī, Imām al-Ḥaramayn (d. 478/1085)
Al-Lawkarī, Abū al-Abbās (fl. 503/1109–10)
Al-Ghazālī, Abū Ḥāmid (450/1058–505/1111)
Al-Nasafī, Abū al-Mu'īn (d. 508/1114–15)
Ibn Bājja (Avempace) (d. 533/1139)
Halevi, Judah (d. 1141)
Al-Baghdādī, Abū al-Barakāt (d. after 560/1164–5)
Ibn Da'ud, Abraham (ca. 1110–80)
Ibn Ṭufayl (d. 581/1185–6)
Suhrawardī (549/1154–587/1191)
Averroes (ibn Rushd) (520/1126–595/1198)
Al-Biṭrūjī (fl. ca. 600/1204)
Maimonides (1135 or 1138–1204)
Al-Rāzī, Fakhr al-Dīn (d. 606/1210)
Al-Baghdādī, 'Abd al-Laṭīf (d. 628/1231)
Ibn 'Arabī (560/1165–638/1240)
Ibn Yūnus, Kamāl al-Dīn (d. 639/1242)
Ibn al-Qifṭī (d. 646/1248)
Falaquera, Shem-Tov (d. ca. 1295)
Al-Abharī, Athīr al-Dīn (d. 663/1264)
Ibn Abī Uṣaybi'a (d. 668/1270)
Al-Ṭūsī, Naṣīr al-Dīn (d. 672/1274)
Al-Kātibī, Najm al-Dīn al-Qazwīnī (d. 675/1276)
Ibn Kammūna, Sa'd al-Dīn (d. 1277)
Al-Bayḍāwī (d. 685/1286 or 691/1292)
Al-Shahrazūrī, Shams al-Dīn (d. after 688/1289)
Albalag, Isaac (late 13th c.)
Al-Shīrāzī, Quṭb al-Dīn (d. 710/1311)
Al-Ḥillī, al-'Allāma (d. 726/1325)
Ibn Taymiyya (d. 728–9/1328)
Gersonides (Levi ben Gerson) (1288–1344)
Al-Iṣfahānī, Maḥmūd (d. 749/1348)
Al-Ījī (d. 756/1355)
Ibn al-Khaṭīb (d. 776/1375)
Al-Taftāzānī, Sa'd al-Dīn (d. 792/1390)
Ibn Khaldūn (732/1332–808/1406)
Crescas, Ḥasdai (d. ca. 1411)

Iṣfahānī, Ibn Torkeh (Ṣā'in al-Dīn) (d. ca. 836–7/1432)
Dashtakī, Ṣadr al-Dīn (d. 903/1497)
Dawwānī, Jalāl al-Dīn (d. 907/1501)
Al-Dimashqī, Muḥammad b. Makkī Shams al-Dīn (d. 937/1531)
Dashtakī, Ghiyāth al-Dīn Manṣūr (d. 949/1542)
Mīr Dāmād (d. 1041/1631)
Mulla Ṣadra (Ṣadr al-Dīn al-Shīrāzī) (979/1571–1050/1640)
Al-Lāhījī (d. 1072/1661)
Sabziwārī (d. 1289/1872)

PETER ADAMSON AND RICHARD C. TAYLOR

1 Introduction

The history of philosophy in Arabic goes back almost as far as Islam itself. Philosophically interesting theological disputes were underway within two centuries of the founding of Islam in 622 C.E. At the same time some important scientific, medical, and philosophical texts from the Greek tradition were being studied and used in the Syriac tradition, with Aristotelian logic being employed in theological debates. By the third century of the Muslim calendar (the ninth century C.E.), a great translation movement centered in Baghdad was in full bloom. In response, Muslim, Christian, and Jewish philosophers writing in Arabic began to make important contributions to a tradition of philosophizing that continues alive to the present day. Debates and contests on logic, grammar, theology, and philosophy by Muslims, Christians, and Jews took place at the caliphal court. The structure and foundation of the cosmos, the natures of entities in the physical world, the relation of human beings to the transcendent divine, the principles of metaphysics, the nature of logic and the foundations of epistemology, and the pursuit of the good life in ethics – in sum, the traditional issues of philosophy, old wine, albeit in new skins – were debated with intensity, originality, and penetrating insight.

This was the beginning of what one might call the classical or formative period of philosophy in Arabic, which goes from the ninth to the twelfth centuries C.E. During this period, authors working in Arabic received and reinterpreted the philosophical inheritance of the Greeks, especially Aristotle. This process culminated at the end of the classical period with the massive body of commentaries on Aristotle by Averroes. But the formative period involves more than just the continuation of the Greek philosophical tradition. Most important for the later Islamic tradition was the towering achievement of Avicenna. He was one of many thinkers to grapple with the ideas put forward by the tradition of theology in Islam (*'ilm al-kalām*). Post-classical philosophy in Arabic would in turn be dominated by the need to respond both to Avicenna and to the *kalām* tradition. While Averroes' project of explicating and exploiting the works of Aristotle continued in Latin and Hebrew, other concerns drove the development of post-classical philosophical inquiry.

In fact interesting philosophical ideas have appeared in the Islamic world across a wide range of traditions and over a period of many centuries. There is much of philosophical interest not only in the obviously "philosophical" writings of authors like Avicenna, and in the complex tradition of *kalām*, but also in works on the principles of jurisprudence (*'uṣūl al-fiqh*), Qur'ānic commentary, the natural sciences, certain literary (*adab*) works that are relevant to ethics, contemporary political philosophy, and so on. It goes without saying that the present volume cannot hope to cover such a broad range of topics. For reasons made clear below, this *Companion* focuses on the formative, classical period of philosophy in Arabic, though we hope to convey a sense of the richness and complexity of the tradition as a whole. In the present volume we take account especially of three sorts of complexity that confront any student of the classical period: the nature of the philosophical corpus received in the Arabic-speaking world, the nature of Arabic philosophy in the classical period itself, and the classical period as a foundation for a continuous indigenous tradition of later philosophy.

THE GREEK INHERITANCE

One should not suppose that early Arabic philosophers, any more than scholastic Christian philosophers, worked primarily through a direct and independent reading of Aristotle. The most obvious reason is that the outstanding "Aristotelian" philosophers in Islam all had to read Aristotle in translation. This was made possible by the aforementioned translation movement in the eighth–tenth centuries C.E., which in a short space of time rendered a vast array of Greek scientific and philosophical works into Arabic. It was made possible by, among other things, the previous tradition of translation and intellectual endeavor in Syriac, the ideologically motivated support of the ʻAbbāsid caliphs, and, at a more mundane level, the invention of paper.[1] The translation movement was the single most important impetus and determinant for the Arabic philosophical tradition. It began to establish the technical vocabulary that would be used (including the word *falsafa* itself, which is a calque from the Greek *philosophia*) and, like the Latin translation movement centuries later, it set forth the challenge of interpreting a Greek tradition that included much more than just Aristotle. The authors of the classical period also read commentaries on Aristotle and independent works by Neoplatonists like Plotinus and Proclus, as well as Greek science (especially medicine, but including a wide range of sciences from physics to astrology).

We hope to draw attention to the decisive impact of the translation movement by calling this a companion to Arabic, and not Islamic, philosophy. It is *Arabic* philosophy because it is philosophy that begins with the rendering of Greek thought, in all its complexity, into the Arabic language. Note that it is not "Arab" philosophy: few of the figures dealt with here were ethnically Arabs, a notable exception being al-Kindī, who was called the "philosopher of the Arabs" precisely because he was unusual in this regard. Rather, philosophy spread with the Arabic language itself throughout the lands of the expanding Islamic empire.

Related to this are two more reasons why it is sensible to call the tradition "Arabic" and not "Islamic" philosophy. First, many of those involved were in fact Christians or Jews. Some of the most important translators (above all Ḥunayn b. Isḥāq and his son) were Christians, as were such philosophers as Abū Bishr Mattā and Yaḥyā b. ʻAdī, who along with the Muslim al-Fārābī were pivotal figures in the Baghdad Peripatetic movement of the tenth century C.E. The intertwining of the Jewish and Islamic philosophical traditions begins with ninth–tenth century philosophers like Isaac Israeli and Saadia Gaon, and is evident in the work of the famous Maimonides (see chapter 16).

Second, certain philosophers of the formative period, like al-Kindī, al-Fārābī, and Averroes, were interested primarily in coming to grips with the texts made available in the translation movement, rather than with putting forward a properly "Islamic" philosophy. This is not to minimize the importance of Islam for any of the figures dealt with in this volume: even the Aristotelian commentator *par excellence* Averroes, who was after all a judge and expert on Islamic law, dealt explicitly with the relationship between *falsafa* and Islam. And once Avicenna's philosophy becomes absorbed into the Islamic *kalām* tradition, we can point to many self-consciously "Islamic" philosophers. Still the term "Arabic" philosophy identifies a philosophical tradition that has its origins in the translation movement.[2] It is important to pay attention to the motives and procedures of this movement – which texts were translated, and why? How were they altered in translation? – rather than assuming the relatively straightforward access to the Greek tradition we now take for granted. Some sense of this complex and often rather technical set of issues is conveyed below (chapters 2 and 3).

THE CLASSICAL PERIOD

Arabic philosophy in the formative classical period was not exclusively, or even always primarily, "Aristotelian." We can certainly identify a dominantly Peripatetic tradition within the classical period. It began in the tenth century C.E. with the school of the aforementioned Abū Bishr Mattā in Baghdad, and al-Fārābī was its first great representative. This tradition tended to see the practice of philosophy as the task of explicating the works of Aristotle, and thus reflected the Greek commentary tradition, especially the commentaries produced by the Neoplatonic school at Alexandria. Al-Fārābī imitated them in writing his own commentaries on Aristotle. His lead was followed by the philosophers in Muslim Spain, or Andalusia (see chapter 8), and the Arabic Peripatetic tradition reaches its apex in the work of Averroes (chapter 9).

Yet the Greek inheritance included not only Aristotle and his commentators, but also original works by Neoplatonists. In fact it is impossible to draw a firm line between the impact of Aristotelianism and the impact of Neoplatonism on Arabic philosophy. It is customary to mention in this regard the so-called *Theology of Aristotle*, which is in fact an interpretive paraphrase of the *Enneads* of Plotinus. But even more important was the already well-established Neoplatonism of the Aristotelian tradition itself: with the exception of Alexander of Aphrodisias, all the important Greek commentators on Aristotle were Neoplatonists. Neoplatonism was thus a major force in Arabic philosophy, and we have accordingly emphasized it in the present volume. Chapters below show that the philosophical curriculum inherited by the Arabic tradition was itself an artifact of Neoplatonism (chapter 2), as well as how al-Fārābī made use of this curriculum (chapter 4). A chapter on al-Kindī emphasizes the influence of the Neoplatonists in early Arabic thought (chapter 3), while its later manifestations are made clear in the chapters on the Ismāʻīlīs, Avicenna, Suhrawardī, and on Ibn ʻArabī and Mulla Ṣadrā (chapters 5, 6, 10, 11).

A third important strand of the classical tradition is the impact of *kalām* on Arabic philosophical works. This too begins already with al-Kindī. And even those philosophers (al-Fārābī and Averroes) who were dismissive of *kalām* as, at best, a rhetorical or dialectical version of *falsafa*, felt the need to respond to *kalām* authors. They were provoked by the independent ideas of the *mutakallimūn*: an example of the productive interchange between *falsafa* and *kalām* can be found here regarding physics (chapter 14). And they were provoked by direct attacks on the philosophical tradition from the *kalām* viewpoint. In this regard the outstanding figure is al-Ghazālī, still one of the great theological authorities in Islam, and of particular interest to us for both his adoption and his critique of philosophical ideas (chapter 7). If not for space restrictions, one could certainly have expanded this volume to include other authors who were critical of the *falsafa* tradition, such as Ibn Taymiyya. Several additional chapters would perhaps have been needed to do any justice to the philosophical significance of *kalām* in its own right.[3] But some of the main themes, for example the problems of divine attributes and human freedom, are explored here in discussing the reaction of philosophers to *mutakallimūn*.

All these factors are important for understanding the most important achievement of the classical period: the self-consciously original system of Avicenna, the greatest philosopher in this tradition. In recognition of this we have here devoted a double-length chapter to his thought (chapter 6). It shows that Avicenna needs to be understood in the context of the classical period as we have described it: he is heir to the Neoplatonic tradition in his understanding of Aristotle, and engages directly with problematics from the *kalām* tradition as well. Indeed, one way of viewing Arabic philosophy is as the tradition that leads up to and stems from the work of Avicenna. Like Kant in the German tradition or Plato and Aristotle in the Greek tradition, Avicenna significantly influenced everything that came after him in the Arabic tradition.

THE POST-AVICENNIAN TRADITION

Admittedly, defining the Arabic philosophical tradition in this way has the disadvantage that it tends to obscure those aspects of earlier Arabic philosophy that Avicenna pointedly ignored.[4] It is however a very useful way to understand later Arabic philosophy. From the time of Avicenna's death in the eleventh century, all philosophical work of note in Arabic responded to him, often critically. We have already alluded to the critiques leveled from the *kalām* point of view. Equally, Averroes criticized him from an Aristotelian point of view, though Avicenna was a major influence for other Andalusians like Ibn Ṭufayl (see chapter 8). An important development of the late classical period was yet another critique and adaptation of Avicenna: the idiosyncratic thought of Suhrawardī, which inaugurated the tradition known as Illuminationism (chapter 10).

The systems of Avicenna and Suhrawardī, an ongoing tradition of *kalām*, and the mysticism of figures like Ibn ʿArabī provided the major impetus to thinkers of the post-classical era. At this point the translation movement was no longer the immediate spur to philosophical reflection; this was rather provided by indigenous Muslim authors. The post-classical era presents us with a forbidding corpus of philosophical work, much of it unedited and unstudied by Western scholars. In the present volume it has been possible only to scratch the surface of this corpus, focusing on a few aspects of the later tradition that are relatively accessible, that is, supported by further secondary literature and some editions and translations. We hope that, by devoting some attention to these later developments, we may encourage the reader to inquire further into this period. It has been remarked that the "Golden Age" of Arabic philosophy could be said to begin only in the *post*-Avicennian era, with a vast number of thinkers who commented or at least drew on Avicenna's works.[5] A companion to Arabic philosophy might look much different once this material is more fully understood. For now, we have devoted particular attention to the reception of Avicenna. Emphasis is placed on Avicenna's inheritance as well as his sources (chapter 6). Another chapter takes up the contentious issue of whether the strand of later Avicennism represented by the great Persian thinker Mulla Ṣadrā can really be called "philosophical," given the mystical aspects of Ṣadrā's system (chapter 11). It shows that we can understand mysticism as the practical complement of Ṣadrā's quite technical and theoretical metaphysical reflections. The last chapter takes our historical narrative down to the present, tracing the themes of later Arabic and Persian philosophy from their roots in Illuminationism and Ṣadrā's version of the Avicennian system (chapter 19). Together, chapters 10, 11, and 19 make the case that the later Illuminationist tradition, which is often treated as dominated by mysticism and symbolic allegory, actually has rational, philosophical analysis at its core.

This, then, is a rough guide to the historical coverage we aim to provide in this *Companion*.[6] Though such a historical summary is needed to orient the reader, it must be said that our aims here remain first and foremost philosophical. That is, we want the reader to come away not just with a grasp of how this tradition developed, but above all with an appreciation of the main ideas that were put forward in the course of that development. Of course many of these are canvassed in the chapters devoted to particular thinkers. But in order to press the point home we have included five chapters on general areas of philosophy ordered according to the late ancient philosophical syllabus, which came down to the Arabic tradition (cf. chapters 2 and 4): Logic, Ethics,[7] Natural Philosophy or Physics, Psychology, and Metaphysics.[8] While some repetition with earlier chapters has been unavoidable, these thematic chapters explore certain topics not dealt with elsewhere (see especially the chapters on logic and physics) and put other topics in a broader context tracing philosophical developments through the tradition. Many of the themes raised will be familiar to students of Christian and Jewish medieval philosophy. This is, of course, not accidental, since as already mentioned Christian and Jewish philosophers in the Middle Ages were thoroughly engaged with the Arabic tradition. The impact of Arabic philosophy on scholastic Latin philosophy is an enormous topic in its own right, one that has been explored to some extent in other *Companions*.[9] Chapter 18 explains the historical background of this influence, detailing the transmission of Arabic philosophical work into Latin, just as chapter 2 explains the transmission of Greek philosophy into Arabic.

Arabic philosophy is of course far too complex to be explored comprehensively in a volume of this size. While the foregoing gives our rationale for the focus and scope of the volume, we are not dogmatic: it is easy to think of philosophers in this tradition who would have merited a chapter of their own in this volume, and easy to think of ways of expanding the scope both historically and thematically. However, in the first instance our goal here is not to be thorough. It is rather to invite readers to the study of Arabic philosophy, giving them a basic grounding in some of the main figures and themes, but also a sense of what is most philosophically intriguing about this tradition.

NOTES

1 See Gutas [58].

2 For this way of defining the tradition, see D. Gutas, "The Study of Arabic Philosophy in the Twentieth Century," *British Journal of Middle Eastern Studies* 29 (2002), 5–25.

3 Useful studies of *kalām* for those interested in its philosophical significance include the following: B. Abrahamov, *Islamic Theology: Traditionalism and Rationalism* (Edinburgh: 1998); R. M. Frank, "Remarks on the Early Development of the Kalam," *Atti del terzo congresso di studi arabi e islamici* (Napoli: 1967), 315–29; R. M. Frank, "The Science of Kalām," *Arabic Sciences and Philosophy* 2 (1992), 7–37; D. Gimaret, *Théories de l'acte humain en théologie musulmane* (Paris: J. Vrin, 1980); van Ess [44]; Wolfson [48].

4 These include the Neoplatonism of the Ismā'īlīs, and of al-'Āmirī and the school of al-Sijistānī (for citations on this see below, chapter 3 n. 33), in addition to such unorthodox thinkers as Abū Bakr al-Rāzī, whose unique system had little influence on the later tradition (for bibliography on al-Rāzī see below, chapter 13 n. 8).

5 See Gutas, "The Study of Arabic Philosophy," and also Gutas [94]. For an even more daunting assessment of the number of later philosophical works, see Wisnovsky [261].

6 Two overviews of the Arabic tradition have appeared recently in other *Companions*: see Druart [13] and Kraemer [27].

7 Our understanding that metaphysical and epistemological principles are foundational in Arabic philosophy for ethical and political ideas is not shared by all contributors to this volume. A different methodological approach inspired by the thought of Leo Strauss is central to the writings of a number of colleagues, among them Muhsin Mahdi and Charles

Butterworth, who have contributed editions, translations, and books and articles of analysis to the field. Chapter 13 by Charles Butterworth follows that approach. For other work in this vein, see the bibliographical citations at the end of the volume under "Ethics and Politics."

8 See for instance Ammonius, *Commentary on the Categories*, 5.31–6.22. Ethics is actually a propaedeutic science in the late ancient curriculum, but Ammonius states that logic is to be studied first, because Aristotle uses it in the course of developing his arguments in the *Ethics*. Psychology is for Aristotle a part of natural philosophy, though it was often treated as a bridge between physics and metaphysics. We separate it off because of its distinctive importance in the Arabic tradition. See further L. G. Westerink, "The Alexandrian Commentators and the Introductions to their Commentaries," in *Aristotle Transformed: The Ancient Commentators and their Influence*, ed. R. Sorabji (London: 1990), 325–48. For versions of the curriculum in the Arabic tradition see below, chapters 2 and 4, Gutas [56], and Rosenthal [39], 52–73.

9 See especially D. Burrell, "Aquinas and Islamic and Jewish Thinkers," in *The Cambridge Companion to Aquinas*, ed. N. Kretzmann and E. Stump (Cambridge: 1993), 60–84, and also the *Companions* to Duns Scotus and Medieval Philosophy.

2 Greek into Arabic: Neoplatonism in translation

SALIENT FEATURES OF LATE ANCIENT PHILOSOPHY

Plotinus: a new reading of Plato

During the imperial age, in many centers of the Roman world, philosophy was taught in close connection to the doctrines of the great philosophers of the past: Plato, Aristotle, Epicurus, Zeno. Not only in Rome, Athens, Alexandria, but also in Pergamon, Smyrna, Apamea, Tarsus, Ege, Aphrodisias in the east of the empire, Naples and Marseille in the west, a "school" of philosophy disseminated either Platonism, Aristotelianism, Stoicism, or Epicureanism. Against this background, the thought of Plotinus represented a turning point in the history of philosophical ideas which was to play a decisive role in the creation of *falsafa* and to influence indirectly philosophy in the Middle Ages, in both Latin and Arabic.

Coming from Alexandria, where he studied Platonism under the guidance of Ammonius Saccas, Plotinus arrived in Rome (244 C.E.) and opened a school. From his explicit claims, as well as the content of his treatises, we know that he was a Platonist and taught Platonism, but also took into account the doctrines of the other philosophers, especially Aristotle. As we learn from the biography that Porphyry prefaced to the edition of Plotinus' works, in the daily meetings of the school the treatises of Aristotle, accompanied by their commentaries – especially those by Alexander of Aphrodisias – were read before Plotinus presented his lecture. This was nothing new: it was customary among the Platonists of that age to compare Plato and Aristotle, either in the hope of showing that they did not disagree on the basic issues or with the aim of arguing that Aristotle's criticisms were erroneous and merely polemical. Still, Plotinus cannot be ranged under the heading either of the "anti-Aristotelian" or of the "pro-Aristotelian" Platonists. He is neither, because some of his key doctrines are grounded in Aristotle's thought – as is the case with his identification of divine Intellect and self-reflexive thinking. At the same time he does not hesitate to criticize Aristotle sharply on other crucial issues, for instance Aristotle's doctrine of substance and his related account of the "categories" of being, whose incompatibility with Platonic ideas about being and knowledge was obscured in the accounts of the "pro-Aristotelian" Platonists.

Plotinus' Platonism is rooted in the Platonic tradition and in the doctrines of what we call Middle Platonism, but he initiated a new age in the history of philosophical thought. As a Platonist, he is convinced that soul is a reality apart from body and that it knows the real structure of things, whereas sense-perception uses bodily organs and only grasps a changing, derivative level of reality. Still, Plotinus is fully aware of Aristotle's criticisms and crafts a doctrine of soul that takes them into account. Soul is closely related to the body to which it gives life, but this does not imply that its cognitive powers depend upon bodily organs: a "part" of soul constantly has access to the intelligible structure of things and provides the principles of reasoning. However, soul is by no means only a cognitive apparatus: it counts also as the immanent principle of the rational organization of the body, as its life, and it links together the two worlds of being and becoming that Plato distinguished from one another in the *Timaeus*. Plotinus makes soul – both of the individual living body and of the body of the universe – a principle rooted in intelligible reality, and yet also the immanent cause of the rational arrangement of visible reality.

The nature of intelligible reality itself is also explored by Plotinus. On the one hand, he takes for granted the Platonic distinction between intelligible and visible reality; on the other hand, he directly addresses the objections raised by Aristotle against the theory of participation, Plato's chief explanation of the relationship between being and becoming. In Plotinus' eyes, Aristotle failed to follow his own methodological rule of making use in each field of the epistemic principles appropriate to it. Since Aristotle conceived of the Platonic Forms as if they were individuals like those of the visible world, he raised a series of objections – among them, the famous Third Man argument – that are completely beside the point if one takes into account their real nature. Plotinus' interpretation of the Platonic intelligible world would be of paramount importance for the development of *falsafa*. The Forms are not general concepts arbitrarily endowed with substantiality. They do not share in the nature of the things named after them (the intelligible principle that makes things triangular is not a triangle). Nor do they simply duplicate items in the sensible world without explaining them, as Aristotle had charged. On Plotinus' interpretation, which owes much to Aristotle's own account of the divine Intellect in book Lambda of the *Metaphysics*, the Forms are the intelligible principles of all that exists, identical in nature with the divine Intellect. This Intellect is both the Platonic Demiurge of the *Timaeus* myth and the *nous* that Aristotle located at the peak of that well-ordered totality which is the cosmos. Assuming the Platonic identification of intelligible reality with true being, Plotinus makes this intelligible being coincide with the divine intellectual principle described in the *Timaeus*. But he also endorses the Aristotelian account of the highest level of being as a motionless, perfect, and blessed reality whose very nature is self-reflexive thinking. Being, Intellect, and the Forms are, in Plotinus' interpretation of Greek philosophy, one and the same thing: in his eyes, Parmenides, Plato, and Aristotle were in substantial agreement on this point, even though it was Plato who provided the most accurate account of it.

On other crucial issues, however, Plotinus thinks that there was no such agreement. In particular, Aristotle was at fault when he argued that this divine Intellect is the first principle itself. Plotinus accepts Aristotle's analysis of the highest level of being as self-reflexive thinking, although he contends that such a principle cannot be the first uncaused cause of all things. What is absolutely first must be absolutely simple, and what eternally thinks itself cannot meet this requirement. Not only must it be dual as both thinker and object of thought, but as object of thought it is intrinsically multiple, since it is identified with the whole range of Platonic Forms. For this reason, Plotinus is unhappy with Aristotle's account of the first principle as self-reflexive thinking; but he is unhappy also with the traditional Middle Platonic solution to the problem of naming Plato's first principle. It is well known that this question is left unanswered in Plato's dialogues. At times Plato suggests that there is a principle of the Forms, but he never addresses this problem directly. Possibly under the influence of Aristotle's theology, the Middle Platonists tended to identify the Good (which counts in the *Republic* as the principle of the Forms) with the Demiurge of the *Timaeus*, that divine Intellect which is said to be "good." Plotinus instead interprets the Good of book VI of the *Republic* as being identical with the "one" discussed in the second half of the *Parmenides*: if it is said "to be," it must be admitted to be multiple. For this reason the One lies, according to Plotinus, "beyond being," like the Good of the *Republic*. Even though the One was also conceived of as the first principle in second-century Neopythagoreanism, the move of conflating the Good of the *Republic* with the "one" of the *Parmenides* is unprecedented in the Platonic school, and allows Plotinus to claim that the core of his philosophy, namely, the doctrine of the three principles One-Good, Intellect, and Soul, is an exegesis of Plato's own thought. This doctrine will play a pivotal role in the formation of Arabic philosophy and lastingly influence it.

Post-Plotinian Platonism: from the "harmony between Plato and Aristotle" to the late antique corpus of philosophical texts

As we learn from Porphyry, for ten years after the opening of the school Plotinus taught only orally, writing nothing. Then, Plotinus began to write treatises and did so until his death in 270 C.E. Thanks to Porphyry, we know about Plotinus something which is usually very hard to know about an ancient philosopher: the precise chronology of his writings. The sequence itself does not show any concern for propaedeutics, and this is confirmed by Porphyry's remarks in the *Life of Plotinus* about the "disorder" of these discussions and the resulting disconcertion of Plotinus' audience. His treatises must have appeared irksome to use and put in order, even apart from their intrinsic complexity. Porphyry himself reports that he composed summaries and notebooks on them, and we still possess a sort of companion to Plotinian metaphysics by him, the *Launching Points to the Realm of Mind*. The *Enneads*, an edition of Plotinus' treatises that Porphyry compiled some thirteen years after Plotinus' death, is an imitation of Andronicus of Rhodes' systematic arrangement of Aristotle's works, as Porphyry himself tells us.

Porphyry was also influenced by the traditional Middle Platonic reading order of Plato's dialogues. His arrangement of the Plotinian treatises in the *Enneads* clearly echoes the model that has Platonic education begin with the question of the essence of "man," dealt with in the *First Alcibiades*. In fact, as Pierre Hadot has shown, the Porphyrian arrangement is by no means neutral: the ascent from ethical to cosmological topics (*Enneads* I–III) and then to metaphysical issues (*Enneads* IV–VI) is reminiscent of the subdivision of the parts of philosophy into ethics, physics, and metaphysics (or theology), a pattern derived from the tradition of pre-Plotinian Platonism in which Porphyry had been educated in Athens by Longinus, before he came to Rome.[1] Henri Dominique Saffrey has pointed out that Porphyry also felt the need to counter Iamblichus' claim that salvation cannot be reached through philosophy alone, but requires "theurgy," the rituals of the purification and divinization of soul revealed by the gods themselves.[2] According to Iamblichus, revelations from the gods and the rituals of Egyptian religion convey a more ancient and perfect truth than philosophy does. More precisely, philosophy itself is a product of this original revelation, because the gods taught Pythagoras, and all Greek philosophy followed in Pythagoras' footsteps. Since soul is sunk in the world of generation and corruption, only divinely revealed rituals can give it true salvation. But Porphyry makes his edition of the Plotinian writings culminate in the treatise *On the One, or the Good* (VI 9 (9)). Here we are told that soul can know the First Principle as the result of its philosophical research about the causes and principles of all things. Plotinus' authority supports Porphyry's final allegiance to the tradition of Greek rationalism. By the same token, the *Enneads* become an ascent from the anthropological-ethical questions dealt with at the beginning to the final claim that our individual soul can reach the First Principle itself, the One or Good.

Porphyry was responsible for more than this systematic reshaping of Plotinus' thought. He also made a move of paramount importance in the history of medieval thought, both in the West and the East: he included Aristotle's works, and especially the logical treatises (the *Organon*), in the Neoplatonic curriculum. For the first time, a Platonist wrote commentaries on Aristotle.[3] Porphyry also provided an introduction to Aristotle's logic, the well-known *Isagoge*.[4] The aim of showing that the two great masters of Greek philosophy were in agreement (as runs the title of the lost work *On the Fact that the Allegiance of Plato and Aristotle is One and the Same*) might have had something to do with this exegetical activity. Indeed, it has also been argued that on this point Porphyry deliberately parted company with Plotinus – who did not conceal his opposition to some crucial tenets of Aristotle's thought – and that this explains Porphyry's move from Rome to Sicily.[5] Two centuries later, when Boethius came to the idea of translating into Latin all the Aristotelian and Platonic writings in order to show their mutual harmony, he was endorsing a model traceable to Porphyry, and still practiced in Boethius' day in Greek Neoplatonic circles. Boethius' project does not begin with Plato (as would seem natural to us for chronological reasons) but with Aristotle and, more precisely, with the *Organon*, introduced by Porphyry's *Isagoge*. Something very similar happens in the Arabic-speaking world: the *Isagoge* is considered the beginning of the philosophical instruction even in the time of Avicenna.[6]

To account for this similarity requires following the transmission to the Arabic-speaking world of the model outlined by Porphyry, and developed in the schools of late antiquity. In the Greek-speaking world, it is possible to follow the main lines of the development of a proper curriculum of philosophical studies in the form of a series of guided readings. But it is less certain how this pattern was transmitted to the Arab philosophers. We have just seen that Porphyry gave a significant impetus toward the creation of a curriculum which included Aristotle as a part of the progressive learning of the philosophical truth. Iamblichus too agreed that Aristotle and Plato were the two great representatives of ancient Greek wisdom and commented upon Aristotle's *Categories* and *Prior Analytics*. In addition, we learn from a later Alexandrian source that he worked out a "canon" of the main Platonic dialogues to be read in sequence. Two dialogues represented in his eyes the sum of Plato's teaching about cosmos and the gods: the *Timaeus* and the *Parmenides*.[7] The approximately 100 years which separate Iamblichus' teaching in Apamea and the renewal of the Platonic studies in Athens, in the first decades of the fifth century, are silent about the curriculum of the Platonic schools. But with Syrianus, the teacher of Proclus, we meet a full-fledged curriculum of philosophical studies, which included both Aristotle and Plato. Studying Aristotle was seen as a preliminary, meant to lead from logic to physics to metaphysics, and the subsequent exposition of supreme theological truth was entrusted to Plato. As we learn from Marinus of Neapolis, Syrianus first taught Proclus Aristotle for two years, before moving on to Plato.[8] Even though there is no direct evidence that Syrianus' courses on Plato's dialogues followed the sequence of the Iamblichean "canon," the fact that all the Platonic commentaries by Proclus are devoted to dialogues from this sequence, with the three major ones devoted to its beginnings and end (*First Alcibiades, Timaeus, Parmenides*),[9] suggests that the Platonic education in Athens was imparted according to this model, while basic education was provided through a guided reading of Aristotle's corpus.

In fifth–sixth-century Athens, philosophy appears more and more as a systematic whole, its study guided by a canon of authoritative works, including both Aristotle and Plato. The peak of the philosophical curriculum is no longer metaphysics, but theology, i.e., a philosophical discourse about the divine principles, whose sources lie first and foremost in the revelations of late paganism[10] and then in Plato's dialogues, allegorically interpreted as conveying his theological doctrine. But Proclus did not just comment upon Plato's main dialogues. He also wrote a huge treatise on systematic theology, the *Platonic Theology*,[11] and collected all the theological truths, in the form of axioms, into a companion modeled on Euclid's *Elements of Geometry*: the *Elements of Theology*.[12] Both the *Platonic Theology* and the *Elements of Theology* begin with the One, the First Principle. Departing from Plotinus, who was convinced that the suprasensible causes were but three – the One-Good, Intellect, and Soul – the two Proclean works expound the procession of multiplicity from the One as the derivation of a series of intermediate principles, first between the One and the intelligible being, then between the intelligible being and the divine Intellect (and intellects), and then between the divine Intellect and the divine Soul (and souls). For Proclus, an entire hierarchy of divine principles lies both outside the visible universe and within it, and the human soul, fallen into the world of coming-to-be and passing away, can return to the First Principle only through the "appropriate mediations."[13] The pagan cults, offered as they are to the intra-cosmic and the hypercosmic gods, vindicate true religion against Christianity and show how soul can ascend toward the "appropriate mediations." Philosophy, insofar as it celebrates the truly divine principles of the visible cosmos, is prayer.

At the end of the fifth century and during the sixth, within a Christian environment both in Alexandria and in Athens, the Neoplatonic schools continued to comment upon Aristotle and Plato.

To some extent, one may also venture to say that it was one and the same school, unified by travel and personal ties between the two cities.[14] Yet there is a difference of emphasis. The focus of the philosophical debate in sixth-century Alexandria appears to have shifted significantly toward Aristotle,[15] even though the Neoplatonic pagan philosophers continued to adhere to the theological doctrines worked out within the school. Ammonius, who received his education in Athens and lectured in Alexandria chiefly on Aristotle,[16] had as his pupils both John Philoponus and Simplicius. The latter went also to Athens, where he studied under the guidance of Damascius.[17] Simplicius' exegetical work allows us to grasp the continuity and innovations of the philosophical curriculum in late antiquity. The anthropological-ethical propaedeutics supplied in Iamblichus' canon by the *First Alcibiades* are for him provided instead by Epictetus' *Encheiridion*, upon which he comments at length.[18] The Aristotelian commentaries that have come down to us[19] follow the post-Plotinian tradition of reading Aristotle's logic and cosmology as fitting perfectly with Plato's metaphysical doctrine. But, departing from the model inherited by Syrianus, theological discussion is no longer entrusted to the allegorical commentary on Plato's dialogues, upon which Simplicius does not comment. A plausible explanation for this fact is the pressure of the Christian environment. Especially after 529, the date of a ban on public teaching by philosophers of pagan allegiance,[20] it would have been daring to give courses on the "theological" dialogues by Plato, whose interpretation, especially after Proclus, was strongly committed to polytheism.[21] To this, another explanation might be added for the prima facie astonishing fact that late Neoplatonism is mostly focused on commenting on Aristotle, rather than on Plato: the pivotal role played by Aristotle in the debate between pagans and Christians, best exemplified by the argument between Simplicius and John Philoponus over whether the cosmos is eternal or created.

John Philoponus is to some extent a dilemma for historians. His twofold activity as Neoplatonic commentator of Aristotle and as Christian theologian and polemicist against both Aristotle and Proclus[22] is a much-debated problem.[23] This point is directly relevant to the formative period of *falsafa* in two ways: first, Philoponus' anti-eternalist arguments were to have a paramount importance for al-Kindī (see chapter 3); second, the polemic itself is proof of the fact that philosophical debate, in the last stages of the Neoplatonic schools, had Aristotle as its main, albeit not exclusive, focus. The last Neoplatonic commentators in Alexandria wrote on Aristotle (Elias, David, Stephanus of Alexandria). At the end of antiquity, especially in the Alexandrian area which was to fall under Islamic rule shortly thereafter, Aristotle was seen as the unexcelled master of scientific learning in logic, physics, cosmology, natural science, and psychology. The architecture of theoretical knowledge was no longer crowned by the theological interpretation of Plato's dialogues. Between the second half of the sixth century and the first decades of the seventh, in Alexandria, Aristotle is not yet credited with a Neoplatonic theology, as he would be in ninth-century Baghdad in the circle of al-Kindī. But everything is ready for his taking on the mantle of "First Teacher."

THE TRANSMISSION OF NEOPLATONIC PHILOSOPHY TO THE ARABIC-SPEAKING WORLD

The schools

In 529, as a consequence of Justinian's closing of the Platonic school, Simplicius, Damascius, and five other philosophers left Athens and went to Persia, at the court of Chosroes I Anūshirwān,[24] where they remained until 532. This was by no means the first penetration of Greek philosophy in the east: indeed, the fact that the Sassanian emperor was deeply interested in philosophy was the reason for the Neoplatonic philosophers to join him in Ctesiphon. Priscianus Lydus, one of the philosophers who came from Athens, wrote a treatise for him, and one of Paul the Persian's writings on Aristotle's logic is dedicated to him.[25] But, notwithstanding the favorable attitude of the Sassanian court toward Greek learning,[26] the first dissemination of philosophy in the Mesopotamian area did not occur in Pahlavi, as a consequence of the interest of the Sassanian dynasty in the foreign sciences, but in Syriac, as a consequence of the necessities of theological discourse.

Before Arabic, the first Semitic language into which the Greek philosophical texts were translated was Syriac – originally an Aramaic dialect, which was soon used for literary and philosophical works.[27] In the biblical school at Edessa, the exegetical works of Theodor of Mopsuestia were translated from Greek into Syriac within the first half of the fifth century, either by Qiore (died 428) or by Hibas (died 475).[28] According to the testimony of Jacob of Edessa (died 708), together with the biblical commentaries by Theodor, Aristotle's *Categories* arrived in the school to be translated into Syriac and serve the purposes of exegesis and teaching.[29] But soon Aristotle's logical works were commented upon in themselves, along the lines of the movement which Sebastian Brock has called a process "from antagonism to assimilation" of Greek learning.[30] The key figure in the transmission of Aristotle's logic, along with its Neoplatonic interpretation, is Sergius of Resh'aynā (died 536), a physician and philosopher who received his education in Alexandria and, in addition to writing commentaries on and introductions to Aristotle's logical works, translated into Syriac many treatises by Galen, the writings of the pseudo-Dionysius the Areopagite, possibly the *Centuries* by Evagrius Ponticus, and the treatise *On the Principles of the All* attributed to Alexander of Aphrodisias. Henri Hugonnard-Roche has shown the close relationship between Sergius' presentation of Aristotle and the Alexandrian curriculum.[31] He also remarks that, while in the Neoplatonic curriculum the Aristotelian corpus was meant to provide an introduction to Plato's dialogues, for Sergius it is the sum of philosophy as demonstrative science.[32] In this, Sergius is following in the footsteps of the Alexandrian developments outlined above.

Another center of learning, the Nestorian school in Nisibi founded by the bishop Barsawma (died 458), gave room to Greek philosophy. Paul the Persian, whom we have already met at the court of Chosroes I Anūshirwān toward the middle of the sixth century, may have had something to do with this school. What lies beyond doubt is that, like Sergius, he inherited the late Neoplatonic classification of Aristotle's writings best exemplified at Alexandria, as is shown by two extant writings by him.[33] Other Syriac commentators on Aristotle, like Proba (sixth century), who commented upon the *Isagoge*, *De Interpretatione*, and *Prior Analytics*,[34] endorsed the model worked out by Sergius of Resh'aynā, creating in this way a Syriac tradition of Aristotelian logic – translations, companions, commentaries – which was to play an important role in the rise and development of *falsafa*. Later on, in the seventh century, a school appended to the monastery of Qenneshrīn (Chalcis) became a center of Greek learning under the impetus of the bishop Severus Sebokht (died 667). Here too, Aristotle's logical works, introduced by Porphyry's *Isagoge*, appear as the core of demonstrative science. Athanasius of Balad (died 687), Jacob of Edessa, and George of the Arabs (died 724)[35] provided new translations of the logical corpus created in late antiquity, i.e., the *Isagoge* and the *Organon*. Even under the 'Abbāsid rule, in the eighth and ninth centuries, the Christians of Syria were the unexcelled masters of Aristotelian logic: the caliph al-Mahdī (reigned 775–85) asked Timoteus I, the Nestorian *katholikos*, to provide a translation of the *Topics*.[36] In ninth-century Baghdad, and even later on, Syriac-speaking Christians carried on a tradition of logical learning in close relationship with the Arab *falāsifa*.[37]

Max Meyerhof, relying on al-Fārābī,[38] worked out the so-called path "from Alexandria to Baghdad" in order to account for the transmission of Greek science and philosophy to the Arabic-speaking world.[39] Dimitri Gutas has pointed out that al-Fārābī's account is to be taken less as a historical report than as an attempt at gaining credit for Islamic culture as the legitimate heir of Greek learning, worthy of being the repository of that heritage which the Byzantine rulers were no longer able to understand and exploit because of their allegiance to the Christian faith.[40] But this should not obscure the intrinsic dependence of the rising Syriac and Arabic philosophical tradition on the Alexandrian model of philosophy as systematic learning, organized around a corpus of Aristotelian texts introduced by Porphyry's *Isagoge*. Such a model is still at work in the Arabic literary genre of the "introductions to philosophy"[41] and shows the close relationship between the rise of *falsafa* and the way in which philosophy was conceived of in the Neoplatonic schools at the end of antiquity. Obviously, Alexandria, Antioch, Edessa, Nisibi, Qenneshrīn, and Jundīsābūr were not the only centers where philosophy was studied and taught: many others disseminated Greek learning, such as Marw, in Khurāsān, and Ḥarrān.[42] One cannot claim that the Alexandrian model was exclusive or even dominant everywhere. But the available data points towards its being the main pattern for the understanding of what philosophy was, and how it was to be learnt, in the Arabic tradition.

The translations

The rise of the 'Abbāsid dynasty and the foundation of Baghdad (762 C.E.) mark a turning point in Islamic culture. A proper movement of translation began and developed into a systematic assimilation of Greek scientific and philosophical learning.[43] A comprehensive account of the scientific fields covered by the activity of the translators, of the stages of assimilation of Greek materials, and of the different styles of translations has been provided by Gerhard Endress.[44] Against this background, the role of Greek Neoplatonism appears to be crucial: the fact that Plotinus' *Enneads* and Proclus' *Elements of Theology* were among the first works translated into Arabic had long-term consequences for the entire development of *falsafa*. These two basic texts of Greek Neoplatonism were translated into Arabic by the same group that also produced the first Arabic translations of Aristotle's *Metaphysics* and *De Caelo*: the circle of al-Kindī (ninth century). We owe to Endress the discovery of a series of features that single out a group of early translations, all of them related in one way or another to al-Kindī, covering many crucial texts of Greek cosmology, psychology, metaphysics, and theology.[45] Later on, the translation of other works and the development of an autochthonous tradition of philosophical thought would partly modify the picture of what philosophy is and how it relates to the Qur'ānic sciences. Still, some general assumptions typical of this first assimilation of Greek thought into an Islamic milieu would remain the trademark of *falsafa*, both in East and West: (1) philosophy is a systematic whole, whose roots lie in logic and whose peak is rational theology; (2) all the Greek philosophers agree on a limited, but important, set of doctrines concerning the cosmos, the human soul, and the first principle; (3) philosophical truths do not derive from the Qur'ān, even if they fit perfectly with it. All this results from the combined reading of Aristotle, Alexander of Aphrodisias, Plotinus, and Proclus, whose works are meant to convey a consistent set of doctrines.

The bio-bibliographical sources mention many Neoplatonic texts known to readers of Arabic, even though the information at times is not reliable or incomplete. Still, the picture is impressive: Arabic speakers acquainted themselves, to different degrees, with the Arabic or Syriac versions of the works of Plotinus, Porphyry, Iamblichus, Themistius, Syrianus, Proclus, pseudo-Dionysius the Areopagite, Simplicius, Philoponus, and Olympiodorus. Some of the Arabic translations of Neoplatonic works have come down to us. Table 2.1 will give some idea of the Neoplatonic writings available in Arabic.[46]

Table 2.1

Authors	Works translated into Syriac and/or Arabic (transl. extant)	Works mentioned as translated into Syriac and/or Arabic (transl. not extant)	Works mentioned in the Arabic sources, without any mention of a translation into Syriac and/or Arabic
Plotinus	*Enneads* IV–VI, Arabic (Ibn Nāʻima al-Ḥimṣī)		
Porphyry	*Isagoge*, Syriac (within 536); Arabic Abū ʻUthmān al-Dimāshqī) *Philos. History* (fragm.), Syriac	*Isagoge*, Syriac transl.; Arabic transl. (Ayyūb ibn Qāsim al-Raqqī); comm. on the *Physics*; *Nic. Eth.*; *Introd. to the Categorical Syllogisms*, Arabic (Abū ʻUthmān al-Dimashqī); *On the Intellect and the Intelligible*, Syriac; *Istafsār* (?), Syriac	Comm. on the *Categories*; summary of the *De Int.* (?); summary of Aristotle's philosophy; letter to Anebo
Iamblichus	Commentary on the *Carmen Aureum*, Arabic		Comm. on the *Categories* (?); comm. on the *De Int.*
Themistius	Comm. on *Met.* Lambda, Arabic (Abū Bishr Mattā ibn Yūnus); on the *De Caelo*, Arabic (Yaḥyā ibn ʻAdī); on the *De Anima*, Arabic	Comm. on the *De Gen. Corr.*; on the *Nic. Eth.*, Syriac	Comm. on the *Categories*; on the *Prior* and *Post. Anal.*; on the *Topics*; comm. on the *Physics*; book to Julian; letter to Julian
Syrianus		Comm. on *Met.* Beta	
Proclus	*Elements of Theology*; *XVIII Arguments on the Eternity of the Cosmos*; *Arguments for the Immortality of the Soul*, Arabic	Comm. on the *Carmen Aureum*, Syriac; on a section of Plato's *Gorgias*, Syriac; on a section of treatise *On Fate*, Syriac; on the *Phaedo* (Abū ʻAlī ibn Zuʻrā)	*Definition of the Origin of Natural Phenomena*; *Ten Doubts about Providence*; *The Indivisible Atom*

ps.-Dionysius	*De Div. Nom.*, *Cael. Hier.*, *Myst. Theol.*, *Eccl. Hier.*, *Ep.*, Syriac		
Ammonius			Comm. on the *Categories*; on the *Topics*, I–IV; exposition of Aristotle's doctrines about the Creator; aims of Aristotle in his books; Aristotle's proof of Oneness
Simplicius		Comm. on the *De Anima*, Syriac and Arabic	Comm. on the *Categories*
Philoponus	Comm. on the *Physics* (fragm.); *De Aet. Mundi contra Proclum* (fragm.); *Against Aristotle on the Eternity of the World* (fragm.), Arabic	Comm. on the *Physics*, Arabic (Basil and Ibn Nā'ima al-Ḥimṣī); *Refutation of Proclus' Arguments for the Eternity of the World; On the Fact that the Power of Physical Realities is Finite*	Comm. on Aristotle's Ten Items; refutation of Nestorius; other refutations; exposition of Galen's medical works
Olympiodorus		Comm. on the *Sophist* (Isḥāq ibn Ḥunayn); exposition of the *Meteorologica* (Abū Bishr Mattā ibn Yūnus and al-Ṭabarī); comm. on the *De Anima*	Ambiguous entry on the *De Gen. Corr.*
David/Elias	*Prolegomena*, Arabic		
Stephanus			Comm. on the *Categories*; comm. on the *De Int.*
Anonymous	Paraphrasis of Aristotle's *De Anima*, Arabic		

ARABIC NEOPLATONISM: A KEY TO UNDERSTANDING *FALSAFA*

Around the forties of the ninth century, when al-Kindī was the tutor of Aḥmad, the son of the ruling caliph al-Mu'taṣim (reigned 833–42), Plotinus' *Enneads* IV–VI were translated into Arabic by a Christian from Emessa, Ibn Nā'ima al-Ḥimṣī. We get this information from the *incipit* of the Prologue to the so-called *Theology of Aristotle*, actually a rearranged Arabic version and paraphrase of part of the *Enneads*. From this Prologue we learn also that the Arabic version was "corrected" by al-Kindī himself for the prince. The question thus arises why al-Kindī would expose him – and obviously an entire milieu interested in philosophy – to such a teaching. The Prologue provides the answer: the treatise drawn from the *Enneads* is presented as the theological complement of Aristotle's *Metaphysics*.

> Since it is established, by the agreement of the leading philosophers, that the pre-existing initial causes of the universe are four, namely, Matter, Form, the Active Cause, and Perfection, it is necessary to examine them . . . Now we have previously completed an explanation of them and an account of their causes in our book which is after the *Physics* . . . Let us not waste words over this branch of knowledge, since we have already given an account of it in the book of the *Metaphysics*, and let us confine ourselves to what we have presented there, and at once mention our aim in what we wish to expound in the present work . . . Now our aim in this book is the discourse on the Divine Sovereignty, and the explanation of it, and how it is the first cause, eternity and time being beneath it, and that it is the cause and originator of causes, in a certain way, and how the luminous force steals from it over mind and, through the medium of mind, over the universal celestial soul, and from mind, through the medium of soul, over nature, and from soul, through the medium of nature, over the things that come to be and pass away.[47]

What we are told here is that another account will follow the *Metaphysics* and deal with the transmission of God's causality to the things falling under generation and corruption, through the mediation of two suprasensible principles – Intellect and the World Soul – and nature. After having recalled the subject matter of Aristotle's *Metaphysics*, the author of the Prologue (in all likelihood, al-Kindī himself)[48] presents the reader with another discipline, rational theology, which is intrinsically connected to metaphysics and yet distinct from it, and which deals with the One, Intellect, and World Soul. Obviously, there is no trace of these principles in Aristotle's *Metaphysics*, and it has been argued that for al-Kindī's circle Plotinus' *Enneads* represented the needed complement to the account of the prime mover given in *Metaphysics* Lambda.[49] However, the reader of the *Theology of Aristotle* may be disappointed to see that the project outlined in the Prologue is not carried on in the *Theology* itself, and that parts of the *Enneads* and extensive interpolations are combined in what appears to be a baffling disorder. Only upon closer examination does the structure of the *Theology* appear: created out of Porphyry's edition,[50] skipping the "propaedeutic" of *Enneads* I–III and translating only treatises belonging to *Enneads* IV–VI (on Soul, Intellect, and the One), the *Theology* is likely to be an abortive attempt at producing a systematic work on rational theology, whose subject matters are announced in the Prologue according to their ontological dignity – the First Cause, Intellect, the World Soul – but whose order of exposition is constrained by the actual order of the *Enneads*.

The ideal order outlined in the Prologue presents the reader with an exposition of the way in which the prime mover acts: its sovereignty is real, its causality reaches all creatures through Intellect and the World Soul. The *Theology*, on the other hand, presents the reader first with the Plotinian topic of the descent of soul into the body and with the idea of soul as the mediator between the visible and invisible realms. Then, a description of the intelligible world and of Intellect as the first creature, and an account of the action of the True One follow, in a rough, hesitant order. Plotinus' description of *nous* as the first image of the One is reshaped into the idea of "creation through the intermediary of intellect." Plotinus' *nous* also provides the author of the *Theology* with a model for God's creation and providence. The True One is credited with a mode of action designed to explain how an immutable principle can cause anything to exist: the Neoplatonic analysis of how Forms act is expounded as a description of God's causality and providence "through its very being (*bi-anniyyatihi faqaṭ*),"[51] which involves no change at all.

Philosophical topics that did not exist as such before Plotinus and were created out of his rethinking of Platonism – the amphibious life of soul, which eternally belongs to both worlds, seeing the intelligibles and animating the living body; the identity of the Forms and Intellect; the absolute simplicity and ineffability of the First Principle – reappear in the formative period of *falsafa*. They equal, in the eyes of many Islamic philosophers, the doctrine of the Greeks dealing with divinity, crowning the study of "what is after the physics." And it is Aristotle, the First Teacher, who is credited with such a rational theology. This is so not only in the *Theology of Aristotle*, but also in the rearrangement of the Arabic translation of Proclus' *Elements of Theology*, the *Book of Aristotle's Exposition of the Pure Good* (*Kitāb al-īḍāḥ li-Arisṭūṭālis fī al-khayr al-maḥḍ*),[52] whose origin within the circle of al-Kindī has been demonstrated by Gerhard Endress. This rearrangement, which has also been credited to al-Kindī himself,[53] will become in twelfth-century Toledo, thanks to Gerard of Cremona's translation into Latin, the *Liber Aristotelis de Expositione Bonitatis Purae* (*Liber de Causis*). The Latin Aristotelian corpus too will then culminate in Neoplatonic rational theology.

The project of crowning Aristotle's metaphysics with a rational theology based on the Platonic tradition is an application of the late Neoplatonic model of philosophy as a systematic discipline, covering topics from logic to theology. We do not know whether this pattern reached the circle of al-Kindī as such or whether it was in a sense recreated. What we can say is that the attribution of a Neoplatonic rational theology to Aristotle has its origins in post-Plotinian Platonism, and in the primacy that the Alexandrian commentators gave to Aristotle without renouncing the main Neoplatonic tenets regarding the One, Intellect, and Soul. For this reason, *falsafa* cannot be properly understood if its roots in the philosophical thought of Late Antiquity are not taken into account.[54]

NOTES

This chapter is dedicated to Richard M. Frank, in gratitude.

1 P. Hadot, "La métaphysique de Porphyre," in *Porphyre*, Entretiens Hardt XII (Vandœuvres: 1965), 127–57.

2 H. D. Saffrey, "Pourquoi Porphyre a-t-il édité Plotin? Réponse provisoire," in Porphyre, *La vie de Plotin*, vol. II, ed. L. Brisson et al. (Paris: 1992), 31–57.

3 Porphyry commented upon the *Categories* (*Commentaria in Aristotelem Graeca* [hereafter *CAG*] IV 1), *On Interpretation*, the

Sophistical Refutations, the *Physics*, and the *Nicomachean Ethics*. The fragments are edited in *Porphyrii Philosophi Fragmenta*, ed. A. Smith (Stuttgart: 1993).

4 Porphyre, *Isagoge*, ed. A. de Libera and A.-Ph. Segonds (Paris: 1998).

5 C. Evangeliou, *Aristotle's Categories and Porphyry* (Leiden: 1988); H. D. Saffrey, "Pourquoi Porphyre a-t-il édité Plotin?"

6 In his autobiography, Avicenna says that his teacher al-Nātilī taught him logic, starting with the *Isagoge* (see D. Gutas, *Avicenna and the Aristotelian Tradition: Introduction to Reading Avicenna's Philosophical Works* [Leiden: 1988], 25).

7 L. G. Westerink, J. Trouillard, and A.-Ph. Segonds (eds.), *Prolégomènes à la philosophie de Platon* (Paris: 1990), 39.16–26.

8 Marinus, *Proclus ou sur le bonheur*, ed. H. D. Saffrey, A.-Ph. Segonds, and C. Luna (Paris: 2001), sect. 13. Syrianus was also the first Platonist to comment at length upon Aristotle's *Metaphysics* (*CAG* VI 1). In his commentary, he systematically had recourse to Alexander of Aphrodisias' exegesis: see C. Luna, *Trois études sur la tradition des commentaires anciens à la "Métaphysique" d'Aristote* (Leiden: 2001). See also my "Commenting on Aristotle: From Late Antiquity to Arab Aristotelianism," in W. Geerlings and C. Schulze (eds.), *Der Kommentar in Antike und Mittelalter: Beiträge zu seiner Erforschung* (Leiden: 2002), 201–51.

9 Proclus' commentaries on the *First Alcibiades* (ed. Segonds, 1985), *Cratylus* (ed. Pasquali, 1908), *Republic* (ed. Kroll, 1899), *Timaeus* (ed. Diehl, 1903–6), and *Parmenides* (ed. Cousin, 1864) have come down to us.

10 H. D. Saffrey, "Accorder entre elles les traditions théologiques: une caractéristique du néoplatonisme athénien," in E. P. Bos and P. A. Meijer (eds.), *On Proclus and his Influence in Medieval Philosophy* (Leiden: 1992), 35–50.

11 H. D. Saffrey and L. G. Westerink, *Proclus: Théologie platonicienne*, vols. I–VI (Paris: 1968–97).

12 Proclus, *The Elements of Theology*, ed. E. R. Dodds (Oxford: 1963).

13 Proclus, *Elements of Theology*, proposition 132, 118.2–4.

14 This is the case with Ammonius, the teacher of the school of Alexandria, whose father Hermias was a fellow disciple of Proclus at Syrianus' classes, and who studied in Athens before getting the chair in Alexandria. In turn, Damascius was educated in Alexandria by Ammonius, but succeeded Proclus as the head of the Platonic school in Athens.

15 Against K. Praechter, who in 1910 argued for a doctrinal difference between the Neoplatonic circles of Athens and Alexandria, I. Hadot, *Le problème du néoplatonisme alexandrin: Hiéroclès et Simplicius*

(Paris: 1978), called attention to the fact that the two circles focused on different steps of the curriculum. The lack of theological speculation in the works of the Alexandrian Neoplatonists does not imply that they held different metaphysical doctrines; they simply addressed preliminary topics without direct theological import.

16 See the entry "Ammonius" by H. D. Saffrey and J.-P. Mahé in Goulet [20], vol. I, 168–70.

17 See P. Hoffmann, "Damascius," in Goulet [20], vol. II, 541–93.

18 Simplicius, *Commentaire sur le "Manuel" d'Epictète*, ed. I. Hadot, vol. I (Paris: 2001). Now translated in Simplicius, *On Epictetus' Handbook*, trans. T. Brennan and C. Brittain, 2 vols. (London: 2003).

19 *Categories*: *CAG* VIII 1; *Physics*: *CAG* IX and X; *De Caelo*: *CAG* VII.

20 See Hoffmann, "Damascius."

21 H. D. Saffrey, "Le chrétien Jean Philopon et la survivance de l'école d'Alexandrie au VIe siècle," *Revue des études grecques* 67 (1954), 396–410.

22 Against eternalism John Philoponus wrote *De Aeternitate Mundi contra Proclum* (ed. Rabe, 1899) and a treatise against Aristotle, lost but quoted by both Simplicius and al-Fārābī. See Philoponus, *Against Aristotle on the Eternity of the World*, trans. C. Wildberg (London: 1987).

23 R. Sorabji (ed.), *Philoponus and the Rejection of Aristotelian Science* (London: 1987); K. Verrycken, "The Development of Philoponus' Thought and its Chronology," in R. Sorabji (ed.), *Aristotle Transformed: The Ancient Commentators and their Influence* (London: 1990), 233–74, and "Philoponus' Interpretation of Plato's Cosmogony," *Documenti e studi sulla tradizione filosofica medievale* 8 (1997), 269–318; U. M. Lang, *John Philoponus and the Controversies over Chalcedon in the Sixth Century* (Leuven: 2001).

24 Agathias, *Hist.* II.31.2–4 (81.8–21 ed. Keydell); see also Hoffmann, "Damascius," 556–9; M. Tardieu, "Chosroès," in Goulet [20], vol. II, 309–18.

25 J. Teixidor, "Les textes syriaques de la logique de Paul le Perse," *Semitica* 47 (1997), 117–38; "La dédicace de Paul le Perse à Chosroès," in J. D. Dubois and B. Roussel (eds.), *Entrer en matière: les Prologues* (Paris: 1997), 199–208.

26 Gutas [58].

27 For instance, Bardaisan (154–222) wrote in Syriac. Cf. J. Teixidor, "Bardesane de Syrie," in Goulet [20], vol. II, 54–63.

28 J. Teixidor, "Introduzione," in *Storia della scienza*, IV, I, *La scienza siriaca* (Rome: 2001), 7.

29 K. Georr, *Les Catégories d'Aristote dans leurs versions syro-arabes* (Beirut: 1948); Endress [54], 407–12; H. Hugonnard-Roche, "L'intermédiaire syriaque dans la transmission de la philosophie grecque à

l'arabe: le cas de l'*Organon* d'Aristote," *Arabic Sciences and Philosophy* 1 (1991), 187–209.

30 S. Brock, "From Antagonism to Assimilation: Syriac Attitudes to Greek Learning," in N. G. Garsoïan, T. F. Mathews, and R. W. Thomson (eds.), *East of Byzantium: Syria and Armenia in the Formative Period* (Washington, D.C.: 1982), 17–39; "The Syriac Commentary Tradition," in Burnett [50], 3–18.

31 H. Hugonnard-Roche, "Les *Catégories* d'Aristote comme introduction à la philosophie dans un commentaire syriaque de Sergius de Resh'aynā (†536)," *Documenti e studi sulla tradizione filosofica medievale* 8 (1997), 339–63; "Note sur Sergius de Resh'aynā, traducteur du grec en syriaque et commentateur d'Aristote," in Endress and Kruk [55], 121–43.

32 H. Hugonnard-Roche, "La tradizione della logica aristotelica," in *Storia della scienza*, IV, I, 18.

33 See Gutas [76].

34 A. Elamrani-Jamal and H. Hugonnard-Roche, "Aristote: l'*Organon*. Tradition syriaque et arabe," in Goulet [20], vol. I, 502–28; H. Hugonnard-Roche, "Les traductions syriaques de l'*Isagoge* de Porphyre et la constitution du corpus syriaque de logique," *Revue d'histoire des textes* 24 (1994), 293–312.

35 D. Miller, "George, Bishop of the Arab Tribes, *On True Philosophy*," *Aram* 5 (1993), 303–20.

36 See Gutas [58], 61–9.

37 H. Hugonnard-Roche, "Remarques sur la tradition arabe de l'*Organon* d'après le manuscrit Paris, Bibliothèque Nationale, ar. 2346," in Burnett [50], 19–28.

38 Al-Fārābī's testimony comes from the lost work *The Blossoms of Philosophy*. See Endress [54], 411 and Gutas [58].

39 M. Meyerhof, "Von Alexandrien nach Bagdad: Ein Beitrag zur Geschichte des philosophischen und medizinischen Unterrichts bei den Arabern," *Sitzungsberichte der Berliner Akademie der Wissenschaften, Philologisch-historische Klasse* (1930), 389–429.

40 See Gutas [58].

41 C. Hein, *Definition und Einteilung der Philosophie: von der spätantiken Einleitungsliteratur zur arabischen Enzyklopädie* (Frankfurt a. M.: 1987).

42 In the account mentioned above, n. 38, al-Fārābī reports that the two pupils of the last teacher of philosophy in Antioch were from Marw and from Ḥarrān, and that when they left Antioch, they took the books with them. It has been claimed that Ḥarrān was the place where Simplicius settled after having left Ctesiphon and where he wrote his commentaries on Aristotle (M. Tardieu, "Les calendriers en usage à

Ḥarrān, d'après les sources arabes, et le commentaire de Simplicius à la *Physique* d'Aristote," in I. Hadot [ed.] *Simplicius: sa vie, son œuvre, sa survie* [Berlin: 1987], 40–57), but this claim has been convincingly criticized by J. Lameer, "From Alexandria to Baghdad: Reflections on the Genesis of a Problematical Tradition," in Endress and Kruk [55], 181–91, and by C. Luna, review of R. Thiel, *Simplikios und das Ende der neuplatonischen Schule in Athen*, in *Mnemosyne* 54 (2001), 482–504.

43 See Gutas [58].

44 See Endress [54], continuation in W. Fischer (ed.), *Grundriss der arabischen Philologie*, vol. III (Wiesbaden: 1992), 3–152.

45 See Endress [53]; Endress [67].

46 Due to space limitations, I cannot give the exact reference for each item in *Kitāb al-Fihrist* by Ibn al-Nadīm, which is the main source of this table. Some items are not recorded in it: Plotinus' *Enneads* IV–VI (ed. Dieterici, 1882, and Badawī, 1966); Iamblichus' commentary on the *Carmen Aureum* (ed. H. Daiber, *Neuplatonische Pythagorica in arabischem Gewande: der Kommentar des Iamblichus zu den "Carmina Aurea"* [Amsterdam: 1995]); pseudo-Dionysius the Areopagite (see S. Lilla in Goulet [20], vol. II, 727–42, at 729); the *Prolegomena* by David-Elias (see Hein, *Definition und Einteilung der Philosophie*); the anonymous *In De Anima* (see R. Arnzen, *Aristoteles' De Anima: eine verlorene spätantike Paraphrase in arabischer und persischer Überlieferung* [Leiden: 1998]).

47 English translation by G. Lewis, in *Plotini Opera*, ed. P. Henry and H.-R. Schwyzer, vol. II (Paris: 1959), 486–7.

48 See my "*Pseudo-Theology of Aristotle*, Chapter I: Structure and Composition," *Oriens* 36 (2001), 78–112.

49 F. W. Zimmermann, "The Origins of the So-called *Theology of Aristotle*," in Kraye, Ryan, and Schmitt [60], 110–240.

50 H.-R. Schwyzer, "Die pseudoaristotelische *Theologie* und die Plotin-Ausgabe des Porphyrios," *Museum Helveticum* 90 (1941), 216–36.

51 I have argued in favor of the influence of pseudo-Dionysius the Areopagite on this formula in "L'influence du vocabulaire arabe: *causa prima est esse tantum*," in J. Hamesse and C. Steel (eds.), *L'élaboration du vocabulaire philosophique au Moyen Age* (Turnhout: 2001), 51–97.

52 Ed. Bardenhewer, 1882 and Badawī, 1955. English translation in Thomas Aquinas, *Commentary on the Book of Causes*, trans. V. A. Guagliardo, C. R. Hess, and R. C. Taylor (Washington, D.C.: 1996).

53 See my "Al-Kindī et l'auteur du *Liber de Causis,*" in D'Ancona [51], 155–94, and my "*Pseudo-Theology of Aristotle,* Chapter I."

54 My warmest thanks are due to Peter Adamson and Richard C. Taylor for correcting the English of this paper. Steven Harvey read a first draft of it and made many useful remarks; my warmest thanks are due to him too. I am solely responsible for any weaknesses.

3 Al-Kindī and the reception of Greek philosophy

The previous chapter has given some sense of the enormous impact of the translation movement during the 'Abbāsid caliphate, which rendered Greek works of science and literature into Arabic.[1] The translation of what we would now consider to be properly philosophical works was only a small part of this movement. Translation of philosophy went hand in hand with the translation of more "scientific" texts, such as the medical writings of Galen and the astronomical and mathematical works of Euclid, Ptolemy, and others. Under the 'Abbāsids the most important group of translators, in terms of sheer output and the quality of their translations, was that of the Christian Ḥunayn ibn Isḥāq (808–873 C.E.), and his son Isḥāq ibn Ḥunayn (died 910 C.E.). Ḥunayn and his school produced many translations, including of works by Plato and Aristotle (especially the logical corpus); particularly important to Ḥunayn himself were translations of Galen, which formed the basis for Ḥunayn's own treatises on medicine.[2]

A second, slightly earlier group was that gathered around the person of Abū Yūsuf Ya'qūb ibn Isḥāq al-Kindī (died about 870 C.E.). Al-Kindī's circle did not produce as many translations as the Ḥunayn circle, yet some of the works they did translate were of immense importance in determining the Arabic reception of Greek philosophical thought. It is quite likely that the choice of which texts to translate was guided in part by the philosophical concerns of al-Kindī and his collaborators. The translations took various forms. Some stay close to the text yet are awkward compared to Ḥunayn's productions, which were marked by superior method (e.g., the collation of numerous manuscripts) and a more advanced and consistent technical terminology.[3] An example is the translation of Aristotle's

Metaphysics written in al-Kindī's circle.[4] Other translations were relatively loose paraphrases of their source texts. Here considerable liberties were taken with the Greek sources, whose Arabic versions might be differently arranged and even include original elaborations written by members of the translation circle. Examples include a paraphrase of Aristotle's *De Anima*,[5] the famous *Theology of Aristotle*, and the *Book on the Pure Good* (known in Latin as the *Liber de Causis*).

The approach used in these interpretive paraphrases gives us an initial indication of the aims of the translation movement as far as al-Kindī was concerned. Al-Kindī himself did not make translations, and it is quite possible that he could not even read Greek. Rather, he oversaw the work of the translators, and drew on the results in his own writings.[6] Al-Kindī described his own project as the attempt to "supply completely what the ancients said . . . and to complete what they did not say comprehensively, in accordance with the custom of language and the practices of the time" (103.9–11). This required the production of a new philosophical vocabulary in Arabic, a process that began in al-Kindī circle translations and that al-Kindī furthered in his original compositions. For example, a treatise *On the Definitions and Descriptions of Things*, which is most likely by al-Kindī, provides an overview of the new Arabic philosophical terminology, with definitions based on Greek sources. As we will see, al-Kindī's advertisement of Greek thought also meant showing the relevance of philosophical ideas for solving contemporary problems, including problems emerging from Islamic theology (*kalām*).

The works in which al-Kindī pursued these goals were treatises of varying length, in the form of epistles addressed to his sponsors (most frequently the son of the caliph al-Mu'taṣim). Al-Kindī's output was vast. A list of his works shows that he wrote hundreds of treatises in a startling array of fields, ranging from metaphysics, ethics, and psychology (i.e., the study of the soul), to medicine, mathematics, astronomy, and optics, and further afield to more practical topics like perfumes and swords.[7] Most of these treatises are lost, and those that remain are a reminder of the fragility of the historical record of this early period of Arabic thought: many of his philosophical works survive only in a single manuscript.

Because of al-Kindī's avowed dependence on Greek philosophy, the specificity of the topics he deals with in his treatises, and the occasional inconsistency between his extant writings, it can be difficult to see a novel and coherent system emerging from the Kindian corpus. This is hardly surprising, given that al-Kindī was attempting to integrate numerous disparate strands of Greek philosophy, especially Aristotelianism and Neoplatonism. The fact that he was even able to undertake such a task with his relatively limited resources can only be explained by the fact that, as we will see, the way had been prepared for him by the late ancients. It was above all their example that al-Kindī followed in writing his own philosophical works.

METAPHYSICS AS THEOLOGY

Among these works the most complex and important is *On First Philosophy*, which is a treatise in four parts (it seems originally to have contained more material, which is now lost), dedicated to the subject of metaphysics.[8] The first part, which includes the statement of purpose quoted above, is nothing less than a defense of Hellenism. Al-Kindī argues that Greek thought is to be welcomed, despite its foreign provenance, because our own inquiry into the truth is greatly assisted by those who have achieved truth in the past. Al-Kindī also does not omit to point out the relevance of Greek metaphysics for his Muslim audience. The study of metaphysics includes, and is even primarily, the study of God: "the noblest part of philosophy and the highest in degree is first philosophy, by which I mean the science of the First Truth, Who is the cause of all truth" (98.1–2). This distillation of metaphysics into theology affected the way that generations of philosophers read Aristotle: later Avicenna said that reading al-Fārābī freed him from his misunderstanding of Aristotle's *Metaphysics*, and it has been plausibly suggested that the misunderstanding in question was the Kindian interpretation that the work deals primarily with God.[9] Al-Fārābī, followed by Avicenna, held that first philosophy is the study of being qua being, and only incidentally of God. Al-Kindī, by contrast, does not leave room for a sharp distinction between theology and metaphysics.

Indeed, the surviving part of *On First Philosophy* ends climactically with a statement of God's nature. The path al-Kindī takes to that statement is somewhat surprising, however. Although allusions to Aristotle proliferate in *On First Philosophy*, the work as a whole contains two major elements, neither of which looks especially Aristotelian. The first of these is in fact a rejection of Aristotle's thesis that the world is eternal. Al-Kindī's arguments here are drawn from the avowedly anti-Aristotelian polemics of the late Greek Christian Neoplatonist commentator John Philoponus.[10] These arguments attempt to show that the created world cannot be infinite. Time – and therefore motion, since time is the measure of motion – must have a beginning. In this al-Kindī differs from the subsequent Aristotelian tradition in Arabic. Avicenna and Averroes in particular are well known for having defended Aristotle's thesis of the eternal world.

The other major element of *On First Philosophy* is a discussion of oneness (*waḥda*). Al-Kindī first shows that in the created world, all things are characterized by both multiplicity and unity. For example, things that have parts are both many (because the parts are numerous) and one (because the parts form a whole). None of these things are a "true unity," by which al-Kindī means something that is one in every respect, and not multiple in any way. Rather, the created things have a source of unity, something that is "essentially one," which again means utterly one, and not at all multiple.[11] Al-Kindī elaborates by drawing on Aristotle's *Categories* (and also on an introduction to that work, the *Isagoge*, written by the Neoplatonist Porphyry) to provide us with a comprehensive list of the sorts of thing that can be said (*maqūlāt*). These include accidents, species, genera, and various others. Now, whatever is said of something, argues al-Kindī, must involve multiplicity. Sometimes this is obvious, as in the examples "this elephant weighs two tons" and "this elephant is twenty years old," where we have as predicates weight and time, both of which are divisible by measurement (in this case into two and twenty, respectively). But it is also the case for statements like "this is a body" and "this animal belongs to the species *elephant*." Here we have two further kinds of multiplicity: first "body," which is divided into many, because bodies have many parts, and then "elephant," which is divided into many, because there are many elephants. No concept or predicate that can be ascribed to something is compatible with absolute oneness.

Because God, the source of all unity, is the true One in question, the argument entails a very rigorous negative theology. Anything that can be said of something else will be inapplicable to the absolutely one. As al-Kindī says, "the true One possesses no matter or form, quantity or quality, or relation, and is not described by any of the other categories; nor does He possess genus, difference, individual, property, common accident, or motion . . . He is therefore nothing but pure oneness (*waḥda faqaṭ maḥd*)" (160.13–16). This seems to be something of a counsel of despair for would-be theologians: the conclusion is apparently that nothing at all can be known or said about God. Yet there is a more positive basis for theology lurking here, because after all al-Kindī is willing to say at least two things about God: that he is "one," and that he is the source of the oneness in created things. (As we will see shortly, this is pivotal in al-Kindī's understanding of God as a Creator. He believes that for God to bestow oneness on something is to make that thing exist, in other words, to create it.) We might, then, extrapolate to a general method for talking about God. Whatever characteristic God has, he has it absolutely, and in no way possesses its opposite; he is also the source of that characteristic for other things. In this case, because God is one, he cannot be multiple in any way and is the cause of all oneness.

In another work, *On the True, First, Complete Agent and the Deficient Agent that is [only an Agent] Metaphorically*, al-Kindī uses the same method to affirm that God is an "agent" (*fā'il*, which also means "efficient cause"). In fact he is strictly speaking the *only* agent, because he alone acts without being acted upon. In other words, he is fully and absolutely active, and in no way passive, just as he is absolutely one and in no way multiple. Created things, meanwhile, are only "metaphorically" agents, because they can only transmit God's agency in a chain of causes (similarly, in *On First Philosophy* al-Kindī says that created things are only "metaphorically" one, because they are also many). The idea here seems to be that God acts through intermediary causes: God acts on something, then that "acts" on something else, and so on. But these secondary causes really do not "act" at all, they only serve to convey God's action to the next link in the chain.

We seem to be quite distant here from the author who was the most important influence on al-Kindī, namely Aristotle. If anything, al-Kindī's characterization of God seems more reminiscent of the Platonic theory of Forms. Plato had stressed that, unlike physical things, the Forms excluded their opposites: a heavy elephant is light compared to a mountain, but the Form of Heavy is in no way light. Similarly God, the true One and agent, is in no way multiple or passive. Yet al-Kindī did not know Plato well and what he did know likely came to him only indirectly. By contrast, al-Kindī knew Aristotle quite well and uses Aristotelian concepts and terminology constantly, both in *On First Philosophy* and elsewhere. But often he deploys these concepts to defend views and devise arguments that are not to be found in Aristotle. Thus if we go straight from Plato and Aristotle to al-Kindī, it will seem that there is very little continuity between Greek and early Arabic philosophy.

Yet this is an entirely misleading impression, and one dispelled by noting that Aristotle came down to al-Kindī filtered through the works of the late ancients. We have already mentioned a few of these figures, and their impact on Arabic philosophy has been discussed in the previous chapter. But the importance of late ancient thought for al-Kindī is so great that it will be worth reviewing here some of the authors who bridge the gap between Aristotle and al-Kindī. First, there are the schools of Hellenistic philosophy: the Stoics, Skeptics, and Epicureans. The latter two schools seem to have left no trace in al-Kindī's philosophy and the Stoics only faint traces in al-Kindī's ethics: in his work of consolation, *On the Art of Dispelling Sorrows*, al-Kindī uses an allegory from Epictetus' *Handbook*, comparing our earthly life to a sojourn on land that interrupts a sea voyage.[12]

The major influence is rather the Greek Neoplatonic tradition, which runs roughly from the career of Plotinus (205–70 C.E.) until 529 C.E., when the Platonic school was closed in Athens. Al-Kindī knew versions of the *Enneads* of Plotinus and *Elements of Theology* of Proclus, which were rendered into Arabic as the above-mentioned *Theology of Aristotle* and *Book on the Pure Good*, respectively. Both of these were later thought to have been written by Aristotle, but al-Kindī was probably aware that they were not genuinely Aristotle's. Still he saw Aristotle and Neoplatonism as compatible, and this for two reasons. Firstly, since al-Kindī was in the business of advertising the power and truth of Greek philosophy, he was predisposed to see all of ancient thought as a single, coherent system. Convinced of the truth of Aristotle's philosophy and the truth of Neoplatonism, he could hardly admit that the two were incompatible with one another.[13] Secondly, he was exposed to Aristotle together with some of the vast corpus of commentaries written on him, by the

Aristotelian Alexander of Aphrodisias but also by Neoplatonists such as Porphyry and John Philoponus.[14]

Al-Kindī's apparently unorthodox interpretation of Aristotle is thus in fact a sign of the continuity of Greek and Arabic thought, since it is based on Neoplatonic interpretations of and reactions to Aristotle. We have already seen several examples of this. Perhaps the most important is a point that is easily taken for granted: al-Kindī believes that God is an *efficient* cause, not just a final cause, and he seems to think that Aristotle would agree. (An efficient cause acts to produce its effect, whereas a final cause exercises causality only by being the object of striving or desire.) In this al-Kindī is, perhaps unwittingly, adopting the interpretation of the Neoplatonist Ammonius, who wrote an entire work urging that Aristotle's God is an efficient as well as final cause.[15] This is a crucial contribution to the history of Arabic philosophy on al-Kindī's part, because it makes it possible to see the God of Aristotle (a pure, immaterial intellect, and an unmoved cause of motion) as compatible with two other rival theologies. First, we have the Neoplatonic theory, according to which the One or God "emanates" the world from himself, in an outpouring or overflowing of generosity and power that is mediated by Intellect. Second, there is God as the Creator of Islam and the other revealed religions. However we interpret this notion of God as "creating," it would seem to involve efficient and not merely final causality.

In fact al-Kindī affirms all three of these portrayals of God, Aristotelian, Neoplatonic, and creationist. He says that God is an unmoved mover, but also that God gives from himself to his creation. Here he uses the term *fayḍ*, "emanation," and as we saw in *On the True Agent* he affirms the Neoplatonic idea that God acts on the world through intermediary causes. God's act is creation, which he defines as "bringing being to be from non-being" (118.18), and God is the principle of being, "the true being" (*al-anniyya al-ḥaqqa*) (215.4), just as he is the principle of agency and of oneness. In fact these various characterizations of God seem to be closely related, if not equivalent. When God creates, he emanates oneness or being onto a thing, where these two are synonymous at least in God ("his oneness is nothing other than his being," 161.14, cf. 160.4–5). He puts the point in a more Aristotelian way when he says that God creates something by "bringing it forth (*kharaja*) into actuality" (257.10, 375.13). The view is presented with a good deal of technical terminology, but it has an intuitive plausibility. When God creates an elephant, for example, he makes the elephant *be*, which is to make it be *one* in a certain way, namely "one elephant," not an elephant that merely could exist but an elephant that *actually* does exist.

This interpretation of divine creation, at once Aristotelian, Neoplatonic, and Islamic, would echo through the rest of the Arabic tradition. Aspects of it are anticipated by late ancient authors. The notion of God as a First Principle that is paradigmatically one and the source of oneness for all other things, is found in both Plotinus and Proclus, on whom al-Kindī drew in *On First Philosophy*. This idea of God as the principle of being is found, not in Plotinus, but in the Arabic version of his works, the *Theology of Aristotle*, as well as in the *Book on the Pure Good*.[16] And John Philoponus' polemics against Aristotle provided a source for the definition of creation as the manifestation of being from non-being.

In his most extensive discussion of creation, which appears incongruously enough in a survey of Aristotle's corpus (*On the Quantity of Aristotle's Books*), al-Kindī again draws on Philoponus' *Against Aristotle on the Eternity of the World*.[17] In the course of his attack on Aristotle, Philoponus had spoken of creation as God's bringing something to be from non-being (*mê on*), and al-Kindī repeats the point. Al-Kindī's argument for this conception of creation in *On the Quantity of Aristotle's Books* follows Philoponus' strategy of using Aristotle against himself. A basic Aristotelian principle is that all change involves contraries. For something to become hot, it must first have been cold. Al-Kindī applies this principle to God's act of creation, reasoning that it too must involve a passage from one contrary to another. In this case, what God creates receives being, as we have seen. It must then be that what is created was previously in a state of "not-being." This gives al-Kindī a further reason to hold, with Philoponus, that there must be a first moment of creation. If there were not, and the world were eternal, then the world would always have being, and there would be no need for God to "create" the world at all – that is, to bring it from not-being to being.

PSYCHOLOGY

Nor was this the only set of issues on which Philoponus influenced al-Kindī. Among al-Kindī's most historically significant works is the brief *On the Intellect*.[18] Again, the treatise is incomprehensible without reference to late ancient authors. It reflects their understanding of Aristotle's theory of intellect, as presented in the third book of his *De Anima* (*On the Soul*). To take account of the various things that Aristotle says there about intellect, late ancient authors such as Alexander, Themistius, and Philoponus had distinguished between several stages or kinds of intellect. It seems that this taxonomy of intellects reached al-Kindī from Philoponus, though al-Kindī does not agree with Philoponus' account in all its details.

Al-Kindī presents the theory that there is a separate, immaterial "first" intellect, which is not identified with God as was sometimes done by the late ancients. Individual human intellects are distinct from this first intellect. They start out "in potency," that is, with an ability to grasp universal concepts. But this ability is realized only when the first intellect, which is always thinking about all the universals, "makes our potential intellect become actual," in other words makes the human intellect actually think about a given universal concept. Why can't human intellects reach these concepts on their own, without the help of the first intellect? Al-Kindī's answer is that just as, for example, wood is potentially hot and needs something actually hot such as fire to actualize that potential hotness, so the intellect that is only potentially thinking about something needs a cause to make it actually think. That cause must actually be thinking about the same concept, just as fire must actually be hot to cause heat. The cause of the actualization in the case of thinking is the first intellect. Once this has happened the concept is stored in one's mental library, which al-Kindī calls the "acquired intellect" – and from then on one can think about it whenever one wishes.

This short treatise has perhaps more significance as a precursor of the more famous treatments of intellect found in al-Fārābī, Avicenna, and Averroes, than it does in helping us understand al-Kindī's other works. Al-Kindī does not often invoke the technical distinction between kinds of intellect in his other works. Yet another distinction made in *On the Intellect* is of fundamental importance for al-Kindī's general theory of human knowledge. As is clear from the foregoing, al-Kindī does not think that humans can obtain general or universal concepts directly from sense perception. That is, I cannot acquire the universal concept of elephant just by looking at a single elephant, or even a herd of elephants. When I look at an elephant, al-Kindī thinks that I only receive a "sensible form," in other words the visual representation of the elephant. This is to be distinguished from the purely immaterial concept that is the species of elephant, which al-Kindī also calls a "form," but a universal form. The distinction between sensible and universal form appears in *On First Philosophy* as well as in *On the Intellect*, and it again allows al-Kindī to have his cake and eat it too in his response to the Greek philosophical tradition. He can remain faithful to Aristotle's empiricist epistemology by saying that we do learn about the world by receiving (sensible) forms through the bodily organs. But at the same time he accepts a more Neoplatonic epistemology. According to this epistemology there is a separate intellect that is always thinking about all universal forms, and humans come to grasp these latter forms by virtue of a relationship with that separate intellect.

This theory of knowledge is crucial for al-Kindī's treatment of soul. His psychology is set out in several works, but especially the *Discourse on the Soul*, which, in a pattern now becoming familiar to us, promises a treatment of the soul based on Aristotle, but moves on to a distinctly un-Aristotelian treatment of the topic at hand. The soul, says al-Kindī, is a "simple substance" (273.4), immaterial and related to the material world only by having faculties that are exercised through the body.[19] Echoing Plato's *Phaedo*, but also with allusions to Pythagoreanism and the *Theology of Aristotle*,[20] al-Kindī stresses that these faculties (the irascible and desiring faculties) are apt to lead the soul astray and plunge it further into association with the body. The soul's good is to concentrate on its "intellectual" aspect. If it does this it may, especially after death, come to be in a purely "intelligible world," and "in the light of the Creator" (275.12–13). I can be assured that my soul will in fact survive to take part in such an afterlife because its distinction from my body shows that the death of my body will not mean the death of my soul. Rather, as an immaterial and simple substance, my soul is immortal.

Thus, just as al-Kindī's epistemology rests on the distinction of sensible from intellectual forms, so his eschatology exhorts us to reject the sensible and pursue the intelligible. His major ethical work, *On the Art of Dispelling Sorrows*,[21] emphasizes this dichotomy:

> It is impossible for someone to attain everything he seeks, or to keep all of the things he loves safe from loss, because stability and permanence are

nonexistent in the world of generation and corruption we inhabit. Necessarily, stability and permanence exist only in the world of the intellect (*'ālam al-'aql*). (I.5–9)

Here al-Kindī, characteristically synthesizing disparate strands of ancient thought, combines a Stoic idea with a Neoplatonic idea. The Stoic idea is that we should not base our happiness on things in the physical world, because they are liable to be taken away from us. Rather, we should only value what is permanent, namely – and here is the Neoplatonic idea – the intellectual world, with its immaterial, universal forms. Again, al-Kindī anticipates later Arabic philosophy even as he echoes Greek thought, by claiming that philosophy itself is the highest good for humankind. For philosophy is the study of universal forms and takes us away from our desires for the transient things of this world. The afterlife al-Kindī offers us is nothing more nor less than an enduring grasp of these forms: a philosopher's vision of paradise.[22]

NATURAL SCIENCE

These considerations might lead one to expect that al-Kindī would have little interest in the strictly physical sciences. But nothing could be further from the truth. Like other Neoplatonizing Aristotelians, al-Kindī believes that empirical science is an integral part of philosophy. This is at least in part because knowledge of the sensible world allows us to study God indirectly: as he says, "in things evident to the senses there is a most manifest indication" of God and his providence (214.9). In fact a large proportion of al-Kindī's lost works dealt with the physical sciences, to judge by their titles, and several that have been preserved do so as well. Two such sciences are particularly well represented in the extant corpus: cosmology and optics.

Cosmology and Astrology

Like his successors in the Arabic philosophical tradition, al-Kindī accepts the cosmology handed down from Ptolemy and Aristotle, according to which the earth is at the center of a spherical universe. It is surrounded by spheres in which the planets are embedded (starting with the moon and the sun, both of which are considered to be planets), and ultimately by the sphere of the fixed stars. There is some hint in al-Kindī that the soul will become associated with the planetary spheres after death: he ascribes such a view to Pythagoras in the *Discourse on the Soul*. But for al-Kindī the most important role played by the heavens is that they are the instrument of divine providence. In an epistle devoted to explaining a passage in the Qur'ān that says the heavens "prostrate themselves" or "bow down" before God (*On the Bowing of the Outermost Sphere*), al-Kindī argues that the stars must be alive, because they engage in a perfect and regular circular motion around the earth. Indeed, he argues, the stars are possessed of rational souls, and their motion is the result of their obedience to the command of God.

This motion commanded by God is, as al-Kindī puts it in the title of another work, *The Proximate Agent Cause of Generation and Corruption*. In other words, the heavens are the immediate cause for all the things that come to be and perish in the world of the four elements, the world below the moon. (The non-proximate, or remote, original cause is of course God himself.) Al-Kindī proves this empirically: he says that we can all see that weather and the seasons depend on the motions of the heavens, most obviously that of the sun, and also points out that the appearance and character of people varies depending on where in the world they live. This, too, is to be ascribed to heavenly influence. Al-Kindī has two incompatible explanations of how this influence is brought about. In *Proximate Agent Cause*, he draws on Alexander of Aphrodisias[23] to argue that the rotation of the heavenly spheres literally causes friction when they move around each other and the sublunar world. This friction stirs up the four elements, earth, air, fire, and water, combining them to yield the production of all things in the natural world.

But in another work preserved only in Latin, entitled *On Rays*, al-Kindī gives a different explanation. This time he tries to subsume the explanation of heavenly influence within a general account of action at a distance. He says that many causes exercise their activity via "rays," which travel along straight lines. For example, fire warms things by sending rays of heat in all directions. In the case of the stars, the strongest influence from a star will be on the place on the earth directly under it along a straight line. Clearly this explanation differs from that given in the more Aristotelian *Proximate Agent Cause*, and in fact the two texts have fundamentally different views of physical interaction: *On Rays* explains interaction at a distance, while *Proximate Agent Cause* tries to reduce what is apparently action at a distance to action by contact, namely the rubbing of spheres that produces friction. This contrast will reappear in al-Kindī's treatment of optics.

However their influence is explained, it seems that for al-Kindī the heavens are the direct cause of everything that happens in the natural world. While their most obvious effects, such as the change of seasons, can be predicted by anyone, there is also a science that predicts less obvious events by analyzing the motion of the stars. This is astrology. Many of al-Kindī's works, both extant and lost, were devoted to applied astrology, and promised to help solve questions such as "How can I find buried treasure?" "What is the most auspicious time for me to take a journey?" and "How long will the Arabs rule?" The contingencies of textual transmission magnified the astrological side of al-Kindī's thought in subsequent centuries, so that medievals reading him in Latin thought of al-Kindī largely as an astrologer. But they were not wrong in seeing astrology as an important part of his thought, and it is no coincidence that the greatest of Arabic astrologers, Abū Ma'shar al-Balkhī, was a student or associate of al-Kindī.[24]

Perhaps the most important aspect of al-Kindī's interest in the heavens, from a philosophical point of view, is his assertion that their motions are the instruments of divine providence. Here we have simultaneously an affirmation of the universality of that providence, insofar as all things in our world are brought about by the stars and the stars are made to move by God, and an affirmation of the idea that God's providence can be grasped and even predicted through a rational, empirical science (for this is what al-Kindī believed astrology to be). At the same time his cosmology seems to be an application of the distinction made in *On the True Agent*. God is the originative source of action, and this action is merely transferred by his proximate effect, the heavens, to the more remote effects, namely us and the sublunar world in which we live.

Optics

In the case of optics, it is easier to see how al-Kindī's view responds directly to the Greek philosophical tradition, even as he in some respects anticipates the achievements of the great Ibn al-Haytham (died 1041).[25] Essentially al-Kindī is caught between two authorities:

Aristotle and Euclid. Al-Kindī draws on both of them in numerous works on vision, the most important of which (again, preserved only in Latin) is *On Perspectives*, a reworking and expansion of Euclid's *Optics*.[26] The conflicting influence of Aristotle and Euclid in optics is at least as thorny a problem for al-Kindī as the conflicting metaphysical views of Aristotle and the Neoplatonists. For Aristotle, vision occurs when a sensible form is transmitted to the eye through a transparent medium, like air. The medium can only transmit the sensible form when it is filled with light. Thus four things are required for vision: a sensible object, an eye, a transparent medium between eye and object, and light filling the medium. The optics of Euclid, by contrast, offered geometrical constructions explaining optical phenomena on the basis that vision and light always proceed along straight lines. Such constructions are used, for example, to explain how mirrors reflect images or light at certain angles, and why shadows fall at certain lengths. The explanatory power of these constructions raises problems for the Aristotelian theory. Al-Kindī repeats an example taken from Theon of Alexandria to illustrate the difficulty: if we look at a circle from the side, we see a line, not a circle. But according to Aristotle's theory, a circle should only transmit its own (circular) form through the medium. Aristotle cannot explain why things look different from different angles.

For this and other reasons, al-Kindī rejects the Aristotelian theory of vision, which is an "intromission" theory: something (a sensible form) must come into my eye from outside. Instead al-Kindī accepts an "extramission" theory, according to which our eyes send visual rays out into the world.[27] When these rays strike illuminated objects, we see the objects. The advantage of this theory is that the rays are straight lines, which accommodates the Euclidean geometrical model of sight. Al-Kindī applies the same model to the propagation of light, and makes the significant advance of proposing that light proceeds in straight lines and in all directions, from every point on a luminous surface. This fits well with *On Rays*, which says that things interact at a distance by virtue of rays that convey causal power.[28] In his works on vision al-Kindī prefers this model of action at a distance to the Aristotelian model of action by direct contact (the eye touches the medium, which touches the object, and this allows the form to go from object to medium to eye). Nevertheless, as we saw above, he is still willing to speak elsewhere of the reception of "sensible forms" in the case of vision and the other senses.

AL-KINDĪ AND ISLAM

Thus in the physical sciences, we see tensions analogous to those found in al-Kindī's metaphysics. Inconsistencies may result, but al-Kindī always follows the same method of drawing on the ancients and trying to smooth over such tensions as he is able. While it is thus impossible to appreciate al-Kindī's works without knowledge of the Greek tradition, it would be incorrect to say that the *only* interest of his works is his reception and modification of Greek thought. As indicated above, al-Kindī tries to present Greek philosophy as capable of solving problems of his own time, including problems prompted by Islamic theological concerns. The most obvious sign of this is that al-Kindī uses philosophy to gloss Qur'ānic texts. *On the Bowing of the Outermost Sphere* explains why the Qur'ān (55:6) says that the heavens and trees "prostrate themselves" before God. Al-Kindī uses this as an opportunity to lay out the idea, discussed above, that the heavens are the instrument of divine providence. He prefaces this with a short lesson on how to deal with ambiguous terms in interpretation of Scripture.

Another instance of Qur'ānic exegesis is the aforementioned digression on creation in *On the Quantity of Aristotle's Books*. Here part of Qur'ān 36, which includes the declaration: "when God wills something, his command is to say to it: 'Be!' and it is," is the occasion for al-Kindī to argue that creation is bringing being from non-being. He also provides a few remarks contrasting the prophet to the philosopher. Philosophers must engage in long study, first mastering introductory sciences like mathematics. Prophets, by contrast,

> do not need any of this, but [only] the will of him who bestows their message upon them, without time, occupation in study, or anything else . . . Let us consider the answers given by the prophets to questions put to them about secret and true matters. The philosopher may intend to answer such questions with great effort, using his own devices, which he has at his disposal due to long perseverance in inquiry and exercise. But we will find that he does not arrive at what he seeks with anything like the brevity, clarity, unerringness (*qurb al-sabīl*), and comprehensiveness that is shown by the answer of the Prophet. (373.7–15)

This is al-Kindī's most important statement about the nature of prophecy. At first glance it seems to put the philosopher at quite a disadvantage relative to the prophet. But on closer inspection we may rather be surprised at how limited is the superiority of the prophet. This superiority is due only to two things: the ease and certainty with which he achieves the truth, and the way he presents it (his statement is briefer, clearer, and more complete). The crucial implication is that the *content* of the philosopher's and the prophet's knowledge are the same.[29] Certainly this makes sense of what al-Kindī does in both this text and *On the Bowing of the Outermost Sphere*: he gives a philosophical explanation of a truth that is expressed more succinctly and elegantly in the Qur'ān.

Another significant text for al-Kindī's ideas about prophecy is his epistle *On Sleep and Dream*. Here al-Kindī draws on the psychology he has presented in other works, with its division of the soul's faculties into those of sensation and of intellection. Associated with the sensory faculties is the faculty Aristotle called "imagination" (al-Kindī uses both the Arabic term *quwwa muṣawwira*, i.e., the faculty that receives forms, and a transliteration of the Greek term *phantasia*, 295.4–6). Imagination receives and entertains sensible forms in the absence of their "bearers" – for example, it allows us to picture an elephant even when there is no elephant in the room. It also allows us to combine sensible forms to produce a merely imaginary image, like a man with feathers. In sleep, when the use of the senses ceases, the imagination may still be active, resulting in the images we call dreams. Having established this, al-Kindī goes on to explain the phenomenon of the prophetic dream (*ru'yā*). Persons possessed of particularly "pure" and well-prepared souls can actually receive the forms of sensible things in their imagination before those things happen, and thus see into the future. This happens most easily when the senses are not active, that is, when we are dreaming. Now, al-Kindī does not connect any of this to specifically *religious* prophecy, nor does he say that God is the source of the prophecy involved in dreams (as he does in *On the Quantity of Aristotle's Books* with regard to Muḥammad's prophecy).[30] But it is very tempting to compare this work of al-Kindī's to other naturalistic explanations of the miraculous abilities of prophets, as criticized by al-Ghazālī in *The Incoherence of the Philosophers*.

Beyond the specific question of prophecy, the relevance of al-Kindī's works for Islamic theology often remains implicit. But many themes discussed above need to be understood against the background of ninth-century Islam just as much as sixth-century Greek thought. From this point of view al-Kindī's most important interlocutors are not Aristotelian commentators, but practitioners of *kalām*, or rational theology, and especially the Muʿtazilites. Titles of some of his lost works show that al-Kindī engaged in detailed refutation of some Muʿtazilite views, especially their atomist physics. Yet al-Kindī seems to have been in agreement with several broader positions that later writers would use, somewhat anachronistically, to define the Muʿtazilite "school" of the third/ninth century.[31] For example, the issue of divine attributes is a chief point of contact between al-Kindī's *falsafa* and the *kalām* of the Muʿtazilites. For both, a tendency toward negative theology is motivated by the need to assert God's absolute oneness. For the Muʿtazilites, a plurality of attributes distinct from God's essence would violate *tawḥīd*, or divine oneness. For, suppose that God is both good and merciful, and that his goodness and his mercy are distinct from one another and from God himself. Then we have not one but three things: God, his goodness, and his mercy. This violates the requirement of Islam that nothing else "share" in God's divinity. In *kalām* of the time this is often expressed by saying that nothing other than God can be "eternal," where "eternal" is taken to imply "uncreated." Thus the Muʿtazilites also insisted that the Qur'ān was created, and not eternal alongside God himself, as some thought because the Qur'ān is God's word. This contrast helps us to make sense of the otherwise jarring juxtaposition of the argument against the eternity of the world and the proof of God's absolute oneness in al-Kindī's *On First Philosophy*. As we have seen, al-Kindī likewise takes the thesis that the world is eternal as tantamount to the thesis that the world is uncreated. Thus proving that the world is not eternal is closely related to showing the absolute uniqueness and oneness of God.[32]

Al-Kindī's position as the first self-described philosopher of the Islamic world makes him a transitional figure in several respects. His philosophy is continuous with the ancient tradition, even as it begins to respond to a very different intellectual milieu. To some extent al-Kindī's reception of Greek philosophy set the agenda for *falsafa* in the generations to come: for instance, his treatment of intellect and theory of creation resonate throughout Arabic philosophy. Above all, the attempt to assimilate Greek thought in al-Kindī's circle proves the wider points that translation is always interpretation and that philosophers can be at their most creative when they take up the task of understanding their predecessors. It would seem that al-Kindī aspired only to transmit Greek philosophy and display its power and coherence. The best indication of his success is the very tradition of philosophy in Arabic that he inaugurated.[33] But a corollary to this understanding of his project is that he had no intention of being innovative or creative in the way I have described. He meant to be unoriginal, and in this respect, he failed.

NOTES

1 See further Gutas [58].

2 For a useful overview of Ḥunayn's career see A. Z. Iskandar, "Ḥunayn Ibn Isḥāq," in *The Dictionary of Scientific Biography* (New York: 1978), vol. XV (suppl. I), 230–49. A classic study of an epistle in which Ḥunayn describes his activities translating Galen is G. Bergsträsser, "Ḥunayn Ibn Isḥāq über die syrischen und arabischen Galenübersetzungen," *Abhandlungen für die Kunde des Morgenlandes* 17.2 (1925).

3 The shortcomings of the al-Kindī circle translations were obvious enough to cause complaint. For instance, al-Ṣafadī says that two of al-Kindī's translators, Ibn Nāʿima al-Ḥimṣī and Ibn al-Biṭrīq, slavishly translated their sources word for word, whereas the Ḥunayn circle would translate the sentence as a whole, and preserve its meaning. The passage is translated in Rosenthal [39], 17.

4 The translation is one of those used by Averroes in his long commentary on the *Metaphysics*: Averroes, *Tafsīr mā baʿd al-ṭabīʿa*, ed. M. Bouyges (Beirut: 1973). See further A. Martin, "La *Métaphysique*: tradition syriaque et arabe," in Goulet [20], vol. I, 528–34.

5 See R. Arnzen, *Aristoteles "De Anima": Eine verlorene spätantike Paraphrase in arabischer und persischer Überlieferung* (Leiden: 1998). This work may simply reflect the paraphrase of its Greek source.

6 Al-Kindī's works are cited from vol. I of al-Kindī [70], with page and line number given. (Improved editions, with facing-page French translations, are appearing in a new series of volumes, al-Kindī [71], with two volumes having appeared so far.)

7 The list is found in Ibn al-Nadīm, *al-Fihrist*, ed. R. Tagaddod (Tehran: 1350 A.H./1950 A.D.), at 315–20, and trans. B. Dodge (New York: 1970), at 615–26.

8 See the translation and commentary in Ivry [68].

9 See Gutas [93], 238–54.

10 See H. A. Davidson, "John Philoponus as a Source of Medieval, Islamic and Jewish Proofs of Creation," *Journal of the American Oriental Society* 89 (1969), 357–91.

11 Compare this to the proof of the One as first principle in the final proposition of the *Book on the Pure Good* (*Liber de Causis*).

12 For this work see H. Ritter and R. Walzer, *Uno scritto morale inedito di al-Kindī* (Rome: 1938) and Druart [66].

13 An example of this tendency is al-Kindī's *Brief Statement on the Soul,* which says of two remarks on the soul putatively from Plato and Aristotle, "someone could think that there is a difference between these two statements" (281.10), but goes on to explain how there is in fact no disagreement between the two.

14 As Cristina D'Ancona has remarked, "one tends to forget that the intermingling of Aristotle and Neoplatonism occurred primarily in the *Aristotelian* works read within a Neoplatonic framework and only secondarily in works like the so-called *Theology of Aristotle,*" in her review of Arnzen, *Aristoteles "De Anima," Oriens* 36 (2001), 340–51, at 344.

15 Simplicius, *Commentary on the "Physics"*, ed. H. Diels, *CAG* IX–X (Berlin: 1882, 1895), 1363.

16 See the studies collected in D'Ancona [51]; R. C. Taylor, "Aquinas, the *Plotiniana Arabica* and the Metaphysics of Being and Actuality," *Journal of the History of Ideas* 59 (1998), 241–64; and my *The Arabic Plotinus: A Philosophical Study of the "Theology of Aristotle"* (London: 2002), ch. 5.

17 As shown in Adamson [62].

18 See Jolivet [69], which shows that *On the Intellect* depends on Philoponus.

19 In *That There Are Separate Substances*, al-Kindī proves that the human soul is immaterial by showing that it is the species of the human and therefore an intelligible object. This is another application of the distinction between sensible and intellectual forms: the soul is a form of the latter kind. The terminology allows al-Kindī to remain nominally faithful to Aristotle's definition of soul as the "form of the body."

20 See C. Genequand, "Platonism and Hermeticism in al-Kindī's *fī al-Nafs,*" *Zeitschrift für Geschichte der arabisch-islamischen Wissenschaften* 4 (1987/8), 1–18, and my "Two Early Arabic Doxographies on the Soul: Al-Kindī and the 'Theology of Aristotle,'" *The Modern Schoolman* 77 (2000), 105–25.

21 See above, n. 12.

22 For a different understanding of *On the Art of Dispelling Sorrows* see below, chapter 13.

23 As shown in S. Fazzo and H. Wiesner, "Alexander of Aphrodisias in the Kindī-Circle and in al-Kindī's Cosmology," *Arabic Sciences and Philosophy* 3 (1993), 119–53.

24 See my "Abū Ma'shar, al-Kindī and the Philosophical Defense of Astrology," *Recherches de philosophie et théologie médiévales* 69 (2002), 245–70.

25 See D. C. Lindberg, "Alkindi's Critique of Euclid's Theory of Vision," *Isis* 62 (1971), 469–89.

26 Al-Kindī [71], vol. I, 438–523.

27 This theory may be compared with that of Plato, *Timaeus*, 45b–46c.

28 For a study comparing *On Rays* and *On Perspectives*, see P. Travaglia, *Magic, Causality, and Intentionality: The Doctrine of Rays in al-Kindī* (Turnhout: 1999).

29 For a similar interpretation see Endress [15], 8.

30 This may be contrasted to the Arabic version of Aristotle's *Parva Naturalia*, which does explicitly name God as the source of prophetic dreams: see S. Pines, "The Arabic Recension of the *Parva Naturalia*," *Israel Oriental Studies* 4 (1974), 104–53, at 130–2.

31 So-called "Mu'tazilites" often argued bitterly with one another and were not yet a unified school with a single body of doctrines. The best source of information on *kalām* in this period is van Ess [44].

32 For further discussion of al-Kindī's relationship to the Mu'tazilites, see Adamson [62].

33 Here it may be helpful to say something about al-Kindī's direct legacy. Abū Ma'shar, the astrologer who has already been mentioned above, was a significant associate, and two of his students were al-Sarakhsī (on whom see F. Rosenthal, *Aḥmad b. aṭ-Ṭayyib as-Sarakhsī* [New Haven, CT: 1943]) and Abū Zayd al-Balkhī. Abū Zayd lived long enough to be the teacher of the fourth/tenth-century philosopher al-'Āmirī, who drew on al-Kindī and the works produced in his circle. Al-Kindī also directly influenced other Neoplatonic thinkers in this later period, like Ibn Miskawayh. But around the same time al-Fārābī did not favor al-Kindī's synthesis of Greek thought, as mentioned above. Avicenna's preference for the Farabian view over the Kindian may explain why al-Kindī receives scant attention in the later tradition, dominated as it was by the task of responding to Avicenna. For the tradition through Abū Zayd and al-'Āmirī, see E. Rowson, "The Philosopher as *Littérateur*: Al-Tawḥīdī and his Predecessors," *Zeitschrift für Geschichte der arabisch-islamischen Wissenschaften* 6 (1990), 50–92, and E. Rowson, *A Muslim Philosopher on the Soul and its Fate: Al-'Āmirī's "Kitāb al-Amad 'alā l-abad"* (New Haven: 1988). For fourth/tenth-century Neoplatonism see also J. Kraemer, *Philosophy in the Renaissance of Islam: Abū Sulaymān al-Sijistānī and his Circle* (Leiden: 1986).

DAVID C. REISMAN

4 Al-Fārābī and the philosophical curriculum

LIFE AND WORKS

The philosophy of al-Fārābī stands in marked distinction to that of al-Kindī but is no less representative of the major trends of thought inherited by the Islamic world. His tradition is consciously constructed as a continuation and refinement of the neo-Aristotelianism of the Alexandrian tradition, adapted to the new cultural matrix of the Near East. The Neoplatonic element of al-Fārābī's thought is most obvious in the emanationist scheme that forms a central part of his cosmology, though that scheme is much more developed than that of earlier Neoplatonists in its inclusion of the Ptolemaic planetary system. His theory of the intellect appears to be based on a close reading of Alexander of Aphrodisias and develops the concept of an Active Intellect standing outside the human intellect. Above all, al-Fārābī's legacy to later thinkers is a highly sophisticated noetics placed within a rigorous curriculum of instruction in Aristotelian logic. Al-Fārābī was above all a systematic and synthesizing philosopher; as such, his system would form the point of departure on all the major issues of philosophy in the Islamic world after him.

The status accorded al-Fārābī's intellectual legacy here stands somewhat at odds with what we can reconstruct of his life with any certainty. With the exception of a few simple facts, virtually nothing is known of the personal circumstances and familial background of al-Fārābī.[1] The great variety of legends and anecdotes about this second major philosopher of the Islamic period is the product of contending biographical traditions produced nearly three centuries after his death. Documentary evidence (in the form of manuscript notations and incidental biographical information in his works) provide the most solid pieces of evidence we have.

Our most authoritative sources agree that his name was Abū Naṣr Muḥammad b. Muḥammad. His familial origins are recorded as alternately in Fārāb, Khurāsān or Faryāb, Turkistān. Al-Fārābī tells us himself that he studied logic, specifically the Aristotelian *Organon* up to the *Posterior Analytics*, with the Christian cleric Yuḥannā b. Haylān in Baghdad, where al-Fārābī spent the larger part of his life and composed the majority of his works. Al-Fārābī's chief student was the Christian Yaḥyā b. 'Adī and he wrote a treatise on astrology for the Christian Abū Isḥāq Ibrāhīm al-Baghdādī. This association with Christian scholarly circles in Baghdad links al-Fārābī to the Syriac neo-Aristotelian tradition which in turn was heir to the Alexandrian scholarly world of the centuries preceding Islam. In Baghdad, al-Fārābī must also have had some contact with personalities of the 'Abbāsid court, since he composed his *Great Book on Music* for Abū Ja'far al-Karkhī, the minister of the Caliph al-Rāḍī (reigned 934–40).

From a series of notes detailing the composition of his work *The Principles of the Opinions of the People of the Excellent City*, we know that al-Fārābī left Baghdad in 942 C.E. for Damascus, Syria, where he completed the work. He also spent some time in Aleppo, the seat of the Hamdānid prince Sayf al-Dawla. Around 948–9 al-Fārābī visited Egypt, then under the control of the Fatimids. Shortly after, he must have returned to Damascus, since we know that he died there in 950–1, "under the protection of" Sayf al-Dawla.[2]

These biographical facts are paltry in the extreme but we must resist the urge to embellish them with fanciful stories, as the medieval biographers did, or engage in idle speculation about al-Fārābī's ethnicity or religious affiliation on the basis of contrived interpretations of his works, as many modern scholars have done. Rather, the very paucity of any substantial biographical information about al-Fārābī in the immediate period after his death suggests that any intellectual influence he may have exerted during his life was almost nugatory. However, this does not mean that the program of philosophical education adumbrated in al-Fārābī's works and indeed his very real and often original intellectual contributions are not of paramount importance to understanding the development of philosophy in the Islamic world. Al-Fārābī's status would be rehabilitated a half-century later by Avicenna, the next great philosopher of the Islamic east, on whom al-Fārābī's interpretation of Aristotle would have a profound effect. Al-Fārābī's particular method of philosophical education would be carried on by the Baghdad school of scholarly interpretation of Aristotle, chiefly through his student Yaḥyā b. ʿAdī. Finally, al-Fārābī's works formed the point of departure for numerous later scholars of Andalusia, including Ibn Bājja and, in his youth, Averroes. However, as has been said before, al-Fārābī appears to have gone through life unnoticed;[3] this being the case, we must focus on the legacy of his thought.

Al-Fārābī's works can broadly be divided into three categories.[4]

(1) Introductory works (prolegomena) to the study of philosophy, including "pre-philosophical ethics,"[5] as well as basic introductions to the study of logic, and the works of Plato and Aristotle. This category includes the historical and educational ethics "trilogy" *The Attainment of Happiness – The Philosophy of Plato – The Philosophy of Aristotle* (as well as the supplementary *Harmony of Plato and Aristotle*) and the logical "trilogy" *Directing Attention to the Way to Happiness – Terms used in Logic – Paraphrase of the "Categories."* A number of other works fill out this group of elementary textbooks, including his *Prolegomena to the Study of Aristotle's Philosophy*. This genre has its roots again in the Alexandrian tradition of teaching philosophy. For instance, in the *Prolegomena* we find nine of the ten traditional points enumerated in that tradition for basic instruction before taking up a serious study of philosophy.[6] Also important here is al-Fārābī's *Enumeration of the Sciences*, which would enjoy great popularity in the Muslim and Latin Christian worlds after al-Fārābī.

(2) Commentaries on and paraphrases of the *Nicomachean Ethics* and the entire Aristotelian *Organon*, along with the by-then common introduction (*Isagoge*) of Porphyry, paraphrased in numerous ways by al-Fārābī. An important characteristic of this group of writings is al-Fārābī's extension of the logical curriculum beyond the traditional end in the midst of the *Prior Analytics*, as taught in the later Alexandrian school and continued by Christian logicians writing in Syriac.

(3) Original works in which al-Fārābī's syncretistic approach to philosophy presents a unified presentation of all aspects of philosophy, accompanied again by an idealized approach to its study. The best known of these works are *The Principles of the Opinions*, mentioned above, and *The Principles of Beings* (also known as *Governance of Cities*).

The al-Fārābīan corpus is almost single-mindedly driven by the combined goals of rehabilitating and then reinventing the scholarly study of philosophy as practiced by the Alexandrian school of neo-Aristotelianism. In this regard, he is rightly called the "second master" (after Aristotle) and he is self-proclaimed heir of that tradition. There is also distinct emphasis on situating that curriculum of philosophical study within the new cultural context of the Islamic empire. Al-Fārābī's conscious articulation of his inheritance of the Alexandrian curriculum of philosophy is found in a "mythologizing" account of the transmission of that school to its new cultural setting. In his *Appearance of Philosophy*, al-Fārābī tells us:

Philosophy as an academic subject became widespread in the days of the [Ptolemaic] kings of the Greeks after the death of Aristotle in Alexandria until the end of the woman's [i.e., Cleopatra's] reign. The teaching [of it] continued unchanged in Alexandria after the death of Aristotle through the reign of thirteen kings . . . Thus it went until the coming of Christianity. Then the teaching came to an end in Rome while it continued in Alexandria until the king of the Christians looked into the matter. The bishops assembled and took counsel together on which [parts] of [Aristotle's] teaching were to be left in place and which were to be discontinued. They formed the opinion that the books on logic were to be taught up to the end of the assertoric figures [*Prior Analytics*, I.7] but not what comes after it, since they thought that would harm Christianity. [Teaching the] rest [of the logical works] remained private until the coming of Islam [when] the teaching was transferred from Alexandria to Antioch. There it remained for a long time [until] only one teacher was left. Two men learned from him, and they left, taking the books with them. One of them was from Ḥarrān, the other from Marw. As for the man from Marw, two men learned from him . . . , Ibrāhīm al-Marwazī and Yuḥannā ibn Ḥaylān. [Al-Fārābī then says he studied with Yuḥannā up to the end of the *Posterior Analytics*.][7]

There are a number of important points to be made about this account, many of which provide the basis for an interesting study of the historiography of philosophy in the early medieval period. For our purposes, we may observe first that al-Fārābī makes absolutely no reference to his predecessor al-Kindī (d. after 870) or his elder contemporary Abū Bakr al-Rāzī (d. ca. 925–35). Clearly, al-Fārābī did not consider their approach to philosophy a viable or accurate one. Second, there is a conscious stylization of the rebirth of the philosophical curriculum after the restrictions placed on the study of logic by the Christians; in the Islamic period, al-Fārābī studied beyond the *Prior Analytics*, thus learning from his teacher Yuḥannā the demonstrative syllogism of the *Posterior Analytics*. As we will see, the valorization of the demonstrative method for philosophy is a singularly important element in al-Fārābī's view. Finally, al-Fārābī's account is designed to link his own work with a long history of studying philosophy, thus lending pedigree to the "new" curriculum of philosophy he envisioned for its practitioners under Islamic rule.

METAPHYSICS AND COSMOLOGY

To provide a concise and accurate account of al-Fārābī's philosophy remains problematic for a number of reasons. First, it is only in the past three decades or so that his works have received modern critical editions and much evaluation and scholarly discussion remains to be done. Second, al-Fārābī presents his philosophy as a unified treatment of all reality in which ontology, epistemology, and cosmology converge in an idealized historical and above all normative account of the universe. The piecemeal studies of very discrete aspects of his thought to date have not yet accounted for all aspects of this synthesis. Below, I endeavor to account for this whole in a general fashion, with reference to some of the more important studies of the past few decades, and following in the main the outline of his *Principles of Beings*.[8]

Al-Fārābī's cosmology integrates an Aristotelian metaphysics of causation with a highly developed version of Plotinian emanationism situated within a planetary order taken over from Ptolemaic astronomy.[9] The combination of the first two elements is not surprising, given the development of Neoplatonism prior to al-Fārābī. The latter element, drawn from Ptolemy's *Planetary Hypotheses*, is perhaps al-Fārābī's original contribution, although this is surmised only in the absence of any identifiable source prior to him. Al-Fārābī presents six "principles" (*mabādi'*) of being in the system: (1) the First Cause, (2) the Secondary Causes, i.e., incorporeal Intellects,

(3) the Active Intellect governing the sublunar world, (4) Soul, (5) Form, and (6) Matter. The emanationist scheme presented by al-Fārābī is a hierarchical descent from the First Cause through "Secondary Causes," or Intellects associated with the nine celestial spheres, to a final tenth Intellect which governs the sublunar world.

In al-Fārābī's presentation, Aristotle's causation of motion, which accounts for the revolutions of the spheres, is developed into a causation of being and intellection, in which each stage in the process imparts reality to the next and is structured according to a descending act of intellection. The First Cause (al-Fārābī says "one should believe that it is God") is the incorporeal First Mover, in that the celestial spheres move out of desire for It. This First Cause, in thinking itself, emanates the incorporeal being of the first intellect. In turn this first intellect thinks of the First Cause and of itself; this "multiplicity" of thought produces, in the first intellection, the second intellect and, in the second intellection, the substantiation of a soul and body for the next stratum. This process of emanating intellect, soul, and body descends through the nine intellects of the spheres. The first intellect is associated with the first heaven, identified as the outer sphere of the universe, rotating in a diurnal motion and moving the other spheres within its confines. The second intellect is associated with the sphere of the fixed stars which, in its own rotation, produces the precession of the equinoxes. Each intellect thereafter is associated with one of the "planets" known in al-Fārābī's time: Saturn, Jupiter, Mars, the Sun, Venus, Mercury, and the Moon. The final intellect, which al-Fārābī calls the Active or Agent Intellect (*al-'aql al-fa''āl*), governs the world of generation and corruption, namely, the four elements (earth, air, fire, water), minerals, plants, and both non-rational animals and rational animals (humans).[10]

This may be viewed as a very bizarre system indeed, but in its subtle complexity it accounts for nearly every element of al-Fārābī's philosophy and nicely incorporates the astronomical knowledge of his day. By placing the emanationist scheme within a tidier Ptolemaic astronomy, al-Fārābī's system does away with the philosophically messy fifty-five or more incorporeal movers of Aristotelian metaphysics. By positing an emanation of being and intellection, the system accounts not only for incorporeal and corporeal gradations of being in a manner consistent with logical division, but also for the process of intellection, and thus ultimately noetics. The crucial element in the scheme in this last regard is the presence of the Active Intellect governing this world, of which we will have more to say below. Other interpretations of al-Fārābī's reasons for adopting an emanationist scheme that he knew was non-Aristotelian have been suggested,[11] but it is clear that without such a system, al-Fārābī felt there was no means by which humans could know, however remotely, the divine, nor account for the diversity presented to humans in their analysis of the universe. Another interesting observation is that al-Fārābī did not hesitate to refer to the various supralunar incorporeal beings in terms recognizable to monotheists. For instance, he says that one ought to call the Intellects the "spirits" and "angels," and the Active Intellect the "Holy Spirit," i.e., the angel of revelation. This is a stroke of rhetorical genius, designed to make palatable to the monotheists of his day (i.e., not exclusively Muslim) the older Greek order of celestial gods.[12]

It is worth concentrating on a few of al-Fārābī's arguments concerning the First Cause (*al-sabab al-awwal*), since they provide us with interesting insights into the manner in which metaphysics and epistemology come to be combined in his thought. In the *Principles of the Opinions*, al-Fārābī tells us that

> The First cannot be divided in speech into the things which would constitute Its substance. For it is impossible that each part of the statement that would explain the meanings of the First could denote each of the parts by which the substance of the First is so constituted. If this were the case, *the parts which constitute Its substance would be causes of Its existence, in the way that meanings denoted by parts of the definition of a thing are causes of the existence of the thing defined*, e.g., in the way that matter and form are causes of the existence of things composed of them. But this is impossible with regard to the First, since It is the First and Its existence has no cause whatsoever.[13]

The negative theology by which al-Fārābī approaches his discussion of the First Cause is designed to demonstrate that It cannot be known through the classical process of dialectical division (*diairesis*) and definition (*horismos*) and hence cannot directly be known by the human intellect. Moreover, we find an additional element here in which logical analysis reflects ontology. The things *said* in defining a being are those things that *actually constitute its substance*. This is a realist trend that can be traced to Porphyry's *Isagoge* and informs the centuries of debate about the place of the Aristotelian *Categories* in metaphysics. In the above quotation, al-Fārābī gives as examples only the Aristotelian material and formal causes. Elsewhere in the same work, al-Fārābī draws on the Porphyrian "tree" of genera and species:

> [The First Cause] is different in Its substance from everything else, and it is impossible for anything else to have the existence It has. For between the First and whatever were to have the same existence as the First, there could be no difference (*mubayana, diaphora*) and no distinction at all. Thus, there would not be two things but one essence only, because, if there were a difference between the two, that in which they differed would not be the same as that which they shared, and thus *that point of difference between the two would be a part of that which substantiates the existence of both*, and that which they have in common the other part. Thus *each of them would be divisible in speech, and each of the two parts would be a cause for the substantiation of its existence*, and then it would not be the First but there would be an existent prior to It and a cause for Its existence – and that is impossible.[14]

Here, al-Fārābī is demonstrating that the components of definition, namely, the genus and the difference of a thing, are of no use in discussing the First Cause, but again (as we see in the italicized statements above), al-Fārābī has a clear conception that these elements not only allow one to talk about things (albeit not the First Cause!) but also to identify their ontological reality. Furthermore, the idea that the genus and difference of a thing *precede* (not temporally but causally) the thing defined is a transferal of the status of the Aristotelian causes (e.g., the example of matter and form in the first quotation) to the predicables of Porphyry's *Isagoge*.

The entire hierarchical edifice of al-Fārābī's emanation of being and intellect can be analyzed in terms of this classification by division into genera and species. Setting aside the First Cause, which alone is one, deficiency and multiplicity serve as the essential properties in the descending levels of substances. The incorporeal substances, i.e., the Intellects of the spheres, do not require a substrate for substantiation but are nonetheless deficient in the sense that their being derives from something "more perfect" (the First Cause). Moreover, they exhibit a multiplicity in the act of intellection: they intellect not only themselves (like the First Cause) but also the intellect that causally precedes them. However, these Intellects are more perfect than the human intellect in that, first, they are always actually intellecting and second, the object of that act of intellection is what is intelligible in itself, always separate from matter. The souls of the spheres, that is, their forms, thus have only the faculty of intellection which, in the desire to emulate what precedes them, serves to set in motion each of the associated spheres. A disjunction occurs at the level of the Active Intellect governing the sublunar world. Whereas the preceding intellects produce both a following intellect and its soul and celestial sphere, the Active Intellect affects only the human intellect in the world below it. Matter and form in the sublunar world, on the other hand, are produced by the differing motions of the celestial spheres.[15]

At the sublunar level, in the world of generation and corruption, complexity informs every species of being. Form (*ṣūra*) and matter (*mādda*) are the lowest principles of being and together (in need of one another, since neither subsists in itself) constitute corporeal substance. Matter is the pure potentiality to be something. Form causes corporeal substance actually to be that something. Al-Fārābī uses two familiar tropes: in the case of a bed, wood is the potential and form gives it its essential definition as a bed; and in the case of sight, the eye is the matter and vision is the form. At its simplest, the forms of the four elements earth, air, fire, and water constitute one species, since the matter that can be, say, earth, can also be water. The "mixture" of the elements produces a gradation of corporeal substances: mineral, plant, non-rational animal, and rational animal.

PSYCHOLOGY AND THE SOUL

Al-Fārābī's treatment of the corporeal soul and its "faculties" or "powers" (sing. *quwwa*) draws on a basic Aristotelian outline but is also one informed by the commentary tradition (particularly, it seems, pseudo-Alexander of Aphrodisias and Plotinus) that stands between him and the "first master." A number of basic faculties constitute the human soul: the appetitive (the desire for or aversion to an object of sense), the sensitive (perception by the senses of corporeal substances), the imaginative (which retains images of sensible objects after they are perceived and combines and separates them to a variety of ends), and the rational.[16] The graduated level of souls, from plant to animal to human, reserves the faculty of reasoning, the ability to intellect (*'aqala*),[17] for the human soul, which also exercises the others. This faculty, also called the "rational soul," alone survives the death of the body.

Al-Fārābī's vision of the world around him is fittingly complex, but the various elements are logically structured and the whole is informed by a teleological principle; each level of being is characterized by the quest for the perfection appropriate to it, a perfection which in each case mirrors that of the First Cause, by seeking to be like it. What constitutes human perfection? Since continuous and actual intellection is the goal of rational beings, and since man possesses an intellect, the goal, or "ultimate happiness (*sa'āda*)," of man is that continuous and actual act of intellecting.

The integration of metaphysics and noetics in al-Fārābī's system assures humans that they *can* know the structure of the universe and, ultimately, the principles that inform that structure.[18] However, there are two caveats to this. First, a person is not born with an actual intellect; that intellect must be developed in a very precise manner if it is to achieve the perfection of its being. Second, the inequality of being and intellect observable in the vertical emanationist hierarchy is replicated at the horizontal level: not all humans can develop their intellect in the same manner or to the same degree.

Because the human intellect is associated with corporeal matter, it represents only the potential, in the earliest stages of cognition, to achieve the perfection unique to it. The task of the Active Intellect is to initiate that process leading to perfection. As al-Fārābī says: "The action of the Active Intellect is the providence of the rational animal, to seek its attainment of the highest grade of perfection appropriate to man, which is supreme happiness, that is, that man arrive at the level of the Active Intellect."[19]

Al-Fārābī identifies the incorporeal Active Intellect as the agent that brings the human material intellect (*'aql bi-al-quwwa, in potentia*) into action, in other words, causes humans to think.[20] This is an amplification of standard Aristotelian causality developed in the preceding centuries of commentary on the basis of the recondite comments of Aristotle in his *De Anima* (III.5). In addition to locating that agent outside of the human intellect, al-Fārābī also employs the common metaphor of light to explain this process. He says:

> The relation of the Active Intellect to man is like that of the sun to vision. Sun gives to vision light, and by the light acquired from the sun, vision actually sees, when before it had only the potential to see. By that light, vision sees the sun itself, which is the cause for it actually seeing, and furthermore actually sees the colors which previously were [only] potentially the objects of vision. The vision that was potential thereby becomes actual. In the same manner, the Active Intellect provides man with something that it imprints in his rational faculty. The relation of that thing to the rational soul is that of light to vision. Through that thing the rational soul intellects the Active Intellect. Through it, the things that are potentially intelligible become actually intelligible. And through it, man, who is potentially intellect, becomes actually and perfectly an intellect, until it all but reaches the level of the Active Intellect. So [man] becomes an intellect *per se* after he was not, and an intelligible *per se* after he was not, and becomes a divine [substance] after being a material one. This is what the Active Intellect does.[21]

Condensed in this metaphorical presentation is a process of actuating man's reason which al-Fārābī develops in detail. The human intellect is initially "material," that is, humans at first have only the potential to think. But they also possess senses and the ability to retain the objects of sense in the "imaginative" faculty. The initial act of a human is to sense the objects of the world and to store images of those particular things. The process of thinking, however, requires the ability to convert those particular material things to universal "intelligibles" (*ma'qūlāt*), in order for one to develop the connections that form the basis of the logical process of defining and ordering the objects of the world. This conversion is effected by an external agent identified as the Active Intellect governing the sublunar world.

What is the nature of this initial alteration, in which the material intellect becomes an actual intellect (*'aql bi-al-fi'l*)? The metaphor of the effect of the sun's light on vision is, perhaps, the only means of approximating what occurs.[22] The Active Intellect brings about a change in the material intellect of the human in which the particular objects of sense are stripped of their material properties and "converted" into intelligibles that have no connection to matter. Al-Fārābī gives examples of these "primary intelligibles": the principle that the whole is greater than the part; the principle that objects equal in magnitude to another object are equal to one another. By intellecting such primary intelligibles, the intellect becomes an actual intellect.[23] Furthermore, as we see in the above passage, the human intellect now intellects the Active Intellect. In knowing something, the intellect becomes that thing, according to the Aristotelian dictum.[24] To what degree this systematization of Aristotle's epistemology, through its combination of causality and identity, is al-Fārābī's original contribution or is culled from the commentary tradition remains open to debate.

While the process of actualizing the human intellect would appear mechanistic in its earliest stage, al-Fārābī is committed to a human voluntarism at the next stage of the process, the development of what he calls the "acquired intellect" (*'aql mustafād*). As al-Fārābī states in explaining his understanding of Aristotle's philosophy: "man is one of the beings not given their perfection at the outset. He is rather one of those given only the least of their perfections and, in addition, principles for laboring (either by nature or by will and choice) toward perfection."[25] Indeed, even within his discussion of the act of sensing and imagining (i.e., those actions man shares with animals), volition plays a significant role, albeit at the basest level of desire or aversion. The particular type of will associated with the actual intellect al-Fārābī terms choice (*ikhtiyār*), through which man actually chooses to behave in a manner that is moral or immoral, and it is through his choice that man can seek or not seek happiness.

It is at this juncture that al-Fārābī's "curricular works," especially those concerning "pre-philosophical ethics,"[26] find their place in his program for the development of the philosopher. In them, al-Fārābī, following broadly the outlines of Aristotle's ethical works (particularly the *Nicomachean Ethics*), undertakes the definition of "happiness" through a dialectical discussion of contrasting views: what is thought to constitute happiness and what actually is happiness. The good that leads to happiness is produced either by nature or by will. In the former case, al-Fārābī sees the role of the celestial bodies as contributing, in an involuntary manner, to what leads to good or obstructs the way to good. As he says: "individual human beings are made by nature with unequal powers and different propensities."[27] Voluntarily choosing good and evil, by contrast, is directly the provenance of the human will. That education is necessary is obvious to al-Fārābī:

> not everyone is disposed to know happiness on his own, or the things that he ought to do, but needs a teacher and a guide for this purpose. Some men need little guidance, others a great deal of it. In addition, even when a man

is guided by these two [that is, happiness and the actions leading to it], he will not, in the absence of external stimulus and something to rouse him, necessarily do what he has been taught and guided to do. This is how most men are. Therefore they need someone to make all this known to them and rouse them to do it.[28]

It is at this practical level of human commitment to choosing the good that the human actual intellect initiates the process of becoming "like" the Active Intellect. By habituating themselves to virtuous actions (the Aristotelian "mean") and, equally important, to the correct mode of deliberating about what constitutes good action, humans develop what al-Fārābī calls the faculty of the rational intellect directed toward practical things (*quwwa ʿaqliyya ʿamaliyya*), that is, things humans can do or affect or produce.[29] Another aspect of the rational faculty is that termed the "theoretical" faculty (*quwwa ʿaqliyya ʿilmiyya*). This is usually defined negatively, that is, as the faculty concerned with objects of knowledge that humans cannot do or affect or produce.[30] It is clear, however, that al-Fārābī has in mind the faculty of the rational intellect (*quwwa nāṭiqa*) directed not simply to the beneficial, that is, what is virtuous in individual and social behavior and thought, but rather to what constitutes true happiness: philosophy, or knowledge of the existing things that by nature are simply to be known.

The broad division between practical and theoretical philosophy was well established in philosophical curricula by al-Fārābī's time. Practical sciences covered ethics, "governance of the household" (economics), and "governance of cities" ("politics"), all of which lead to happiness in the arenas of individual action and social interaction. Theoretical sciences included mathematics (the quadrivium), what is called "physics" or natural philosophy (the study of the world and its constituent parts, including man's soul, i.e., psychology), and the supreme science containing the principles of investigation of all other sciences: metaphysics. Study of the theoretical sciences leads to the ultimate human happiness: the perfection of the human soul. Again, it is significant that the philosophical curriculum was ordered on the basis of the two different objects of knowledge themselves informed by the very structure of the universe. On the basis of this division in the objects of knowledge, al-Fārābī catalogs the two levels of epistemology (classified by the Aristotelian practical and theoretical sciences), again consciously links them to his ontology (these sciences comprise what is actually real), and finally orders them in the evolution of human thought, both historically (this was the sequence in the progression of human knowledge) and on an individual level (this is the way humans learn to think).

LOGIC AND THE EDUCATION OF THE PHILOSOPHER

In both classes of the practical and theoretical sciences, al-Fārābī's curriculum emphasizes the necessity of studying logic, the supreme tool of scientific inquiry and the only means by which humans can perfect the ability to deliberate well about different objects of thought, and more significantly, guard the mind against error. The larger bulk of al-Fārābī's extant works concern the various types of logical inquiry and discourse. This is fitting, given the central place occupied by the Aristotelian *Organon* in the commentary tradition of the Alexandrian neo-Aristotelians and indeed in the Baghdad Aristotelian school, founded by al-Fārābī's teachers.[31]

Al-Fārābī's commentaries and paraphrases of logic encompass the entire Aristotelian *Organon* (*Categories*, *De Interpretatione*, *Prior* and *Posterior Analytics*, *Topics*, *Sophistical Refutations*, *Rhetoric*, and *Poetics*) along with Porphyry's *Isagoge*, the customary introduction to the whole, and finally, original works that focus on the relationship between logic and language.[32] This comprehensiveness represents a culminating stage in the process of updating the tradition of studying logic in the Christian Syriac intellectual context. Where before, students stopped midway through the *Prior Analytics*, al-Fārābī's new curriculum emphasized knowledge of the entirety of the syllogistic and non-syllogistic arts with a special emphasis on the demonstrative syllogism as the means to certain truth.

It is only relatively recently that editions of al-Fārābī's logical works have been published, and so comprehensive study of his contributions to the field remain to be undertaken. However, recent scholarship has emphasized two aspects of al-Fārābī's thought in this area: his treatment of logic and grammar; and his conception of what constitutes certainty in human thought and the relation of that view to how he ordered the levels of logical discourse.[33]

Al-Fārābī's attention to the relative valorizations of logic and grammar is a product of his inheritance of the neo-Aristotelian tradition of teaching philosophy, in which discussions about grammar and logic had already been combined.[34] It has also been suggested that al-Fārābī's concern here was a direct response to a debate in his time over the relative disciplinary merits of logic and Arabic grammar. This debate was presented in idealized form as a rhetorical battle between the logician Abū Bishr Mattā b. Yūnus, who argued for the universal applicability of logic as a type of meta-language, and the grammarian al-Sīrāfī, who scorned the "foreign" science of logic, given that the Arabs had Arabic grammar to aid them in guarding against methodological errors.[35] Modern scholarship on this issue has grown considerably in recent years, and whether or not al-Fārābī is really concerned with developing Aristotelian logic as a type of universal grammar remains itself open to debate. In any case, it would appear at the very least that al-Fārābī was trying to "naturalize" the *Organon* in the Arabic language by explaining its technical terms in the plain language of his day. In all of his introductory works on logic, al-Fārābī provides examples of the transfer of terms from their daily usage to the technical senses they require for logic. Furthermore, he argues that "the relation of grammar to language and expressions is like the relation of logic to the intellect and the intelligibles."[36] An additional example of al-Fārābī's "naturalization" of logic can be seen in his explanation of the analogical reasoning employed by the jurists and theologians of his day in terms of Aristotelian rhetoric.[37]

A much broader, and potentially more fruitful, discussion of al-Fārābī's treatment of logic concerns his theory of certitude (*yaqīn*) and the graded ranks of the different syllogisms in terms of their value for arriving at scientific certitude and explaining such according to people's varying abilities. In most basic form, al-Fārābī identifies two actions of the human mind, "conceptualization" (*taṣawwur*) and "assent" (*taṣdīq*).[38] Conceptualization occurs when the mind conceives simple concepts (terms) with the aim of defining their essential nature. Assent is directed toward complex concepts (premises) and results in the affirmation of their truth or falsity. "Perfect assent" is the mental judgment that produces complete certitude, not only that the object of thought is truly such a thing but also that one's knowledge of it is equally true and cannot be otherwise.[39] Again, we see al-Fārābī's assimilation of epistemology and ontology: in perfect form, al-Fārābī's certitude assures us that the knowledge of a thing is that thing itself. Now, clearly not all conceptualizations and assents produce this level of certainty, and it is here that al-Fārābī's "context theory" of Aristotelian syllogistic plays a role.[40] Al-Fārābī divides the books of the *Organon* according to their subjects. The *Categories*, *De Interpretatione*, and the *Prior Analytics* are applicable to all modes of discourse. The following books, treating syllogisms in the following sequence, cover the full range of mental assent and verbal explanation: demonstrative (*Posterior Analytics*), dialectical (*Topics*), rhetorical, sophistic, and poetic. With al-Fārābī, the original, descriptive classification of logic, which he inherited from the neo-Aristotelian tradition, is transformed into epistemological fact: these are the five types of syllogisms in which the human mind thinks.[41] This epistemological division is then synthesized with psychology, in which these modes of thinking are associated with the rational and imaginative faculties of the soul. Finally, this epistemology is transformed into an ontological classification: the objects of these modes of thought conform to the hierarchy of beings.

Logic is the sole methodology underpinning the divisions of the sciences, and the demonstrative syllogism (*qiyās burhānī*) is the sole means for arriving at "perfect assent," or complete certitude. The remaining classes of syllogism serve either to train the mind for demonstration or to provide the means to protect against error, in one's own thought processes as well as others'. This valorization of demonstration raises another interesting question: while perfect philosophers are capable of attaining the truth through demonstrative proof, what about the remainder of people, who are either incapable or unwilling to tread the path to happiness? Here al-Fārābī again "naturalizes" Aristotelian logic in his monotheistic environment. Philosophers think in demonstrative syllogisms, the premises of which they receive as "secondary intelligibles" from the Active Intellect in that process which leads to the human "acquired" intellect, the ultimate happiness of the human. For others, the role of prophecy, in both its religious and social function, serves to transform demonstrative truth into a rhetorical form understandable by the remainder of people.

It is within this context of the social function of the syllogistic arts and al-Fārābī's description of the different levels of truth (and thus being) afforded by the different classes of syllogisms that we can understand the presentation of what scholars have called his "political" philosophy. In the most original exposition of al-Fārābī's syncretism, found in *Principles of Beings* and the *Principles of the Opinions*, al-Fārābī follows up his presentation of cosmology and psychology with a detailed discussion of the different types of society in which humans live. In his presentation of the various social formations and their constituent parts, al-Fārābī presents a gradation of human society, from the most excellent, in which the harmony he depicts in his cosmological hierarchy is reflected, to the worst, in which material chaos has replaced that harmony. Al-Fārābī is not outlining an independent discipline of "political philosophy" in these discussions.[42] Rather, he is attempting to account for the multiple realities produced by "correct" or "incorrect" thinking, that is, the variant worlds as perceived and thus formed by demonstrative, dialectical, rhetorical, sophistic, or poetic modes of thought. In one sense, then, al-Fārābī assesses the apparent variability of the world of humans by means of an ordered philosophical system. In another sense, his presentation of these social orders is also commensurately rhetorical, employed for the sake of those incapable of pursuing philosophy: demonstrative truths concerning the true order of beings are here refashioned for the masses. The systematization inherent in al-Fārābī's philosophy is here masterful: it accounts for human society within the larger presentation of its cosmology; it sets forth an educational curriculum by which the divine order al-Fārābī saw in the universe could be replicated; and it articulates that curriculum of absolute truth in metaphorical terms that could be understood by those not capable, or not willing, to pursue the rigorous path to happiness through the development of "correct thinking."

Al-Fārābī was perhaps the most systematic of all the early philosophers writing in Arabic. His genius lies neither in the radical eclecticism of al-Rāzī nor in the self-proclaimed brilliance of Avicenna, but it is nonetheless present, in his revitalization of the numerous trends of thought that preceded him, in his conscious systematization of those disparate elements into a philosophically consistent whole, and above all, in his thoughtful but insistent articulation of the path to human happiness:

> Man is a part of the world, and if we wish to understand his aim and activity and use and place, then we must first know the purpose of the whole world, so that it will become clear to us what man's aim is, as well as the fact that man is necessarily a part of the world, in that his aim is necessary for

realizing the ultimate purpose of the whole world. Therefore, if we wish to know the object toward which we should strive, we must know the aim of man and the human perfection on account of which we should strive.[43]

NOTES

1 The brief biographical treatment presented here, eschewing repetition of the literary legends associated with al-Fārābī, follows D. Gutas, "Biography," in Yarshater [78], 208–13.
2 Ibid., 210b.
3 Ibid., 212b.
4 For English translations of the works of al-Fārābī see A. Hyman, "The Letter Concerning the Intellect," in A. Hyman and James J. Walsh (eds.), *Philosophy in the Middle Ages* (Indianapolis: 1973), 215–21; M. Mahdi, *Alfarabi's Philosophy of Plato and Aristotle* (Ithaca, N.Y.: 1969); F. Najjar, "Alfarabi: The Political Regime," in Lerner and Mahdi [189], 31–57; Walzer [77]; Zimmermann [79]. For translations of some of his short logical works, see below, n. 32.
5 I adapt here P. Moraux's term "vorphilosophische Sittlichkeit" as discussed in Gutas [76].
6 Gutas [76], 115–16.
7 I have modified the translation by Dimitri Gutas in Gutas [57].
8 Thus, what follows is a summary of his *Principles of Beings* (*al-Siyāsa al-madaniyya al-mulaqqab bi-mabādi' al-mawjūdāt*, ed. F. Najjar [Beirut: 1964]), unless otherwise noted.
9 The presence of an emanationist system in al-Fārābī's thought has generated some scholarly contention among earlier generations of interpreters of al-Fārābī; see the corrective analysis in Druart [74], Druart [75], and T.-A. Druart, "Metaphysics," in Yarshater [78], 216–19. I am not entirely convinced by Druart's own explanation (conceived as a question of loyalty or disloyalty to Aristotelianism) for the presence or absence of emanationism in one or another of al-Fārābī's works. A distinction in al-Fārābī's works between those we might call "curricular," designed to present a historical overview of philosophy to students, and those in which he develops his own synthesis of earlier trends of thought, appears to me to be a more fruitful avenue of investigation. Druart's consideration of chronology in the above works, however, does appear equally reasonable.
10 See the account in Davidson [208], 45ff.
11 See Druart's articles in n. 9 above.
12 See the remarks in Walzer [77], notes to part III, 3.
13 Translation from Walzer [77], 67, with modifications and italics.

14 Ibid., 58–61, with modifications and italics.

15 On this topic, see Druart [73].

16 The level of functional complexity, situated within a Galenic anatomy, can increase, depending on al-Fārābī's presentation in a given work; see Alon [72], vol. II, under "Faculty," for other treatments.

17 Hence, the use of the neologism "to intellect" here and in most writings on the theory of the intellect in Arabic philosophy rather than, for example, "to understand intellectually," which does not capture the connotations of the Arabic.

18 I base the following account of human intellection on Davidson [208], ch. 3.

19 *Principles of Beings*, 32. Scholars have devoted some attention to what precisely this means in relation to the question of human immortality and, above all, whether or not al-Fārābī endorsed the notion of conjunction between the Active Intellect and the human intellect. The issue is raised in relation to later philosophers' record of al-Fārābī's views (especially those of Ibn Bājja and Averroes). See S. Pines, "The Limitations of Human Knowledge according to al-Fārābī, Ibn Bajja, and Maimonides," reprinted in *The Collected Works of Shlomo Pines*, vol. V, ed. W. Z. Harvey and M. Idel (Jerusalem: 1997), 404–31; and Davidson [208], 70–3.

20 For the background of this development in the commentaries on Aristotle's *De Anima*, see Davidson [208], ch. 2. A recent study has gone so far as to claim that al-Fārābī did not even read Aristotle's *De Anima*, and took (or developed) his theory of the intellect from the commentary tradition alone: M. Geoffrey, "La tradition arabe du *Peri nou* d'Alexandre d'Aphrodise et les origines de la théorie farabienne des quatre degrés de l'intellect," in *Aristotele e Alessandro di Afrodisia nella tradizione araba*, ed. C. D'Ancona and G. Serra (Padova: 2002), 191–231.

21 *Principles of Beings*, 35–6.

22 Elsewhere al-Fārābī uses the metaphor of the seal and the wax; see Hyman, "Letter Concerning the Intellect," 215.

23 "Primary intelligibles" are indemonstrable, as can be seen from the examples above; "secondary intelligibles" are based on sense data but stripped of their material aspects.

24 *De Anima*, 430a20. See Davidson [208], 19, who further notes that this does not mean that the intellect is thereby affected or altered as a result.

25 "Philosophy of Aristotle," in Mahdi, *Alfarabi's Philosophy of Plato and Aristotle*, 76.

26 I include al-Fārābī's *Directing Attention to the Way to Happiness* here.

27 Najjar, "Alfarabi: The Political Regime," 35.

28 Ibid., 35–6; modified.

29 For the various terms al-Fārābī uses for this faculty, see Alon [72], vol. II, 604f.

30 Alon [72], vol. II, 606.

31 It has also been noted that al-Fārābī's valorization of logic as the instrument of philosophy represents an important development in the history of the study of Aristotelian logic, since previously, in the educational curriculum of Alexandria, logic was closely related to medicine. See Gutas [57], 174.

32 Many of al-Fārābī's short introductory works on logic have been translated by D. M. Dunlop: "Al-Fārābī's Introductory Sections on Logic," *Islamic Quarterly* 2 (1955), 264–82; "Al-Fārābī's *Eisagoge*," *Islamic Quarterly* 3 (1956), 117–38; "Al-Fārābī's Introductory *Risālah* on Logic," *Islamic Quarterly* 3 (1956), 224–35; "Al-Fārābī's Paraphrase of the Categories of Aristotle," *Islamic Quarterly* 4–5 (1957), 168–97, 21–54. Fritz Zimmermann has translated al-Fārābī's texts on Aristotle's *De Interpretatione*, in Zimmermann [79].

33 My account of the broad contours of al-Fārābī's logic follows Deborah Black, "Logic," in Yarshater [78], 213–16.

34 He followed, for instance, Paul the Persian (see Gutas [56], 248) and Sergius of Resh'aynā; see H. Gätje, "Die Gliederung der sprachlichen Zeichen nach al-Fārābī," *Der Islam* 47 (1971), 1–24. Al-Fārābī's treatment and its place in intellectual history is a widely debated topic; P. E. Eskenasy, "Al-Fārābī's Classification of the Parts of Speech," *Jerusalem Studies in Arabic and Islam* 11 (1988), 55–82, summarizes the different views nicely.

35 For a summary of this debate and its relation to al-Fārābī's works, with multiple references, see Street [182], 22ff.

36 *Introductory Treatise on Logic*, translation from Street [182], 23.

37 See Lameer [175].

38 On these terms (derivative of Aristotle, *De Anima*, III.6), see H. A. Wolfson, "The Terms *Taṣawwur* and *Taṣdīq* in Arabic Philosophy and their Greek, Latin and Hebrew Equivalents," *The Moslem World* 33 (1943), 114–28, and "The Internal Senses in Latin, Arabic and Hebrew Philosophic Texts," *Harvard Theological Review* 28 (1935), 69–133.

39 See Black's remarks at Yarshater [78], 214–15.

40 Street [182], 23–4.

41 Gutas [56], 257.

42 For a clear presentation of the history of errors concerning al-Fārābī's so-called "political philosophy," see D. Gutas, "The Study of Arabic Philosophy in the Twentieth Century," *British Journal of Middle Eastern Studies* 29 (2002), 5–25, esp. 19–25.

43 *Philosophy of Aristotle*, ed. M. Mahdi (Beirut: 1961), 68–9.

5 The Ismā'īlīs

The Ismā'īlī attitude toward philosophy and the philosophers was decidedly ambiguous. They tried consistently to deny that philosophers, in particular the ancient Greeks, possess an authority in any way superior to that of the legislating prophets of their own tradition. Despite an admirable skill with, and even mastery of, mathematics, physics, and logic, the practitioners of philosophy, in their view, had achieved almost nothing that they had not taken from a prophetic source. Ismā'īlī rejection of philosophy, however, covered less the content of that philosophy than the contributions claimed for individual thinkers. For the Ismā'īlīs, the philosophers, on their own, were capable of little except personal speculations that yielded them mere opinions – often mutually contradictory ones at that. Anything that was true in philosophy depended in the end on the sure guidance of divinely inspired prophets; without it the work of philosophers, no matter how brilliant and profound, produced a result ultimately lacking validity and real value.

Nevertheless, Ismā'īlī thought in its formative period would be simply unintelligible without philosophy, most especially Neoplatonism, which so permeates the works of the main figures that what they said is incomprehensible otherwise than by reference to a classical Greek background. These writers had clearly imported and used various elements of philosophy, not merely in vague generalities, but in specific terms and a technical language that derived more or less directly from translations of ancient texts. Although the works they wrote to explain their Ismā'īlism were not as a whole strictly speaking philosophical, many portions of them are in reality small treatises of philosophy.

In addition, the Ismāʿīlīs maintained the absolute primacy of intellect within the created realm, a position rare in Islam outside of the mainstream philosophers. For them the first created being is intellect and it is the sum and essence of all subsequent being; it governs and rules the universe. Revelation is not, and cannot be, in conflict with universal reason. Religious law does not constitute a separate source of truth, but rather is a manifestation of reason. The two are, in a sense, identical. The role of the legislating prophet – the lawgiver – is to fashion an incarnation of intellect suitable for the physical world. Sacred law is intellect incarnate. The lawgiver converts what is theoretical into a practical instrument for the control and then amelioration of human society, moving it thereby to its collective salvation. Scripture therefore signifies intellect and is subservient to it.

This understanding of intellect and its role is most certainly philosophical and it reveals clearly an influence of the Greek legacy. Therefore the Ismāʿīlīs who explored the details and the ramifications of doctrines that flow from this premise are philosophers even if they refuse to accept that name for themselves. They might insist that their teachings have a prophetic origin in some distant past but the particulars of their arguments – their form and language – owe more to the history of philosophy and to its reception in the Islamic world.

THE HISTORICAL CONTEXT

The Ismāʿīlīs are a branch of the Shīʿa.[1] Their existence as a separate movement began in deep obscurity about the middle of the ninth century. The technical term for such a movement is *daʿwa*, an appeal on behalf of a special cause or in favor of a specific line of imāms. For its first half-century only a few names of its agents – in Arabic called *dāʿī*s – are known. A *dāʿī* is a summoner, a missionary for converts, and a preacher of doctrine. By the start of the tenth century matters become much clearer. Yet even so, doctrines other than those concerning the imāmate remain uncertain. The movement had by then also split into factions, one supporting the leader who would shortly become the first caliph of the Fāṭimid dynasty (ruled from 909 to 1171), and the other a group of dissenters who refused to acknowledge the imāmate of these same caliphs. The latter group, who existed for the most part exclusively in the eastern Islamic lands, were known as the Qarmatians.

Ismā'īlīs then, like the rest of the Shī'a, all drew on a common fund of doctrine that had been assembled and propagated by several generations of Shī'ite scholars and authorities, particularly but not solely previous imāms. Strictly among the Ismā'īlīs, interesting early evidence for the study of philosophy by key members of the *da'wa* appears in a memoir by Abū 'Abdallāh Ibn al-Haytham.[2] This North African writer was Shī'ī prior to the advent of the Fāṭimids and, once they had achieved victory, he quickly joined their cause. His account reveals important details of his own background, which included a fairly complete education in Greek philosophy. He says that he owned and had read the works of both Plato and Aristotle, for example.[3] His conversations with the *dā'īs* in charge of the new government show, as well, that both he and at least one of them had read a range of philosophical works and that they could discuss, at will, specifics of Aristotelian logic and other Aristotelian doctrines.[4] Ibn al-Haytham became a *dā'ī* himself. The other *dā'ī* was the brother of the mastermind of the Fāṭimid triumph in North Africa; he had worked for the Ismā'īlī *da'wa* for close to twenty years.

At the same time or slightly later, in the east, in Khurāsān and in north-central Iran, another set of writers began to explain Ismā'īlī doctrine in a philosophical manner.[5] They converted an older Shī'ite cosmology by reinterpreting it Neoplatonically. As a prime example, cosmic figures in the older Islamic myth became universal intellect and universal soul in the newer version. The one *dā'ī* most responsible for this development was Muḥammad al-Nasafī (d. 943), who was active in Khurāsān.

Unfortunately, al-Nasafī's major work, *The Result* (*al-Maḥṣūl*), has not survived, leaving any reconstruction of the beginnings of Ismā'īlī philosophy hampered by its absence. Still, some passages from it occur in later works. It also soon became the subject of controversy within the eastern *da'wa*. A contemporary, Abū Ḥātim al-Rāzī (d. 934), a *dā'ī* operating in the area of Rayy, felt called upon to write a detailed "correction" of it. That work, the *Iṣlāḥ* – at least a major portion of it – is available.[6] Thus, there is sufficient material to construct a general picture of the contributions of al-Nasafī, albeit often by extrapolating what he might have said from the refutation by his opponents.

Al-Nasafī was, moreover, not alone in Khurāsān. His predecessors and successors wrote treatises containing philosophical doctrine. An important disciple, a *dāʿī* known only as Abū Tammām, composed a work called *Kitāb al-shajara* that has been preserved in several versions. Falsely ascribed to someone else, its second half was published under the title *Kitāb al-īḍāḥ*.[7] One other member of this same Khurāsānī school is Abū Yaʿqūb al-Sijistānī, who was to become, in the next generation, the most important advocate of Ismāʿīlī Neoplatonism.

Abū Ḥātim is famous for another of his works, the *Distinction of Prophecy* (*Aʿlām al-nubuwwa*), which is his account of a debate he held with the renowned physician-philosopher Abū Bakr al-Rāzī, a fellow townsman.[8] Abū Bakr had boldly argued that the prophets have had no advantage over the great philosophers and that in fact their so-called revelation is generally incoherent and of little value. He was the champion of philosophy exclusively, and was thus uninterested in the reconciliation of scripture and reason. Abū Ḥātim, like many other Ismāʿīlī writers, was deeply offended by this man and what he stood for. His record of this debate is, nonetheless, a major source for our knowledge of Abū Bakr's thought.

The development of Ismāʿīlī philosophy was thus ongoing, with considerable internal disagreement and agitation. Moreover, these Iranian writers were not supporters of the Fāṭimids, at least not initially. However, the Fāṭimids eventually adopted a conciliatory attitude to the eastern Ismāʿīlīs and, in the second half of the tenth century, began to accept their works, though often in an edited or abridged version. Al-Sijistānī finally recognized the leadership of the Fāṭimids and, as appears quite likely, revised his own older treatises appropriately. By the end of the century the major eastern philosophers, among them al-Nasafī, al-Rāzī, Abū Tammām, and al-Sijistānī, were a fully honored part of the Ismāʿīlī heritage. They, but most especially al-Sijistānī, were the authorities of record; their statements of Ismāʿīlī doctrine defined its main tenets.

It is especially important here to understand the real nature of their philosophical sources. Given the fragmentary condition of the earliest evidence, however, and the generally poor state of editions of nearly all Ismāʿīlī works from the period, that investigation remains quite tentative.[9] But it is clear that the writers just mentioned had access to a number of Neoplatonic texts, in addition to other Greek classics in translation.[10] They knew such treatises as the so-called *Theology of Aristotle* along with the other material derived from Plotinus' *Enneads*. Some version of the *Liber de Causis* and the other Arabic versions of Proclus[11] had likely reached them as well. In these cases, however, the connection is not (at least not thus far) textually explicit but rather implicit in the use of shared language and technical terms and concepts.

For two other crucially important pseudo-epigraphic texts the link is, by contrast, more obvious. One is now known as the *Pseudo-Ammonius*, a collection of opinions, in the main Neoplatonic, said to have been advocated by various ancient Greek philosophers on several topics such as creation *ex nihilo* and the identification of God with being.[12] Traces of this work show up in Arabic discussions of the history of Greek thought. It is quoted in passages from al-Nasafī and Abū Tammām and is certainly the source for Abū Ḥātim al-Rāzī's chapters that purport to prove the failure of the philosophers to attain the truth on their own. Lacking the sure guidance of the divinely inspired prophets, says Abū Ḥātim, they flounder about in error, each asserting an opinion and nothing more. There is therefore little doubt that Abū Ḥātim used this work and that it served as a basis for Ismā'īlī knowledge of Neoplatonic doctrine. The one manuscript of it available now,[13] moreover, begins with a statement to the same effect. The Arabic work that we have now may thus have been a product of the Ismā'īlī *da'wa*, perhaps a collection of notes taken by a *dā'ī* (such as Abū Ḥātim or al-Nasafī) from one or more translations of an ancient author (one possibility would be the Ammonius mentioned near the beginning of it). For the Ismā'īlīs its primary purpose was to invalidate the work of philosophers, and it is therefore less a source in itself than evidence of other sources of theirs.

The other text is equally problematic. In the *Longer Version of the Theology of Aristotle*, which incorporates all of the shorter version, but adds many passages that appear in it alone, there are sections, mostly quite brief, that match portions of some Ismā'īlī works in both wording and in doctrine.[14] The additions in question do not go back to Plotinus. The doctrines expressed in them are, or rather become, however, characteristic of the Ismā'īlīs in the Fāṭimid period. Yet they surely also come from an older, possibly ancient, source and are not in themselves a product of Ismā'īlī interests.

Because so much of his writing survives, al-Sijistānī, who died not long after 971, is for us the major representative of the earliest Ismā'īlī philosophy. Until the beginning of the eleventh century, the *da'wa* produced no other important figures, unless it is appropriate to place in this interval the Brethren of Purity (Ikhwān al-Ṣafā') and to accept them as being somehow Ismā'īlī. Their famous encyclopedia, the *Epistles* (*Rasā'il*), displays certain affinities with Ismā'īlī Neoplatonic doctrine and it is commonly supposed that this secretive society was connected to the Ismā'īlī movement. There is, however, dispute about both the dates of their activities and their affiliation. The best evidence places them about this time and various statements in their *Epistles* closely match certain doctrines of the Ismā'īlīs. However, what they advocate in regard to the imāmate does not; they cannot have been supporters of the Fāṭimids. Instead they represent vaguely on this one issue the position of the Qarmatians.[15]

Strictly within the Fāṭimid context the next great authority chronologically is Ḥamīd al-Dīn al-Kirmānī, a towering figure whose writings dominate the era of the caliph al-Ḥākim (reigned 996–1021). As is typical for all of these Ismā'īlī *dā'ī*s, there exists little information about al-Kirmānī's life, except that he lived and worked in Iraq and visited Cairo. He dedicated all of his writings to al-Ḥākim, the last of them in the year 1021 when this ruler disappeared.[16]

Al-Kirmānī belonged to a philosophical tradition different from the others; the major influence on him is not the Neoplatonism of the *Theology* and related texts, but al-Fārābī. Accordingly, al-Kirmānī's own approach is much more Aristotelian. For example, he adopted a version of the scheme of multiple intellects that correspond each in turn to the heavenly spheres – a doctrine favored by his contemporary Avicenna, as well. He speaks of the active intellect and not the universal intellect; he has little or no real notion of a universal or world soul. Needless to say, his views on many issues were in conflict with those of al-Sijistānī and the other earlier figures. In fact he wrote an important treatise precisely to analyze and then recast previous Ismā'īlī doctrine in a mode more in tune with his own. That work, the *Riyāḍ*,[17] attempts to reconcile the positions espoused by, first, Abū Ḥātim al-Rāzī in his critique of al-Nasafī and, second, those of al-Sijistānī, who had tried to come to the aid of al-Nasafī.

The points of contention are largely philosophical: for example, is universal soul perfect from its inception or does it need to acquire perfection in the course of time? Inadvertently, al-Kirmānī provides, in this instance, a rare internal view of the development of Ismā'īlī philosophical doctrine.

Al-Kirmānī's attempt to readjust the course of Ismā'īlī thought failed in the short run. Nevertheless, his work constitutes one of the high points of Ismā'īlī philosophical interest. Subsequent Fāṭimid era authorities ignored him and preferred instead the doctrines of al-Sijistānī. The two prime examples are Nāṣir-i Khusraw (d. ca. 1077) and al-Mu'ayyad fī al-Dīn al-Shīrāzī, the former a *dā'ī* who wrote exclusively in Persian but who often seems to be translating passages from al-Sijistānī, and the latter the head of the *da'wa* from 1058 to 1077, whose massive output of sermons and doctrinal lessons has yet to be studied in detail.

With the end of the Fāṭimid dynasty in 1171, the main center of Ismā'īlī activity moved either to Alamut in northern Iran or to the Yemen. The Ṭayyibī *da'wa* in the Yemen maintained throughout the later medieval period a vigorous scholarly tradition of collecting, studying, and writing. The survival of nearly all earlier Ismā'īlī texts depended on the Ṭayyibīs; and scholars in this *da'wa* continued to produce new works that build on the older philosophical doctrines. In them the *Epistles* of the Brethren of Purity assume an important place, as do the writings of al-Kirmānī, who was much favored by the later Yemenis.

THE PHILOSOPHICAL DOCTRINES OF THE MAJOR FIGURES

Muḥammad al-Nasafī

A major concern of al-Nasafī[18] was to define the transcendence of God in such a way that he, the Originator, stands totally outside his creation. To do so al-Nasafī relied on a special vocabulary, which he shared with others of his time. The verb *abda'a* (to originate) yields the active participle *Mubdi'*, God as Originator, who brings into being both thing (*al-shay'*) and not-thing (*al-lā-shay'*). He originates from nothing (*lā min shay'*); beforehand he is and there is nothing else, no knowledge or form. All knowledge and forms are originated; they cannot be other than originated being; and they are not in God's being (*huwiyya*) in any sense. Non-being and nothingness, like being, follow being; they are negations of an existent.

God's command (*amr*), which is also called the word (*kalima*) and is the very originating itself, causes originated being, which is intellect. The command thus serves as an intermediary between him and first originated being – that is, between God and intellect. But, although the act of the agent here is prior ontologically to its effect, from the perspective of the effect, the action is the effect. The command is intellect. This notion appears to derive from a passage in the *Pseudo-Ammonius* that states that the agent (*mu'aththir*) produces an effect (*athar*) that becomes the patient (*mu'aththar*). Thus the command of God, which is this effect, has no separate identity other than the being it brings into being.

Originated being (the *mubdaʿ*) is intellect. The Creator has given existence to the universe all at once by the origination of intellect as a whole and by seeding in it the forms of the world. Intellect like its cause is eternal; in intellect the forms are also eternal. If this were not so, they would not endure and there would be no possibility of reverting to this eternity. If intellect were not perfect and eternal, the order in the world would cease and it would perish. Intellect in turn emanates the forms to what follows after and below it. Intellect becomes thus the intermediary between its own cause and the world. Its immediate effect is soul, which, unlike intellect, is not perfect. Soul requires the benefit of intellect in order to acquire perfection in the future. One result is time. In its search for these benefits, soul produces motion; in finding them it rests. These two tendencies result from soul's relationship with intellect; they in turn generate prime matter and specific form, which together provide the foundation of the compound, material world.

Mankind, the first thing formed in the soul, is the fruit of soul's endeavor to master intellect. Knowledge was hidden in the rational human soul, which is a part of universal soul, in the same way a tree is concealed in its seed. Just as the seed cannot develop without water, likewise this knowledge in the human – its rationality – will not sprout or grow without the water of prophecy.

Abū Ḥātim al-Rāzī

Like his contemporary, Abū Ḥātim gave great importance to terms based on *abdaʿa*: God is the *Mubdiʿ*, the Originator. He originates all existing being at once; the first of them is the sum of existing being(s). Also, as with al-Nasafī, the originating (*ibdāʿ*) is God's command and his word. Once originated, it and all aspects of it are one and the same being; they are first intellect. Hence no aspect or attribute of the originating or what it creates applies in any way to the Originator; he cannot be described with any term that pertains to created beings.

To this point Abū Ḥātim's doctrine of God and creation is much like that of al-Nasafī, or for that matter al-Sijistānī, or even the *Longer Theology*. His concept of time, however, is new. In his system time and intellect are one being. Since there is no time prior to origination and since origination and intellect are the same being, time and intellect, he argues, are the same. Soul proceeds from intellect (he uses the verb *inbaʿatha*); intellect then bestows beingness in its entirety on soul. Soul receives all and also time. Although its reality requires time, soul is nevertheless perfect. For Abū Ḥātim its discursive mode of being is not a defect, nor is its subservience to intellect. The two are together in a higher, spiritually pure realm, uncontaminated by any portion of, or contact with, the physical heavens or the mundane world. They are alike in the sense that male and female are both one species even though one is above the other. Intellect and soul are both of the highest rank and nobility; there is no nobility higher. As the foundation of the higher, spiritual world, they are the source of perfect nobility, light, mercy, knowledge, the ultimate in all ways, containing no darkness or murkiness at all.

The foundation of the lower world is prime matter and form, whose temporal mode of being is not connected to that higher world. Nonetheless, an effect (*athar*) of that lofty world does govern this one, like the effect of a craftsman on his product. The kinds of soul are vegetative, animal, rational, and, only in man, a fourth that is not of this world but is an effect of that other higher world. Thus human soul is not a part of universal soul, nor does it participate in that soul. Nothing of this world is directly connected to the world of intellect and soul. However, humans, for the sake of whom the mundane world exists, accept the effect of the higher realm. And man is the fruit of this world. The world and all that is in it was originated for his sake. It reaches completion and its end is when man is complete. At that point the world will disappear.

Despite some differences, both al-Nasafī and Abū Ḥātim offered a fairly clear Neoplatonic interpretation of the issues just outlined.

Unfortunately, beyond this brief sketch, the evidence for the full range of either man's doctrines is at present missing. What we know about what they said is tantalizing, but it remains only that.

Abū Ya'qūb al-Sijistānī

Whereas the material for al-Nasafī and al-Rāzī is slight and any picture of their ideas must, by the nature of the evidence, remain superficial, for al-Sijistānī[19] it is relatively abundant.[20] It is true, nonetheless, that even he never composed a complete work of philosophy. Instead there are individual chapters and sections in his works – many in fact – that are by themselves treatises of philosophy. Frequently, within a single composition, he provides a discussion of a philosophical issue in one chapter followed by another on a topic that can only be classed as Ismā'īlī doctrine.[21]

Al-Sijistānī's philosophical teachings range over a descending and ascending scheme – from the simple and universal to the complex and particular, from the one to the many, and back again. For him the study of creation reveals the structure of the universe: the perpetual stability of the higher and the constant flux of the lower worlds. Human soul is entangled in the latter; its salvation and eventual eternity resides in the former. Creation proceeds from God to the foremost among created beings, the intellect, which is the first to have existence and is nearest to God himself. Next is soul, followed by nature, the latter in reality only a lower form of soul. After nature there is a shift from the sublime and spiritual to the mundane and corporeal. Nature generates the physical world, the earthly habitat of plants, animals, and above all of humans. For al-Sijistānī, as for the Ismā'īlīs in general, the upward return is of even greater concern. They see it as a historical process, the collective salvation of mankind. A second hierarchy, parallel to intellect, soul, and nature, provides the law and the truth that lead humans away from this world into the next, from the physical and sensate to the sublime and spiritual, in reverse back to pure intellect.

In al-Sijistānī's statements about this process there are several doctrines that are characteristic of him. His doctrine of the One is primarily concerned to preserve its absolute unqualified transcendence. God is not the first in any sense; he is not the outer limit. For al-Sijistānī God is not a substance; he is not intellect, he has no being, he is not a cause, he has no that-ness (*inniyya*). All such attributions are false in his case. Al-Sijistānī devoted separate chapters in his works to refute carefully those who hold to any of these propositions. Among his opponents are both the philosophers and the vast majority of Islamic theologians. He comments that the philosophers claim that God is a substance that is somehow related to something else. But one cannot say, for example, that God is a thing not like other things. Al-Sijistānī's point is that denying all physical attributes of God is but one step toward distinguishing him from all created being. Attempting to understand God by intellectual means, even approximations, is also, despite its abstract theoretical form, a kind of anthropomorphism. The intellect, human or otherwise, simply cannot know God.

Most Neoplatonists assume that the intellect's role is, in part, to contemplate the One and to realize some apprehension of it (possibly to attempt a union with it). But these Ismāʿīlī philosophers insist that intellect is incapable of attaining this goal. To express his doctrine al-Sijistānī advocated the use of a double negation, a kind of *via negativa duplex*. One must say that God is not a thing, not limited, not describable, not in a place, not in time, and so on; but then add to these negations a second set. Thus one also states that God is *not* not a thing, *not* not limited, *not* not describable, *not* not in a place, *not* not in time. He aims to remove God from intelligibility altogether. Simple negation is an understandable act that yields an intellectual result; double negation is not.

Yet curiously al-Sijistānī next insists that creation, or more precisely "origination" – he also uses the Arabic verb (*abdaʿa*) – occurs in response to the "will" of God. God thus "commands" that the universe exist. His concern here to preserve the act of God's originating the world from any comparison with other types of agency is not surprising. In relying exclusively on the term "originate" (*abdaʿa*) for God's creating something from nothing, he joins both his predecessors in the Ismāʿīlī *daʿwa* and others such as Isaac Israeli and al-Kindī. He is careful to call all other creating by another name. Soul, for example, gushes (*inbajasa*) or proceeds (*inbaʿatha*) from intellect. Emanation is not the same as origination. But even so he stands out in his attempt to insert an intermediary between God and intellect and to label it in such a way as to emphasize both its distinctness and its connotation of will and purpose. It is also the word, the *logos* (*al-kalima*). Yet its real status is that of a nonexistent and, once the command is issued by God, that very command thereafter is intellect and nothing more. Once the world has come into being, the order that gave it existence is an aspect of intellect itself. Moreover, there cannot and will not be another command; the first is eternal and outside of time and sequence. God's origination determined that there should be cosmos rather than chaos. If God exists the cosmos can never be chaos.

The object of the command is, in the first instance, intellect, which is the sum and principle of all being, the form of all things, both manifest and hidden. It is the wellspring of all spiritual and physical light. Al-Sijistānī also employs the peculiarly Ismāʿīlī term, "the preceder" (*al-sābiq*), to indicate that intellect precedes all other beings. Yet some aspect of intellect enters all subsequent being as well. Soul gushes from it when intellect turns upon itself in contemplation; soul in turn engenders nature within itself. Whereas intellect is perfect, soul is not. Rather it needs the benefit of intellect to attain a degree of that possible perfection. Soul is in motion, intellect at rest. As soul moves it creates time. However, insofar as soul is unmindful of its own mentor, it sinks, often becoming enthralled with the natural world it has made within itself. It must be reminded of its origin; its forgetfulness requires a revelation that corrects its orientation, turning its attention upward again rather than downward.

Most aspects of al-Sijistānī's doctrine of intellect and soul follow Neoplatonic precedent. Significantly, he resolutely maintains the indivisibility of both. For him there are no separate intellects, such as, for example, show up on the planetary scheme of al-Fārābī and Avicenna. His intellect is universal and individual human mind participates in it. Likewise the soul is universal and our souls are a part of that universal.

A key problem is prophecy. Prophecy is not philosophy and philosophers are not prophets. In fact the major lawgiving prophets all belong to the same lineage. They share a similar extraordinary faculty that is not available to other humans. But, at the same time, they are, as al-Sijistānī puts it, men who are "the deputies of intellect in the physical world." Based on their perfect access to the realm of intellect, their role is to convert reason into language and to convey it to other humans. This function requires that such prophets have unrestricted and unencumbered benefit of intellect, that their physical selves be so harmoniously undisturbed by worldly desire or bodily interference that they can, at will, take what they find in intellect and bring it back down to earth, so to speak. In so doing they formulate laws and compose Scripture; the product of this effort is an incarnation of intellect.

In order to govern the world of flux and constant change, the timeless reality of what is truly real must inspire a representative who acts here. The task is to warn the soul away from the terrestrial realm and to teach it, as it exists in the collective souls of individual humans, how to return to its higher self. For the Ismāʿīlīs Muḥammad was the final legislator; his is the ultimate law. At a future point a messiah will bring an end to human history. In the meanwhile a sacred line of imāms, descended from Muḥammad, and thus of the same lineage, provide guidance; they each preserve the standard of his legislation by an inherited knowledge of what his words actually signify. They all have the ability to trace meaning back from the literal exoteric expression to its abstract esoteric source in the universal timeless intellect.

Ḥamīd al-Dīn al-Kirmānī

Al-Kirmānī[22] entered the Ismāʿīlī *daʿwa* about one full generation after al-Sijistānī's death. The earliest date in his writings is 1008.[23] As mentioned previously, al-Kirmānī adopted a kind of Farabian scheme to an Ismāʿīlī purpose and in so doing hoped to convince the *daʿwa* to move in the same direction.

Nevertheless, for al-Kirmānī, in contrast to al-Fārābī, God is not the first being, First Cause, or necessary being (*wājib al-wujūd*). The beginning of a causal series is, despite its primacy in that series, still a part of that same series. That beginning is intellect – the first intellect – and not God. God is rather that on which the series itself depends. He is the very principle of existence but is not an existent being. God is also not a substance. He is neither corporeal nor incorporeal; neither potentially something (*bi-al-quwwa*) nor actually something (*bi-al-fiʿl*); he has no need; nothing is similar to him; he has no relationship, no contrary, no equal, is not in time and not subject to time, and he is neither eternity nor subject to eternity.

Al-Kirmānī's point is that God is utterly unknown and unknowable. As much as the intellect might want to grasp or to comprehend and understand him, it cannot. To try only increases its distance from him. God can no more be seen by the intellect than the sun by the naked human eye. He simply cannot be perceived by the methods of intellect. And languages cannot signify God as he really is, since the signifier must have a referent that exists and can be known. God, however, is unknown; one cannot signify with language, or with abstractions in the mind, something that is unknown. Following al-Sijistānī, al-Kirmānī advocates a process of double negation. A true declaration of God's unique oneness, *tawḥīd*, tolerates no compromise, even of the most intellectually sophisticated. The proper procedure then is to deny all physical and mental images that seek to understand God. None are valid. What this method achieves is the removal of God from the sphere of human speculation and imagination. But what of standard, religiously based discourse about God? Al-Kirmānī's answer is that what humans speak about when they talk of God is actually the intellect at its highest and ultimate first level. It is not really God and should never be confused with the true Lord Creator, but it is as close as humans can come. It suggests God but is not him.

Creation occurs initially by origination and what came into being by *ibdāʿ* is first intellect, which is, subsequently, the absolute first of the cosmos: the first being, the First Cause, the first mover. It is the one, the first cause and effect, the innovation and innovated, perfection and perfect, eternal and eternity, existent and existence, all at once. Though one, it thinks, is thought, and is what is thought. First intellect, i.e., the first being in the cosmic order, is the eternal unmoved mover. In the Aristotelian model, the unmoved mover is God, the cause of all causes. Therefore, al-Kirmānī's recognition that this intellect serves as the God that humans know and understand confirms the philosophers' position but with a profound change. Their God is the first intellect, yet it is not really God but rather an intellectual image actually quite distinct from the real God. Nevertheless, this first intellect, although it bears some relationship to the cosmos that it now causes, is absolutely unique. It is the first thing among things; the mover of all motions; and it is the actuality that brings all potentiality into actuality.

There are, in all, five kinds of intellect: a first, a second, and three types in the human mind – acquiring, potential, and actual. The first is prior to all others. It is one in essence but multiple in its relationships and thus it gives rise to a dual being, the second intellect, a being of more complexity than the first. The process of going from the first to the second broadens creation by creating a multiplicity.

The second intellect arises from the first because the first unintentionally radiates its joy at being itself. It is so pleased and rapturous with its own being that it blushes, thereby generating an image that becomes a separate second intellect which is a reflection of itself. This process is called "procession" or "emanation" (*inbaʿatha, inbiʿāth*). The second, in contrast to the first, has a rank and position merely by being second and thus not alone or unique. It is subject to procession; it is *inbiʿāthī* rather than *ibdāʿī*, although, in so far as it is intellect pure and simple, it continues to have *ibdāʿī* qualities. It is actual and not potential; it encompasses and preserves its own essence like the first. But, unlike its own immediate source, the second both must and can conceive from what it came; it envisions the first intellect as well as it contemplates itself, thus producing a double aspect that gives it its fundamental duality. In its imitation of intellect as agent, it is what al-Kirmānī calls soul – a soul, however, unrelated to human soul and clearly parallel to the universal soul of Neoplatonism only in name. The second aspect of second intellect derives from the first in its capacity as effect. In the second intellect it constitutes an intellect in potentiality rather than in actuality. And, in contrast to the higher aspect, it takes on the characteristics of prime matter, an unrealized potential in which it, with form, produces bodily being. By itself the *ibdāʿī* aspect of second intellect preserves its essence as intellect while, in its acquisitive mode, it is simply form to this material being. As a whole it is potential life.

From these two aspects of second intellect, there issue a further procession of intellects and a parallel series of material entities. The former are the eight additional intellects of the cosmic system and the latter are the material forms of the spheres, out of which generate the corporeal beings of the terrestrial world. Al-Kirmānī assigns the intellects of these spheres the role of governing and regulating the physical world. They are also intimately related to the progress of religious revelation and the development of sacred law. Each of these secondary intellects – called the *thawānī* by the philosophers, he notes – observe their own veneration and service to God by their perfect unchanging circular motion like pilgrims circumambulating the Kaʿba. This perfection is an emulation of or a desire for assimilation to the first intellect. Arrayed in rank order strictly determined by how many intellects precede, each must acknowledge and attempt to comprehend all those before it, and this increasingly complex requirement burdens the next with an imperfection more serious than that of its predecessor. As the number increases, the complexity of the images required to comprehend those previous to each imposes a certain need and impotence. Relative to human society, the tenth intellect is the closest and most directly involved in the governance of terrestrial affairs.

Al-Kirmānī's concept of soul in the individual human makes perfectly clear that humans do not possess either a soul or intellect directly comparable to the celestial beings. Human soul does not have existence prior to the body in which and with which it acquires its being. Such a soul at the beginning is formless and devoid of knowledge although it is, nevertheless, the first perfection of its natural body. Intellect in this situation is a rational quality of the soul, a kind of soul, or an aspect of it. This soul, as a substance, has the possibility of surviving its body. But, for its knowledge of the world, neither soul nor its rational faculty can function without depending on physical sensations. It commences with an instinctual comprehension of the surrounding world, an instinct it shares with the other animals. But it also possesses a possible second perfection, a purely rational existence in which its substance ceases to be attached to body. Human souls for the present cannot exist without a body, but that will not always be the case. On the basis of what it acquires in the way of knowledge and good deeds, soul is a living substance with the ability of enduring beyond the dissolution of the material body.

This soul has three aspects to its single self: growth, sensation, and rational discrimination. The third category is potentially intellectual. It develops through seven stages: conception, growth, sensation, imagination, rationality, intellectuality, and finally a "second procession" (*munbaʿath thānī*), the last stage being its final move from corporeal existence into an eternal state without body. Even with a rational faculty, however, it commences without knowing what is in its best interest. It lacks knowledge like, he says, a blank sheet of paper and thereafter undergoes a progressive development in which it assumes a different form. At the start, from the perspective of true *ibdāʿī* and *inbiʿāthī* beings, it is sick, and its illness is not due to its body but rather its own imperfection. On its own, it cannot learn anything that does not strictly depend on information gleaned from the senses. However, there are intelligent forces that can deal with these souls and convince them to accede to the regimen that will bring them knowledge from outside. They must have a teacher.

As with celestial souls, human souls contain, however slight and weak they may be, some *ibdāʿī* and *inbiʿāthī* qualities. In a way they resemble distantly the intellect and soul of that higher world, and in turn that world preserves a remote interest in the souls of this realm. Accordingly the heavenly members of the hierarchy retain a providential responsibility for human beings. The tenth and final intellect of the heavenly world, acting on behalf of the whole system, has the greatest responsibility. It generates its own intellectual representative in that lower world, who, in turn, receives the emanations of all the higher angels – i.e., the separate intellects. This person must be human but, as al-Kirmānī is careful to point out, it also must be someone who is *truly* human, a person whose human quality is most perfectly and exclusively intellectual and thus not merely animal. Only such a person actually resembles the angels in their *inbiʿāthī* and *ibdāʿī* qualities. Such rare and unique individuals are the great prophets and founders of religions, and above all the messiah of the future who will, at the end of time, finally represent the actualization of intellect among humans. For now the imām is the perfection of intellect in any one period; he is the ultimate teacher in this world because he most completely knows the truth. The prophets were, in fact, the intellects of their time; they were the earthly image of true first intellect, which is the Divine in so far as he is an intelligible being.

The philosophical base of Ismāʿīlī doctrine, especially as propounded by the figures just discussed, was perfectly obvious to their Islamic opponents, many of whom explicitly cite such a connection in refuting it. The *daʿwa* vainly attempted to control access to the writings of these *dāʿī*s, but prominent authorities knew them nonetheless. Moreover, despite a stated rejection, many may have been more influenced by what they learned than they willingly admit. Avicenna (d. 1037), for example, confessed that his father and brother were

Ismāʿīlīs and that he was first made aware of their teachings by his own family.[24] The great Sunnī theologian al-Ghazālī (d. 1111) commented frequently on the philosophical appeal of the Ismāʿīlīs.[25] The vehemently anti-philosophical critic Ibn Taymiyya (d. 1328) reports that he came upon and had read al-Sijistānī's *Maqālīd* among other works of theirs.[26] And, finally, the famous Egyptian, Mamluk-era historian al-Maqrīzī (d. 1442) states quite clearly that he had located genuine books by members of the *daʿwa* and that he derived his knowledge of Ismāʿīlī doctrines from them. He, too, had no doubt about the essential role of philosophy in their thought.[27]

NOTES

1 The best general account of the Ismāʿīlīs is Daftary [80]. But see also W. Madelung, "Ismāʿīliyya," in [16].

2 W. Madelung and P. E. Walker, *The Advent of the Fāṭimids: A Contemporary Shīʿī Witness* (London: 2000).

3 Ibid., 111–12.

4 Ibid., 136–55.

5 The first to work out the details of the life of these Iranian *dāʿīs* was S. M. Stern in his "The Early Ismāʿīlī Missionaries in North-West Persia and in Khurasan and Transoxiana," *BSOAS* 23 (1960): 56–90, reprinted in Stern [83], 189–233. Since his pioneering effort some additional information has come to light. See Walker [84], 1–24; and Daftary [80], 120–3, 164–8, and 234–42.

6 Ed. H. Mīnūcheher and M. Mohaghegh (Tehran: 1998).

7 *Kitāb al-īḍāḥ*, ed. A. Tamer (Beirut: 1965). For the identity of the real author, Abū Tammām, see Walker, "Abū Tammām and his *Kitāb al-shajara*: A New Ismāʿīlī Treatise from Tenth Century Khurasan," in *JAOS* 114 (1994): 343–52.

8 Ed. Ṣ. al-Sawy and G.-R. Aavani (Tehran: 1977).

9 With a few exceptions the works of the Ismāʿīlī philosophers remain either unpublished or printed in editions so unreliable as to make these investigations hazardous and critical judgment about them extremely difficult.

10 For a general assessment of the sources of Ismāʿīlī thought in this regard, see Walker [84], ch. 2.

11 On these texts see chapter 2 above, D'Ancona [51], and Endress [53].

12 See the edition and study by U. Rudolph in his *Die Doxographie des Pseudo-Ammonios: Ein Beitrag zur neuplatonischen Überlieferung im Islam* (Stuttgart: 1989).

13 Istanbul, Aya Sofya 2450.
14 The comments offered here and in Walker [84] about the *Longer Theology* depend on an as yet unpublished preliminary edition of the text by Paul Fenton (shared privately by him). For a description see his "The Arabic and Hebrew Versions of the *Theology of Aristotle*," in Kraye, Ryan, and Schmitt [60], 241–64.
15 On the Ikhwān al-Ṣafā', for whom there is a substantial bibliography, see especially Netton [82]. Although this edition is otherwise all but identical with the older edition, see Netton's recommendations for the most important of recent studies, xii–xiii.
16 On al-Kirmānī's life and works, see Walker [87].
17 Printed in an unreliable edition by 'Ā. Tāmir (Beirut: 1960).
18 The summary of the philosophical doctrine that follows here draws upon and to a certain extent depends on Walker [84], ch. 3.
19 The summary that follows is based, in the main, on Walker [84], part II (67–142). On al-Sijistānī see also Walker [85] and Walker [86].
20 The most important writings of al-Sijistānī are the following: *Ithbāt al-nubūwa* (or *al-nubūwāt*) (*Prophecy's Proof*), ed. 'Ā. Tāmir (Beirut: 1966); *Kashf al-maḥjūb* (*Revealing the Concealed*), ed. H. Corbin (Tehran: 1949), French trans. by H. Corbin: *Le dévoilement des choses cachées* (Paris: 1988); *Kitāb al-iftikhār* (*The Boast*), ed. I. Poonawala (Beirut: 2000); *Kitāb al-maqālīd* (*The Keys*), MS. Hamdānī Library; *Kitāb al-yanābī'* (*The Wellsprings*), ed. and partially trans. into French by H. Corbin, *Trilogie ismaélienne* (Tehran: 1961), English trans. in [85]. For an English translation of the table of contents of these works, see Walker [86], appendix (104–18).
21 A good example is his *al-Yanābī'*, on which see the preceding note.
22 The following summary of al-Kirmānī's thought is based largely on Walker [87], ch. 5. For an even more detailed analysis of these and other doctrines see de Smet [81].
23 On the works of al-Kirmānī, see Walker [87], ch. 2. Those of special philosophical importance are *Kitāb al-riyāḍ*, ed. A. Tamer (Beirut: 1960); *Kitāb rāḥa al-'aql*, ed. M. Kāmil Ḥusayn and M. Ḥilmī (Cairo: 1953), ed. M. Ghālib (Beirut: 1983); *al-Aqwāl al-dhahabiyya*, ed. Ṣ. al-Sāwī (Tehran: 1977); *al-Risāla al-waḍī'a fī ma'ālim al-dīn*, ed. M. 'Ā. al-Ḥurayrī (Kuwait: 1987); and several short treatises available in *Majmū'at rasā'il al-Kirmānī*, ed. M. Ghālib (Beirut: 1987).
24 Gohlman [91], 18–19.
25 See, for example, his *Faḍā'iḥ al-bāṭiniyya*, ed. A. Badawi (Cairo: 1964), 4, 9, 18, 36, 40.
26 See his *Dar' ta'āruḍ al-'aql wa al-naql*, ed. M. R. Salim (Cairo: 1971–), vol. V, 323. For this and other such passages see the important study

by Y. J. Michot, "A Mamlūk Theologian's Commentary on Avicenna's *Risāla Aḍḥawiyya*, Part I," *Journal of Islamic Studies* 14 (2003), 149–203, at 178 and esp. app. II, 199–203.

27 See for example his *Khiṭaṭ* (Bulaq: 1853), vol. I, 395, and P. E. Walker, "Al-Maqrīzī and the Fāṭimids," *Mamluk Studies Review* 7 (2003), 95.

6 Avicenna and the Avicennian Tradition

The scope of this chapter is dauntingly broad, since Avicenna was the central figure in the history of Arabic-Islamic philosophy. Before Avicenna, *falsafa* (Arabic Aristotelian and Neoplatonic philosophy) and *kalām* (Islamic doctrinal theology) were distinct strands of thought, even though a good deal of cross-fertilization took place between them. After Avicenna, by contrast, the two strands fused together and post-Avicennian *kalām* emerged as a truly Islamic philosophy, a synthesis of Avicenna's metaphysics and Muslim doctrine.

To talk about the sources, evolution, and influence of Avicenna's ideas is, in fact, to talk about over two thousand years of philosophical activity. Avicenna's sources begin with Aristotle in the fourth century B.C.E. and include the late antique Greek Aristotle commentators, both Peripatetic and Neoplatonist. Avicenna himself was extremely prolific: between 40 and 275 titles have been attributed to him by bibliographers ranging from his student Jūzjānī to the late Egyptian scholar Georges Anawati, with approximately 130 reckoned to be authentic by the Iranian scholar Yaḥyā Mahdavī.[1] What is more, his ideas evolved during the course of his career, with the result that, as with Plato's and Aristotle's thought, Avicenna's philosophy will often resist our attempts to systematize it, and his position on a number of important philosophical issues will appear frustratingly underdetermined. As for Avicenna's impact, it was felt acutely in both the Islamic world and in Christian Europe. After several of his major philosophical and medical works were translated into Latin at the end of the twelfth century, Avicenna came to exert great influence on European scholastic thought, an influence that was overshadowed only by that of the Andalusian Aristotle commentator Abū al-Walīd ibn Rushd, or Averroes (d. 1198). In post-classical Islamic intellectual history, by contrast, Avicenna's influence was unparalleled, and Averroes played only a minor role.[2] Avicenna's innovations in metaphysics – his most important philosophical contributions – were debated in the works of *mutakallimūn* (i.e., those engaged in constructing *kalām*) from both the mainstream Sunnī and smaller Shī'ī branches of Islam right up to the advent of Islamic modernism at the end of the nineteenth century.

How best to proceed, then, in light of the complex and wide-ranging history of Avicenna's sources, thought and legacy? To start with, I shall not discuss the transmission of Avicennism into medieval Latin philosophy, but leave that instead to Charles Burnett in chapter 18.[3] Second, I shall not discuss at any length the doctrines of the Ismā'īlīs, of Suhrawardī, or of Mullā Ṣadrā, but leave those instead to Paul Walker, John Walbridge, and Sajjad Rizvi in chapters 5, 10, and 11, respectively. Finally, I shall not examine Avicenna's logic, even though his innovations in that field shaped the subsequent logical tradition in Islam as profoundly as his metaphysical innovations did; I shall leave that task to Tony Street in chapter 12.

What I *shall* do is focus on the history of three basic philosophical issues, the examination of which throws light on how Avicenna appropriated ancient and late antique Greek philosophy, how his ideas changed during his lifetime, and how some of those ideas came to be naturalized in subsequent Islamic intellectual history by Sunnī and Shī'ī *mutakallimūn*. The three issues are first, Avicenna's theory that a human rational soul comes into existence with the birth of the body which it governs and uses, yet survives the body's death; second, his distinction between essence and existence; and third, his analysis of God as the only being which, by virtue of itself and nothing else, necessarily exists, in contrast to all other beings, which necessarily exist only by virtue of another, namely, their cause.[4]

At the bottom of each of these three issues lurks a problem of metaphysics. The metaphysical problem underlying the first issue is one of "applied" ontology, so to speak: what is the soul, and how does it cause the body in which it inheres? The second problem is also ontological, but much more general: what are the most fundamental components of reality? The third question is one of theology and cosmology: what is God, and how does he cause the universe? Before plunging into these deep and frigid waters I should take a moment to describe Avicenna's upbringing.

BACKGROUND AND EDUCATION

Abū ʻAlī al-Ḥusayn ibn ʻAbdallāh ibn Sīnā, known in the West by his Latinized name Avicenna, was born some time before the year 980, in a village called Afshana near the city of Bukhārā, in what is now Uzbekistan. Avicenna's father originally came from the city of Balkh (next to Māzār-i Sharīf in what is now Afghanistan) and had moved to Bukhārā during the reign of Nuḥ ibn Manṣūr, a prince of the house of the Sāmānids, who ruled northeastern Iran and parts of Transoxania during the latter part of the tenth century. Avicenna's father was appointed the governor of an important village, Kharmaythan, which was situated near a smaller village, Afshana, where he lived with his wife and where Avicenna and his younger brother were born. The family moved to Bukhārā – the big city – when Avicenna was a young boy, and there Avicenna studied the Qur'ān and Arabic literature (*adab*) with two different teachers, exhibiting even at the age of ten the intellectual independence that would characterize his studies for the next ten years or so.

Avicenna's first encounter with philosophy came through listening in on discussions his father had with Ismā'īlī missionaries. The Ismā'īlīs were a subsect of the Shī'īs, themselves the largest minority sect in Islam, the majority being the Sunnīs. The disagreement between Shī'īs and Sunnīs arose over the Prophet Muḥammad's succession. Following Muḥammad's death in 632, one group gelled around the figure of 'Alī, Muḥammad's cousin and son-in-law, and came eventually to be called Shī'a 'Alī, the "Party of 'Alī." However it was not 'Alī but Muḥammad's companion Abū Bakr who emerged as the Prophet's successor, or caliph, and 'Alī and his descendents, along with their followers, the Shī'īs, ended up being largely excluded from political power during the centuries that followed.

When Avicenna's father was a young man, in the middle of the tenth century, three centuries of Shī'ī disappointment and frustration seemed finally to be ending. A Persian Shī'ī family, the Buwayhids, captured the imperial capital Baghdad in 945, fatally weakening the already sickly caliphate of the Sunnī 'Abbāsid family, who had ruled there since 750. More importantly for Avicenna's father, a North African Shī'ī family called the Fāṭimids conquered Egypt in 969 and set up an anti-caliphate in Cairo, from which Ismā'īlī–Shī'ī missionaries fanned out across Iraq and Iran, gaining converts and hoping to lay the ground for an Ismāʿīlī revolution.

Despite the difficulties – even persecution – that Ismāʿīlīs faced in Khurāsān and Transoxania, it could well have seemed to Avicenna's father that things were finally going the Shīʿīs way, and perhaps as a result of this perception he became one of those who, as Avicenna put it, "responded positively to the missionary of the Egyptians and was reckoned to be an Ismāʿīlī."[5] With his Ismāʿīlī friends Avicenna's father used to discuss Ismāʿīlī theories about the nature of the soul and the intellect, theories which Avicenna listened to but which, he baldly asserts, he refused to accept. Whether the young boy spurned his father's attempts to bring him into the fold of the Ismāʿīlīs as an act of pre-adolescent rebellion or out of genuine philosophical dissatisfaction, it seems not to have spoilt their relationship, since Avicenna's father then arranged for him to be tutored in Islamic jurisprudence by a Ḥanafī, that is, a member of one of the four Sunnī – as opposed to Shīʿī – schools of legal thought.[6]

His religious education more or less complete, Avicenna was then tutored in philosophy by a journeyman sophist named Nātilī, with whom the ten-year-old read the Arabic translation of Porphyry's *Isagoge*, the standard introduction to logic (and to philosophy generally) in the late antique and medieval Islamic worlds. Quickly realizing – and demonstrating – that he was far cleverer than his teacher, Avicenna embarked, with his father's blessing, on a course of intense self-education, guided less and less by Nātilī, who left town in search of a more educable pupil. All by himself Avicenna read the works of Euclid and Ptolemy on arithmetic and geometry, and moved through the texts that made up the Aristotelian corpus, starting with logic, then natural philosophy, and finally metaphysics. It is very important to note that in addition to the Arabic versions of Aristotle's texts, Avicenna read many of the Greek commentaries on those texts, commentaries which had also been translated into Arabic in the ninth and tenth centuries.[7]

Using the word "read" to describe what Avicenna did when he sat down with a pile of philosophical texts and commentaries is a bit misleading. Unlike most of us Avicenna read in a very active way: he took notes, of course, but more than that he reduced all the arguments articulated in a philosophical text to their constituent premises, and then put those premises in the correct syllogistic order so that the conclusions they produced were valid, at least in those cases where the author's argument was cogent. In other words, Avicenna not only read and took notes on the Aristotelian texts and commentaries, he analyzed them. In the process he produced for himself a large set of files that he could turn to whenever he needed to remind himself of the structure of a particular argument.

Avicenna read widely as well as intensively. His skill as a physician brought him into the orbit of his father's employer, Prince Nūḥ ibn Manṣūr, who gave the young polymath permission to conduct research in the Sāmānids' library in Bukhārā in return for Avicenna's attendance upon him. In that library Avicenna encountered a vast trove of literature, with each of the library's rooms dedicated to a different field of inquiry. There, Avicenna claims, he read works of the ancients (*al-awā'il*) which he had never come across before nor was ever to see again later in his life; absorbed what was useful in them; and in so doing completed the course of self-education he had begun eight years earlier:

> When I reached my eighteenth year I was done with all these sciences. And while at that time I had a better memory for [such] knowledge, I am more mature today; otherwise the knowledge [itself] is one and the same thing, nothing new having come to me afterward [i.e., after the age of eighteen].[8]

WHAT IS THE SOUL AND HOW DOES IT CAUSE THE BODY?

It is hard to imagine that the ten-year-old Avicenna was turned off by Ismā'īlī ideas about the soul and the intellect because he had himself already come up with, or simply encountered, a more plausible theory. Avicenna was precocious, but not that precocious. Nevertheless the mature Avicenna's theory of the soul was markedly different from that of his father's friends, the Ismā'īlīs. Like Aristotle and Alexander of Aphrodisias (fl. 205 C.E., the first great commentator on Aristotle), Avicenna believed that the human rational soul comes into existence at the same time as the body in which it inheres; and Avicenna is also crystal clear in rejecting transmigration, a theory closely associated with Plato and Plotinus (d. 270 C.E., the founder of the school of Neoplatonism), a version of which was followed by some Ismā'īlī thinkers. On the other hand, Avicenna did believe – this time like Plato and Plotinus – that the human rational soul continues to exist even after the death of the body in which it formerly inhered.[9]

At first glance Avicenna's position looks like a conscious and rather crude attempt to reconcile Aristotle and Alexander with Plato and Plotinus. Upon closer analysis, Avicenna's position turns out to be a reflection of his hermeneutical context. By the time Avicenna was composing his first philosophical treatises, the ancient way of interpreting Aristotle's works, that associated with Alexander, had been superseded by a new method, one associated with Ammonius (fl. ca. 490 C.E.), son of Hermeias, as well as with Ammonius' students such as Asclepius (fl. 525 C.E.) and more importantly, John Philoponus (d. ca. 570 C.E.). After five centuries of successful development, the new, Ammonian method had come to be seen as such a natural approach to reading Aristotle, that in 1000 C.E. Avicenna would have been unaware that his view of the soul differed in any significant way from that of Aristotle. In other words, Avicenna's position on the human rational soul's separability ought not to be seen as an attempt to stuff a square Plato into a round Aristotle, but instead as the product of the fusion of two hermeneutical projects, a fusion that had been going on for five hundred years or so before Avicenna was born.

By "fusion of two hermeneutical projects" I mean the following. First, Aristotle's very large body of work is not entirely consistent on issues as widely discussed and as fundamental as the relationship between body and soul. As a result, the first commentators on Aristotle, such as Alexander, played a crucial role in constructing a single coherent Aristotelian doctrine out of the sometimes incompatible doctrines and assertions found in Aristotle's many writings. (Elsewhere I refer to this project – the attempt to reconcile Aristotle with Aristotle – as the "lesser harmony.")[10] Later on, building on the work of Porphyry (d. 309 C.E.) and other early Neoplatonists, philosophers such as Proclus (d. ca. 485 C.E.) were engaged in another, more ambitious harmonization project: reconciling Aristotle with Plato (which I call the "greater harmony"). But Proclus' efforts at reconciling Plato and Aristotle found expression in a few enormous independent treatises (e.g., *The Platonic Theology*) as well as in his lengthy commentaries on Platonic works such as the *Timaeus*, *Parmenides*, and the *Republic*. What Proclus left to his student Ammonius was the task begun tentatively by Proclus' own teacher Syrianus

(d. ca. 437 C.E.), the task of folding the greater harmony into the lesser harmony. In practice this meant composing commentaries on Aristotle's treatises in such a way that those passages in which Aristotle articulates ideas that are most reconcilable with Plato's ideas are spotlighted and then joined together to form the basis of a newly systematized Aristotelian philosophy – one that was identifiable at some deep level with Proclus' newly systematized Platonic philosophy. The task of advancing the Ammonian synthesis – of folding the greater harmony into the lesser harmony – was in turn passed along to Ammonius' students Asclepius and Philoponus, several of whose commentaries on Aristotle were translated into Arabic in the ninth and tenth centuries.[11]

The notion that the soul exists before the birth of the body to which it comes eventually to be attached, and also survives its death, had its first major elaboration in Plato's work, and specifically in his *Phaedo*. Plotinus expanded upon and systematized this theory in his *Enneads*, bits and pieces of which were translated into Arabic in the ninth century, reworked, attributed to Aristotle, and entitled *Theology of Aristotle* (*Uthūlūjiyā Arisṭūṭālīs*). According to the version of Plotinian psychology found in the *Theology of Aristotle*, the soul has two tendencies, one upward towards the world of intellect, the other downwards towards the world of matter.[12] The birth of a baby, or perhaps even conception, represents the moment when descending soul, having (as it were) "split off" from the Universal Soul, finds itself individuated in a particular body which is disposed to receive it. During its lifetime of attachment to the body the soul is constantly tempted by the possibility of indulging in bodily pleasures, and some souls give in. Other souls take the longer view, having realized that the more time spent doing philosophy, and the less time spent engaging in self-gratification, will ultimately reduce the number of cycles of death and rebirth before the final moment when, the perfect number of cycles having been completed, the soul can join the other permanent inhabitants of the intelligible world, never again to be dragged down into the world of matter. This theory, or at least important aspects of it, was embraced by Ismāʿīlī thinkers of the tenth century (such as Abū Yaʿqūb al-Sijzī, a.k.a. al-Sijistānī, fl. ca. 960) as well as by others who have been associated with the Ismāʿīlīs (such as the "Brethren of Purity" – *Ikhwān al-Ṣafāʾ*, fl. ca. 980), and it is probably quite close to the picture Avicenna's father is said to have painted during his philosophy sessions with fellow Ismāʿīlīs, given that al-Sijzī had been active in Bukhārā just before that period.

In *De Anima*, II, by contrast, Aristotle defines the soul – describes it, to be precise – as the "first *entelekheia* of a natural instrumental body possessing life potentially." One of the challenges facing the Greek commentators on the *De Anima* was figuring out exactly what Aristotle meant by *entelekheia*, a term which he invented and which he also used to define change (*kinêsis*) in *Physics*, III. The consensus amongst scholars nowadays is that we ought to translate *entelekheia* as "actuality," thereby making it more or less synonymous with the Greek term *energeia*; and that we ought to worry less about what Aristotle thinks an *entelekheia is* than what he thinks the soul and change are *entelekheia*s *of*. Early Greek commentators such as Alexander and Themistius (fl. 365 C.E.) were more determined to fix upon an acceptable meaning for *entelekheia*, and specifically a meaning that made sense in both of Aristotle's definitions. To that end Alexander and Themistius turned to another Greek term, *teleiotês*, when they wished to gloss *entelekheia*. The commentators reckoned that the range of meanings associated with *teleiotês* was broad enough to cover Aristotle's use of *entelekheia* to define the soul in the *De Anima* as well as his use of *entelekheia* to define change in the *Physics*. Alexander focused on the sense of "completeness" and "completion" conveyed by *teleiotês*, that is, the sense in which *teleiotês* was to be construed as the abstract noun associated with the adjective *teleion*, "complete," a term which Aristotle helpfully defined in *Metaphysics*, V.16. Themistius added a new sense to the range of meanings associated with *teleiotês*, one which I have called "endedness" for lack of a more elegant word; it refers to the sense in which a thing is either directed at or serves as a *telos*, or "end."

As with Alexander's emphasis on completeness and completion, which was motivated by a desire to come up with a set of meanings broad enough to square Aristotle's use of *entelekheia* to define the soul with his use of *entelekheia* to define change, Themistius' inclusion of the notion of endedness in the semantic range of *teleiotês* was also motivated by a hermeneutical commitment to the lesser harmony, to the project of reconciling Aristotle with himself. But it also gave the later commentators of the Ammonian synthesis a tool with which they could fashion an interpretation of Aristotle's theory of the soul that was more easily reconcilable with Plato's.

When the Ammonian commentators on Aristotle's texts, and particularly on the *De Anima*, found themselves confronted by Aristotle's definition of the soul as an *entelekheia* – a term which Plotinus had derided as connoting too much inseparability from the body – they soon realized they could turn to Themistius for help. Remember that Themistius added the notion of endedness – being directed at an end or serving as an end – to the mix of meanings associated with *teleiotês*, the term which Alexander had first used to gloss Aristotle's opaque *entelekheia*. With Themistius' understanding of *teleiotês* in hand, the Ammonians could direct attention away from the problem of *what the soul is* (i.e., what the soul is in relation to the body), and toward the problem of *how the soul causes* (i.e., how the soul causes the body). The Ammonian commentators had little room to maneuver if their focus was entirely confined to what the soul *is*. After all, Aristotle had said the soul *is* an *entelekheia* – that is, the soul is a state of being, namely, the state of being actual as opposed to the state of being potential – and had also implied that the soul's relation to the body was analogous to the relationship of form to matter. The analogy of form to matter led Alexander to reason that the soul, according to Aristotle, is inseparable from the body just as form is inseparable from matter (although form and matter are of course distinguishable conceptually – *kata ton logon*).

The Ammonian commentators' move from analyzing the soul–body relationship in terms of the relationship between two states of being – actuality and potentiality – to analyzing it in terms of the relationship between cause and effect, consisted in their focusing on other passages in the *De Anima* where the soul is described as causing the body not only as its formal cause, but also as its efficient and final cause. These passages presented the Ammonians with an exegetical opportunity because earlier Neoplatonists such as Plutarch of Athens, Syrianus, and Proclus, had argued quite persuasively that Aristotle's formal and material causes were crucially different from his efficient and final causes. Following these earlier thinkers, the Ammonians held that the formal and material causes are *inseparable from* or *immanent in* their effects. The efficient and final causes, by contrast, are *separate from* or *transcendent of* their effects.[13]

The Ammonians then reasoned as follows: since Alexander, the most authoritative Aristotelian commentator, had glossed Aristotle's *entelekheia* with *teleiotês*, and since Themistius had added endedness – being directed at or serving as a *telos*, or final cause – to the semantic range of *teleiotês*, the most likely way in which the soul causes the body is therefore the way in which a final cause acts on its effect. And given the fact that final causes are separate from or transcend their effects, so the soul, as a final cause, will be separate from or transcend its effect, the body.

In an attempt to come to grips with Aristotle's assertion that the soul causes the body not just as a final cause but as an efficient and formal cause as well, an Ammonian commentator could retreat a little from the strong version of this argument – that the soul causes its effect *only* as a final cause, and that therefore the soul is *always* separate from or transcends its effect – and maintain instead that the *primary* way in which the soul causes the body is as a final cause. The soul causes the body as an efficient and a formal cause as well, but only in a secondary sense, since the soul's formal causation and efficient causation of the body can, with some aggressive interpreting of Aristotle's texts, be reduced to its final causality of the body. What this meant in practice for late Ammonians such as Avicenna is that the intellect – the part of the soul that seemed the surest candidate for separability – was seen to act as a final cause on its effects, namely, the lower faculties of the soul; for these lower faculties are used by the intellect as instruments to help it think about universal intelligibles and thereby come as close as possible to attaining its own final cause, namely the eternality of the active intellect, which is always thinking about universal intelligibles. In other words, my intellect uses my soul's lower faculties of motion and sensation, which in turn use the parts of my body they are associated with, be they muscles in the limbs or the sense organs. My intellect might use my faculty of motion to convey me to the library, where I can read an Avicennian text and thereby come to think about universal intelligibles; or my intellect might use my faculty of sensation to observe repeated instances of individual things, and thereby lay the ground for its apprehension of abstracted universals. The ultimate goal of the intellect's employment of the soul's lower faculties, and of the soul's lower faculties' employment of the muscles or sense organs they are associated with, remains the realization of individual immortality, the kind of immortality that is available – in the sublunary world at least – only to human rational souls, since the souls of animals and plants can attain immortality only as species, by means of sexual reproduction, and not as individuals.

The advantage of this line of analysis is that it allowed Ammonian commentators to focus on those passages in the Aristotelian corpus where Aristotle, while not expressly advocating the idea, allowed for the possibility that the intellectual part of the soul survived the death of the body.[14] To the earlier commentators such as Alexander these passages seemed little more than Aristotle's passing fancies, off-the-cuff remarks that were so clearly contradicted by other, more canonical passages that it would be irresponsible for a commentator to cite them in an effort to undermine Aristotle's core doctrine of the soul's inseparability. But to the Arabic heirs of the Ammonian synthesis the soul's separability, understood in a restricted sense as the transcendence of the intellectual part of the soul and its survival after the body's death, was an interpretation of Aristotle's ontology of the soul that was justifiable on textual as well as theoretical grounds. In fact, a sign of the Ammonian synthesis' powerful momentum can be detected in some of the early Arabic translations of Aristotle's works, those undertaken in the beginning and middle of the ninth century. In the Arabic version of the *Metaphysics* and in the earliest version of the *De Anima*, as well as in many of the early Arabic paraphrases and summaries of those works, the Greek terms *entelekheia*, *teleiotês*, and *telos* were most often rendered into Arabic using the same term, *tamām*. The upshot is that when viewed in its proper context, as the product of a thousand-year history of shifting interpretive projects, Avicenna's theory that the soul comes into existence with the body but that it survives the body's death – or at least that the intellectual part of the soul survives the body's death – is in no sense contradicted by his close reading of and deep commitment to the Arabic Aristotle's texts and theories.

Even though the interpretive tradition to which Avicenna was heir determined the overall contours of his position that the soul was in some way separable from the body, he also offered some original arguments of his own. The most famous of them is his discussion of the "floating man," which turns out to be less an argument than a mnemonic device. At the end of the first book of the *De Anima* (*Kitāb al-nafs*) part of his great philosophical *summa*, *The Healing* (*al-Shifā'*), Avicenna asks that we move beyond the stage of considering the soul in the context of its relationship to the body, in which context we speak of it as "soul" and define it as the first perfection of a natural instrumental body. What is required, Avicenna says, is that we get some sense of what the substance we call "soul" is once we take the body out of the equation. With this aim in mind he offers a thought experiment: imagine that you have come into being fully mature and are floating in completely still air, with limbs splayed so that they do not touch each other, with your eyes covered in a membrane that prevents you from seeing anything, and with your other sense organs similarly unable to apprehend any object. In that state of total sensory deprivation, with no awareness of anything physical, would you affirm your own existence? Avicenna says yes, of course you would: in that state you would never doubt the existence of your self, even though you would not be able to affirm the existence of any part of your body. The substance that we call "soul" when placed in relation to "body," and which we further define as the first perfection of a natural instrumental body, turns out to be this "self" (*dhāt*). What is more, one's instinctive knowledge that one *would* affirm the existence of one's self in such a state of total sensory deprivation constitutes a "hint" or "indication" (*ishāra*) of the soul's essential immateriality.[15]

Much has been made of the apparent similarity between Avicenna's floating man and Descartes' *cogito*, and some have even wondered whether this passage might prove to be one of the textual sources of the *cogito*. Others have argued (and I agree) that the similarity, though striking, turns out on closer inspection to be quite superficial, since the context and purpose of the floating man were so different from those of the *cogito*.[16] Avicenna's floating man was not even meant to serve as a "proof" of anything: it is only a hint of what the soul is outside of the context of its relationship to the body, a hint that reminds us of the soul's essential immateriality. Avicenna's hope was that when his advanced students were stuck in the middle of some complex proof of the soul's separability from the body, they would not fall prey to sophistical arguments whose goal was to convince them that the soul was an atom, or some type of material object. With Avicenna's floating man always ready to remind them of the conclusion they must reach, their argumentative path would be surer. Avicenna extended this method of hinting and indicating to cover all of his basic philosophical positions in his last major work, entitled *The Pointers and Reminders* (*al-Ishārāt wa al-tanbīhāt*), which, like the floating man passage, was written with his most advanced students in mind.

Up to now I have concentrated on a theory – the human rational soul's survival of its body's death – that highlights the philosophical continuity between Avicenna and earlier thinkers. Avicenna's theory of the soul's separability is, in a sense, the culmination of what I earlier called the Ammonian synthesis, that is, the project of the Aristotle commentator Ammonius and his students, to integrate the greater harmony (i.e., reconciling Plato and Aristotle) of Neoplatonists such as Proclus into the lesser harmony (i.e., reconciling Aristotle with himself) of early Aristotle commentators such as Alexander.[17] As far as subsequent Islamic intellectual history is concerned, however, Avicenna's theory – that after death *only* the rational soul survives – was something of a cul-de-sac. It is true that most post-Avicennian thinkers agreed with Avicenna's claim that the soul survives death. It is also true that these thinkers embraced important aspects of Avicenna's psychology, for example his ideas about the structure of the soul's faculties and about the role of intuition in epistemology. But most maintained, in contrast to Avicenna, that the body enjoyed some kind of afterlife too. (The extent to which one's future body is identical to one's current body, and the sense in which "body" can be understood metaphorically, as something immaterial, posed philosophical challenges for them.) Eschatology was the motivation here, since Avicenna's idea contradicts the Islamic doctrine of bodily resurrection.

The Muslim thinker who came out most famously against Avicenna's denial of bodily resurrection was the Sunnī thinker al-Ghazālī (d. 1111), author of an elegant synopsis of Avicenna's philosophy entitled *The Aims of the Philosophers* (*Maqāṣid al-falāsifa*), a work that bears a very close connection to Avicenna's Persian *summa*, *The Book of Knowledge for [Prince] 'Alā' [al-Dawla]* (*Dānishnāma-yi 'Alā'ī*). With the *Aims* in hand, al-Ghazālī had a ready source of raw material from which to draw in his frontal attack on Avicenna, *The Incoherence of the Philosophers* (*Tahāfut al-falāsifa*). In the *Incoherence*, al-Ghazālī focused on three of Avicenna's theses whose logical implications warranted condemnation as disbelief (*takfīr*): the denial of bodily resurrection, which is entailed by Avicenna's thesis that after the body's death, only the soul survives; the denial of God's knowledge of particular things, which is entailed by Avicenna's thesis that God knows particulars only in a universal way; and the denial of the world's temporal originatedness, which is entailed by Avicenna's thesis that the world, though caused by God, is co-eternal with him.

Partly as a result of al-Ghazālī's attack, Avicenna's thesis that after death *only* the soul survives – and his theses that God knows particulars in a universal way and that the world is co-eternal with God – found little sympathy amongst later Muslim thinkers. That is not to say that all of Avicenna's ideas were dead ends, or worse, to restate the often-repeated claim, now discredited, that al-Ghazālī's attack succeeded in extinguishing philosophical activity in post-classical Islamic intellectual history. On issues other than these three, the conceptual connections between Avicenna and both earlier and later Sunnī *mutakallimūn*, his supposed enemies, are in fact much closer than we have been led to believe. What I shall next focus on is Avicenna's distinction between essence and existence, a quasi-innovation which shows how Avicenna both received and appropriated previous Sunnī *kalām* discussions, in this case about the difference between a thing and an existent.[18]

ESSENCE AND EXISTENCE

It is difficult for us nowadays to sympathize much with medieval philosophers, for whom the basic elements of reality were not physical objects, however tiny (molecules, atoms, neutrons, etc.), but rather ontological categories (substance, thing, existent, etc.). Generally speaking, Muʿtazilī *mutakallimūn*, who formed the first school of Islamic doctrinal theology, were of the opinion that "thing" (*shay'*) was the most broadly applicable category in reality, and that "thing" was in turn divisible into the subcategories "existent" (*mawjūd*) and "nonexistent" (*maʿdūm*).

There are two main reasons why the Muʿtazilīs were committed to the ontological primacy of "thing." The first is that the early Arabic grammarians were virtually unanimous in holding that "thing" refers to all that can be placed in relation to a predicate. In other words "thing" is the most universal subject, one that cannot be subsumed under any broader category or genus. The second reason was that the Qur'ān, in a pair of widely cited verses, describes God's creative act as consisting in God's saying "Be!" to a *thing*, at which point the thing then *is*.[19] To the Mu'tazilīs this was a clear indication that a thing can be either nonexistent or existent: a thing is nonexistent before God says "Be!" to it, and it is existent after God says "Be!" to it. Yet the Mu'tazilīs were never quite sure what a nonexistent thing might look like, and attacks on their ontology came to revolve more and more around their seeming inability to solve the problem of the "thingness of the nonexistent" (*shay'iyya al-ma'dūm*). What exactly does a Mu'tazilī mean when he asserts that a thing *is* nonexistent? Where exactly "is" a nonexistent thing? In God's mind, perhaps? If outside God's mind, then where? Is there one single and undifferentiated nonexistent Thing somewhere, out of which an individual thing is siphoned into existence once God says "Be!" to it? Or is there a multiplicity of nonexistent things, each ready and prepared for the moment when God says "Be!" to it? The Mu'tazilīs gave a fairly clear answer at least to the question of the existential status of mental objects. Universal concepts, such as "horseness," and fictional entities, such as a unicorn, are things, but because universal concepts and fictional entities are found only in the mind and not in the extramental world, they are, strictly speaking, nonexistent things. Objects that it is impossible to conceive of, such as square circles, are not even nonexistent things.

Sunnī *mutakallimūn* of the Ash'arī and Māturīdī schools, who began to eclipse the Mu'tazilīs in prominence at the end of the tenth century, held an opposing view. They believed in a strong identification of thing and existent, not merely holding that the domain of things is coextensive with the domain of existents (that is, every thing will also be an existent, and every existent will also be a thing), but also holding that the meaning of "thing" and the meaning of "existent" are one and the same. The Sunnī *mutakallimūn* reckoned that this strong identification between thing and existent enabled them to argue more clearly and forcefully for God's creation of the world out of absolutely nothing. This was because the Mu'tazilī doctrine that God created existent things out of nonexistent things (or out of a single nonexistent Thing) could be taken to imply that these pre-existent things (or Thing) in some sense kept God company before the creation of the world; and this in turn would undermine the Mu'tazilīs' fundamental tenet that God alone possessed the attribute of eternality. To the Sunnīs, by contrast, nothing meant *no thing*: nothing had no ontological value whatsoever, unlike the Muʿtazilīs nonexistent thing.

The fly in the Sunnīs' ointment was the status of mental objects. On the one hand mental objects could be considered to be existents just as extramental, concrete objects were. In that case an existent in the mind such as "horseness" or a unicorn will deserve to be called an existent just as much as this horse here in the stable does, and the boundary between mental existence and concrete existence will become blurry. The alternative – preferred by most Sunnīs – was to deny that mental objects have any kind of existence whatsoever. The problem then becomes avoiding the inference that since neither universal concepts such as "horseness," nor fictional entities such as unicorns, nor impossibilities such as square circles, exist concretely in the extramental world, all will be *equally* nonexistent, a conclusion that seems counterintuitive, given that "horseness" and unicorns, which you or I are able not only to make assertions about but also conceive of, seem fundamentally different from square circles, which we can make assertions about but certainly cannot conceive of.

Generally speaking, and most explicitly in his *Book of [Grammatical] Particles* (*Kitāb al-ḥurūf*), the tenth-century philosopher al-Fārābī adopts the Muʿtazilī view, holding that "thing" is the supreme genus, which can be distinguished into the species "existent" and the species "nonexistent." But al-Fārābī does allow that existent has a function which thing does not: as the copula in an assertoric proposition (i.e., a proposition with no modal qualifier such as "possibly" or "necessarily"). Al-Fārābī claims that in place of the copula "is" in the proposition "Zayd is a just man," one can use "existent" instead: "Zayd [is] existent [as] a just man." But, al-Fārābī argues, one cannot replace the "is" here with "thing," since "Zayd [is] thing [as] a just man" makes no sense. The rules of Arabic grammar make al-Fārābī's point less confusing than it might at first appear, but even so, he does seem to be straining to find some way to distinguish his own position from that of the Muʿtazilīs. Nevertheless al-Fārābī's theory reveals that there is a role for the term "existent" – as a copula – that "thing" cannot play, and that regardless of the extent of their respective domains "thing" and "existent" do have two very different meanings.

Avicenna's own set of positions on this issue comes across as a series of compromises between the Mu'tazilīs' and al-Fārābī's elevation of thing as the supreme genus, and the Sunnīs' strong identification of thing and existent; but also one that takes into consideration al-Fārābī's point that thing and existent cannot have the same meaning, given the different uses each term can be put to. In *Metaphysics* 1.5 of his *Healing*, when Avicenna speaks in terms of things and existents – when he speaks, that is, in the old ontological idiom of the *mutakallimūn* – his position is clear: "thing" and "existent" are extensionally identical but intensionally different. In other words, Avicenna maintains that while the domains of things and existents are coextensive, their meanings are distinct. Even though there will never be a thing which is not also an existent, nor an existent which is not also a thing, this is not to say that "thing" means nothing other than "existent" and that "existent" means nothing other than "thing." When we speak of an object as a "thing," we are referring to a different aspect of that object than when we speak of the object as an "existent." Nevertheless, Avicenna stresses that "thing" and "existent" are co-implied (*mutalāzimāni*): you cannot find a thing which is not also an existent, nor an existent which is not also a thing.

According to Avicenna, how do "thing" and "existent" differ in meaning? When we refer to an object as a thing, or, to be more precise, when we speak of an object's thingness (*shay'iyya*), what we are referring to is a differentiating quality which sets that object apart from another thing: a quality which "makes" the object one thing as opposed to another thing. Thus the thingness of a cat – its catness – is what sets it apart from a horse, whose thingness, of course, is horseness. When we speak of an object as an existent, however, we are not referring to *what* the object is – i.e., one thing as opposed to another thing – but rather *that* the object is – i.e., an existent.

Holding that thing and existent are co-implied forced Avicenna to maintain that mental objects such as horseness, and concrete objects such as this horse here in the stable, will both warrant being called existents. A mental object – e.g., horseness – is "an existent in the mind" (*mawjūd fī al-dhihn*), whereas a concrete object – e.g., this horse here in the stable – is "an existent amongst [concrete] individuals" (*mawjūd fī al-a'yān*). Avicenna, in short, committed himself to the existence of mental objects in a way that earlier *mutakallimūn* had balked at.

But Avicenna's ideas were more slippery than this, by which I mean that in various different works, written for different audiences and at different points in his career, he advocated positions on this question which, in the end, must be seen as inconsistent. Part of the reason for this is that Avicenna straddled two worlds: the world of *falsafa* and the world of *kalām*. His discussions of the relationship between thing and existent are clearly informed by previous *kalām* debates: both the terminology and the issues at stake are identical. But when Avicenna adopts the language of the Arabic Aristotle and of al-Fārābī, a slight conceptual shift is detectable. Instead of analyzing the relationship between thing and existent, Avicenna speaks of the relationship between essence (*māhiyya*, literally "whatness") and existence (*wujūd*). The term he uses for essence, *māhiyya*, comes from the Arabic version of the various logic texts that constitute the *Organon*, in which a definition, when properly constructed, is held to indicate the essence (*māhiyya*) of a thing.

An example of his inconsistency is that in *Metaphysics* 7.1 of *The Healing*, Avicenna implies that it is not *thing* and existent which are co-implied, but instead *one* and existent, and that *thing* is equally applicable to both one and existent. Such a position sounds dangerously close to the Mu'tazilīs' and al-Fārābī's views, since thing seems now to be a genus under which existent is subsumed. Even if we permit Avicenna to deny having advocated an ontological scheme – analogous to the Mu'tazilīs' and al-Fārābī's – in which "thing" is extensionally broader than existent, thing will at least be seen now to enjoy a logical priority over existent, that is, to be viewed as more basic than existent.

Even more anxiety-provoking is the fact that in a famous passage from *Isagoge* 1.2 of *The Healing*, Avicenna implies that thing and existent may not even be extensionally identical. There he says that the essences of things (*māhiyyāt al-ashyā'*) will sometimes be found in concrete objects in the extramental world, and at other times they will be conceived of in the mind. However, essence has *three* aspects: as a concrete, extramental existent; as a mental existent; and a third aspect, in which it is unrelated to either concrete or mental existence. A commentator could fairly infer from Avicenna's assertion that essence is not only logically prior to existence, it is also extensionally broader than existence. After all, Avicenna now holds that there are essences which are *neither* mental nor concrete existents; therefore every existent will also be an essence, but not every essence will be an existent. It appears, then, that Avicenna fluctuated between the Sunnī and the Mu'tazilī positions, between thinking on the one hand that thing and existent are extensionally identical, and on the other hand that essence is extensionally broader than existence, or at the very least that essence is logically prior to existence.

By now it will have become clear that Avicenna's discussions of the relationship between essence and existence are quite underdetermined. In fact three different Avicennian positions have been articulated: (I) thing and existent, and by implication essence and existence, are extensionally identical and intensionally distinct, with neither enjoying any kind of priority over the other; (II) essence and existence are extensionally identical and intensionally distinct, but essence enjoys a logical priority over existence; and (III) essence is extensionally broader than existence and each is intensionally distinct from the other. Adding to the confusion is Avicenna's use of so many different terms for essence – not only the two already mentioned, *māhiyya* (whatness) and *shay'iyya* (thingness), but also *dhāt* (self), *ḥaqīqa* (inner reality), *ṣūra* (form), and *ṭab'* (nature), amongst others – that it is sometimes unclear to a reader if he or she is actually in the middle of a discussion of the relationship between essence and existence. In spite of this ambivalence most subsequent treatments of the distinction in Islamic intellectual history came to use the pair of terms *māhiyya* and *wujūd* for essence and existence, respectively.

The result is that Avicenna can be judged to have succeeded in moving the discussion of general ontology from one that revolved around the old, *kalām* distinction between thing and existent, to one that revolved around the new, Avicennian distinction between essence and existence. In other words, Avicenna's contribution here lay in his framing of the distinction, rather than in his having invented the distinction out of thin air. By "framing the distinction" I do not mean that Avicenna merely supplied the basic terms used in subsequent discussions, *māhiyya* and *wujūd*. I also mean that Avicenna laid down a limited number of positions on the distinction, positions that would eventually form the core of a radically expanded spectrum of positions.

To illustrate the framing role that Avicenna played, I shall point to a number of post-Avicennian philosophers, two of whom staked extreme, though opposing, positions on the essence/existence distinction, with the others fighting over the middle ground. At one end of the spectrum, Suhrawardī (d. 1191) maintained that essence was primary and basic, that is to say, real in the most basic sense, while existence got lumped together with other unreal products of conceptual distinction-making. For Mullā Ṣadrā (d. 1640), existence was primary and real, whereas essence was a mental construct. These two opposing positions came to be termed, respectively, *aṣāla al-māhiyya* (literally, the "foundationality" of essence) and *aṣāla al-wujūd* (the "foundationality" of existence).

As I mentioned at the beginning of this chapter, I shall not go into detail in discussing Suhrawardī's and Mullā Ṣadrā's theories, because that is a task better left to the experts who have written chapters 9 and 10, respectively. My point in bringing these two thinkers up is simply to point out that each of them advocates a position on essence and existence that is so radically different from Avicenna's that to call either an Avicennist, or part of the Avicennian tradition, would be to make the adjective "Avicennian" so elastic that it ends up covering all (or at least the vast majority of) philosophical activity in post-classical Islamic intellectual history; and this would be to render it a trivial term.

The middle ground between Suhrawardī's and Mullā Ṣadrā's extreme positions was fought over by many generations of *mutakallimūn*, including the Twelver-Shī'ī al-Ṭūsī (d. 1274) and the Sunnī-Ash'arī al-Rāzī (d. 1210). In his *Commentary* on the title ("On Existence and its Causes") of the Fourth Section (*Namaṭ*) of Avicenna's *Pointers*, al-Ṭūsī articulated a much milder version of essentialism than Suhrawardī had, holding that essence and existence were co-implied, but that existence should in fact be seen as nothing more than an accident (*'araḍ*) of essence. Al-Ṭūsī reckoned that in the case of all beings other than the First Cause, existence is extensionally identical but intensionally distinct from essence. Yet existence is only an accident of essence – a necessary accident, to be sure, but an accident nonetheless. Therefore al-Ṭūsī's position echoes Avicenna's position (II), that though extensionally identical, essence is logically prior to existence.[20]

Al-Rāzī's theory is more difficult to pin down. As I mentioned above, the classical position of Sunnī *mutakallimūn* had been that thing and existent – and by implication, essence and existence – were not just extensionally identical, they were intensionally identical as well. That is to say, essence meant nothing more or less than existence, and vice versa. But by al-Rāzī's time Avicenna's distinction between essence and existence had become so much a standard part of philosophical discourse that Sunnī *mutakallimūn* could not afford simply to reassert their old position of hard identity between essence and existence. This was partly because the compositeness which a distinction between essence and existence entailed had become so useful in proving God's existence: every being is a composite of essence and existence; every composite requires a composer to bring its composite parts together; therefore every composite is caused; and in order to avoid an infinite regress of composites and composers, and hence of effects and causes, we will need to terminate at some being which is not composed; this being is God.

Given the usefulness of holding that essence and existence are intensionally distinct, it is not that surprising that post-Avicennian Sunnī *mutakallimūn* softened their earlier, rock-hard identification of essence with existence, an identification that had been the basis of their pre-Avicennian ontology. At one point in his *Commentary* on Avicenna's *Pointers* al-Rāzī advocates Avicenna's position (I), namely, that while extensionally identical, essence and existence are intensionally distinct.[21] Similarly, in his *Commentary on the Nasafite Creed*, the Sunnī-Māturīdī *mutakallim* al-Taftāzānī (d. 1390) resists embracing Avicenna's position (I) too openly, but the idea that essence and existence are intensionally distinct though extensionally identical is clearly implied in his comments.[22]

Most striking of all is the position advocated by the Sunnī-Ash'arī *mutakallim* al-Iṣfahānī (d. 1348), in his commentary on his fellow Ash'arī *mutakallim* Bayḍāwī's (d. ca. 1316?) *Rays of Dawnlight Outstreaming* (*Ṭawāli' al-anwār*). There al-Iṣfahānī admits openly (following al-Bayḍāwī) that his own, post-Avicennian position that existence is additional to essence radically departs from the school founder's (i.e., al-Ash'arī's) own doctrine. In fact al-Iṣfahānī's view seems to be based upon Avicenna's position (III), namely, that essence is extensionally broader than existence; and that existence is therefore not a necessary accident (*'araḍ lāzim*) of essence, as al-Ṭūsī had held, but something extra, an add-on (*zā'id*) to essence.[23]

What I am getting at is that in post-Avicennian Islamic intellectual history, the spectrum of positions arising from Avicenna's distinction between essence and existence was centered around the doctrines articulated by Shī'ī and Sunnī *mutakallimūn*, and stretched in opposing directions by the positions of Suhrawardī and Mullā Ṣadrā, two philosophers who, at least on this crucial issue, fall outside the bounds of what could strictly be said to be the Avicennian tradition. With respect to the distinction between essence and existence, it is the Shī'ī and Sunnī *mutakallimūn* who propel the Avicennian tradition forward. The realization that Shī'ī and Sunnī *mutakallimūn* are the true Avicennians comes as a bit of a shock, given our expectation that philosophy and *kalām* are naturally and perpetually opposed trends in Islamic intellectual history – an expectation fed by generations of Western scholars, sometimes citing al-Ghazālī's supposedly fatal attacks; sometimes regurgitating the stale taxonomies presented by pre-modern Muslim doxographers who applied to their categories *mutakallim* and *faylasūf* the Aristotelian notion that species are eternally differentiated one from the other by essential, unchanging characteristics; and sometimes blithely superimposing onto Islamic intellectual history a distinction between two categories, "philosophy" and "theology," which itself arose as a result of the institutional separation between faculties of arts and faculties of divinity in medieval European universities.[24]

THE NECESSARY OF EXISTENCE IN ITSELF

Let me take stock. Thus far I have focused on two issues, or rather two clusters of philosophical issues, that illustrate how Avicenna received and appropriated two different textual traditions. The first textual tradition had at its core the problem of the soul's relationship to the body. The authors whose opinions shaped Avicenna's own theory were Aristotle and his late antique Greek commentators, particularly those commentators who were involved in the Ammonian synthesis, that is, the attempt to fold the larger project of reconciling Aristotle and Plato into the smaller project of reconciling Aristotle with Aristotle. The second textual tradition centered on the challenge of determining the most basic elements of reality – thing and existent, essence and existence – and offering a coherent theory of how these basic elements of reality relate to each other. The authors whose opinions shaped Avicenna's own response to this challenge were the tenth-century Muslim *mutakallimūn*, both Mu'tazilī and Sunnī, and the philosopher al-Fārābī.

In the first case, that of the soul, Avicenna's theory comes across as a natural product of the Ammonian tradition that came before. Though Avicenna's thought experiment of the floating man is original, it is not an indispensable part of his theory of the soul's separability, a doctrine that had been worked on with great effort by previous Ammonian philosophers. Certain aspects of Avicenna's psychology proved influential in subsequent Islamic intellectual history. But his crucial insistence that *only* the rational soul survives death, and his consequent denial of the Islamic religious doctrine of bodily resurrection, had a short shelf-life among subsequent Muslim thinkers, who were anxious about the degree of allegorizing exegesis such a theory would force them to resort to, given the Qur'ān's crystal-clear description of the physical pains and pleasures that await us in the afterlife.

As for essence and existence, Avicenna once again took an already existing problem (though one that was not nearly as well developed as that concerning the soul–body relationship), namely, classical *kalām* debates over whether or not – and if so, how – "thing" and "existent" are to be distinguished. But Avicenna refashioned that old distinction in two parallel ways: on the one hand, by abstracting existence (*wujūd*) from existent (*mawjūd*); and on the other hand, by abstracting thingness (*shay'iyya*) from thing (*shay'*), and then by replacing thingness with the Aristotelian-Fārābian term for essence or quiddity (*māhiyya*). In contrast to Avicenna's theory of the soul, the essence–existence distinction was enormously important in post-classical Islamic intellectual history. Subsequent Muslim thinkers found in Avicenna's various – and somewhat inconsistent – attempts to distinguish between essence and existence a set of well-defined terms as well as the central span of a spectrum of possible positions on the issue, a spectrum bounded at either end by Suhrawardī's radical essentialism and Mullā Ṣadrā's radical existentialism.

The third and final cluster of issues that I will discuss centers around Avicenna's most original contribution to Islamic philosophy, namely, his distinction between (A) "that which, in itself, necessarily exists" (literally, "[the] necessary of existence in itself" – *wājib al-wujūd bi-dhātihi*) and (B) "that which, through another (i.e., through its cause), necessarily exists" (literally, "[the] necessary of existence through another" – *wājib al-wujūd bi-ghayrihi*); and his further identification of (B) with (C) "that which, in itself, possibly exists" (literally, "[the] possible of existence in itself" – *mumkin al-wujūd bi-dhātihi*). (I shall be using the more literal renderings – e.g., "necessary of existence in itself" – instead of the more elegant renderings – "that which, in itself, necessarily exists" – because the more literal renderings better flush out Avicenna's philosophical choices and dilemmas.) By Avicenna's reckoning, God is the only being that fits into category (A), while all other beings fit into category (B–C).

Like his distinction between essence and existence, Avicenna's distinction between (A) and (B–C) proved to be hugely influential in post-classical Islamic intellectual history, and later on in this section I shall briefly describe how subsequent *mutakallimūn*, both Sunnī and Shī'ī, appropriated Avicenna's distinction for their own ends and naturalized it in their *kalām*. But first I must turn to Avicenna's sources, in order to determine the ways in which Avicenna's distinction between (A) and (B–C) was really innovative. For unlike Avicenna's theory of the soul, in which his original contribution was the invention of a thought experiment devised simply to reinforce, in the minds of advanced students, an already argued-for conclusion; and unlike Avicenna's distinction between essence and existence, in which Avicenna inherited a series of rather terse articulations from preceding Mu'tazilī and Sunnī *mutakallimūn* and then refashioned them into something approaching a theory, Avicenna's distinction between (A) and (B–C) was made almost from scratch, using materials that were still quite raw in the year 1000, when Avicenna first articulated it. In this section I shall first review those sources; discuss the reasons why Avicenna felt the need to come up with his new distinction; go over the two major tendencies in his use of the distinction; and finally survey the most important ways in which later Muslim intellectuals appropriated and naturalized the distinction.

Sources

The raw materials which Avicenna drew from to construct his distinction can be found mostly in the Arabic Aristotle, and particularly in the Arabic versions of *Metaphysics*, V.5, Aristotle's discussion of "the necessary" (*to anankaion* = *al-muḍṭarr*), and of *De Interpretatione*, XII–XII, Aristotle's discussion of the modal qualifiers "necessary [that]" (*anankaion* = *wājib*), "possible [that]" (*dunaton* = *mumkin*) and "impossible [that]" (*adunaton* = *mumtani'*). In *Metaphysics*, V.5, the chapter devoted to "the necessary" in Aristotle's "Philosophical Lexicon," as *Metaphysics*, V is often called, Aristotle offers several different meanings for the necessary. The first two are quite similar: (1) necessary in order to live or exist (e.g., "breathing" and "eating"), and (2) necessary in order to live or exist well (e.g., "taking one's medicine"). The two types of necessity are related in that they both refer to what Aristotle elsewhere (e.g., *Physics*, II.9) calls "hypothetical" necessity, that is, the necessity that obtains when some goal (living; living well) is postulated or hypothesized. According to Aristotle this type of necessity governs natural things, whose matter is necessary not in any absolute sense (*haplôs*), but only given (*ex hupotheseôs*) the natural thing's specific form and purpose. The third kind of necessity (3) is compulsion: the taxi I was in got a flat tire, and as a result I was compelled to miss my train. This kind of necessity applies to intentional acts, acts that end up being frustrated by some compelling factor.

The fourth type of necessity (4) refers to the bundle of qualities – simplicity, immutability, eternality – that divine things possess. It is this type of necessity that Aristotle sees as basic, as that to which all other types of necessity ultimately refer. The fifth and final type of necessity is complex. It can be seen to refer (at least in the Arabic version of *Metaphysics*, V) to two types of necessity: the necessity *possessed by* a premise that is unshakably true (5a′), as well as the necessity *possessed by* a conclusion that follows from two necessary premises in a valid syllogism (5a″); and also to the necessity *with which* a conclusion *follows* from two necessary premises in a valid syllogism (5b). Thus in the syllogism:

All dachshunds are dogs
All dogs are animals
____
All dachshunds are animals

necessity (5a′) obtains in the two premises and necessity (5a″) obtains in the conclusion, while necessity (5b) obtains in the act of inferring the conclusion from the premises. Put another way, necessity (5a′)

refers to the necessity that a cause possesses (in this case, the causes are the premises) and necessity (5a″) refers to the necessity that a cause produces in its effect (in this case, the effect is the conclusion). Necessity (5b), by contrast, refers to the necessity that obtains in the cause's act of causing or producing its effect: given the (5a′) necessity possessed by the cause (or the premises), the (5a″) necessity of the effect (or conclusion) follows by (5b) necessity. In a way, (5a′) and (5a″) both refer to *necessity*, whereas (5b) refers to *necessitation*.

At the conceptual level, as opposed to the lexical or terminological level, *Metaphysics*, V.5 provided Avicenna with most of the raw material he needed to fashion his distinction between (A) "[the] necessary of existence in itself" (*wājib al-wujūd bi-dhātihi*) and (B) "[the] necessary of existence through another" (*wājib al-wujūd bi-ghayrihi*). But before explaining how and why Avicenna appropriated this material I shall first describe the terminological sources of Avicenna's distinction, since, as mentioned above, the term used in the Arabic translation of the *Metaphysics* for *anankaion* ("necessary") is *muḍṭarr* and not *wājib* as in Avicenna's distinction. Instead, the most likely terminological source of Avicenna's distinction is *De Interpretatione*, XII–XIII, the chapters of the *De Interpretatione* in which Aristotle is concerned with the nature of modality. That is to say, Aristotle wants to determine as precisely as he can what it is we mean when we say that a proposition is necessary, possible, or impossible; or, put another way, what it is we mean when we say that it is necessary, possible or impossible that predicate P (e.g., "dog") holds of subject S ("dachshund"). Why should Aristotle want to do this? The reason is that in the next treatise of the *Organon* Aristotle is very concerned with the implications of necessity. In the *Prior Analytics*, Aristotle begins by investigating the structure and behavior of assertoric syllogisms, but quickly turns to the structure and behavior of modal syllogisms, i.e., those syllogisms whose premises and conclusion contain modal qualifiers such as "necessarily" or "necessary [that]."

In the course of rendering *De Interpretatione*, XII–XIII into Arabic the translator made two important lexical moves. First, he started to use the more existential Arabic root *w-j-d* (as in *wujūd*, "existence"), instead of the more copulative *k-w-n*, to translate Aristotle's copulative uses of the Greek verb *einai*, "to be." The second move was using *w-j-b* instead of *ḍ-r-r* to translate *anankaion*, "necessary." In my opinion the move from *k-w-n* to *w-j-d* in translating *einai* is evidence that the translator worried about Aristotle's uncertainty over whether possibility is one-sided (i.e., opposed in a contradictory way only to impossibility) or two-sided (opposed in a contradictory way to impossibility *and* to necessity); and that the greater existential weight conveyed by the root *w-j-d* (in contrast to the more copulative *k-w-n*) helped the translator come down on the side of two-sided possibility. This is because *w-j-d* appeared to be usable both as a copula in propositions, where the logical mode *mumkin* – "possible [that S is P]" – is the contradictory of the mode *mumtani'* – "impossible [that S is P]"; and as an existential signifier in descriptions of real beings, in which the existential state *wājib* – "necessary [of existence]," here meaning "a being which is uncaused" – is the contradictory of the existential state *mumkin* – "possible [of existence]," here meaning "a being which is caused." In other words, the translator chose *w-j-d* because that Arabic root better ensured that *mumkin* was able to perform the dual role that Aristotle seemed to expect of *dunaton*, as meaning both "possible" (i.e., the contradictory of "impossible") and "contingent" (i.e., the contradictory of "necessary").

As for the translator's move from *ḍ-r-r* to *w-j-b* in translating *anankaion*, my sense is that whereas *ḍ-r-r* could have conveyed the (5a′) and (5a″) senses of necessity – that is, the necessity possessed, respectively, by the premises and by the conclusion in a valid syllogism – only *w-j-b* could also have conveyed the (5b) sense of inferential necessity – of necessitation, that is. This is because the Arabic verb *wajaba/yajibu* was the standard term one turned to when one wanted to say that a conclusion "follows necessarily from" its premises.

The result of these two shifts in translation patterns is that Avicenna was provided with an Aristotelian text in which the phrases *wājib al-wujūd* ("necessary of existence") and *mumkin al-wujūd* ("possible of existence") were both prominently used. However, the last remaining pieces of raw material – the qualifiers *bi-dhātihi* ("in itself") and *bi-ghayrihi* ("through another") – though they appeared in al-Fārābī's *Commentary on the "De Interpretatione,"* seem in fact to have come to Avicenna from *kalām* treatments of the problem of God's attributes, a topic I shall turn to now, in my discussion of the two main problems that Avicenna was trying to solve by coming up with his new distinction.

Objectives

The first problem dealt with by Avicenna's new distinction was: how is a duality – conceptual, if not real – in God to be avoided? Like the Mu'tazilīs, the Neoplatonists had insisted on a strict understanding of God's oneness – as simplicity, and not merely as uniqueness. Yet the efforts by commentators of the Ammonian synthesis to reconcile Plato's and Aristotle's theories of God's causality ultimately produced a God who was a composite of efficient causality and final causality. God as efficient cause was either the Demiurge of Plato's *Timaeus*, who creates the world out of matter but in view of the transcendent Forms; or it was the Neoplatonists' One, who is the original source of the downward procession (*proödos*) of existence (*to einai*) to each thing in the universe. God as final cause was either the Unmoved Mover of Aristotle's *Physics* and *Metaphysics*, who serves as a goal, impelling the eternal circular motion of the heavens; or it was the Neoplatonists' Good, who is the ultimate destination of the upward reversion (*epistrophê*) of each thing toward the well-being (*to eu einai*) that is peculiar to its species. For Avicenna it was simply not good enough to assert, as some Greek Neoplatonists had, that in God no *real* duality is entailed by his being both an efficient cause and a final cause, and that what appears to us to be a *conceptual* duality between God's two causal roles is a reflection of the fact that human minds are just too feeble to apprehend the real identity of efficient and final causality in God. Avicenna's discomfort with this dodge may have been exacerbated by the fact that the Ammonians had actually papered over a more fundamental disjunction. After all, God's final causality and his efficient causality not only served as explanations of the ways in which God causes the universe, they also expressed in what were then seen as scientific terms the two basic qualities that God should possess: on the one hand being utterly separate from and transcendent of the world (a quality more compatible with God's being a final cause), and on the other hand being creatively involved with and productive of the world (a quality more compatible with God's being an efficient cause).

Avicenna was able to take a fresh approach to this first challenge because by his time the Ammonian synthesis had pretty much run out of steam. By this I mean that Avicenna, born and raised and educated at the periphery of the Islamic world, had no professional teachers to instill in him the hermeneutical commitments of the Ammonian synthesis. As a result Avicenna felt under little obligation to adhere to the original interpretive premises that had caused earlier Ammonians to cut philosophical corners in order to harmonize Plato and Aristotle – or more specifically, in order to advance the Ammonian project of folding the greater harmony into the lesser harmony. These hermeneutical commitments were still operative in works as recent as those of Avicenna's predecessor al-Fārābī, who had received his philosophical education in the Aristotelian school in metropolitan Baghdad.[25]

Because of Avicenna's peripheral education – because he was almost entirely self-educated, in fact – he inherited the old set of problems created by the Ammonian synthesis yet without any motivation to keep him working within its rules; without any motivation, that is, to keep him from simply discarding or moving beyond those old Ammonian problems. True, some of the problems Avicenna inherited had already been solved within the context of the Ammonian synthesis, a prominent example being the question of the soul's relationship to the body, as I discussed earlier. But the conceptual duality entailed by God's being both a final and efficient cause remained an unsolved problem.[26]

The way that Avicenna side-stepped the Ammonians' commitment to God's troublesome combination of efficient and final causality was to propose a new formula to describe God: "[the] necessary of existence in itself." Avicenna's new formula enjoyed the enormous advantage of being syntactically amphibolous. That is to say, "necessary of existence in itself" can be construed both intransitively and transitively, and therefore can be understood as referring to a being who is transcendent of the world and productive of it at the same time. Understood intransitively, Avicenna's God satisfies the criteria of Aristotle's type (4) necessity, when type (4) necessity is viewed as the grab-bag of intransitive divine qualities, such as simplicity, immutability, and eternality; as well as the criteria of Aristotle's type (5a′) necessity, that is, the necessity with which a predicate holds of a subject, when that subject-predicate combination is viewed in itself, as a stand-alone proposition. Understood transitively, Avicenna's God also satisfies the criteria of Aristotle's type (4) necessity, when type (4) necessity is understood as the basic necessity from which all other necessities derive; as well as the criteria of Aristotle's type (5a′) necessity, the necessity with which a predicate holds of a subject, when that subject-predicate combination is viewed not as a stand-alone proposition but rather as a premise in a syllogism – when it is viewed, in other words, as productive of the necessity of a conclusion. And in this latter, transitive case, the effect which is produced corresponds to Aristotle's (5a″) necessity, the necessity that a conclusion possesses but which is produced by the (5a′) necessity of the premises. This effect of the transitive necessary of existence in itself is the necessary of existence through another.

The second problem that Avicenna's new distinction helped to solve was: how is one to distinguish between God and other eternal things? The elaborate pleromas constructed by various Neoplatonic thinkers – cosmologies that reached their peak (or depth) of complexity in the works of Proclus – cried out for a simple and basic way to differentiate the First Cause from the monads and henads and gods and intellects all crowding round it. Amongst the Sunnī *mutakallimūn*, the problem was expressed in terms of finding a way to distinguish between God's self (*dhāt*) and God's eternal attributes (*ṣifāt*), such as his knowledge (*'ilm*), power (*qudra*), and life (*ḥayāt*).

The Sunnīs had insisted on the reality, eternality, and distinctiveness of the divine attributes. This was in contrast to the Mu'tazilīs, who refused to grant the divine attributes any separate reality, arguing that while the attributes can be distinguished from each other and from God's self (*dhāt*) at a purely conceptual level, in reality they are all identical to God's self. By the Mu'tazilīs' reckoning, a cluster of eternal, real, and distinct attributes violated Islam's cardinal tenet of God's oneness (*tawḥīd*). If, for example, the divine attributes were really distinct from God's self, then there would be a plurality of eternal entities, and God's oneness, understood as his *uniqueness*, would be infringed upon. If, on the other hand, the divine attributes were not really separate from God's self but were instead contained within it, yet were still distinct enough to be really differentiated one from the other, then God's oneness, understood as his *simplicity*, would be violated. Solving this second problem – finding a watertight way to distinguish between God and other eternal things – was clearly in

Avicenna's mind when he composed his first philosophical treatise, which I shall discuss in the next subsection.

Evolution

How did the various ways in which Avicenna articulated, justified, and employed his distinction between (A) "necessary of existence in itself," and (B) "necessary of existence through another" – (C) "possible of existence in itself," evolve over his career? Is there as much evidence of inconsistency and uncertainty as there was with his distinction between essence and existence? The answer to the second question is no: the ways Avicenna expressed, argued for and employed his distinction between (A) and (B–C) are more coherent – and hence his overall theory is less underdetermined – than the ways in which he expressed, argued for, and employed his distinction between essence and existence. Nevertheless, in answer to the first question, two trends in his approach to the distinction between (A) and (B–C) can be detected, trends that are clearly distinct at the beginning of his career but which became increasingly interwoven as his career progressed.

Avicenna's distinction between (A) and (B–C) first appears in his earliest philosophical *summa*, the *Philosophy for ʿArūḍī* (*al-Ḥikma al-ʿArūḍiyya*), dating from around 1001, when Avicenna was just twenty-one years old, and commissioned by a neighbor of his in Bukhārā. In that work, most of which remains unedited, Avicenna introduces two ways of distinguishing between different types of necessary existence: *necessary of existence in itself* as opposed to *necessary of existence through another*; and *necessary of existence at all times* as opposed to *necessary of existence at some time and not at other times*. Avicenna plumps for the former way of distinguishing between different types of necessary existence, because he thinks the "in itself" vs. "through another" method will better warrant an identification of the necessary of existence in itself with the *uncaused* and the necessary of existence through another with the *caused* than the "at all times" vs. "at some times and not other times" method will.

The reason why Avicenna makes this choice is that he has in mind the second major challenge discussed in the previous subsection, namely, finding some way to distinguish between God and other eternal things, or, put another way, finding some way to distinguish between something eternal which is uncaused and something eternal which is caused. In Avicenna's case, the eternal things that are caused consist in the celestial spheres, the celestial souls that motivate them, and the celestial intellects whose serene (and motionless) eternality serves as the object of the celestial souls' desire. For Neoplatonists such as Proclus, as mentioned above, this category (eternal but caused) comprises the full complement of gods, henads, monads, and intellects. For the Sunnī *mutakallimūn*, "eternal but caused" (or better, "eternal but not uncaused") applies to the eternal divine attributes, each of whose individual reality was distinct enough from God's self to raise warning flags about the consequences of creating a pleroma of eternal and divine – though not causally self-sufficient – things. Since the problem facing Avicenna revolved around differentiating between eternal things, the "necessary at all times" vs. "necessary sometimes" distinction was of little help, since the qualifier "at all times" covers all eternal things, instead of distinguishing between them.

By contrast, the "in itself" vs. "through another" method of distinguishing between types of necessary existence was better equipped to ensure the distinctness of God, the only uncaused being, from *all* caused beings, be they eternal (such as the celestial spheres, souls, or intellects) or temporally originated (such as you or I). In the *Philosophy for ʿArūḍī* Avicenna justified his identification of the necessary of existence in itself with the uncaused, and his identification of the necessary of existence through another with the caused, by asserting that the necessary of existence in itself, unlike the necessary of existence through another, is not divisible into two modes or states (*ḥālatayni*). His reasoning was that whatever is divisible into two modes or states will be a composite of those two modes or states, and since every composite requires a composer and is therefore caused, everything divisible into two modes or states will be caused. By contrast, everything simple – here meaning not even conceptually divisible – will be uncaused. But what do the two modes or states refer to? Here Avicenna is unclear. The two modes or states could refer to (1) the fact that a being which is necessary of existence through another is *also* possible of existence in itself, and will therefore be divisible into those two modes of being (i.e., B *and* C). This is in contrast to a being which is necessary of existence in itself, which is only ever conceivable as being necessary of existence in itself (i.e., only A), and hence is indivisible into two modes of being. The problem with this interpretation is that Avicenna also asserts in this passage that whatever is subject to change will possess neither mode in itself. But whatever is necessary of existence through another and possible of existence through itself *does* possess one of those two states in itself, namely, being possible of existence.

Alternatively, the two modes or states could refer to (2) the state of nonexistence and existence which obtain in the necessary of existence through another, with nonexistence obtaining before the necessary of existence through another comes into being and also after it passes away, and existence obtaining while the necessary of existence through another actually exists. The problem with this interpretation is that it cannot account for beings which are caused but also eternal, since they are never nonexistent and hence never divisible into the states of nonexistence and existence. A final alternative is that the two modes or states into which the necessary of existence through another is divisible refer to (3) the state of potentiality (or imperfection) and the state of actuality (or perfection) that simultaneously obtain in something subject to change. After all, a log is conceptually divisible into two states: actuality (i.e., as actual wood) and potentiality (i.e., as potential fire). This interpretation works a bit better than interpretation (2) in accounting for eternal things which are caused, for even though the celestial spheres are never nonexistent, they are subject to change and therefore exhibit potentiality (they move in an eternal circular motion); and even though the celestial souls are never nonexistent, they are perfectible (they yearn to be assimilated into the celestial intellects that are paired with them). Nevertheless, interpretation (3) still fails to account for the celestial intellects, which by Avicenna's reckoning are all fully actual and perfect, uninfected by any potentiality or imperfection whatsoever. The result is that interpretation (3) will fail to account for *all* eternal but caused things.

Perhaps because of his frustration at not coming up with a satisfactory way to justify his assertion that the necessary of existence through another will be divisible into two modes or states and therefore be caused, Avicenna changed tack entirely in his next work, the *Origin and Destination* (*al-Mabda' wa-al-ma'ād*), written around 1013, when he was 33 or so. In contrast to the *Philosophy for ʿArūḍī*, where Avicenna begins with a distinction between the necessary of existence in itself and the necessary of existence through another, and then moves to identify the necessary of existence through another with the possible of existence in itself, Avicenna starts his discussion in the *Origin and Destination* by distinguishing the necessary of existence and the possible of existence, and only after doing that moves on to identify the possible of existence with the necessary of existence through another. What advantage did this new approach give to Avicenna? How did it provide a way for him to unblock the logjam that had frustrated him in the *Philosophy for ʿArūḍī*?

By 1013, when he wrote the *Origin and Destination*, Avicenna apparently felt that the distinction between the necessary of existence and the possible of existence was sufficiently intuitive that he could simply assert that the necessary of existence is *by definition* that whose nonexistence is inconceivable, whereas the possible of existence is *by definition* that whose nonexistence is conceivable. (The impossible of existence, which we need not worry about too much, is *by definition* that whose existence is inconceivable.) Once he had laid out this assumed basis for the distinction, Avicenna then claimed that we can conceive of the existence of something which is possible of existence only in the context of a relation which that possibly existent thing has, namely, the relation it has with its cause. It is in virtue of this relation with its cause, Avicenna asserts, that the possible of existence is *also* necessary of existence through another; in itself – that is, conceived of in isolation from its relation to its cause – it remains only possible of existence.

The advantage of the *Origin and Destination*'s approach to the distinction is that in it Avicenna felt under no obligation to argue that the causedness of the necessary of existence through another results from its being composed of two modes or states, and this in turn freed him from having to explain precisely what those two modes or states might be. In the *Origin and Destination*, the causedness of the possible of existence stems from its relation to its cause, a relation whose nonexistence is inconceivable once we posit the actual existence of something which is possible of existence. On the other hand, the *Origin and Destination*'s approach could be faulted for assuming too much – for assuming, that is, that everyone would find its ontological or definitional approach to the distinction to be so intuitive that the distinction could now bear all the cosmological weight that would be piled on top of it. After all, the distinction did serve as the axis of Avicenna's analysis of all reality in the universe.

In his middle period, the period when he wrote his greatest philosophical work, *The Healing*, Avicenna continued to appeal to the *Origin and Destination*'s definitional, assumed basis for his distinction. But in the *Metaphysics* of *The Healing*, a crucial thought seems to have occurred to him. As discussed above, Avicenna argues in *Metaphysics* 1.5 that thing and existent – and by implication, essence and existence – are extensionally identical but intensionally distinct. Every thing will also be an existent, and every existent will also be a thing, but to be a thing and to be an existent have different meanings. In the very next chapter, *Metaphysics* 1.6, Avicenna distinguishes between the necessary of existence, the possible of existence, and the impossible of existence, following the definitional approach he took in the *Origin and Destination*, although the phrases he uses are slightly different. Slightly later on in this chapter, Avicenna introduces the term *māhiyya*, essence, into the discussion: that whose essence is insufficient for it to exist will be caused, whereas that whose essence is sufficient for it to exist will be uncaused. The new distinction Avicenna draws here is less important for what it lays out than for what it represents, because it is here, I believe, that it occurs to Avicenna to use his essence vs. existence distinction to provide the conceptual divisibility – and hence compositeness, and hence causedness – of any being that is necessary of existence through another and possible of existence in itself, a conceptual divisibility that he had groped for unsuccessfully twenty-five years earlier in the *Philosophy for 'Arūḍī*.

In fact it is only toward the end of the *Metaphysics* of *The Healing* that Avicenna actually appeals to the essence vs. existence distinction in this way. In *Metaphysics* 8.4, a chapter devoted to proving God's existence as well as his uniqueness, Avicenna argues that God is the only being that is necessary of existence in itself because only God is not divisible into essence and existence, unlike all other beings, which are composites of essence and existence, and hence caused, and hence merely necessary of existence through another and possible of existence in themselves. In God, Avicenna asserts, essence and existence are intensionally as well as extensionally identical: God's essence refers to nothing other than his existence.

Although this appears on the surface to be a crucial move, and despite the fact that later Muslim thinkers were intensely preoccupied with determining the extent to which essence and existence really were identical in God, Avicenna's new argument, at least in the context of the *Metaphysics* of *The Healing*, is not an indispensable component of his general discussion there of the distinction between the necessary of existence in itself and the possible of existence in itself. This is because, as I already mentioned, that general discussion is still framed in the terms Avicenna first set out in the *Origin and Destination*, namely, that the basis for the distinction was definitional.

In his last major work, the *Pointers and Reminders*, the two trends in Avicenna's articulation, justification, and use of the distinction all come together in a terse synthesis. As he had in the *Metaphysics* of *The Healing*, Avicenna discusses the distinction between necessary and possible existence very soon after he discusses the distinction between essence and existence. But in the *Metaphysics* of *The Healing*, Avicenna's general discussions of essence and existence (1.5) and of necessary, possible, and impossible existence (1.6) were separated by seven long sections from his proofs of God's existence and of God's uniqueness as the only being that is necessary of existence in itself (8.4). In the *Pointers and Reminders*, by contrast, Avicenna moves straight from his discussions of essence and existence and of necessary, possible, and impossible existence (interspersed with some comments on the different categories of causes) to his proofs of God's existence and of God's uniqueness. As a result the distinction between essence and existence is pressed into immediate service, now playing a fundamental role in the proofs of God's existence and of his uniqueness as the only being that is necessary of existence in itself.

Legacy

As I mentioned above, Avicenna's distinction between essence and existence is more underdetermined, more variously interpretable, than his distinction between the necessary of existence in itself and the necessary of existence through another – possible of existence in itself. This is not to say that the latter distinction was passed on to subsequent thinkers in a fully crystallized form. On the contrary, it created a number of philosophical problems, opportunities, and challenges to subsequent *mutakallimūn*. One problem was that God's being necessary of existence might imply a conceptual duality in him, since there is a sense in which "necessary of existence" can be understood as a species (albeit a species with only one individual member) whose genus is "existent" (or "substance") and whose specific difference is "necessary." Just as the species "human" is notionally divisible into – and hence a composite of – the genus "animal" and the specific difference "rational," so too the species "necessary of existence" will be notionally divisible – and hence a composite of – the genus "existent" (or "substance") and the specific difference "necessary."[27] But once he was understood as a composite, God no longer had any basis – any non-definitional basis, that is – to claim sole occupancy of the category "uncaused being." A second problem is, should God's existence be understood as an attribute (*ṣifa*) which is somehow additional to his self or essence, in the way that Sunnī *mutakallimūn* understood God's attributes of knowledge (*'ilm*), power (*qudra*) and life (*ḥayāt*)? Should God's existence be seen instead as an accident of – and thus caused by – his essence? Or should God's essence and existence be taken to be wholly identical?[28]

A third loose end is that Avicenna seems to take for granted that (B) "necessary of existence through another" and (C) "possible of existence in itself" are convertible: that every existent that is (B) will also be (C), and vice versa. The convertibility of (B) and (C) is certainly plausible, even intuitive, in the case of concrete, extramental existents (*mawjūdāt fī al-a'yān*). But what about mental existents (*mawjūdāt fī al-dhihn*)? The answer I give will depend on other interpretive commitments I have made. If, for example, my overriding concern is to uphold Avicenna's position (I) on essence and existence – that essence and existence are intensionally distinct but extensionally identical – then I shall tend to maintain that the existence of an essence in the mind deserves to be called "existence" just as much as the existence of an essence in the concrete, extramental world does. (This is because I want to avoid holding the Mu'tazilite position that essences in the mind can be construed as non-existent). And this tendency will further lead me in the direction of assuming that Avicenna's distinction between (A) "necessary of existence in itself" and (B–C) "necessary of existence through another" – "possible of existence in itself" will be just as applicable to mental beings as it is to concrete existence. An important question arises, however: what is the cause that makes a mental being "necessary of existence through another"? If the mental being is a universal such as "Horse" or "Cat," then the active intellect seems the likeliest candidate to serve in the role of cause, since it is the source of all forms in the sublunary world: it is the source of substantial forms in the case of concrete beings such as the individuals *this horse* and *that cat*, and it is the source of intelligible forms in the case of mental beings such as the universals "Horse" and "Cat." But what about "Unicorn" and "Phoenix," which are universals that it is possible to conceive of, and which thus possess mental existence, yet which are unrealizable as concrete, extramental beings – as the individuals *this unicorn* or *that phoenix*? A further step leads us to the problematic status of "Pentagonal House" (to use an example Avicenna cites in a different context), which is a universal that it is possible to conceive of, and which thus possesses mental existence, but which (unlike "Unicorn" or "Phoenix") might well exist someday as a concrete, extramental being – as the individual *this pentagonal house* – even though up to now (at least as far as Avicenna was concerned) such a house has never existed concretely.

In the case of mental beings that are either unrealizable or as yet unrealized in the concrete world – mental beings such as "Unicorn," "Phoenix," or "Pentagonal House" – it is harder to determine which cause makes them "necessary of existence through another." Perhaps the cause is still the active intellect; if that is so, the individuals *this unicorn* and *that phoenix* will be unrealizable as concrete beings (and *this pentagonal house* is as yet unrealized as a concrete being) simply because the sublunary world happens to contain no matter that is suitably disposed to receive those forms from the active intellect. However, in the case of the intelligible forms "Unicorn," "Phoenix," or "Pentagonal House," as opposed to the substantial forms that would inhere in *this unicorn* or *that phoenix* or *this pentagonal house*, there *are* suitably disposed receptacles – human intellects – that can and do receive what issues from the Active Intellect. Alternatively, one might reasonably claim that in the case of "Unicorn," "Phoenix," and "Pentagonal House," it is merely one of my soul's internal senses that serves as the cause that makes them "necessary of existence through another" – my faculty of "rational imagination", say, which can separate, juggle, and combine different pieces of abstracted sense data.[29] Of course, if I am not so committed to promoting Avicenna's position (I) on essence and existence, I shall be tempted to avoid all the foregoing problems by clearly restricting the distinction between (A) and (B–C) to concrete, extramental beings.[30] But then I am still left with the original problem: (B) and (C) will not be convertible, since there will be as yet unrealized entities – "Pentagonal House," for example – that are possible of existence in themselves but that are not (yet) necessary of existence through another.

Despite this problem, Avicenna's analysis of God as the necessary of existence presented a golden opportunity to Sunnī *mutakallimūn* struggling with the troublesome consequences of their theory that God's attributes were, in some real sense, distinct from God's self. Before Avicenna came along, Sunnī *mutakallimūn* had treated eternality (*qidam*) as the most important meta-attribute – the kind of attribute that is predicable both of God's self *and* of God's attributes. (This position emerged because the Sunnīs, in contrast to the Mu'tazilīs, were committed to the traditionalist notion that the Qur'ān, conceived of as God's attribute of speech, was not created, and hence was eternal.) But if all – or even some – of God's attributes are eternal, then a risk arose of seeming to allow for a multiplicity of uncreated, eternal things, which in turn infringed upon God's uniqueness as the sole possessor of eternality, that ultimate criterion of divinity which set him apart from all other beings, which are temporally originated (*muḥdath*).

The post-Avicennian Sunnī *mutakallimūn* realized that necessity of existence could also be conceived of as a meta-attribute, and one with fewer problematic implications than eternality. God's self is necessary of existence, as are God's attributes; yet the attributes are not necessary of existence in themselves, since they are merely attributes and thus, strictly speaking, not "selves" but only predicated of selves. Instead, God's attributes are necessary of existence in (or with – the Arabic preposition *bi*-means both) *his* self.[31] Other Sunnī *mutakallimūn* realized that necessity of existence could be construed as a mode of the copula that bound the attribute (understood as a predicate) to God's self (understood as subject).[32]

Any *mutakallim*, Sunnī or Shī'ī, interested in taking up Avicenna's new distinction still faced one crucial challenge. The Qur'ān describes God as possessing not only the attribute of causal power (*qudra*), but also the attribute of will (*irāda*). One theme that runs through much of the first part of Ghazālī's *Incoherence of the Philosophers* is that Avicenna's conception of the relationship between God and the world – a relationship between a being which is necessary of existence in itself, and all other beings, which are necessary of existence through another – robbed God of any true agency. It is not enough, according to al-Ghazālī, to conceive of God merely as a cause; we must also conceive of God as an agent and thereby make some room for God's will. Al-Ghazālī reckoned that Avicenna expected too much from Muslim intellectuals, by forcing them in effect to reduce all the names and acts of God so clearly and powerfully described in the Qur'ān to one single, simple name – the necessary of existence in itself – and to one single, simple act – self-intellection. What would be left of Islamic doctrine after such a radical reduction?

In particular, Avicenna's conception of the relationship between God and the world entailed the denial of God's most important act, namely, his having created the world at some moment in the past. This is because Avicenna's distinction between the necessary of existence in itself and the necessary of existence through another was expressly designed *not* to map onto the *mutakallimūn*'s distinction between the eternal (*qadīm*) and the temporally originated (*muḥdath*). Remember that one of Avicenna's objectives was that his new distinction would be able to differentiate between an uncaused being – God – and all other, caused beings, eternal *or* temporally originated.

The balancing act that preoccupied post-Avicennian *mutakallimūn*, both Sunnī and Shī'ī, was to make good use of Avicenna's compelling and innovative analysis of God as the only being which is necessary of existence in itself, while at the same time ensuring that they had not thereby committed themselves to the idea that God necessitated the world's existence. That is to say, the Sunnī and Shī'ī *mutakallimūn* were entirely comfortable appropriating and naturalizing Avicenna's analysis of God as the necessary of existence in itself, as long as that formula was understood in an intransitive and not a transitive way: it should point to God's transcendence of and separateness from the world, but not indicate the manner in which God was causally involved with the world. The *mutakallimūn* felt that Avicenna's distinction was useful because it provided the basis for an excellent proof of God's existence, and more generally because it provided what appeared to be a watertight method of differentiating between God's existence and the world's existence. But as an analysis of the *way* God causes the world's existence, it required serious qualification, since it could be taken to imply that God's causation of the world was no more than an involuntary act of necessitation, rather than a voluntary act of agency.

At first glance, then, one of the great challenges of naturalization facing the Sunnī and Shī'ī *mutakallimūn* of the post-Avicennian era was to find some way to avoid throwing out the baby – the idea that God is the only being that is necessary of existence in itself – when they threw out the bathwater – the idea that God eternally necessitates the world's (eternal) existence. In fact, this was done with relative ease. The Sunnī-Māturīdī *mutakallim* al-Nasafī (d. 1114–15), for example, incorporated Avicenna's distinction into a section of his *Manifesto of the Proofs* in which the compositeness of all beings other than God – their being composed of motion and rest, or of substance and accident – point to their *not* being necessary of existence in themselves.[33] And the Shī'ī *mutakallimūn* Ḥillī (d. 1326) and Lāhījī (d. 1661) in their comments on al-Ṭūsī's *Outline of Dogma* (*Tajrīd al-i'tiqād*, also known as *Outline of Kalām – Tajrīd al-kalām*), both insist that asserting that God is necessary of existence in itself does not entail God's necessitation (*ījāb*) of the world's existence.[34] Ṭūsī himself had earlier tried to interpret Avicenna's God as only an efficient cause and not a final cause as well, probably because the efficient cause (*al-'illa al-fā'iliyya*) seemed the closest of Aristotle's four causes (the efficient, final, formal, and material) to the idea of "agent" (*fā'il*), and thus most easily naturalized into a philosophical discourse in which God acts with will.[35]

Subsequent chapters in this volume on metaphysics and psychology will treat the issues introduced here in a way more congenial to those whose interest in Avicenna's ideas is solely (or primarily) philosophical. My goal in this chapter has been to locate Avicenna in the *history* of philosophy: to unearth the philosophical challenges that most demanded Avicenna's attention; to describe the spectrum of responses open to him at that time, given the raw materials he probably had in front of him; and to explain why he chose one option over another. Avicenna, it turns out, is situated at the end of one period of synthesis – the Ammonian synthesis – and at the beginning of another, a new synthesis of Avicenna's metaphysics and Muslim doctrine. A daunting amount of scholarly work remains to be done on the 800-year history of efforts by post-Avicennian *mutakallimūn* to appropriate and naturalize Avicenna's metaphysics into their *kalām*.[36] But I hope that I have given a hint here of the richness of the sources to be mined, and made the beginnings of a case for viewing these *mutakallimūn* – Sunnī as well as Shī'ī – as the torchbearers of the Avicennian tradition in Islamic intellectual history.

NOTES

1 See Gohlman's remarks in his edition and translation of Avicenna, Gohlman [91], 13, 91–113, and 143–52; G. C. Anawati, *Mu'allafāt Ibn Sīnā* (Cairo: 1950); and Y. Mahdavī, *Fihrist-i Muṣannafāt-i Ibn-i Sīnā* (Tehran: 1954). Bibliographies of Avicenna's works can also be found in Janssens [95] and Daiber [1]; a chronology of the major works is proposed by Gutas [93]. Avicenna's major works include *The Healing* (*al-Shifā'*), covering the exact sciences, logic, natural philosophy, and metaphysics; *The Salvation* (*al-Najāt*), a summary drawn from *The Healing* and from a number of Avicenna's earlier works; and *The Pointers and Reminders* (*al-Ishārāt wa-al-tanbihāt*), a late work composed for his advanced students and requiring a great deal of decompression, and which was consequently much commented upon by subsequent Muslim thinkers.

2 At least until a number of twentieth-century Arab intellectuals made Averroes a hero of Arab (or more generally, Muslim) rationalism; on this see A. von Kügelgen, *Averroes und die arabische Moderne: Ansätze zu einer Neubegründung des Rationalismus im Islam* (Leiden: 1994).

3 On the textual transmission of Avicenna's works into Latin, see d'Alverny [248]; for a study of how a number of Avicenna's psychological theories were received and appropriated by Latin thinkers, see now Hasse [251].

4 I chose these three issues not only because they are basic but because I have worked at length on them already and am therefore confident of my analysis. Readers interested in seeing a detailed treatment of them, as well as textual evidence supporting my views, should consult Wisnovsky [105].

5 Avicenna, *Autobiography*, 18.4 (English trans. at Gohlman [91], 19).

6 See D. Gutas, "Avicenna's *Madhhab* with an Appendix on the Question of the Date of his Birth," *Quaderni di studi arabi* 5–6 (1987–8), 323–36.

7 Avicenna, *Autobiography* 22.6–7 and 24.6–7 (English trans. at Gohlman [91], 23 and 25); see also Ibn Khallikān, *Wafayāt al-a'yān wa-anbā' abnā' al-zamān*, ed. M. 'Abd al-Ḥamīd, 6 vols. (Cairo: 1949), vol. I [#182], 420.10–11.

8 Avicenna, *Autobiography*, in Gohlman [91], 36.8–38.2 (my trans.).

9 See Avicenna, *al-Najāt*, ed. M. Ṣ. al-Kurdī (Cairo: 1913), 300.2–310.7 (English trans. at Avicenna [205], 56–64); Avicenna, *Kitāb al-shifā': ṭabī'iyyāt (6): al-nafs*, ed. F. Rahman (as *Avicenna's "De Anima": Arabic Text*) (Oxford: 1959), 5.3–5.5.4, 223.11–234.11; French trans. J. Bakoš (as *Psychologie d'Ibn Sīnā (Avicenne) d'après son œuvre ash-Shifā'*) (Prague: 1956), 158–66; Avicenna, *Liber de Anima seu Sextus de Naturalibus* (medieval Latin trans.), ed. S. van Riet, 2 vols. (Leiden: 1968 and 1972), 105.40–126.26.

10 For a fuller discussion of the "lesser" and "greater" harmonies see Wisnovsky [105].

11 On Philoponus Arabus see R. Wisnovsky, "Yaḥyā al-Naḥwī (John Philoponus)," in *Encyclopedia of Islam* [16], vol. XI, 251–3.

12 On the complex relationship between the *Theology of Aristotle* and the *Enneads*, see now P. Adamson, *The Arabic Plotinus: A Philosophical Study of the "Theology of Aristotle"* (London: 2003).

13 This distinction is stated most canonically by Ammonius' student Asclepius, *In Metaph.* [= *CAG* VI 2] 5.1 (*ad* 1013a17), 305.2–17. See Wisnovsky [232] for a discussion of the history of this exegetical trend.

14 E.g., Aristotle, *De Anima*, I.4, 408b18–19; *De Anima*, II.1, 413a3–9; *De Anima*, III.4, 429a22–5; *Parts of Animals*, I.1, 641a32–641b10; *GA*, II.3, 736b28–30; *Metaphysics*, VI.1, 1026a5–6; and *Metaphysics*, XII.3, 1070a24–6.

15 *Al-Shifā': kitāb al-nafs* 1.1, 15.17–16.17 (medieval Latin trans., ed. van Riet, 36.43–37.68; French trans. by Bakoš, 12–13).

16 On Avicenna's floating man, and on its relation to Descartes' *cogito*, see Marmura [214] and Druart [89], who refer to earlier works. See also below, chapter 15.

17 For another example of how Avicenna can be fruitfully compared with another philosopher of the Ammonian synthesis, see A. Stone, "Simplicius and Avicenna on the essential corporeity of material substance," in Wisnovsky [104], 73–130.

18 On this problem generally, see Wisnovsky [231].

19 Qur'ān, 16:40: "Our statement to a thing, when we wish it [to be], consists merely in our saying to it 'Be!', and then it is" (*inna-mā qawlunā li-shay'in idhā aradnāhu an naqūla lahu kun fa-yakūnu*); and 36:82: "His command, when he wishes a thing [to be], is merely that he say 'Be!' and then it is" (*inna-mā amruhu idhā arāda shay'an an yaqūla kun fa-yakūnu*).

20 Naṣīr al-Dīn al-Ṭūsī, *Sharḥ al-ishārāt*, in *Sharḥay al-ishārāt* (Qom: 1983 or 1984), 189.16–19 (inside box on the page).

21 Fakhr al-Dīn al-Rāzī, *Sharḥ al-Ishārāt*, in *Sharḥay al-ishārāt*, 192.5–13 (outside box).

22 Sa'd al-Dīn al-Taftāzānī, *Sharḥ al-'aqā'id al-nasafiyya* (Cairo: 1916), 16.2–17.3 (top part of inside box); trans. E. Elder, *A Commentary on the Creed of Islam* (New York: 1950), 11–12.

23 Maḥmūd al-Iṣfahānī, *Maṭāli' al-anẓār sharḥ ṭawāli' al-anwār* (Cairo: 1902), 39–41; English trans. by E. Calverley and J. Pollock, *Nature, Man and God in Medieval Islam* (Leiden: 2002), vol. I, 192–7.

24 In fact many historians of medieval European thought are now actively engaged in re-examining the traditional distinction between philosophy and theology; see the articles contained in J. Aertsen and A. Speer, eds., *Was ist Philosophie im Mittelalter? Akten des X. Internationalen Kongresses für mittelalterliche Philosophie* (Berlin: 1998).

25 That al-Fārābī saw himself as part of the tradition of the Ammonian synthesis is evident throughout his treatise *On the Harmony between the Opinions of the Two Philosophers, Plato the Divine and Aristotle*, but particularly in his claim that Ammonius' arguments about God's being both an efficient and final cause were so well known that they did not require citation: al-Fārābī, *Kitāb al-jam' bayna ra'yay al-ḥakīmayni Aflāṭūn al-ilāhī wa-Arisṭūṭālīs*, ed. F. Dieterici, *Alfārābī's philosophische Abhandlungen* (Leiden: 1890), 24.24–25.1.

26 On the history of this issue see Wisnovsky [233].

27 E.g., al-Shahrastānī, *Kitāb al-muṣāra'a*, ed. W. Madelung and trans. T. Mayer, *Struggling with the Philosopher: A Refutation of Avicenna's Metaphysics* (London: 2001), 8.6–11.2; 24.3–31.2; and 43.3–46.10 (trans. 23–5, 33–7, and 44–6).

28 E.g., al-Rāzī, *Sharḥ al-ishārāt*, 200.3–204.7.

29 To some extent this dilemma is symptomatic of Avicenna's ambivalence over the degree of genuine agency enjoyed by humans during the act of intellection; on this see now D. Hasse, "Avicenna on Abstraction," in Wisnovsky [104], 39–72.

30 See al-Bayḍāwī's (and following him, al-Iṣfahānī's) description of the position of the "philosophers" (here probably referring to Avicenna) at *Maṭāli' al-anẓār: Sharḥ ṭawāli' al-anwār* 36 (English trans. by Calverley and Pollock, vol. I, 176–7).

31 E.g., al-Taftāzānī, *Sharḥ al-'aqā'id al-nasafiyya*, 52.2–60.5 and 69.2–72.10 (top part of the inside box; English trans. by Elder, 36–40 and 49–53). For a Shī'ī counterargument, see Ḥaydar Āmulī (d. after 1385), *Jāmi' al-asrār*, ed. H. Corbin and O. Yahia (Paris: 1969), 139.7–142.11.

32 See Imām al-Ḥaramayn al-Juwaynī (d. 1085), *al-'Aqīda al-Niẓāmiyya*, ed. M. Z. al-Kawtharī (Cairo: 1948), 16.19ff., 14.12ff., and 25.3ff.; and *Kitāb al-irshād*, ed. and French trans. J.-D. Luciani (as *El-Irchad*

par Imam el-Haramein) (Paris: 1938), 17.16ff. and 94.3ff.; al-Sanūsī (d. 1490), *al-ʿAqīda al-sanūsiyya*, in Ibrāhīm al-Bājūrī (d. 1860), *Ḥāshiya ʿalā matn al-Sanūsiyya* (Cairo: 1856), 57.8–58.2 (marg.); Ibrāhīm al-Laqānī (d. ca. 1631), *Jawhara al-tawḥid* (Cairo: n.d.), 28.1 and 31.1; and al-Faḍālī (d. 1821), *Kifāya al-ʿawāmm fī ʿilm al-kalām*, in Ibrāhīm al-Bājūrī, *Ḥāshiya ʿalā Kifāya al-ʿawāmm* (Cairo: 1906), 31.1–33.1; 38.2–4 and 44.1 (all top section of page).

33 Abū al-Muʿīn al-Nasafī, *Kitāb tabṣira al-adilla*, ed. K. Salāma (Damascus: 1993), 61.1–63.3.

34 ʿAllāma al-Ḥillī, *Kashf al-murād fī sharḥ Tajrīd al-iʿtiqād* (Beirut: 1979), 305.1–306.12; al-Lāhījī, *Shawāriq al-ilhām fī sharḥ Tajrīd al-kalām* (Iṣfahān: reprint of lithograph from 1878/1893), 494.13–504.26.

35 Al-Ṭūsī, *Sharḥ al-ishārāt*, 194.13–17 (inside box). I argue against al-Ṭūsī's interpretation in Wisnovsky [233].

36 For a concise overview, see now Gutas [94]; see also Wisnovsky [261]. Some work on the naturalization of Avicenna's metaphysics in Shīʿī *kalām* has been done; see, for example, Schmidtke [259], esp. 180–6, and Schmidtke [260], esp. 37–114, and now A. al-Rahim, "The Twelver-Shīʿī Reception of Avicenna in the Mongol Period," in Reisman [103], 219–31. On the Sunnī side, by contrast, little is available apart from van Ess' (German) translation of and commentary on the first part of the Sunnī *mutakallim* al-Ījī's (d. 1355) *Book of Stations*: see J. van Ess, *Die Erkenntnislehre des ʿAḍudaddīn al-Īcī: Übersetzung und Kommentar des 1. Buches seiner Mawāqif* (Wiesbaden: 1966), and even this concentrates more on epistemology than metaphysics. But see also Y. Michot, "L'avicennisation de la sunna, du sabéisme au leurre de la Ḥanīfiyya: à propos du *Livre des religions et des sectes*, II d'al-Shahrastānī," *Bulletin de philosophie médiévale* 35 (1993), 113–20, and J. Michot, "La pandémie avicennienne au VIe/XIIe siècle: présentation, editio princeps et traduction de l'introduction du *Livre de l'advenue du monde* (*Kitāb ḥudūth al-ʿālam*) d'Ibn Ghaylān al-Balkhī," *Arabica* 40 (1993), 287–344.

MICHAEL E. MARMURA

7 Al-Ghazālī

The writings of al-Ghazālī (d. 1111) mark a critical stage in the history of Arabic philosophy. He is noted for his classic, *The Incoherence of the Philosophers* (*Tahāfut al-falāsifa*), an incisive critique largely of the metaphysics and psychology of Avicenna (d. 1037). At the same time, he is also noted for adopting Avicennian philosophical ideas. This at first sight seems paradoxical, if not downright inconsistent. In fact, he adopted them after reinterpreting them in terms of his Ash'arite occasionalist perspective (to which we will shortly turn), rendering them consistent with his theology. This reinterpretation is not without intrinsic philosophical interest.

Al-Ghazālī was a renowned Islamic lawyer (*faqīh*), speculative theologian (*mutakallim*), but above all an Islamic mystic (*ṣūfī*). In his autobiography, written a few years before his death, he states that it was the quest after certainty that motivated his intellectual and spiritual journey and that he finally found this certainty in direct mystical experience, *dhawq*, a technical Ṣūfī term that literally means "taste."[1] Although trained in the Ash'arite school of speculative theology, *kalām*, to which he contributed two works, he was also critical of this discipline. This has raised the question of whether his mysticism was at odds with his theology, which included the reinterpreted, assimilated, Avicennian philosophical ideas. A close reading – in proper context – of his writings during the period in which he became a mystic suggests that this is not really the case. As we hope to indicate, his mysticism and his theological–philosophical affirmations tend to complement each other.

LIFE AND CAREER

Born in 1058 in the city of Ṭūs or its environs in northeast Persia, al-Ghazālī had a traditional Islamic education in *madrasas*, religious colleges that focused on the study of religious law. After studying in Ṭūs, then Jurjān, he went (around 1077) to Nīshāpūr where he studied with the renowned Imām al-Ḥaramayn al-Juwaynī, a jurisconsult of the school of al-Shāfi'ī (d. 820) and a leading theologian of the *kalām* of al-Ash'arī (d. 935). It is probable that during his studies in Nīshāpūr he had some exposure to philosophy: its intensive study came later when in Baghdad.

Al-Juwaynī died in 1085. Al-Ghazālī seems to have remained in Nīshāpūr for some six years. He acquired the reputation of being a brilliant scholar who contributed works on Shāfi'ī law. In 1091, the vizier Niẓām al-Mulk appointed him as professor of law in the Niẓāmiyya at Baghdad. This was the most prestigious of a number of colleges that took their name from their founder, Niẓām al-Mulk, the vizier of the Seljuk Turkish sultans, for the teaching of Shāfi'ī law. These sultans wielded real power in Baghdad, but their power was legitimized by the 'Abbāsid caliph. The Seljuk Turks had adopted Islam in its Sunnī (orthodox) form and were hence in conflict with the Shī'ite Fāṭimid anti-caliphate in Cairo. The Niẓāmiyya colleges were intended in part to counteract Fāṭimid religious doctrine. One of the books al-Ghazālī wrote when he came to Baghdad, *The Scandal of the Esoterics* (*Faḍā'iḥ al-bātiniyya*), commissioned by the 'Abbāsid caliph, al-Mustaẓhir (d. 1118), was a theological attack on Fāṭimid doctrine.

Al-Ghazālī taught at Baghdad from 1091 until 1095. Probably early during this period, he underwent a period of skepticism. For in his quest after certainty, as he tells us in his autobiography,[2] he could no longer trust the senses. How could one trust the strongest of these senses, sight? We look at the shadow and see it static, but later find out that it has moved and has been moving all the time, gradually, imperceptibly. Again, we look at the sun and it appears to us to be the size of a coin, but astronomical proof shows that it is greater than our earth. This skepticism extended to reason. If the senses cannot be trusted, can one trust reason? Here again, al-Ghazālī found no guarantee that the primary principles of reason – the principle of the excluded middle, for example – can be trusted. For one cannot demonstrate their truth without circularity, without assuming them. This skepticism, he tells us, was an illness that afflicted him for two months, until God restored to him belief in reason.

The four years of teaching at the Niẓāmiyya were also the years of al-Ghazālī's intensive studies of philosophy and his writing of a number of works relating to it. Of these, the most important was his *The Incoherence of the Philosophers*. He also wrote *The Aims of the Philosophers* (*Maqāṣid al-falāsifa*), a work of exposition that closely followed Avicenna's Persian work, *The Book of Knowledge for [Prince] 'Alā'ī [al-Dawla]* (*Dānishnāma-yi 'Alā'ī*). The *Aims* became known in its Latin translation to the medieval West, but was mistakenly thought to be an expression of al-Ghazālī's own philosophy. In introducing it and at the end of this work, al-Ghazālī states that he wrote it to explain the Islamic philosophers' theories as a prelude to his refuting them in the *Incoherence*. Curiously, however, the *Incoherence* neither mentions nor alludes to it. It is possible that he initially wrote it to summarize for himself the philosophical theories he was studying and that later, when he decided to circulate it, he added the statements that he wrote it as a prelude to the *Incoherence*. This, however, is speculation. Another work of this period, explicitly related to the *Incoherence*, is *The Standard for Knowledge* (*Mi'yār al-'ilm*). It was expressly written as an appendix to the *Incoherence*. This is essentially an exposition of Avicenna's logic, the most comprehensive of several expositions of this logic he wrote.

To this period also belongs his most important theological work, *Moderation in Belief* (*al-Iqtisād fī al-i'tiqād*). It is an Ash'arite work which al-Ghazālī held in high regard. Written after the *Incoherence*, it is closely related to it. The purpose of the *Incoherence*, as al-Ghazālī clearly states, is to refute the philosophers, not to affirm true doctrine.[3] The affirmation of doctrine is embodied in the *Moderation* and in a shorter complementary Ash'arite work, the *Principles of Belief* (*Qawā'id al-'aqā'id*), incorporated in his later voluminous work, *The Revival of the Sciences of Religion* (*Iḥyā' 'ulūm al-dīn*),[4] written after he left Baghdad to follow the Ṣūfī path.

This decision followed a spiritual crisis. As he tells it in his autobiography, he realized that his motivation in pursuing his career as teacher and writer was worldly success. It was not an authentic religious impulse. He also hints at a deeper reason, namely, a dissatisfaction with the purely doctrinal and rational approaches to religion. These bypassed the most essential aspect of the religious life – the directly experiential, the *dhawq* we referred to earlier. He had read the works of Ṣūfīs and wanted to follow their practice. This meant seclusion and devotion unencumbered by worldly concerns. He decided to leave Baghdad and the prestigious teaching position he held. To do so without opposition from the authorities, he gave as his reason his intention to go on pilgrimage to Mecca. After making appropriate arrangements for the welfare of his family, he traveled to Syria and secluded himself in the mosque in Damascus. He then went to Jerusalem and the Dome of the Rock, and also visited Hebron. He then visited Mecca and Medina.

He spent some eleven years away from teaching as he became a Ṣūfī. During this period he wrote his magnum opus, the *Iḥyā'*, which strove to reconcile traditional Muslim belief with Ṣūfism. In related works, al-Ghazālī tended to interpret what the Ṣūfīs termed the "annihilation" (*al-fanā'*) of the self in God as "closeness" (*qurb*) to the divine attributes, a view more acceptable to traditional Islamic belief. The *Iḥyā'* included homilies designed to nurture Islamic piety, in part to encourage an ascetic way of life as a necessary requirement for those intent on following the Ṣūfī path. In 1106, he resumed his teaching of Islamic law first at Nīshāpūr and then at Ṭūs, where he died in 1111. His return to the teaching of law saw the writing of his major work on Islamic law, namely, *The Choice Essentials of the Principles of Religion* (*al-Mustasfā min uṣūl al-dīn*). After the writing of the *Iḥyā'*, al-Ghazālī wrote a number of important shorter works which include among others the following: *The Highest Goal in Explaining the Beautiful Names of God* (*al-Maqṣad al-asnā fī asmā' Allāh al-ḥusnā*); *The Decisive Criterion for Distinguishing Belief from Unbelief* (*Faysal al-tafriqa bayn al-Islam wa al-zandaqa*); *The Book of Forty* (*Kitāb al-arba'īn*), which sums up some main ideas of the *Iḥyā'*; the two mystical works, *The Alchemy of Happiness* (*Kīmīā-ye sa'ādat*) in Persian and *The Niche of Lights* (*Mishkāt al-anwār*); his autobiography, *The Deliverer from Error* (*al-Munqidh min al-ḍalāl*); and his last work, *Restraining the Commonality from the Science of Kalām* (*Iljām al-'awām 'an 'ilm al-kalām*).

Al-Ghazālī's religious thought is multi-faceted and is expressed in a variety of contexts. One way to approach it is to discuss it first in terms of the relation of his Ash'arite theology to philosophy and then in relation to his mysticism.

GHAZĀLĪ AND THE ASH'ARITES

The work in which al-Ghazālī expresses his Ash'arite theology in detail is the *Moderation in Belief*. It is significant that he expressed his high regard for this work long after he had become a Ṣūfī, in *The Book of Forty* (written after the *Iḥyā'*), in which he proclaims that the *Moderation in Belief* contains the essentials of the science of the theologians, in effect, the Ash'arite theologians (*al-mutakallimīn*). He then adds that it goes deeper than the Ash'arite works of *kalām* in ascertaining the truth and "is closer to knocking at the door of gnosis" (*abwāb al-ma'rifa*) than the "official discourse" (*al-kalām al-rasmī*) encountered in their books.[5] It is significant that he did not regard it as one of the "official" Ash'arite works and that he held it to be superior to such works in ascertaining what is true.

The cornerstone of Ash'arite theology is its doctrine of the divine attributes. Al-Ghazālī endorses and expands on this doctrine. For the Ash'arites, the divine attributes of life, knowledge, will, power, speech, hearing, and seeing are co-eternal with the divine essence and intimately related to it, but are not identical with it. They are attributes "additional" (*zā'ida*) to the divine essence. This point is quite basic, particularly for understanding al-Ghazālī's rejection and condemnation of the philosophical doctrine of an eternal world. For if these attributes are identical with the divine essence, then the divine act would be an essential act, an act which proceeds as the necessary consequence of the very essence or nature of God. Now for Avicenna, with whom al-Ghazālī is contending, God is the supreme essential cause for all the existents that successively emanate from him, the totality of which is the world. According to Avicenna, the priority of the essential cause to its effect is ontological, not temporal. The essential cause coexists with its effect. Hence, for Avicenna, the world as the necessitated effect of the eternal essential cause is necessarily eternal.

This consequence meant for al-Ghazālī the negation of the divine attribute of will. To be sure, for al-Ghazālī, whatever the divine eternal will chooses and decrees must come about. In this sense the existence of what it decrees is necessary. It is not, however, necessitated by the divine essence. Not being identical with the divine essence, the eternal will does not have to decree the creation of the world. It does so "freely," so to speak, by an eternal voluntary act.

According to al-Ghazālī, by this act it decrees the world's creation out of nothing (*ex nihilo*) at a finite moment in time in the past from the present.

Whatever the divine will decrees comes about through the attribute of divine power. This brings us to the relation of the divine attributes of life, knowledge, will, and power to each other. These are conditionally related. There can be no knowledge without life, no will without knowledge, and no power without will. Each, that is life, knowledge, will, and power, is respectively a necessary condition for the other. This does not, however, mean that they "cause" each other. They are eternal coexisting uncaused attributes. Moreover, the eternal will decrees that all created existents and events follow a uniform course. Al-Ghazālī refers to this uniform course as *ijrā' al-'āda*, God's ordaining things to flow according to a habitual course. But this habitual course is not in itself necessary. It can be disrupted without contradiction. The eternal will that decrees this uniform, habitual course decrees also its disruptions at certain moments of history. These disruptions are the miracles that God creates on behalf of his prophets and holy men.

The divine attribute of power is the sole cause of all created things and events.[6] It is also pervasive. By this al-Ghazālī means that divine power is one, not divisible into many powers, and is the cause of each and every created existent and event. Our world consists of bodies, composed of indivisible atoms and accidents that inhere in them. The atoms, the accidents, the bodies they compose, and all sequences of events are the direct creation of this pervasive divine power. The uniform course of events constitutes an order which includes what we habitually regard as causes and effects. But while these behave as though they are real causes and effects, in fact they are not. They are concomitant events that are not necessarily connected with each other and are causally connected only with the one cause, divine power. This brings us to what is meant by saying that this theology is occasionalist. Events habitually regarded as causes are merely the occasions for divine, direct, real causal action. They follow an order that parallels the order (in all its details) of what Avicenna regards as real causes and effects, so that normally one can draw "demonstrative" inferences from the chains of occasionalist/habitual causes and effects.[7]

At the heart of Ash'arite occasionalism is their doctrine of "acquisition" (*kasb*). Human acts, like all other events, are the direct creation of divine power. This power creates in us power we experience as the cause of our deliberate actions. But just as the events we normally regard as causes and effects are concomitants, created by divine power, so are those acts we normally believe to be our deliberate acts. They are acts concomitant with the events we normally regard as the "effects" of this power. These "effects," however, are not of our doing. They are created for us by divine power. In other words, the power created in us has no causal efficacy. Whatever we believe to have been "acquired" by our own power is in reality acquired on our behalf by divine power. Al-Ghazālī insists that the created power in us exists only with the acquisition the divine power creates for us. Created power does not temporally precede the human act. It and the act are created simultaneously. Moreover, divine power cannot enact the impossible. It cannot enact in us created power without first creating in us respectively life, knowledge, and will. Each of these, however, is the direct creation of divine power.

If this then is the case, how can we differentiate our spasmodic movements from those movements we normally regard as deliberate? The classic Ash'arite answer, which al-Ghazālī endorses, is that in the case of the spasmodic movement, such a movement is created without the created power, whereas what is normally regarded as the deliberate movement is created with it. This is how they differ. We ourselves experience this difference. This, however, does not resolve the question of how this theory can account for human moral responsibility, premised on the doctrine of the freedom of the human will. Al-Ghazālī is hardly unaware of this problem. But he supports this theory of acquisition, suggesting that a resolution of its difficulties is attained when, through mystical vision, its place in the cosmic scheme of things is understood.

THE *INCOHERENCE*

Al-Ghazālī's Ash'arite occasionalist perspective given in the *Moderation in Belief* is reiterated in different contexts in the *Iḥyā'*, as we shall point out. This perspective forms the background of the *Incoherence* and helps us better understand some of its arguments.

Now it is true that al-Ghazālī regarded the *Incoherence* as a work of refutation and did not intend it to be an exposition of Ash'arite theology. He thus declares quite plainly that he is not writing the book from any one specific doctrinal position (*Incoherence*, 7). Moreover, on two notable occasions he adopts some of the views of his philosopher opponents to show that even in terms of their own theories, the literal scriptural assertions they deem impossible are in fact possible. In this he is quite consistent with his declaration that the primary intention of the *Incoherence* is to refute, not to build up doctrine.

Al-Ghazālī, however, in one of his later works,[8] declared the *Incoherence* as belonging to the genre of *kalām* works – this not inconsistently. For he held the main task of Ash'arite *kalām* to be the defence of what he conceived to be Islamic Sunnī doctrine. The *Incoherence* constitutes such a defence, even though it does not set out to formulate a doctrine (*Incoherence*, 7). At the same time, there are many assertions and hidden premises in this work that when extracted convey a specific theological view, namely, the Ash'arite. As we will indicate, an Ash'arite assertion is introduced as part of al-Ghazālī's method of refuting. Hence when the chief critic of this work, Averroes, in his *Incoherence of the Incoherence* (*Tahāfut al-tahāfut*) repeatedly refers to al-Ghazālī's stance in the *Incoherence* as Ash'arite, he is to a good extent justified. But before turning to the Ash'arite base that underlies much of the arguments of the *Incoherence*, a brief word about this work is necessary.

In the *Incoherence*, al-Ghazālī singled out for criticism the philosophies of al-Fārābī and Avicenna. These two, he holds, are the best exponents of the philosophy of Aristotle. Here, however, we have to be reminded that while these two were Aristotelians, they were also Neoplatonists, each constructing an emanative scheme that has its own peculiarities. Their respective emanative schemes, though similar, are not identical. Moreover, their theories of the soul and eschatologies are also not identical. Al-Ghazālī's critique has as its more direct object the philosophy of Avicenna. Nonetheless, many of these criticisms apply to aspects of al-Fārābī's thought. In the *Incoherence* al-Ghazālī sometimes refers specifically to Avicenna, but in general he simply refers to his opponents as "the philosophers."

The *Incoherence* is aimed at refuting those philosophical ideas deemed by al-Ghazālī to contravene Islamic religious belief. It thus addresses itself to twenty philosophical theories, three of which it holds to be utterly opposed to Islamic religious belief, those upholding them to be infidels, to be grouped with heretical innovations that some Islamic sect or another had held. The three theories he condemns as utterly opposed to Islamic teaching are the theory of a pre-eternal world, the theory (specifically Avicennian) that God knows only the universal aspects of terrestrial particulars, and Avicenna's doctrine of the immortal, immaterial soul that denies bodily resurrection. To refute such theories, all that al-Ghazālī needs to show is that contrary to the philosophers' claims, these theories have not been demonstrated. He certainly endeavors to do this, but he also argues that some of them are self-contradictory.

CAUSALITY

The Ash'arism of the *Incoherence* is best seen in discussions where the concept of causality is involved. The First Discussion is devoted to the question of the world's origin, and consists of a debate of four philosophical proofs for the world's pre-eternity. The debate of the first proof is the longest. The philosophers' proof, which al-Ghazālī regards as their strongest, is premised on the theory of divine essential causality. According to the philosophers, a world created in time would mean the delay of the effect of a necessitating cause (namely God) when there can be no impediment or any other reason to account for such a delay. After presenting the philosophers' argument in its most forceful way, al-Ghazālī begins his refutation by asking whether the philosophers can demonstrate the impossibility of the contradictory of its conclusion, namely, the Ash'arite doctrine that the world is created at that moment of time which the eternal divine will has chosen and decreed for its creation (*Incoherence*, 17). He argues that they can do this neither syllogistically nor by an appeal to what is self-evidently necessary. If the denial of the conclusion cannot be proven to be untrue, then its premise that the divine essential cause necessitates its effect remains unproven. At the conclusion of this multi-faceted debate, he refers to the philosophers' theory that the cause for the occurrence of temporal events is the circular movement of the celestial spheres. He denies this, affirming the Ash'arite view that all temporal events are "the initial inventions" of God (*mukhtara'a li-al-Lāhi ibtidā'an*; *Incoherence*, 30).

In the Third Discussion, al-Ghazālī discusses the use of the term "agent." Agency belongs only to a living, willing, knowing being. When the opponent appeals to correct Arabic usage, as, for example, when it is said that fire kills, al-Ghazālī insists that this is merely metaphorical usage: fire as such in reality has no action (*Incoherence*, 58–9) – a point repeated in the Seventeenth Discussion.

While the Seventeenth Discussion is devoted to causality, its real purpose is to show that some of the miracles, reported in the Qur'ān and the prophetic traditions but considered by the philosophers as impossible, are possible.[9] Al-Ghazālī begins the discussion with the Ash'arite declaration: "the connection between what is habitually believed to be a cause and what is habitually believed to be the effect is not necessary for us." With any two things, he continues, that are not identical, where neither the affirmation or negation of the one entails the affirmation or negation of the other, the existence or nonexistence of the one does not entail the existence or nonexistence of the other. He then gives as examples, "the quenching of thirst and drinking, satiety and eating, light and the appearance of the sun, death and decapitation." The connection of these and other such observable things is due to the prior decree of God, who creates them side by side. The connections between them are not in themselves necessary and they are hence capable of separation. It is thus within divine power, for example, to create death without decapitation and to continue life after decapitation (*Incoherence*, 166).

Al-Ghazālī then takes his well-known example of the contact of a piece of cotton with fire. What we see is the occurrence of the burning of cotton at the point of contact with the fire. We do not see its being burnt by the fire. What we witness are two concomitant events. He then asserts that the one who enacts the burning by creating blackness in the cotton, producing separation in its parts, and rendering it cinder and ashes, is God, either directly or through the mediation of his angels (*Incoherence*, 167). (We will be turning to the question of what al-Ghazālī means by angelic mediation when discussing aspects of the *Iḥyā'*.)

As the discussion of causality proceeds, al-Ghazālī puts in the mouth of his opponents a major objection. From the denial of necessary causal connection in natural events, they argue, repugnant impossibilities will ensue. There will be no order in the world.

All occurrences would be sheer possibilities whose contraries can equally occur. A man, for example, will be confronted by wild beasts and raging fires but will not see them because God has not created sight for him. All kinds of similar absurdities will then follow (*Incoherence*, 169–70). To this al-Ghazālī replies that if things whose existence is possible are such that there cannot be created for an individual knowledge of their nonexistence, the impossibilities the opponents mention would follow. These things they mention, however, he goes on, are mere possibilities that may or may not occur. God, al-Ghazālī then asserts, creates in us the knowledge that he did not enact these possibilities. (Implicit in this answer is al-Ghazālī's concept of *ijrā' al-'āda*, God's ordaining events to proceed along a uniform, orderly, habitual course.) As such, the philosophers' objection amounts to nothing more than sheer vilification (*Incoherence*, 170).

Still, to avoid being subject to such vilification, al-Ghazālī proposes another causal theory (*Incoherence*, 171–4). He will concede that when fire touches two similar pieces of cotton it will burn both. A measure of causal efficacy is thus allowed in things. But it is allowed only if the divine act remains voluntary, not necessitated by his essence, and divine power is such that it can intervene in nature to allow the miracle. Thus, for example, a prophet placed in a fiery furnace may be miraculously saved, either by God's changing the character of the fire or by creating a cause that impedes its action.

Now al-Ghazālī tells us that both theories, the Ash'arite, and the modified philosophical theory that allows a measure of causal efficacy in natural things, are possible. But in what sense are both possible? As they are mutually exclusive, one denying causal efficacy in things, one allowing it, they cannot be compossible. What al-Ghazālī probably means is that either theory, independently of the other, is internally consistent and that each allows the possibility of those miracles deemed impossible by the philosophers. This parallels his argument in the Twentieth Discussion where he concedes the possibility of the human soul's being immaterial and proceeds to argue that even if this is granted, bodily resurrection, denied by Avicenna, is still possible. In the *Moderation in Belief*, where al-Ghazālī reaffirms the Ash'arite doctrine of a material soul, he refers us back to the *Incoherence*, saying:

We have treated this problem in detail in the *Incoherence* adopting in refuting the philosophers' doctrine the view that affirms the immortality of the soul – which according to them has no position in space – and that allows the resumption of its management of the body, regardless of whether or not such a body is the same as the original human body. This, however, is a consequence [we made logically incumbent on them to accept] that does not agree with what we believe. For that book was written for the purpose of refuting their doctrine, not for the purpose of establishing true doctrine.[10]

Turning back to the second causal argument, we find no reaffirmation of it in the *Moderation in Belief*, nor in the *Iḥyā'* and subsequent writings. All the indications are that it was introduced in the *Incoherence* for the sake of argument, to show that even if one concedes a measure of causal efficacy in things, one can still accept the miracles rejected by the philosophers.

The *Moderation in Belief* affirms the Ash'arite occasionalist position forcefully and unequivocally. It reaffirms it by a detailed refutation of the doctrine of generation (*al-tawallud*) espoused by the Mu'tazilite school of *kalām*, a doctrine al-Ghazālī in the *Incoherence* identified with the philosophers' causal theory (*Incoherence*, 230). This refutation is concluded with the announcement that "all temporal things, their substances and accidents, those occurring in the entities of the animate and the inanimate, come about through the power of God . . . He alone holds sole prerogative of inventing them. It is not the case that some creatures come about through others; rather, all come about through [divine] power" (*Moderation*, 99). Then in a discussion of the term *ajal*, the predestined term of life of an individual human, the question arises in the case of decapitation whether or not it is decapitation that causes death. Al-Ghazālī answers:

It ought to be said that [the decapitated individual] died by his *ajal*, *ajal* meaning the time in which God creates in him his death, regardless of whether this occurs with the cutting of the neck, the occurrence of a lunar eclipse, or the falling of rain. All these for us are associated things, not generated acts, except that with some the connection is repeated according to habit (*bi-al-'āda*) but with some they are not repeated. (*Moderation*, 224–5)

The divine eternal will has so ordained it that (barring a miracle, also preordained by this will), death always follows decapitation, even though the real cause of death is divine power. This is brought home in al-Ghazālī's endorsement of Avicenna's Aristotelian demonstrative logic, where the necessary connection in natural events in effect is denied, substituting for it the habitual uniform course, in itself contingent, but which, decreed by the divine will, is the norm. It is this habitual uniform course that is the ultimate justification for scientific inference, for scientific knowledge.

In the *Standard for Knowledge*, the logical treatise appended to the *Incoherence*, al-Ghazālī accepts the Avicennian claim that certain empirical premises yield certainty. How can this be, he poses as an objection, "when the theologians have doubted this, maintaining that it is not decapitation that causes death, nor eating satiation, nor fire burning, but that it is God who causes burning, death, and satiation at the occurrence of their concomitant events, not through them?" In response al-Ghazālī writes:

> The theologian admits the fact of death, but inquires about the manner of connection between decapitation and death. As for the inquiry of whether this is a necessary consequence of the thing itself, impossible to change, or whether this is in accordance with the custom (*sunna*) of God, the exalted, due to the fulfillment of His will that can undergo neither substitution nor change, this is an inquiry into the mode of connection, not into the connection itself.[11]

Now, Avicenna no less than al-Ghazālī maintains that observation by itself shows only concomitance. In addition to the observation of regularities, he argues, there is "a hidden syllogism," namely, that if these past regularities were accidental or coincidental they would not have continued always or for the most part. From this, Avicenna draws the conclusion that the regularities derive from the inherent causal properties of things. Al-Ghazālī accepts the existence of such "a hidden syllogism" but draws from it the different conclusion, namely, that this regularity derives from the decree of the eternal will.[12]

OCCASIONALISM IN THE *IḤYĀ'*

When we turn to al-Ghazālī's writing after his following the Ṣūfī path, particularly his monumental *Iḥyā'*, we find confirmation of the Ash'arite occasionalist perspective. We meet this confirmation in different contexts of the *Iḥyā'*. We find it, as expected, in *The Principles of Belief*, which outlines and defends the Ash'arite articles of faith, particularly in its endorsement of the doctrine of *kasb*. Sometimes we find it unexpectedly in contexts where it appears as though a comment made in passing. A passage in the *Book of Love* (*Kitāb al-maḥabba*) from the *Iḥyā'* is a case in point:

> How is it imaginable that the human would love himself and not love his Lord through whom is his sustenance? It is known that inasmuch as the one afflicted by the heat of the sun loves the shade, [such a person] would necessarily love the trees through which the shade subsists. Everything in existence in relation to the power of God, exalted be He, is like the shade in relation to the trees and light in relation to the sun. For all [things] are the effects of His power and the existence of all [things] follows His existence, just as the existence of light follows [the existence] of the sun and shade [the existence] of the trees. Indeed, this example is sound relative to the imaginings of the common people. For they imagine that the light is the effect of the sun, emanates from it and exists by it.
>
> This, however, is pure error, since it has been revealed to the masters [of those who know by means] of the heart (*li-arbāb al-qulūb*) by a revelation that is clearer than what is observed by sight that the light comes about "by invention" (*ikhtirā'n*) from the power of God, exalted be He, when it happens that the sun and opaque bodies face each other, just as the sun, its eye, its shape and form occur through the power of God, exalted be He. But the purpose of examples is to explain, the truth not being sought in them. (*Iḥyā'* IV.293, 22–9)

What we have here is the use of the common belief in the efficacy of natural things – proclaimed a pure error – as an example to illustrate a point. The sun and the opaque body it faces are not the real causes. They are merely the habitual or occasional causes. This point becomes more explicit in al-Ghazālī's discussion of astrology in the *Iḥyā'*. The discussion first occurs in *The Book of Knowledge*. Astrology, according to al-Ghazālī, is inferring (and predicting) temporal events from astral causes, this, in principle, being similar to the physician's inferring from the pulse what malady will take place. This, he affirms, "is knowledge of the currents [of events according] to the custom (*sunna*) and habit (*'āda*) of God, exalted be he, in his creation" (*Iḥyā'* I.30). Some prophets in the past have been endowed with this astral predictive ability. The religious law, however, blames the practice of astrology, because it is harmful to most people. The main source of this harm is that when told that "these effects occur subsequent to the movement of the stars, they come to believe that the stars are the things that are efficacious" (*Iḥyā'* I.31). For the perception of the weak, as distinct from those well grounded in knowledge, is confined to the intermediaries, not realizing that the celestial orbs are compelled entities behaving in subjection to divine command.

This is complemented by a discussion of astrology in *The Book of Patience and Gratitude* (*Kitāb al-ṣabr wa al-shukr*). Al-Ghazālī writes:

> You must not think that belief in the stars, the sun, and moon [as being] compelled by the command of God, praised be He, in matters for which [the former] are rendered causes in accordance with [divine] wisdom is contrary to the religious law – [this] by reason of what has come down in it by way of prohibiting belief in the astrologers and astrology. Rather, prohibition concerning the stars consists of two things.
>
> One of them is that [these heavenly bodies] enact their effects, independently, and that they are not compelled under the management of a Manager that created and subdued them. This would be infidelity (*kufr*).
>
> The second is to believe the astrologers in the detail of what they inform about the effects, the rest of creation not sharing in the apprehension [of such effects]. This is because [the astrologers] state [things] out of ignorance. For the knowledge of the stars' determination [of events] was a miracle to some prophets, peace be on them, but this science became obliterated. What remains is a mixture where truth and error are not distinguished. For the belief that the stars are causes (*asbāb*) for effects (*āthār*) that come about by the creation of God, exalted be He (*bi-khalq al-Lāhi ta'ālā*), in the earth, plants, and animals, does not belittle religion. (*Iḥyā'* IV.114, 20–8)

The key expression in this last paragraph is "by the creation of God." The *asbāb*, "causes," are not the things that bring about those effects in the earth, plants, and animals. The effects come about by God's creation. But then, what does al-Ghazālī mean by "causes" (*asbāb*), "intermediaries" (*wasā'iṭ*), and things acting through God's "compulsion" (*taskhīr*)? One has to look carefully at the context and extract his meaning from it. Read in proper context, when al-Ghazālī speaks of "causes" other than God, what he is referring to are the habitual causes. Some of these (but not all) constitute conditions for the creation of the habitual effects – the creation of will, knowledge, and life in humans are conditions preceding the creating of human power, for example. And when he speaks of intermediaries, "compelled to act," particularly angelic intermediaries, at first sight he seems to be endowing these with causal efficacy. But some of his statements indicate the opposite of this.

In the chapter on divine unity, the *Basis of Trust* (*Iḥyā'* IV.240ff.), al-Ghazālī tells us that it is revealed to the gnostic that "there is no agent except God . . . and that he has no partner sharing his act." The same act, however, is sometimes attributable to the servant in the sense that he is the locus of divine action, but to God in terms of causal efficacy, that is, in terms of "the connection of the effect to the cause and the created thing to his creator" (*Iḥyā'* III.123). It is in terms of this that in the Qur'ān the act is sometimes attributed to God, sometimes to the servant, sometimes to angels. But if God is the only true agent, "no partner sharing his act," one must conclude that the angel, like the human servant, is the locus of divine action and is an intermediary only in this sense.

Al-Ghazālī's occasionalism pervades the *Iḥyā'*. How then does this tally with al-Ghazālī's criticisms of Ash'arite *kalām*, in the *Iḥyā'* and elsewhere?[13] The main reason that underlies his many criticisms is epistemological. Al-Ghazālī holds that the main function of Ash'arite *kalām* is the defence of traditional Islamic belief against "heretical innovations." This function is not unimportant. For a firm hold of this traditional belief which entails utter devotion to the one God and the piety that attends it is the basis for salvation in the hereafter for all Muslims; and for those pursuing the mystical path, the necessary foundation for their ascent towards gnosis. But the act of defending traditional belief is only a means to an end. When *kalām* is taken as an end in itself it leads to the error that it constitutes what is experientially religious. Moreover, even the most sincere and religiously motivated theologians who direct their thought to attaining "one of the realities," can be veiled by beliefs "that solidify in their souls, and become fixed in their hearts, becoming a veil between them and the apprehension of realities" (*Iḥyā'* III.13, 19–20).

This brings us to the main concern of al-Ghazālī in his mystical writings, namely "the apprehension of realities." These realities belong to the divine world of the unseen (*'ālam al-malakūt*). Direct experience of them involves mystical vision. It is this mystical vision that yields certainty. Now, for al-Ghazālī, while Ash'arite *kalām* can be a veil preventive of this mystical vision, it can also constitute a move toward it. This brings us back to his statement about his major Ash'arite work, the *Moderation in Belief*. He states that this work not only supersedes the official Ash'arite *kalām* works in ascertaining what is true, but is "closer to knocking at the doors of gnosis." In what way, then, can Ash'arism be close to knocking at the doors of gnosis?

There is one Ash'arite doctrine in particular which al-Ghazālī relates to the mystic vision. This is the doctrine of acquisition, *kasb*, which is at the heart of the causal question. The basic premise of this doctrine – repeatedly and unequivocally affirmed in the *Iḥyā'* – is that each and every human act is the direct creation of divine power. To formulate intellectually the doctrine of *kasb* is one thing. To understand what it means in the cosmic scheme of things is another. Al-Ghazālī tells us quite plainly that this understanding is attainable only through mystical vision. What we have here are in effect two different, but complementary, levels of knowing.

To return to more mundane matters, it is al-Ghazālī's discussions of causality that are of special significance for the history of Arabic philosophy. Although theologically motivated, his argument that necessary causal connections in nature are provable neither logically nor empirically remains philosophical. In his adoption of Avicennian demonstrative logic (by reinterpreting causal sequences on occasionalist lines), al-Ghazālī brings home the point that science rests on the belief in nature's uniformity. This belief he shares with Avicenna. What he does not share with him, as already indicated, is the justification of this belief.

NOTES

1 Al-Ghazālī [110], 101–2.
2 Ibid., 65–8.
3 Al-Ghazālī [111], 7, 46; hereafter *Incoherence*.
4 Al-Ghazālī, *Iḥyā' 'ulūm al-dīn*, 4 vols. (Cairo: 1377 A.H./1957 C.E.), hereafter *Iḥyā'*.
5 Al-Ghazālī, *Kitāb al-arba'īn fī uṣūl al-dīn* (*The Book of Forty on the Principles of Religion*), ed. M. M. Abū al-A'lā (Cairo: 1964), 22 (hereafter *Arba'īn*).

6 See the author's "Al-Ghazālī's Chapter on Divine Power in the *Iqtiṣād*," *Arabic Sciences and Philosophy* 4 (1994), 279–315. For a rival interpretation of Ghazālī on this point, see Frank [108] and Frank [109]; my response to Frank's interpretation is presented in Marmura [118]. See also the review of Frank [109] in A. Dallal, "Ghazali and the Perils of Interpretation," *Journal of the American Oriental Society* 122 (2002), 773–87.

7 For a discussion of al-Ghazālī's reinterpreation and adoption of Avicenna's demonstrative logic, see Marmura [116].

8 Al-Ghazālī, *Jawāhir al-Qur'ān* (*Jewels of the Qur'ān*), ed. M. R. R. al-Qabbani (Beirut: 1986), 39.

9 The literature on the discussion of causality in this chapter is extensive. See, for example, in chronological order, Fakhry [107]; H. A. Wolfson, "Nicolas of Autrecourt and Ghazali's Argument against Causality," *Speculum* 44 (1969), 234–8; B. Kogan, "The Philosophers al-Ghazālī and Averroes on Necessary Connection and the Problem of the Miraculous," in Morewedge [32], 113–32; L. E. Goodman, "Did al-Ghazālī Deny Causality?" *Studia Islamica* 47 (1978), 83–120; I. Alon, "Al-Ghazālī on Causality," *Journal of the American Oriental Society* 100 (1980), 397–405; B. Abrahamov, "Al-Ghazālī's Theory of Causality," *Studia Islamica* 67 (1988), 75–98; S. Riker, "Al-Ghazālī on Necessary Causality," *The Monist* 79 (1996), 315–24; B. Dutton, "Al-Ghazālī on Possibility and the Critique of Causality," *Medieval Philosophy and Theology* 10 (2001), 23–46. See also my own studies of the question in Marmura [116], [117], [118], and [119].

10 Al-Ghazālī, *al-Iqtiṣād fī al-i'tiqād* (*Moderation in Belief*), ed. I. S. Çubukçu and H. Atay (Ankara: 1962), 215 (hereafter *Moderation*). It is not clear whether in the *Iḥyā'* Ghazālī continues to adhere to this doctrine of the soul; there are suggestions of a shift from this doctrine toward an immaterial one. But this is not definite; see Gianotti [112].

11 Al-Ghazālī, *Mi'yār al-'ilm* (*The Standard for Knowledge*), ed. S. Dunya (Cairo: 1961), 190–1. See also above, n. 6.

12 Ibid., 188–9, 191.

13 For a detailed discussion of this question, see Marmura [119].

8 Philosophy in Andalusia: Ibn Bājja and Ibn Ṭufayl

From the first incursion of Islam into Spain in 710 until the eventual success of the Christian reconquest in 1492, the Iberian peninsula was partially or wholly under Muslim rule, the westernmost outpost of a sprawling Muslim empire. For many decades the intellectual and cultural climate of "al-Andalus" was thus subsidiary to that of the East. Philosophy was no exception: it came first from the East, but in time acquired an autonomous life. This is reflected in the history of Andalusian philosophy, which at first followed in the footsteps of al-Fārābī and Avicenna, but soon developed along two very different paths. On the one hand, the Andalusians took up al-Fārābī's project of reconstructing and further developing the thought of Aristotle, a process that would culminate in the commentaries of Averroes. On the other hand, Andalusian philosophers were attracted by Ṣūfism. Most prominently, the mystic Ibn 'Arabī hailed from al-Andalus. But as will be indicated below, even authors who worked within the *falsafa* tradition were not immune to the appeal of the Ṣūfīs. This chapter will illustrate these competing traditions in the thought and writings of the two most significant Muslim philosophers of al-Andalus prior to Averroes: Ibn Bājja (known as Avempace to the Latins) and Ibn Ṭufayl.

IBN BĀJJA (AVEMPACE)

In his account of the study of the sciences in al-Andalus, Abū al-Qāsim Ṣā'id ibn Ṣā'id (d. 1070) mentioned those who were interested in philosophy in the broad sense up to his time.[1] Most were physicians, while others were devoted to the natural sciences and logic. Those who cultivated natural philosophy and metaphysics were few and their writings have not reached us, except those of Sulaymān Ibn Jabirwāl, known also as Ibn Gabirol or Avicebron (1021–58),[2] whom he records among the Jewish scholars.

Abū Bakr ibn al-Ṣā'igh, Ibn Bājja, could not be mentioned by Ibn Ṣā'id since he was born in Saragossa in a year between 1085 and 1090. At the time, Saragossa was the capital of the kingdom of the Banū Hūd and the petty king 'Imād al-Dawla might have protected Ibn Bājja, but he stayed in power only until 1110. He was then overthrown by 'Alī ibn Yūsuf ibn Tāshufīn (1107–43), the ruler of the North African dynasty of the Almoravids, who replaced him with his brother-in-law, Abū Bakr ibn Ibrāhīm al-Ṣahrawī, better known as Ibn Tīfilwīt, as governor of the province.[3]

Ibn Bājja had poetical talent and mastered the *muwashshaha* genre.[4] His panegyrics were rewarded with the generosity of his patron and his intelligence earned him an appointment as a vizier, but Ibn Tīfilwīt died soon, in 1116, fighting against the Christians; Ibn Bājja composed elegies in his memory. Eventually, the Christian king Alfons I of Aragon conquered Saragossa on December 18, 1118, and Ibn Bājja had to flee. He first found shelter in Xàtiba at the court of the emir Abū Isḥāq Ibrahīm ibn Yūsuf ibn Tāshufīn, brother of the caliph and governor of the Eastern part of al-Andalus. Ibn Bājja remained for the rest of his life within the Almoravid circle and served for about twenty years in Granada as vizier of the governor Yaḥyā ibn Yūsuf ibn Tāshufīn. We know that in 1136 he was in Seville and that his disciple, Abū al-Ḥasan ibn al-Imām, also a vizier, accompanied him. Ibn Bājja wanted to go to Oran but he died in Fez in May 1139 (Ramadan 533 A.H.). Ibn Ma'yūb, a servant of his enemy the physician Abū al-'Alā' ibn Zuhr, was suspected of poisoning him with an eggplant. Ibn Zuhr was not his only foe; the personal enmity of Ibn Khāqān against him is well known to us since he attacked Ibn Bājja in the entry he devoted to him in his collection of poetry, accusing him even of depriving God of his attributes (*ta'ṭīl*). The Almoravids bestowed favor on Ibn Bājja and other non-religious scholars, among them Mālik ibn Wuhaib, who was his main teacher. The positive environment for study created during the time of the petty kingdoms, as described by Ibn Ṣā'id, lasted during that of the Almoravids in spite of the opposition of the preeminent scholars of religious law (*fiqh*).

Information about Ibn Bājja's philosophical background is found in an elaborate study of Ibn Bājja's writings by the late Jamāl ad-Dīn al-'Alawī,[5] who tries to establish their chronology and, on this basis, a developmental account of his thought. Al-'Alawī takes into consideration a letter Ibn Bājja sent to his friend Abū Ja'far Yūsuf ibn Ḥasday in which he explained that he first learned the mathematical sciences, music, and astronomy. He went on to the study of logic using the books of al-Fārābī and finally devoted himself to physics, the philosophy of nature. On the basis of his order of learning, al-'Alawī divides Ibn Bājja's writings into three stages. His writings on music, astronomy, and logic belong to the first stage; those on natural philosophy to the second; and those most representative of his thinking – the *Rule of the Solitary*,[6] the *Epistle of Conjunction*,[7] and the *Farewell Message*[8] – to the third and last stage.

Philosophy and the classification of sciences

We may accept al-'Alawī's thesis for the purpose of analyzing Ibn Bājja's thought. Ibn Bājja followed other Andalusians in turning to al-Fārābī for logic, writing commentaries on his works without pretending to be an independent logician. There are extant annotations on the *Categories*, *De Interpretatione*, and both *Analytics*, and also on the *Introduction* (a summary of Porphyry's *Isagoge*) and the *Five Sections*, two short texts of al-Fārābī.[9]

Porphyry's *Isagoge* was translated into Arabic by Abū 'Uthmān Ya'qūb al-Dimashqī and his translation was used by al-Fārābī in his *Kitāb Īsāghūjī*, which he also calls *Kitāb al-madkhal* (*Introduction*).[10] Ibn Bājja links the book to another by al-Fārābī, his *Classification of the Sciences*.[11] In his *Isagoge*, Porphyry had established five universal "meanings" or "sounds" – genus, species, differentia, property, and accident – as the foundations of logic, the highest development of which is the syllogism. Ibn Bājja goes in another direction. He is more concerned with the arts that employ syllogisms, and places his own classification of the sciences before the exposition of the five universals: "it is in the nature of the syllogistic arts to employ the syllogism once they are assembled and completed, and not to have an action as their end."[12] The syllogistic sciences are five, the first and most important of which is philosophy, since it embraces all beings "insofar as it knows them with *certain* science." Thus two requirements are to be followed: certainty of knowledge and universality of scope, and these requirements hold for the five divisions of philosophy: metaphysics, physics, practical philosophy, mathematics, and logic.

Metaphysics aims at those beings that are the ultimate causes; they are neither a body nor in a body. Physics or natural science aims at the natural bodies, the existence of which does not depend on human will at all. Practical philosophy – which Ibn Bājja calls "voluntary science" – aims at beings produced by the human will and choice. Mathematics deals with beings abstract from their matters and is divided into arithmetic, geometry, optics, astronomy, music, the science of weights, and engineering, the "science of devices," which studies:

> how to bring into existence many of the things proved theoretically in mathematics, where the worth of the device consists in removing the hindrances that perhaps hindered their existence. There are numerical devices (like algebra), geometrical ones (like those for measuring the surface of bodies impossible to access), astronomical devices, optical devices (like the art of mirrors), musical and mechanical devices.[13]

Logic is the fifth and last division of philosophy and focuses on the properties that beings acquire in the human mind; "because of such properties and their knowledge [logic] becomes an instrument for apprehending the right and the truth in beings."[14] Ibn Bājja remarks that for this reason some people consider logic to be only an instrument and not a part of philosophy, but insofar as these properties have real existence, logic can be integrated into philosophy. He concludes that logic is both part and instrument of philosophy.

Since a distinguishing feature of philosophy is the use of the apodictic syllogism (*burhān*), the only one that yields certain knowledge, not all syllogistic sciences can be considered parts of philosophy. Ibn Bājja enumerates four such non-philosophical arts. Dialectic relies only on opinion, and negates or asserts something through methods of general acceptance. Sophistry aims at beings insofar as it misrepresents them and deceives us: it makes the false look true, and the true, false. And following the tradition initiated by the Greek commentators on Aristotle, Ibn Bājja includes the *Rhetoric* and the *Poetics* in the logic.[15]

Nevertheless the classification of the sciences is not complete because the aforementioned arts are all theoretical and arts like medicine or agriculture were not considered. Ibn Bājja does not admit these practical arts as syllogistic sciences: although they make use of syllogisms, they employ them only "for the purpose of certain activities [or tasks]" and neither medicine nor agriculture, in their final shape, can be built on syllogisms. By contrast, Ibn Bājja insists, the rules of optics or mechanics can be organized by means of syllogisms. To sum up, according to Ibn Bājja, sciences are first divided into those built on syllogisms and those organized without syllogisms. Syllogistic sciences divide into philosophy, dialectic, sophistic, rhetoric, and poetics. Philosophy subdivides into demonstrative logic (the *Prior* and *Posterior Analytics*), mathematics, natural philosophy, metaphysics, and practical philosophy.

For Ibn Bājja the main purpose of the *Isagoge* is to explain the concepts that underlie the ten Aristotelian categories, so that the essence of the *Kitāb al-madkhal* must be a theory of the individual and the universal, which develops into an analysis of simple and composite universal meanings, or intelligibles. Ibn Bājja shows that the five predicables are not primitive concepts, but constitute correlations between two universals falling within the rules of individuals and classes. He says: "Genus, species, property, and accident are correlates (*iḍāfa*) which are inherent to the intelligibles regarding the quantity of their subjects."[16] Genus, species, and property are essences (*māhiyyāt*) inhering in a shared subject; by contrast, the accident is not an essence and exists outside the subject. The specific difference is related only to the individual and may be grasped without reference to the universal.

Ibn Bājja's annotations to al-Fārābī's *Kitāb al-madkhal* are more innovative than they might seem at first. He is concerned to point out that the *Isagoge* should not be limited to the exposition of the five "sounds" – maybe six, if the individual is added[17] – and that a science is needed to lay the foundations for the *Organon*. He conceives this science as a formal theory of individuals and classes, integrated into the Porphyrian division and the principles of definition and description, and thinks that this science should establish the ten categories. Unfortunately he did not carry out his ideas and his words are only a sketch of the theory.

Philosophy of nature

Among Ibn Bājja's contributions to the philosophy of nature, those concerning movement are of great import; they are found mainly in his *Commentary on the Physics*. Shlomo Pines introduced the term "dynamics"[18] to define his views, which no doubt were influenced by the tradition linked to John Philoponus (d. ca. 566).[19] Commenting on Aristotle's *Physics*, book VII, Ibn Bājja considers the claim that everything is moved by something else, and says:

> It is evident that the rest of the whole because of the rest of one of its parts, takes place insofar as the movable is other than the mover, and when the influence of the latter ends, it comes to rest. Its influence ends because the mover ceases to act either on its own or because something else exerts resistance on it. Whenever the mover ceases to act on its own, this happens due either to its destruction, or to exhaustion (*kalāl*) of the power of the mover, or because the cause disappears, or because the movement is complete, since the movable has reached the end toward which it was moving.

The movements involved here are so-called "violent" movements, as opposed to "natural" ones, discussed below. Ibn Bājja sketches a theory of dynamics based on a notion of "power" different from the Aristotelian notion of *dunamis*: they are mechanical forces which can join another force or counteract it by offering resistance. There is a minimum amount of moving power for each movable.[20] For instance, to move a boat a minimum of power is needed, otherwise "one grain of sand could move the boat." When two opposing powers are equal, there is no movement, but when one power "overcomes" the other, the body moves until it suffers "exhaustion" (*kalāl*), because any body moved "violently" creates a contrary power stronger than the one imposed by the mover, and also because the imposed force becomes "exhausted." The moving power is also subject to time and distance factors and the mobile can offer almost no resistance, so that absolute terms of proportionality do not apply.

Ibn Bājja analyzes "natural" movements too, such as a stone's falling through air and water. These movables need a moving power capable not only of moving them but also of displacing the medium they pass through. Dust particles stay suspended in the air because, although they possess enough power to go down, the power is insufficient to displace the air. Ibn Bājja differs here from Aristotle, who thought the medium to be necessary for any natural movement, and expresses the view that the medium is not a necessary condition, but only provides resistance. The different velocity with which the stone passes through the air or the water is only caused by the different density of the medium, it is not connatural to the medium. As a proof that movement without any medium, namely, through a void, is possible, Ibn Bājja adduces the movement of the spheres:

> There [in the heavens] there are no elements of violent movement, because nothing bends their movement, the place of the sphere remains the same and no new place is taken by it. Therefore circular movement should be instantaneous [if it were determined by the medium through which it moved]. But we observe that some spheres move slowly – such as the sphere of fixed stars – and others fast – the daily movement – and that there is neither violence nor resistance among them. The cause for the different velocities is the difference in nobility (*sharf*) between mover and movable.[21]

The role of the medium is not essential, but is only a kind of resistance, and thus movement in the void is both theoretically possible and confirmed by the observation of the spheres. Ibn Bājja contradicts Aristotle and advances a doctrine that Galileo will prove to be right.[22] Once again he gives us only an outline, without undertaking a deeper inquiry.

His theory of movement is the backbone of his philosophy of nature, and has a further projection into metaphysics. In his epistle *On the Mobile*,[23] Ibn Bājja refers to his commentary on Aristotle's *Physics* where it has been proved that there is a First Mover causing the eternal movement as well as numerous intermediate movers. The souls of living beings count among those movers. But man's soul is characterized by the "deliberative movement" which is possible because he is rational, and thus deliberates in order to achieve an end. For the righteous soul this end is "absolute goodness" (*al-khayr 'alā al-iṭlāq*), and man is able to know the good abstract from matter, not only the good embedded in matter. While the soul is in a body, the body is the instrument in which he moves toward this end, but movement ceases once the soul has left the body and has become identical with the pure forms: a process that we will examine in the next section.

The metaphysics of forms

Ibn Bājja wrote several independent treatises on metaphysics, but no commentary on Aristotle's *Metaphysics* is extant, a fact already noted by his disciple ʻAlī ibn al-Imām. Ibn Bājja's treatise on the *Union of the Intellect with Man* begins with an annotation on *Metaphysics*, V.6, on the meaning of "one" or unity,[24] but nothing else, and we may raise the question why he did not write a full commentary on the *Metaphysics*, given its importance. One reason could be that the Aristotelian work does not fit well into the Neoplatonic conception of philosophy, and of metaphysics as a means of ascent to the highest principle and human happiness. Al-Fārābī had taught that there is a descending procession from the One, and a corresponding ascent available to the philosopher, while Avicenna linked philosophy to the transcendent when he asserted that philosophy has to achieve direct intellectual vision of the Necessary Being and the forms that emanate from him.

Ibn Bājja takes up Aristotle's theory of form but gives it a new meaning, which is central to his system. Like his predecessors al-Fārābī and Avicenna, he believes in an emanationist system in which there is a First Being from whom the heavenly intelligences emanate as far as the last one, the Active Intellect, which endows material bodies with their forms. The most simple bodies are the four elements: fire, air, water, and earth. Their forms are only pairs of the opposite qualities hot–cold, moist–dry: for instance, water is cold and moist. For Ibn Bājja these qualities are essentially powers, powers that can cause motion.[25] From these simple elements all natural beings are generated and they receive more and more elaborate forms, the most complex being souls. The simplest of souls is the nutritive soul, the perfection of the body of a plant; it is followed by the sensitive soul, belonging to animals, by the imaginative soul, which is a perfection of men and animals that can make images out of earlier sensations,[26] and finally, by the rational soul. All are active forms, i.e., powers and faculties, but only the rational soul goes beyond the limits of the corporeal.

In his *Treatise on the Spiritual Souls*,[27] which is the final section of his book *Rule of the Solitary*, Ibn Bājja enumerates those forms that are free of matter, in descending order:

> The spiritual forms are of various kinds: the first kind are the forms of the circular [i.e., heavenly] bodies, the second are the active intellect and the acquired intellect, the third are the material intelligibles (*maʻqūlāt*), the fourth are the intentions (*maʻānī*) existent in the faculties of the soul, i.e., existent in common sense, in the imaginative faculty, and in the memory.[28]

"Spiritual" therefore applies broadly to every form that is not joined to matter and is not separable from individual substance; the terminology and doctrine echo those of Alexander of Aphrodisias. Spiritual forms divide into universal and particular forms: particular forms are found in the common sense, and are thus in a sense corporeal, whereas universal forms are found only in the Active Intellect. Particular spiritual forms may be true or false instantiations; they are true only if their predicates exist in corporeal forms of individuals. Forms thus have three degrees of existence: universal spiritual, particular spiritual, and particular embodied forms.

Spiritual forms may produce a "state" (*ḥāl*) in the soul, either a state of perfection, as is produced by beauty, the fine arts, or noble ascent, or of imperfection, produced by the opposite vices. Spiritual forms, therefore, play a role in every aspect of human activity. Even the inspiration received by the prophets belongs to the category of particular spiritual forms, which do not pass through the common sense, but are received directly from the Active Intellect. As for the Ṣūfīs, their experiences belong to the level of the particular spiritual forms, where common sense, imagination and memory are active. But they mistake them for universal spiritual forms, and wrongly believe that the coincidence of the three faculties is the source of supreme happiness.[29]

Man has to organize his various faculties – from the rational down to the nutritive – and there are categories of men according to the prevalence of each of the three faculties. In some of them, corporeality prevails, in a select few, spirituality does – Ibn Bājja counts some ascetics and Ṣūfīs among the latter – but for most the situation is mixed. Man is moved by spiritual forms that may be as basic as clothing, housing, or food, but clothing, for instance, acts on two levels, the protective and the ornamental. Virtues are attached to the spiritual forms found in the imaginative faculty, because the purpose of virtuous actions is generating positive feelings and admiration in the souls of those who see them. The spirituality of most men is, however, limited to particular forms, and only philosophers attain the highest degree of spirituality, the immaterial and universal intelligibles (*akhlaṣ al-rūḥāniyyāt*). Although philosophers have to take due care of the corporeal and particular spiritual forms, in order to live, and live honorably, their main concern is the universal separated forms:

> Spiritual acts render him more noble, and the intellectual acts render him divine and virtuous. The man of wisdom is therefore necessarily a man who is divine and virtuous. Of every kind of activity, he takes up the best only . . . when he achieves the highest end – that is, when he apprehends the simple substantial intelligences (*'uqūl*) that are mentioned in the *Metaphysics*, *On the Soul*, and *On Sense and the Sensible* – he then becomes one of these intelligences. It would be right to call him simply divine, and he will be free from the mortal sensible qualities, as well from the [particular] spiritual qualities.[30]

"Divine" here does not mean identical with God, but having Godlike qualities, although his enemies could interpret such words as being heretical. The philosopher has reached the highest point of human wisdom, where it continues into the divine world.

Political philosophy

If we now contrast Ibn Bājja with his master al-Fārābī, we realize that the philosopher has attained this degree of perfection while *solitary*, without living in the virtuous city. At the beginning of *The Rule of the Solitary*, Ibn Bājja explains the meaning of "rule" (*tadbīr*) as the organization of actions toward an end; the proper "rule" is political, an organization of the lives of the citizens in order to help them to their perfection. Al-Fārābī, following Plato, had distinguished four kinds of defective or sick cities or societies: the ignorant, the wicked, the weakened, and the miscarried, as opposed to the perfect city, whose success requires philosophers.[31] Following him, Ibn Bājja defines the virtuous city as one where its inhabitants do not need physicians and judges: "love being the strongest bond between them, there is no contention at all."[32] In the virtuous city all actions are right: people avoid harmful foods and excessive drink, take physical exercise, and always act honestly. The imperfect cities, however, do need doctors, judges, and also "weeds" (*nawābit*). "Weeds" are men whose views are not the views of the majority; their idiosyncratic opinions may be true or false, and those whose opinions are correct are the cause for the coming-to-be of the perfect city in which there is no disagreement. The solitary "weed" is the agent whose "rule" is discussed by Ibn Bājja, who realized that the cities or societies of his time belonged to the corrupted types and could not be rehabilitated. He abandoned al-Fārābī at this point and, as Steven Harvey puts it, was convinced that intellectual happiness is possible but political happiness is not.[33]

The political philosophy of Ibn Bājja has attracted much interest in recent times.[34] Nevertheless it is not as essential to his thought as the doctrine of forms. Ibn Bājja was a disciple of al-Fārābī but was also a careful reader of the available Aristotelian corpus; we might say that Aristotelianism entered al-Andalus through him. His doctrine of spiritual forms seeks to harmonize emanationism with a hylomorphic vision of nature. The Aristotelian forms become powers moving bodies, *intentiones* moving men, essential constituents of mankind, and separated substances. Insofar as man is spiritual form, he can know the intelligibles, although he needs the assistance of the active intellect. Only the active intellect can be apprehended without an accompanying spiritual form:

> The intellect that itself is its own intelligible has no spiritual form that is its subject; the intelligible that this intellect apprehends is the intellect that is one and not multiple, because it has been liberated from the relation that links form to matter. This sort of vision is the afterlife, and is unified, ultimate human happiness.[35]

Ibn Bājja's philosophy does not seek to interpret or to transform the universe but to make man truly happy. Happiness can in part be achieved by means of a "noble" life away from corporeal forms, like that lived by the ascetics and the Ṣūfīs. But this is not enough: the true way leads through the perfection of the rational faculty and the acquisition of philosophical knowledge.

IBN ṬUFAYL

In his prologue to the *Story of Ḥayy ibn Yaqẓān*, Abū Bakr Muḥammad ibn Ṭufayl al-Qaysī (d. 1185) draws a different picture of the state of philosophy in Andalusia from that given by Ibn Ṣā'id. Ibn Ṭufayl belongs to the generation that follows Ibn Bājja and mentions him with great admiration, but complains that "most of his extant books are incomplete and their final sections are missing."[36] Ibn Ṭufayl names no one of his own generation, since according to him, they have not reached the level of perfection, or he has not yet appreciated their true value. Given that two such great thinkers as Ibn Maimūn or Maimonides (1125–1204) and Averroes (1126–98) belong to Ibn Ṭufayl's generation, he must have written these lines before 1159, when Averroes finished the summaries of Aristotle's natural philosophy that first gave him renown. That he would know about Maimonides is not likely, because of the persecution and eventual emigration to Egypt of Maimonides and his family.

One century after Ibn Ṣā'id, Ibn Ṭufayl informs us also about the available books and prevailing trends of philosophy in al-Andalus. Besides Ibn Bājja three authors are well known: al-Fārābī, for his logical works, but also such treatises as his *Book of Religion, Book of Politics*, and commentary on Aristotle's *Ethics*; Avicenna, for his encyclopedic *al-Shifā'* (*The Healing*), but also "his book on the *Oriental Philosophy*"; and al-Ghazālī, for his *Incoherence of the Philosophers, Balance of Actions, The Jewel, The Niche for Lights, Intellectual Knowledge, Inspiration and Reconciliation, The Highest Aim*, and the *Deliverer from Error* (but surprisingly, not his major work, the *Revival of the Religious Sciences*). If we add a major number of Aristotle's writings, we realize that Ibn Ṭufayl and his contemporaries had access to sufficient sources for his philosophical enterprise.

About Ibn Ṭufayl's life not very much is known.[37] His family came from Porchena (Almería) but he was born in the village of Guadix near Granada around 1110–16, when al-Andalus was under Almoravid rule. He became physician and secretary to Abū Sa'īd, a son of the caliph 'Abd al-Mu'min (1130–63) and the governor of Granada. Later he became physician to his brother, the new caliph Abū Ya'qūb Yūsuf (1163–84), and served the Almohad cause also with his poetry, calling the Muslims to join the Almohad forces against the Christians. Abu Ya'qūb and Ibn Ṭufayl were close friends, and he introduced many scholars to the cultivated caliph, among them Averroes, who replaced him as court physician when he retired in 1182. Ibn Ṭufayl died in 1185 in Marrakech and the next caliph Abū Yūsuf (1184–98) attended his funeral.

We cannot say that he was an outstanding figure in medicine on the basis of the only medical work that has survived mostly intact: his poem or *Urjūza* of medicine extant as a manuscript of the Qarawiyyin library of Fez. Ibn Ṭufayl's medical education is linked to his knowledge of the other sciences of the Greeks, including philosophy, which he learned from Ibn Bājja's works and from the authors mentioned above. 'Abd al-Wāḥid al-Marrākushī affirmed in 1224 that Ibn Ṭufayl was author of "books on philosophy, natural sciences, and metaphysics" and mentions his *Ḥayy ibn Yaqẓān*, which expounds "the origin of the human species according to the view of [the philosophers]," and also an *Epistle on the Soul*. The same source, al-Marrākushī, informs us that Ibn Ṭufayl was very keen "to harmonize wisdom with the Islamic sciences."[38]

Recent investigation has stressed Ibn Ṭufayl's involvement with Ṣūfism, which sheds important light on his thought. Al-Andalus was at that time burgeoning with Ṣūfīs, of whom the most influential was Muḥyī al-Dīn ibn 'Arabī (d. 1240). Ṣūfīs challenged official Islam, as represented by Malikite jurists and Ash'arite theologians, with their ascetic practice and mystical teachings. They wanted to reach a state of perfection and happiness while being in this world, a state indescribable even in poetic language. Ibn Ṭufayl approves of this aim, but sees that people follow different paths in order to reach it. On the one hand, Ibn Bājja insisted on the path of pure reason; Ibn Ṭufayl believes that he reached this state, but does not accept this sort of "speculation and thinking" as sufficient. On the other hand, the Ṣūfīs achieve the state by non-rational means, but since many of them lack education, they speak of it only in a confused fashion. The right path is the one Ibn Ṭufayl finds in Avicenna's "oriental wisdom," which requires philosophical education and Ṣūfī training.[39]

To explain his doctrine, Ibn Ṭufayl had several choices, including poetry. One was the scholarly genre of Avicenna's encyclopedic works. Another option was the allegorical genre of Avicenna's *Epistle of Ḥayy ibn Yaqẓān*,[40] in which a wise man representing the Active Intellect goes on an allegorical journey. Ibn Ṭufayl instead chose the form of a novel, or better, a tale, so as to add verisimilitude to the account. He gave it the same title as the Avicennian allegory and added to it "on the secrets of the oriental wisdom," another reference to Avicenna. The three characters of the tale bear names borrowed from Avicennian works: the protagonist Ḥayy ibn Yaqẓān, and his equals Absāl and Salāmān.[41] Since the development of the story corresponds to the order and division of knowledge, it seems advisable to retain its order of exposition here. (Ibn Ṭufayl does not devote a chapter to logic, but logical method is applied by the protagonist in the first part of his research.)

The search for the origins of human life

The tale begins with the birth of the protagonist, and Ibn Ṭufayl leaves us the choice between two versions: first, that the sister of a jealous island king secretly marries a neighbor called Yaqẓān ("the Awake") and bears him a child. Out of fear that her brother would kill the newborn, she places him in an ark upon the ocean, which is carried to another deserted island and runs ashore. The child's cries of hunger are heard by a gazelle that has lost her fawn, and this gazelle raises him. This echoes the story of Moses in Exodus as transmitted by the Qur'ān (20:39). The second version is the one preferred by Ibn Ṭufayl, the scientist and physician. On the island there is a depressed moist place where a mass of clay begins to "ferment"; the process generates a very small bubble[42] divided into two parts, separated by a fine membrane and filled with subtle *pneuma*, a substance able to receive the soul that God creates. Avicenna's influence may be seen from the fact that the soul emanates from God and is compared with the sun's light. As usual, Ibn Ṭufayl does not mention his sources, and prefers to introduce Qur'ānic quotations, for instance "the soul coming from your Lord" (17:85).

Once the soul is attached to the embryonic bubble all the faculties are subordinated to its authority. Altogether, three bubbles are generated, yielding three organs: the heart is the most important as the center of natural heat, the liver supplies it with fuel, and the brain tells it what to take in and expel. Following Galen, Ibn Ṭufayl should have included the testes, but he suppresses allusions to sexuality. Once all the organs were built, the enveloping mud dries and breaks up, and the child is born. From here on, both versions about Ḥayy's origin merge together.

Ibn Ṭufayl divides the life of his hero into stages of seven years.[43] In his first septennial, Ḥayy grows with the gazelle and her brood. He learns their language and also the singing of the birds and sounds of other animals. Ibn Ṭufayl evokes here a happy coexistence of man and nature, a recurrent theme in the narrative. Ḥayy realizes his inferiority in front of the animals, which are stronger, faster, and better protected by nature than he is. Here Ibn Ṭufayl draws on the *Encyclopedia* of the Brethren of Purity, and its discussion of the superiority of animals.

The death of the gazelle gives the physician Ibn Ṭufayl an opportunity to digress on the heart as the center of life. Ḥayy ventures to dissect the dead gazelle, finds her heart, and observes that it has two cavities, the one to the right full of coagulated blood and the other to the left empty. Ḥayy infers that her death was caused because the substance filling it disappeared, and that such a substance is superior, and master and mover of the body. He then generalizes the conclusion as being valid for all beings. We observe that Ḥayy systematically applies a logical method to discover the essence and the cause of what he sees.

Ḥayy comes to the conclusion that the departed substance is fiery and spends his third septennial watching nature in search of the principle of life. When a wildfire breaks out, he is amazed by the qualities of fire and decides to keep it alive in his cave. Despite its practical utility, he focuses on the theoretical aspects of fire: by analogy Ḥayy reasons that fire and the substance evaporated in the left side of the heart of the gazelle belong to the same category, but he needs proof, and decides to undertake vivisection of an animal. Upon opening the heart, he finds in the left cavity a white vapor, very hot, whose disappearance causes the animal's death. He infers that this was the animal *pneuma*, or spirit, ruling the body.

The fourth septennial of Ḥayy's life is devoted to analysis of the sublunary world. He observes three realms within it: animal, vegetable, and mineral, and then looks for a character common to all kinds. He finds it to be corporeality, and that every body is distinguished by being either heavy or light. Ibn Ṭufayl lets his character adopt the Aristotelian doctrine that all sublunary beings are composed of two principles, matter and form, but follows Avicenna in rejecting a purely potential prime matter. Matter is always informed by the three dimensions and is always united to corporeal form (Arabic 70, English 125). Yet he observes the simplest bodies and sees that their essences can desert them. Water is cold and heavy (note, not cold and moist, as Aristotle said) and can become hot, and even light. As soon as it loses one of its primary qualities, it loses its "watery form" and acquires another form. Ḥayy discovers that all forms in nature are of this kind: they are generated temporally and "*by necessity of the intellect*, he knew that every generated being needs a generator and by means of this consideration, the agent of the form was drawn in his soul" (Arabic 73, English 127, emphasis added).

Ḥayy's reasoning, however, is twofold. For him form is only a disposition or ability to cause some motions and not others. Assuming this definition, whatever bestows the form upon the corporeal matter bestows also the actions proper to such a form. Therefore the true agent is not the immediate one, but the "creator of the form," a doctrine Ibn Ṭufayl confirms by citing the Qur'ān. Ḥayy is twenty-eight years old when he deduces the necessity and the existence of a first efficient Cause, and thereafter he endeavors to identify it. Since the sublunary world is wholly subject to the process of coming-to-be and passing-away, he focuses on the supralunary world. Ḥayy observes the circular movements of the heavenly bodies, and concludes that together they constitute one spherical body of limited dimensions, and that the universe is similar to a living being. Ibn Ṭufayl shows contempt for the sublunary world with a curious comparison to the belly of the universe: the animal belly "contains excrement and fluids, in which other animals are frequently generated, as they are generated in the macrocosm" (Arabic 80, English 130).

The search for the Creator and union with him

On the issue of whether the universe is eternal, Ibn Ṭufayl has a difficult choice between al-Ghazālī, the Ash'arite theologian, who was well respected by the Almohads, and his philosophical exemplar Avicenna. Ḥayy tries to answer questions that we know al-Ghazālī had raised against the philosophers in *The Incoherence of the Philosophers*, but without success. When this inquiry "leaves him exhausted" he escapes the antinomy by showing that the consequences of both positions are the same. He does this by first assuming the hypothesis that the world is created in time and coming to the necessity of an agent who could bring it into existence, and who cannot be a body. Then he assumes the hypothesis of an eternal world, realizes that its movement is eternal too, so that it needs an eternal mover, and concludes that such a mover must be incorporeal. Ibn Ṭufayl's arguments both draw on other philosophers, but he is original in adopting this conciliatory position.

Ibn Ṭufayl refers to two further demonstrations of God's existence. One is based on the composition of matter and form in all sublunary beings and on the fact that they "subsist only because of form." Ḥayy infers that if these beings need the form to exist, the Agent bestowing the form upon them bestows their existence and is their Creator. The second demonstration is based on the limited and finite nature of the world and its parts, and its need for an infinite power to sustain its existence. Ibn Ṭufayl admits that their relationship is one of temporal simultaneity, although the cause is ontologically prior to the effect. Both arguments belong to the emanationist tradition, represented by al-Fārābī and Avicenna, but in order to endorse the position that the universe is caused and created by this Agent without time, Ibn Ṭufayl prefers to quote the Qur'ān: "When he wants anything he only has to say 'Be' and it is" (36:82).[44] At this stage of knowledge Ḥayy has reached the age of thirty-five, and fulfilled his fifth septennial.

During the next two periods of seven years, Ḥayy mainly concentrates his efforts on reaching mystical union with the Creator by considering the divine essence and attributes. As we read in Avicenna, God is the Necessary Existent. His existence has no other cause and he is the cause of all other existents. Ibn Ṭufayl emphasizes God's incorporeality in order to establish the incorporeality of the human soul. God's incorporeality belongs to his essence and whatever knows an incorporeal essence must also be incorporeal:

> It became evident to him [Ḥayy] that he apprehended this Being by means of his own essence and that the knowledge of His essence was engraved in his own. It became evident to him that the essence by means of which he apprehended [God] was something incorporeal, for which none of the corporeal attributes was acceptable.[45]

But we should not be too enthusiastic about the conclusion, and he admonishes the reader that not all souls are immortal. As al-Fārābī already made clear,[46] those souls that never reach any knowledge of the Necessary Being while attached to their bodies do not survive the death of the body. As for the souls who know God but deviated from him, they will survive but will be punished, eternally or for a limited time according to their sins. The souls of those men who knew the Necessary Existent and devoted themselves to him will survive and be eternally blessed enjoying his vision, because their own perfection consists of the vision of the Necessary Being.

Ibn Ṭufayl's arguments lead to the conclusion that the state of mystical union man is longing for will be possible in the afterlife, but he also wants to allow for its possibility in this life. His hero achieves this state – we are not informed how – and wants not only to reach it but also to enjoy it in a continuous way.

The breaking point: Ṣūfism prevails

Ḥayy has enjoyed the vision of the Necessary Being for an instant, but cannot achieve it permanently because his senses, his imagination, and his body hinder him. He does not give up his endeavor and searches for beings capable of continuous access to the Necessary Being in order to imitate them, finding that only the heavenly bodies show continuity and regularity in their movements. From this observation he draws the following analogy: if he has been able to reach a fleeting intuition despite his body, the stars and the heavenly spheres in which they reside are no doubt capable of a continuous vision. Ḥayy needs to know if his own nature is like theirs and sees that the spiritual animal in it resembles these heavenly bodies, insofar as he is a self-mover, and unlike the four elements has no form that would make him move up and down; he can also move circularly. He infers that if he imitates the heavens, he may acquire their ability to see the Necessary Being permanently.

This requires conscious preparation. Since man's nature is threefold, having purely animal, spiritual animal (like the heavens), and purely spiritual aspects, Ḥayy must subordinate the first aspect to the second and then both of these to the spiritual. This means leading an ascetic life but also a life respecting the divine order set in nature, for instance, abstaining from meat in his diet. As for the second stage of becoming close to a heavenly body, he must perform three kinds of actions, directed toward the inferior world, toward himself, and toward the Necessary Being: he must be compassionate toward the inferior world of plants and animals, with regard to himself he must be extremely clean and spin around quickly, just as the heavens rotate, and he must concentrate his thought on the Creator, in order to lose his personality and dissolve within him.

We should notice that Ibn Ṭufayl simply assumes that the heavenly spheres are intelligences, and that they are the pattern to be imitated. Even if such a doctrine is accepted, there remains the central issue of how to enjoy a permanent vision of the Necessary Being.

Ibn Ṭufayl explains that Ḥayy goes to the point of losing his individual consciousness and obliterating himself, so that:

> He devoted himself entirely to the vision of the Truth, and when he succeeded, everything, the heavens, the earth and everything between them, vanished from his memory and his intellect. All spiritual forms, and corporeal faculties, and all the powers separated from matter which are the essences that know the true Being, and even his own essence vanished.[47]

The reader may here expect the end of the tale but Ibn Ṭufayl has prepared a surprise for us: after arriving at this point, Ḥayy leads us through a celestial promenade. Without any logical or empirical justification we are informed that Ḥayy first sees the outermost sphere the essence of which is like "the image of the sun reflected on a polished mirror," where the sun symbolizes the Necessary Being. Thereafter he contemplates the following spheres, those of the fixed stars and the planets, and the corresponding intelligences. Eventually he descends into the sublunary world, where the Active Intellect endows matter with different forms. Although human souls also proceed from the Active Intellect, their destiny varies. Ḥayy sees souls of bodies that have passed away, many of them "like dirty mirrors": the souls of the damned, suffering endless torture. Others shine with infinite beauty and happiness, and the soul of Ḥayy is among them. Many souls simply vanish along with their bodies.

The resulting knowledge is the same in content as the fruits of his inquiry before mystical union, but it is qualitatively different, because now Ḥayy *contemplates* and sees (*shāhada, ra'ā*) divine reality, with no need of discursive reasoning; the objects appear to him under a new perspective, with intense clarity.[48] But Ḥayy wakes up from his visionary experience and finds himself thrown again into this world. Repetition of his exercises allows him to reach the mystical state more easily and for increasingly longer periods of time. At this stage he has completed his seventh septennial.

Conclusion: the defense of Ṣūfī and philosophical activity

Ibn Ṭufayl now deals with issues on which he could be accused of heterodoxy, allowing Ḥayy to discover Islam. This occurs in the form of Ḥayy's meeting with Absāl and Salāmān, residents of a neighboring island. Although at the beginning Ibn Ṭufayl does not refer to their religion as Islamic, it becomes soon evident:

> One of them, Absāl, tried to penetrate the hidden meaning [of the revealed religion] and to unveil its mystical content . . . Salāmān adhered to the external meaning and refrained from any allegorical interpretation. Both nevertheless zealously complied with the external practices, the examination of their conscience and fighting the passions.[49]

Because of the sharp differences between the two, Absāl decides to move to the island where Ḥayy lives, to pursue allegorical interpretation of the Holy Book. Ḥayy first sees him at prayer and immediately recognizes Absāl as a fellow human being. Mastering Absāl's language, Ḥayy is able to communicate to him all the knowledge he has acquired without any teacher, without any revealed book, solely by means of human reason. Ḥayy and Absāl, symbols of natural reason and revealed wisdom, illustrate the agreement of both kinds of knowledge.

Ḥayy embraces Islam (which is still not identified explicitly), its doctrines and practices, but has two main objections to it: why does the Prophet employ images and allegories instead of expressions revealing the divine truth, and why does the Prophet allow his followers to strive for material goods (Arabic 146–7, English 161)? The use of images and the search for wealth both prevent men from coming close to God. These objections lead to the final section of the book: in order to move Muslims to the true Islam, Ibn Ṭufayl needs to address political issues as well. Ḥayy goes with his friend Absāl to the island where Salāmān rules, but fails completely in his endeavor to lead the citizens to the right path. We need not assume that the Almohad sultan is the sole addressee; the ending could apply to all Muslim rulers, so that Ibn Ṭufayl levels a general critique at Muslim society, as did the Ṣūfīs.

Although al-Marrākushī said that the aim of Ibn Ṭufayl in this work was to prove the harmony between Islam and human wisdom, the issue is treated only in passing, leaving the impression that the work is mainly apologetic, designed to justify philosophy and Ṣūfism. The main objective is no doubt the achievement of mystical union, and the development of both the tale and the philosophical doctrine culminate in this. Nevertheless the belief underlying all his thought seems very different: Ibn al-Khaṭīb (d. 1375) counted Ibn

Ṭufayl among those who consider that human reason (*fiṭra*) has the capacity to know the Truth by means of logical demonstrations, who think that prophets are not necessary, and that the knowledge of God resides in the soul.[50] On this interpretation Ḥayy is the symbol for humankind and his story shows how human reason must proceed: using the logical method and correct reasoning. Yet his goal remains mystical union, and philosophy helps man achieve this only insofar as it could tell Ḥayy: "I have brought you to a point where you have to take another guide." Ibn Ṭufayl sees philosophy as establishing the need for mystical union, as explaining how it is possible, and even as something necessary to avoid confusion on the way, but he does not admit that the mystical state is a part or result of the philosophical inquiry itself.

Therefore we may agree with Ibn al-Khaṭīb on the implicit purpose of Ibn Ṭufayl's *Epistle of Ḥayy Ibn Yaqẓān*, namely, the autonomous capacity of human intelligence, but insist that this capacity has to include Ṣūfī practice as well as logical reasoning. Moreover Ṣūfism is presented as the essential means to attaining the state of mystical experience. Still, because after achieving this state mankind will contemplate the same immaterial forms it had discovered by reasoning, but now in a direct vision, it is tempting to think that this vision is the fruit of rationality, and that Ṣūfism is superfluous to this purpose.

Ibn Bājja and Ibn Ṭufayl thus shared a firm belief in the power of the human mind, as well as a mistrust in the society of al-Andalus, which was losing territory against its Christian enemies even as it lost interest in the sciences, including philosophy. As we have seen, there are major differences between them: Ibn Bājja adhered to Aristotelianism, while Ibn Ṭufayl preferred Avicenna's innovative philosophy. Ibn Bājja sustained the possibility of attaining happiness as a result of intellectual activity, Ibn Ṭufayl found it in Ṣūfī experience. They both placed man in the center of their concerns, as they wanted to help him to achieve his perfection – that is, his happiness – within a framework not opposed to religion but independent of it. They differed over how this perfection might be reached, and even what it would consist in.

They both were influential: the fact that Ṣūfīs in al-Andalus and elsewhere would henceforth try to integrate philosophical elements into their doctrines is thanks in no small part to Ibn Ṭufayl. As for

Ibn Bājja, there can be little doubt that his influence upon the young Averroes was decisive for the latter's understanding of Aristotle, and above all, for making many major issues of philosophical inquiry clear to the Cordovan Aristotelian.

NOTES

1 *Ṭabaqāt al-umam*, ed. H. Mou'nes (Cairo: 1998), 96–108.
2 On whom see J. M. Millás, *Selomó Ibn Gabirol, como poeta y filósofo* (Grenada: 1993), S. Pessin, "Jewish Neoplatonism: Being Above Being and Divine Emanation in Solomon Ibn Gabirol and Isaac Israeli," in Frank and Leaman [234], 91–110, and further references given there.
3 On Ibn Bājja's life, see J. Lomba, *Avempace* (Zaragoza: 1989); D. M. Dunlop, "Remarks on the Life and Works of Ibn Bājja, Avempace," in *Proceedings of the Twenty-Second Congress of Orientalists* (Leiden: 1957), 188–96. His full name was Abū Bakr Muḥammad ibn Yaḥyā ibn al-Ṣā'igh ibn Bājja at-Tūjībī.
4 *Muwashshaha* is a genre of poetry composed of a main body in classical Arabic and a final part in vernacular Arabic or Romance.
5 *Mu'allafāt Ibn Bājja* (Beirut: 1983), esp. 77–81.
6 Partial edn. and Engl. trans. by D. M. Dunlop, *Journal of the Royal Asiatic Society* (1945), 61–81. Full edn. and Spanish trans. by M. Asín Palacios, *El régimen del solitario* (Madrid: 1946). New edn. by Fakhry in Ibn Bājja [128], 37–96. Partial English trans. by L. Berman, "The Governance of the Solitary," in Lerner and Mahdi [189], 122–33. New Spanish trans. by J. Lomba (Madrid: 1997). Edn. and Italian trans. by M. Campanini, *Il regime del solitario* (Rome: 2002).
7 Arabic edn. and Spanish trans. by M. Asín Palacios, "Un texto de Avempace sobre la unión del intelecto con el hombre," in *Al-Andalus* 7 (1942), 1–47. Ed. in Ibn Bājja [128], 153–73.
8 "Carta del adiós," *Al-Andalus* 8 (1943), 1–87. Ed. in Ibn Bājja [128], 113–43.
9 *Ta'ālīq Ibn Bājja 'alā manṭiq Arisṭū*, ed. M. Fakhry (Beirut: 1994). Ed. M. T. Dānesh-Pažūh, *Al-manṭiqiyyāt li-al-Fārābī*, vol. III (Qom: 1990), 3–219.
10 Edn. and English trans. by D. M. Dunlop in *Islamic Quarterly* 3 (1956), 117–38.
11 *Iḥṣā' al-'ulūm*, ed. A. González Palencia, *Clasificación de las ciencias* (Madrid: 1953).
12 *Ta'ālīq*, 27.
13 *Ta'ālīq*, 28.

14 Ibid.
15 For this traditional view of the *Organon* see Black [170].
16 *Ta'ālīq*, 50.
17 The addition of this sixth term is attributed to the Brethren of Purity. See Netton [82], 47–8.
18 Pines was first to underline the different meaning of *quwwa* in Ibn Bājja and Aristotle: see his "La dynamique d'Ibn Bājja," in *Mélanges Alexandre Koyré*, vol. II (Paris: 1964), 442–68; repr. in Pines [36], 450–74.
19 See M. Wolff, "Philoponus and the Rise of Preclassical Dynamics," and F. W. Zimmermann, "Philoponus' Impetus Theory in the Arabic Tradition," in R. Sorabji (ed.), *Philoponus and the Rejection of Aristotelian Science* (London: 1987), 84–120 and 121–9.
20 *Sharḥ al-samā' al-ṭabī'ī*, 114. Simplicius already spoke of this minimal amount; see *CAG* X, 1108–10.
21 *Sharḥ al-samā' al-ṭabī'ī*, 116.
22 A. Maier, *Studien zur Naturphilosophie der Spätscholastik*, 5 vols. (1943–58), esp. vol. V (Rome: 1958); E. A. Moody, "Galileo and Avempace: The Dynamics of the Leaning Tower Experiment," *Journal of the History of Ideas* 12 (1951), 163–93 and 375–422.
23 Ed. J. al-Dīn al-'Alawī, *Rasā'il falsafiyya li-Abī Bakr Ibn Bājja* (Beirut: 1983), 135–9. The epistle is a late work, where Ibn Bājja refers to the *Rule of the Solitary*, the *Epistle of Farewell*, and other writings.
24 Ibn Bājja [128], 155–6. See also his epistle on unity and on the one, in *Rasā'il falsafiyya*, ed. al-'Alawī, 140–9. The obvious precedent is al-Fārābī's treatise on unity, *Kitāb al-wāḥid wa al-waḥda*, ed. M. Mahdi (Casablanca: 1989).
25 The doctrine is expounded in the *Book on Coming-to-Be and Passing-Away*: 1 edn. of M. Ṣ. Ḥ. Ma'ṣūmī in the journal *Majallat majma' al-lugha al-'arabīya bi-Dimashq* 42 (1967), 255–74 and 426–50. Ed. and Spanish trans. by J. Puig Montada (Madrid: 1995).
26 See the *Book of the Soul*, ed. M. Ṣ. Ḥ. Ma'ṣūmī in *Majallat majma' al-lugha al-'arabīya bi-Dimashq* 34 (1959), 655–6; his Engl. trans. (Karachi: 1961), 106–7.
27 *Al-qawl fī al-ṣuwar al-rūḥāniyya*, in Ibn Bājja [128], 49–96.
28 Ibid., 49. (For the notion of "intentions" (*ma'ānī*), see below, chapter 15.)
29 Ibid., 55.
30 *Rule of the Solitary*, ed. Fakhry, 79–80; trans. Berman, 131–2.
31 See Walzer [77], 252–5. The Platonic antecedent is *Republic* 445d–573c.
32 *Rule of the Solitary*, ed. Fakhry, 41; trans. Berman, 126.
33 Harvey [126].

34 See the introductory study of M. Campanini in the aforementioned version of the *Rule of the Solitary*, with references to studies by E. I. J. Rosenthal, O. Leaman, S. Harvey, and others.

35 *Ittiṣāl al-'aql bi-al-insān*, ed. Fakhry, 166.

36 Ed. and French Ibn Ṭufayl [129], at 12–13. English trans. in Goodman [131]. Partial trans. by George N. Atiyeh in Lerner and Mahdi [189], 134–62. Citations are to Gauthier's edition followed by citation of the Goodman translation.

37 Modern studies of import are Gauthier [130], Conrad [123], and 'Ā. al-'Irāqī, *Al-mītāfīzīqā fī falsafa Ibn Ṭufayl* (Cairo: 1995).

38 *Al-Mu'jib fī talkhīṣ akhbār al-Maghrib*, ed. R. Dozy (Leiden: 1881), 172–5; ed. M. S. al-'Aryān and M. al-'Arabī al-'Ilmī (Cairo: 1949), 239–42. French trans. by E. Fagnan, *Histoire des Almohades de Merrākechi* (Algiers: 1893), 207–9.

39 To be precise: this is how Ibn Ṭufayl interprets Avicenna, a false interpretation according to D. Gutas, "Ibn Ṭufayl on Ibn Sīnā's Eastern Philosophy," *Oriens* 34 (1994), 222–241.

40 Ed. A. F. Mehren, *Traités mystiques d'Abou Ali al-Hosain ben Abdallah ben Sina ou Avicenne*, fasc. 1: *Risāla Ḥayy Ibn Yaqẓān* (Leiden: 1889), 1–23. French trans. by A-M. Goichon, *Le récit de Ḥayy Ibn Yaqẓān*, (Paris: 1959). Spanish trans. by M. Cruz Hernández, *Tres escritos esotéricos de Avicenna: Risāla de Ḥayy Ibn Yaqẓān, R. del pájaro, Qaṣīda del alma* (Madrid: 1998).

41 The story of Salāmān and Absāl is printed in Avicenna, *Tis' rasā'il fī al-ḥikma wa al-ṭabī'iyyāt wa qiṣṣat Salāmān wa Absāl*, ed. Ḥ. 'Āṣī (Beirut: 1986), 125–39, and is ascribed to Ḥunayn ibn Isḥāq.

42 For the Aristotelian origins of the doctrine see R. Kruk, "A Frothy Bubble: Spontaneous Generation in the Medieval Islamic Tradition," *Journal of Semitic Studies* 35 (1990), 265–82.

43 The kind of division of human life into periods of seven years is of ancient origin: it is already attested in Solon's elegy, which organized the life of man in ten septennials, see fr. 19 (27) in E. Diehl, *Anthologia Lyrica Graeca*, 3rd edn. (Leipzig: 1949), 38–40. A book on the subject ascribed to Hippocrates, *De Septimannis*, was known in Arabic; cf. H. Roscher, *Die hippokratische Schrift von der Siebenzahl in ihrer vierfachen Überlieferung* (Paderborn: 1913).

44 There is a third proof from the wisdom and beauty found in creation, which requires a Creator from whom wisdom, beauty, and all other qualities emanate (Arabic 89, English 134).

45 Arabic 92, English 135–6. Ibn Ṭufayl's words evoke Descartes' reasoning toward the end of the third *Meditation*: "superest tantum ut examinem qua ratione ideam istam a Deo accepi."

46 Walzer [77], 270–3.

47 Arabic 120, English 148–9. The phenomenon is known in the mystic terminology as *fanā'*. See for instance its definition by an early mystic, al-Junayd (d. 910) in A. H. Abdel-Kader, *The Life, Personality and Writings of al-Junayd* (London: 1962), 31–9 (Arabic) and 152–9 (English).

48 The intrusion of the mystical stage in the story is problematic: Ḥayy first arrives at his state of mystical dissolution by means of ascetic practices, so that his philosophical effort is only of auxiliary value. And now he gains knowledge of the immaterial world with no effort. What need is there, then, for philosophy? Ibn Ṭufayl relies here on a faulty interpretation of Avicenna's doctrine of intuition, where intuition is not contrasted to rational thought.

49 Arabic 136–7, English 156.

50 Ibn al-Khāṭib, *Rawḍa al-ta'rīf bi-al-ḥubb al-sharīf*, ed. 'A. al-Qādir Aḥmad 'Aṭā' (Cairo: n.d.), 275–6; ed. M. al-Kattānī (Beirut: 1970), 280–3. Ibn al-Khaṭīb was, of course, against the view, but the philosophers of the Enlightenment will celebrate it. Leibniz saw it as fully compatible with a deep understanding of the Divinity: see his letter to Abbé Nicaise, in *Die philosophischen Schriften von G. W. Leibniz*, ed. C. J. Gerhard, vol. II (Berlin: 1879), 563 (Letter 12, Feb. 15, 1697).

RICHARD C. TAYLOR

9 Averroes: religious dialectic and Aristotelian philosophical thought

Abū al-Walīd Muḥammad ibn Aḥmad ibn Muḥammad ibn Rushd (ca. 1126–98), who came to be known in the Latin West as Averroes, was born at Cordoba into a family prominent for its expert devotion to the study and development of religious law (*shar'īa*). In Arabic sources al-Ḥafīd ("the Grandson") is added to his name to distinguish him from his grandfather (d. 1126), a famous Malikite jurist who served the ruling Almoravid regime as *qāḍī* (judge) and even as *imām* (prayer leader and chief religious authority) at the magnificent Great Mosque which still stands today in the city of Averroes' birth and where Averroes himself served as Grand *Qāḍī* (chief judge). When the governing regime changed with the success of 'Abd al-Mu'min (r. 1130–63), founder of the Almohad (*al-Muwaḥḥidūn*) dynasty, the members of the family continued to flourish under a new religious orientation based on the teachings of the reformer, al-Mahḍī ibn Tūmart (d. ca. 1129–30). Although insistent on the strict adherence to religious law, Ibn Tūmart's teachings were at the same time equally insistent on the essential rationality of human understanding of the existence and unity (*tawḥīd*) of God and his creation as well as the rationality of the Qur'ān and its interpretation. This approach was embraced – even exploited – by Averroes in his own writings on dialectical theology and thereby played a role in the development of his thought on the nature of religious law and revelation in relation to philosophy founded on the powers of natural reason. Considerations of family, history, and contemporary religious doctrine play roles in the thought of other philosophical thinkers presented in this volume, but in the case of Averroes his times and his various appointments at Seville and Cordoba as *qāḍī* seem to have melded in special ways with his understanding of Aristotle and al-Fārābī. Over the short period of 1179–81 he propounded publicly his controversial views on religion and natural reason in four important dialectical works: the so-called *Decisive Treatise*, the *Explanation of the Sorts of Proofs in the Doctrines of Religion* (*al-Kashf 'an al-manāhij*), a *Ḍamīma* or *Appendix on Divine Knowledge* usually understood as attached to the *Decisive Treatise*, and his famous *Incoherence of the Incoherence* written as a commentary on and response to al-Ghazālī's *Incoherence of the Philosophers*. In these compositions, Averroes is a thinker dynamically engaged with religious issues, working out a coherent account of matters of relevance to both religion and philosophy. The dynamism of his thought is also apparent in another way in philosophical works where he changed views on a number of issues, among them the nature of divine causality in the world and the vexing problem of providing a coherent and cogent account of human knowing and the role of the receptive human material intellect.

The philosophical works of Averroes range in size from short treatises on specific issues of logic, physics, psychology, *et alia* to his three sorts of commentaries on major works of the Aristotelian corpus. His *Short Commentaries*, usually considered early, consist of epitomizing accounts of Aristotelian doctrines, often substantially based on discussions in the accounts of commentators of the Greek tradition.[1] The *Middle Commentaries* more often have the form of a clarifying and simplifying paraphrase of the Aristotelian text, and for that reason are thought likely to arise in response to the request of his patron, Abū Ya'qūb Yūsuf, for help in understanding the works of Aristotle. The late *Long Commentaries*, consisting of the entire text of Aristotle divided into sections followed by detailed commentary, are generally thought to contain his most mature thought. The first of these was the *Long Commentary on the "Posterior Analytics"* (ca. 1180–3). Following in measured succession were Long Commentaries on the *De Anima* (ca. 1186?), on the *Physics* (1186), on the *De Caelo* (1188), and on the *Metaphysics* (1190). As will be discussed below, Averroes himself held that truth, not as grasped *per accidens* by the methods of persuasion or dialectic, but in its fullest sense as *per se*, is to be found in his "books of demonstration,"[2] that is, in his philosophical works and in particular his commentaries on Aristotle which he held to be substantially composed of philosophical demonstrations. Through translations into Hebrew the work of Averroes had a very substantial influence on the development of medieval Jewish philosophical thought. The works translated included the *Decisive Treatise*, the *Incoherence of the Incoherence*, several *Short Commentaries*, *Middle Commentaries* on the *Physics*, *De Caelo*, *De Anima*, *Metaphysics*, and more, and the *Long Commentaries* on the *Posterior Analytics* and *Physics*.[3] It is particularly significant that the *Long Commentarie*s on the *De Anima* and on the *Metaphysics* were not included, since these contain his final positions on soul, intellect, and personal immortality as well as on God and the nature of metaphysical science. Yet it is because of translations from Arabic into Latin in the thirteenth century that Averroes is a widely recognized figure in the history of philosophy today. This early wave of translations, many by Michael Scot, who worked in Toledo and in Sicily at the court of Frederick II, were for the most part of philosophical commentaries and did not include his works of dialectical argumentation relevant to religion. Averroes' thought continued to draw the attention of Western thinkers, and interest was reinforced by a second wave of translations and the printing of his translated works with those of Aristotle.[4] No such intense interest in the works and thought of Averroes was maintained in the Arabic philosophical milieu of the Middle Ages.

RELIGIOUS DIALECTIC AND PHILOSOPHY

Much philosophical confusion has arisen regarding the interpretation of the religious and philosophical thought of Averroes, oftentimes due to factors extraneous to his own work. Since the emergence of interest in Averroes broadly in the Arab world following the appearance of Renan's 1852 work, in some cases the writings and figure of Averroes have been used in blatant manipulation, with little if any regard to the genuine sense of his thought, to champion many diverse causes from socialism and Marxism to nationalism and more recently to promote the harmony of religion and rationality in the face of rising anti-rational Islamic fundamentalism.[5] In other cases, however, confusion has been due to the lack of access to or consultation of the complete corpus of his works, while in still others it has been due to confusion in the interpretation of doctrine and texts. This latter has been particularly evident in regard to the issue of the relation of philosophy and religion and the imputation to Averroes himself of the doctrine of "Double Truth" that is often claimed to have arisen in the Latin West.[6] Careful consideration of Averroes' methodology as expounded and employed in his dialectical works will show that imputation to be incorrect and will also valuably set the stage for consideration of his strictly philosophical work.

In the *Incoherence of the Incoherence* Averroes makes it clear that the discussions of philosophical topics recounted in that work should not be regarded as definitive accounts of his views. He also remarks on the nature of statements set forth in that work:

> All this is the theory of the philosophers on this problem and in the way we have stated it here with its proofs, it is a persuasive not a demonstrative statement. It is for you to inquire about these questions in the places where they are treated in the books of demonstration, if you are one of the people of complete happiness (*al-sa'āda al-tāmma*) and if you are one of those who learn the arts the function of which is proof. For the demonstrative arts are very much like the practical; for just as a man who is not a craftsman cannot perform the function of craftsmanship, in the same way it is not possible for him who has not learned the arts of demonstration to perform the function of demonstration which is demonstration itself: indeed this is still more necessary for this art than for any other – and this is not generally acknowledged in the case of this practice only because it is a mere act – and therefore such a demonstration can proceed only from one who has learned the art. The kinds of statements, however, are many, some demonstrative, others not, and since non-demonstrative statements can be adduced without knowledge of the art, it was thought that this might also be the case with demonstrative statements; but this is a great error. And therefore in the spheres of the demonstrative arts, no other statement is possible but a technical statement which only the student of this art can bring, just as is the case with the art of geometry. Nothing therefore of what we have said in this book is a technical demonstrative proof; they are all non-technical statements, some of them having greater persuasion than others, and it is in this spirit that what we have written here must be understood.[7]

Demonstrative statements have a formal structure, insofar as they are the necessary conclusions of demonstrative arguments which are technically sound and yield knowledge for the one who formed the arguments and drew the conclusions. As Averroes knew well, Aristotle held demonstrations to be valid syllogisms based on premises which are true, primary, and immediate as well as more known than, prior to, and causes of the conclusion (*Posterior Analytics*, I.2, 71b18–24). Syllogisms based on invalid technical form or on premises not meeting these criteria are not demonstrative and not productive of knowledge, however persuasive they may be. While demonstrations may build upon conclusions of other demonstrations, these statements based on non-demonstrative arguments may turn out to be true, but they would be so in a merely accidental way and not *per se*. For the practitioner of demonstration conclusions are necessary and known and, as such, are also persuasive; for the practitioner of rhetorical or dialectical argument statements cannot be known to be true on the basis of the reasoning given in the account. The syllogism used for these sorts of arguments will be a dialectical syllogism, a rhetorical syllogism, or a sign, says Averroes in his *Long Commentary on the "Posterior Analytics,"* and as such cannot be considered altogether evident or true (*al-yaqīn alladhī fī al-ghāya / secundum maximam veritatem*).[8] Yet, as he indicates in the quoted passage from the *Incoherence of the Incoherence*, there is no necessity that statements be demonstrative in order for them to be persuasive.

In his *Faṣl al-maqāl* or Decisive Treatise, the full title of which can be rendered, "Book of the Distinction of Discourse and the Establishment of the Relation of Religious Law and Philosophy,"[9] persuasion is explained as having to do with the movement of the soul in assent (*taṣdīq*). Not all forms of assent are dependent in a compelling way on the truth of the statement to which assent is given. Following the lead of al-Fārābī regarding what are called "modes of thought" by David Reisman in an earlier chapter of the present collection,[10] Averroes distinguishes human beings with respect to their native capacities and their methods of assent:

> [T]he natures of men are on different levels with respect to assent. One of them comes to assent through demonstration; another comes to assent through dialectical arguments, just as firmly as the demonstrative man through demonstration, since his nature does not contain any greater capacity; while another comes to assent through rhetorical arguments, again just as firmly as the demonstrative man through demonstrative argument.[11]

Nothing in dialectical arguments as such compels assent, though it may be the disposition of a given person to be swayed by dialectical arguments based on assumed principles and so to assent with fullest personal conviction to a certain statement or proposition. Likewise in rhetorical arguments as such there is nothing to compel assent, though it may be the disposition of a given person to be swayed by emotive appeals and displays and, again, to assent with fullest personal conviction to a certain statement or proposition. In these cases assent voiced or otherwise evinced is not founded on the truth or falsity of a statement or proposition as the criterion of its appropriateness. If the conclusion of a dialectical or rhetorical argument happens to be true, it is not because of the argument itself but because of extraneous considerations. The truth of the conclusions, then, has to be considered *per accidens*, not *per se*. It is only demonstration properly so called which attains truth with necessity in its conclusion and necessarily causes knowledge.

It is in this context that Averroes' distinction of characters of individuals with respect to their intellectual abilities has to be understood. He does not assert that there are different truths for these diverse classes of human beings. Those for whom the rhetorical mode of argumentation is most fitting require the guidance of others if they are to assent to what happens to be the truth, since neither the premises nor the argument form as such contribute to the truth of the conclusion. Those for whom the dialectical mode of argumentation is most fitting are those who are misled particularly regarding the starting points and foundations of arguments; for them to hit upon the truth in their conclusions would require the guidance of others who in fact know the truth of the premises. There is then no doctrine of "Double Truth" in Averroes such that religion has its truth and philosophy has yet another. Instead, Averroes holds for a unity of truth when he writes in his *Decisive Treatise*, "Truth does not contradict truth but rather is consistent with it and bears witness to it."[12]

This principle of the unity of truth plays a central role in Averroes' arguments, for otherwise it would be possible to hold there to be true propositions set forth in religion by dialectical argumentation founded on interpretation of religious scripture but which are at the same time incompatible with true propositions set forth in philosophy founded on demonstration. Averroes does not hold for actual incompatible truths to be present in the discourses or argued conclusions of religion and philosophy. Rather, he openly acknowledges that, in spite of the distinct ways assent is brought about in diverse classes of human beings, primacy has to be given to the philosophical method of demonstration.

We affirm definitely that whenever the conclusion of a demonstration is in conflict with the apparent meaning of Scripture [or Religious Law], that apparent meaning admits of allegorical interpretation according to the rules for such interpretation in Arabic. This proposition is questioned by no Muslim and doubted by no believer. But its certainty is immensely increased for those who have had close dealings with this idea and put it to the test, and made it their aim to reconcile the assertions of intellect and tradition. Indeed we may say that whenever a statement in Scripture [or Religious Law] conflicts in its apparent meaning with a conclusion of demonstration, if Scripture [or Religious Law] is considered carefully, and the rest of its contents searched page by page, there will invariably be found among the expressions of Scripture [or Religious Law] something which in its apparent meaning bears witness to that allegorical interpretation or comes close to bearing witness.[13]

Moreover, philosophically established truths can be used to correct theological excesses in scriptural interpretation such as the commonly held religious notion of creation *ex nihilo* and the origination of time. In the *Incoherence of the Incoherence* Averroes sets forth the understanding of the metaphysical dependence of the world on God in accord with the account of God as creator by way of final causality which he argues in his philosophical works. God is the creator of the universe insofar as he draws it from potentiality into the actuality of existence and also conserves it. Such is the case without entailing a temporal origination of the world and a starting moment of time. God does so by being "the cause of the composition of the parts of the world, the existence of which is in their composition," so that "he is the cause of their existence" and properly called agent of the existence of the world.[14] Since there cannot be two incompatible truths, in this case Averroes finds that the dialectical theologians moved from incorrect premises in their refusal to accept the literal account of Scripture because

in their statements about the world [they] do not conform to the apparent meaning of Scripture but interpret it allegorically. For it is not stated in Scripture that God was existing with absolutely nothing else: a text to this effect is nowhere to be found.[15]

Thus, Averroes holds that the truth of religion and the truth of philosophy are one and the same. In the *Incoherence of the Incoherence* Averroes holds that

> the religions are, according to the philosophers, obligatory, since they lead toward wisdom in a way universal to all human beings, for philosophy only leads a certain number of intelligent people to the knowledge of happiness, and they therefore have to learn wisdom, whereas religions seek the instruction of the masses generally.[16]

Not unlike al-Fārābī, Averroes holds that the role of religion is the education of human beings in proper social mores and conduct for their fulfillment and happiness. Yet it is necessary for those of the demonstrative class of philosophers to understand common religious propositions critically.

We have already seen that Averroes' account of the compatibility of the eternity of the world and Scripture is founded on a precise philosophical understanding of the issue. This issue of the eternity of the world *a parte ante* was one of the three positions for which al-Ghazālī accused the philosophers of *kufr*, unbelief. The remaining two were the denial of God's knowledge of particulars and the denial of resurrection and the afterlife. In both cases Averroes treads carefully in his responses, but those responses are in accord with the methodology indicated here. To the first he responds that divine knowledge cannot be understood on the model of human knowledge, which both in knowing particulars and in knowing universals is posterior to things. Since divine knowledge is the cause of things, not caused by things, the consequence is that God's knowledge cannot be characterized by human notions of universal or particular knowledge. In the *Ḍamīma* he holds that demonstration shows that it is not by some originated knowledge analogous to that of human beings that God can be said to know particulars or universals. Recognizing the limits of inquiry on this issue, he says, "This is the furthest extent to which purification [of concepts] ought to be admitted."[17] He later adds that

> there must be another knowledge of beings which is unqualified, the eternal Glorious Knowledge. And how is it conceivable that the Peripatetic philosophers could have held that the eternal Knowledge does not comprehend particulars, when they held that It is the cause of warning in dreams, of revelation, and of other kinds of inspiration?[18]

This issue of God's knowledge will be considered again below in a strictly philosophical context. But what the careful student should note here is that Averroes has affirmed that divine knowledge exists and that it is the cause of things. These assertions are acceptable to him on the basis of philosophical demonstration, as we shall see, and they are acceptable as statements of dialectical religious discourse. As he puts it, "demonstration compels the conclusion that [God] knows things, because their issuing from him is solely due to his knowing." Yet, "demonstration also compels the conclusion that God does not know things with a knowledge of the same character as originated knowledge."[19] But given that divine knowledge is a *tertium quid* unlike human particular or universal knowledge, "the limits of inquiry on this issue" as dealt with here in the context of dialectical arguments strictly preclude the explanation of exactly what it means to say that God knows things.

Averroes' critical interpretation of religious issues in accord with philosophical demonstration is also found in his treatment of al-Ghazālī's condemnation of the philosophers for denying resurrection and the afterlife (*al-ma'ād*). In the *Decisive Treatise* he outlines his understanding of Scripture to contain three sorts of texts: those which must be read literally, those which the demonstrative class may interpret allegorically, and those over which there is disagreement. Scholars who err in regard to this third sort of text should be excused because of the acknowledged difficulty and disagreement. The issue here is of the third sort. If an expert scholar should hold for an allegorical interpretation of Scripture on resurrection and the afterlife with respect to its character (*fī ṣifati al-ma'ād*), not with respect to its existence (*fī wujūdihi*), he should be excused "provided that the interpretation given does not lead to denial of its existence."[20] As we shall see, in his mature philosophical work Averroes allows no provision for continued existence after death for individual human beings, though he does hold that human life continues for other members of the species insofar as the species itself exists eternally. Hence, we see here again there is no question of two incompatible truths but rather one truth which may be differently conceived by people of the different classes of intellectual ability and assent. Those of the dialectical and rhetorical classes may give assent to the proposition of future life in accord with their ability to conceive that life as one of personal immortality and continued existence for individuals *post mortem*. The philosopher, however, gives assent to the proposition of future life, but does so without understanding it to refer to personal immortality, simply because the demonstrative methods of philosophical psychology yield only the notion of a future life for the human species, not the persistence of particular individuals.[21]

His argumentation for the existence of God in his *Explanation of the Sorts of Proofs in the Doctrines of Religion* is founded on statements from the Qur'ān but follows the same model.[22] In this work of dialectical theology Averroes applies his own teachings on the different classes of human beings to his analysis of methods of Scripture. Complex syllogistic explanation is not the appropriate method of persuasion for the common folk and so is not found in the Qur'ān. Rather, the Qur'ān's arguments for God are rhetorical and also dialectical insofar as they are based on commonly held presuppositions of a religious sort. The argument from providence (*'ināya*) for humans holds that the beings of the world exist for sake of human welfare and that this must be so only by a willing agent. The Qur'ān provides the premise and affirms the conclusion that the existing God is this agent. The argument from creation (*khalq*) has the premises that it is self-evident that animate things differ from inanimate and that the existence of the animate requires something to provide a determination (*qaṭan*) for life, namely God, the creator. The providential movement of the heavens for the benefit of our world equally gives indication of the creator. Thus, since everything created has to have a creator, observation of the universe and our world together with these premises yields the conclusion that God exists. For Averroes these arguments are suitable religious arguments, and they also happen to coincide with his philosophical argumentation which holds for a form of divine providence as well as for a form of divine creation. This understanding and also his rationalist approach to the issues of religion can be considered to coincide harmoniously with the rationalist elements of the theology of Ibn Tūmart, something which may have emboldened Averroes to set forth his views publicly in the four works discussed.[23]

ARISTOTELIAN PHILOSOPHICAL THOUGHT

Of Aristotle Averroes wrote, "I believe that this man was a model in nature and the exemplar which nature found for showing final human perfection."[24] He sought so much to follow the lead of

Aristotle (*Prior Analytics*, I.32) in attempting to convert arguments to syllogistic figures that he asserts in his *Middle Commentary on the "Prior Analytics"* that all speech and discourse should be reduced to syllogisms for critical analysis since "the nature of the reality on which demonstration rests" is truth and its self-consistency.[25] While the effort to return to genuine Aristotelian principles is increasingly evident in his later works on physics and metaphysics, Averroes struggled over the years to provide coherent interpretations of texts and issues in the works of Aristotle, employing translated works of the Greek commentary tradition by Alexander, Themistius, and others as aids to understanding much as do philosophers studying Aristotle today. His best-known struggle was with Aristotle's teachings on the intellect.

The Greek and Arabic philosophical traditions clearly saw that Aristotle in *De Anima*, III.5 posited a transcendent active intellect as a cause in the transformation of intelligibles in potency garnered via sensation into intelligibles in act known in human understanding. Yet they were also acutely aware that Aristotle had nowhere fulfilled his promise at III.7, 431b17–19, to return to consideration of the receptive powers of intellect to determine whether thinking of separate immaterial objects (intelligibles in act) is possible for human beings when they themselves are confined to the material conditions of body. While a complex and important issue for all thinkers of these traditions, for Averroes the issue of the nature, function, and metaphysical status of the receptive human power called material intellect (following Alexander of Aphrodisias) was one to which he returned repeatedly for refinement and development in at least five distinct works in addition to the three philosophical commentaries where his fullest accounts are to be found.[26]

In his *Short Commentary on the "De Anima"* (ca. 1158–60), Averroes was under the influence of Ibn Bājja, who held that the name, material intellect, denoted an intellectual receptive potency with human imagination as its subject. After the external and internal sense powers apprehend the intentions (*ma'ānin*) or intentional forms of things, these particulars are received into the imagination, a power of soul which has no need of a bodily instrument for its activity.[27] Causally established in the things of the world by way of these intentions, these forms come to be intelligible in act through the immaterial power of the agent intellect which exists separately from the soul. On this understanding, receptive material intellect is understood as "the disposition which is in the forms of the imagination for receiving intelligibles,"[28] brought to exist there thanks to the agent intellect which thereby brings the individual to intellectual understanding of intelligibles predicable as universal concepts. Averroes was initially so pleased with this account he called it "true" and "demonstrative." This notion of the imagination as the subject for the material intellect accounts for the personal intellectual activities of each individual person. As an immaterial disposition attached to imagination, the material intellect seemed to transcend body and the particularity characteristic of bodily powers sufficiently to account for the understanding of intelligibles in act.

With the appearance of the *Middle Commentary* (ca. 1174), Averroes had substantially rethought his views on the nature of imagination as a power transcending the body. Imagination is now conceived as a power too mixed with the body to permit it to be subject for a disposition which must be so unmixed as to be open to the reception of any and all intelligibles without distortion or interference. As completely unmixed, the material intellect cannot properly be considered to have a subject which is a body or a power in a body. Apparently using the celestial bodies, souls, and intellects as his model, Averroes now conceives the material intellect as a disposition with the soul as subject, but with the special understanding that it is in its subject without being in a composed union with it, not involving the sort of composition found in the being of material substances or accidents. Instead the material intellect is made by the agent intellect to exist in association with each individual after the manner of the celestial soul, which has an association with a celestial body but exists separately. In this sense, then,

> the material intellect is something composed of the disposition found in us and of an intellect conjoined to this disposition. As conjoined to the disposition, it is a disposed intellect, not an intellect in act; though, as not conjoined to this disposition, it is an intellect in act; while, in itself, this intellect is the Agent Intellect, the existence of which will be shown later. As conjoined to this disposition, it is necessarily an intellect in potentiality which cannot think itself but which can think other than itself (that is, material things), while, as not conjoined to the disposition, it is necessarily an intellect in act which thinks itself and not that which is here (that is, it does not think material things).[29]

Thus, in the *Middle Commentary* the material intellect is a power made to exist in immaterial association with individual human beings by the separate agent intellect. This allows for sensed intentions intelligible in potency to be transformed by the intellectual power of the agent intellect and deposited in individual and immaterial receptive intellects belonging to distinct human beings.

The final position of Averroes on intellect is found in his *Long Commentary* (ca. 1190), where he rejects the notion of a plurality of individual material intellects, argues for a single eternal material intellect for all humankind, expounds a new teaching on the cogitative power, excludes human immortality, explains how the agent intellect is "our final form" and formal cause, and establishes principles essential for his account of the hierarchical relationship of intellects leading up to the First Cause or God. While in the earlier commentaries Averroes was concerned over the requirement that the material intellect be unmixed, the driving force behind his new views is found in two key principles generated out of his concern for the metaphysics and epistemology of the intelligibles received in the material intellect. The first concerns the material intellect itself. Insofar as the material intellect is "that which is in potency all the intentions of universal material forms and is not any of the beings in act before it understands any of them,"[30] it is not possible for the material intellect itself to be a particular or definite individual entity (*aliquid hoc* or *al-mushār ilā-hi*), since the received intelligible would be contracted to the particular nature of its subject, the material intellect. The material intellect then must be an entity unique in its species. It must be an existing immaterial intellect, yet it must also be receptive in nature. Averroes marks the unusual nature of the material intellect by calling it "a fourth kind of being" other than matter, form, or a composite of these.[31] The second concerns the intelligibles themselves. The problem with the accounts of the earlier commentaries was that their plurality of immaterial receptive intellects meant a plurality of intelligibles in act without the same intelligible being understood by each human being. If two humans are thinking of the same intelligible, for example, a teacher and a student, then they cannot be thinking about two different intelligibles. Indeed, a third intelligible, over and above those in their individual intellects, would be required to explain why they are in fact thinking about the same intelligible. Consequently, it is necessary that the intelligible in act exist separately from particular or definite individual entities in the single transcendent material intellect shared by all human beings.[32]

This new teaching on the material intellect necessitated not only a more complex account of the relations of the agent and material intellects but also a rethinking of the nature of individual human knowers for Averroes. The result was the development of a more robust account of the internal sense powers and a detailed exposition of the role of the cogitative power (*fikr* / *cogitatio*) in the generation of intelligibles in the material intellect as well as in the knowing of intelligibles on the part of individual human beings. In the process of coming to have knowledge, the perishable bodily powers of common sense, imagination, cogitation, and memory work together to spiritualize or denude the intentions apprehended via sense of accidents and attributes extrinsic to the nature of the thing. Though none of these are properly called intellect, cogitation can be said to share in the powers of intellect insofar as it has the task of discerning and separating off the extraneous before depositing the still particular denuded form in memory. This brings about the state called the intellect in a positive disposition (*al-ʿaql bi-al-malaka* / *intellectus in habitu*). This disposition allows us to renew our connection with the material intellect and thus to think again about something we have thought about already earlier. The intelligibles in act or theoretical intelligibles thus attained may be said to have two subjects: the subject of truth, consisting of the cogitative and other internal powers of the individual soul, is cause of the intention presented to the material intellect; the subject for the existence of the intelligible in act is the material intellect where its existence is realized.

Even if the metaphysical natures of the agent and material intellects must be understood as distinct in existence from perishable individuals, the powers of these intellects must be understood as present in human souls and as essentially connected with human rationality. Our individual voluntary effort at coming to have knowledge remains grounded in a particular intention, but is also what generates in the individual the form presented to the separate intellects for abstraction and intellectual apprehension. This takes place when the "light" of the agent intellect shines on the presented form and the material intellect so as to allow for the abstraction of the intelligible from what has been presented to it and for the impressing of the generated intelligible on the receptive material intellect. Like the potentially transparent medium for sight made actually transparent by light in Aristotle's doctrine of light and vision, the material intellect is actualized as receptive intellect by the "light" of the agent intellect. Averroes describes this as a process in which intentions intelligible in potency are made intelligible in act, that is, they are "transferred" in "being from one order into another."[33] In this natural process of conjoining (*ittiṣāl*), the agent intellect and material intellect are united with the knower such that the agent intellect is "our final form," that is, our formal cause and perfection, and the material intellect is our intellect. In this process the agent intellect is "form for us," both because we are the ones who individually initiate the process of knowing,[34] and also because in knowing, the agent intellect is intrinsic to us, not something external emanating intelligibles out of itself. In the formation of knowledge from experience, the agent intellect does not give intelligibles from its own nature to some distinct entity, but only functions as an abstractive and imprinting power, actualized as such only in the presence of denuded intelligibles provided by individual human beings. Since humans are deliberate initiators of the process of knowing, the agent intellect is their formal cause and the material intellect is the receptive power as shared human intellect actualized in abstraction.[35] Yet the individual human knower, who is bodily and identified with the perishable cogitative power, perishes at death, while the immaterial separate intellects continue in their existence eternally functioning as powers of knowing for other transitory members of the equally eternal human species.

Averroes understood the new doctrine of the material intellect in the *Long Commentary on the "De Anima"* to have important ramifications for his metaphysical teachings in his *Long Commentary on the "Metaphysics"*; the two works refer to each other. In contrast to Avicenna, who held that metaphysical argument for the establishment of the existence of the Necessary Being begins with consideration of primary concepts, Averroes held that the only suitable philosophical way to the existence of God is through Aristotle's arguments of the physics for an eternal cause of the motions of the heavens. Since physics concerns bodies and powers in bodies, this science which proves the existence of an eternal immaterial cause for the motion of the universe could not include in its subject matter the nature of this immaterial entity. For Averroes, the role of philosophical psychology's epistemological arguments was to show the identity of intellect and immateriality in the natures of the agent and material intellects. Thus he could conclude that the immaterial entity reached by physics is in fact intellectual in nature. And with its establishment of the material intellect as an incorporeal receptive potency for intelligibles, philosophical psychology also showed that immaterial separate intellect could possess potency in some form.

This was also used by Averroes in his metaphysics to hold for a hierarchy of specifically distinct intellectual substances ranked according to potency in relation to God, the First Cause and First Form, whom he characterized as "pure actuality" (*fi'lun maḥḍun*).[36] While Averroes made liberal use of the language of creation in characterizing God, his metaphysical teaching expounded an Aristotelian account of an eternal universe drawn into existence by the final causality of the pure actuality of the First Cause, which is being in its highest form. All other entities (including the hierarchy of immaterial intellects moving the heavens) contain some note of potency at least insofar as their being and knowing necessarily contain reference to something extrinsic, namely, the pure actuality of being of the First Cause. The First Cause alone contains no reference to anything outside itself. What is more, as pure immaterial actuality of intellect, the First Cause is the highest actuality of thought with itself as its sole object, as Aristotle had held. As such, the knowledge of the First Cause is a noetic and metaphysical identity with its being. As noted earlier in considering his religious dialectic, for Averroes divine knowledge is neither universal nor particular and as such is not to be identified with any of the modes of knowledge known to human beings. Unlike human knowledge, for Averroes divine knowledge is creative of things, not posterior to them. In the context of Averroes' philosophical thought this can be understood to mean that the actuality and activity of the First Cause as the self-knowing pure actuality of being is responsible for its being the primary referent for all other beings, and thereby the cause of the existence of all beings as the ultimate final cause against which others are measured and toward which all beings are drawn. Hence, in knowing itself, it is knowing the cause of all other beings, and it is in the same activity causing all other beings.

Although perhaps somewhat similar in language of dependence, this doctrine is altogether different from that of Avicenna, who also held God to be the highest instance of the purity of being and actuality. While Averroes did set forth a doctrine of emanation of a hierarchy of intellects in his early *Short Commentary on the "Metaphysics,"*[37] he rejected that in his mature thought in favor of the view recounted above and also rejected the tripartite Avicennian distinction of being into necessary in itself, possible in itself, and possible in itself but necessitated by another. Averroes objected to this view because it allowed only the First Cause to be considered necessary in its own right. Following Aristotle, he understood the heavens and their movers not to be possible in themselves but rather necessary beings in their own right insofar as they are not subject to corruption. In his *Long Commentary on the "Metaphysics"* Averroes also rejects the Avicennian distinction between existence and essence, insisting that Avicenna was confused by theological considerations contaminating his philosophical metaphysics in thinking that one and being are dispositions added to the essence of a thing, rather than seeing man, one man, and existing man as modes of signifying one reality.[38]

The works of Averroes were not widely influential in the history of Arabic philosophy, though they were appreciated by Moses Maimonides and some were known by Ibn Khaldūn. No school of Averroist thought arose in the Arabic tradition to continue his work, perhaps because of his failure to gain favor for his philosophically driven analysis of religious issues. But his works lived on in translations into Hebrew and Latin. In the Jewish tradition his translated works – the Middle Commentaries generally rather than the Long – were studied intensely and gave rise to their own supercommentary tradition (see below, chapter 17). In the Christian West, Latin translations of many of his *Long Commentaries* were available to thinkers of the thirteenth century, where they served to play a fundamentally important role in teaching the Latins how to read Aristotle with sympathy and insight (see below, chapter 18). The insights of Averroes and his detailed comments on Aristotle were initially welcomed in the Latin tradition.[39] Yet with deeper critical study and growing familiarity with and reflection upon the texts and issues, it soon became apparent that the commentaries of Averroes contained philosophical arguments and teachings on issues such as the eternity of the world and the nature of the soul which were incompatible with Christian belief in creation *ex nihilo* and the personal immortality of the human soul. Around these issues the so-called "Latin Averroist" controversy arose in reaction to works by Siger of Brabant and Boethius of Dacia. In this context the much-discussed and seldom-understood "Double Truth" doctrine often wrongly attributed to Averroes himself was thought by Latin religious authorities to be held by certain philosophers in the Parisian Arts Faculty. This and the other issues mentioned reasserted themselves in various contexts up to the time of the Renaissance, when the works of Averroes enjoyed a second Latin life with new translations, for the most part from Hebrew versions, and with the publication of printed editions of works of Aristotle with the Commentaries of Averroes as well as other works of Averroes.

Understood in this fashion, Averroes has generally come to be regarded by some as first and foremost a rationalist philosopher whose loyalty to Islam must either be based on some form of fideism or must be disingenuous. Yet this dilemma and its dangerous horns should be rejected for a more sympathetic understanding of Averroes as a devotee of the most sophisticated and dominant religion of his historical culture, Islam. A distinguished scholar and religious *qāḍī*, Averroes' devotion to Islam and its religious practices was never significantly questioned in a way prominent to historical scholarship. Rather, it is apparent that Averroes held the world and its First Principle, God, to be through and through rational in nature, such that human rational endeavors are understood to be the keys to the most complete knowledge and happiness open to human beings. His philosophical thought includes important roles for religion in the development of human powers toward their fulfillment in the highest intellectual insight into God and his creation, even as it gives critical assessment to the truth and efficacy of religious arguments and statements.

NOTES

1 Druart [141].

2 Averroes, *Tahāfut al-tahāfut*, ed. M. Bouyges, S.J. (Beirut: 1930), 427–8; Averroes [140], 257–8.

3 See G. Endress, "*Averrois Opera*: A Bibliography of Editions and Contributions to the Text," in Aertsen and Endress [134], 339–81.

4 See C. Burnett, "The Second Revelation of Arabic Philosophy and Science: 1492–1562," in C. Burnett and A. Contadini (eds.), *Islam and the Italian Renaissance* (London: 1999), 185–98.

5 See E. Renan, *Averroès et l'averroïsme*, in *Œuvres complètes de Ernest Renan*, ed. H. Psichari, vol. III (Paris: 1852); A. von Küglegen, *Averroes und die arabische Moderne: Ansätze zu einer Neubegründung des Rationalismus im Islam* (Leiden:1994). Also see von Küglegen, "A Call for Rationalism: 'Arab Averroists' in the Twentieth Century," *Alif* (Cairo) 16 (1996), 97–132.

6 See O. Leaman, *Averroes and his Philosophy* (Oxford: 1988) and O. Leaman, *A Brief Introduction to Islamic Philosophy* (Oxford: 1999).

7 Averroes, *Tahāfut*, 427–8; Averroes [140], 257–8. Translation slightly modified; Arabic added.

8 Averroes, *Sharḥ al-burhān li-Arisṭū*, in A. Badawī (ed.), *Ibn Rushd, Sharḥ al-burhān li-Arisṭū wa-talkhīṣ al-burhān* (*Grand Commentaire et Paraphrase des "Secondes Analytiques" d'Aristote*) (Kuwait: 1984), 184; Latin *In Aristotelis Opera Cum Averrois Commentariis* (Venice: 1562; repr. Frankfurt a. M.: 1962), vol. I, pt. 2, bk. 1, Comment 9, 32rA. At 32vD Averroes quotes Aristotle's text that true conclusions can be made from false premises, though those conclusions are *per accidens*. The next Comment argues that the conditions for demonstration must be met completely.

9 In this translation I follow A. El Ghannouchi, "Distinction et relation des discours philosophique et religieux chez Ibn Rushd: *Fasl al maqal* ou la double vérité," in *Averroes (1126–1198) oder der Triumph des Rationalismus: Internationales Symposium anlässlich des 800. Todestages des islamischen Philosophen*, ed. R. G. Khoury (Heidelberg: 2002), 139–45; see 145.

10 See chapter 4 above; and al-Fārābī, *Taḥṣīl al-sa'āda*, in *Rasā'il al-Fārābī* (Hyderabad: 1926/1345 A. H.), 29–36; "The Attainment of Happiness," in *Alfarabi's Philosophy of Plato and Aristotle*, trans. M. Mahdi (Ithaca, NY: 1969), sect. iii, 34–41. Cf. Walzer [77], ch. 17, 276–85.

11 Averroes [139], 49. Translation slightly modified.

12 For detailed discussion of this rendering of Aristotle, *Prior Analytics*, I.32, 47a8–9, see Taylor [148].

13 Averroes [139], 51.

14 Averroes, *Tahāfut*, 151–2; Averroes [140], 90. Creation *ex nihilo* is also denied in the *Long Commentary on the "Metaphysics"*: Averroes, *Tafsīr mā ba'd al-ṭabī'a*, ed. M. Bouyges (Beirut: 1949), 1497–1505;

Engl. trans. at Averroes [137], 108–12; Latin in *In Aristotelis Opera cum Averrois Commentariis*, vol. VIII, 304rD–305vI.

15 Averroes [139], 57.

16 Averroes, *Tahāfut*, 582; Averroes [140], 360.

17 Averroes [139], 75.

18 Ibid.

19 Ibid.

20 Averroes [139], 61.

21 Taylor [216].

22 Ibn Rushd (Averroes), *al-Kashf 'an al-manāhij al-adilla fī 'aqā'id al-milla* (Beirut: 1998), 118–19; English trans. Averroes [136], 79ff.

23 See M. Geoffroy, "L'Almohadisme théologique d'Averroès (Ibn Rushd)," *Archives d'histoire doctrinale et littéraire du moyen âge* 66 (1999), 9–47.

24 Averroes [135], 433. My translation. For other texts, see S. Harvey, "The Quiddity of Philosophy according to Averroes and Falaquera: A Muslim Philosopher and his Jewish Interpreter," in J. A. Aertsen and A. Speer (eds.), *Was ist Philosophie im Mittelalter?* (Berlin: 1998), 904–13. Also see Taylor [146].

25 Ibn Rushd (Averroes), *Middle Commentary on Aristotle's "Prior Analytics"* (Arabic), ed. M. M. Kassem, with C. E. Butterworth and A. Abd al-Magid Haridi (Cairo: 1983), 226.

26 These are (1) the *Epistle on the Possibility of Conjunction*, trans. K. P. Bland (New York: 1982); (2) *Epistle #1 On Conjunction* and (3) *Epistle #2 On Conjunction*, ed. and trans. in M. Geoffroy and C. Steel (eds.), *Averroès, La béatitude de l'âme: éditions, traductions et études* (Paris: 2001); (4) *De Separatione Primi Principii*, in C. Steel and G. Guldentops, "An Unknown Treatise of Averroes against the Avicennians on the First Cause: Edition and Translation," *Recherches de théologie et philosophie médiévales* 64 (1997), 86–135; and (5) the *Commentary on the "De Intellectu" of Alexander*, in M. Zonta, "La tradizione guideo-araba ed ebraica del *De intellectu* di Alessandro di Afrodisa e il testo originale del *Commento* di Averroè," *Annali di Ca' Foscari* 40.3 (2001), 17–35.

27 *Epitome de Anima* (Arabic text), ed. S. Gómez Nogales (Madrid: 1985), 108. Gómez Nogales has also translated his edition as *La psicología de Averroes: comentario al libro sobre el alma de Aristóteles* (Madrid: 1987).

28 *Epitome de Anima*, 124.

29 Averroes [138], 111–12.

30 Averroes [135], 387. The account which follows is based on 387–8.

31 Averroes [135], 409.
32 Averroes [135], 411–12.
33 Averroes [135], 439.
34 "[W]ithout the imaginative power and the cogitative [power] the intellect which is called material understands nothing" (Averroes [135], 450).
35 "[T]hat in virtue of which something carries out its proper activity is the form, while we carry out our proper activity in virtue of the agent intellect, it is necessary that the agent intellect be form in us" (Averroes [135], 500). Also see 439. On "our final form," see 444–5, 485–6, 490.
36 In the *Long Commentary on the "Metaphysics"*: Averroes, *Tafsīr mā ba'd al-ṭabī'a*, 1599.7.
37 See Davidson [208], 220ff.
38 Averroes, *Tafsīr mā ba'd al-ṭabī'a*, 313ff.; see also 1279ff.
39 See C. Bazán, "Was There Ever a 'First Averroism'?" in *Miscellanea Mediaevalia* 27 (Berlin: 2000), 31–53.

JOHN WALBRIDGE

10 Suhrawardī and Illuminationism

SUHRAWARDĪ AND HIS CAREER

One is tempted to romanticize Suhrawardī.[1] Indeed, there is no particular reason to avoid romanticizing him as a personality. He lived the life of a wandering wise man, and his story involved a prince, a magic gem, the fabulous Saladin, and a tragic early death. We can see him as his contemporaries saw him – probably as he saw himself – as a figure out of philosophical folklore, the like of whom had not been seen since Apollonius of Tyana. However, in my view it is a grave error to examine his philosophy, Illuminationism, through romantic spectacles, for Suhrawardī, despite his own attempts to mystify his project, was a hardheaded philosophical critic and creative thinker who set the agenda for later Islamic philosophy. Al-Ghazālī's attempt to make religion independent of reason and Averroes' Aristotelianism left little trace in later Islamic thought, but Suhrawardī's critique of Avicenna's ontology and of Aristotelian epistemology and his solutions to these problems were his successors' starting points. The modern description of his philosophy as "theosophy" does not do justice to the rigor and philosophical influence of his thought.[2]

Suhrawardī was probably born around 1154 in the village of Suhraward near Zanjān in northwestern Iran.[3] We know nothing of his family or ethnic background. He first appears in Marāgha, a nearby city, where he studied logic and philosophy with Majd al-Dīn al-Jīlī, a scholar of moderate prominence who also was the teacher of the famous theologian Fakhr al-Dīn al-Rāzī. Later he studied with Fakhr al-Dīn al-Mārdīnī, either in Mārdīn in southeastern Anatolia or in Isfahan. Mārdīnī was a prominent teacher of medicine and the rational sciences and apparently a Ṣūfī. In Isfahan he studied Ibn

Sahlān al-Sāwī's *Baṣā'ir*, an innovative text on logic, with the otherwise unknown Zahīr al-Fārisī (or al-Qārī). He seems to have spent his twenties wandering in central Anatolia and northern Syria in search of patronage. His books written in this period are dedicated to various local dignitaries.

At some point in these wanderings Suhrawardī abandoned the Avicennian Peripatetic philosophy that he had learned from his teacher and became a Platonist. It was, he tells us, his mystical exercises and a dream of Aristotle that led to his conversion. He does not explain in detail the mystical experiences, though they seem to have been connected with the apprehension of the Platonic Forms.[4] As for the dream, Aristotle appeared to him one night, shining with light. Suhrawardī had been struggling with the problem of knowledge. Aristotle explained that the key to understanding knowledge was self-consciousness – the basis of the doctrine of knowledge by presence, of which I will say more presently. After he had finished his explanations, Aristotle began praising Plato. Startled by the extravagence of the praise, Suhrawardī asked Aristotle whether any of the Islamic philosophers had reached that rank. It was only the ecstatic mystics like Bisṭāmī and Tustarī who were worthy of the great philosopher's notice.[5]

In 1183 he came to Aleppo, which had just been captured by Saladin. It is said that he entered the city in clothes so shabby that he was mistaken for a donkey driver. He took up residence at a *madrasa*, where the director quickly realized that he was a man of learning and tactfully sent his young son with a gift of decent clothes. Suhrawardī brought out a large gem and told the boy to go to the market and have it priced. The boy came back and reported that the prince-governor, a teenaged son of Saladin, had bid 30,000 dirhams for it. Suhrawardī then smashed the gem with a rock, telling the boy that he could have had better clothes had he wished.[6] Suhrawardī was soon under the protection of the prince. He finished his most important work, *The Philosophy of Illumination*, three years later on September 15, 1186, on an evening when the sun, the moon, and the five Ptolemaic planets were all in conjunction in Libra.[7]

Suhrawardī's ascendancy over the prince, al-Malik al-Ẓāhir, aroused the jealousy of various local scholars. The magical powers and mystical attainments that he is said to have flaunted cannot have helped relations. Complaints reached the ear of Saladin.

Suhrawardī's philosophy would have sounded like Ismāʿīlism to Saladin and his conservative religious advisors, and Aleppo was of great strategic importance, especially with the looming threat of the Third Crusade. Accordingly, Saladin ordered Suhrawardī's execution, and the young prince reluctantly acceded. Suhrawardī probably died in 1191, though the accounts are contradictory.[8] The circle of disciples who had accompanied him scattered, and not even their names are recorded.

SUHRAWARDĪ'S WRITINGS AND THE TRANSITION FROM PERIPATETIC TO ILLUMINATIONIST PHILOSOPHY

There is a major difficulty in interpreting Suhrawardī's thought. He is known as *Shaykh al-Ishrāq*, which means – we will tentatively (and tendentiously) say – "the master of illumination" or, less dramatically, "the founder of the Illuminationist school." The question is, what might that mean? In the introduction to *The Philosophy of Illumination* Suhrawardī says:

> Before I wrote this book and during the times when interruptions prevented me from working on it, I wrote other books in which I have summarized for you the principles of the Peripatetics according to their method . . . I also have composed other works, some in my youth. But the present work has another method and a shorter path to knowledge than their method. It is more orderly and precise, less painful to study. I did not first arrive at it through cogitation, but rather it was acquired through something else. Subsequently I sought proof for it so that should I cease contemplating the proof, nothing would make me fall into doubt.[9]

Combining this statement with what we know about Suhrawardī's surviving works, we can divide them into four classes:

(1) juvenilia;
(2) mystical works, notably a number of allegories;
(3) works expounding the principles of the Peripatetics according to their methods;
(4) *The Philosophy of Illumination.*

Probably half or less of the bulk of Suhrawardī's writings has been published and only *The Philosophy of Illumination* and the allegories have received serious scholarly attention, so anything we can say about his works as a whole is necessarily tentative. So far, Suhrawardī's statement about his works has been understood in two quite different ways.

The approach popularized by the late Henry Corbin, the scholar most responsible for bringing Suhrawardī to the attention of world scholarship, focuses on the mystical and mythical elements of Suhrawardī's thought. The "Peripatetic" works are simply an exercise for those unable to pursue serious mystical – or to use the term popularized by Corbin, "theosophical" – investigations. Therefore, the works of Suhrawardī worthy of serious attention are the mystical allegories and *The Philosophy of Illumination* less its first book, which deals with logic and the critique of the Peripatetics. By this account, Suhrawardī was a reviver of the wisdom of the ancient Persians, as indicated by his use of light and darkness as fundamental philosophical concepts and by his invocation of various Zoroastrian sages and gods. Thus, Corbin translated the title of *The Philosophy of Illumination* as "Le livre de théosophie orientale" and spent a good deal of time talking about the importance of "spiritual geography" in Suhrawardī's thought.[10]

This was not how Suhrawardī was understood by most of his successors in the Islamic world. For both followers like Quṭb al-Dīn al-Shīrāzī and critics like Mullā Ṣadrā, he was a philosopher who had made certain specific contributions in metaphysics, ontology, and epistemology. Suhrawardī had begun with a critique of the standard philosophy of the day, the Peripatetic system of Avicenna, and attacked it on several major points. First, while attempting to clarify the murky Aristotelian conception of being, Avicenna had made a distinction between essence and existence and then assumed that a real distinction must correspond to this mental distinction. Suhrawardī attacked this assumption, arguing that conceptions such as existence were *iʿtibārī*, products of the mind. Suhrawardī's successors accepted his critique of Avicenna, but disagreed as to whether his solution was adequate. Mullā Ṣadrā, for example, held that in fact it was essence, the differences among things, that was *iʿtibārī*. Second, Suhrawardī criticized Avicenna's Aristotelian conception of knowledge by abstraction of forms. Instead, he argued that knowledge was essentially the unmediated presence of the thing known to the conscious knower. This theory was the basis of his use of mysticism as a philosophical tool. This criticism and solution was generally accepted by his successors. Finally, Suhrawardī argued that philosophical cosmology required the assumption that existents could differ in intensity as well as in kind. Again, this theory was immensely influential among his successors.

Suhrawardī made various other criticisms of the prevailing Avicennian Peripateticism: a reassertion of the doctrine of Platonic Forms, an attack on the Peripatetic theory of essential definition, and an attack on the Peripatetic theory of matter, for example. These were obviously philosophical positions, understood as such by Suhrawardī's successors. Moreover, *The Philosophy of Illumination*, by universal agreement the most important of Suhrawardī's works, was understood by his successors through a series of philosophically oriented commentaries, notably the commentary of Shahrazūrī, its adaptation by Quṭb al-Dīn al-Shīrāzī, and the annotations by Mullā Ṣadrā. These commentaries translated its novel philosophical terminology into the standard philosophical language of Avicenna so that, for example, "barrier" becomes "body" and "managing light" becomes "soul."[11] The legitimacy of this procedure was not, so far as I know, questioned from within the Islamic philosophical tradition, though it has been by some modern scholars.

Whether or not they were correct to label Suhrawardī a "theosophist," Corbin and his followers were quite correct in stressing the importance of the passages in Surhawardī's writing concerning his philosophical genealogy. Suhrawardī clearly saw himself as the reviver of the most ancient tradition of philosophy. Modern scholars for the most part would see the genealogy of Islamic philosophy as going back to Aristotle as understood by his later commentators with some Neoplatonic influence through stray texts like the *Theology of Aristotle*. There was perhaps some slight influence from other Greek philosophical schools and from other nations in politics and ethics. Later on, there was influence from Ṣūfism, with Suhrawardī being one of the important instances.

Suhrawardī saw things differently. There were three ancient sources of philosophical thought: the Egyptians, the Indians and Chinese, and the ancient Persians. The mainstream of Islamic philosophy derived ultimately from Egypt, from the philosopher-prophet Hermes Trismegistus, also called Enoch or Idrīs.[12] Empedocles had studied in Syria and Pythagoras in Egypt and Mesopotamia. The two of them were the founders of the tradition of "divine philosophy" in

Greek philosophy. Socrates and Plato were under their influence, and Aristotle was, of course, the student of Plato. The followers of Aristotle took his philosophy in two directions. The Aristotelians best known in the Islamic world were those who pursued only the superficial aspects of his thought. Their champion was Avicenna, and Suhrawardī himself had belonged to their school. However, there were also Aristotelians – including Aristotle himself in his later years – who carried on the divine philosophy of Plato, which is represented in such works as the *Theology*. In the meantime, there was also a Pythagorean tradition that survived in Egypt and was associated with the alchemists of Panopolis. Its Islamic representatives were the Ṣūfī alchemist Dhū al-Nūn al-Miṣrī and his student Sahl al-Tustarī. Second, there was the tradition of the ancient Persians, represented by various pre-Islamic Persian sages and by the ecstatic Persian Ṣūfīs Abū Yazīd al-Basṭāmī, al-Ḥallāj, and al-Kharaqānī. The exact position of the Chinese and Indians, the third source of philosophy, is less clear. Probably, Suhrawardī saw them mostly as having parallel traditions of wisdom whose influence on Islamic philosophy, such as it might be, was either through the Iranians or through Pythagoras, who was thought to have journeyed in the East and to have had followers in India. Suhrawardī was thus the first of the Muslim philosophers to reunite these various traditions, and it is clear from the language he uses that Plato was the central hero of his philosophy.[13]

Though there is much of the mythical in Suhrawardī's account of the history of philosophy, it deserves some consideration both on historical and philosophical grounds. First some comments and clarifications. The Ionian physicists are ignored, although they were known to Muslim philosophers through doxographies, Aristotle, and the Galenic tradition. There are also no Christians or Muslims, except for the Ṣūfīs, and these do not include the individuals usually listed as the founding fathers of Islamic mysticism. The Persians are not historical Zoroastrian priests but legendary Persian kings and viziers, understood as sages. The connections to the Orientals – Persians, Indians, and Chinese – are much vaguer than those to the Greeks. As for the Greeks, Suhrawardī's "divine philosophers" are what the doxographers called "the Italian School." The historical Socrates and Plato obviously had connections to both the Ionians and the Italians, but I think that Suhrawardī was correct to say that Plato should be thought of primarily as a successor of Empedocles and Pythagoras rather than of Thales and the Ionians. Moreover, the view that the Egyptian alchemists preserved a pre-Platonic philosophical tradition that they passed on to the Muslims has recently found a scholarly defender.[14] Both the occult sciences and medicine transmitted Greek thought to the Muslims in parallel to the translations of Aristotle and other philosophers.[15]

Suhrawardī's interest in his philosophical genealogy, its "Oriental" connections, and many of its details are characteristic of the whole Pythagorean/Platonic/Neoplatonic tradition. Plato, Porphyry, Iamblichus, and Renaissance and early modern Neoplatonists like Bruno were all interested in ancient wisdom, Oriental wisdom, and particularly Egyptian wisdom. They were all interested in the allegorical interpretation of classic texts. There was a consistent interest in occult sciences and their practical application. Members of this tradition believed that truth is primarily to be found in an intelligible world, accessible to us only through some sort of intellectual or mystical intuition and accessible only imperfectly. The product of such intuition can be conveyed only through language that is symbolic to one degree or another. The mythical systems of other peoples presumably represent the intuitions of their sages. Ancient Egypt, with its rich mythology and evocative hieroglyphs, exercised a unique fascination.[16]

THE NOMINALIST INTUITION AND THE CRITIQUE OF AVICENNA

The explanation that a philosopher gives of the universe and our knowledge of it depends very much on how he is inclined to see the world when he starts out; one is born a Platonist or Aristotelian, it is said. For Suhrawardī the relevant fact is that the world stands present to us as distinct manifest concrete things having particular qualities. It may be that it is only after rigorous training that we learn to see everything that is before us – he is a mystic, after all – but even our knowledge of God and the metaphysical foundations of the universe is not a matter of laborious construction and deduction but of learning to see what is always before us. We see what is concrete, and it is the concrete thing that is real, not the metaphysical ingredients whose existence we might infer. Thus in metaphysics Suhrawardī rejects realism with regard to universals, holding that everything that exists is a particular; in this he may be compared to nominalists like Ockham. And in epistemology he holds that knowledge consists in immediate awareness; in this he may be compared to empiricists like Berkeley and Hume. Like the nominalists and empiricists he is suspicious of metaphysical constructs and thus is more zealous as a philosophical critic than as a constructor of systems. Given the way that Suhrawardī has usually been portrayed, these claims need to be defended.[17]

The place to start is where Suhrawardī himself claimed to have started – with the doctrine that later came to be known as "knowledge by presence." The dominant epistemological theory among Muslim philosophers of Suhrawardī's time was that of Avicenna, which in turn derived from the theory of cognition in Aristotle's *De Anima*. In this Peripatetic epistemology, as Suhrawardī would have called it, our senses are affected by external stimuli. The resulting forms are imprinted somehow in the sense organs and then are combined in the brain and manipulated in various ways to produce the objects of sensation and imagination. Objects of pure thought – the concept of triangle, for example – cannot simply be imprinted in the brain since any imprinted triangle must necessarily be the image of some particular triangle with particular angles and sides of particular length. Such abstract ideas must therefore be in the immaterial mind, which has the capacity to become the idea of triangle. The idea of triangle comes into being in the immaterial intellect through the contemplation of the particular triangles presented to it by the senses and the related material faculties of the brain. The intellect is thus able to recognize the pure essences of things in the material images presented to it by the senses and the brain. These then become the raw materials of the sciences and real knowledge.[18]

There are difficulties, however, as anyone who has wrestled with Aristotle's accounts of cognition can testify. The theory explains how we know universals once we know them but not how we come to know universals nor how we know particulars beyond the level of sensation. The obvious problem is that the theory seems to require that we can recognize the essences of natural kinds by inspection and know immediately what those essences consist in. This is plausible if we are talking about triangles, but Aristotle developed the theory for natural science and biology. We should thus know that human beings are rational animals by meeting various human beings and know by inspection that bats and horses belong to the same class, mammals, but that bats and birds are in quite different classes. This implausibility has always dogged the Peripatetic scientific project, despite Aristotle's attempt to address the problem in *Posterior Analytics*, II.19. From an Islamic point of view the greater difficulty is that we cannot have intellectual knowledge of particulars. We know geometry as immaterial minds, but we know the things around us as material beings, in the same way that animals do. We might live with the implausibility of knowing the diagram in a geometry book in a completely different way than we know the theorem illustrated, but the theory also implies that God cannot know particulars. Averroes responded that God knew things through their causes, but this does not seem too convincing.[19]

Suhrawardī started over with the phenomenon of vision, the noblest of the senses and the usual, if not always acknowledged, starting point for theories of knowledge. There had been for centuries two contradictory theories of vision – extramission and intromission. In the one a cone went out from the eye and contacted the objects of vision; in the other something came in from the things seen and affected the eye. The former lent itself to mathematical optics but was physically implausible. The latter was more plausible physically, even if no one had quite worked out the details, but it had mathematical problems. Both theories had difficulties explaining how light made it possible to see things. (The theory of Ibn al-Haytham, or Alhazen, which is more or less correct, was not yet widely known.) Suhrawardī pointed out that both theories missed a fundamental point, that we see *things*, not the images of things. We see a large mountain that is far away, not a small image in the eye. We see whiteness whether or not it is brightly illumined. Actually, vision is simple, Suhrawardī tells us. It consists of a sound eye being in the unveiled presence of something illumined. Light is simply that which makes something manifest. Most important, vision requires a self-aware being. The other senses are analogous. Obviously, a completely worked out Illuminationist theory of vision would require us to take account of the mechanics of perspective and the eye, but Suhrawardī has made an important point, that the critical element in sensation is that there is awareness by a conscious being of the thing that is the object of sensation. That awareness is what distinguishes a human being seeing from a movie camera.[20]

He then extends this theory to knowledge in general. In the famous dream, Aristotle had told him that the key to understanding knowledge was self-knowledge. Knowledge, like vision, consists in the unveiled presence of the object of knowledge before the self-aware knower. Later Illuminationists refer to this as the unity of the knower, knowledge, and object of knowledge, but this formulation misses the point that I think is important – that knowledge is of particular things that can be apprehended directly. Being a mystic, Suhrawardī did not think that the objects of the senses were the only things that could be apprehended. We can, with suitable training, apprehend the immaterial beings – the angels and Platonic Forms. Nevertheless, these too are particulars (on Forms as particulars, see further below). The whole theory is nominalism of a thoroughly radical sort.[21]

This nominalism is the basis for his attack on the Peripatetic theory of essential definition. Aristotle, followed by his Islamic disciples, had held that the essences of things are made known by essential definitions, *ḥudūd* in Arabic. Such definitions consist of the genus plus the differentia – "man is a rational animal," for example. Other kinds of definitions might succeed in identifying a natural kind – "man is a laughing biped" – but they do not make the essence known. If we know the differentia, we effectively already know the thing, but in practice we can never know whether we have exhausted the differentia of a particular kind. Moreover, many Peripatetic definitions turn out to be more obscure than what they define. "Black gathers vision," but, of course, anyone who can see knows what black is. If he doesn't, it can be pointed out to him. Since Aristotle and Avicenna identify essential definition as the way by which concepts must be conveyed, Suhrawardī concludes that the Peripatetics have made it impossible to know anything.[22]

THE METAPHYSICS OF ILLUMINATIONIST NEOPLATONISM

The ontological counterpart of Suhrawardī's critique of Peripatetic epistemology is the doctrine of *i'tibārāt 'aqliyya* or beings of reason.[23] *I'tibār* means taking something into account or considering something. Beings of reason for Suhrawardī are those concepts that result from the mind's contemplation of the thing, not from the apprehension of the concrete qualities of the thing. If we say that a particular horse has four legs or is brown, these are concrete qualities, properties that we meet in the actual horse in the real world. However, if we say that the horse is existent, one, or contingent, these are properties that have to do with how we think about the real horse. When properties are made into nouns, brownness and four-leggedness refer to something concrete while existence, unity, and contingency do not – or, if they do, they all refer to the same thing, the horse itself.[24]

The target of this analysis is, as usual, the Peripatetics. Avicenna had made a distinction between the essence – or, more properly, quiddity – of a thing and its existence. He pointed out that you could ask two quite different questions about a thing: "Is it?" and "What is it?" The first addressed its existence and the second its quiddity.[25] The Aristotelian roots of this distinction are obvious, and it is clearly a useful clarification of Aristotle, employing the distinction between the Arabic participle and infinitive. The distinction is legitimate. The difficulty is that Avicenna seems to assume that a real distinction corresponds to the mental distinction, that if we can distinguish the existence from the quiddity of a thing, the thing must contain both existence and quiddity. The move is the more natural since it reflects an Aristotelian tendency to explain things as combinations of substrates and forms. There are difficulties. Bemused European philosophers pointed out that the distinction implied that existence was an accident.[26] The problem, as Suhrawardī relentlessly points out, is that it leads to insuperable problems of regression. One can ask the same questions about the quiddity and the existence. Is there a quiddity and existence of the existence and of the quiddity? What about the existence of the existence of the existence? Similar arguments can be made against the other beings of reason: unity, contingency, necessity, and the like.

Suhrawardī gives a parallel critique of the Peripatetic doctrine of hylomorphism, the theory that material bodies are compounds of matter and form, with form being a composite of forms of different kinds: species, accidents, elements, and qualities of various sorts. Suhrawardī finds this all quite implausible and argues instead for a simpler explanation, that bodies are just self-subsistent magnitude and qualities. It is a theory that has its origins in Plato's *Timaeus* and reappears occasionally thereafter in the history of philosophy, notably in Descartes. It is not particularly central to the Illuminationist project, for the theory is abandoned by Suhrawardī's commentator Quṭb al-Dīn Shīrāzī, but it is characteristic of Suhrawardī's ontologically parsimonious critique of the Peripatetics.[27]

In modern times, Suhrawardī is best known for the metaphysics of light that appears in the second book of *The Philosophy of Illumination*. The relation of this system to the critique of the Peripatetics in the first half of that book is reasonably clear: the Peripatetic doctrines that he refutes concern the fundamental epistemological and metaphysical issues where his new system differs from that of Avicenna.[28] It is less clear how the metaphysics of *The Philosophy of Illumination* relates to his so-called Peripatetic works, some of which were written at roughly the same time as this work. The usual account is that these other works are intended for those incapable of understanding the true Illuminationist philosophy and are therefore of at best limited significance for understanding Suhrawardī's thought. I am inclined to doubt it, since his later followers seem to have made no such distinction, but the solution waits on serious study of Suhrawardī's other philosophical works.

Whatever may be the relation of the second part of *The Philosophy of Illumination* to his other work, its philosophical doctrine is reasonably clear with careful reading and the advice of the early commentators.[29] Suhrawardī begins by identifying his fundamental concepts: light and darkness, independent and dependent. Light, he explains, is the most self-evident of entities, "that which is manifest in itself and manifests others," says one of the commentators, citing a well-known definition of light.[30] The independent entity is that whose existence or perfections do not rest upon another. Darkness and the dependent are the opposite. Moreover, light and darkness can be either self-subsistent or in another. This corresponds to a distinction that he made earlier between substance, that whose existence is not diffused throughout another, and states, which exist diffused throughout another. These distinctions yield four classes of entities:

(1) Self-subsistent or immaterial lights, which the commentators identify with intellects.
(2) Barriers or substantial darknesses, which are bodies.
(3) Accidental lights, which are physical light and various other self-manifesting accidents.
(4) Dark accidents, those properties that are not manifest in themselves.

Everything that exists falls into one of these four classes. Light is active; darkness, whether substantial or accidental, is passive.

(1) Immaterial lights are intellects or minds. The key concept here is "self-evident" or "manifest." Immaterial lights are manifest both to other things, like all light, and to themselves, which is to say that they are self-aware and aware of other things. Therefore, anything that is alive must be an immaterial light. They are, we must be clear, lights, not light. Suhrawardī is not thinking of a substratum of luminous matter or chunks of light that are emitted from something luminous, cross the intervening space, and fall on something else. He is thinking of distinct luminous individual incorporeal things whose essence is to be manifest. They are more like Leibnizian monads than like the undifferentiated primal reality of existence that we find in some later philosophers like Mullā Ṣadrā and Sabziwārī. They are individualized by differences in intensity and by luminous and dark accidents; Suhrawardī has earlier argued that things can differ by the intensity of their being. If they are above a certain level of intensity, their ability to manifest other things includes the ability to bring other things into being and to sustain their existence. His concept of immaterial light can be identified with the ordinary Peripatetic concept of intellect but with two new features: first, if immaterial lights are sufficiently intense, they can create, and, second, they are manifest to other immaterial lights, so that we can, in principle, see God and the celestial intellects/lights. (2) Dark barriers or bodies are more or less the opposite. They are neither manifest in themselves, nor do they manifest another. Therefore, they can be seen only with the aid of accidental light and be known only by incorporeal lights, and they are alive only insofar as they are associated with an incorporeal light. They are passive, not active, so that both their activities and they themselves are the effects of lights. (3) Accidental lights are physical lights and the luminous accidents that occur in both barriers and in immaterial lights. Like immaterial lights, accidental lights are manifest and manifest other things, but since they subsist in something else, they are not self-aware or alive. (4) Dark accidents are the qualities of physical things that are not manifest in themselves, as well as certain states in immaterial lights.

All these entities are connected through illumination and their presence to each other. The immaterial lights must be causally primary, since an accident in itself cannot be the cause of a substance nor can a passive darkness be the cause of light with its activity. The more intense immaterial lights can be the efficient and sustaining causes of other immaterial lights less intense than themselves. They can also be the cause of both luminous and dark accidents in lower lights due to the lower light's contemplation respectively of the luminosity of the higher light and its own relation of dependence. Thus, immaterial lights can differ in intensity and in luminous and dark accidents. Finally, the immaterial lights can be the cause of barriers, bodies, through their aspect of dependence on another. The immaterial lights are also the ultimate cause of the luminous accidents in physical bodies – which is to say, physical light – as well as their dark accidents. If we work our way up this causal chain of entities we reach first immaterial lights and finally an immaterial light that is not caused by another immaterial light, the Light of Lights or God.

From this set of entities and relationships, Suhrawardī derives his cosmology. First – in an ontological, not a temporal sense – there is the Light of Lights. Its illumination results in another immaterial light, and this second light's illumination results in a third immaterial light. Suhrawardī calls this the vertical order of lights. At some point, there is a double effect, both an immaterial light resulting from the luminosity of the higher light and a material sphere resulting from its dependence on and separation from the Light of Lights. This is the outer sphere of the universe. At each step down from here, there is another immaterial light and another sphere. At some point, there also begin to be material lights associated with the spheres. Moreover, immaterial lights begin to multiply on the lower levels since there can also be lights reflecting the various luminous and dark accidents of the higher lights. These can be of equal intensity but differ by accidents and are called the horizontal order of lights though, of course, they can be of many different levels. They are, Suhrawardī tells us, the Platonic Forms, the "archetypes of the talismans." Since the lights become weaker at each successively lower stage, there comes a point when the immaterial light cannot create another sphere, and we have reached the earth. The lowest immaterial lights are the souls of living beings in this world.

These classes of lights interact with the material world in various ways. The lights that are the souls of the spheres drive the planets. The paths of the planets and the pattern of the stars are determined by the incomprehensible complexity of the horizontal order of immaterial lights. The lights that are the Platonic Forms care for the various kinds of things in the world, giving them their characteristic manifolds of qualities, acting as the efficient causes of the formal causes of material things. The souls or managing lights rule individual living things.

There is a puzzle connected with the human soul. Souls are immaterial lights, but unlike the lights that rule the sphere or that are the Platonic Forms, human and animal souls apparently come into being. Suhrawardī, like the other philosophers of the Platonic tradition, believed that the soul is essentially independent of the body and thus survives its death. Like most important Islamic philosophers, Suhrawardī seems to have believed that the world had no beginning in time, and it is difficult to imagine how he would have explained the creation of the world in time in terms of his cosmological system. The questions are: when do souls come into being, how many of them are there, what happens to them after death, and what is their relation to the souls of animals? Plato believed in both the fall of the soul and reincarnation. The fall of the soul is the doctrine that the soul originally existed in a higher world then ventured down into this world and became entangled in matter. A version of Plotinus' account was transmitted in the *Theology of Aristotle*, a work that Suhrawardī was surely familiar with.[31] The fall of the soul is a theme of most of Suhrawardī's allegories, but it is not clear whether it is a metaphor or his actual doctrine. In *The Philosophy of Illumination* he gives an elaborate account of reincarnation attributed not to Plato but to the Buddha and the Oriental sages. In this account, which Suhrawardī cites but does not explicitly endorse, the human soul is the "gate of gates" for souls, which is to say that at conception a human soul is emanated and then at death this soul passes into animals suited to its particular moral character. The soul is repeatedly reborn in animals of various kinds until all of its vicious characteristics have been purged, whereupon it is free to rise to the world of light. His commentator Quṭb al-Dīn believed that this was Suhrawardī's own view, which seems quite likely since there is no evidence of a source for this supposedly quoted text. It is not unreasonable that he should have believed in reincarnation, for it was a characteristic doctrine of Platonists of all periods, but it was a very unusual position for a Muslim.[32]

A related issue is the doctrine of *'ālam al-mithāl*, the world of immaterial images. This metaphysical doctrine, which was to be of great importance in the later tradition, was a way to account for a variety of phenomena in which forms could not be explained as being embedded in matter. These included the images in mirrors and the imagination, dreams, miracles of certain sorts, and various eschatological events and entities. In such cases there is a material locus (*maḥall*), but the images are manifested through it, not embedded in it. It was a concept of considerable power, for it allowed philosophers to accept the literal reality of religious phenomena that were not physically plausible, such as the events of the Day of Judgment. It was far preferable to the radical allegorizing that philosophers such as Averroes had used to explain such things. The concept was still rudimentary and undeveloped in Suhrawardī, but it developed rapidly in the hands of his successors, notably Quṭb al-Dīn Shīrazī, who wrote an essay on it.[33]

There is a point that needs to be emphasized about this cosmological system. It is made up solely of concrete, apprehendable individuals and their concrete, apprehendable accidents. It is true that some of these entities can only be apprehended at the end of an arduous course of mystical training, but in principle the immaterial lights are as concrete and manifest as the sun. The metaphysical apparatus needed to sustain this system is minimal. There is no hierarchy of Peripatetic forms in concrete individuals – elements, species, genera, essential accidents, etc. – only the substances and their accidents. The regularity of nature is maintained by the direct action of the immaterial lights. Rabbits, liverworts, and granite boulders remain what they are and breed true because there are immaterial lights, angelic minds, Platonic Forms, or whatever they should be called, that act through their radiated light to make them do so. It is a system as resolutely parsimonious as anything Ockham or Hume could devise.

THE POLITICS OF ILLUMINATIONISM

Suhrawardī saw himself as the inheritor of a Pythagorean and Platonic tradition, a tradition many of whose figures ran afoul of political authority. Pythagoras is said to have died of grief or starved after the philosophical republic he had established in southern Italy was overthrown by a democratic revolution. Empedocles was exiled. Socrates was executed, nominally for corrupting the religion of the young but probably for his connections with former students like

Alcibiades and Critias who betrayed the Athenian democracy. Plato attempted to educate the young tyrant of Syracuse but had to make his escape when the venture failed. According to legend, he escaped slavery only because one of his old students recognized him and bought him at auction. There is considerable confusion in the sources about Suhrawardī's death and its causes, but the general picture seems plain enough. His offense seems to have been his influence over al-Malik al-Ẓāhir, the son of Saladin who was prince-governor of Aleppo. Jealous clerics accused him of various heresies, including a claim to prophethood, and Saladin, the zealous defender of Muslim orthodoxy, ordered him executed.

There is a philosophical background to this, however. In the introduction to *The Philosophy of Illumination*, Suhrawardī had distinguished between the discursive and intuitive philosophers, whom we may identify with the Peripatetics and the Illuminationists. Philosophers could be proficient, deficient, or intermediate in each kind of philosophy, but divine providence insured that at the least the world was never without a philosopher proficient in intuitive philosophy. This proficient intuitive philosopher was the true king, the man that the Ṣūfīs called the Pole, and he might rule either openly or secretly. If there was in any age a philosopher proficient in both discursive and intuitive philosophy and if political power was actually in his hand, "he will be the ruler by right and the vicegerent of God . . . When the government is in his hands, the age will be luminous."[34] This is not a particularly developed political doctrine, but it is a recognizable mystical variant of the Platonic doctrine of the philosopher-king. Saladin would have found it disturbingly similar to the political doctrines of the Ismāʿīlīs, philosophically inclined sectarians whom he had suppressed with considerable difficulty in both Egypt and Syria. Since the Third Crusade was bearing down on him and Aleppo sat astride his lines of communication to the east, it is scarcely surprising that he saw Suhrawardī as dangerous and acted decisively to end his influence over his son.

THE ILLUMINATIONIST SCHOOL

When Suhrawardī was killed, his disciples fled, or so we are told by the biographers. This fact does have philosophical significance since it determined the reception of Suhrawardī's thought. Suhrawardī was certainly not forgotten, for he was a colorful figure who died young. Historians and biographers of the following generation were interested in him, and there were contemporaries and even teachers who survived to talk about him. What seems not to have survived was a living tradition of interpretation of his work. In *The Philosophy of Illumination* he refers to a successor, "he who arises with the Book," as holding the keys to the meaning of his Illuminationist philosophy. Moreover, he insisted that *The Philosophy of Illumination* could only be understood by someone who had undergone a course of mystical discipline.[35] This seems rather an exaggeration, since the book is actually quite clearly written. Nevertheless, certain matters do remain obscure, notably the exact relation between *The Philosophy of Illumination* and his books written in "the Peripatetic mode."

The earliest surviving evidence of scholarly interpretation of Suhrawardī's *Philosophy of Illumination* dates from the mid- to late seventh/thirteenth century – a generation or two after the death of the unnamed fugitive disciples. This is Shams al-Dīn al-Shahrazūrī's *Commentary on the "Philosophy of Illumination."* Shahrazūrī definitely states in the introduction to the book that it was based on the study of Suhrawardī's text (and mystical inspiration), so it is quite clear that he did not have access to an oral tradition of interpretation of Suhrawardī. Quṭb al-Dīn's commentary, published in 1295, in turn is based almost exclusively on Shahrazūrī's.[36] The one other direct evidence of early scholarly interest in Suhrawardī is what Ziai and I refer to as the "corrected text" of *The Philosophy of Illumination*, the text used as the basis of Quṭb al-Dīn's commentary. This edition corrects various lapses in the text used by Shahrazūrī, which was also known to Quṭb al-Dīn through a manuscript that had been read to Suhrawardī for correction. Though we can hardly be certain, this edition has an academic feel to it. To this list can be added Sa'd al-Dīn ibn Kammūna (d. 1284), a philosopher of Jewish background, who published a commentary on one of Suhrawardī's "Peripatetic" works around 1270.[37] These three commentators are also the principal early exponents of Suhrawardī's philosophy. Thereafter, Suhrawardī's works attracted readers, citations, and occasional commentators, though none of them seem to have become school texts, with the relatively elementary *Temples of Light* being the work most commented on.[38]

Suhrawardī's later readers almost always treated him as a philosopher. The early commentators had, in effect, translated the light metaphysics of *The Philosophy of Illumination* back into standard philosophical terminology. The light metaphysics was admired, but it influenced mostly poets and ecstatics, not philosophers. The problems that interested later Islamic philosophers were the points on which he had critized Avicenna: existence as a being of reason, the Platonic Forms, knowledge by presence, and a few other points. These were decisive issues and shaped the agenda of later Islamic philosophy. Philosophers debated whether quiddity was primal, the position of Suhrawardī and Mīr Dāmād, or existence, the view defended by Mullā Ṣadrā and Sabziwārī, among others. Intense, highly sophisticated debates raged on these issues, and they continue to this day in the madrasas of Qom.

There was a popular and nationalistic side to Suhrawardī's heritage. His reference to exotic Oriental sages and terms drew the attention of commentators. More important, they drew the attention of Zoroastrian scholars in India, who found it convenient to interpret Suhrawardī's claim that his philosophy corresponded with that of the sages of ancient Persia as meaning that his philosophy was the secret wisdom of the Zoroastrian sages. Thus, a popularized form of his philosophy enjoyed a vogue in India in the shape of a forged ancient Persian scripture, the *Dasātīr*. Ultimately, Henry Corbin's influential interpretation of Suhrawardī derives from the Zoroastrian authors of the *Dasātīr* and related texts.[39]

Suhrawardī was revived once again in twentieth century-Iran under the nationalist Pahlavi shahs. As in Turkey, the nationalist rulers of Iran sought to free their native language from the influence of Arabic. In any case, knowledge of Arabic was declining precipitously among younger Iranians who preferred to study European languages. The two trends combined to produce a demand for Persian prose classics – there was no lack of Persian poetry – and literary heroes of Persian nationalism. Suhrawardī with his exquisite Persian allegories fitted perfectly. His allegories were widely read and in the eyes of many Persian scholars and philosophers came to be considered the centerpiece of his philosophy. This seems wrong on the face of it, since the content of the allegories is quite elementary and they do not contain his more advanced doctrines. I am convinced they were intended for popular readers and for students.[40]

Suhrawardī represents a decisive moment in Islamic philosophy, the break with the Peripatetic philosophy of Avicenna. Suhrawardī attacked certain key Peripatetic doctrines, notably the reification of metaphysical abstractions like existence, defending instead a sort of rigorous Platonic nominalism. Philosophically, his influence was decisive, setting the agenda for later Islamic philosophy. What is the nature of consciousness and how does it shape what we can know? How do we experience knowing, whatever the mechanics of sensation and abstraction may be? His questions are those of the Platonists and the mystics, the nature of the intelligible world and of inwardness. Others, most especially Mullā Ṣadrā, the greatest of Muslim scholastics, went on to build great palaces of the mind upon the foundations he laid. The clerical philosophers of the holy cities of Mashhad and Qom still wander their corridors, and the questions that trouble their thoughts are still, in great part, those asked by Suhrawardī.

NOTES

1 This chapter is largely based on three books that I have written on Suhrawardī and his school: Walbridge [154], [155], and [156]. Representative books expressing other interpretations of Suhrawardī include Corbin [150], Corbin [7], Nasr [151], and Aminrazavi [149]; and also Ziai [158].

2 "Theosophy" in this context has nothing to do with the modern religious sect. The term was applied to Suhrawardī's philosophy by his most influential Western interpreter, the late Henry Corbin, who also produced the main modern edition of Suhrawardī's works. Corbin's interpretation of Suhrawardī really reflects his own philosophical project, which had roots in modern perennialism, Masonic thought, and twentieth-century continental philosophy, notably Heidegger and Jung. Corbin's view of Suhrawardī has been supported by Seyyed Hossein Nasr, Mehdi Aminrazavi, and most other recent scholars who have written about Suhrawardī. This "theosophical interpretation" of Suhrawardī is part of a larger account of the history of Islamic philosophy stressing mystical elements and rooting it in ancient Iranian thought and mythology. My differences with this interpretation will be made clear below, but the reader should be aware that I represent a minority opinion.

3 For a list of primary sources on Suhrawardī's life, see Suhrawardī [152], 165 n. 1. The most important source is Shahrazūrī's *Nuzha al-arwāḥ*,

a biographical dictionary of ancient and Islamic philosophers, one version of which is translated in Suhrawardī [153], ix–xiii. Most modern works on Suhrawardī contain a brief biography, more or less based on Shahrazūrī's.

4 Suhrawardī [152], para. 166.

5 Suhrawardī, *Talwīḥāt*, para. 55, pp. 70–4. I translated it in Walbridge [155], at 225–9, where references are given to other translations and discussions of the dream.

6 Walbridge [155], 52–3.

7 Suhrawardī [152], para. 279.

8 The circumstances of Suhrawardī's death and the reasons for it are discussed in Ziai [159] and Walbridge [155], 201–10.

9 Suhrawardī [152], para. 3.

10 See Suhrawardī, *Le livre de la sagesse orientale: Kitāb ḥikmat al-ishrāq*, ed. Christian Jambet (Paris: 1986), and the introductions to Suhrawardī, *Majmū'a-yi muṣannafāt-i shaykh-i ishrāq: Œuvres philosophiques et mystiques*, ed. H. Corbin, 3 vols. (Tehran: 1976–7), along with the works of Corbin mentioned in n. 1 above.

11 See Walbridge [154], 194–5.

12 Idrīs was a prophet casually mentioned in Qur'ān 19:56 and 21:85. On the general question of Hermes, including his identification with Enoch and Idrīs, see Walbridge [156], 17–24.

13 See Walbridge [155], 27–35.

14 P. Kingsley, *Ancient Philosophy, Mystery, and Magic: Empedocles and Pythagorean Tradition* (Oxford: 1995).

15 Walbridge [155], 39–54.

16 Walbridge [156], 5–16.

17 Walbridge [154], 40–55, Walbridge [155], 21–3.

18 See Avicenna [205], Yazdi [157].

19 Al-Ghazālī's argument and Averroes' reply are found respectively in al-Ghazālī [111], chs. 11 and 13, and the corresponding sections of Averroes [140], and more concisely in al-Ghazālī [110], trans. R. J. McCarthy as *Freedom and Fulfillment: An Annotated Translation of Al-Ghazālī's "al-Munqidh min al-Ḍalāl" and Other Relevant Works of al-Ghazālī* (Boston, MA: 1980), and Averroes [139].

20 Suhrawardī [152], paras. 101–5, 115; Walbridge [155], 157–64.

21 Walbridge [155], 164–81.

22 Suhrawardī [152], paras. 14–15, 70–1; Ziai [158], 77–127; Walbridge [155], 143–8; Walbridge [154], 101–4.

23 This term does not have a standard translation, so far as I know, nor is there an exact Western philosophical equivalent. "Transcendentals," in the medieval sense, comes close; "second intentions" is a little more

distant and ought to be reserved for the corresponding term in logic, *ma'qūlāt thāniyya*. In Walbridge [154], I used "intellectual fictions," a term I coined myself. In this article I use "beings of reason," a medieval term that I owe to my friend Paul Spade. On the general question of existence and whether it is *i'tibārī*, see T. Izutsu, *The Concept and Reality of Existence* (Tokyo: 1971), 99–102.

24 Suhrawardī [152], paras. 56–68.

25 Avicenna [88], 29–36.

26 Thomas Aquinas, *Commentary on Aristotle's "Metaphysics,"* trans. J. P. Rowan (Notre Dame, IN: 1995), paras. 556–8.

27 Suhrawardī [152], paras. 72–88; Walbridge [154], 98–100; J. Walbridge, "Suhrawardī on Body as Extension: An Alternative to Hylomorphism from Plato to Leibniz," in T. Lawson (ed.), *Reason and Inspiration: Essays in Honour of Hermann Landolt* (London: forthcoming). The physical portions of Suhrawardī's so-called Peripatetic works are mostly unpublished, though Ibn Kammūna, *al-Tanqīhāt fī sharḥ al-talwīḥāt*, ed. H. Ziai and A. Alwishah (Costa Mesa, CA: 2002) contains an extensive discussion of bodies, matter, and form.

28 See Walbridge [154], chs. 32–9.

29 Suhrawardī's science of lights is in the second part of his *Philosophy of Illumination*. I have summarized it in Walbridge [154], 40–78, and more concisely in Walbridge [155], 19–26.

30 Quṭb al-Dīn Shīrāzī, *Sharḥ ḥikma al-ishrāq*, ed. A. A. Harātī ([Tehran]: 1895–7), 283.

31 Walbridge [154], 130–41. *The Theology of Aristotle*, trans. G. Lewis in *Plotini Opera*, ed. P. Henry and H.-R. Schwyzer (Paris: 1959), vol. II, 219.

32 Suhrawardī [152], paras. 229–36; Walbridge [154], 141–9; Walbridge [156], 73–80. See further P. E. Walker, "The Doctrine of Metempsychosis in Islam," in W. B. Hallaq and D. P. Little (eds.), *Islamic Studies Presented to Charles J. Adams* (Leiden: 1991), 219–38.

33 For the text and translation see Walbridge [154], 196–271.

34 Suhrawardī [152], para. 5. See also Ziai [159]; Walbridge [155], 201–10.

35 Suhrawardī [152], para. 6, 279–80.

36 Shams al-Dīn al-Shahrazūrī, *Sharḥ ḥikma al-ishrāq*, ed. H. Ziai (Tehran: 1993), English viii–21, Arabic passim. Quṭb al-Dīn intersperses commentary with the text while Shahrazūrī comments on blocks of text.

37 Ibn Kammūna, *al-Tanqīhāt*. See H. Ziai, "Ebn Kammūna," in E. Yarshater (ed.), *Encyclopaedia Iranica* (New York: 1999).

38 See, for example, B. Kuspinar, *Ismāʿīl Anḳaravī on the Illuminative Philosophy* (Kuala Lumpur: 1996). Unfortunately, few of these texts have been published and almost none translated into Western languages.

39 *The Desatir, or Sacred Writings of the Ancient Persian Prophets . . .*, 2 vols. (Bombay: 1818). H. Corbin, *Encyclopaedia Iranica*, s.v. "Āẕar Kayvān"; Walbridge [156], 91–105.

40 Suhrawardī [153]; Walbridge [155], 97–116; Walbridge [156], 105–10.

SAJJAD H. RIZVI

11 Mysticism and philosophy: Ibn ʿArabī and Mullā Ṣadrā

In a monotheistic culture of the "examined and contemplative life," the central intellectual challenge for a thinking, experiencing believer is to address the question: how can I know God? and concomitantly, how can I know what God means?[1] In the classical period, Muslim thinkers approached this question by delineating four possible paths toward realizing, understanding, internalizing, and implementing the "truth" or "reality."[2] These four ways are succinctly and importantly examined in the famous "autobiography" of the theologian and Ṣūfī Abū Ḥāmid al-Ghazālī (d. 1111), *al-Munqidh min al-ḍalāl* (*The Deliverer from Error*):[3] the imitation of infallible authoritative example (*taʿlīm*, following the infallible Shīʿite Imām), acceptance of prophetic traditions and norms (*taqlīd* of the *Sunna*), rational and discursive argument (*ʿaql, naẓar*), and ineffable "pure" experience or "taste" (*dhawq*). So the first question that needs to be considered is the method of acquiring truth and certainty. In the context of this chapter, the options that I shall consider are reason and experience. In al-Ghazālī's account, the use of philosophical reason is denounced for its failure to conform to "revealed truths,"[4] while mystical experience is lauded: the difference is, as he puts it, that reason is an indirect means of acquiring truth through the verification of arguments, while "taste" experiences and directly takes on the state of truth, effecting a critical complementarity between knowledge and action.[5] "Taste" has the added advantage of being a Qurʾānic concept and became the commonplace nomenclature for experience in Ṣūfī circles. Thus it would seem that early on in Islam, we find reason and experience pitted against each other.[6]

However, our focus is upon the reconciliation of reason and experience in the later Iranian traditions of philosophy in Islam, and on the recovery of a sense of philosophy that combined rational discourse with intuitive experience. A second, ontologically prior question is the diagnosis of the need for truth, a recognition of human ignorance and "sickness" of the soul and mind that is devoid of truth and certainty and is misled by unworthy passions and false beliefs. This is the second theme that I want to pursue in this chapter: the discovery of a method for inquiring into "truth" that is therapeutic and even salvific. The aim of this chapter is to explain the relationship between mysticism and philosophy in the later Islamic tradition, focusing on the particularly illuminating relationship between the Ṣūfī thought of the Andalusian Ibn ʿArabī (d. 1240), the "rationalizing mystic" *par excellence* of Islam, and the Illuminationist philosophical tradition of Iran, represented by Mullā Ṣadrā al-Shīrāzī (d. 1640), the Iranian "mystical philosopher" *par excellence.*

I want to consider mysticism and philosophy in later Islamic history within the context of a Neoplatonic intellectual paradigm. The late antique Neoplatonic traditions recognized numerous "ways" to the truth, including that of the "rationalizing mystic" who is capable of articulating a philosophical and discursive language for his experiences that are non-propositional, non-conceptual, and even lacking in "cognitive content" insofar as human reason can comprehend it. Philosophy is here envisioned as a "way of life" and, significantly, as a path to salvation. Similarly in Islam, there were traditions of learning, thinking, and articulated experience that considered it possible to rationalize and express the "ineffable" apophatically and ironically, and considered inquiry to be a matter of soteriological "realization" (*taḥqīq*).[7] Here I have in mind particularly late Islamic forms of Neoplatonism that are akin to the thought and praxis of Iamblichus (d. ca. 325) and Damascius (d. ca. 538),[8] the last head of the Platonic Academy in Athens. Muslim thinkers followed their Neoplatonic predecessors in a Pythagoreanizing insistence on the necessity of "spiritual practices" and theurgy for philosophical inquiry,[9] a method of acquiring wisdom and ethical perfection and salvation.[10]

It is often said (still!) that al-Ghazālī's critique and condemnation of Neoplatonized Aristotelianism (*falsafa*) led to the demise of philosophical inquiry in Islam. What it did effect was rather a shift in both the conception of philosophy and the context of philosophical inquiry: *falsafa* was absorbed into the sophisticated philosophical theology that was *kalām*, but also and more significantly in the Islamic East, it was reconciled with mystical intuition and gnosis (*ʿirfān*), providing it with a language in which to articulate the results of mystical experience and mediate its religious and ineffable language. Islamic philosophy, consistent with its late antique predecessor, was never a merely theoretical inquiry seeking knowledge for its own sake, but was rather a transformative practice that combined both "rational" and "arational" (*alogos*) elements.[11] *Falsafa*, or *ḥikma* ("wisdom") as it was increasingly named, provided a metalanguage for explaining and analyzing the "pure consciousness experiences" that were the inner, ineffable, and infallible domain of the mystic. This transformation also affected the self-definition and conceptualization of mysticism, urging upon mystics the need for rationalizing, verifying, and especially "communicating" their mystical experience. The goal of philosophy was not only to provide an account of experience, but a (Platonic) method: a practice and an ethics that would reveal how one might emulate the moral paradigm of the Good.

IBN ʿARABĪ AND MULLĀ ṢADRĀ

Shaykh Muḥyī' al-Dīn ibn ʿArabī is perhaps the most famous of medieval Islamic mystics.[12] Born into a noble Arab family in Murcia, he turned to the visionary and contemplative life early on and sought out spiritual masters. His visions of Ṣūfī masters and Qur'ānic prophets impelled him to travel and blend his developing spiritual insight with a practical "journey for truth": this combination of the spiritual and practical is stressed in the hagiographical tradition about Ibn ʿArabī. He finally settled in Damascus, a prolific author surrounded by many disciples, and died there in 1240. His major works, especially *Fuṣūṣ al-ḥikam* (*Ring-settings of Wisdom*) and *al-Futūḥāt al-Makkiyya* (*The Meccan Revelations*) were widely disseminated and became the core texts of an interpretive community in the Islamic East, especially in Iran.[13] Ibn ʿArabī described himself as one of the Ṣūfīs, who are "realized selves" (*muḥaqqiqīn*) possessing true insight, open to divine disclosures and revelations (*kashf*) in their souls, and to the experience of the "truth" (*Fut.* III, 34). He considered himself to be above most Ṣūfīs and disdained philosophers.[14] However, his superiority, as he saw it, lay in his use of intellectual insight. Though he did not consider himself a philosopher (*faylasūf*), later detractors accused him of being one and his school tradition developed a more markedly philosophical explanation for his mystical thought.[15] What he proposed most explicitly was a gnostic practice that would lead the seeker to an experience of the Truth. He would claim that this experience was ineffable but then would churn out quires explaining its states, a classic expression of apophasis (negative theology) by a "rationalizing mystic." Whilst many have claimed that Ibn 'Arabī was a Neoplatonist philosopher and monist, whose works constitute a mystical philosophy or even a "theosophy" (that most unfortunate of labels), there is little sense of a philosophical system or method in his articulation either of rational knowledge or mystical experience.[16] Rather, it is best to describe him, as Merlan did the later Neoplatonists, as a "rationalizing mystic":[17] the God that one experiences ultimately in rationalistic mysticism is not above and beyond Being but is identical to thought and being-thought-itself; there is absolute transparency between the knower, the known, and knowledge itself.[18] Thus mystical experience, despite being a form of cognition that transcends all concepts, is yet communicable and accessible to some diminished discursive representation.

Similarly, a central feature of the method of Illuminationist (*ishrāqī*) philosophy is its integration of spiritual practice into the pursuit of wisdom. A philosophical attempt at reforming Avicennism, the tradition however retains a stress upon philosophical discourse, and in its ontology posited metaphysical variance and plurality rather than the monism of the school of Ibn 'Arabī. Thus one finds in the work of Mullā Ṣadrā a compromise between the demands of philosophy and mysticism, between monorealism and metaphysical pluralism. A precocious talent born into a noble family of Shīrāz, Ṣadr al-Dīn Muḥammad, later known as Mullā Ṣadrā, was one of the major intellectual figures of Safavid Iran and the culmination of an Illuminationist tradition which he irrevocably transformed. Having studied in Iṣfahān, the Safavid capital of Shah 'Abbās, he retired to write and teach, first in Qom and then in his native Shīrāz. He died in 1641 on his return from the ritual pilgrimage to Mecca, his seventh that he had undertaken by foot. A keen commentator on Scripture as well as the philosophical texts of the Avicennian and Illuminationist schools, he was also profoundly influenced by the Ṣūfī thought of Ibn ʿArabī. All these elements are illustrated in his major work, *al-Ḥikma al-mutaʿāliya fī al-asfār al-ʿaqliyya al-arbaʿa* (*The Transcendent Philosophy/Wisdom of the Four Journeys of the Intellect*), commonly known as *al-Asfār al-arbaʿa* (*The Four Journeys*).[19] His philosophical and hermeneutic method of achieving truth and realizing it had a profound effect in later Islamic philosophy such that the "school of Mullā Ṣadrā" has become the hegemonic philosophical tradition of the Islamic East (see below, chapter 19). Characteristically reconciling the demands and methods of reason and experience, it would be best to describe him as a "mystical philosopher," a thinker who develops a philosophical system, method, and mode of argument based upon the mystical experience of Reality. Indeed, the key feature of his work is the use of experience as a means of understanding, the grounds for explaining, the truth. Mullā Ṣadrā himself often praises Ibn ʿArabī as a great spiritual master who has realized truths, while Avicenna the discursive philosopher did not quite make the grade of a "sage" (*Asfār* IX, 108).

MYSTICISM AND/OR PHILOSOPHY

The late antique philosophical traditions recognized the soteriological and practical nature of philosophizing. Philosophy provided an account of the soul and its salvation in its return to the One (or the Principle/Cause) and freedom through discipline and training against false beliefs and emotions. Thus, philosophy is the therapy of the soul, an art for the diseased soul, dealing both with beliefs and emotions, a familiar concept in Hellenistic and Neoplatonic philosophy.[20]

But for our purposes, philosophy as an art that heals through the rehearsal of arguments that respond to the specific needs of the sick soul in a particular situation is insufficient. The practice of philosophy as an inquiry must be supplemented and reconciled with philosophy as a way of life and a commitment. This requires certain disciplines and "spiritual exercises" (*riyāḍāt*). These practices are of three types: physical practices including dietary restrictions and self-mortification, contemplative practices such as meditation, and discursive practices such as dialogue and pedagogy.[21] Dialogue and philosophical analysis itself could be therapeutic because they could uncover false propositions and isolate the demands of emotion.[22] Divorcing the inquiry from the exercises would be akin to the state of interest in the Indian philosophical school (*darshana*) of Yogā nowadays, in which most practitioners think of Yogā as merely physical exercise, and are often unaware of both the "spiritual" element of the exercises and the philosophical inquiry that complements it.[23]

Thus philosophy in this holistic sense is a training of the soul, stripping it of the "pluralizing tendencies" that emerge from acquiring false beliefs and emotions. It is an interesting point to note that the Stoics had a term to express the philosophical supervision and vigilance of the soul, namely *prosokhê*,[24] and the Ṣūfī tradition that Ibn 'Arabī and Mullā Ṣadrā inherited had an elaborate theory for the supervision of the soul to avoid sins, temptations, and false beliefs. Adepts were required to be ever-vigilant and disciplined over their selves. The process involved a daily regime: at dawn, when the Ṣūfī awoke, he would make a compact (*mu'āhada*) with himself that he would avoid both the temptations of the soul and body and would avoid all that distracted him from the contemplation of the ultimate reality. Continual watchfulness over the self during the day was termed *murāqaba*. Finally, before sleeping, or generally at times of introspection, the Ṣūfī would judge and consider his actions, both physical and mental, a process known as *muḥāsaba*.

However, it was the Platonic emphasis on *theosis* (or *ta'alluh* as it was understood in the Arabic tradition),[25] of "becoming god so far as is possible" (*homoiôsis theôi kata to dunaton anthrôpoi*) as the ultimate goal of philosophy that was taken up by the return to Pythagoreanizing Neoplatonism of the later Iranian traditions. In Plato's *Theaetetus*, Socrates says:

> Of necessity, it is mortal nature and our vicinity that are haunted by evils. And that is why we should try to escape from here to there as quickly as we can. To escape is to become like god so far as is possible and to become like god is to become just and holy, together with wisdom.[26]

Thus philosophy is a soteriological path, a salvific practice that extricates man from the evils of everyday life and holds out the promise of achieving divinity by emulating the moral paradigm of the divine, the Good.[27] Philosophical perfection, for Mullā Ṣadrā, results in social order and salvation (*Asfār* I, 21.5). This emulation is reflected in the *ḥadīth* famous among Ṣūfīs that demands of the godly that they "acquire the virtues of God" (*takhallaqū bi-akhlāq Allāh*).[28] The connection between this saying and *theosis* is made explicit by Ibn

'Arabī, and he says "that is Ṣūfism" (*Fut.* II, 72.9, 126.8, 267.11). The result of *theosis* is holiness, the attribute of living a good, virtuous life, and justice, the attribute of recognition of moral norms and wisdom, the state of seeing things "as they truly are."[29] Becoming like God, the process of assimilation to the One, is merely the proper return of the rational soul to its principle, a soteriology as well as an ethics.[30] *Ta'alluh*, according to Ibn 'Arabī, ensures that man is a theomorphic being, the true viceregent of God on earth who can exhibit divine virtue.[31] That individual can display attributes of perfection, which are divine traits and exhibit true value in moral agency (*Fut.* II, 72.9, 126.8, 241). But there are critical limits: man cannot arrogate for himself the role of God, since as Ibn 'Arabī says (*Fut.* II, 224.7), no existent has independence, but everything reverts to God (quoting Qur'ān 11.123, inter alia).

One can recognize this important Platonic theme in Mullā Ṣadrā's definition of philosophy in the *Four Journeys* (*Asfār* I, 20.7–10), his major work:

> Know that philosophy is the perfecting of the human soul (*istikmāl al-nafs al-insāniyya*) through cognition of the realities of existents as they truly are (*kamā hiya*), and through judgments about their existence ascertained through demonstrations (*bi-al-barāhīn*) and not understood through conjecture (*bi-al-ẓann*) or through adherence to authority (*bi-al-taqlīd*) according to man's capability. Through philosophy, man ascribes a rational order to the world and acquires a resemblance to the Creator according to the measure of human capacity (*al-tashabbuh bi-al-Bārī' ḥasab al-ṭāqa al-bashariyya*).

There are seven discrete elements within this definition that need to be drawn out. First, philosophy is a transformative practice designed to perfect the soul. The perfection of the soul results in *tashabbuh bi-al-Bārī'* (becoming like God). Second, philosophy is about a veridical cognition of realities "as they truly are," which suggests that the central question within philosophical discourse is that of existence. Third, philosophical discourse is conducted rationally through the formulations of arguments and demonstrations, which are valid Aristotelian syllogisms. Fourth, knowledge about existence is certain; it cannot be a rehearsed theological argument nor can it be a mere guess. Fifth, the limits of human reason and discourse are due to the inadequacy of language and the ineffability of the One. Sixth, philosophical understanding results in rational ordering of the cosmos and recognizing it as the macrocosmic manifestation of the One, a central metaphysical doctrine in Ṣūfī thought. Because God is a rational and determined Creator (an idea already found in Plato's *Timaeus*),[32] man's assimilation to him means that he begins to see that created order in the cosmos. Finally, we return to the theme of *theosis* (*ta'alluh*).[33] Following the *Theaetetus*, wisdom is the end of *theosis*; the sage is elevated above the masses. Through his practice of philosophy combined with spiritual practices,[34] the sage acquires the qualities of generosity, good humour, fine judgment, pronounced taste (*dhawq*), and the experience of spiritual disclosure (*Asfār*, VI, 6.19–7.2).

The Avicennian tradition recognized the need to combine discursive and intuitive, experiential thought in a higher synthesis for which Avicenna himself coined the phrase *ḥikma muta'āliya* (transcendent philosophy), which is the term that Mullā Ṣadrā, and many within the school of Ibn 'Arabī, use for their method of philosophizing.[35] The contemplative ideal was present in Islamic thought before it was given an explicitly mystical tone by Ibn 'Arabī. Dā'ūd al-Qayṣarī, a preeminent commentator on Ibn 'Arabī's *Fuṣūṣ al-Ḥikam*, describes *ḥikma muta'āliya* as the only true mode of inquiry and as non-discursive philosophizing that can achieve knowledge of God.[36] However, Mullā Ṣadrā insists that true philosophy is a reconciliation of discourse and intuition (*Asfār* VI, 5–8). Indeed, the successful philosopher is one who can bring together his rational effort with the grace of intuition that is received from above in the form of divine knowledge from on high (*'ilm ladunnī*).[37] Experience is the ground for philosophy and philosophical discourse is a means for making sense of that experience (*Asfār* IX, 108).[38] In the *Four Journeys* (*Asfār* III, 326), he says:

> Our arguments are based upon direct experience and inner revelation and not the blind following of the Law without proof, demonstration, or logical inference. Mere inner revelation (*mukāshafa*) is insufficient on the path [to truth] without demonstrations, just as mere discourse (*baḥth*) without inner revelation is a great flaw along the path.

Ibn 'Arabī had earlier derided the possibility of pure thought and discourse to understand truth (*Fut.* II, 382.24–5, 389.6–7). Thought cannot comprehend God, but constitutes a "veil," since the affirmation of one's thought leads to an expression of one's independence as a being; hence one cannot appreciate the exclusivity and unity of Reality (*Fut.* II, 85.7). Discourse blinds man and leads to discord while contemplation and inner revelation are non-discursive and fail to achieve accord (*Fut.* III, 82.15–16). But man must exercise his reason since it is an instrument of divine grace and he has been commanded in the Qur'ān to use it (*Fut.* II, 319.13ff., III, 436.7, 250, inter alia). Ibn 'Arabī even praises Plato as a true "sage (*ḥakīm*) with mystical tastes" and not as a "mere philosopher" (*Fut.* II, 523). True sagacity results from inner revelation and is an expression of prophetic wisdom.[39] Elsewhere, he quotes approvingly the famous "doffing metaphor" concerning the soul's beatific experience of the One in the intelligible world that originates in Plotinus' *Enneads*, IV.8.1, which was translated into Arabic as the *Theology of Aristotle* (see above, chapter 2). However, it seems that both Ibn 'Arabī and the Illuminationist tradition correctly recognized this as a Platonic doctrine.

Finally, philosophy is a disciplined and taught spiritual practice. As an ethical mode of life in the world, it cannot be blind to the need for moral perfection and normative practice. Philosophy delivers the good life and the Good itself for man but only if he is guided and develops a moral character. Mullā Ṣadrā says:

> The perfection of man lies in the perception of universal realities and disposition toward cognition of the divine and transcendence above material matters and self-purification from the constraints of carnal and passionate appetites. This can only be acquired through guidance, teaching, discipline, and the formation of a righteous character.[40]

The Ṣūfī tradition also upholds the importance of spiritual training as a method for the intuitive disclosure of reality. As such, both Ibn 'Arabī and Mullā Ṣadrā posit a spiritual hierarchy depending on the varying dispositions to accept truth that are found among people. In *Īqāẓ al-nā'imīn* (*The Awakening of the Dormant*), a work heavily influenced by the thought and terminology of Ibn 'Arabī, Mullā Ṣadrā discusses five levels of humanity in descending order of their ability to cognize reality:

> On the first level are people of inner revelation who know the Truth by forsaking themselves and negating their being . . . They constantly contemplate His signs.
>
> On the second are the excellent philosophers who perceive Him in a purely rational sense . . . Their ratiocination creates images through

conjecture and their imagination produces forms appropriate to the most subtle and noble rational forms [of things]. Yet they know that those rational forms are above those conjectural and imaginative forms.

On the third are the common people of faith . . . The most that they are capable of are conjectural conceptions [about the Truth].

On the fourth level are those who follow authority and are submissive. They are not even capable of conjecture, let alone imagination.

On the fifth level are those who rely upon physical forms [to know] the Truth.[41]

The hybrid discourse of Sadrian language is expressed in this hierarchy that is in terms of levels of knowledge and insight, as well as grace and disclosure, packed within the larger quest for truth and recognition of God that is faith.

ONTOLOGY: THE GRADES OF UNITARY REALITY

It is often said that the prime doctrine of rationalized mysticism in Islam of the school of Ibn 'Arabī is that of the unity of Being (*waḥda al-wujūd*): it underlies ontology, epistemology, and soteriology (theory of salvation) in this tradition.[42] This doctrine expresses a desire for experiencing Being. The mystic's quest is to discover and experience God qua ultimate reality (*ḥaqīqa al-ḥaqā'iq*) and in this endeavor, he ultimately discovers and finds (*wajada*) the unity that is God. Ibn 'Arabī in his *magnum opus*, *al-Futūḥāt al-Makkiyya* (*The Meccan Revelations*), in chapter 237 on Being, says (*Fut.* II, 537.33–538.4):

Being of the Ultimate Reality (*wujūd al-ḥaqq*) is identical to what is found through my ecstasy,

And I was annihilated in Being and through Being
The rule of ecstasy is that everything is annihilated through it
Yet the eye of ecstasy cannot know the hidden reality.
Pure consciousness of Being in every facet,
Through a mystical state or not is from it [Being].

Know that Being, according to the initiates, is the pure consciousness of the Ultimate Reality (*wijdān al-ḥaqq*) through ecstasy (*wajd*). They [the initiates] say that if you are not seized by ecstasy, and if, during this state, you do not contemplate the Ultimate Reality, then you are not [really] in ecstasy, because the fact of contemplating it should annihilate from you your self-contemplation and the contemplation of that which is present to you. [Thus] you are not seized by ecstasy if you have not "found" Ultimate Reality in that state. Know that the Being of the Ultimate Reality is not known (*ma'lūm*) in ecstasy, because the ecstasy is coincidental and what is coincidental is unknown and may have arisen through some other state.

Since being and what is "found" through pure experience are the same (and rendered by the same term in Arabic, *wujūd*, which literally means "what is found"), only God is worthy of the name "being" (*wujūd*). Ibn 'Arabī (*Fut.* I, 328.15 and III, 566.30, inter alia) carefully articulates the view that "the ultimate reality is identical to what is found (*al-wujūd*)." Crucially, the method of finding must be "ecstatic," through a mystical experience, and this is made explicit by linking the experience in the passage above to the Ṣūfī institution of sessions of "audition" (*samā'*). True *samā'* involves ecstasy and true ecstasy responds to *samā'* as humans respond to the speech of God articulated in it (*Fut.* ch. 172 on the station of audition, II, 366.27–32). Thus mystical intuition and rationalization follow from an appreciation of the meaning of revelation both through Scripture and through "nature." A key feature of his method is the Qur'ānicity of his rationalization. Ibn 'Arabī's language is thickly Qur'ānic and he refers to Qur'ān 24:39.

But two questions arise: in what sense is God identical to Being, and does it follow that nothing else exists (including the very mystic who is recognizing this reality)? These two questions are connected through the idea that Being as such only refers to God insofar as he is a pure, unconditioned, unqualified, and hidden Being. He is solitary in being.[43] Yet this does not mean plural phenomena are unreal, but only that they are self-disclosures and theophanies of the single Being. Existents (or things "found" in the universe, *mawjūdāt*), therefore, to use the Avicennian language employed by Ibn 'Arabī, are contingents that have no existence or Being in themselves but exist through the grace of Being in which they participate. They are thus manifestations of Being, differentiated from one another insofar as they are either sensible (*maḥsūs*) or intelligible (*ma'qūl*), and by virtue of the varying "dispositions" that God has placed within them to act as a mirror for his Being (*Fut.* II, 160.1–8).

The doctrine of the unity of being or monism has important repercussions for the two other sets of doctrines: an apophatic mystical theology (and resultant skepticism), and a soteriology or theory of salvation. Firstly, then, the recognition that there is a single Being, and that our phenomenal experience of pluralism is an illusory perception of the manifest disclosures of that Being, results in a problem of language. If only God is worthy of the title of Being, then there is nothing else that we can use as an analogy to grasp Being. Thus for us humans, being in itself is rendered meaningless, or at the very least we cannot fully comprehend either what Being is or communicate our "experience" of it. Our being is "not-being" (*Fut.* III, 362). The second, soteriological result is that our state of ignorance and "existential poverty" with respect to Being[44] places us in a humbled position in which the pride of saying "I exist" gives way to the uncertainty of "I am not sure that I exist." Mullā Ṣadrā, while accepting the doctrine of the unity of being with qualifications (see below), appropriates this idea of existential poverty into his account of the modality of contingency, of all that is made necessary by another (*al-wājib bi-al-ghayr*) (i.e., by the Necessary Being). He uses the term "contingency of poverty" (*imkān faqrī*). This follows from the tradition stemming from Ibn 'Arabī that considers all existents that depend on another, and "annex their existence from the other" (that is, they have relational existence, *al-wujūd al-iḍāfī*), as being "essentially privative."[45] Ibn 'Arabī himself draws upon Qur'ān 35:15, "O mankind! You are poor before God," to articulate his theory of the existential indigence of all that is not the divine essence. Further, once one realizes that there is a single Being that is the goal (*ghāya*) of every existent, then one knows that every existent, whether microcosmic man or macrocosmic universe, is itself merely a "mirror" of that Being. It is the ethical implication of this that restricts the possible vice of pride that may result from *ta'alluh* (*Fut.* I, 196).

Though we speak here of monism, the doctrine of the unity of being does not entail a hypostatic continuity and unity of God, cosmos, and man. The three "realities" are not one person, a gross misunderstanding of Ibn 'Arabī that Mullā Ṣadrā calls the doctrine of the hypostatic unity of being (*waḥda al-wujūd al-shakhṣiyya*).[46] The schools of Ibn 'Arabī and Mullā Ṣadrā make a distinction between Being (*wujūd*), which is solely applicable to God, and existence (*mawjūd*), which applies to all that there is insofar as they are theophanies of divine names and acts. God is existent (*mawjūd*) insofar as he is disclosed to us, but Being insofar as he is unknown and unseen (*ghayb*). There is a unity of Being but existence is not a singular reality. It is our self-conceptualization as existing entities that assists us in recognizing divine existence, since our awareness of our selves is the basis for the central cosmological proof for God.[47] Contingency is an essential feature of the cosmos (*Fut.* III, 275, 443; *Asfār* II, 318ff.). Using the language of philosophy, Ibn ʿArabī expresses it thus (*Fut.* II, 69.3–4):

> The existence attributed to each created thing is the existence of the Reality, since the contingent does not possess being. However, the entities of contingents are receptacles for the manifestation of Being.

We acquire existence from him, and the contingency of our existence is the basis of both epistemology and ontology in this tradition.

Thus far, we discern a distinction between Being, the absolute prerogative of the One, and existence, a derivative mode of being that applies to contingent beings. Whilst this distinction may also be articulated in terms of the Avicennian distinction between existence and essence in contingent beings (the Necessary does not bear this distinction), in our thinkers this distinction is not connected to the notion of essence, because of the critical (Sadrian) doctrine of the "ontological primacy of being" (*aṣāla al-wujūd*). A major question of post-Avicennian thought is whether, given Avicenna's distinction between existence and essence, it is existence or essence that is actual and ontologically prior (see above, chapter 6). Since both of our thinkers regard essences as inert, mental notions that are empty (i.e., without reference in reality), existence or Being must be the actual principle (*Asfār* I, 61–3).

Being is thus taken as primary, and phenomenal existence as the arena of its unfolding. This is reflected in a doctrine of three levels of unfolding Being, which expresses the God–cosmos relationship. Ṣadrā sees this doctrine also as a mystical explanation for his own theory of metaphysical variance around a singular Being: the "modulation of being" (*tashkīk al-wujūd*). Beyond the three degrees of existence is the unseen and ineffable essence that is the ultimate mystery (*al-dhāt*, *ghayb al-ghuyūb*), as he is the pure Being beyond existence. God qua Absolute Being (*al-wujūd al-muṭlaq*) is utterly unknowable (*Fut.* I, 118, inter alia). Yet the three degrees themselves provide the basis for a more positive theory of theological discourse, insofar as they are equated with the divine attributes. Corresponding to the first degree are the intrinsic attributes, which refer to the essence in which there is no duality (*al-aḥadiyya*) and in which the divine essence is emanated to the other attributes through the Most Holy Emanation (*al-fayḍ al-aqdas*). The second and third levels correspond to two types of extrinsic attributes. The second level consists in those manifestations of the divine in which God is said to see, hear, and so forth. This level marks the onset of alterity and duality (*al-wāḥidiyya*). The third and final level is the emanation of the attributes through the Holy Emanation (*al-fayḍ al-muqaddas*), and the divine creative command and Breath of the Merciful (*Nafas al-Raḥmān*). It is only at this third, lowest level that God is considered as related to the world, as it is this level that explains the coming into existence of the cosmos.

The Breath of the Merciful (*Nafas al-Raḥmān*)[48] is the process by which Being becomes manifest and things obtain their existence in the cosmos according to the level of their "disposition" to receive the manifestation of Being in themselves.[49] It is also this creative breath that issues and sustains the cosmos (*Fut.* II, 123.26). It is Being that is spread out (*munbasiṭ*) and manifest. It is identical to the primordial cloud of being (*al-'amā'*), the "dust" (*al-habā'*), prime matter, and the primal element discussed in Presocratic thought (*Fut.* II, 431–2, 310, 390; *Asfār* II, 329, 331.9, 333.17). Prime matter as the foundational substrate is an uncaused cause of all things that we perceive in phenomenal reality.[50] The breath is the exoteric and subaltern aspect of divine Being: it is the reality that is created and creates (*al-ḥaqq al-makhlūq bi-hi*) (*Asfār* II, 328.10).[51] It is identical to the reality of realities (*ḥaqīqa al-ḥaqā'iq*) that bestows "reality" to each existent in the cosmos (*Fut.* II, 432–3, IV, 311). As such it is known as the "universal reality" (*al-ḥaqīqa al-kulliyya*) (*Fut.* I, 119, III, 199). This level of Being unfolding is the key source for existence in this world and the variety of names given to it reflects an attempt to reconcile different creation myths and accounts of the primordial substance and source of existence. With respect to its principle, it is a passive substance, an inert potency requiring divine Being to actualize it; but with respect to its objects, it is that which creates. As an intermediary, it links divine Being with existents in this world whilst retaining an ontological distinction between the two. The recipients of the breath and its loci are described by Mullā Ṣadrā (*Asfār* II, 328.4–5) in terms characteristic not only of the Ibn 'Arabī school but also the Illuminationists: they are the "temples of contingency" (*hayākil al-mumkināt*) and "tablets of quiddities" (*alwāḥ al-māhiyyāt*). It is the Breath of the Merciful that gives existence to things that we experience in this world. It seems that Mullā Ṣadrā wishes to modify his monism whilst retaining a link between the three levels of being, descending from the One, through its first level of manifestation, through to the secondary manifestation in existents in this world. In an Avicennian system, arguably the work of the Breath is carried out by essences before they are actualized in this world, but Mullā Ṣadrā's insistence upon the unreality of essences necessitates the substitution of some mode of being which he finds in Ibn 'Arabī's notion of the Breath of the Merciful.

But we still have the problem of the reality of existents in this world. They do not possess existence in themselves but may be conceptualized as existent by grasping them through universals. In *Fuṣūṣ al-ḥikam* Ibn 'Arabī writes:

> Know that universal entities, even though they do not possess existence in themselves, are intelligible and knowable insofar as one can ascribe existence to them. They can be considered to exist in themselves but [in themselves] they can be neither divisible nor differentiated. They exist in themselves through every individual of a species that is ascribed to them, such as individual humans in relation to humanity, but they neither differentiate nor are multiplied by multiple individuals, remaining intelligible [only]. (*Fuṣūṣ* I, 52.15–53.4)

Phenomenal existence insofar as it is multiple and conceptual is not true Being, but rather it is granted its existence through true Being. This is a corollary of the idea that essences in themselves do not exist in concrete reality but are merely notional and intentional. So, contrary to what one might expect, the distinction between (necessary) Being and (contingent) existence is not provided by the existence–essence distinction as articulated by Avicenna. For the Avicennian distinction in the later tradition was read as a purely notional/mental distinction. Ibn 'Arabī says in *Inshā' al-dawā'ir*, in perpetuation of this Averroist reading of the Avicennian doctrine:

> Know that existence and nonexistence are not added to an existent or a nonexistent, but are identical to the existent and the nonexistent. It is only estimation that imagines that existence and nonexistence are attributes that refer to an existent and a nonexistent . . . Existence and nonexistence are merely expressions for the affirmation and the negation of a thing.[52]

What is actual and is found exists. Existence is thus neither an accident nor a mere property of an entity. Mullā Ṣadrā similarly has little use for the Avicennian distinction, but takes from Ibn 'Arabī the importance of the foundational reality of existence, the notion of *aṣāla al-wujūd* that we encountered above, in opposition to the Illuminationist rejection of existence (expressed by Suhrawardī: see chapter 10) as a mere concept that has no basis in what is actual.[53] Mullā Ṣadrā considers that the term "existence" applied to the cosmos and other than God is meaningful only because the concept has grades of sense and reference, a point whose ontology has been expressed above in the notion of degrees of reality (*Asfār* I, 37–8). While the ground of Being remains God qua the Ultimate Reality, all that exists manifests Being in grades of manifestation, distinguished through a logic of "intensification" (*ishtidād*). As Mullā Ṣadrā says (*Asfār* VI, 277.1–3),

> Existence has degrees of existentiality, and Being possesses different modes, some of which are more perfect and more noble, and others which are more imperfect and more base, such as the divine realm, the intelligible realm, the psychic realm, and the natural realm of existence.

Mullā Ṣadrā is thus not caught between monism and pluralism, but rather seeks to escape the paradigms offered by Ibn 'Arabī by attempting to produce a synthesis based on the notion of grades of intensity within a singular reality. Different intensities mean different degrees of content in our experience of things, corresponding to greater and lesser degrees of the manifestation of Being.

EPISTEMOLOGY: *VIA NEGATIVA* AND REALIST SKEPTICISM

One epistemological result of monism and the recognition of the utter existential poverty of the self is the elevation of the idea that "one does not know," of "ignorance" that is typical of apophasis in the Platonic tradition. In the Neoplatonic tradition, there are two types of knowledge: philosophical insight and self-knowledge (intuition). But they are not necessarily opposed to each other. Similarly in the thought of Ibn 'Arabī, direct experience (*dhawq*) and disclosure (*kashf*) is contrasted with reflection and reason (*'aql*), while necessary and certain knowledge is contrasted with probabilistic understanding (*Fut.* I, 319.28–35). But in Mullā Ṣadrā, they are complementary, as we have seen above in his definition of the quest for truth.

The Socratic maxim "I know that I do not know" is quoted approvingly by Ibn 'Arabī and is linked to unwitting self-awareness (*Fut.* II, 84.11, III, 22.12). Similarly, true knowledge is ignorance (*Fut.* I, 728.18–20). Ibn 'Arabī says (*Fut.* II, 552.25–27):

> He who has not knowledge imagines that he knows Reality/God but that is invalid, since a thing cannot be known except through the positive attributes of itself, and our knowledge of this is impossible, so our knowledge of Reality is impossible. So glory be to He who is known by the fact that He cannot be known. The knower of God does not try to get beyond his rank. He knows that he is one of those who do not know.

A further reason why knowledge of Reality is so elusive is that knowledge of Reality would be infinite, since Reality itself is infinite and is manifest through infinite relationships. Knowledge of these relationships would require that our finite minds grasp infinity, but this is impossible (*Fut.* II, 671.5).

Being and existence are elusive for Mullā Ṣadrā too. This is a paradoxical result of the doctrine common in medieval philosophy that existence is an immediate notion that arises naturally in the mind – it is both the most common and immediate of notions and yet a true understanding of its very reality is hidden and undisclosed (*Asfār* I, 260). Thus Mullā Ṣadrā says in the *Four Journeys*:

> The Pure One is the cause of all things and not all things. Rather it is the principle of everything and not everything. All things are in it and not in it. All things flow from it and subsist and are sustained by it and return to it. (*Asfār* VII, 272–3)

This paradoxical nature of the relationship between Being and its existents results in a problem. If Being is elusive and yet immediate, how can one know whether one has grasped it? For Mullā Ṣadrā, the desire to "grasp" an existent in the mind is to reify and essentialize it. As such it no longer remains concrete "existence" but becomes an essence in the mind (*Asfār* I, 37). Thus one cannot know existence through intellection.

A further result of the experiential path and the doctrine of monism is that the perception of the heart dominates over the perception of the mind, or intellection, in Ibn 'Arabī; for it is only the heart (following a famous saying of the Prophet) that can embrace Reality (*Fut.* III, 129, 250). This contrast mirrors the contrast between learned knowledge and its limitations and gnosis of reality (*ma'rifa*), which is a result of grace and disclosure in the heart: it is practical, pious, and leads to truth along a mystical path (*Fut.* II, 316.9–10).

SOTERIOLOGY: A SALVATIONAL PSYCHOLOGY

The philosophical focus of our two thinkers is the notion and reality of Being. Everything follows from its inquiry. It forces us to investigate its nature, its origins, and its culmination. The soul as a psychic being needs to understand its ontological beginning and end. It is a key tenet of Neoplatonism that the physical world is not the proper abode of the soul. The soul must revert to its origin and principle the One, the ultimate source of its being, and thus be saved from the vicissitudes and confines of the material and the base. It is the practice of philosophy, the combination of discursive and non-discursive thought with intuition and experience of the One, that transforms and moves the soul toward this goal. It is in this sense that later Islamic philosophy combines the practice of philosophizing and mystical experience to effect a soteriological change in the soul. As such, later Islamic philosophy in its approach to philosophy and mysticism represents a strong continuity with late antique Neoplatonic traditions.

A healthy soul, one that moves toward its salvation and goal, is a soul unfettered and unobstructed by divisions within itself. It is a unity that has a plurality of functions and faculties, a psychological expression of the metaphysics of monism and the gradation of phenomenal realities in the thought of Mullā Ṣadrā. While the soul may be pulled in different directions by its desires, beliefs, and faculties, the training of philosophy is designed to reintegrate it and discipline it. Philosophy is a transformative discipline designed to create a particular kind of self/soul.

Two crucial practices and ideas provide the means of the integration of the soul. The first is love (the *eros* of the Platonic tradition).[54] The second is focus upon immutable moral principles and objective norms,[55] provided by the desire to seek the return to the One and the beatitude of experiencing the presence of the One. As we have seen, the practice of mysticism and quest for the experience of Reality is a process whereby one can escape this world and be "saved." Philosophical discourse and practice for Mullā Ṣadrā is precisely the means for this salvation. Thus a key feature of the later traditions of philosophy in Islam after their encounter with mysticism is a reappropriation of the soteriological elements in the Neoplatonic tradition. These were among the elements of Neoplatonism most conducive to a reconciliation with a religious worldview, a worldview that seeks to understand the nature of reality by discerning both a meaning for humanity, and an account of salvation and sustenance in an everlasting life.

NOTES

1 Making sense of revelation and its product, revealed texts, is a central hermeneutic concern of Muslim mystics and philosophers. There are established genres of Ṣūfī and philosophical exegeses of the Qur'ān and the prophetic dicta, and both Ibn 'Arabī and Mullā Ṣadrā wrote such exegeses as primary expressions of their mystical intuition and philosophy. For a more general attempt by philosophers to make sense of the "given" of revelation, see J. E. Gracia, *How can we Know what God Means?* (London: 2002); W. Alston, *Divine Nature and Human Language: Essays in Philosophical Theology* (Ithaca, NY: 1989); and R. Swinburne, *Revelation: From Metaphor to Analogy* (Oxford: 1992).

2 The same word in Arabic renders these two terms, *al-ḥaqīqa*, and thinkers have played upon the ambiguity of the Arabic term.

3 Al-Ghazālī, *al-Munqidh min al-ḍalāl*, ed. F. Jabre (Beirut: 1959), 16–40; cf. E. Ormsby, "The Taste of Truth: The Structure of Experience in al-Ghazālī's *al-Munqidh min al-ḍalāl*," in W. Hallaq and D. Little (eds.), *Islamic Studies Presented to Charles J. Adams* (Leiden: 1991), 133–4.

4 Al-Ghazālī, *al-Munqidh*, 25–7.

5 Al-Ghazālī, *al-Munqidh*, 40.10–11.

6 See, for example, O. Leaman, "Philosophy versus Mysticism: An Islamic Controversy," in M. McGhee (ed.), *Philosophy, Religion and the Spiritual Life* (Cambridge: 1992), 177–87; W. Chittick, "Mysticism versus Philosophy in Earlier Islamic Philosophy," *Religious Studies* 17 (1981), 87–104.

7 My intellectual debt to the seminal work of Pierre Hadot and André-Jean Voelke (and to a certain extent, Martha Nussbaum) for this conception of philosophy as therapy of the soul, and as praxis oriented toward

salvation, should be clear enough not to need indication. But for references, see P. Hadot, *Philosophy as a Way of Life*, trans. M. Chase (Oxford: 1995), esp. 49–70, 81–125, 264–75, and *What is Ancient Philosophy?* trans. M. Chase (Cambridge, MA: 2002), esp. 15–21, 55–233.

8 See S. Rappe, *Reading Neoplatonism: Non-discursive Thinking in the Texts of Plotinus, Proclus, and Damascius* (Cambridge: 2000); H. D. Saffrey, *Le néoplatonisme après Plotin II* (Paris: 2000), 129–41; D. Taormina, *Jamblique: critique de Plotin et Porphyre* (Paris: 1999), esp. 133ff.

9 Of particular significance here are two texts of Iamblichus, *On the Pythagorean Life* and his commentary on the Pythagorean *Golden Verses*, the latter of which was available in Arabic. See H. Daiber (ed.), *Neuplatonische Pythagorica in arabischem Gewande: der Kommentar des Iamblichus zu den* Carmina Aurea: *ein verlorener griechischer Text in arabischer Überlieferung* (Amsterdam: 1995).

10 Cf. Walbridge [155]. Of course, one might say that this is more accurately a Platonic intention of philosophy, and indeed this is how it was understood in Islam, as an expression of the thought of the "divine Plato" (*al-Aflāṭūn al-ilāhī*). For an argument that the goal of Platonic philosophy is, through providing metaphysical foundations, the articulation of *phronêsis* and ethics of *eudaimonia*, see J. M. Rist, *Real Ethics: Rethinking the Foundations of Morality* (Cambridge: 2002), esp. chs. 1 and 2; for an alternative reading of the Platonic texts, see J. Annas, *Platonic Ethics, Old and New* (Ithaca, NY: 2000).

11 Hadot, *What is Ancient Philosophy?* 81.

12 The best spiritual and intellectual biography of him is C. Addas, *Quest for the Red Sulphur: The Life of Ibn ʿArabī*, trans. P. Kingsley (Cambridge: 1993).

13 Ibn ʿArabī [163] and [164]. Hereafter cited as *Fuṣūṣ* and *Fut.* respectively.

14 Like al-Ghazālī, he often attacks philosophers for holding heretical views. See Ibn ʿArabī, *Fut.* III, 401.20, 536.16–18.

15 On the accusation, see Alexander Knysh, *Ibn ʿArabī in the Later Islamic Tradition: The Making of a Polemical Image in Medieval Islam* (Albany, NY: 1999), 113–17.

16 Rosenthal [169], 5–7.

17 Given Ibn ʿArabī's fondness for the *coincidentia oppositorum*, this term is very apt for him. See H. Corbin, *Creative Imagination in the Sufism of Ibn ʿArabī*, trans. R. Manheim (Princeton, NJ: 1969), 205–15.

18 Philip Merlan, *Monopsychism, Mysticism, Metaconsciousness: Problems of the Soul in the Neoaristotelian and Neoplatonic Traditions* (The Hague: 1963), 20–1.

19 Mullā Ṣadrā [166]; hereafter *Asfār*.

20 R. Sorabji, *Emotion and Peace of Mind* (Oxford: 2000), 17–19; Hadot, *Philosophy as a Way of Life*, 87–90.
21 Hadot, *What is Ancient Philosophy?* 6.
22 Sorabji, *Emotion and Peace of Mind*, 159–60.
23 This quite apposite example is suggested by Sorabji, *Emotion and Peace of Mind*, 161.
24 Sorabji, *Emotion and Peace of Mind*, 13; Hadot, *Philosophy as a Way of Life*, 84.
25 On which see Annas, *Platonic Ethics*, ch. 3; D. Sedley, "The Idea of Godlikeness," in G. Fine (ed.), *Plato, II: Ethics, Politics, Religion and the Spiritual Life* (Oxford: 1999), 309–28, and J. Domanski, *La philosophie: théorie ou manière de vivre* (Paris: 1996), 5–9.
26 Plato, *Theaetetus*, 176a6–b3, trans. Sedley, "The Idea of Godlikeness," 312.
27 See Plato, *Laws*, 716c.
28 Evinced by Mullā Ṣadrā, *Asfār* I, 21.6, 22.4; cf. Ibn ʿArabī, *Fuṣūṣ* 55.
29 Hadot, *What is Ancient Philosophy?* 69.
30 Sedley, "The Idea of Godlikeness," 320.
31 See Ibn ʿArabī, *Fut.* I, 118.9, II, 187.17–18. However, instead of explicitly referring to *ta'alluh*, Ibn ʿArabī prefers talking about acquiring divine virtue because becoming godlike may easily be misunderstood in a strictly monotheistic society.
32 The connection was suggested by Walbridge [155], 90–1.
33 Cf. *Asfār* III, 446.
34 *Asfār* I, 22. The complementarity of philosophical discourse and spiritual practices is stressed in the Illuminationist tradition. Suhrawardī himself makes this explicit in Suhrawardī [152], 162.11–15.
35 Avicenna used the term in *al-Ishārāt wa al-tanbīhāt*, ed. M. Shihābī (Tehran: 1996), vol. III, 399.21, in his discussion of the separable intellects. His commentator Naṣīr al-Dīn al-Ṭūsī (d. 1274) explained that this method of philosophy combined discourse (*baḥth*) with intuition (*kashf*) and experience (*dhawq*) – see vol. III, 401.3. Avicenna's student, Bahmanyār, also stressed the significance of contemplation as a higher cognitive form than mere discourse – see *Kitāb al-taḥṣīl*, ed. M. Muṭahharī (Tehran: 1996), 816.16–17.
36 S. J. D. Āshtiyānī, *Sharḥ-i muqaddima-yi Qayṣarī bar Fuṣūṣ al-ḥikam* (Tehran: 1991), 280.
37 Mullā Ṣadrā, *Mafātīḥ al-ghayb*, with scholia of ʿAlī Nūrī, ed. M. Khājavī (Tehran: 1984), 41.
38 Ibn ʿArabī says that *al-Futūḥāt al-Makkiyya* (*The Meccan Revelations*) is based on mystical experience and divine revelation (*kashf*); see *Fut.*, II, 389, 432.

39 The inadequacy and superfluity of reason is indicated in his gloss upon the Qur'ānic description of the Prophet Muḥammad as *ummī* (understood to mean "illiterate"). Knowledge is acquired not from the books of philosophers but from prophetic experience and disclosure. See Ibn 'Arabī, *Fut.* II, 595.32, 644.

40 Mullā Ṣadrā, *Asrār al-āyāt wa anwār al-bayyināt*, with marginalia of 'Alī Nūrī, ed. M. Khājavī (Tehran: 1984), 132.5–7.

41 Mullā Ṣadrā, *Īqāẓ al-nā'imīn*, ed. M. Mu'ayyadī (Tehran: 1982), 69.2–19.

42 Ibn 'Arabī himself never used the term, but the concept is made explicit from commentaries on his work, especially the *Fuṣūṣ*, and from the work of his disciples and followers, beginning with his stepson Ṣadr al-Dīn al-Qunawī (d. 1274). See Chittick [160], 3.

43 The solitude of Being that the divine qua unconditioned reality possesses explains the desire and need for it to create something by which it may be known, the prime creation myth of the school of unity of being expressed in the divine words expressed on the tongue of the Prophet Muḥammad, "I was a hidden Treasure (*kanzan makhfiyyan*) but was not known. So I loved to be known and I created the creation and made myself known to them. Then they came to know me." Love thus becomes the impulse for creation. See Ibn 'Arabī, *Fut.* II, 232.11–12, inter alia, and *Kitāb al-awrād al-usbū'* (Istanbul: 1299 A.H.), trans. P. Beneito and S. Hirtenstein as *The Seven Days of the Heart* (Oxford: 2000), 115, in which he supplicates that God may bring him to contemplate the "solitude of your Being" (*waḥdat wujūdika*).

44 The existential poverty is asserted through the recognition that man does not even possess his own existence and that when he seeks out his existence or that of any phenomenal object, he only finds God (as in Qur'ān 24:39). See Ibn 'Arabī, *Fut.* ch. 328 on the Muḥammadan Presence (*al-ḥaḍra al-Muḥammadiyya*), III, 105.8–25.

45 See 'Abd al-Razzāq Kāshānī, *Iṣṭilāḥāt al-ṣūfiyya*, ed. A. Sprenger, repr., *A Glossary of Sufi Technical Terms* (London: 1991), 28.

46 *Asfār* I, 68–9.

47 Ibn 'Arabī, *al-Tadbīrāt al-Ilāhiyya*, in *Kleinere Schriften des Ibn 'Arabī*, ed. J. Nyberg (Leiden: 1919), 208: "God is found [exists, *mawjūd*] and we are existents (*mawjūdāt*). If we did not conceive of our own existence, we would not have been able to cognize the importance of Being nor affirm that the Creator exists. He created in us the faculty of knowledge so we realized that he possesses the attribute of knowledge and that he is knowing, and similarly through our life we knew that he possesses life."

48 Ibn 'Arabī, *Fut.* II, 60, 426–7, III, 77, 150, 354, 420, 444. For a discussion of the pseudo-Empedoclean aspects of this doctrine, see D. de Smet, *Empedocles arabus: une lecture néoplatonicienne tardive* (Brussels: 1998).

49 Ibn 'Arabī, *Fuṣūṣ* I, 112, 219; *Fut.* II, 394, 426. The Breath of the Merciful is a reference to the creative breath when God blew his spirit into Adam; see Qur'ān 15:29.

50 Ibn 'Arabī, *al-Tadbīrāt al-Ilāhiyya*, 122–3.

51 This term is first used by Ibn Barrajān (d. 1191) of Seville as attested by Ibn 'Arabī, *Fut.* II, 60.12, 104.6.

52 Ibn 'Arabī, *Inshā' al-dawā'ir*, in *La production des cercles*, trans. P. Fenton and M. Gloton, ed. J. Nyberg (Paris: 1996), 5.10–16 in the Arabic.

53 Suhrawardī [152], 45–51.

54 See Rist, *Real Ethics*, 95ff.

55 Rist, *Real Ethics*, 117.

TONY STREET

12 Logic

A chapter on logic in an introductory book on Islamic philosophy could legitimately be expected to cover a range of topics, from the argument techniques used by ninth-century theologians and jurists to the semantical analyses of the fourteenth-century grammarians.[1] But by the late tenth century, the Arabic word commonly translated as "logic," *manṭiq*, had come to refer almost exclusively to Peripatetic traditions of distinguishing a good from a bad argument, and those are the traditions to which this chapter is limited. This means that the Arabic logical writings examined here are, like their medieval Latin counterparts, concerned with a problematic arising from the Aristotelian texts; more than medieval Latin logic, however, the dominant tradition of Arabic logic is mainly at one remove from those texts, as will be exemplified below.

Even with this limitation, the writings which fall under the chapter's remit stretch from 750 to the present day, covering the whole course of subjects developed in the *Organon*. For practical purposes, I impose the further limitation of referring the material covered back to *al-Risāla al-shamsiyya*, the *Logic for Shams al-Dīn* by Najm al-Dīn al-Kātibī (d. 1276).[2] I do so because down to the twentieth century it was commonly the first substantial text on logic which a Sunnī Muslim would study in the course of a *madrasa* education.[3] Because the problematic considered by the *Shamsiyya* acquired its precise form in Avicenna's writings, and acquired its commonly accepted resolution by the late thirteenth century, I will not consider any logical work written after this time. This should not be taken to imply that original work in logic came to an end in 1300, but rather that other problems had taken center stage.

I begin this chapter by making a few comments on the pitfalls awaiting the historian of Arabic logic. I then sketch in broad terms historical aspects of the tradition to which the *Shamsiyya* belongs, and the way that tradition came to be represented in the *madrasa* curriculum. I describe the contents of the *Shamsiyya* to give some idea of the range of topics covered by the average student of logic. I then note certain elements of al-Kātibī's treatment of the modal syllogistic and examine its predecessors. I conclude by attempting a broad characterization of later Arabic logic.

PRELIMINARY CONSIDERATIONS

Whereas the study of medieval Western logic is now an established field of research, contributing both to modern philosophy of logic and to the intellectual history of the Middle Ages, the study of logic in the precolonial Islamic world is still barely in its infancy. That fact alone makes it difficult to write an introductory chapter on the field: we are as yet unclear what contributions of the logicians writing in Arabic are particularly noteworthy or novel. It is also a dangerous temptation in this state of relative underdevelopment to cast an eye too readily on the work of the Latin medievalist, and to import the methods, assumptions, and even the historical template that have worked so well in the cognate Western field.

This temptation must be resisted at all costs. There are many important differences between the scholarly ideals and options of the Latin West and the Muslim East; there are, also, many differences between the various fortunes encountered by rigorous logical activity in the two realms over the centuries. A glance at the historiographical preliminaries of Bochenski's *History of Formal Logic* prompts the following observations.[4] First and foremost, Aristotle ceases by the end of the twelfth century to be a significant coordinate for logicians writing in Arabic – that place is filled by Avicenna. The centrality of Avicenna's idiosyncratic system in post-Avicennian logical writings and the absence of Aristotelian logic in a narrowly textual sense meant that Arabic texts dealing with Avicenna's system were left to one side by the medieval Latin translators. Instead, other, less influential texts by Averroes and al-Fārābī were translated, because they did concentrate on Aristotle and spoke to thirteenth-century Western logical concerns. Even at the outset, then, the insignificance of Aristotle's logical system in the Avicennian tradition worked to distort Western appreciation of the relative importance of particular logicians writing in Arabic.

A second difference is that the whole range of Aristotelian logical texts were available in Arabic by about 900, and so the broad periodization of medieval Latin logic into *logica vetus* and *logica nova* is inappropriate as a way of periodizing logic written in Arabic;[5] by the time serious logical work began, the complete *Organon* was available. Avicenna's work marks the watershed for any helpful periodization. Thirdly, Bochenski's analysis of what preconceptions and historical meanderings clutter the way to the proper study of medieval Western logic (the collapse of acute logical study with the demise of scholasticism, the ahistorical reductivism of post-Kantian logic, the institutionalization of a psychologistic logic in neoscholasticism)[6] do not apply to the study of the logic of medieval Muslim scholars – even in the early twentieth century, it is clear that at least some scholars were still in contact with the acute work of the thirteenth century. There had been far less of a rupture in logical activity over the intervening centuries. On the other hand, there have been post-colonial efforts to find later Western logical achievements foreshadowed in early Arabic logic, and this has damaged the prospects for appraisal of the work by leading to a disproportionate focus on minor traditions.[7]

Finally, only some of the characteristics Bochenski finds which distinguish medieval Western logic from the logic of late antiquity apply to the logic being written in Arabic at roughly the same time.[8] It too is highly formal and metalogical in its treatment, and pedagogically central; but no doctrine like supposition was developed, and there seems to have been far less concern with antinomies. One may say – nervously, given the current state of research – that Arabic logic is somewhat closer to the logic of late antiquity in its concerns and methods than medieval Latin logic. That said, one must guard against an obvious alternative assumption, which is that Arabic logic is by and large just one or other of the systems of late antiquity.[9] We already have enough control over Avicenna's logic to know that is false.

THE TRADITION OF LOGIC AND THE *MADRASA*

The average learned Muslim from the late thirteenth century on acquired some logic as part of his intellectual arsenal. Very often, that logic had been acquired from the lovely little textbook, the *Shamsiyya*, perhaps the most studied logic textbook of all time. The *Shamsiyya* belonged to and reflected a tradition which had its own peculiar features. Further, the *Shamsiyya* had found a home in the *madrasa* curriculum in the face of opposition from some quarters. I examine aspects of each of these matters in the following subsections.

The form and substance of the tradition

As a religious community, Islam had first come in contact with a living logical tradition when the Muslim armies coming out of the peninsula in the seventh century took control of the Fertile Crescent where Christian communities had made logic an important part of their studies. The logic they studied was a shortened version of what had been taught in the Alexandrian curricula of the sixth century, limited to the *Categories*, *On Interpretation*, and the assertoric syllogistic of the *Prior Analytics* (which is to say, up to the end of the seventh chapter of the first book).[10] There are various reasons given for why the Christians stopped at that point (al-Fārābī was later to write that it was due to a synodal decree, but there are good reasons to doubt that was the reason),[11] but probably it was because that was the simplified basic logic they received. It was that basic logic which was translated from Syriac into Arabic in the second half of the eighth century.

The first Arabic translations of logic were executed, then, at the beginning of the ʻAbbāsid regime. No universally valid generalization can be made about how the translations proceeded, but by and large logical summaries were translated, then texts or fragments of texts from the *Organon*, then commentaries on those texts of the *Organon*; again, by and large, translations went from Greek to Arabic by way of the Syriac. Even the earliest translations are, however, an exception to that process; the earliest surviving text translated, by Ibn al-Muqaffaʻ (d. 757) in the 750s, was indeed a summary, but we know that it was made at roughly the same time as a translation of the *Topics*.[12] The early efforts gave way to better translations by better-organized translators, and by the mid-ninth century there were highly skilled translators working in the circle of al-Kindī (d. ca. 870) and, somewhat later, in the circle of Ḥunayn ibn Isḥāq

(d. 873). Though some of the logic texts translated were still descendants of the Alexandrian summaries, more and more texts of the *Organon* were translated and retranslated. The *Organon* texts were ultimately furnished with commentaries by scholars of late antiquity like Alexander, Ammonius, and Themistius. Ḥunayn had particular veneration for Galen, and many Galenic logical works now lost were available to the Arabs.

It was not until the rise of the Baghdad Peripatetics, marked by the activities of Abū Bishr Mattā ibn Yūnus (d. 940) and al-Fārābī (d. 950), that logicians started to focus closely on the *Organon* itself. Al-Fārābī came to conceive his task as clearing away misinterpretations of the Aristotelian text, many the result of the Syriac summaries, and reviving true Peripatetic doctrine after a period of rupture. The Baghdad Peripatetics who carried on the work of Abū Bishr and al-Fārābī were able by about 1000 to produce a heavily annotated version of the *Organon* which was accurate enough for close exegesis.[13] The Farabian tradition, both in Baghdad until the mid-twelfth century and in Spain where it ended somewhat after the time of Averroes (d. 1198), would always be concerned with this kind of exegesis.

At the same time the final version of the Arabic *Organon* was being achieved, a young philosopher from Khurāsān, Avicenna (d. 1037), had set about changing forever the course of Islamic philosophy. Avicenna claimed for himself, by virtue of his Intuition (*ḥads*), the ability to judge the Peripatetic tradition, and to be in a position to say what philosophical doctrines Aristotle should properly have come to.[14] One aspect of his philosophical activity particularly relevant for present purposes led him to reinterpret sections of the *Prior Analytics*, and it is his reinterpretation which served as the object of study and debate among later scholars in his tradition rather than the original Aristotelian system.

The leaders of this Heroic Age of Arabic logic, al-Fārābī and Avicenna, dealt with the books of the *Organon* one by one. But after them, a major change in focus occurred in the tradition, here described by Ibn Khaldūn (d. 1406), the first (and still greatest) historian of Arabic logic.

> The later scholars came and changed the technical terms of logic; and they appended to the investigation of the five universals its fruit, which is to say the discussion of definitions and descriptions which they moved from the *Posterior Analytics*; and they dropped the *Categories* because a logician

is only accidentally and not essentially interested in that book; and they appended to *On Interpretation* the treatment of conversion (even if it had been in the *Topics* in the texts of the ancients, it is nonetheless in some respects among the things which follow on from the treatment of propositions). Moreover, they treated the syllogistic with respect to its productivity generally, not with respect to its matter. They dropped the investigation of [the syllogistic] with respect to matter, which is to say, these five books: *Posterior Analytics*, *Topics*, *Rhetoric*, *Poetics*, and *Sophistical Fallacies* (though sometimes some of them give a brief outline of them). They have ignored [these five books] as though they had never been, even though they are important and relied upon in the discipline. Moreover, that part of [the discipline] they have set down they have treated in a penetrating way; they look into it in so far as it is a discipline in its own right, not in so far as it is an instrument for the sciences. Treatment of [the subject as newly conceived] has become lengthy and wide-ranging – the first to do that was Fakhr al-Dīn al-Rāzī (d. 1210) . . . The books and ways of the ancients have been abandoned, as though they had never been.[15]

By the time al-Kātibī wrote the *Shamsiyya*, at the height of the Golden Age of Arabic logic, the discipline had changed from ranging over all the subjects covered in the *Organon* to concentrating on narrowly formal questions. And, as did all at his time, al-Kātibī wrote on those questions as developed by Avicenna.

The study of logic

This is how the *Shamsiyya* acquired the form and focus it has. How did it come to be studied in the *madrasa* – how, in short, did Islam embrace a Greek-derived science at its educational heart? At the time of the translation movement, some Muslim religious scholars were open to the study of logic, some less so. One of the most commonly cited examples of antipathy to logic in Muslim intellectual circles is that expressed by a grammarian, Abū Sa'īd al-Sīrāfī, in a debate that took place in the 930s with one of Baghdad's leading Peripatetics, the Abū Bishr Mattā mentioned above. The debate touched on a number of complex issues, but most significantly for present purposes it serves to show how doubtful scholars were about claims for the utility of Greek logic. Al-Sīrāfī taunted Abū Bishr about his trust in logic: "The world remains after Aristotle's logic as it was before his logic . . . you can dispense with the ideas of the Greeks as well as you can dispense with the language of the Greeks."[16]

Al-Fārābī, spurred by Abū Bishr's humiliation, set about showing how logic complemented the Islamic sciences. This he did by showing that logic underpinned and guaranteed the arguments deployed in theology and law. In his book *The Short Treatise on Reasoning in the Way of the Theologians*, "he interpreted the arguments of the theologians and the analogies of the jurists as logical syllogisms in accordance with the doctrines of the ancients."[17] In *The Short Treatise*, we find analyses of the paradigmatic argument, of the argument used by Muslim theologians called "reasoning from the seen to the unseen," and of the "juristic argument" itself.[18] This programmatic defence of logic was adopted by an important Muslim jurist, Abū Ḥāmid al-Ghazālī (d. 1111), who prefaced his most famous juristic digest with a short treatise on logic, saying that knowledge of logic was indispensable for a proper control of jurisprudence.[19] Logic was thereafter widely recognized as a necessary part of a scholar's training. The way that recognition had been won led subsequent writers of logic manuals to consecrate at least a part of their manuals to the reduction of juristic argument forms to the syllogism, a reflex carried over from this early time when Muslim scholars contested the place of logic in Islamic society.

The Farabian strategy succeeded in making logic a commonly studied discipline, but dissenting voices could still be heard. A famous condemnation of logic, issued by Ibn al-Ṣalāh (d. 1245), lets us see how pious doubts arose about the discipline.

> As far as logic is concerned, it is a means of access to philosophy. Now the access to something bad is also bad. Preoccupation with the study and teaching of logic has not been permitted by the Lawgiver. The use of the terminology of logic in the investigation of religious law is despicable and one of the recently introduced follies. Thank God, the laws of religion are not in need of logic. Everything a logician says about definition and apodictic proof is complete nonsense. God has made it dispensable for those who have common sense, and it is even more dispensable for the specialists in the speculative branches of jurisprudence.[20]

But as a formal system, logic is unobjectionable, and an influential jurist and famous hater of logic, Ibn Taymiyya (d. 1328), was prepared to concede that point, albeit rather mockingly:

> The validity of the form of the syllogism is irrefutable . . . But it must be maintained that the numerous figures they have elaborated and the conditions

they have stipulated for their validity are useless, tedious, and prolix. These resemble the flesh of a camel found on the summit of a mountain; the mountain is not easy to climb, nor the flesh plump enough to make it worth the hauling.[21]

CONTENTS OF THE *SHAMSIYYA*

There is much in the structure of the *Shamsiyya* that is familiar to anyone who has looked at medieval Latin treatises on logic, particularly the division of the three main parts of the treatise (parts 2, 3, and 4) into Terms, Propositions, and Syllogism.[22] There are other deep similarities, especially the way logic is defined, and the way the treatment of universals is developed. Much of the material would work perfectly well as an introduction to logic in the medieval Western tradition; it is, like its Latin counterparts, ultimately descended from the Aristotelian texts.

1. Introduction
   (a) What logic is
   (b) Subject matter of logic
2. Terms
   (a) Utterances
   (b) Individual concepts
   (c) On universals and particulars
   (d) Definition
3. Propositions
   (a) Introduction: definition of proposition and its parts
   (b) On the categorical proposition
      i. Parts thereof, and kinds
      ii. On quantification
      iii. On equipollence and existence
      iv. On modal propositions
   (c) On the hypothetical proposition
   (d) On rules governing propositions
      i. Contradiction
      ii. Simple conversion
      iii. Obversion
      iv. Equivalences among hypothetical propositions
4. Syllogisms
   (a) Definition of "syllogism," and its kinds
   (b) Syllogisms with mixed premises
   (c) On conjunctive syllogisms with hypothetical propositions

   (d) On repetitive syllogisms
   (e) Further matters to do with syllogistic
      i. Linked syllogisms
      ii. Reduction
      iii. Induction
      iv. Example
5. Conclusion
   (a) Syllogistic matter
   (b) On the parts of the sciences

Still, some points in the *Shamsiyya* would not serve to introduce material treated by its Latin contemporaries, most especially the division of the syllogistic, the division of different kinds of discourse, and the modal logic.

The division of the syllogistic in nearly all works belonging to the dominant Avicennian tradition reproduces a division set out by Avicenna and claimed by him to be one of his own innovations.

According to what we ourselves have verified, syllogistic divides into two, conjunctive (*iqtirānī*) and repetitive (*istithanā'ī*). The conjunctive is that in which there occurs no explicit statement [in the premises] of the contradictory or affirmation of the proposition in which we have the conclusion; rather, the conclusion is only there in potentiality, as in the example we have given. As for the repetitive, it is that in which [the conclusion or its contradictory] occurs explicitly [in the premises].[23]

The division probably relates to epistemic questions to do with perfecting syllogisms, and ramifies through to the analysis of the proof by reduction to an impossibility, both topics too complex to be explored here. Averroes criticized it as a division, and he and al-Fārābī used an alternative division common in the Latin tradition.[24]

Another strange aspect of the *Shamsiyya* relative to its Latin contemporaries is its section devoted to syllogistic matter (*al-mādda al-qiyāsiyya*). This was referred to above in the quote taken from Ibn Khaldūn, who said that the later logicians "dropped the investigation of [the syllogistic] with respect to matter, which is to say, these five books: *Posterior Analytics*, *Topics*, *Rhetoric*, *Poetics*, and *Sophistical Fallacies* (though sometimes some of them give a brief outline of them)" – the brief outline became a way to deal with the later parts of the Alexandrian arrangement of the *Organon*. The syllogism was taken to be what formally underlies all arguments, but propositions making up those arguments may differ; these differentiated stretches of discourse manipulated by the syllogism in turn determine what kind of argument is produced, be it demonstrative, dialectical, rhetorical, poetical, or sophistical. There was dispute about the criteria to differentiate syllogistic matter, but in the Avicennian tradition to which the *Shamsiyya* belongs, the criteria were epistemological.[25]

THE MODAL SYLLOGISTIC

With that we come to the modal syllogistic, perhaps the most foreign of the *Shamsiyya's* doctrines. It is not obvious from the table of contents given above just how much of the *Shamsiyya* is given over to the modals; one needs to realize that the sections on contradiction, conversion, obversion, and syllogisms with mixed premises are all on modal logic, amounting to over eight pages of the twenty-eight and a half pages of Sprenger's printing. In other words, nearly one-third of an introductory treatise is given to modal logic. Throughout its treatment of the modals, a distinction between the *dhātī* and *waṣfī* readings of the proposition crops up again and again. Whence comes this distinction, unknown in the West?

To answer this question, we need to return to the Aristotelian system. Let us consider the following famous problem. Aristotle wants this syllogism to be valid:

(1) Every *c* is *b*, every *b* is necessarily *a*, therefore every *c* is necessarily *a*.

but he wants to reject the next syllogism:

(2) Every *c* is necessarily *b*, every *b* is *a*, therefore every *c* is necessarily *a*.

The "necessarily" in the first, valid, syllogism, seems to belong to the predicate term "*a*"; that is, the full predicate of the second and third propositions in (1) is "necessarily *a*." This is what is referred to among medieval Latin writers as a *de re* reading of the modal proposition. At the same time, Aristotle wants the proposition

(3) Every *a* is necessarily *b*.

to convert as

(4) Some *b* is necessarily *a*.

which suggests that he reads "necessarily" in this case as belonging to the whole proposition rather than merely to the predicate term; he is taking the proposition (3), in short, as "necessarily, every *a* is *b*." Taking the proposition to assert that "every *a* is *b*" is necessary is to take it in what is known among medieval Latin writers as a *de dicto* reading. The problem is that if the *de dicto* reading is adopted, then syllogism (1) is no longer valid; if the *de re* reading is adopted, the conversion of (3) no longer goes through as (4). Aristotle never refers to the distinction between *de re* and *de dicto* readings, and seems to propose a uniform reading for his modals throughout the exposition.[26] Is he right to do so?

The Farabian tradition

At this point, I will take a considerable detour through the earliest Arabic treatment of the modal logic, so I can examine the way the Farabian tradition tried over two and a half centuries to refine a solution to the problem. When al-Fārābī began his work in the early tenth century, he had the relevant chapters of the *Prior Analytics* (chs. 8–22 of book I, translated by an otherwise unknown collaborator working with Ḥunayn ibn Isḥāq, probably finished some time between 850 and 875), and a mass of commentatorial material translated three or four decades later, probably including Alexander, Ammonius, Themistius, and others. We have lost the work in which al-Fārābī set out his exegesis, but his approach to one particular problem was explicitly adopted and extended by Averroes (d. 1198).[27] By and large, the Farabians wanted to give a way to make sense of the difficult passages in Aristotle's modal syllogistic, and proffered ways of construing the text to do that. Their interests were exclusively textual, in the sense that it is hard to picture a freestanding system that would make the distinctions their exegetical posture led them to make. They did not make use of the distinction between *de re* and *de dicto* readings. But they accepted the validity of syllogism (1), the invalidity of syllogism (2), and tended to focus their concerns on the proper converse of (3). One concrete counterexample to the inference of (4) from (3) that Farabian logicians dealt with was:

(5) Every literate being is necessarily a human being,

which, given the way things are, seems to be true, but which would convert to the untrue

(6) Some human being is necessarily literate.

Developing a distinction found in Aristotle between terms taken to be *per se* (*bi-al-dhāt*) and *per accidens* (*bi-al-'araḍ*) – too complex for the present chapter – the Farabians would hold "literate being" to be merely *per accidens*, expressing a peculiarity had only by the predicate, human being, but not had necessarily by any. So (5) is only true as a *per accidens* necessary proposition because one of the terms is only *per accidens*. "Human being," by contrast, is said of things essentially, that is, *per se*. Aristotle only intends to be able to infer (4) from (3) if (3) is a *per se* necessary proposition, with *per se* terms like

(7) Every human being is necessarily an animal.

A simplified version of this approach was adopted by medieval Latin logicians, notably Robert Kilwardby (d. 1279), though we are unable to say what source he may have followed. Here is his statement of the argument:

When it is said: "Every literate being is necessarily a human being," this subject is not something which can be said *per se* of this predicate, but since "literate being" is not separated from that which belongs to a human being itself, the proposition is conceded to be necessary, but when a proposition is necessary in this way it is necessary *per accidens*. Therefore, when Aristotle says that necessary propositions are convertible, he means only that the propositions which are necessary *per se* are convertible.[28]

In another essay, Averroes gave a statement of a series of problematic passages in Aristotle, followed by a declaration of why he wanted to find a solution to them:

These are all the doubts in this matter. They kept occurring to us even when we used to go along in this matter with our colleagues, in interpretations by virtue of which no solution to these doubts is clear. This has led me now (given my high opinion of Aristotle, and my belief that his theorization is better than that of all other people) to scrutinize this question seriously and with great effort.[29]

Nothing could better characterize the way the Farabian approaches the Aristotelian text; and it is this approach which Avicenna rejects.

The Avicennian tradition

Which is not to say Avicenna had little respect for Aristotle, or that his syllogistic is presented without reference to the system of the *Prior Analytics*. But Avicenna was sure he knew the system which Aristotle was trying to put forward, and used that system as a way to judge when to depart from the literal sense of the text. On a related point, he said:

You should realize that most of what Aristotle's writings have to say about the modal mixes are tests, and are not genuine opinions – this will become clear to you in a number of places.[30]

The Avicennian approach to the problem of interpreting Aristotle was to accept (1), reject (2), and then simply reject the claim that (3) converts as (4). The counterexample Avicenna used was *every laughing being is necessarily a human*. It is obvious that it will convert to *some humans are laughing*,

but it does not necessarily convert as a necessary, for it may be that the converse of the necessary is possible; it may be that J (such as *laughing*) necessarily has B (such as *man*), but that B (such as *man*) does not necessarily have J (such as *laughing*). Whoever says otherwise, and has sought to find a stratagem for it, do not believe him.[31]

One of the stratagems expressly ruled out by Avicenna is the Farabian.[32] In other words, Avicenna did not seek to exclude certain propositions from the Aristotelian rule, he just changed the rule. The Farabians changed their system to fit the text, Avicenna changed the text to fit his system.

That said, Avicenna did develop his own stratagems to save Aristotle's text. One of these stratagems is the *waṣfī/dhātī* distinction whose origin we seek, which he introduced when discussing propositions in a necessary mode, but which he first used in discussing propositions with no explicit modality (what he called "absolute" propositions).[33] Here is the introduction of the different readings:

Necessity may be (1) absolute, as in *God exists*; or it may be connected to a condition. The condition may be (2) perpetual for the existence of the substance (*dhāt*), as in *man is necessarily a rational body*. By this we do not mean to say that man has been and always will be a rational body, because that would be false for each given man. Rather, we mean to assert that while he exists as a substance, as a human, he is a rational body. Or the condition may be (3) perpetual for the subject's being described (*mawṣūfan*) in the way it is, as in *all mobile things are changing*; this is not to be taken to assert that this is the case absolutely, nor for the time [the subject] exists as a substance, but rather while the substance of the moving thing is moving. Distinguish between this condition and the first condition, because the first has set down as the condition the principle of the substance, "man," whereas here the substance is set down with a description (*ṣifa*) that attaches to the substance, "moving thing." "Moving thing" involves a substance (*dhāt wa jawhar*) to which movement and non-movement attach; but "man" and "black" are not like that.[34]

How did Avicenna use this distinction? A *dhātī* reading is like the *de re* reading mentioned above, whereas the *waṣfī* reading takes a proposition like *every a is necessarily b* as properly *every a is necessarily b while a*. The distinction is probably best explained by example. *All who are sitting may be standing* is true as a *dhātī* reading; each person who sits can at a later time stand, all other things being equal. Under this reading, all men are necessarily rational, all young men may be old men, all bachelors may be married men, and all who are sleeping are waking. In the *waṣfī* reading, *all men are necessarily rational* is still true, but *all who are sitting may be standing* taken as a *waṣfī* (which is to say, *all who are sitting may be standing while sitting*) is false. False too are the propositions claiming that all bachelors may be married men, and that all who are sleeping are waking.

The right way to understand Aristotle's syllogistic was as a system involving propositions in the *dhātī* reading and, so understood, the converse of (3) is not (4). Was there a way to have Aristotle's claim make sense? By taking (3) in the *waṣfī* reading. In fact, according to Avicenna, the move from (3) to (4) was not the only place where Aristotle needed to be read charitably, nor was it the only place the *waṣfī* reading could help. He also thought it could preserve the Aristotelian stipulations for the contradictories and converses of absolute propositions. Naṣīr al-Dīn al-Ṭūsī (d. 1272), one of Avicenna's great thirteenth-century commentators, tells us why Avicenna developed the distinction:

What spurred him to this was that in the assertoric syllogistic Aristotle and others sometimes used contradictions of absolute propositions assuming them to be absolute; and that was why so many decided that absolutes did contradict absolutes. When Avicenna had shown this to be wrong, he wanted to give a way of construing [those examples from Aristotle].[35]

THE NATURE OF LATER ARABIC LOGIC

It is from Avicenna's exercise in exegetical charity that al-Kātibī and his predecessors found the distinction they deployed so extensively. It is instructive to examine how al-Kātibī used the distinction, and some of the results to which he came, because that in turn illustrates certain characteristic aspects of later Arabic logic.

Firstly, al-Kātibī never brought the *dhātī/waṣfī* distinction to bear on any problem in Aristotle's *Prior Analytics*, nor, for that matter, on any problem in Avicenna's logic. Al-Kātibī was setting down a system of modal logic, not writing a commentary on someone else's system. But the system he put forward was based closely on Avicenna's. In other words, the system to which immediate reference was made by the later logicians writing in Arabic – al-Kātibī is representative in this respect – was Avicenna's, not Aristotle's.

Secondly, on looking at the specific deductions in al-Kātibī's treatment, one finds the following: if the premises are in the *dhātī* reading, then syllogism (1) is valid, and syllogism (2) invalid. The converse of (3) in the *dhātī* reading is not (4), but nor is it the one-sided possible that Avicenna took it to be. Al-Kātibī took its converse instead to be a proposition in the *waṣfī* reading, *some b is at least once a while b* – I will not go into his proof for the conversion here. So although the system was based closely on Avicenna's, it was not Avicenna's. It was rather a modification of that system, and the modifications were in some cases extensive. Among other things, they made the system completely useless for one of the tasks Avicenna had in mind when he produced it, which was to use it to make sense of Aristotle's *Prior Analytics*.

We may say that later Arabic logic is Avicennian, then, but that claim should be understood fairly specifically. Firstly, it is Avicennian in that the base system taken as the object of debate and repair is Avicennian. And secondly, it is Avicennian in its attitude to past authority – just as Avicenna had rejected Aristotle's doubtful claims, so too the later logicians writing in Arabic felt free to reject Avicenna's doubtful claims.[36] Further, they did not share his interest in the work of the First Teacher. But by developing, extending, and repairing the various logical insights of Avicenna as exposited through his conversation with Aristotle's *Organon*, these later logicians offered up vast quantities of material on important logical problems. It is the task of present and future generations of scholars to begin to take stock of the quality of this material.[37]

NOTES

Thanks are due to Henrik Lagerlund, John Marenbon, Rob Wisnovsky, and the editors of this volume for reading this chapter and offering various helpful suggestions.

1 For information on these interesting topics, see respectively J. van Ess, "The Logical Structure of Islamic Theology," in von Grunebaum [184], 21–50; and B. Weiss, "*Ilm al-Waḍ'*: An Introductory Account of a Later Muslim Philological Science," *Arabica* 34 (1987), 339–56.

2 The whole of the *Shamsiyya* is available in translation, though a new translation is overdue. See A. Sprenger (ed. and trans.), *Bibliotheca Indica: A Collection of Oriental Works*, no. 88: *First Appendix to the Dictionary of Technical Terms used in the Sciences of the Mussulmans, containing the Logic of the Arabians* (Calcutta: 1854); this partial translation is completed in Rescher [178], 39–45. Rescher added to his translation a somewhat faulty analysis of the logic; he corrected it later in his study with A. vander Nat [180].

3 In Shī'ite seminaries, the commentary by al-'Allāma al-Ḥillī (d. 1325) on the *Tajrīd al-manṭiq* of Naṣīr al-Dīn al-Ṭūsī (d. 1274), the *Jawhar al-naḍīd fī sharḥ Kitāb al-tajrīd*, served in the role of introductory logic text.

4 I. M. Bochenski, *A History of Formal Logic*, trans. I. Thomas (Notre Dame, IN: 1961); see esp. "On the History of the History of Logic," 4–10.

5 See, e.g., K. Jacobi, "Logic: The Later Twelfth Century," in P. Dronke (ed.), *A History of Twelfth-Century Western Philosophy* (Cambridge: 1988), 227–51, at 236ff. Cf. S. Pines, "A Parallel in the East to the *Logica Vetus*," in Pines [37], 262–6, and Gutas [57].

6 Bochenski, *History*, 6–9.

7 As an example, see the introduction of the otherwise extremely valuable Jabre et al. [174], v–ix.

8 Bochenski, *History*, 152.

9 Made for example by Madkour [176], at 268–9.

10 See, e.g., Gutas [56], 246.

11 See Gutas [57].

12 Gutas [58], 61.

13 Peters [61], 7–30; cf. Lameer [175], ch. 1. See also H. Hugonnard-Roche, "Remarques sur la tradition arabe de l'*Organon* d'après le manuscrit Paris, Bibliothèque nationale, ar. 2346," in Burnett [50], 19–28; and the review of the chapter by J. Lameer, "The *Organon* of Aristotle in the Medieval Oriental and Occidental Traditions," *Journal of the American Oriental Society* 116 (1996), 90–8.

14 Gutas [93], 197–8; see the revised treatment of *ḥads* by Gutas in "Intuition and Thinking: The Evolving Structure of Avicenna's Epistemology," in Wisnovsky [104], 1–38.

15 Ibn Khaldūn, *Prolégomènes d'Ebn-Khaldoun: texte arabe,* part 3, ed. M. Quatremère (Paris: 1858), 112–13; cf. the translation by F. Rosenthal in his *The Muqaddimah of Ibn Khaldun* (London: 1958), vol. III, 142–3.

16 D. S. Margoliouth, "The Discussion between Abū Bishr Mattā and Abū Sa'īd al-Sīrāfī on the Merits of Logic and Grammar," in *Journal of the Royal Asiatic Society* (1905), 79–129 at 115–16; cf. Endress [172], 163–299.

17 Al-Fārābī, *Kitāb al-qiyās al-ṣaghīr*, in *al-Manṭiq 'inda al-Fārābī*, ed. R. al-'Ajam, vol. II, 68; cf. A. I. Sabra, review of N. Rescher's *Al-Fārābī's Short Commentary on Aristotle's Prior Analytics*, in *Journal of the American Oriental Society*, 85 (1965), 241–3, at 242a.

18 Lameer [175], chs. 6, 7, and 8.

19 *Al-Mustaṣfā min 'ilm al-uṣūl* (Cairo: 1938). I tend to think the legal use of logic was the most important factor in its acceptance, although other factors are cited (e.g., by Ibn Khaldūn) like the theological use of logic.

20 I. Goldziher, "The Attitude of Orthodox Islam toward the 'Ancient Sciences'," in M. Swartz (ed. and trans.), *Studies on Islam* (Oxford: 1981), 185–215, at 205–6.

21 W. B. Hallaq, *Ibn Taymiyya against the Greek Logicians* (Oxford: 1993), 141.

22 Cf. Bochenski, *History*, 159–62. It is worth noting that – to the best of my knowledge – there was no treatment in the Arabic manuals paralleling the treatment in the later Latin manuals of obligations and insolubles, among other things, but one could find parallel treatments of these topics outside the logic manuals.

23 Avicenna, *al-Ishārāt wa al-tanbīhāt*, ed. S. Dunya, 2nd edn. (Cairo: 1971), 374; cf. S. Inati, *Ibn Sina: Remarks and Admonitions,*

part 1: *logic* (Toronto: 1981), a somewhat problematic translation which records the Arabic pagination in the margin.

24 *Discourse on the Categorical and Hypothetical Syllogistic, with a Criticism of the Conjunctive Syllogistic of Avicenna*, in *Rasā'il falsafiyya: Maqālāt fī al-manṭiq wa al-'ilm al-ṭabī'ī li-Abī al-Walīd Ibn Rushd*, ed. J. 'Alawī (Casablanca: 1983), 187–207.

25 Black [170], 97ff.

26 A succinct statement of the problem is given in H. Lagerlund, *Modal Syllogistics in the Middle Ages* (Leiden: 2000); see ch. 1 generally, and esp. 12–14.

27 *A Criticism of Avicenna's Doctrine of the Conversion of Premises*, in 'Alawī, *Maqālāt*, 100–5, at 104–5; Averroes defends al-Fārābī's approach which had been attacked by Avicenna, though al-Fārābī came to the problem from the other direction, by considering the converse of the contingent proposition, *every human being may or may not be literate*. In fact, matters are much more complicated than I indicate in the text, because Averroes kept shifting his position on the modal syllogistic (see Elamrani-Jamal [171]; it is the last attempt by Averroes that I refer to here). For details of this extremely technical system, see now Thom [183], ch. 5.

28 Quoted in Lagerlund, *Modal Syllogistics*, 28; I have very slightly modified the translation.

29 'Alawī, *Maqālāt*, 181.

30 Avicenna, *al-Shifā', al-qiyās*, ed. S. Zayed (Cairo: 1964), 204. For the full system developed by Avicenna, see now Thom [183], ch. 4.

31 Avicenna, *al-Ishārāt*, 334–5.

32 Avicenna, *al-Shifā', al-qiyās*, 209–10; this is the attack against which Averroes defended al-Fārābī.

33 See Lameer [175], 55ff. for the reasons the term "absolute" was adopted.

34 Avicenna, *al-Ishārāt*, 264–6. *Mawṣūf* and *ṣifa* come from the same Arabic radicals as *waṣfī*, the "descriptional."

35 Al-Ṭūsī, *Sharḥ al-Ishārāt*, printed with Avicenna, *al-Ishārāt*, 312.

36 An attempt at characterizing the attitude and practice of post-Avicennian philosophers is made in Gutas [94].

37 Some suggestions for further reading: aside from the books referred to in the footnotes, the following are particularly useful. For an introductory overview that stretches to cover aspects of non-Aristotelian logic, and which is very helpful for historical context, see the entry *Mantiḳ* by R. Arnaldez in *Encyclopaedia of Islam* [16]. For a rapid historical sketch, overview of the genres of logical writing, and extensive bibliography, see Gutas [173]. For a longer historical survey, concentrating on the period 900–1300, see Street [182]. For a treatment of whether logic

in this tradition is itself a science, see the splendid Sabra [181]. For bibliographical guidance, the first port of call is Daiber [1], under "logic." For the research on the various books of the *Organon* in Arabic, see the entries on Aristotle's *Organon* in Arabic in Goulet [20]. For studies on the most central logician of those writing in Arabic, see Janssens [95]. For the technical terms used by the logicians, see now esp. the *Encyclopaedia of Arabic Terminology of Logic*, prepared by Jabre et al. [174].

CHARLES E. BUTTERWORTH

13 Ethical and political philosophy

No one within the tradition of medieval Islamic political philosophy contests the notion that human beings are political by nature. Indeed, in a now famous passage of his *Muqaddima*, Ibn Khaldūn (1332–1406) cites a corollary of that adage – namely, "human social organization is necessary" – with approval, using it to focus on what the philosophers mean by "regime" (*siyāsa*), especially "political regime."[1] As contrasted to the way the term is understood by the jurists and theologians, the philosophers understand the "political regime" to encompass

> what is incumbent upon each of the inhabitants of the social organization with respect to his soul and moral habits so that they may entirely dispense with judges. They call the social organization that obtains what is required "the virtuous city" and the rules observed with respect to that "the political regime." They are not intent upon the regime that the inhabitants of the community set down through statutes for the common interests, for this is something else. This virtuous city is rare according to them and unlikely to occur. They speak about it only as a postulate and an assumption.

Two considerations make it probable that Ibn Khaldūn is referring to al-Fārābī (870–950) here. First, al-Fārābī is cited more frequently than any other philosopher in the *Muqaddima*. Second, he was well known as the author of the *Book of the Political Regime* (*Kitāb al-siyāsa al-madaniyya*). Linking ethical training or soulcraft with the political or statecraft is the hallmark of al-Fārābī's philosophy. His prowess in directing attention to the political, in making it central to every investigation, so dominates his writing that he has long been seen as the founder of political philosophy within the medieval Islamic tradition.[2]

Indeed, setting the political above all else seems so central to al-Fārābī and those who follow his lead that it may well provide a measure by which to categorize the numerous thinkers within the medieval Arabic/Islamic philosophical tradition who have written on ethics. Al-Fārābī's two best-known predecessors, al-Kindī (d. after 870) and al-Rāzī (864–925), present an ethical teaching void of reflection on the political, while his successors – especially Avicenna (980–1037) and Averroes (1126–98) – join with him in linking ethics and politics. To defend such sweeping claims, we will examine the ethical teaching of these first two philosophers and what keeps it from being linked to a political teaching until the advent of al-Fārābī, as well as how he so persuasively manages to bring these two pursuits together, then note the way Avicenna and Averroes preserve that bond.

AL-FĀRĀBĪ'S PREDECESSORS

Al-Kindī

Al-Kindī was acclaimed "the philosopher of the Arabs"; renowned for his excursions into Greek, Persian, and Indian wisdom and for his detailed knowledge of astronomy; held to be most knowledgeable in medicine, philosophy, arithmetic, logic, and geometry; supposedly skilled as a translator and editor of Greek philosophical works; a sometime tutor and an astrologer in the courts of two caliphs; and a highly prolific author. Only a few of his works, however, have anything to do with ethics. And the teaching set forth in them is not very far-reaching.

In his *Epistle on the Number of Aristotle's Books and What is Needed to Attain Philosophy* al-Kindī speaks in passing of ethics and even of Aristotle's writings on ethics. But he does not investigate the ethical teaching set forth by Aristotle nor ethics *per se* except as a kind of appendix to metaphysics.[3] The same holds for al-Kindī's *Epistle on the Utterances of Socrates*, which consists mainly of anecdotes about the kind of ascetic moral virtue so often attributed to Socrates.[4] It is only in the *Epistle on the Device for Driving Away Sorrows* that he reflects at any length on ethics or moral virtue.[5]

In *On the Number of Aristotle's Books*, al-Kindī argues that Aristotle's philosophy offers insufficient guidance for the attainment of man's goal, human virtue. He presents Aristotle's practical teaching as depending upon a knowledge of metaphysics, yet evinces doubt as to whether such knowledge is accessible to human beings. At the same time, he characterizes the only other science that can claim to offer such knowledge, divine science, as being beyond the reach of most human beings and without practical content. Clearly, another science is needed, perhaps a human one that presupposes neither metaphysical knowledge nor divine inspiration – one on the order of the practical reasoning presented in the *Epistle on the Device for Driving Away Sorrows*.

It is very limited in scope, and the devices presented in it for driving away sorrow are of utter simplicity. Al-Kindī reasons about a human phenomenon from the perspective of things we all know and have observed or even experienced. He calls upon that experience to set forth his teaching about the nature of sorrow. Even when he urges the reader to consider the activity of the Creator (R-W X.1–15, AB 22:1–23:4) or to entertain the notion that there is a homeland beyond earthly existence (R-W XI.53–7 and XIII.17, AB 27:13–17 and 31:12), he does so on the basis of common opinion rather than on the basis of any divinely revealed texts. And the asceticism he eventually urges is grounded upon common-sense arguments about true human needs, not upon an appeal to otherworldly goals.

From the very outset, al-Kindī assigns firm limits to the treatise and, in closing, restates them. He understands his task as that of indicating arguments that will combat sorrow, indicate its flaws, and arm against its pain. Noting that anyone with a virtuous soul and just moral habits would reject being overcome by vices and seek protection against their pain and unjust dominion, implying thereby that sorrow is to be counted among the vices, al-Kindī says simply that what he has presented here is "sufficient" (R-W Prologue. 6–7 and 3–6, AB 6:7–8 and 3–7). Admitting at the end of the treatise that he has been somewhat prolix, he excuses himself on the grounds that the paths to the goal sought here are almost unlimited and insists that reaching it provides what is sufficient. That goal is identified as furnishing the admonitions to be erected firmly in the soul as a model in order to gain security from the calamities of sorrow and arrive at "the best homeland," namely, "the lasting abode and the resting place of the pious" (R-W XIII.19–21 and 16–17, AB 31:14–32:3 and 31:11–12). Fundamental to the exposition provided here is al-Kindī's exhortation to pay less attention to the things prized by fellow human beings and to concentrate on what is most important for a human life directed to something beyond sensual pleasure.

Al-Kindī begins by explaining what sorrow is, his supposition being that one cannot cure a sickness or ease a pain without knowing its cause (R-W I.1–2, AB 6:9–10). In his eyes, the answer is quite simple: "sorrow is a pain of the soul occurring from the loss of things loved or from having things sought for elude us" (R-W I.2–3, AB 6:11–12). Since it is clear that no one can acquire all the things he seeks nor avoid losing any of the things he loves, the only way to escape sorrow is to be free from these attachments. Dependent as we are upon our habits to attain happiness or avoid misery, we must school ourselves to develop the right kind of habits: ones that lead us to delight in the things we have and to be consoled about those that elude us. Thus, the cure of the soul consists in slowly ascending in the acquisition of praiseworthy habits from the minor and easily acquired to the harder and more significant, while inuring the soul to patience over things that elude it and consoling it for things lost (R-W IV.11–19, AB 12:1–10).

The argument up to this point is, nonetheless, more theoretical than it is practical. Al-Kindī has explained why people become sad and how they can avoid sorrow by changing their habits and their perspective on the world. In short, thus far he has set forth no practical device for driving away sorrow once it arises. He has not done so, because these changes are simply too radical; they demand too much of human beings. Moreover, it is far from clear that we can avoid sorrow while living as normal human beings. This, it would seem, is the point of the exhortation that closes the theoretical part of the epistle, namely, that "we ought to strive for a mitigating device to shorten the term of sorrow." The devices to follow will keep us from misery; they may even allow us happiness insofar as they help us overcome the effects of sorrow, but not escape the losses that occasion it.

Al-Kindī then enumerates ten devices, but digresses at one point to relate anecdotes and a parable as well as to reflect upon the way the Creator provides for the well-being of all creatures. The digression, especially the allegory of the ship voyage, moves the discussion to a higher level of analysis by indicating that our sorrows come from possessions. All of them, not merely the superfluous ones, threaten to harm us. Our passage through this world of destruction, says al-Kindī, is like that of people embarked upon a ship "to a goal, their own resting place, that they are intent upon" (R-W XI.1–3, AB 23:5–7).

When the ship stops so that the passengers may attend to their needs, some do so quickly and return to wide, commodious seats. Others – who also tend quickly to their needs, but pause to gaze upon the beautiful surrounding sights and enjoy the delightful aromas – return to narrower, less comfortable seats. Yet others – who tend to their needs, but collect various objects along the way – find only cramped seating and are greatly troubled by the objects they have gathered. Finally, others wander far off from the ship, so immersed in the surrounding natural beauty and the objects to be collected that they forget their present need and even the purpose of the voyage. Of these, those who hear the ship's captain call and return before it sails, find terribly uncomfortable quarters. Others wander so far away that they never hear the captain's call and, left behind, perish in horrible ways. Those who return to the ship burdened with objects suffer so, due to their tight quarters, the stench of their decaying possessions, and the effort they expend in caring for them, that most become sick and some die. Only the first two groups arrive safely, though those in the second group are somewhat ill at ease due to their more narrow seats.

Noting at the end of the allegory as at the beginning that the voyage resembles our passage through this world, al-Kindī likens the passengers who endanger themselves and others by their quest for possessions to the unjust we encounter along the way (R-W XI.48–9, AB 27:7–8).[6] Conversely, the just must be those who attend to their needs or business quickly and do not permit themselves to become burdened with acquisitions or even to be side-tracked into momentary pleasures. All the passengers are bound for their homeland, but it is not clear where that is. At one point, al-Kindī claims that we are going to "the true world" (R-W XI.48, AB 27:7) and at another that the ship is supposed to bring us to "our true homelands" (R-W XI.54, AB 27:14). There is no doubt, however, that whether the destination be one or many, it can be reached only by acquiring the habits that eschew material possessions. Beyond that, al-Kindī says nothing, nor does the rest of the epistle shed light on this issue.

The allegory emphasizes the voyage and the conduct of the passengers. As one who calls to the passengers, the captain may be compared to a prophet. Like a prophet, he calls only once. Those who do not heed the call are left to their misery, even to their perdition. Yet the content of the call is empty: it merely warns about the imminent departure of the ship. The captain offers no guidance about what to bring or leave; he merely calls. Perhaps more precision is not needed. The allegory is presented merely as a likeness of our earthly voyage.

The goal pursued in this treatise is less that of learning about our end than learning how to make our way here comfortably. Al-Kindī has already spoken about the habits we need to acquire to accomplish this goal, but thus far his advice has seemed unduly ascetic. The allegory shows that we have nearly complete freedom over the way we conduct ourselves on our voyage. How we use it determines whether we reach our goal comfortably or suffer throughout the voyage and perhaps perish. To voyage without troubling ourselves or others, we must be almost insensitive to our surroundings.

In this sense, the *Epistle on the Device for Driving Away Sorrows* confirms al-Kindī's teaching about human virtue in the *On the Number of Aristotle's Books*. As long as we know of no purpose for human existence, virtue – above all, moral virtue – must be our goal. The virtue praised here comes closest to moderation, but is also similar to courage. And in pointing to the way others commit injustice by amassing possessions, al-Kindī alerts us – albeit in a limited way – to the requisites of justice.

The primary lesson is that these kinds of virtuous habits provide comfort during our earthly voyage and preserve us so that we may eventually arrive at the true world and our homeland, wherever it may be. Apart from pointing to our lack of wisdom as a problem, the epistle tells us nothing about that most important virtue. Nor does al-Kindī make any attempt here to tell us how we can act to improve our condition and that of those around us. His teaching provides strategies for coping, especially with personal loss, and accepts the milieu in which we live as a fixed variable – that is, as something not worth trying to alter. We learn to put up with it, even to come to terms with it in such a way that we improve our own life. At best, al-Kindī offers here a muted call for citizen education – teaching others the importance of making their possessions fewer – but he sets forth no broader political teaching.[7]

Al-Rāzī

Abū Bakr al-Rāzī was mainly a physician and teacher of medicine, but he also served as a sometime advisor to various rulers and was a prolific author. Indeed, his writings included over 200 books, treatises, and pamphlets. Though his writing apparently led to a paralysis of the hand and impaired eyesight, he nonetheless continued writing with the help of secretaries and scribes.[8]

It is difficult to form an appreciation of al-Rāzī's ethical teaching because so few of his writings have come down to us and because the major source for our knowledge of what he believed is an account his arch-enemy, the Ismā'īlī missionary Abū Ḥātim al-Rāzī, presented of their different positions. Fortunately, we do have an important work al-Rāzī wrote late in his life, the *Book of the Philosophic Life*.[9] In it, seeking to justify his conduct against contradictory criticisms leveled against him by unnamed individuals he describes as "people of speculation, discernment, and attainment," he reflects on the importance of devoting oneself to philosophy and to the significance of taking Socrates as a model for such a way of life. His critics accuse al-Rāzī of turning away from the life of philosophy because he socializes with others and busies himself with acquiring money, activities shunned by the Socrates known to them, but also blame the ascetic life of Socrates for its evil practical consequences. In other words, al-Rāzī is as wrong to have turned away from Socrates as he was to have followed him in the first place.

Al-Rāzī answers these charges and provides insight into his fuller teaching without ever exploring why Socrates made his famous conversion, that is, changed from a youthful asceticism to a mature involvement in all too human activities. Even though he could present the turn as evidence that Socrates also deemed it wrong, al-Rāzī treats Socrates' asceticism as merely a zealous excess of youth (sects. 4–29, 99:14–108:12). Since Socrates abandoned it early on, he sees no need to consider whether a life so devoted to the pursuit of wisdom that it ignores all other concerns is laudable or whether the good life is the balanced one he describes as his own at the end of the treatise. Al-Rāzī refrains from blaming Socrates for his ascetic practices because they led to no dire consequences. He sees no reason to blame asceticism simply.

Still, the issue cannot be ignored, for it points to the broader question of whether the pursuit of philosophy must be so single-minded that it takes no account of the needs of men or, differently stated, whether the proper focus of philosophy is nature and the universe or human and political things. Al-Rāzī does not immediately distinguish between the two, for he identifies practicing justice, controlling the passions, and seeking knowledge as characteristic of the pursuit of philosophy and praiseworthy in Socrates' life. By emphasizing that Socrates abandoned asceticism so as to participate in activities conducive to human well-being, al-Rāzī avoids examining whether it is wrong *per se* or against nature. He judges it instead in terms of its results – in quantitative terms, rather than in qualitative ones – and deems it wrong only when following it threatens the well-being of the ascetic or of the human race. Such a tactic also allows al-Rāzī to avoid having his critics impugn him for being sated with desires just because he does not imitate Socrates' earlier asceticism.

The point is eminently sensible, but al-Rāzī weakens it by contending that however much he may fall short of Socrates' early asceticism (a position he has now made defensible), he is still philosophical if compared to non-philosophic people. He would have been on more solid ground had he acknowledged that asceticism is always a threat to the world we live in and then praised the salubrious consequences of the life of the reformed Socrates. By phrasing his defense in quantitative terms, he fails to give an adequate account of the balanced life. What al-Rāzī needed to do was show that Socrates' earlier asceticism kept him from pursuing philosophy fully insofar as it prevented him from paying attention to the questions related to human conduct.

He does not because it would take him away from his major goal: setting forth the argument that completes his depiction of the philosophic life. It in turn depends upon his full teaching, and he offers a summary of it by listing six principles, all taken from other works (sects. 9–10, 101:5–102:5). Nonetheless, he develops only two in the sequel. One, phrased almost as an imperative, asserts that pleasure is to be pursued only in a manner that brings on no greater pain (sects. 11–14, 102:6–103:13), and the other insists upon the way the divinity has provided for all creatures (sects. 15–22, 103:14–106:6).

This latter principle necessarily obliges humans not to harm other creatures. In his elaboration of this principle, al-Rāzī leads the reader to issues of political importance: the natural hierarchy between the different parts of the body and between the various species, then a presumed hierarchy among individuals within the human species. Such distinctions allow him to formulate a provisional definition of morality, something he calls the upper and lower limits (sects. 23–8, 106:7–108:3). Briefly, accepting differences in birth and habit as fixed and as necessarily leading to different pursuits of pleasure, al-Rāzī urges that one not go against justice or intellect (understood naturally and according to revelation) on the one hand nor come to personal harm or excessive indulgence in pleasure on the other. The point is that since some people can afford more ease than others, the rule must be flexible. Though he urges that less is nonetheless generally better, the disparities caused by differences in fortune provoke him to no suggestions about the need to strive for a more equitable distribution of wealth or to regulate the way it is passed on. Completely eschewing such excursions into politics and political economy, al-Rāzī notes merely that the less wealthy may have an easier time of abiding by the lower limit and that it is preferable to lean more toward that limit.

All of this is captured in what al-Rāzī calls the sum of the philosophic life, "making oneself similar to God . . . to the extent possible for a human being" (sect. 29, 108:4–12). This summary statement is extraordinarily subtle and inventive. It consists of four basic parts. Al-Rāzī begins by asserting certain qualities of the Creator. He then seeks a rule of conduct based on an analogy between the way servants seek to please their sovereigns or owners and the way we should please our Sovereign Master. Next he draws a conclusion from that analogy about the character of philosophy. And he ends with the declaration that the fuller explanation of this summary statement is to be found in his *Book of Spiritual Medicine*.[10]

The interested reader must turn to it, al-Rāzī says, because it sets forth (a) how we can rid ourselves of bad moral habits and (b) the extent to which someone aspiring to be philosophic may be concerned with gaining a livelihood, acquisition, expenditure, and seeking rulership. In other words, the definition of the philosophic life set forth here raises questions that al-Rāzī identifies there as relating to moral virtue, especially moral purification, and human affairs – economics as well as political rule. Insofar as philosophy may be defined as seeking knowledge, struggling to act justly, and being compassionate as well as kindly, it does encompass matters falling under moral virtue or ethics, household management or economics, and political rule. Allusion to the *Book of Spiritual Medicine* only underlines what has already been made clear by al-Rāzī's introduction of the two principles from his larger teaching. As he notes almost in passing, confident that the reader discerns how divine providence for all creatures warrants some serving others, it is perfectly justifiable to distinguish between human beings in terms of how essential they are to the well-being of the community.

While allowing al-Rāzī to defend himself against his nameless critics, such reflections go beyond mere exculpation to an explanation of philosophy itself (sects. 30–7, 108:13–110:15). Thus, in the concluding words of this treatise, as part of his final self-justification, he asserts that philosophy consists of two parts, knowledge and practice, and that anyone who fails to achieve both cannot be called a philosopher. His own role as a philosopher is vouchsafed: his writings testify to his knowledge, and his adherence to the upper and lower limits proves his practice (sects. 38–40, 110:16–111:7). Yet he clearly prizes knowledge more and subordinates practice, especially political practice, to it in both of these ethical writings.

AL-FĀRĀBĪ'S MORAL AND POLITICAL TEACHING

Widely referred to as "the second teacher," that is, second after Aristotle, al-Fārābī is renowned as much for his teaching as for those with whom he studied – logic with Yuḥannā ibn Ḥaylān, Arabic with Ibn al-Sarrāj, and philosophy with Abū Bishr Mattā ibn Yūnus – and his travels: he is known to have sojourned in Bukhārā, Marv, Baghdad, Damascus, and Cairo. There is also some speculation, albeit now contested, that he spent time in Byzantium. His writings, extraordinary in their breadth and deep learning, extend through all of the sciences and embrace every part of philosophy. He wrote numerous commentaries on Aristotle's logical treatises, was knowledgeable about the Stagirite's physical writings, and is credited with an extensive commentary on the *Nicomachean Ethics* that is no longer extant. In addition to writing accounts of Plato's and Aristotle's philosophy prefaced by his own adaptation of it to the challenges posed by Islam in the *Philosophy of Plato and Aristotle*, he composed a commentary on Plato's *Laws*.

Of al-Fārābī's many works that illuminate his ethical and political teaching, *Selected Aphorisms* (*Fuṣūl muntaza'a*) reveals most clearly how he looks to Plato and Aristotle, the ancients, for guidance in practical and theoretical philosophy. Indeed, in the subtitle he declares his reliance upon them and then goes on in the work itself to weave together in a most novel manner key themes from Plato's *Republic* and Aristotle's *Nicomachean Ethics*. The goal of the work, as described in the subtitle, is to set forth:

> Selected aphorisms that comprise the roots of many of the sayings of the ancients concerning that by which cities ought to be governed and made prosperous, the ways of life of their inhabitants improved, and they be led toward happiness.[11]

The emphasis here is on the partial character of the treatise: it contains selected aphorisms that encompass the foundations, principles, or grounds of several – that is, not all – of the sayings of the ancients. In the ninety-six aphorisms comprising the work (four contested aphorisms found only in the most recent and least reliable of the six manuscripts are best ignored), al-Fārābī begins with, then develops, a comparison between the health of the soul, and that of the body. Quite abruptly, he starts his exposition by defining the health of each and then explains how the health of the more important of the two – that of the soul – may be obtained and its sickness repulsed. The first word of the *Selected Aphorisms* is simply "soul," while the last is "virtue."

As he moves from "soul" to "virtue," al-Fārābī first enters upon a detailed examination of the soul, then provides an account and justification of the well-ordered political regime it needs to attain perfection. At no point does he speak of prophecy or of the prophet or legislator. He is equally silent about the philosopher and mentions "philosophy" only two times, both in the antepenultimate aphorism (94) – the same one in which he mentions, for the only time, "revelation." On the other hand, al-Fārābī speaks constantly throughout these aphorisms of the statesman (*madanī*) and of the king.

Al-Fārābī calls upon the ancients in this work to identify the political order that will achieve human happiness. The individual who succeeds in understanding how a political community can be well ordered – whether a statesman or king – will do for the citizens what the physician does for individual sick persons and will accomplish for the citizens who follow his rules what the prophet accomplishes for those who follow his. Nonetheless, to attain such an understanding, one must first be fully acquainted with the soul as well as with political life. More precisely, the virtuous political regime is the one in which the souls of all the inhabitants are as healthy as possible: "the one who cures souls is the statesman, and he is also called the king" (4).

This is why such a patently political treatise contains two long discussions of the soul – one, very similar to the *Nicomachean Ethics*, explains all the faculties of the soul except for the theoretical part of the rational faculty (6–21), while the other analyzes this theoretical part and its companion, the practical part, by discussing the intellectual virtues (33–56) – as well as an investigation of the sound and erroneous opinions with respect to the principles of being and to happiness (68–87). These three groups of aphorisms constitute a little less than two-thirds of the treatise. Void of formal structure or divisions, the treatise unfolds in such a manner that each moral discussion is preceded and followed by other groups of aphorisms that go more deeply into its political teaching. Thus, the discussion of the soul in general is preceded by a series of analogies between the soul and the body as well as between the soul and the body politic (1–5), and is followed first by a discussion devoted to domestic political economy (22–9) and then by an inquiry into the king in truth (30–2). The second discussion of the soul, preceded by these three aphorisms, is followed by an inquiry into the virtuous city (57–67). This in turn precedes the investigation of sound and erroneous opinions, itself followed by the account of the virtuous regime (88–96). Subsequent to each moral digression, the tone of the discussion seems to become more elevated, almost as though the moral teaching were the driving force for the political teaching of the treatise or were at least giving it direction.

In the analogies that open the treatise, al-Fārābī not only compares the body to the soul as though it were better known than the body, but goes further and boldly defines what constitutes the health and sickness of each. The health of the soul consists in its traits being such that it can always do what is good and fine as well as carry out noble actions, whereas its sickness is for its traits to be such that it always does what is evil and wicked as well as carry out base actions. The description of the health and sickness of the body is nearly identical to that of the soul's, with one important difference: the body is presented as doing nothing without first having been activated by the soul. Then, after the good traits of the soul have been denoted as virtues and the bad traits as vices (2), al-Fārābī abandons this analogy.

His juxtaposition of the physician to the statesman or king insofar as the first cures bodies and the second cures souls obliges al-Fārābī to move beyond the individual level. He defines the health of the body as the "equilibrium of its temperament," as distinct from the health of the city, defined as the "equilibrium of the moral habits of its people." The change thus introduced is by no means insignificant: whereas the focus of bodily health is always the individual body, so that the physician is concerned with individuals as such, the statesman or king aims at the equilibrium of the city and is concerned with the totality or at least the plurality of its inhabitants – not with each one as an individual. If the statesman or king can arrive at his ends only by establishing (or re-establishing) an equilibrium in the moral habits of all the inhabitants, so much the better for them. But al-Fārābī no longer speaks explicitly of individuals. Henceforth, he speaks more readily of the community – of the city – and rarely evokes the image of the individual soul. Here, too, he emphasizes the moral habits of the people of the city as compared to the temperament of the individual body. The effect is to underline the greater importance attaching to the statesman/king and his art than to the physician and his art. After all, it is the statesman or king who determines how the healthy body will be employed in the city. It falls not to the physician, but to the statesman or king, to prescribe what actions the healthy citizen, sound of body as well as of soul, ought to carry out.

Differently stated, another consideration that distinguishes the statesman/king from the physician is moral purpose. The physician's task is merely to heal, without asking how restored strength or improved sight will be used, whereas his counterpart must reflect upon how the benefits of the civic or kingly art will affect the persons to whom it is applied – how their souls may be healed so that they carry out actions of service to the city. In this sense, the relationship between "the art of kingship and of the city with respect to the rest of the arts in cities is that of the master builder with respect to the builders" and "the rest of the arts in cities are carried out and practiced only so as to complete by means of them the purpose of the political art and the art of kingship" (4). Because the greater complexity of this art vouchsafes its greater importance, al-Fārābī can insist that such an individual needs to be cognizant of "the traits of the soul by which a human does good things and how many they are" as well as of "the devices to settle these traits in the souls of the citizens and of the way of governing so as to preserve these traits among them so that they do not cease" (5).

Again, this manner of beginning his discussion of "the science of morals" permits al-Fārābī not only to associate it with politics, but also to subordinate the moral part of the soul to the intellectual part – in effect, the statesman/king discerns how to legislate for the city by means of the intellectual part (see 32, 34–9, 41–5, and 52–3) – and then to establish a hierarchy among the moral habits themselves. The latter belong to the appetitive part of the soul and comprise moderation, courage, liberality, and justice (8). With the exception of justice, al-Fārābī says little of these virtues. (Though justice is investigated at some length in aphorisms 61–6 and just war considered in aphorism 67, one cannot fail to notice how this enumeration of the moral virtues confuses the teaching of the ancients in that Aristotle's generosity takes the place of Plato's wisdom as one of the four cardinal virtues.)

By the end of aphorism 21, that is, by the end of the first extensive discussion of the soul, all of the moral virtues except for justice have been discussed in some detail: al-Fārābī has explained what these habits are qua balanced traits of the soul and indicated how to bring them about. (It is not completely accurate to say that justice has been totally neglected in this account, for in aphorism 26 he indicates how the statesman/king must seek the health of each part of the city with an eye to the way its health or sickness affects the whole city, just as the physician must look to the health of the whole body when treating a particular limb or organ.) As this section closes, al-Fārābī seems to restate the parallel between the physician and the statesman/king, but does so by introducing a new term: instead of talking about the statesman (*al-madanī*), he now speaks of the "governor of cities" (*mudabbir al-mudun*). The change in terminology is minor, but it permits or calls for a new inquiry, one that explains the groupings formed by human beings. As he explains in aphorism 23, the way people live – ephemeral as such matters are – influences their characters. More important than these accidental matters, however, is what cities aim at, the common goal pursued by their citizens.

Al-Fārābī's consideration of this problem leads him to make distinctions that elevate the tone of the discussion and, above all, to introduce happiness – even ultimate happiness – into the discussion for the first time. Now, then, we need to distinguish between different kinds of rulers; we need to know who truly deserves to be called a king, and that brings us to the fourth section of the treatise. Thus, when we do learn what characterizes this individual, it becomes evident that we need to understand better how he has come to discern human happiness. Differently stated, we need to learn about the intellectual virtues: wisdom and prudence.

Although it is not possible here to follow al-Fārābī step by step through the rest of the treatise, it should now be clear how he successfully fuses statecraft with soulcraft, that is, how his ethical teaching leads necessarily to his political teaching. It should also be clear that both the ethical and political teaching draws upon Plato and Aristotle, even as both adjust them ever so subtly.

AL-FĀRĀBĪ'S SUCCESSORS

Avicenna

Of all the medieval Islamic philosophers, we are best acquainted with the life of Avicenna thanks to the efforts of his devoted pupil and long-time companion, al-Juzjānī, who preserved something resembling an autobiography along with his own biographical appendix.[12] We learn from it that Avicenna was an assiduous and devoted learner from the days of his youth to his death. Nowhere is this dedication to learning more evident than in his massive encyclopedic work, *The Healing* (*al-Shifā'*).

In the first chapter of the introductory volume to its logical part, Avicenna explains the general order of the whole work. After the part on logic is another part devoted to natural science. It is followed by a third part that sets forth mathematics, and the whole compendium concludes with Avicenna's explanation of the divisions and aspects of the science pertaining to metaphysics. From this account of its scope, one might think that Avicenna's *Healing* was devoted solely to theoretical philosophy or science, that it had nothing to say about practical philosophy or science. Indeed, not until the very end of his discussion of metaphysics does he speak of the practical sciences or arts of ethics and politics. As he puts it, this "summary of the science of ethics and of politics" is placed there "until I compose a separate, comprehensive book about them."[13]

Avicenna's fuller teaching reveals, however, that ethical and political science belong after divine science intrinsically and not provisionally. Indeed, they are the human manifestation of divine science – its practical proof. They testify to divine providence for humankind and thus to the truth of revelation more clearly than any of the other sciences investigated in the *Healing*. Yet because the correctness of what they teach can also be verified by Aristotelian or pagan reasoning processes, Avicenna must elucidate the relationship he discerns between pagan philosophy and the revelation accorded the Prophet Muḥammad.

Avicenna's description of Plato's *Laws* as a treatise on prophecy provides a clue to how interrelated he deems philosophy and revelation.[14] Similarly, the attention he gives to the political aspects of prophecy and divine law in the *Healing* leads to reflection upon the most fundamental political questions: the nature of law, the purpose of political community, the need for sound moral life among the citizens, the importance of providing for divorce as well as for marriage, the conditions for just war, the considerations that lie behind penal laws, and the end of human life.[15] Avicenna's political teaching here provides an introduction to the fundamentals of political science and alerts readers to the need to think carefully about the strong affinity between the vision of political life set forth by the pagan Greek philosophers and that exceptional individual who surpasses philosophic virtue by acquiring prophetic qualities.

Averroes

Averroes was an accomplished commentator on Plato and Aristotle, physician, practicing judge, jurist, princely advisor, and spokesman for theoretical and practical problems of his day. His profound accomplishments in jurisprudence, medicine, poetry, philosophy, natural science, and theology were recognized by fellow Muslims as well as by the Jews and Christians who first translated his writings into Hebrew and Latin, but he was known above all for his commentaries on Aristotle – commentaries that range across the whole of Aristotle's corpus. He also wrote a commentary on Plato's *Republic*, this ostensibly because Aristotle's *Politics* was unknown to the Arabs. Moreover, he composed treatises on topics of more immediate concern to fellow Muslims: the *Decisive Treatise* on the relationship between philosophy and the divine law and the *Incoherence of the Incoherence*, an extensive reply to al-Ghazālī's attacks upon al-Fārābī and Avicenna.

In these works, Averroes forcefully pleads that philosophy serves religious and political well-being. It is ever the friend of religion, seeking to discover the same truth as religion and to bring the learned to respect divine revelation. Though persuaded that science and with it philosophy had been completed by Aristotle, Averroes thought philosophy still needed to be recovered and protected in each age. To these goals he addresses himself in all of his works: the commentaries on Aristotle and Plato are intended to recover or rediscover the ancient teaching and explain it to those who can profit from it, while the public writings, written to address issues of the day, seek to preserve the possibility of philosophical pursuits in an increasingly hostile religious environment.

From Averroes' *Commentary on Plato's Republic* we learn, above all, that the simply best regime is one in which the natural order among the virtues and practical arts is respected.[16] The practical arts and the moral virtues exist for the sake of the deliberative virtues, and – whatever the hierarchical relationship between the practical arts and the moral virtues – all of these exist for the sake of the theoretical virtues. Only when this natural order is reflected in the organization and administration of the regime can there be any assurance that all of the virtues and practical arts will function as they ought. In order to have sound practice, then, it is necessary to understand the principles on which such practice depends: the order and the interrelationship among the parts of the human soul. He reaches the same conclusion, albeit much more rapidly, by identifying the best regime in his *Middle Commentary on the "Rhetoric"* as the city whose opinions and actions are in accordance with what the theoretical sciences prescribe.

These principles permit Averroes to identify the flaws in the regimes he sees around him more clearly. They are faulted either because they aim at the wrong kind of end or because they fail to respect any order among the human virtues. Thus he blames democracy for the emphasis it places on the private and for its inability to order the desires of the citizens. In his *Commentary on Plato's "Republic,"* he first emphasizes the need to foster greater concern for the public sphere and to diminish the appeal of the private, then explains man's ultimate happiness in order to indicate how the desires should be properly ordered. A broad vision of the variety within the human soul and of what is needed for sound political life leads Averroes to endorse the tactics – and in some respects, the very principles – of Platonic politics.

The distinctions scholars habitually draw between Plato and Aristotle are precisely the ones al-Fārābī seems to delight in collapsing, overlooking, or simply obfuscating. Pursuing common goals and teachings, his Plato and Aristotle differ only in the paths they take toward them. Above all, they perceive ethical teaching to be first and foremost a political undertaking. From them, al-Fārābī learns that citizen virtue must be the primary concern of the lawgiver. Forming the character of citizens and helping them to achieve the highest of human goods – ultimate perfection – is the end at which, following them, he aims.

Consequently, character formation takes precedence over institutions and even kinds of rule. Determining who rules is less important than insuring that the ruler has the qualities – moral and intellectual – for rulership. And should a single person having the requisite qualities not happen to be found, rulership passes to two or more – assuming they come to have those qualities. This sums up what we learn from al-Fārābī and from those who, like Averroes as well to a certain extent as Avicenna, follow in his footsteps.

Or do we? If this is a correct conclusion to draw from what al-Fārābī has to say in the *Selected Aphorisms* and related writings, does it not conflict with what we know about his teaching in yet others? More important, does it not conflict with what Plato's Socrates has to say about the importance of a philosopher having some notion of the good if he is to rule well and with Aristotle's emphasis on contemplation immediately before calling attention to the need for laws as a means of making good citizens – the one in *Republic*, books VI and VII, the other at the end of the *Nicomachean Ethics*? Differently stated, is not sound theory the basis for sound practice?

The answer to that question separates al-Fārābī and Averroes (and, again, Avicenna to a certain extent) from al-Kindī and al-Rāzī.

Insofar as the latter two subordinate the practical to the theoretical, their ethical teaching is limited to the individual. Even though it is far from certain al-Fārābī and his erstwhile companions succeed in finding an independent ground for practice, they oblige a thoughtful reader to travel that road. In doing so, the reader flirts with becoming a lawgiver much as did Adeimantus and Glaucon under the spell of Socrates. That, in the end, is the significance of linking an ethical teaching with a political one.

NOTES

1 See Ibn Khaldūn, *Muqaddimat Ibn Khaldūn (Prolégomènes d'Ebn-Khaldoun): texte arabe, publié d'après les manuscrits de la Bibliothèque impériale*, ed. M. Quatremère (Paris: 1858; repr. Beirut: 1970), 2.126:16 and 2.127:1–6. For the citation that follows, see 2.127:6–14; the translation is my own.

2 See Mahdi [190].

3 These issues are discussed at greater length in C. E. Butterworth, "Al-Kindī and the Beginnings of Islamic Political Philosophy," in Butterworth [187], 11–60, esp. 23–6.

4 See Butterworth, "Al-Kindī and the Beginnings," 52–6. For anecdotes and sayings involving Socrates in Arabic, see I. Alon, *Socrates in Mediaeval Arabic Literature* (Leiden: 1991), and I. Alon, *Socrates Arabus* (Jerusalem: 1995).

5 There are two editions: H. Ritter and R. Walzer, *Uno scritto morale inedito di al-Kindī* (Rome: 1938), A. Badawī, *Rasā'il falsafiyya li-al-Kindī wa al-Fārābī wa Ibn Bājja wa Ibn 'Adī* (Beirut: 1980), 6–32. Textual references are to the sections and lines of the Ritter and Walzer edition (R-W) by means of Roman and Arabic numerals and to the pages and lines of Badawī's (AB) by means of Arabic numerals alone. For a recent English translation see G. Jayyusi-Lehn, "The Epistle of Ya'qūb ibn Isḥāq al-Kindī on the *Device for Dispelling Sorrows*," *British Journal of Middle Eastern Studies* 29 (2002), 121–35.

6 Both here and in the only other passage about injustice in this treatise (R-W XXXI:6, AB 6:7), at issue is the trouble undue attachment to possessions brings upon ourselves and others.

7 For a different reading of this work see further Druart [66].

8 For al-Rāzī's works, see al-Rāzī, *Rasā'il falsafiyya*, ed. P. Kraus (Cairo: 1939; repr. Beirut: 1973); see further C. E. Butterworth, "The Origins of al-Rāzī's Political Philosophy," *Interpretation* 20 (1993), 237–57; Druart [209]; M. Rashed, "Abū Bakr al-Rāzī et le *kalām*," *MIDEO* 24 (2000), 39–54; P. E. Walker, "The Political Implications of al-Rāzī's Philosophy," in Butterworth [187], 61–94.

9 See al-Rāzī, *Rasā'il falsafiyya*, 98–111 (with an introduction by Kraus on 97–8). For an English translation, see C. E. Butterworth, "Al-Rāzī: The *Book of the Philosophic Life*," *Interpretation* 20 (1993), 227–36. Section references here are to my English translation, which is based on Kraus' edition.

10 The Arabic text of the *Book of Spiritual Medicine* or *Kitāb al-ṭibb al-rūḥānī* is in al-Rāzī, *Rasā'il falsafiyya*, 15–96. Focused primarily on how to acquire moral virtue and avoid vice, the last few pages contain a summary account of the relationship between virtue and political life; see chs. 1–16, 17.14–80.9 with chs. 18–19, 85.1–92.10. In ch. 17, 80.10–84.16, al-Rāzī explains how to earn a living within the strictures of the moral teaching already set forth, while in ch. 20, 92.11–96.9, he investigates why people fear death.

11 For the Arabic text, see Abū Naṣr al-Fārābī, *Fuṣūl muntaza'a*, ed. F. M. Najjar (Beirut: 1971). An English translation may be found in Alfarabi [185], 1–67. The references here to the aphorisms follow Najjar's numbering, reproduced in the translation.

12 Of al-Fārābī's many successors, it is possible here only to focus upon Avicenna and Averroes. For Ibn Bājja and Ibn Ṭufayl, see above, chapter 8. Figures later than al-Fārābī who wrote on ethics include his student, Yaḥyā ibn 'Adī (d. 363/974), and Ibn Miskawayh (d. 421/1030), both of whom wrote works entitled *Tadhīb al-akhlāq*. See Yaḥyā ibn 'Adī, *The Reformation of Morals*, trans. S. H. Griffith (Provo: 2003), and Miskawayh, *Tadhīb al-akhlāq*, ed. C. Zurayk (Beirut: 1966). For an English version of the latter see Miskawayh, *The Refinement of Character*, trans. C. Zurayk (Beirut: 1968). See further R. Walzer, "Aspects of Miskawayh's *Tadhīb al-akhlāq*," in *Studi orientalistici in onore di Giorgio Levi della Vida*, vol. II (Rome: 1956), 603–21, repr. in Walzer [45], 220–35. On Ibn Miskawayh generally see M. Arkoun, *Contribution à l'étude de l'humanisme arabe au IVe/Xe siècle: Miskawayh, philosophe et historien* (Paris: 1970; 2nd edn. Paris: 1982).

13 See Avicenna, *Kitāb al-shifā': al-manṭiq, al-madkhal*, ed. G. Anawati, M. El-Khodeiri, and F. El-Ahwani (Cairo: 1952), 11.12–13; see also 11.1–11.

14 See Avicenna, *Fī aqsām al-'ulūm al-'aqliyya* (*On the Divisions of the Intellectual Sciences*) in *Tis' rasā'il* (*Nine Treatises*) (Cairo: 1908), 108.1–3.

15 See Avicenna, *Kitāb al-shifā': al-ilāhiyyāt*, ed. G. Anawati and S. Zayid (Cairo: 1960), bk. 10, chs. 2–5, 441.1–455.16. For an English translation, see M. Marmura, "Avicenna, *Healing*: *Metaphysics* X," in Lerner and Mahdi [189], 98–111.

16 For what follows, see Averroes [186] and also C. E. Butterworth, *Philosophy, Ethics, and Virtuous Rule: A Study of Averroes' Commentary*

on Plato's "Republic", Cairo Papers in Social Science, vol. IX, Monograph 1 (Cairo: 1986). Unfortunately, Averroes' *Middle Commentary on Aristotle's "Nicomachean Ethics"* has survived only in independent Hebrew and Latin translations; see Averroes, *Middle Commentary on Aristotle's "Nicomachean Ethics" in the Hebrew Version of Samuel Ben Judah*, ed. L. V. Berman (Jerusalem: 1999) and Averroes, *In Libros Decem Moralium Nicomachiorum Expositio*, in *Aristotelis Opera cum Averrois Commentariis* (Venice: 1552; repr. Frankfurt a. M.: 1962), vol. III. A splendid edition and French translation of the *Middle Commentary on Aristotle's Rhetoric* has just appeared; see *Averroès (Ibn Rushd), Commentaire moyen à la "Rhétorique" d'Aristote: édition critique du texte arabe et traduction française*, ed. and trans. M. Aouad, 3 vols. (Paris: 2002).

MARWAN RASHED

14 Natural philosophy

Natural philosophy, or physics, occupies an ambiguous position in the encyclopedia of ancient learning. It is primarily an ontology of the sensible world, and is thus inseparable from metaphysics. Aristotle's physical inquiries, for example, can only be understood in the light of the discussions of substance, potentiality, unity, and the Prime Mover that we find in his *Metaphysics*. But natural philosophy is not *only* an ontology of the sensible world. It does not aim solely at explaining what we might call the "semantics" of the sensible world. It also tries, in some cases, to set up "syntactic" rules that allow us to describe a given idealized category of phenomena. The contrast between ontology and mathematical physics is an example. But as we shall shortly see, the "syntax" need not be mathematical.

In classical Islam, there was a multiplicity of physical theories. We may mention, among others, the atomism of the "rational theologians" (*mutakallimūn*), Avicennian neo-Aristotelianism, Averroist "orthodox" Aristotelianism, and the infinitesimalism of some geometers. Does that mean that any effort to distinguish unitary features of a *single* natural philosophy is doomed to fail? On the contrary, although there was a multiplicity of schools, the physical debate was nonetheless focused on certain fundamental problems. This means not only that certain questions were recognized as particularly significant by all the schools, but also that the answers proposed to them proceeded from some basic intuitions that were held in common. These shared intuitions may thus be viewed as typical of the classical period, even if points of disagreement were more evident to those embroiled in the controversy. This relative coherence across disputing schools is not best understood merely by determining "who influenced whom." Rather, we should direct our attention to the intrinsic necessity, felt by many Islamic thinkers, of revisiting two fundamental (and connected) topics of Aristotelian physics: the status of the *minima* and the distinction between actuality and potentiality.

THE BEGINNINGS: THE DEBATE BETWEEN ABŪ AL-HUDHAYL AND AL-NAẒẒĀM (CA. 830 C.E.)

The beginnings of reflection on physics in Islam are obscure. We know nothing much of relevant discussions, if any, before the ʿAbbāsid period, and even our knowledge of the ninth century relies nearly exclusively on later doxographies.[1] The works of the two Basrian theologians Abū al-Hudhayl and al-Naẓẓām are no exception. But their controversy over the question of the continuum and infinity may be taken as marking the birth of a whole tradition of physics in Islam.[2]

According to the doxographers, Abū al-Hudhayl posited "atoms" or, in his terminology, "indivisible parts" (*al-ajzāʾ allatī lā tatajazzaʾ*). He took them to be:

(1) non-corporeal (rather than incorporeal)
(2) without extension
(3) indiscernible from one another.

The first criterion, unlike the other two, is terminological: indivisibles are not bodies, because they are the *constituents* of bodies. Criteria (2) and (3) are more significant. Abū al-Hudhayl has, so to speak, an "abstract" conception of the indivisibles, different from the corpuscular theories of the ancient atomists and the alchemists of his own day. Indivisible parts are not qualitatively different from one another; they do not differ even in shape. Local motion consists in the fact that a body (that is, an assemblage of indivisibles)[3] occupies one and then some other position. Indivisibles are separated by vacuum, and over any given distance the "atomic density" depends on the width of the intervals of vacuum between the indivisible parts. These parts are discrete and finite in number. We see immediately that such considerations are not intended to explain the world in the way that modern physics does: they hold only at a theoretical (ontological) level. Thus Abū al-Hudhayl never suggests that the thresholds implied by the theory (the length of the maximum possible interval with no atoms in it, the maximum number of atoms in a given length, etc.) could actually be determined, i.e., measured.

Al-Naẓẓām accepts the rejection of the Aristotelian ontology implicit in this model, but refuses its finitist bias. More precisely, he recognizes the validity of premises (1), (2)[4], and (3), but remarks that if, as (2) claims, atoms are deprived of any extension, then *a fortiori* the same must be true of the positions occupied by something moving during its transit. Therefore, the puzzle of how a motion can traverse an infinite number of points cannot be resolved by saying that there is a finite number of material points between the starting point and end point of the motion. There must be an infinite number of indivisible positions on any given stretch AB. And since nothing can move through an infinite number of positions during a finite time, we have to admit that the moving thing "leaps" over some spaces, so that the distance between A and B can be traversed in a finite number of leaps. This theory of the "leap" (*ṭafra*), for which al-Naẓẓām was famous, must not be confused with the atomic or sequential motion of Abū al-Hudhayl, which is more reminiscent of Greek theories.[5] It must be understood as a sort of perpetual miracle taking place in the sensible world. It is God who, *annihilating and recreating* the moving thing a finite number of times at different positions of its transit, allows every local motion to succeed.

This debate deeply influenced later thinkers, who accepted its major premises. The debate does not seem to reflect previous doctrines, at least not directly, though parallels have been drawn to Indian atomism,[6] with which the Basrian theologians may effectively have been partially acquainted,[7] and to the Epicurean theory of the *minima*.[8] But the differences are more striking than the similarities. Nobody before Abū al-Hudhayl had so strongly insisted on the theoretical primacy of motion as opposed to bodily composition, nor had anyone so firmly maintained the undifferentiated nature of the indivisible parts. The comparison with Epicureanism, on this question, is illuminating: the Epicureans found it necessary to distinguish an atom (the smallest possible body) and its *minima* (the smallest bodily parts) primarily in order to save their doctrine of matter. But the *mutakallimūn* tend to assimilate the two, yielding an atomism of position that is essentially dictated by their conception of local motion.

Because – or, from an Aristotelian point of view, in spite – of this emphasis on the question of motion, Basrian atomism has an obvious "geometricizing" character. While it seems improbable to suppose that Abū al-Hudhayl and al-Naẓẓām were conscious of the full implications of this aspect of their theories, it seems nevertheless certain that both authors had some knowledge of basic geometry. In particular, they were undoubtedly aware of the Euclidean definition of the point and the line. We know that Abū al-Hudhayl was acquainted with Sahl b. Hārūn,[9] who was "director" of the House of Wisdom in Baghdad and would have had expertise in geometry. It would be naive to suppose that the similarities between the indivisible parts of the Basrians and the points of the geometers are mere coincidence.

ABŪ AL-HUDHAYL'S FOLLOWERS (CA. 900–CA. 1050 C.E.)

The later *kalām* tradition confirms this close connection. Abū al-Hudhayl's school makes clear the similarities between Euclidean "punctualism" and their master's atomism. Paradoxically, though, the *mutakallimūn* of the period from the time of Abū al-Hudhayl until the contemporaries of Avicenna try to combine their geometrical atomism with a radical finitism. This gives rise to certain difficulties for moderns who are trying to understand *kalām* atomism.

Around 900 C.E., there were two major schools of Mu'tazilite *kalām* (the "Basrians" and the "Baghdadians"), going back ultimately to Abū al-Hudhayl. The apogee of Basrian scholasticism is represented by Abū 'Alī al-Jubbā'ī (d. 915–16 C.E.) and his son Abū Hāshim al-Jubbā'ī (d. 933) – both of them first-class metaphysicians – whereas the leading personality of the Baghdadian school is Abū al-Qāsim al-Balkhī (d. 931). In spite of many points of dispute between the schools, they basically accept Abū al-Hudhayl's atomism.[10] Even more interestingly, his geometrical intuition is explicitly recognized and vindicated: we know from later reports in the *Tadhkira* of the *mutakallim* Ibn Mattawayh (d. 1076–7) that Abū al-Qāsim and Abū Hāshim both assimilated the indivisible parts to Euclidean points.

Of the two mathematical references attributed to Abū al-Qāsim al-Balkhī by Ibn Mattawayh, the first is a negative refutation of an opponent's position, while the other provides positive grounds for his own view. This is probably not fortuitous, but expresses the master's careful dialectical strategy. Against his opponents who believe that space and bodies are continua, that is, infinitely divisible, Abū al-Qāsim presents first an argument regarding the cornicular angle: that is, the angle between a circle and its tangent line.

It is possible that there be an angle narrower than anything, so narrow that it is impossible to draw two straight lines out of it. According to them [sc. Abū al-Qāsim and the other atomists], this must invite us to postulate indivisible parts, because otherwise all angles would have the same property of allowing us to draw straight lines out of them.[11]

It is probable that Abū al-Qāsim, even before suggesting an analogy with what the indivisibles *are*, is criticizing his continuist adversaries' use of the lemma of Archimedes (every magnitude, multiplied a certain number of times, will be greater than every homogeneous magnitude).[12] The point of contention is therefore the question of *homogeneity*. The atomists believe that any two magnitudes are homogeneous: every magnitude is a multiple of the smallest possible magnitude, the minimum. They believe that the case of the cornicular angle points to the existence of this smallest magnitude: any rectilinear angle (an angle between two straight lines), no matter how small, will have a *smaller* cornicular angle inside it. This cornicular angle (from within which no rectilinear angle can be drawn) has a magnitude smaller than that of any rectilinear angle. Thus, on the assumption that all magnitudes are homogeneous, this cornicular angle will be a sort of "minimal part" of any rectilinear angle. The fact that both types of angle are drawn in the unitary domain of *surfaces* makes this assumption not implausible: any two angles drawn on the same surface ought to be homogeneous. The continuists, by contrast, hold that a cornicular angle is not homogeneous to a rectilinear angle, but only to other cornicular angles. Avicenna provides a similar refutation in the *Mubāḥathāt*, insisting on the divisibility of the cornicular angle into smaller cornicular angles.[13]

Arguing positively, Abū al-Qāsim cites the Euclidean definition of the point:

Euclid has mentioned in his book that a point has no part and that the distance from the circle's center to its circumference is the same in every direction. But if the part were divisible, there would be an infinite number of distances.[14]

For the first time in the long history of atomism, an atomist appeals to the Euclidean definition of the point as his authority.[15] This means not only that corpuscularism, as we have seen, is more or less abandoned in favor of an atomism of position, but also that a new articulation of "physics" and geometry comes to the fore. For mathematical realities are no longer *secondary* qualities of the sensible, that is, properties of the sensible objects only insofar as they are grasped through imaginative abstraction.[16] Now, they become directly constitutive of the sensible world. The geometrical point and the indivisible part are not merely analogous: they are identical. The indivisible is a point that belongs not to an already abstracted "extension," but to matter itself. From an Aristotelian point of view, the paradox is that only our imaginative faculty enables us to grasp this basic constituent of matter. Without entering into details, it is worth noting that such a doctrine entails a re-evaluation of the epistemic status of imagination, which, far from being tied only to *abstracta*, becomes our primary access to *reality*. Arabic Peripatetics thus persistently criticized what they saw as the excessive role that imagination played in the ontology of the *mutakallimūn*.[17]

A third passage, less explicit but in a sense even more interesting, appears in the same chapter of Ibn Mattawayh. Surprisingly – and we shall very shortly indicate the polemical charge of the unusual interpretation – the author mentions Aristotle himself as a defender of the indivisibles:

> Aristotle has mentioned in his treatise *On the Heavens and the World* that the line can be divided in length but not in width, that surface can be divided in both directions and that the body can be divided in three directions. It has also been said that according to him and others, the line has only one dimension, the surface two, and the body three.[18]

Ibn Mattawayh alludes here to the first chapter of Aristotle's *De Caelo* (I.1, 268a7–8 = *al-Samā' wa al-'ālam*, ed. Badawī 126.1–3): "magnitude divisible in one direction is a line, in two directions a surface, in three directions a body." It cannot have escaped the author whose argument Ibn Mattawayh is reporting that Aristotle, in the lines immediately preceding, in fact asserted the infinite divisibility of every magnitude (*De Caelo*, I.1, 268a6–7 = Badawī 125.9–126.1): "the continuous may be defined as that which is divisible into parts that are themselves divisible to infinity, body as that which is divisible in all ways." It is probable then that Ibn Mattawayh's source tries to take Aristotle at his own word: if we can distinguish the line from the surface, it is because the "second dimension" (the "width") of the line is a *minimum*. It is not to be thought of as equivalent to some extended division of a line perpendicular to the line we have. But if, on the other hand, this second dimension, which admittedly is minimal, did not exist at all, it would be impossible to speak of the very existence of the line:

> Thus Abū Hāṣhim has said that that agrees with what we say about the [indivisible] part because otherwise, if we did not stop at a limit, it would be necessary for the line and the surface to be like the body: they would have dimensions [divisible] without end, and we could not distinguish [lines, surfaces and bodies] from one another.[19]

Since Abū Hāshim dedicated an entire volume to a critical examination (*taṣaffuḥ*) of the *De Caelo*, and since this book is quoted twice in the *Tadhkira* of Ibn Mattawayh, Aristotle's quotation and the remark of Abū Hāshim probably go back to this treatise.[20] Abū Hāshim has polemically combined two of Aristotle's remarks, the first one postulating the infinite division of magnitudes, the other the unidimensionality of the line. If the line is really unidimensional, it is because there are, "in the heavens and the world" as well as in Euclidean geometry, some minimal entities. Let us note in passing that the "Euclidean" overtones of *De Caelo*, I.1 have struck modern Aristotle scholars as well.[21]

AL-NAẒẒĀM AND THĀBIT IBN QURRA

We have just seen that Abū al-Hudhayl's successors clarified and made more explicit the geometricizing intuition present in his atomism. By contrast, except for some pupils about whom we know practically nothing,[22] al-Naẓẓām does not seem to have had a wide posterity. That is not to say that his ideas about infinity were not an important legacy to natural philosophy. I show elsewhere that his theory of the "leap" as a solution to the puzzle of actual infinity was known to Leibniz and reformulated by him in the light of infinitesimal calculus. Leibniz uses the term "transcreation" (*transcreatio*) to describe God's recreation of a moving thing at each new position, and attributes a similar idea to some *theologi*, which may be an allusion to the *mutakallimūn*.[23]

In the Islamic world, al-Naẓẓām's doctrine of the "leap" was frequently criticized by philosophers and theologians, but it undoubtedly encouraged them to distance themselves from a purely Aristotelian conception of the distinction between potentiality and actuality. In particular, we shall see below how Avicenna tries to introduce more actuality into the traditional conception of the infinite. Al-Naẓẓām's infinitism was soon aided by the ideas of infinitesimalist mathematicians, especially Thābit ibn Qurra (d. 288/901). Thābit was responsible for a decisive event in the history of physics: the conscious combination of a "philosophical" and a "mathematical" theory of actual infinity. Thābit wrote an entire treatise to establish the validity of actual infinity, but, unlike al-Naẓẓām and Leibniz, he never appeals to God in order to explain motion from A to B.

A fragment, quoted by Avicenna, can help us to compare Thābit's doctrine of local motion to al-Naẓẓām's.[24] According to the latter, the soul, which is a "subtle" (*laṭīf*) body, "leaps" toward its origin at the moment of death.[25] Some transmigrationist disciples of al-Naẓẓām extended the model, probably claiming that, since the soul cannot go through the infinite number of points existing between two bodies A and B, it is obliged to leap over the space between them.[26] Thābit, whose treatise on actual infinity begins with an allusion to the problem of the soul's transmigration,[27] explains that when the soul leaves the body to rejoin the astral element, it needs a "subtle body" (*jism laṭīf*) to inhabit during its transit (soul being the form of the body). This doctrine must be understood in its philosophical context, against the background of an important passage of Alexander's lost commentary on Aristotle's *Physics*.[28] Alexander alludes here to some Platonists who have introduced a doctrine of the soul's vehicle (*ochêma*) to explain the motion of something without parts. But Thābit's argument is different. The difficulty, according to him, is not in supposing that something without parts (a point) can move, but that the form of a body can persist in the absence of body. In this departure from al-Naẓẓām and from the philosophical tradition, Thābit's own conception of motion stands out clearly: the mobile that is a point (here, the soul) goes through an actually infinite number of positions in a finite time.

This fragment is the only allusion to non-heavenly motion that the tradition has recorded from Thābit. But it of course has consequences beyond the particular case of the *soul*'s motion. It must be understood in the context of the development of mathematical theories of motion, attested by numerous sources: astral motion in the works of Thābit and al-Bīrūnī,[29] the motion of light in a short treatise of al-Qūhī,[30] the motion of objects in free fall in the *Optics* of Ibn al-Haytham,[31] etc. All these discussions share an implicit rejection of the Aristotelian conception of "extended" motion, in favor of the idea of motion and/or velocity *at an instant*.[32] Natural philosophers could not remain indifferent to this new mathematical approach to physical reality, as we shall now see.

AVICENNA'S DYNAMICS

Avicenna's dynamics are in part an attempt to reassess and reformulate the Aristotelian distinction between the sublunar and supralunar world: the world we live in and the world of the heavens. Avicenna's success in this project depended on an original articulation of dynamics and kinematics that, given its deep influence on generations of Islamic and Latin scholars, may be considered as the single most important authority of preclassical physics.[33] Let us try to understand better the historical significance of his position. I shall argue:

(1) that the central problem of Avicenna's Aristotelian physics is a distinction between different types of *impetus*;[34]
(2) that a coherent doctrine of rectilinear (sublunar) impetus must admit some sort of actual infinity, and that as a consequence Avicenna reformulated the Aristotelian discussion of infinity found in book III of the *Physics*.

The controversy over the "law" of motion

In order to explain Avicenna's position in its context, we have first to say a word about the debate, initiated by Philoponus, over the Aristotelian "law" of motion. Combining some arguments in Aristotle (*Physics*, IV.8, VII.5, and *De Caelo*, I.6 in particular) – which originally have very different purposes[35] – Philoponus and his followers constructed an Aristotelian "law" of motion. It expresses mean speed (S) as a function of force (F, which is weight in the case of free fall) and the resistance of the medium (R):

$$S = F/R.$$

For ontological and empirical reasons, many physicists of antiquity and the Middle Ages reformulated the relation of the force and the resistance. Philoponus, in particular, replaces this "law" he attributes to Aristotle with another one, which does not divide the force by the resistance but postulates that the time t required for an object to fall a certain distance through a medium will be inversely proportional to its weight (W), plus a certain time (x):

$$t = 1/W + x.$$

It is only in the determination of x that the density of the medium plays a role. Thus, the mean speed of a free fall is directly proportional to the weight of the body, but is also partially influenced by the density of the medium.

Philoponus was not the only one who tried to reformulate the Aristotelian "law." Another attempt, surely known to Avicenna, was that made by some *mutakallimūn*. We learn from Ibn Mattawayh that according to Abū Hāshim's followers, any two bodies (they use the example of a feather and a stone) would fall in a void with exactly the same speed.[36] This conclusion results from an ontological consideration (since, as we have seen, the indivisibles are perfectly identical to one another, the *impetus* of each atom must be identical) and a physical observation (some bodies around us fall more quickly than others). It follows that two indivisible parts in free fall, separated from one another, fall with the same speed. Now suppose they are joined through the accident of "composition" (*ta'līf*). The cause of the fall of each atom considered separately (that is, its "weight") is the same. The difference in speed must then be explained by the fact that the body of lesser atomic density does not cut through the medium with the same force as the body of higher atomic density. Hence, we obtain the following law, which anticipates the results of Benedetti and the young Galileo:

$$S = c(W - R)/W,$$

where c is a constant, S the speed, W the weight of the body, and R the resistance of the medium. In a void (where $R = 0$), $S = c$, whatever the value of W, yielding the above-mentioned result that any two bodies fall through a void at equal speed, whatever their weight. It should also be noted that both the weight and the resistance are here conceived of as "impetus" (*i'timād*).

Impetus (mayl)

Avicenna has very precise reasons for rejecting Philoponus' reading of Aristotle:[37] it neglects a fundamental difference between supralunar and sublunar motion. Astral motion always displays the same speed, whereas motion below the heavens is subject to acceleration and deceleration. But what all the "laws" so far proposed take into account is at best the mean velocity of the body, and may describe nothing more than a body's "abstract" aptitude to move through a medium. None accounts for acceleration.

But in the sublunar world, one has to distinguish sharply between the "general" impulsion of a given body towards its natural place (*mayl*-1), and the "concrete" impulsion of this body at a certain instant (*mayl*-2). The contrast is between a stone's invariant tendency to move downward (*mayl*-1) and its actual acceleration downward at a given instant (*mayl*-2), which is the *realization* of natural acceleration. This realization makes it impossible to consider the different moments of the motion as pure potentialities, like the points of a line drawn on a sheet of paper. There are only two options: either we adopt a sequential conception of motion, or we come to terms with actual infinity.

By the time of Avicenna, the first solution had been put forward by the *mutakallimūn*. According to them, if we throw a body vertically, on its way up it might have an impetus (*i'timād*)[38] of intensity 1,000, for example, at the first instant t_0, 900 at the next instant t_1, 800 at t_2, and so on. It will fall back down when the quantity of *i'timād* towards the top imposed by the thrower no longer suffices to counterbalance its natural *i'timād* toward the bottom.[39] Furthermore, these discrete unities of dynamic motion will be separated by minute (and, of course, imperceptible) instants of rest. This last point is sharply criticized by Avicenna in the *Physics* of the *Shifā'*:

According to them [sc. the *mutakallimūn*], it is not impossible that a motion cease, be followed by a rest, and that a motion then be generated again by the *i'timād*. This is most absurd.[40]

Thus, according to Avicenna, a free-fall motion must display perfect kinetic continuity *and* a principle of distinction for each point of its trajectory. Because these points are infinite, and the principle of distinction will be a certain actuality, it now becomes necessary to reconsider the question of actual infinity.

The question of actual infinity

Avicenna has paid much attention to the question of the infinite. Even though he followed Aristotle in maintaining the basic distinction between potential and actual infinity, he refined this distinction by introducing two subcategories. This allowed him to come to terms with contemporary developments in the exact sciences and theology. According to the *locus classicus* on this issue in Aristotle's *Physics* (III.5, 206b12–14), the potential infinite includes the infinite by division (dichotomy) and by addition (counting), whereas the actual infinite is reduced to the special case of past years and events:

Potential infinite	**Actual infinite**
By addition, by division	Recurrent events *a parte ante*

This sort of actual infinity can be allowed, because even though an infinity of years or events may have passed, there is no infinite set of things all present together. In a sense, such an actual infinite is still at least partially potential. But a problem arises once we admit the personal immortality of the soul: the souls of all individual humans that have lived in the past still exist now, and on the assumption that the world is eternal, they form an infinite set of substances. Christian and Muslim Aristotelians must now get to grips with a real actual infinity.

This is one reason, though surely not the whole reason, for Avicenna's introduction of a subtle distinction between two types of infinite sets. Sets of the first type include in themselves their own rule of construction, their "order" (*tartīb*). They are infinitely *extendable* i.e., potentially, but not actually, infinite (e.g., someone counting up through the integers, and never of course reaching infinity). Of the second type are sets with no internal rule of construction. These can be actually infinite.[41] The set of the past souls at any time *t* is an infinite set of this second type. Potential infinity, as it were, becomes tied to an intellectual operation (counting, constructing a geometrical figure, etc.), whereas actual infinity may exist even in the absence of any mind that could think discursively through an infinite order.

Avicenna revisits Aristotle's discussion of infinity not only by upholding the existence of a "strong" actual infinity, but also by showing that a certain type of potential infinity is much closer to actual infinity than orthodox Peripatetics were willing to claim. The decisive step consists in describing sublunar dynamic motion in terms of a potential infinity that has much in common with actual infinity. It is the idea of a *dynamic moment* that allows Avicenna to do this. For every sublunar natural motion, there is an infinity of dynamic states "in actuality." These states are not purely potential, since, unlike the points of a line, they have a principle of distinction (each has a *mayl*-2). But their infinity is not entirely actual, since they are not all present at the same time. Although Avicenna nowhere presents a table such as the following, it may represent adequately the distinctions he introduces in the Aristotelian classification:

"strong" potential infinite	**"weak" actual infinite**
By addition, by division	Recurrent events *a parte ante*
"weak" potential infinite	**"strong" actual infinite**
Sublunar dynamic motion	Souls of past men

It is in his *Glosses* (*Ta'līqāt*) that Avicenna sets out in detail the distinction between sublunar and supralunar motion. In order to do so, he must explain how the *mayl*-2, which is characteristic of sublunar motion, is something *real*:

The cause of the alteration (*al-istiḥāla*) that supervenes on natural bodies endowed with force consists in the places and the positions, insofar as rectilinear motion is produced by nature and the mobile is not in its natural state. And the cause of the renewal [reading *tajaddud* for *taḥaddud*] and repetition of its movements, as well as the cause of the alteration (which tends to the destruction of one force and to the renewal of one another) of its nature, is the existence of "wheres" and actually determined positions (*wujūdu uyūnin wa awḍā'in mutaḥaddidatin bi-al-fi'l*), from the beginning of the movement until it comes to a rest. For nature does not cease, at every instant (*fī kulli ānin*), to be in a new state, different from the previous one. And what makes these to be *states* are the changing *mayls* (*wa hādhihi aḥwālun li-al-muyūli al-mutabaddila*). This case is similar to the alteration of this or that quality, e.g., an extraneous temperature of the water, which does not cease, at every instant, to be altered – increased or diminished – until the water returns to its natural state. The renewed cause of this process is the existence of "wheres" and positions actually determined.[42]

Four points must be emphasized regarding this passage.

(a) The repeated use Avicenna makes of the terms "renewal" (*tajaddud, tajaddada*) and "state" (*ḥāl*) allows us to understand in all its complexity his position relative to contemporary *kalām*, and to the school of Abū Hāshim in particular. With the latter's disciples, Avicenna holds that there is a renewal of the movement at every instant, and that the moving thing, at every instant, is in a different *state*. This state is characterized by a position (Avicenna's *waḍ'* corresponds to the *ḥayyiz* of the *mutakallimūn*) and produced by an impulsion (Avicenna's *mayl*, the *i'timād* of the *mutakallimūn*). These similarities underline the fundamental difference between the two systems: their interpretation of continuity. Whereas between any two Avicennian positions, there exists always a third one (and so on *ad infinitum*), Abū Hāshim and his disciples theoretically maintain a series of discrete positions, even if they take great care not to determine these atomic thresholds quantitatively. Avicenna is quite skeptical about the discontinuity and finitism of the *kalām* theory, but does not seem to reject its notion of *tawallud* ("engendering"), to which his *tajaddud* appears roughly equivalent. One may thus interpret Avicenna's doctrine as a continuist reformulation of the dynamical principles of Abū Hāshim.

(b) This implies that Avicenna distances himself from Aristotle's conception of potential continuity, since every point of the trajectory has a *principle of distinction* dictated by its *mayl*. At a terminological level, this tension is conveyed by the word "alteration" (*istiḥāla*), which Avicenna employs in order to describe the variations of the movement's intensity.

We know that in Arabic Peripateticism, this word is the translation of the Greek *alloiôsis*, change in the category of quality (*poiotês*). This apparent misuse reflects the fact that Avicenna does not find at his disposal, in the Aristotelian terminology, a word perfectly suited to the reality he wishes to describe. The term "alteration" is no longer confined to the transition from a (qualitative) beginning to a (qualitative) end, but can also refer to the instantaneous variability of the movement itself.

(c) Avicenna consciously remains just shy of accepting an actual infinity. He says twice that the successive positions of the mobile are *actually* (*bi-al-fi'l*), not just potentially, determined. Since he obviously accepts that the points, and therefore the positions, on any stretch AB are not finite in number, he must conclude that all the elements of a non-finite set are actually determined. Interestingly, however, Avicenna does not say that they are *actually infinite*. For all the trajectory's states are not realized *together* (*ma'an*).[43]

(d) This passage from the *Ta'līqāt* permits us finally to understand Avicenna's general theory of motion, as it appears in particular in the *Physics* of the *Shifā'* (bk. II, ch. 1).[44] Avicenna stresses there that we can mean two things when we speak of "motion": motion as a trajectory, which pertains to our imaginative faculty and is conceived of only as linking a starting point to an end; and motion as an intermediary state, which must be attributed to each moment of the trajectory. Motion in the second sense characterizes an infinitesimal moment, and nothing else. The present text of the *Ta'līqāt* is the only passage where Avicenna draws such a strong connection between the *mayl*-2 and this second sense of "movement." The *mayl* represents the principle of distinction of each position of the trajectory. Each substance spatially or qualitatively removed from its natural state (e.g., a stone thrown up away from its natural resting place) returns to it, passing through *all* intermediary states. Each of these intermediary states, because it is not the end point of the process, produces a new *mayl*, which adds itself to the impulsion produced by the others. Every moment is thus characterized by its own kinetic intensity.[45]

Avicenna can thus explain the fundamental difference between sublunar and supralunar motion. Unlike the trajectory of the four sublunar elements, the trajectory of a heavenly body has no real principle of distinction for its positions; the principle of distinction exists only in the imaginative faculty of the celestial substance. In other words, Avicenna accepts in this case an interpretation of continuity akin to that of Aristotle, where the potentiality (*dunamis*) is hardly to be distinguished from a purely imaginative existence (cf. *Physics*, VIII.8): "the reason for the alteration of the celestial body is not its positions but its imagination and its renewed volition, one imaginative act after the other."[46]

Avicenna thus seems to stand at the crossroads of two traditions. With the mathematicians, he recognizes that every one of the infinite points on a spatial interval AB, without perhaps being perfectly real, is however notionally and qualitatively distinct from every other point. But with the *mutakallimūn*, he sees in a dynamic of impetus the efficient principle of such a distinction. Thus, starting from a classificatory project of the different types of impetus, Avicenna arrives at a complex – because partially "ontological" – doctrine of instantaneous motion. This combination of the kinematics of the geometers and the dynamics of *mutakallimūn* deeply influenced Avicenna's successors in the East and the West. It is probably Avicenna's main achievement in natural philosophy that after him, for every lucid reader, the discussion of motion must focus on what happens at an infinitesimal level.

POST-AVICENNIAN *KALĀM*: AN OVERVIEW

We have already seen that the great *mutakallimūn* of the tenth century did not hesitate to appeal to the authority of Euclid in defense of their atomism. But because of the finitist principles of their ontology, they limited themselves to assimilating their indivisibles to the points of the geometers. After Avicenna, and probably under the influence of his doctrine of continuity and the infinite, the *mutakallimūn* seem ever more eager to extend their appeal to geometry from the model of the point to that of the line. This shift is made possible only by concentrating, even more than previously, on the question of motion, and above all by putting tacitly aside the finitist considerations that were characteristic of the school of Abū al-Hudhayl.[47] The modern historian is struck by the impression that thinkers after Avicenna, apart from rather verbal polemics on some refined – and sometimes extremely interesting – points, share a more or less common doctrine of motion as a realized set of punctual moments. But whereas orthodox Avicennians insist that the moments of the trajectory belong to a *continuum*, the *mutakallimūn* stress that each kinetic point is *totally and perfectly realized*. What makes the discussion somewhat scholastic is that the latter more than ever avoid emphasizing the finite character of this set of points, while the former, as we have seen, refrain from admitting clearly that what we have here is nothing other than a pure actual infinity. They seem rather to consider sublunar motion as a false potential infinity, or, so to speak, a virtual actual infinity.

By far the most interesting discussion on these topics appears in the sixth book of the *Maṭālib al-ʿāliyya* of Fakhr al-Dīn al-Rāzī (d. 1210). He dedicates lengthy chapters to the opposition between continuism and atomism, and carefully and honestly presents the "geometrical proofs" that each doctrine uses as support. Two aspects of al-Rāzī's approach are striking. First, he is dealing with the foundations of geometry, since the discussion of atomism leads him to discuss such questions as the generation of geometrical objects through motion and the fifth Postulate (in both cases, al-Rāzī levels criticisms at the mathematicians). Second, atomism is no longer simply opposed to geometry,[48] but is taken to be confirmed by at least some geometrical postulates.

It is impossible to summarize here the numerous arguments and counterarguments presented by al-Rāzī. Very broadly, we can distinguish two main intuitions in the argumentation of the atomists. First, they rely on the generation of simple geometrical figures by motion, in particular the generation of the line by the motion of a point. A line perpendicular to a surface, moved in a direction parallel to this surface, will trace a line on the surface. This shows that at every instant, the line is in contact with the surface in one distinct indivisible. Second, they appeal to tangent lines. A line can be in contact with a circle at one single point only if indivisible parts do exist. It is worth noting that these reflections are permitted by the re-evaluation of the epistemic status of the imagination, which as mentioned above is typical of classical *kalām*.

On the other side, the continuists appeal again and again to the incommensurability of the side and the diagonal of the square. If both the side and diagonal contain a finite number of indivisibles – let us say p and q respectively – then the ratio p/q ought to be a rational number. But of course, this is not the case. The only escape for the adversary would be to postulate that there is vacuum between the indivisible parts – which is, mathematically speaking, no escape at all. The rhetoric of these polemics aside, we have already alluded to the fact that the positive argument of the atomists tacitly renounces the traditional finitism of atomism. The "indivisible parts" of the late *mutakallimūn* become more and more akin to "positions" in an Avicennian sense. We ought however to realize that in taking this physical turn, the *mutakallimūn* are simply bringing out a latent aspect of classical (pre-Avicennian) *kalām*, to which Avicenna too had been sensible.

This suffices in any case to show that from the eleventh century C.E. onward, all parties recognize the validity, in sublunar physics, of a theory of infinitesimal positions characterized by dynamic moments. It is probable that these decisive transformations of the Aristotelian doctrine of continuity, and the positing of a new relationship between imagination and reality that made these transformations possible, deeply influenced Latin preclassical physics[49] and European scholars of the sixteenth and seventeenth centuries.

NOTES

1 The exceptions are extremely rare. One thinks of al-Jāḥiẓ, partially transmitted because of his literary skill, and of al-Kindī's philosophical treatises, preserved in *one* Istanbul manuscript.

2 On what follows, see also Rashed [199].

3 The *mutakallimūn* intensely debated the nature of the relation of the minimal body to its indivisibles. See, e.g., Al-Ash'arī, *Maqālāt al-islamiyyīn*, ed. H. Ritter, 3rd edn. (Wiesbaden: 1980), 302.16–306.13; Ibn Mattawayh, *Al-Tadhkira fī aḥkām al-jawāhir wa al-a'rāḍ*, ed. S. N. Luṭf and F. B. 'Un (Cairo: 1975), 47–8, 193.7ff.

4 It is true that al-Naẓẓām objects to Abū al-Hudhayl that parts without extension cannot produce an extended body (see Ibn Mattawayh, *Tadhkira*, 189.4–5). This is not, however, meant to prove that there are no indivisible parts at all, but only that Abū al-Hudhayl has not carried his atomism of motion as far as he could have done. Otherwise, he

would have realized that atomism is properly a theory about motion, or kinetics, and not about "chemical" composition. Briefly put, al-Naẓẓām recognizes the existence of unextended indivisibles, but denies that they play any role in the *constitution* of bodies. They are rather to be understood as *positions*.

5 See D. Furley, *Two Studies in the Greek Atomists* (Princeton: 1967), 117ff.

6 See S. Dasgupta, *A History of Indian Philosophy*, 4 vols. (Cambridge: 1922), vol. I, 326–30; S. Radhakrishnan and C. H. Moore, *A Sourcebook in Indian Philosophy* (Princeton: 1957), 412. Cf. S. Pines, *Beiträge zur islamischen Atomenlehre* (Berlin: 1936), 112–23; for English translation see Pines [198].

7 See M. Aouad and M. Rashed, "L'exégèse de la *Rhétorique* d'Aristote: recherches sur quelques commentateurs grecs, arabes et byzantins, 1ère partie," *Medioevo* 23 (1997), 43–189, at 89–91.

8 See Dhanani [193], 106.

9 See al-Sharīf al-Murtaḍā, *Amālī al-Murtaḍā: Ghurar al-fawā'id wa durar al-qalā'id*, ed. M. A. Ibrāhīm, 2 vols. (Cairo: 1998), vol. I, 182.1ff.

10 There are however some very interesting transformations, in particular concerning atomic motion and the continuity of time.

11 Ibn Mattawayh, *Tadhkira*, 162.8–11.

12 Cf. Euclid, *Elements*, V, def. 4.

13 Ibn Sīnā [Avicenna], *al-Mubāḥathāt*, ed. M. Bīdārfar (Qom: 1413 A.H./1992 C.E.), 363–4, §1136.

14 Ibn Mattawayh, *Tadhkira*, 162.12–14.

15 Euclid, *Elements*, I, def. 1.

16 See in particular W. Detel, *Aristoteles: "Analytica Posteriora"* (Berlin: 1993), 189–232.

17 For a good synthesis of the traditional arguments against the use of imagination by the *mutakallimūn*, see the "warning" (*tanbīh*) in Ibn Maymūn, *Dalāla al-ḥā'irīn*, ed. H. Atay (Ankara: 1974), 209.21–211.25.

18 Ibn Mattawayh, *Tadhkira*, 163.1–4.

19 Ibn Mattawayh, *Tadhkira*, 163.5–8.

20 A list of the preserved fragments is to be found in D. Gimaret, "Matériaux pour une bibliographie des Gubbā'ī," *Journal asiatique* 264 (1976), 277–332, at 312. To this can be added al-Bīrūnī, *Taḥdīd nihāyat al-Amākin li-taṣḥīḥ masāfāt al-masākin*, ed. V. Bulgakov and I. Aḥmad, 2 vols. (Cairo: 1964), 185–6.

21 See the discussion (with further literature) in C. Wildberg, *John Philoponus' Criticism of Aristotle's Theory of Aether* (Berlin: 1988), 28–37.

22 See van Ess [44], vol. III, 418–45 and below.

23 See G. W. Leibniz, *Pacidius Philalethi*, Academy Edition, 6th ser., vol. III (Berlin: 1980), 528–71, at 568.1–3: "Hinc mirifice confirmatur quod praeclare olim a Theologis dictum est conservationem esse perpetuam creationem, huic enim sententiae affine est quod a te [sc. Leibniz] demonstratur mutationem omnem quandam esse transcreationem." We learn from other documents that Leibniz was deeply interested in the theories of the *mutakallimūn*. I present and investigate the relevant material in my French translation of the *Pacidius Philalethi*, to appear in 2004.

24 See Avicenna, *Risālat al-adḥawiyya fī al-ma'ād*, ed. and Italian trans. in Avicenna, *Epistola sulla vita futura*, ed. F. Lucchetta (Padua: 1969), 114–15.

25 Cf. al-Jāḥiẓ, *Kitāb al-ḥayawān*, ed. A.S.M. Harun, 7 vols. (Cairo: 1938–45), vol. V, 113.8ff.

26 See van Ess [44], vol. III, 428–45 and vol. VI, 76–8.

27 See Thābit ibn Qurra, *Answers to the Questions of Ibn Ussayyid*, in A. Sabra, "Thābit ibn Qurra on the Infinite and Other Puzzles," *Zeitschrift für Geschichte der arabisch-islamischen Wissenschaften* 11 (1997), 1–33.

28 See M. Rashed, "A 'New' Text of Alexander on the Soul's Motion," in *Aristotle and After*, ed. R. Sorabji (London: 1997), 181–95.

29 See R. Morelon, *Thābit ibn Qurra: Œuvres d'astronomie* (Paris: 1987), LXXVIII–LXXIX.

30 See Rashed [201], 9–14.

31 See M. Naẓīf, "Ārā' al-falāsifati al-islamiyyīn fī al-ḥaraka wa musāhamatuhum fī al-tamḥīd ilā ba'd ma'ānī 'ilm al-dīnāmīkā al-ḥadīth," *Al-jam'iyya al-miṣriyya li-tārīkh al-'ulūm* 2 (1942–3), 45–64.

32 See H. Bellosta, "Cinematica," *Storia della scienza*, vol. III: *La civiltà islamica* (Rome: 2002), 642–6.

33 See M. Rashed, "Dinamica," *Storia della scienza*, vol. III: *La civiltà islamica* (Rome: 2002), 624–42.

34 See Hasnawi [194], with further bibliography.

35 See M. Wolff, *Fallgesetz und Massbegriff* (Berlin: 1971), and M. Wolff, "Philoponus and the Rise of Preclassical Dynamics," in *Philoponus and the Rejection of Aristotelian Science*, ed. R. Sorabji (London: 1987).

36 See Ibn Mattawayh, *Tadhkira*, 488.9–11 (cf. 473.9–11): "The reason why the fall of the light body differs from the fall of the heavy body is the air that is in the atmosphere. Because otherwise, if we threw a stone and a feather, they would fall in the same time. But the air prevents the light body from falling, whereas the heavy body cuts through it."

37 For more details on this issue, see also A. Sayili, "Ibn Sīnā and Buridan on the Dynamics of Projectile Motion," in *Ibn Sīnā: Ölümün bininci yılı Armaflani 1984'ten ayribasim* (Ankara: 1984).

38 The general equivalence between the notion of *mayl* and *i'timād* was accepted by the ancient scholars themselves (cf. Naẓīf, "Ārā'," 51).

39 Ibn Mattawayh, *Tadhkira*, 596.19–597.13.

40 Avicenna, *al-Shifā': al-ṭabī'iyyāt* [*Physics*], vol. I, *Al-samā' al-ṭabī'ī*, ed. S. Zāyid (Cairo: 1983), 325.19–326.1.

41 Avicenna, *Shifā': Physics*, 212: "We say . . . that it is impossible, in things counted and endowed with a natural or positional order (*la-hā tartībun fī al-ṭab' aw fī al-waḍ'*), that there be a magnitude or a number existing that is actually infinite."

42 Avicenna, *Ta'līqāt*, ed. 'A. Badawī (Bengazi: 1972), 101–14, 105.6–13 in part.

43 More on this criterion in Ibn Sīnā [Avicenna], *Risāla ilā al-wazīr Abī Sa'd*, ed. and French trans. Y. Michot (Beirut: 2000), 32–3.

44 See A. Maier, *Zwischen Philosophie und Mechanik* (Rome: 1958), 12–20, and Hasnawi [195].

45 Because every instant of movement is characterized by a *mayl*-2, it is useful and necessary to reform Aristotle's doctrine and to introduce an instantaneous movement, "the thing of which we have shown that it is really the motion," as Avicenna calls it (see the numerous references collected in Hasnawi [195], 236 n. 44).

46 See Avicenna, *Ta'līqāt* 105.14–15: *wa laysa sababu istiḥālatihi awḍā'ahu bal tawahhumahu wa irādatahu al-mutajaddidata tawahhuman ba'da tawahhumin.*

47 Which explains why the criticisms of the continuists now focus on the alleged finitism of their adversaries.

48 As it was in the Aristotelian tradition. Cf. *Physics*, VI, *De Caelo*, III.4, 303a20–4, III.7, 306a26–b2.

49 For Latin mathematical atomism, probably influenced by the *mutakallimūn* through the refutations of Avicenna, Averroes, and Maimonides, see B. Pabst, *Atomtheorien des lateinischen Mittelalters* (Darmstadt: 1994), 276–85 with further references.

15 Psychology: soul and intellect

Most Arabic philosophers took the general inspiration for their discussions of soul (*al-nafs*) and intellect (*al-'aql*) from the Arabic translations of Aristotle's *De Anima* and *Parva Naturalia* and later Greek commentaries on Aristotle, although a few philosophers, such as al-Rāzī, were of a more Platonic bent.[1] In addition to assimilating Greek sources into their own philosophical psychology, Arabic philosophers were also sensitive to the need to address the competing views of the Islamic theologians (*mutakallimūn*), who upheld an atomistic metaphysics in which all created beings were understood to be mere aggregates of atoms and accidents held together by God's absolute power. This yielded a bundle theory of personal identity which left no room for an immaterial soul. Such a view of human nature was vehemently denied by the philosophers, although it was attractive to the theologians since it allowed them to offer an account of the revealed doctrine of the resurrection of the body.[2]

THE NATURE OF THE SOUL AND ITS RELATION TO THE BODY

Unlike their theological adversaries, all the Arabic philosophers accepted some conception of the soul derived from the Greek tradition. In most cases it was Aristotle's definition of the soul in *De Anima*, II.1, as the first "form" or "actuality" of a body which is potentially alive, that held sway. Under this conception, the soul is simply the animating and organizing principle of a body and is therefore "inseparable from the body."[3] Most of the Arabic philosophers also accepted Aristotle's division of the parts and powers of the soul, according to which "soul" is an ordered genus divided into three species, corresponding to the division of living things into plants, animals, and humans. The lowest power of the soul is the nutritive or vegetative, which is common to all living bodies – plants, animals, and humans alike; next is the sensitive soul, which belongs to animals as well as humans; and finally the intellective or rational soul, which is unique to human beings.

While this Aristotelian account of the soul was accepted by most philosophers in the Arabic tradition, both al-Rāzī and Avicenna took exception to it in some way. In the case of al-Rāzī, the entire Aristotelian view of the soul and its powers was rejected in favor of an account based in large part on Plato's *Timaeus*.[4] Al-Rāzī accepts Plato's tripartite division of the soul into the desiderative, the spirited, and the rational, and he upholds a belief in the transmigration of souls which greatly downplays the divide between humans and other animals. Al-Rāzī also subscribes to the *Timaeus'* conception of a World Soul, from which all animal and human souls in the present world have fallen, a Fall which he recounts in mythic form.[5]

Unlike al-Rāzī, Avicenna does not reject the Aristotelian conception of the soul outright, but he upholds a form of soul–body dualism that is foreign to Aristotle. While Aristotle and most of his Arabic followers allow for the possibility that the human intellect is separable from the body, this holds for them only to the extent that the intellect is separable from the rest of the soul as well. For Avicenna, by contrast, the individual human soul is more than a physical entity and organizing principle for the body. It is a subsistent being in its own right, and a complete substance independent of any relation it has to the body.[6]

This dualistic perspective on human nature is evident in many places in Avicenna's psychology, but the best-known of these is a thought experiment that has come to be known as the "flying man," a precursor of Descartes' famous *cogito, ergo sum* argument in which Avicenna attempts to show that human self-awareness is entirely non-sensory.[7] To conduct the experiment, the reader is asked to imagine herself in a state in which all forms of sensory perception are impossible. This means that one must bracket (1) all previously acquired sense knowledge; and (2) all occurrent sensation. The first is done by imagining oneself as newly created, but as a mature adult with full rational capacities. The second is accomplished by imagining oneself suspended in a void in such a way that one's limbs do not touch each other, thereby cutting oneself off from sensing both external objects and one's own body (hence, the label "flying man"). Avicenna claims that even under these conditions, each of us would undoubtedly affirm her own existence. But that affirmation can in no way depend upon the experience of having a body, for the very state hypothesized in the thought experiment abstracts from all bodily experience.[8]

Despite his dualism, Avicenna recognizes that there are close ties between the soul and the body. The body serves as an instrument for the soul, and it is a necessary condition for its creation and individuation. While this may seem to conflict with Avicenna's claim that the soul is subsistent, Avicenna is forced to uphold this position on metaphysical grounds. Unlike the separate or angelic intelligences, each individual of which constitutes a species unto itself, "humanity" is a single species common to many individuals, and numerical multiplicity within a species is a function of matter. Avicenna places the creation of human souls within the framework of his theory of emanation. Whenever the appropriate material conditions are present in the sublunar world (that is, whenever a human embryo is conceived), the agent intellect concomitantly creates a human soul to inform that body. According to this picture, then, the true cause of the existence of the individual human soul is the agent intellect itself, and the parents merely serve to prepare a material body appropriate for receiving it. The soul and the body are thus made for each other, and the soul has a special attraction to its own body, which aids it in the performance of many of its operations. This, Avicenna argues, also refutes theories advocating the pre-existence of a single World Soul and transmigration, such as those upheld by al-Rāzī.

Despite the soul's dependence upon the body for its initial creation, Avicenna denies that the soul requires the body for its continued existence. Upon the death of the body, the soul retains its individuality in virtue of its own intrinsic substantiality, and because of the persistence of individuating characteristics that defined its embodied life. The very fact of having been born with a particular body and having uniquely individual experiences while in that body affects the soul itself. Different souls thus achieve different levels of perfection through the use they make of their individual bodies, and those differences will remain after death.[9] Thus, Avicenna alone among the *falāsifa* upholds the *personal* immortality of the individual human soul.

SOUL AS A PRINCIPLE OF COGNITION

One of the most important functions of the soul is to serve as the principle of cognition, both sensitive and intellectual. In the Arabic tradition, the divide between the senses and the intellect was a fundamental assumption of all cognitive psychology, and the contribution of the senses to human knowledge was always subordinated to that of the intellect, on the grounds that sensation is always of the particular and operates through a bodily organ, whereas true knowledge is of the universal. Despite their professed devaluation of sense-knowledge, however, some of the most original developments in Arabic philosophy arise from the efforts of Arabic philosophers to explain the nature and mechanics of sense-perception.

Moreover, while a deep chasm is posited between sense and intellect in terms of their cognitive value, the Arabic philosophers offered a general theory of the nature of cognition that was applicable to both sensation and intellection. The ultimate foundation of their theory was Aristotle's description of cognition as the reception of the form of the perceived object without its matter.[10] The result of their attempts to explain and expand upon this remark was the theory that *intentionality* is the mark of cognition.

"Intentionality" is a concept that continues to influence contemporary philosophy of mind, where it refers to the directedness of mental states toward objects, and it has a similar meaning in its original usage in Arabic philosophy. In the technical terminology of the Arabic philosophers, an "intention" (*ma'nan*) – literally a "meaning" or an "idea" – is a form or essence insofar as it is apprehended by any cognitive faculty and serves as an object for that faculty. There are thus different types of intentions corresponding to the various cognitive faculties – color and sound are sensible intentions, for example; images are intentions in the faculty of imagination; and universal concepts are intelligible or understood intentions. The exact origins of the philosophers' concept of intentionality are unclear, and no completely satisfactory explanation has been offered. One important precedent comes from the Islamic *mutakallimūn*, for whom *ma'nan* was one of the technical terms for accidents.[11] As for the

English term "intention," it came to be applied to the Arabic concept through the use of *intentio* as the medieval Latin translation of *ma'nan*. While not a literal rendition of the Arabic, the term nicely reflects one of the few explicit definitions of intentionality offered by Avicenna in his *Interpretation*. According to this definition, *ma'ānin* are "what is intended by the soul" (*maqāṣida li-al-nafs*), that is, they are the things that linguistic expressions are meant to signify.[12] For Avicenna intentionality is interpreted as the mental *existence* of the form or quiddity that is perceived in the soul of the perceiver, and it is closely connected to his metaphysical distinction between essence and existence.[13] While Averroes rejects the metaphysical basis for Avicenna's understanding of intentions, he too upholds the thesis that as sensible, imagined, or intelligible intentions, the forms of the objects that we know can be said to exist in some way in our souls, so that all cognized forms have two "subjects." One subject, the "subject of truth," is the object to which the cognitive act refers, and by which its truth or falsity is determined, ultimately, the extramental thing itself. The other subject, the "subject of existence," is the faculty in which the form exists as an intention, be it the senses, the imagination, or the intellect.[14]

In addition to providing the foundation for the Arabic theory of intentionality, the claim that cognition involves the reception of form apart from matter also led the Arabic philosophers to interpret not only intellectual cognition, but also sensation, as a type of *abstraction* (*tajrīd*). Hence all cognition came to be viewed as a hierarchy of grades of abstraction beginning with the senses and reaching its apex in the intellect. The abstractive hierarchy receives its first explicit formulation with Avicenna, who defines "perception" (*idrāk*) as the "grasping (*akhdh*) of the form of the thing apprehended in some way," adding that "the kinds of abstraction vary and differ in degree."[15] Avicenna identifies four grades of abstraction, with sensation the lowest, intellection the highest, and the two middle grades occupied by the faculties which were known in the Arabic tradition as "the internal senses" (*al-ḥawāss al-bāṭina*).[16]

The doctrine of the internal senses is an attempt to expand and systematize Aristotle's account of the pre-intellectual capacities of the soul that could not simply be explained as functions of the five external senses of vision, hearing, smell, taste, and touch. Among these capacities were the common sense (*koinê aisthêsis*), the imagination (*phantasia*), and memory. The doctrine of the internal senses also drew upon later Greek developments in physiology stemming from the physician Galen. Like the external senses, the internal senses require a bodily organ to perform their operations, usually identified as the brain, following Galen, or less frequently the heart, following Aristotle.

The theory of the internal senses is not yet evident in al-Fārābī's writings of undisputed authenticity.[17] Al-Fārābī presents instead a sparse Aristotelian scheme that includes the common sense power, which is assigned the task of collecting and collating the information provided by the five senses, and the imagination, both of which are localized in the heart rather than the brain. Initially, al-Fārābī assigns two functions to the imagination, the capacity to retain sensible impressions when the external object itself is absent, and the ability to compose and divide these retained impressions into combinations that may or may not represent real objects in the external world. To these two he later adds a third function, "imitation" (*muḥākāt*), by which he seems to mean the depiction of an object by means of an image other than its own. To imitate *x*, then, is to imagine *x* by depicting it under sensible qualities that do not describe its own sensible appearance. Through imitation, the imagination can represent not only sensible bodies, but also bodily temperaments, emotions, and even abstract universals, as happens when evil, for example, is symbolized by the image of darkness.[18] The imitative capacities of imagination are also the foundation for al-Fārābī's characterization of the prophet, that is, the founder of a religion. In virtue of possessing a strong imaginative faculty, the prophet is able to receive an "overflow" of intelligibles into his imagination, where they become subject to symbolic imitation. Through these symbols and images, the prophet can communicate abstract truths in concrete terms that can be understood by simple believers.

The full spectrum of internal sense powers makes its first appearance in the works of Avicenna, who posits five internal sense powers, each assigned to its own location within the ventricles of the brain. Avicenna justifies his positing of each of these sense powers by a set of principles for differentiating psychological faculties. Of these principles, two are fundamental. The first is the claim that the reception and retention of sensibles must be functions of distinct faculties, a principle supported by the observation that in the physical world what receives an imprint easily, for example, water, does not retain that imprint well. The second is the claim that a diversity of objects diversifies faculties. The most innovative and influential part of Avicenna's theory of the internal senses is his assertion that perceptual objects are of two types. One sort of perceptual object is a sensible form, that is, an image of one of the five proper sensibles of color, sound, taste, smell, and texture, or an image of one of the common sensibles, objects perceptible by two or more senses, such as motion, magnitude, and shape. The other sort of object is one that Avicenna calls an "intention" (*ma'nan*), using the same term that Arabic philosophers had adopted to signify the object of any cognitive faculty.

In the context of the internal senses, Avicenna defines an "intention" as a property which is not essentially material or sensible, but which in some way accompanies a sensible form. Avicenna often illustrates this with the example of the sheep's instinctive perception of hostility in the wolf. "Hostility" is not itself a sensible form like color or motion, but it must still be an object of sense perception in some way, for animals perceive intentions of this sort. Indeed, it is our observation of animal behavior and the underlying perceptual capacities that such behavior presupposes that requires the positing of an internal sense faculty for grasping intentions, since animals do not have reason or intellect. Avicenna calls the faculty which grasps intentions "estimation" (*wahm*).[19] Nonetheless, Avicenna does not confine estimation to animals, and humans too have an estimative faculty. Nor does Avicenna limit estimative intentions to affective properties such as hostility and friendliness. Rather, the estimative faculty ultimately functions as the animal analogue to the intellect, directing and controlling all the judgments of the sensitive soul and allowing it to associate sensible descriptions with individual objects, a capacity which Aristotle calls "incidental" perception, for example, my perception of the white thing as Diares' son.[20]

From the principles we have examined, Avicenna deduces four of the five internal sense faculties: the common sense receives, distinguishes, and collates sensible forms from the external senses, and they are then stored in the retentive imagination (*al-khayāl*), sometimes called the formative faculty (*al-muṣawwira*); estimation receives non-sensible intentions, and they are retained in the memorative faculty. Avicenna also posts a fifth internal sense power, the compositive imagination (*al-mutakhayyila*), which is the ability to manipulate images and intentions rather than receive them passively from external objects. Avicenna seems to hold that the compositive imagination is always engaged in the random creation of new images, even unconsciously and during sleep, when it produces dreams. Its random activity can, however, be controlled and directed to specific ends. When the ends are those of the sensitive or animal soul, the director is the estimative faculty. But in humans the compositive imagination can also be placed under rational control, and when this happens, its proper designation is the "cogitative" faculty (*al-mufakkira*). In Avicenna the cogitative faculty – that is, the entity formed by the cooperation between the intellect and the imagination – is responsible for a good deal of what we would ordinarily call "thinking," including the analysis and synthesis of propositions and syllogistic reasoning.[21]

The most innovative element in Avicenna's theory of the internal senses, the positing of the estimative faculty, was also the most controversial for later authors. Averroes eliminates this faculty entirely in animals, arguing that it is superfluous, since sensation and imagination are able in their own right to perceive their objects as pleasant and painful.[22] But Averroes does accept Avicenna's claim that the senses perceive "intentions" as distinct from mere sensible forms. Averroes, however, believes that the perception of intentions is distinctive of human sensation, and he assigns it to the cogitative and memorative faculties. Thus Averroes reduces the total number of internal senses to four: common sense, imagination, cogitation, and memory, substituting cogitation for estimation in humans and rejecting the distinction between compositive and retentive imagination. Moreover, for Averroes intentions are no longer defined as any non-sensible properties conveyed by the senses. Instead, an intention is the property that allows us to grasp the individual as such, and its function is thus limited to explaining incidental perception.

Avicenna and Averroes also offer different versions of the scale of abstraction as it applies to the external and internal senses. For Avicenna, there are two distinct grades of abstraction within the internal senses, corresponding to the retentive imagination (*al-khayāl*) and estimation. Imagination is deemed more abstract than sensation (including both the external senses and the common sense), since the sense powers can only operate through contact with objects that are actually present to them, whereas imagination is able to imagine objects which are no longer physically present. Estimation is the most abstract sense power, however, because its objects, intentions, are in themselves non-sensible properties. Nonetheless estimation remains at the level of sensible abstraction because its objects are always particular and conveyed through sensible forms and qualities. The sheep, for example, does not fear the universal wolf, but always *this* particular wolf that it encounters.

Averroes makes extensive use of the claim that sensation is a form of abstraction in his account of the perceptual capacities of both the external and the internal senses. He claims that sensible forms, such as colors, exist in a nobler and more immaterial way in the soul of the perceiver than they do in extramental objects. Averroes often describes their abstract, perceptual mode of existence as a more "spiritual" one (*rūḥāniyya*), borrowing a term used extensively by his Andalusian predecessor, Ibn Bājja. As a favorite illustration of this point, Averroes notes that the senses are not subject to material limitations such as the inability to be simultaneously affected by contraries. While a physical body cannot be black and white in the same respect at the same time, nor can a very large body be contained within a small one, the eye can actually see black and white at the same time, and despite its own small size it can be visually informed by the entire hemisphere.[23]

Still, Averroes admits that sensible abstraction retains some tinge of materiality, for it perceives particulars rather than universals, and this requires some sort of relation to the matter that makes individual intentions individual. This explains why the senses require media, such as the air, to convey the forms of their objects to them. The medium functions as a sort of connector which preserves a relation between the percipient and its material object, even though the act of sensation itself remains abstract. But since sensation itself is spiritual, the medium must also share some spiritual properties, such as the ability to receive and convey contraries simultaneously. The medium, then, must be quasi-spiritual and included on the hierarchy of abstraction, albeit at a lower grade than the senses themselves.

As for the internal senses, Averroes assigns a distinct grade of abstraction to each power, with cogitation and memory the most spiritual senses because of their concern with the individual intention, which Averroes likens to the "fruit" or "core" of the sensible, in contrast to its external qualities or "rinds." The limit of sensible abstraction, then, is the ability to perceive and identify an individual whole, such as an individual person like Zayd or Socrates, and the perception of the individual as an individual is the sensible analogue to the perception of the universal as universal.[24]

INTELLECT

The framework for all Arabic theories of the intellect was provided by Aristotle's distinction in book III of the *De Anima* between the agent and potential intellects. But the Arabic philosophers also identified a number of additional stages of the intellect, a practice which they inherited from the later Greek tradition. Both al-Kindī and al-Fārābī wrote brief treatises which are concerned with clarifying these various senses of the term "intellect."[25] Later, Avicenna and Averroes would incorporate their own versions of these discussions into their psychological works.[26] Although individual philosophers interpret the scheme differently to fit their own theories of how knowledge is acquired, generally the Arabic Aristotelians identify four meanings of "intellect":

(1) The *agent* intellect of *De Anima*, III.5. The Arabic philosophers all followed the prevailing view of the Greek commentators that the agent intellect, which Aristotle declares to be immortal and eternal, is a separate, immaterial substance, not a faculty in each individual soul. Its function is to act as an efficient cause of human understanding, either by rendering objects intelligible or by actualizing the potential intellect, or some combination of the two.

(2) The *potential* intellect, which is often called the *material* intellect, following the practice of the Greek commentator Alexander of Aphrodisias. For most of the Arabic philosophers this is an innate capacity within the human soul for receiving intelligibles, as discussed by Aristotle in *De Anima*, III.4. Averroes, however, comes to believe that this intellect, like the agent intellect, must also be a separate substance and one for all humans.

(3) The *habitual* or *speculative* intellect, sometimes called the *actual* intellect by al-Fārābī. This is the status of the human potential intellect once it has acquired some intelligibles and

developed a habit or disposition for thinking at will. Avicenna subdivides it into two stages, using the label "habitual intellect" to describe the acquisition of primary intelligibles, such as the principle of non-contradiction, and the label "actual intellect" for the acquisition of secondary intelligibles deduced from them. To add to the terminological confusion, al-Kindī uses the label "acquired intellect" for this stage of development.

(4) The *acquired* intellect (*al-'aql al-mustafād*, Latin *intellectus adeptus*). For most Arabic philosophers this is the habitual intellect when it has perfected itself by acquiring all possible intelligibles. At this stage it becomes a completely actual being akin to the separate intelligences, able to know itself as well as the closest separate intelligence to us, the agent intellect. In Avicenna, the acquired intellect is simply the intellect when it is exercising knowledge that it has previously learned, such as when the grammarian parses a sentence. For Al-Kindī, such an actual exercise of stored knowledge is called the "appearing" or "second intellect."[27]

Averroes adds a fifth type of intellect to these four when he regularly calls the imagination, or more precisely the cogitative faculty, the "passive intellect," the only term found in Aristotle's own *De Anima*.[28] Modern readers take the passive intellect to be identical to the potential intellect, but since Aristotle says that it is perishable, Averroes follows an alternative interpretation among the Greek commentators and reasons that it must be identified with a bodily faculty.

The questions about the intellect that most concerned the Arabic Aristotelians were the nature of the potential intellect and the explanation of how intellectual cognition comes about. While there are some minor discrepancies among al-Fārābī's various writings on the intellect, it is clear that for him the potential intellect is a faculty of the individual human soul on which intelligibles are imprinted through a process of abstraction. Since it is subject to generation and corruption, the human potential intellect is not immortal in its own right. Rather, its immortality depends on the degree to which it actualizes itself by acquiring immaterial intelligibles, a process by which it gradually becomes freed from matter. This, in effect, is what al-Fārābī believes happens when a human being reaches the stage of the acquired intellect. At this stage the individual human intellect becomes entirely one with its immaterial intelligibles, thereby attaining a status similar to that of the agent intellect itself. As a result, the human acquired intellect is also able to have the agent intellect as a further object of knowledge, to "conjoin" (*ittiṣāl*) with it in a union of knower and known. Conjunction with the agent intellect is identified by al-Fārābī as the supreme human end and a necessary condition for achieving immortality. Souls which do not reach the level of acquired intellect in this life thus cannot survive the death of the body, since they remain material and perishable. But the immortality envisioned by al-Fārābī does not seem to be a personal one, and toward the end of his life al-Fārābī came to doubt the viability of even this limited form of immortality. In his now-lost commentary on Aristotle's *Nicomachean Ethics*, known through the reports of Ibn Bājja, Ibn Ṭufayl, and Averroes, al-Fārābī is reported to have abandoned belief in the possibility of conjunction with the agent intellect, on the grounds that it would require the impossible transformation of a material and contingent being into an immaterial and eternal one.[29]

In contrast to al-Fārābī, individual immortality is not a problem for Avicenna since he holds that the soul is subsistent in itself. Avicenna's dualism also sets him apart from the other Arabic philosophers in his account of the roles played by the potential and agent intellects in the acquisition of knowledge. Just as the body is only a preparatory cause that initially occasions the creation of the individual, so too the sense powers play only a preparatory function in the production of intelligibles. Indeed, the function of the agent intellect in the production of human knowledge exactly parallels its function in the creation of human souls: the consideration of the corresponding sense images disposes the soul to receive one universal rather than another, for example, "human being" rather than "horse," in exactly the same way that the species of the parents disposes the matter of their offspring to receive one form rather than another (that is, humans beget humans and horses beget horses). The function of the agent intellect in this process is therefore not to illumine the sense images so that universals can be abstracted from them. The ultimate cause of the production of new intelligible concepts in individual minds is not an act of *abstraction* at all, but rather, a direct *emanation* from the agent intellect:

> For when the intellectual power sees the particular things which are in the imagination, and when the light of the agent intellect in us . . . shines upon them, they become abstracted from matter and its attachments, and are imprinted on the rational soul, not in the sense that they themselves pass from the imagination to our intellect, . . . but rather, in the sense that their consideration prepares the soul so that what is abstract emanates upon it from the agent intellect.[30]

Avicenna's claim that knowledge is ultimately an emanation has a number of important epistemological consequences, one of which is his denial of intellectual memory. On the emanational account of knowledge, intellectual understanding is nothing but the actual existence of the object known in the knower. To think of some concept, *c*, is simply for the form or quiddity of *c* to exist in one's intellect. Since the intellect is not a body which has spatial extension, there is no "place" within the intellect in which an intelligible can be actually stored while it is not consciously being thought. The storehouse for intelligibles, then, is not in the soul, but rather, it is the agent intellect itself, which is always engaged in the contemplation of its own contents. Moreover, "conjunction" with the agent intellect for Avicenna is not a special state through which the intellect becomes immortal, but rather it is the foundation for all learning, which is nothing but "the search for the perfect disposition for conjunction."[31]

Avicenna's account of the agent intellect's role in human understanding also allows him to posit a form of prophecy that is properly intellectual. Avicenna's prophet is blessed with a strong capacity for intuition (*ḥads*), possessing what Avicenna calls a "holy intellect." Avicenna recognizes lesser forms of intuitive ability in which other human beings share, by which they are occasionally able to receive the agent intellect's emanation without the prior aid of the sense faculties or the help of a human teacher. But the prophet's intuition is unique. For him intuition does not come in episodic flashes; rather, he receives *all* intelligibles from the agent intellect in a single instant. Nor is the prophet lacking in *comprehension* of the intelligible truths that he receives in this way, since they are already rationally ordered and logically arranged insofar as they include the middle terms of the syllogisms that demonstrate their truth. For Avicenna, then, the prophet is special not merely in virtue of the bodily faculty of imagination, as was the case for al-Fārābī, but in virtue of the special qualities of his immaterial intellect as well.[32]

Of all the Arabic philosophers, it is Averroes for whom the ontological status of the material or potential intellect and its relation to the individual causes the most vexation. In his three commentaries on the *De Anima* and in related minor works, written at various times over the course of his life, Averroes struggled to make sense of Aristotle's account of the potential intellect in *De Anima*, III.4, changing his interpretation of the text many times.[33] Averroes' task was complicated by the competing theories of his predecessors, the Greek commentators Alexander of Aphrodisias and Themistius, who represented polar opposites on the question of the intellect's ontological status. At issue for Averroes was the basic question of how to interpret Aristotle's claim that the potential intellect must be unmixed with matter in order to acquire knowledge of intelligible universals. What exactly does it mean for the intellect to be "unmixed," and how does this affect the intellect's relation to a human being, whose individuality is a function of matter?

Averroes' first position on the material intellect is represented in the original version of his *Epitome of the "De Anima,"* a work that Averroes reworked at least twice to bring it in line with his changing views. This position, which is closest to that of Alexander, may loosely be termed "materialist." On this view, the material intellect is a special disposition for receiving intelligibles unique to the human imagination, or more precisely, "the disposition which is in the imaginative forms for receiving the intelligibles." Since the imagination is a faculty of the soul, and its contents have spiritual or intentional rather than physical being, Averroes believes at this stage in his thinking that such a position meets Aristotle's fundamental criterion that the intellect is neither a body "nor material in the way that corporeal forms are material."[34]

This solution did not satisfy Averroes for long. In his later writings, in particular his *Long Commentary on the "De Anima"* (which survives only in its medieval Latin version), Averroes moves closer to the position of Themistius, now arguing that the material intellect can be "neither a body nor a power in a body." But Averroes adds a further qualification to his account that sets it radically apart from the views of all his predecessors. For he reasons that if the material intellect is entirely separate from matter and incorporeal, then it cannot be *individuated* by the body as Avicenna held, or as Averroes puts it, "numbered according to the numeration of individual humans." The result, then, is Averroes' much maligned position that has come to be known as the "unicity of the intellect" or, less felicitously, "monopsychism," according to which the material intellect, as well as the agent intellect, is a separate substance and one for all human knowers.[35]

While this position is a sharp departure from Averroes' earlier view on the metaphysical status of the material intellect, it is noteworthy that it shares with that view the recognition that human thought is individuated by the images that accompany universal thoughts, according to Aristotle's dictum in the *De Anima* that the soul never thinks without an image. Moreover, neither Averroes' original materialism, nor the unicity of the intellect, allow for individual immortality. Thus while Averroes allows for the possibility of conjunction with the agent intellect, like al-Fārābī before him it remains an intellectual ideal that has little bearing upon the traditional belief in personal survival after death.[36]

THE SOUL AS A PRINCIPLE OF MOTION: APPETITE AND PRACTICAL INTELLECT

The Arabic philosophers did not entirely neglect Aristotle's observation that the soul is a principle of motion as well as cognition, but they focused most of their attention on the cognitive faculties of the soul. The Arabic Aristotelians treat appetite as a byproduct of cognition that arises when an object is perceived by either sense or intellect as worthy of pursuit or avoidance. The principle that appetite follows upon perception was applied with equal rigor in the intellectual as well as the sensible realm. Perhaps the most important consequence of this is that Arabic philosophers lack a strong conception of the will, understood as an autonomous rational faculty able to resist the dictates of the intellect. Rather, in the Arabic tradition "will" (*irāda*) is a generic term for all appetites, having roughly the same extension as Aristotle's conception of the voluntary, which applies to animals and children as well as to adult humans. The peculiar appetitive faculty associated with the intellect in Arabic philosophy is not will but "choice" (*ikhtiyār*, equivalent to the Greek *prohairêsis*), that is, the ability to decide between alternative courses of action and to base one's choices on a process of rational deliberation.[37]

The Arabic philosophers do not worry whether this view compromises human freedom or moral responsibility. Morality for them is primarily a matter of the interaction between the practical intellect and the lower sense appetites. For Avicenna the practical intellect cooperates with the estimative and cogitative faculties on the one hand, and the theoretical intellect on the other, to engage in moral deliberation and practical reasoning, and to produce generalized ethical principles and rules of conduct. Virtue and vice are thus functions of the practical intellect's success at governing the body. To the extent that the practical intellect is able to control and direct the lower appetites, the agent is virtuous, and to the extent that it fails to dominate, the agent is vicious.[38] Although the practical intellect is thus essential to human morality, it is consistently subordinated to the theoretical intellect in the Arabic tradition. Nowhere is this attitude better captured than in Averroes' *Epitome of the "De Anima,"* where he observes that human rationality in most cases never reaches beyond the capacities of the practical intellect: "This power is a power common to all people who are not lacking in humanity, and people only differ in it by degrees. As for the second power [the theoretical intellect], it is clear from its nature that it is very divine and found only in some people, who are the ones primarily intended by Divine Providence over this species."[39]

NOTES

1 For the Greek background, see Davidson [208], 3–43; Peters [61], 40–7.

2 For a theological critique of the philosophers, see al-Ghazālī [111], 212–29.

3 Aristotle, *De Anima*, II.1, 412a27–8; 412b4–6; 413a4–6. The Greek term *entelecheia*, "actuality," was rendered into Arabic as *istikmāl*, "perfection."

4 For an excellent account of al-Rāzī's psychology, see Druart [209].

5 Al-Rāzī's works containing the myth are lost, and known only by the reports of his critics. For a translation of one report, see Pines [198],

68–9. See further L. E. Goodman, "Razi's Myth of the Fall of the Soul," in Hourani [25], 25–40.

6 Avicenna, *Avicenna's "De Anima": Being the Psychological Part of Kitāb al-shifā'*, ed. F. Rahman (Oxford: 1959), bk. 1, ch. 1, 5–11.

7 See Marmura [214] for a translation of the three versions of the argument.

8 *Avicenna's "De Anima,"* bk. 1, ch. 1, 15–16.

9 Ibid., bk. 5, chs. 3–4. For an English translation of the shorter version of these arguments in Avicenna's *al-Najāt* (*The Salvation*), see Avicenna [205], chs. 12–13. On this topic see also Druart [89] and Druart [210].

10 *De Anima*, II.12, 424a17–19; cf. *De Anima*, III.4, 429a15–18.

11 See R. M. Frank, "*Al-Ma'ná*: Some Reflections on the Technical Meanings of the Term in Kalām and its Use in the Physics of Mu'ammar," *Journal of the American Oriental Society* 87 (1967), 248–59.

12 Avicenna, *al-Shifā': al-'ibāra* (*The Healing: On Interpretation*), ed. M. El-Khodeiri and I. Madkour (Cairo: 1970), 2–3.

13 A precursor to Avicenna's notion of mental existence can be found in al-Fārābī [211], §21, 17–18: "When [the intelligibles] become intelligibles in actuality, they become, then, one of the things existing in the world, and they are counted, insofar as they are intelligibles, among the totality of existing things." English trans. in Hyman and Walsh [26], 216.

14 Averroes [135], bk. 3, comment 5, 400–1; English trans. in Hyman and Walsh [26], 327–8.

15 *Avicenna's "De Anima,"* bk. 2, ch. 2, 58–67; English version in Avicenna [205], ch. 7, 38–40.

16 See Wolfson [217], for a comprehensive though dated account.

17 Al-Fārābī's most complete discussion of the imagination is in Walzer [77], ch. 10, 162–3, and ch. 14, 210–27.

18 This example is given by al-Fārābī in the *Attainment of Happiness*: see *Alfarabi's Philosophy of Plato and Aristotle*, trans. M. Mahdi (Ithaca, NY: 1962), 45.

19 On the topic of *wahm* see Black [207], and D. L. Black, "Estimation and Imagination: Western Divergences from an Arabic Paradigm," *Topoi* 19 (2000), 59–75.

20 *De Anima*, II.6, 418a20–5.

21 Avicenna's basic account of the internal senses is given in *Avicenna's "De anima,"* bk. 1, ch. 5, 43–5, English version in Avicenna [205], 30–1. The theory is developed in greater detail in bk. 4, chs. 1–3.

22 Averroes, *Tahāfut al-tahāfut*, ed. M. Bouyges (Beirut: 1930), 546–7; English trans. at Averroes [140], vol. I, 336.

23 *Talkhīṣ kitāb al-nafs* (*Epitome of the "De Anima"*), ed. A. F. Al-Ahwani (Cairo: 1950), 24; *Talkhīṣ kitāb al-ḥiss wa al-maḥsūs* (*Epitome of "On*

Sense and Sense-Objects"), ed. H. Blumberg (Cambridge, MA: 1972), 23–24; *Epitome of "Parva Naturalia,"* trans. H. Blumberg (Cambridge, MA: 1961), 15–16. For *Talkhīṣ kitāb al-nafs* see also A. Ivry, "Averroes' *Short Commentary* on Aristotle's *De Anima*," *Documenti e studi sulla tradizione filosofica medievale* 8 (1997), 511–52.

24 *Talkhīṣ kitāb al-ḥiss*, bk. 2, 29–35, and bk. 3, 42–3; *Epitome of "Parva Naturalia,"* 18–21 and 26–7.

25 R. J. McCarthy, "Al-Kindī's Treatise on Intellect," *Islamic Studies* 3 (1964), 119–49; al-Fārābī [211].

26 For Avicenna's version see *Avicenna's "De Anima,"* bk. 1, ch. 5, 48–50; *Avicenna's Psychology*, ch. 5, 33–5. The references are scattered throughout Averroes' various commentaries, for example, *Talkhīṣ kitāb al-nafs*, 85–6, 89–90.

27 See McCarthy, "Al-Kindī's Treatise on Intellect," 130–1, 142; Jolivet [69], 12–13, for the textual difficulties surrounding the term "second intellect."

28 *De Anima*, III.5, 430a24–5.

29 Averroes [135], bk. 3, Comment 36, 481; Davidson [208], 70–3. See also above, chapter 4.

30 *Avicenna's "De Anima,"* bk. 5, ch. 5, 235. For an alternative interpretation of Avicenna's views on abstraction, see D. Hasse, "Avicenna on Abstraction," in Wisnovsky [104], 39–72.

31 *Avicenna's "De Anima,"* bk. 5, ch. 6, 244–8.

32 Ibid., 248–50. On intuition see Gutas [93], 159–77, and the further discussion in "Intuition and Thinking: The Evolving Structure of Avicenna's Epistemology," in Wisnovsky [104], 1–38. On prophecy in Avicenna see M. E. Marmura, "Avicenna's Psychological Proof of Prophecy," *Journal of Near Eastern Studies* 22 (1963), 49–56. See further F. Rahman, *Prophecy in Islam* (Oxford: 1958; repr. Chicago: 1979).

33 For the evolution of Averroes' views, see Davidson [208], 258–314. There is some dispute as to the chronological relation between Averroes' long and middle commentaries. See H. A. Davidson, "The Relation between Averroes' Middle and Long Commentaries on the *De Anima*," *Arabic Sciences and Philosophy* 7 (1997), 139–51, and A. Ivry, "Averroes' Three Commentaries on *De Anima*," in Aertsen and Endress [134], 199–216, for the competing views.

34 Averroes, *Talkhīṣ kitāb al-nafs*, 86.

35 Averroes [135], bk. 3, Comment 5, 401–9; English trans. in Hyman and Walsh [26], 324–34. See further D. L. Black, "Memory, Time and Individuals in Averroes's Psychology," *Medieval Theology and Philosophy* 5 (1996), 161–87, and Hyman [143].

36 For Averroes on conjunction with the agent intellect, see A. Ivry, "Averroes on Intellection and Conjunction," *Journal of the American Oriental Society* 86 (1966), 76–85, Black [206], and Averroes [204].

37 See, for example, Walzer [77], ch. 10, 165, 171–3, and ch. 13, 203–11.

38 *Avicenna's "De Anima,"* bk. 1, ch. 5, 46–8; Avicenna [205], ch. 4, 32–3.

39 *Talkhīṣ kitāb al-nafs*, 69. See further A. Ivry, "The Will of God and Practical Intellect of Man in Averroes' Philosophy," *Israel Oriental Studies* 9 (1979), 377–91.

THÉRÈSE-ANNE DRUART

16 Metaphysics

Metaphysics, first philosophy, or divine science has always been a subject of controversy. Too often medieval Arabic metaphysics is regarded as either simply a paraphrase of or a commentary on Aristotle's *Metaphysics*, or a curious and rather unsuccessful blend of Aristotelian metaphysics and Neoplatonism. Cristina D'Ancona has shown the superficiality of this latter approach by highlighting how carefully and creatively the "*falāsifa*" or Hellenizing philosophers used the various Greek sources, such as the works of Aristotle, the *Plotiniana Arabica* (a group of texts based on Plotinus and including the so-called Aristotle's *Theology* derived from *Enneads* IV–VI), and the *Liber de Causis*, adapted from Proclus' *Theology* and known in Arabic as *The Book of the Pure Good*.[1] Yet Greek sources are not enough to explain some developments. In 1979 Richard Frank argued that *falsafa* (the Arabic transliteration of the Greek term for philosophy, highlighting its foreign origin) is not immune to the influence of *kalām* or Islamic theology, which had elaborated an ontology of its own.[2] More recently, though controversially, he has argued that even al-Ghazālī, the famous author of the *Incoherence of the Philosophers* and the staunch protector of orthodox Sunnī Islam, is himself deeply influenced by Avicenna.[3]

The *falāsifa*, too, confused the issues, because some of them, al-Fārābī, Ibn Ṭufayl, and Averroes in particular, claim that there is one philosophical truth reflected in a plurality of simultaneously true religions. "True religions" simply translate into symbolic and, therefore, culturally determined languages what the philosophers know through demonstrations. Such a claim, whether or not it is purely rhetorical, implies that the great philosophers hold basically the same philosophical tenets and that philosophy reached its peak with Aristotle. Al-Fārābī offers a striking example of this attitude in his *The Harmonization of the Two Opinions of the Two Sages: Plato the Divine and Aristotle*.[4] This text illustrates the old Alexandrian tradition that profoundly influenced the *falāsifa*. Its introduction states its aims:

> I see most of the people of our time delving into and disputing over whether the world is generated or eternal. They claim that there is disagreement between the two eminent and distinguished sages, Plato and Aristotle, concerning the proof [of the existence] of the first Creator; the causes existing due to Him; the issue of the soul and the intellect; recompense for good and evil actions; and many political, moral, and logical issues. So I want to embark in this treatise of mine upon a harmonization of the two opinions of both of them and an explanation of what the tenor of their arguments signifies in order to make the agreement between the beliefs of both apparent, to remove doubt and suspicion from the hearts of those who look into their books, and to explain the places of uncertainty and the sources of doubt in their treatises.[5]

Besides the confusion arising from this mix of Aristotelianism and Neoplatonism, there is another source of problems. The *falāsifa* moved from identifying metaphysics solely with some kind of natural theology and, therefore, as a more sophisticated form of *kalām*, to taking into account ontology, i.e., metaphysics, as primarily a study of being qua being. Dimitri Gutas and more recently Amos Bertolacci have highlighted this turning point[6] by a careful study of Avicenna's famous *Autobiography*.[7] In it Avicenna explains that though he read Aristotle's *Metaphysics* forty times and knew it by heart, its content baffled him so much that he gave it up. One day at the book market, by a fluke he was offered at a discount a small treatise by al-Fārābī explaining the purpose of the *Metaphysics*. He bought it and understood then that its main aim was not the study of God.

Let us, therefore, retrace some important steps in this development focusing on the subject matter of metaphysics and on the explanation of causal relationships that are at the core of, for example, the famous dispute between most of the *falāsifa* who claim that the world is eternal, and the theologians who defend creation in time.

AL-KINDĪ

In his *On First Philosophy*, of which sadly only the first part is extant, al-Kindī spells out his conception of philosophy:

Indeed, the human art which is highest in degree and most noble in rank is the art of philosophy, the definition of which is knowledge of the true nature of things, insofar as is possible for man. The aim of the philosopher is, as regards his knowledge, to attain the truth, and as regards his action, to act truthfully . . . We do not find the truth we are seeking without finding a cause; the cause of the existence and continuance of everything is the True One, in that each thing which has being has truth. The True One exists necessarily, and therefore beings exist.[8]

This passage clearly shows how al-Kindī immediately moves from philosophy as knowledge of the true nature of things to knowledge of the cause of both the existence and the continuance of everything. This cause is equated with the True One, i.e., God, since the "True" is one of the Qur'ānic beautiful names of God. Philosophy aims at discovering the existence of God as cause and then at explaining how he creates and maintains everything in existence. As al-Kindī claims a few paragraphs later that Aristotle is the most eminent of the Greek philosophers, we may wonder how he derives his conception of philosophy from Aristotle's texts. Amos Bertolacci and Cristina D'Ancona provide some clues toward an answer.[9]

Al-Kindī only draws on book II and on book XII, chapters 6–10 of Aristotle's *Metaphysics*, which he supplements with references to the *Posterior Analytics* and the *Topics*.[10] Modern scholars have neglected book II since it had been generally considered inauthentic, and even if book II is authentic there are reasons not to consider it part of the *Metaphysics*. In the Arabic tradition, book II is extremely important because it was only much later that just part of book I made it into Arabic and that part was located after book II. Book II, therefore, becomes the official introduction to the whole book. The end of its first chapter includes one of the very few references in Aristotle to a cause of existence. Comparing it with the passage of al-Kindī I have just quoted shows how much book II influenced al-Kindī's conception of philosophy:

It is right also that philosophy should be called knowledge of the truth. For the end of theoretical knowledge is truth, while that of practical knowledge is action . . . Now we do not know a truth without its cause; and a thing has quality in a higher degree than other things if in virtue of it the similar quality belongs to the other things . . . so that that which causes derivative truths to be true is most true. Therefore the principles of eternal things must be always most true; for they are not merely sometimes true, nor is there any cause of their being, but they themselves are the cause of the being of other things.[11]

Putting aside other differences, I want to emphasize that al-Kindī speaks of creation and maintenance in existence.[12] For him God does not simply grant an initial existence that keeps subsisting for as long as it can; he also maintains it in existence. Al-Kindī envisions continuous creation and the utter contingency of all that is created, whereas human agents may build a house that will survive them. As the second chapter of Aristotle's *Metaphysics*, book II, argues against an infinite regress in material, formal, efficient, and final causes as well as against an infinite variety of kinds of causes, the issue of causation assumes great importance.

The other passage of Aristotle's *Metaphysics* that plays some role in al-Kindī's *On First Philosophy* is book XII, chapters 6–10, which establishes the existence and attributes of the Prime Mover, conceived as a final cause. The conception of causation in those chapters is much more limited than the one sketched in book II, and it is left to philosophers in Islamic lands to resolve the differences.

The group of translators who worked around al-Kindī produced and were influenced by the *Plotiniana Arabica*. This influence explains why al-Kindī abandons much of Aristotle's conception of the Prime Mover, giving less importance to the second part of book XII than to book II. God is uncaused and without accident or substrate. He is eternal, incorruptible, and immutable. Chapter 3 establishes the existence of a first cause after complex disquisitions on unity and plurality. The first cause totally transcends any form of plurality and is perfectly one and simple. It is, therefore, neither soul nor intellect. Aristotle's Prime Mover was an intellect, but al-Kindī, following Plotinus, posits that the One is beyond soul and intellect. It is also beyond the categories, and therefore cannot be said to be a substance.

This insistence on God's oneness is another way to link philosophy to Islamic theology, since the latter is known not only as *kalām*, but also as the "Science of Unification" (*'ilm al-tawḥīd*), i.e., the proclamation of God's oneness, emphasizing monotheism and rejection of any Trinitarian conception. In the introduction of *On First Philosophy* al-Kindī defends *falsafa* against some religious people, insisting that truth should be accepted wherever it comes from. He clearly means some theologians whose ignorance of logic does not allow them proper understanding of the Greek heritage. Al-Kindī is scathing:

> [They are strangers to the truth] also due to the dirty envy which controls their animal souls and which, by darkening its veils, obscures their thought's perception from the light of truth; and due to their considering those with human virtue – in attainment of which they are deficient, being on its remote fringes – as audacious, harmful opponents; thereby defending their spurious thrones which they installed undeservedly for the purpose of gaining leadership and traffic in religion, though they are devoid of religion. For one who trades in something sells it, and he who sells something does not have it. Thus one who trades in religion does not have religion, and it is right that one who resists the acquisition of knowledge of the real nature of things and calls it unbelief be divested of [the offices of] religion. (Arabic 15, English trans. 58–9)

As Adamson has shown, despite the vehemence of the attack, al-Kindī articulates his positions on divine attributes, creation, and freedom through a creative adaptation or reaction to the main tenets of one school of theology, the Mu'tazilites.[13] For instance, al-Kindī defends creation in time against the Aristotelian tenet of its eternity not only in using arguments from the Christian Aristotelian commentator John Philoponus, but also in stating the *kalām* view that even non-being is a "thing."[14]

In another text, the very brief *The Agent in the Proper Sense, Being First and Perfect, and the Agent in the Metaphorical Sense, Being Imperfect*, al-Kindī tries to spell out how God's agency transcends that of creatures. True agency implies bringing into existence from utter non-being, and this alone belongs to God. Besides, any other so-called agent is acting under the influence of a superior agent. Only God is a pure agent and a creature can only be called an agent metaphorically, since it cannot bring existence from nothing and depends on a superior cause for the exercise of its own causation. There are two types of such metaphorical agency: (1) the cause is simultaneous with its effect, for example, walking; (2) the effect subsists after the cause ceases to produce the effect, for example, the products of crafts, such as house building.[15] Al-Ghazālī will adopt the view that only God is an agent and Avicenna will use the distinction between the two types of metaphorical agency in order to differentiate physical causes from metaphysical ones.

AL-RĀZĪ

Al-Rāzī, who is sometimes better known as a physician than as a philosopher, shows that *falsafa* included a great diversity of views. An independent thinker, he holds the religiously unorthodox view that revelation is impossible, because it is always addressed to a particular people at a particular time and, therefore, incompatible with God's justice since it excludes other peoples and other times. His metaphysics is strikingly different from that of other *falāsifa*. First, he is very critical of Aristotle and in particular rejects his conception of nature, which he finds anthropomorphic. He therefore abandons some of Aristotle's views on causes. He prefers Plato, whom he knows at least through the Arabic version of Galen's summary of the *Timaeus*. Second, he is influenced by the *Plotiniana Arabica* and some form of Gnosticism.

As we know his metaphysical views almost exclusively through hostile reports, we are not sure how he defended them. For him there are five eternal beings: God, Soul, time, space, and matter. Originally these five coexisted and there was no motion. Soul succumbed to a passionate desire to get enmeshed in matter and in so doing introduced motion, but of a disorderly kind. God, being merciful, took pity on Soul and the world. Endowing Soul with intellect he enabled it to realize its mistake and to organize the disorderly motion. Al-Rāzī certainly does not accept creation out of nothing and in time, as does al-Kindī. His metaphysics seems to limit itself to a natural theology superseding the false claims of any revealed religion. Very conscious of the cultural and religious diversity of the Islamic empire and desirous of a common set of moral values, al-Rāzī will use his metaphysical conception of God's three main attributes of compassion, justice, and intellect to develop a detailed normative ethics. Al-Rāzī defends his conception of philosophy and develops his normative ethics in his short but fascinating autobiography, *The Book of the Philosophic Life*.[16]

AL-FĀRĀBĪ

Al-Fārābī's understanding of Aristotle's Metaphysics

As we saw above, in his autobiography Avicenna says he understood the *Metaphysics* properly only after reading al-Fārābī's *Treatise on the Aims of Aristotle's "Metaphysics"*, most likely because he then realized that the work is primarily about being qua being and only incidentally about natural theology.[17] Yet we still do not know much about al-Fārābī's metaphysics, and its interpretation is very disputed. How and when al-Fārābī himself discovered that the subject matter of metaphysics is being qua being we do not know. Neither do we have much in the way of chronological indications to trace a possible intellectual development. What we do know is that at some stage he used a much more complete translation of the *Metaphysics* than al-Kindī, missing only the beginning of book I, book XI – in fact a collection of duplicates of other passages – and parts of books XIII and XIV. His early training was probably in a more syncretic approach to philosophy, but painstakingly reading Aristotle's own texts made him more aware of the true content of Aristotle's metaphysical enterprise, as the introduction of the *Aims* shows:

> Our intention in this treatise is to indicate the purpose contained in the book by Aristotle known as *Metaphysics* and the primary divisions which it has, since many people have the preconceived notion that the import and contents of this book consists of a treatment of the Creator, the intellect, the soul, and other related topics, and that the science of metaphysics and Islamic theology are one and the same thing . . . The primary object of this science is absolute being and what is equivalent to it in universality, namely, the one.[18]

One remarkable feature of this passage is al-Fārābī's way of singling out "one" from among all the transcendentals. This allows him to integrate Neoplatonic traits in his own conception of metaphysics despite his understanding of Aristotle's *Metaphysics* and his doubts about the authenticity of the so-called *Theology of Aristotle*.[19]

Al-Fārābī's conception of metaphysics

When purporting to present Aristotle's own views, as in *The Philosophy of Aristotle*, al-Fārābī is careful not to include Neoplatonic features, such as emanationism, but raises questions Aristotle did not answer. Where do material forms and matter come from? Is the agent intellect a cause of existence? He finally states that "we do not possess metaphysical science." Not surprisingly this sentence has puzzled Farabian scholars, since al-Fārābī had access to an Arabic translation of Aristotle's *Metaphysics*. Muhsin Mahdi and others interpret it as al-Fārābī's way of hinting that no metaphysics is possible and that the texts in which he uses emanation are simply a sop to placate religious authorities.[20] Yet I think that this is al-Fārābī's polite way of pointing to the inadequacies and the incompleteness of Aristotle's *Metaphysics*.

In texts in which al-Fārābī lays down his program for philosophical education, such as the *Enumeration of the Sciences*, he explains that metaphysics has three parts. The first one studies beings qua beings; the second studies the principles of the theoretical sciences, such as logic and mathematics; the third studies beings that are neither bodies nor in bodies and discovers that they form a hierarchy leading to the First or One, which gives existence, unity, and truth to all other beings. It also shows how all other beings proceed from the One. Al-Fārābī grants one line to the first part, probably because Aristotle has already successfully formulated this part of the science, but one paragraph to the second part explaining the origin of the first intelligibles of each science, and two pages to the third, perhaps because Aristotle said little about these issues. Al-Fārābī suggests ways of realizing an ascent to all immaterial principles followed by a descent explaining how everything arises from these principles. The presentation of the third part shows that al-Fārābī has abandoned al-Kindī's view of the One as beyond being and intellect, and that he equates some features of Aristotle's Prime Mover who is an intellect with those of the Neoplatonic One. He also distinguishes the First or God from the agent intellect. As the First knows only itself, emanation is necessary and eternally gives rise to the world. Al-Fārābī intends to tidy up all the unresolved questions of Aristotle's *Metaphysics* and to develop its theological teaching.

The systematization process reaches its peak in *The Political Regime*, also known as *The Principles of the Beings*. This text, in which al-Fārābī speaks in his own name, begins by stating that there are six hierarchical kinds of principles that explain the subsistence of bodies and their accidents: the First Cause, the secondary causes, the agent intellect, the soul, form, and matter. He then treats of each, beginning with the First and its attributes and explaining how it gives rise by emanation to the secondary causes or intelligences, which themselves give rise to the celestial spheres and the agent intellect. The agent intellect is a giver of forms: it emanates intelligibles. The motion common to all celestial bodies gives rise to prime matter, and their individual motions give rise to all the material forms in succession, beginning with the four elements. We have here a realization of the descent and a derivation of both material and intelligible forms as well as matter, from higher causes, through emanation. Al-Fārābī does not confuse Aristotelianism and Neoplatonism; nor does he philosophically reject the latter in his esoteric teaching while using it as religious camouflage in more popular writings; rather he attempts to complete metaphysics as he understands it.

Al-Fārābī and first intelligibles

In his numerous works on logic, al-Fārābī often speaks of first intelligibles, which are common to all human beings and are the ultimate principles of the various disciplines. The study of such principles belongs not to logic but rather to metaphysics, since such intelligibles are not acquired from experience. We saw earlier that this constitutes the second part of metaphysics. In *The Opinions of the People of the Virtuous City*, another emanationist text, al-Fārābī indicates that such intelligibles are of three kinds: technical, ethical,[21] and theoretical. The agent intellect emanates them as conditions for the intelligibility of experience. Here again, since al-Fārābī admits intelligibles that are not derived from experience and whose origin Aristotle did not explain, he needs to turn to emanation to explain their existence. Interestingly, al-Ghazālī will derive the first principles of medicine and astronomy from prophecy, arguing that they cannot be derived from experience. In the *Long Commentary on the "De Interpretatione,"* al-Fārābī scathingly attacks the theologians who deny human freedom, i.e., the Ash'arites, and claims that human freedom is a first intelligible.[22] Al-Fārābī also thinks that even the intelligibles derived from experience and subsumed under the categories need to be grounded through emanation from the agent intellect.

Al-Fārābī and the categories

One of al-Fārābī's most puzzling texts is the *Book of Letters*.[23] Its title has sometimes been understood as referring to metaphysics since the various books of the *Metaphysics* are indicated in both Greek and Arabic by the name of letters. Yet instead of focusing on the *Metaphysics*, this text quotes extensively from the *Categories* and pays much more attention to interrogative particles – the Arabic word used for letter also means particle – that are linked to the categories, such as the category of time or "when." Aristotle studied the categories not only in the *Categories*, but also (though very briefly) in the *Metaphysics*, and al-Fārābī wants to give a metaphysical grounding to the logical categories. In the *Book of Letters* al-Fārābī indicates that the categories are the ten *summa genera* of intelligibles referring to objects of sense perception. Section V, numbers 11–18 of this text discusses the role of the categories in the different disciplines in the order of the Alexandrian philosophical curriculum and in relation to the various causes.

Mathematics deals with quantity, and though it disengages its objects from their relation to sensible things it can account for its objects without referring to anything outside the categories, since quantities, though intelligible independently of their relation to sensible and material things, can never exist without them. This study limits itself to the formal cause. Physics, on the other hand, considers the categories inasmuch as they are the species and genera of sensible things and considers the four causes (formal, material, efficient, and final), though limiting itself to causes that are not outside the categories, i.e., excluding immaterial causes. Yet, at some stage, it ascends to ultimate efficient causes and to the end for which those things subject to the categories came to be. It then discovers that the grounding of the categories is beyond the categories and realizes that it has reached its own limits. That there are beings beyond the categories is something that Aristotle did not say, and it smacks of Neoplatonism. Let us not forget that al-Kindī too had claimed that God is beyond the categories. Metaphysics will of course deal with causes and beings which are beyond the categories, since they are immaterial, but also with sensible things inasmuch as such beings outside the categories are the efficient and final causes of the sensible individual things comprised by the categories.

The text implies that material things are subject to the four Aristotelian causes and the categories, but that the quest for ultimate causes will lead to the discovery of immaterial causes that are not only final causes of motion as in Aristotle but also efficient causes of existence, and that the physical and metaphysical kinds of causation may be quite different. Avicenna will explicitly and deliberately make that move. Al-Fārābī's metaphysics has not yet been studied in depth, but there is no doubt that it begins to explore some of the important ideas Avicenna highlights in *al-Shifā'* (*The Healing*): the distinction between physical and metaphysical causes, and the need to begin with Aristotle's study of being qua being but then to move to an ascent to causes beyond the categories, and from that to derive the existence of all beings, material and immaterial.

AVICENNA

Thanks to al-Fārābī, Avicenna discovered the subject matter of Aristotle's *Metaphysics*, but also some of the problems Aristotle had not resolved, tackled, or raised. Thinking through these issues he centered his own metaphysics in the *Shifā'* on the distinction between existence and essence. I have selected this text partly because it was translated into Latin and had a great influence on Western philosophy, but mostly because it is a masterpiece in its own right.

Being qua being and its concomitants

At times it has been argued that Avicenna's metaphysics makes of existence an accident of essence. Fifty years ago Fazlur Rahman was already disputing this interpretation, and I would like to emphasize that for Avicenna the overt primary notion is being, not essence (see also chapter 6, above, on this question). In book I, following the Alexandrian tradition, Avicenna first establishes the aim of the discipline, its rank, and its usefulness. He also asserts in I.2 that its subject matter is being qua being and so it will need to study the relation of "thing" and "being" to the categories (I.4). In the next chapter he explains what he means by this mysterious "thing" by asserting that there are three primary concepts: being, thing, and necessary (I.5, first sentence).[24] Priority is given to being and we should notice that "one," so important in both al-Kindī and al-Fārābī, does not play an immediate role. For the Neoplatonic one Avicenna substitutes "thing," an attribute of being not present in Aristotle. Where does it come from? Recently both Robert Wisnovsky and I have argued that this concept is borrowed from *kalām* and used by Avicenna to ground his distinction between essence and existence.[25] *Kalām* is in fact not simply a discipline philosophers outgrow and neglect, but has become at least in part a source of inspiration. In both al-Kindī and al-Fārābī the First Cause was already a cause of being, but its oneness or simplicity was what distinguished it from other beings. As Avicenna rejects the Neoplatonic primacy of oneness over being, he needs now to find something else that would ground this distinction. Strictly speaking, "thing" is not synonymous with essence, but whatever is a thing has an essence or quiddity. In God there is no distinction whatsoever between being and essence, but this distinction applies to all other beings and explains their utter contingency. Because for Avicenna there are two types of existence, concrete individual existence outside the mind and mental existence in the mind, even concepts or universals are things.[26] This leads him to select as his third primary notion a disjunctive attribute of being "necessary," since every being is either necessary, possible, or impossible. Avicenna insists on the impossibility of determining which of these modal concepts is prior, but will use them to establish his proof for the existence of God. There is only one being, God, that is necessary in itself. Any being other than God is possible in itself and as a mere possible always enjoys mental existence in God's mind, though it may become necessary through another when God creates it and maintains it in concrete existence.

The distinction between physical and metaphysical efficient causes

Avicenna integrates into the *Metaphysics* of the *Shifā'* al-Fārābī's point about the different approach to the categories in logic and metaphysics, and devotes book II to substances, book III to some of the accidents, and book IV to the relations between substance and accidents. Book V completes the ontological foundation of logic by examining universals and particulars as well as whole and part.

The time has now come for Avicenna to move to a study of the causes in order to provide a foundation for natural theology. Avicenna's conception of the four causes in metaphysics has finally attracted the attention it deserves and we will refer in our discussion to the excellent scholarship now available. Wishing to connect his examination of causes to the primacy of the concept of being, Avicenna introduces book VI by remarking that cause and effect are among the consequents of being qua being. Any being is either uncaused and, thus, the universal cause of all other beings, or caused. If caused, it may itself be a secondary cause of another, or it may be purely passive and not endowed with any derivative causal power. Chapter 1 gives a very technical presentation of the division of the causes and their states. Avicenna indicates that by "agent" he means a cause that bestows existence separate from itself and is not simply a principle of motion. "The metaphysicians do not intend by 'the agent' the principle of movement only, as do the natural philosophers, but also the principle of existence and that which bestows existence, such as the creator of the world."[27] In fact Avicenna had already extensively studied such physical causes and principles in the first book of the *Physics* of the *Shifāʾ*. But just as al-Kindī had required a cause not only of initial existence but also of maintenance in existence, so Avicenna concludes this section by claiming that "that which is caused requires some thing which bestows existence upon it continuously, as long as it continues to exist."[28]

Very much aware that such a claim goes far beyond Aristotle's conception of the causation of the Unmoved Mover, Avicenna demonstrates in chapter 2 that every cause exists simultaneously with that which is caused by it. According to Wisnovsky this reflects an earlier distinction between immanent and transcendent causes going back to the Neoplatonic commentators on Aristotle.[29] Much attention has been paid to this presentation of efficient causation, which will introduce continuous creation to the West and be picked up, for instance, by Duns Scotus in his distinction between essentially and accidentally related causes.[30] Avicenna carefully explains that what people take to be true agents, e.g., the builder for the house, the father for the child, and fire for burning, are causes neither of the subsistence of their effects nor even of their existence. They simply are accidental or supporting causes that precede the existence of the effect and can constitute an infinite series. The real agents are transcendent and immaterial causes, finite in number, which are simultaneous with their effect and act on the sublunary world by means of the agent intellect who is the bestower of forms. The true agent is always prior in essence to its effect even if it is not prior to it in time, since for Avicenna creation is an eternal process that does not require pre-existing matter, whereas an accidental agent is prior in time to the effect and requires matter to act. A true agent is also superior to its effect, while the accidental agent may be of the same species. The father who is an instrumental cause for the existence of the child is a human being too, but the child's very existence comes through a form bestowed by the agent intellect, the tenth pure intelligence. In this way the universe proceeds indirectly but necessarily from the First by emanation as do all the intelligences, except the first one that proceeds immediately from the First. *Pace* al-Kindī, the First is an intellect, but to avoid his considering lower realities this intellect knows only universals. His causation does not require choice or will.

The priority of the final cause and the distinction between "being" and "thing"

In his analysis of the relations between the various types of causes Avicenna insists on the supremacy of the final cause over the others and, therefore, combines the Neoplatonic insistence on the First as efficient cause with Aristotle's emphasis on the importance of the final cause. But if the First is both an efficient and a final cause, does not this introduce some multiplicity in the One? Wisnovsky has shown how Avicenna solves this problem by means of the distinction between "being" and "thing."[31] Since in every creature essence is distinct from existence, the First is its efficient cause in relation to its being, but its final cause in relation to its thingness. So the distinction between the efficient and final causation of the First is simply relative to the creature and its constitutive composition of essence and existence. This aspect has escaped most commentators because the medieval Latin translation substituted "causality" (*causalitas*) for "thingness," a concept unknown to the translator who probably assumed it was a paleographical error. Indeed, the First ultimately bestows on creatures both their existence and whatever limited causal power they may have, but it is qua efficient cause that the First bestows such causal power and not qua final cause, as the Latin assumes. Besides, according to Wisnovsky, the universe proceeds from the First as efficient cause (bk. IX.1–6) but its reversion or return by attaining its perfection (bk. IX.7 and X.1) originates from the First as final cause.

The material and the formal causes

If Wisnovsky sheds further light on the First as final cause, Bertolacci gives us for the first time an extensive treatment of material and formal causes in Avicenna.[32] Following Wisnovsky he shows that the distinction between immanent causes, i.e., form and matter, and transcendent causes, i.e., efficient and final causes, is more fluid than generally thought. In fact Avicenna accepts Aristotle's view of the identity between formal and efficient causes in artificial production and the identity between formal, efficient, and final causes in some natural processes. Avicenna also admits that in the case of material objects form is an intermediate between matter and the prime cause of its existence and, therefore, has some efficacy. Even matter, at least as subject, is a cause of existence and subsistence for the accidents inhering in it, and therefore it too has some causal efficacy.

Avicenna successfully accomplished the program that al-Fārābī had laid down for metaphysics and grounded the whole enterprise in being qua being and its concomitants "thing" and "necessary," as well as in one of its pair of consequents, cause and effect. The key to the successful completion of this program in a unified and coherent manner is Avicenna's bold introduction of "thing," an ontological notion borrowed from *kalām*, in order to insure a real distinction between essence and existence. This also allows him to highlight, following al-Kindī though in a more muted way, the difference between immaterial and material causation. Such a brilliant and original synthesis gained popularity and insured the continuous influence of Avicenna's thought through the ages in Iran, where it would be combined with Ṣūfism in the Philosophy of Illumination (see chapters 11 and 19). It is no surprise that Avicenna's metaphysics, with its sophisticated and complex understanding of causes, both worried and attracted the theologian and Ṣūfī al-Ghazālī, but angered Averroes who saw it as an unhappy compromise between true philosophy and religion and preached a strict return to pure Aristotelianism in a kind of philosophical fundamentalism. Averroes claims that physics proves the existence of God, and rejects most of emanationism, as well as the notion of necessary being, key to Avicenna's metaphysical proof of the existence of God.

AL-GHAZĀLĪ

Al-Ghazālī, famous for his attack against the *falāsifa* in his *Incoherence of the Philosophers*, shows great philosophical acumen and may have been more influenced by *falsafa* than he wants to acknowledge. In the tradition of al-Rāzī and Avicenna he wrote an intellectual autobiography, *al-Munqidh min al-dalāl*, often known in English as *Deliverance from Error*.[33] In response to a personal intellectual and religious crisis, al-Ghazālī examines the four main categories of truth seekers: the theologians, the philosophers, the Bāṭinites (a Shīʿa group who look for privileged knowledge acquired from an infallible Imām), and the Ṣūfīs. *Kalām* has lost much of its previous prestige and al-Ghazālī dismisses it fairly quickly, as intellectually too limited and unsophisticated in its arguments. He also dismisses the *falāsifa* and the Bāṭinites but promotes Ṣūfism.

His appraisal of philosophy, based on his previous work in the *Incoherence*, is fairly nuanced and complex. He debunks al-Fārābī's claim that philosophers use demonstrative reasoning, as well as his slogan that Plato and Aristotle basically said the same thing. If the philosophers' arguments were truly demonstrative they would not disagree among themselves. Their disagreements divide them roughly into three categories: (1) materialists who denied the existence of the omniscient Creator; (2) naturalists who, impressed by the marvels of nature, discovered the existence of the omniscient creator, but reduced human beings to a mix of humors and ended up denying the immateriality and immortality of the soul as well as the possibility of resurrection; and (3) theists who accepted both the existence of a knowing Creator and the immortality of the soul and refuted the two previous groups. Yet even the theists disagree among themselves, since Aristotle refuted Socrates and Plato. Their disagreements are a sign of the weakness of their arguments. For al-Ghazālī the main proponents of *falsafa* and Aristotelianism are al-Fārābī and Avicenna.

In a somewhat lengthy discussion al-Ghazālī does not hesitate to endorse both logic and mathematics, warning that rejecting them in the name of religion would discredit Islam. But he also worries that the excellence of their proofs, which indeed are true demonstrations, may mislead people into assuming that the other branches of philosophy are as intellectually rigorous. His treatment of Aristotle's conception of physics and nature is extremely brief. It indicates that much of what it studies is as valid and useful as the study of medicine but ends with the same criticism as that of al-Rāzī.[34] The philosophers endow nature, including the celestial bodies, with some kind of agency, whereas no natural body or element is capable of any action by itself or from itself. In other words, he too wants to maintain that all natural things are purely passive and inert, but going further than al-Rāzī he will even deny causal efficacy to soul.

Al-Ghazālī's treatment of metaphysics is more elaborate, though it completely neglects any allusion to being qua being. First, he gleefully indicates that the philosophers, being unable to provide apodeictic arguments, ended up differing greatly and falling into innumerable errors. Hence metaphysics gives rise to the three philosophical claims that should be rejected as unbelief, that is to say, the eternity of the world, the denial of God's knowledge of particulars, and the dismissal of corporeal rewards and punishments in the afterlife. These three issues stem from the philosophers' conception of causation. For al-Ghazālī, at least as presented here, true agency requiring both knowledge of particulars and will is God's privilege. There is only one agent, God, and all other beings are not endowed even with a derivative causal power. He adds that on other topics the metaphysicians did err, but not as seriously, and are close to one school of *kalām*, the Mu'tazilites, who, though not orthodox, should not be tarred as unbelievers. The sympathy al-Ghazālī exhibits for the Mu'tazilites may explain why among the *falāsifa* he singled out al-Fārābī and Avicenna, but omitted al-Kindī, a defender of creation in time and known, as we have seen, for his Mu'tazilite sympathies.

Whether al-Ghazālī truly denies to all creatures any agency, even, *pace* al-Kindī, in a metaphorical sense, is disputed. Richard Frank has argued that he does not and that under the influence of Avicenna he even gave up being a strict Ash'arite theologian, but Marmura has rejected Frank's interpretation (see above, chapter 7). What concerns me here is not so much whether al-Ghazālī did indeed abandon a strict occasionalism typical of his school of *kalām*, but rather his insistence that the core difference between the ontological commitments of the *falāsifa* and the theologians rests in their conception of causation and its implications. For al-Ghazālī all the unorthodox positions of the main *falāsifa* derive from their conception of agency, as highlighted in the *Incoherence*.

The Incoherence

Al-Ghazālī's purpose in this text is simply to show that contrary to their boast the philosophers do not present genuinely demonstrative arguments, particularly in metaphysics. He simply wants to highlight the flaws in their arguments and he does not necessarily endorse any tenet he uses to show such flaws. This makes it difficult to assert what exactly al-Ghazālī thinks on some of these issues. Metaphysical questions occupy sixteen out of the twenty discussions and precede the four discussions concerning the natural sciences. There is no concern shown for being qua being; the focus is natural theology. Why al-Ghazālī adopts an order that is the reverse of the traditional philosophical curriculum is not clear, but he may have been more worried about the metaphysical conception of causation than about the physical one. The metaphysical denies both knowledge of particulars and will to God, and so according to him makes nonsense of agency. Reversing al-Kindī's famous contention that God alone is a true agent and creatures are agents only in a metaphorical sense, al-Ghazālī insists that the *falāsifa* utterly fail to make of God a true agent and attribute agency to him only in a purely metaphorical way. Therefore, "they have rendered his state approximating that of the dead person who has no information of what takes place in the world, differing from the dead, however, only in his self-awareness."[35]

In order to preserve God's oneness al-Kindī had claimed that God is not an intellect, and al-Fārābī and Avicenna, though granting intellect to God, had denied his knowledge of particulars. Besides, God's action is necessary, and therefore they do not endow him with will or choice or freedom. Al-Ghazālī, on the other hand, defines the agent as "one ['man,' a person] from whom the act proceeds together with the will to act by way of choice and the knowledge of what is willed" (III, n. 4), and in the first discussion he defines the will as "an attribute whose function is to differentiate a thing from its similar," i.e., the ability to specify one of two or more indiscernibles (I, n. 41). This ability is required to explain creation in time: since God has will and knowledge, he can specify one among several indiscernible potential instants of time to "begin" his creation. Al-Ghazālī, therefore, highlights the contrast between voluntary agency and natural causation:

> If we suppose that a temporal event depends for its occurrence on two things, one voluntary and the other not, the intellect relates the act to the voluntary. The same goes for the way we speak. For if someone throws another in the fire and [the latter] dies, one says that [the former], not the fire, is the killer. (III, n. 13, trans. modified)

Whether or not al-Ghazālī truly grants some agency to human beings is dubious, but he certainly wishes to grant it fully to God. God's knowledge of particulars and his will and power ground creation in time. This leads al-Ghazālī to reject the Neoplatonic axiom that "from the One only one comes" as totally unable to explain multiplicity. In its name the philosophers had denied to God knowledge of the particulars, though Avicenna endowed him with knowledge of universals that would already compromise his simplicity according to the philosophers' own argument.

Al-Ghazālī's philosophically sophisticated attacks on al-Fārābī and Avicenna were enormously influential. Averroes took them so seriously that he answered them one by one in his *Incoherence of the Incoherence*. However, his careful reading of Aristotle led him to abandon the emanationism that had been present in various forms in al-Kindī, al-Rāzī, al-Fārābī, and Avicenna and to endorse a more genuine Aristotelianism. How philosophy moved from the East of the Islamic empire to the West, and which exact texts of al-Kindī, al-Rāzī, al-Fārābī, Avicenna, and al-Ghazālī were available to Averroes and his predecessors in Andalusia, is not always clear.

FALSAFA IN ANDALUSIA

Ibn Ṭufayl, in his philosophical novel, bypasses Aristotle's conception of metaphysics by completely ignoring being qua being, but presenting a purely rational assent to God leading to a natural mysticism of which the various true religions are pale imitations. Rationalist *falsafa* has abandoned the mantle of *kalām* and adopted a Ṣūfī garb (see chapter 8).

On the other hand, Averroes, gradually provoked by al-Ghazālī's criticisms and by closer and closer readings of Aristotle's own texts, vilifies Avicenna for corrupting *falsafa* and advocates with the zeal of the convert a return to true Aristotelianism purified from Neoplatonism and *kalām* accretions. Though the complex and confusing story of Averroes' various views on psychology and on the material intellect in particular has been studied in detail (on these topics see chapters 9 and 15 above), metaphysical questions have received little attention.[36] For the *Long Commentary on the "Metaphysics"*, which probably presents Averroes' final positions, we have a good Arabic edition but no critical edition of the medieval Latin version.[37] Charles Genequand provided a translation and study of book Lambda or XII, making this the only part so far accessible in English.[38] Averroes considers that the subject matter of metaphysics is being qua being, whose focal meaning is substance characterized by form. He rejects emanationism, so that physics must establish by induction the existence of the Prime Mover as efficient cause since metaphysics is unable to ground it.[39] Metaphysics simply shows that this prime mover is also the formal and final cause of the world. As Laurence Bauloye's recent study of book Beta or III indicates, Averroes leaves aside the distinction between essence and existence and focuses on being as substance and form.[40]

Scholars of Greek philosophy are still trying to work out a satisfying integration of various trends in Aristotle's *Metaphysics*, particularly between metaphysics as the study of the most universal, i.e., being qua being, and the study of God and other immaterial beings. Islamic philosophers too wrestled with this issue. They either more or less dropped the study of being qua being, as al-Kindī, al-Rāzī, and Ibn Ṭufayl did, or they tried to integrate these trends in completing Aristotle's metaphysics. Al-Fārābī points to the difficulties and inconsistencies and adumbrates an integration through Neoplatonic influences. Avicenna reaches a full integration by rethinking all the issues and also borrowing a new notion, this time from *kalām*, "thing." Al-Ghazālī's attacks against the *falāsifa* and emanation in particular, as well as the close reading required for paraphrases and literal commentaries, awoke Averroes from his dogmatic slumber and changed him into a reformist who preached a return to uncontaminated Aristotelianism.

NOTES

1 D'Ancona Costa [9]. See also P. Adamson, *The Arabic Plotinus: A Philosophical Study of the "Theology of Aristotle"* (London: 2002).
2 Frank, R. M., "*Kalām* and Philosophy: A Perspective from One Problem," in Morewedge [31], 71–95.
3 Frank [108]. Reviewed in Marmura [118].
4 *L'harmonie entre les opinions de Platon et d'Aristote*, Arabic ed. F. M. Najjar and French trans. D. Mallet (Damascus: 1999). English trans. by C. E. Butterworth in Alfarabi [185], 115–67.
5 Trans. from Alfarabi [185], 125, with one modification.
6 Gutas [93] and Bertolacci [223].
7 Ed. and trans. Gohlman [91].
8 For the Arabic text see Al-Kindī [71], vol. II, 1–133; English translations are taken from Ivry [68], with this passage at 55.
9 See Bertolacci [222], and C. D'Ancona, "Al-Kindī on the Subject-Matter of the First Philosophy: Direct and Indirect Sources of *Falsafa al-ūlā*, Chapter One," in J. A. Aertsen and A. Speer (eds.), *Was ist Philosophie im Mittelalter?* (Berlin: 1998), 841–55.
10 On translations of the *Metaphysics* into Arabic, see A. Martin, "La *Métaphysique*: tradition syriaque et arabe," in Goulet [20], 528–34.
11 *Metaphysics*, 993b20–30, trans. W. D. Ross, *The Complete Works of Aristotle*, ed. J. Barnes (Princeton, NJ: 1984), vol. II, 1570.
12 On al-Kindī's metaphysics see Adamson [63].
13 Adamson [62].
14 For the dispute over whether non-being is a thing, see also above, chapter 6.
15 Arabic 169–71; English translation in A. Altmann and S. M. Stern, *Isaac Israeli* (Oxford: 1958), 68–9.
16 Abū Bakr Muḥammad ibn Zakariyyā al-Rāzī, *The Book of the Philosophic Life*, trans. C. E. Butterworth, *Interpretation* 20 (1993), 227–36. For further references to al-Rāzī see above, chapter 13.
17 Ed. in F. Dieterici, *Alfārābīs philosophische Abhandlungen* (Leiden: 1980). English trans. in Gutas [93].
18 Trans. Gutas [93], 240–2.
19 See Druart [74].
20 Mahdi [190], 201.
21 See T.-A. Druart, "Al-Fārābī, Ethics, and First Intelligibles," *Documenti e studi sulla tradizione filosofica medievale* 8 (1997), 403–23.
22 For this work see Zimmermann [79].
23 *Alfarabi's Book of Letters (Kitāb al-Hurūf)*, ed. M. Mahdi (Beirut: 1969).
24 Marmura [227].

25 Wisnovsky [231] and Druart [224]. Adamson [62] shows the importance of "thing" in al-Kindī's conception of creation in time.
26 See Black [220].
27 Translation of VI.1 and 2 by A. Hyman in Hyman and Walsh [26], 247–55, at 247.
28 Ibid., 251.
29 Wisnovsky [233].
30 See Marmura [226], Marmura [228], and Wisnovsky [232].
31 See Wisnovsky [105], Wisnovsky [233], and above, chapter 6.
32 See Bertolacci [221].
33 Al-Ghazālī [110], English translation in al-Ghazālī, *Deliverance from Error*, ed. and trans. R. J. McCarthy (Boston: 1980).
34 For a diatribe against Aristotelian physical theory that has been ascribed to al-Rāzī, see al-Rāzī, *Rasā'il falsafiyya*, ed. P. Kraus (Cairo: 1939), 116–34, with Italian translation and commentary in G. A. Lucchetta, *La natura e la sfera: la scienza antica e le sue metafore nella critica di Rāzī* (Bari: 1987).
35 Al-Ghazālī [111], no. 58; further citations are to the English translation in this edition.
36 On Averroes' revisions of his positions and writings, see Druart [141].
37 For the Arabic text see Averroes, *Tafsīr mā ba'd al-ṭabī'a*, ed. M. Bouyges (Beirut: 1973).
38 Averroes [137].
39 On Averroes' views on causation and emanationism, see Kogan [144].
40 Averroes, *Grand Commentaire (Tafsīr) de la "Métaphysique," Livre Bêta*, intro. and trans. L. Bauloye (Paris: 2002). See further Bauloye [218] and [219].

STEVEN HARVEY

17 Islamic philosophy and Jewish philosophy

THE BEGINNINGS OF MEDIEVAL JEWISH PHILOSOPHY

The broadest periodization of medieval philosophy, in general, and of medieval Jewish philosophy, in particular, begins with Philo in the first century and comes to an end with Spinoza in the seventeenth century. This is the well-known periodization of Harry A. Wolfson, who explains:

> [We] describe this period as mediaeval, for after all it comes between a philosophy which knew not of Scripture and a philosophy which tries to free itself from Scripture, [so] mediaeval philosophy is the history of the philosophy of Philo.[1]

Wolfson was in a sense correct. The problems and concerns of Philo were to a great extent those of the medieval philosophers.[2] Yet, while it is helpful to think of the philosophy of Philo as the "Foundations of Religious Philosophy in Judaism, Christianity, and Islam," virtually all datings of medieval philosophy begin centuries later and in the case of medieval Jewish philosophy nearly a millennium later. The resistance of scholars to beginning medieval Jewish philosophy with Philo is not simply a result of their discomfort with beginning the medieval period in the first century. More importantly, if one begins medieval Jewish philosophy with Philo, there is no continuity. From Philo to the ninth century, there are no writings that may be considered Jewish philosophy.[3] Moreover, although Wolfson can speak of the recurrence of Philonic views in post-Philonic Islamic and Jewish philosophy, Philo – as far as we know – was not translated into Arabic or Hebrew and accordingly had no direct influence upon Jewish philosophers until the Renaissance. For these reasons it seems preferable to begin medieval Jewish philosophy in the ninth and early tenth century – the same time that Islamic philosophy begins – with figures such as Dāwūd al-Muqammaṣ (early ninth century), Isaac Israeli (d. 955), and Saadia Gaon (882–942).

It is not a coincidence that philosophy emerges in Islam and Judaism in the same period and in the same lands. The sudden awakening of interest in philosophy among Jews may be attributed directly to the translation movements of the ninth and tenth centuries, centered in Baghdad, that translated numerous Greek philosophic and scientific works into Arabic; the ascendancy of Mu'tazilite *kalām* under the caliph al-Ma'mūn in the first third of the ninth century in Baghdad; and the influence of the first Muslim philosopher, al-Kindī, in the first half of the ninth century, also in Baghdad. Thus, for example, al-Muqammaṣ was a *mutakallim* whose views were similar to those of contemporary Mu'tazilite theologians; Israeli was a Neoplatonist philosopher, influenced directly or indirectly by al-Kindī;[4] and Saadia, while much indebted to the structure and arguments of the Mu'tazilites, was an eclectic thinker whose major theological-philosophic work, *Kitāb al-amānāt wa al-i'tiqādāt* (*Book of Beliefs and Opinions*), reveals a familiarity with the teachings of a variety of philosophic and theological schools.

THE DIVERGENT PATHS OF MEDIEVAL ISLAMIC AND JEWISH PHILOSOPHY

In short, the same factors that occasioned the birth of philosophy in Islam in the ninth century made possible the renewed interest in philosophy among Jews. Shlomo Pines, one of the leading scholars of Jewish philosophy of the past century, has thus written:

> Approximately from the ninth to the thirteenth centuries, Jewish philosophical and theological thought participated in the evolution of Islamic philosophy and theology and manifested only in a limited sense a continuity of its own. Jewish philosophers showed no particular preference for philosophic texts written by Jewish authors over those composed by Muslims.[5]

Yet while it is true that philosophy appears in the medieval period at the same time among Jews as it does among Muslims and that "Jewish philosophical and theological thought participated in the evolution of Islamic philosophy and theology," it would be a mistake to assume that Jewish philosophy and Islamic philosophy pursued parallel tracks from their beginnings in the ninth century to the turn of the thirteenth century. In fact, their histories are in some crucial respects quite different. This may be seen from the following thumbnail sketches of the histories of medieval Islamic philosophy and Jewish philosophy.

Islamic philosophy began in the ninth century with al-Kindī, the "philosopher of the Arabs," a well-known and prolific author. After al-Kindī, philosophy in Islam spread in different directions with various Islamic sects finding Plotinus' teachings, particularly as disseminated in the so-called *Theology of Aristotle*, a key to understanding their own theological doctrines. Here mention may be made of the Ismāʿīlīs and their adoption and explication of Neoplatonic teachings. The central role of al-Kindī in the development of Islamic philosophy, through his own writings, through the many important Greek philosophic and scientific works that were translated for him and his circle, and through his efforts to legitimize the philosophic teachings of the ancients, is becoming more and more evident.[6] Yet despite al-Kindī's undisputed place in the history of Islamic philosophy, he is often passed over in medieval Arabic listings of the leading Islamic philosophers.[7] It is al-Fārābī (ca. 870–950) who is recognized as the first outstanding Islamic philosopher. He is the founder of the tradition in Islamic philosophy rooted in the orderly study of Aristotelian logic, physics, and metaphysics, and indebted to Plato in matters of political philosophy. While al-Kindī was familiar with Aristotle's writings, he was no Aristotelian; and while al-Fārābī's writings exhibit Neoplatonic features, he was no Neoplatonist.[8] Al-Fārābī was followed by Avicenna in the East and Ibn Bājja, Ibn Ṭufayl, and Averroes in the twelfth-century Spanish West. There are significant differences among these thinkers, but all belong to the tradition of Islamic philosophy founded by al-Fārābī. While it would not be accurate to claim, as many have done, that philosophy in Islam dies with the death of Averroes at the end of the twelfth century, there is a sense in which this is true. The great tradition of Islamic philosophy inaugurated by al-Fārābī comes to an abrupt end or is at least muted. Later philosophers in Islam will fail to appreciate the importance of Aristotelian logic and the orderly study of Aristotelian natural science and in some cases will dilute their philosophy with heavy doses of mysticism or esoterica.

Medieval Jewish philosophy begins, as we have seen, in the late ninth, early tenth century with Isaac Israeli and, a bit later, Saadia Gaon.[9] These are two very different thinkers. Israeli is a Neoplatonist philosopher very much indebted to al-Kindī, yet, as Husik has pointed out, "he never quotes any Jewish works, and there is nothing in his writings to indicate that he is a Jew and is making an effort to harmonize Judaism with philosophy and science."[10] In contrast, Saadia is intent on proving rationally the theological truths of Judaism and showing the weaknesses and inadequacies of those arguments that gainsay those truths. He thus explains:

> We inquire into and speculate about matters of our religion with two objectives in mind. One of these is to have verified in fact what we have learned from the prophets of God theoretically. The second is to refute him who argues against us in regard to anything pertaining to our religion.[11]

For Saadia, philosophy is thus at the service of religion, but for him logical reasoning is also a valid source of truth in its own right. As a source of truth, no less so than Scripture, the teachings of reason – when properly understood – may be expected to accord with those of Judaism. When this agreement is seen, our beliefs become concretized and no doubts remain.

This view of reason is maintained by later thinkers even in anti-rationalistic tracts such as Judah Halevi's *Kuzari*, which says, "Heaven forbid that there should be anything in the Bible to contradict that which is manifest or demonstrated."[12] Jews like Saadia thus turned to philosophy to strengthen Jewish belief, while others like Israeli turned to philosophy for the sake of knowledge. Whatever the motivations, what is remarkable is that few Jewish philosophers or philosophic theologians from Saadia and Israeli to the second half of the twelfth century exhibit any influence by or interest in al-Fārābī, Avicenna (980–1037), Ibn Bājja (d. 1139), or any of the other Islamic philosophers in the Farabian tradition of *falsafa*. In fact, although Halevi's *Kuzari* (1140) is in part a critique of that stream of Aristotelian philosophy that was espoused by the Islamic *falāsifa*,[13] it is hard to know what occasioned this particular critique. As Pines has shown, his portrayal of the teachings of the philosophers is based on those of Ibn Bājja and Avicenna,[14] but which Jewish philosophers of Halevi's day were influenced by or even well read in these philosophers? Halevi's young friend Abraham ibn Ezra was certainly influenced by some of Avicenna's writings – for example, in his treatment of God's knowledge of particulars and in the distinction between necessary and possible existence – but he is the exception and in any case can hardly be classified as a philosopher in the Farabian mold. Similarly, the other known Jewish philosophers in Spain at the time – the most important of whom was Solomon ibn Gabirol (1021–58 or 1070) – may all be classed as primarily Neoplatonist thinkers, who show little interest in the *falāsifa*. All this changes with Abraham ibn Da'ud (ca. 1110–80), who, as Husik writes, was "the first Jewish philosopher who shows an intimate knowledge of the works of Aristotle and makes a deliberate effort to harmonize the Aristotelian system with Judaism."[15] Ibn Da'ud's debt to al-Fārābī and, in particular, Avicenna has recently been delineated,[16] yet his place as the first Jewish philosopher in the *falāsifa* tradition is quickly overshadowed by Maimonides (1138–1204), the best-known and perhaps greatest of the medieval Jewish thinkers. Maimonides' own philosophic teachings are rooted in the writings of al-Fārābī, Avicenna, and Ibn Bājja.

After Maimonides, Hebrew replaces Arabic as the primary language of Jewish philosophic discourse. The works of the *falāsifa* are translated into Hebrew, and the Aristotelianism of Maimonides and Averroes becomes the dominant school of the leading thirteenth- and fourteenth-century Jewish philosophers. Most philosophers of this period do not strive for originality, but rather seek to expound the true teachings of philosophy and science. One major exception is Gersonides (1288–1344), who focused in his *Wars of the Lord* on those problems that he believed had not been treated philosophically and correctly.[17] His target is often Maimonides, the Jewish philosopher he admired most, whose views he claims are not always based on philosophic principles, but sometimes on "theological considerations."[18] Another major exception is Ḥasdai Crescas (d. ca. 1411) who criticized Maimonides, the Jewish philosopher whom he most respected, for being "seduced by the discourses of the philosophers."[19] Crescas' philosophic critique of Aristotelian/Maimonidean science was based on principles of Aristotelian science. The core of the post-Maimonidean philosophic enterprise within Judaism thus accepted Aristotle and the Islamic *falāsifa* as the leading philosophic authorities. While there were Neoplatonic trends within post-Maimonidean Jewish philosophy, these were peripheral, had little impact, and need not concern us.[20] Jewish interest in philosophy did not die out, but simply waned until Spinoza heralded in a new period in the seventeenth century.

These two thumbnail sketches suggest that while philosophy began in the medieval period in Islam and in Judaism at the same time and in similar fashion, it developed in different ways or at different paces in the two religious communities. The tradition of Aristotelian philosophy in Islam begins with al-Fārābī in the first half of the tenth century, continues with Avicenna in the East, and moves to Spain in the early twelfth century with Ibn Bājja. It virtually comes to an end with Averroes' death in 1198. This tradition does not appear in Judaism until Ibn Da'ud and Maimonides in the second half of the twelfth century. Until this time Jewish philosophy is mostly built upon the foundations of *kalām* or Neoplatonism. Averroes and Maimonides were contemporaries. Averroes is the last great representative of the Aristotelian tradition in Islam. Maimonides ushers in this tradition within Judaism. Averroes and Maimonides would become the two leading philosophic authorities among the Jews in the centuries that followed them. It is in these centuries that the Islamic *falāsifa* would make their mark, in Hebrew translation, on medieval Jewish thought. In what follows I will illustrate this impact of the *falāsifa* through select examples.

HOW DID THE *FALĀSIFA* COME TO INFLUENCE HEBREW PHILOSOPHY?

As we have seen, Islamic theology and philosophy, from their very beginnings, exercised a direct influence upon contemporary Jewish thought. Yet we have also seen that while the Mu'tazilites and the Muslim Neoplatonists impacted on their Jewish contemporaries, al-Fārābī and his school of *falāsifa* were all but neglected until the second half of the twelfth century. In this light, how can their dominant role in post-Maimonidean Hebrew philosophy be explained?

The answer lies in Maimonides. He was immediately recognized as the outstanding thinker of his time, and in his *Guide of the Perplexed* he expounded the Aristotelianism of the *falāsifa*. Yet perhaps the single most telling document regarding the influence of the *falāsifa* on post-Maimonidean Hebrew thought is Maimonides' well-known letter to Samuel ibn Tibbon in which he recommends which philosophers to study and which to avoid. The two most noticeable features of this part of Maimonides' letter to Ibn Tibbon are that he does not recommend a single Jewish thinker or a single Neoplatonic work. Aristotle is the supreme philosopher, but he can only be understood fully through the commentaries of Alexander of Aphrodisias, Themistius, and Averroes. Apart from Aristotle, Maimonides reserves his praise and recommendations for the Islamic *falāsifa*. Everything the scholar al-Fārābī wrote is "fine flour," the books of Avicenna, while not equal to those of al-Fārābī, are useful and should be studied and reflected upon, and Ibn Bājja was a great philosopher, whose words and compositions are all straightforward. Maimonides' recommendations in this letter to a remarkable extent determined the philosophers and the philosophic texts that were to be translated from Arabic into Hebrew.[21] The Arabic philosophic texts that were translated became the philosophic texts that were accessible and hence studied by the medieval Jewish thinkers who read no Arabic. Thus, for example, Aristotle, the Philosopher whose books could not be fully understood without commentary, was translated into Hebrew in only a few instances, while all or nearly all of Averroes' thirty-six commentaries on his works were systematically translated into Hebrew. Post-Maimonidean Jewish philosophers thus studied Aristotelian philosophy and science through the commentaries of Averroes.[22]

THE INFLUENCE OF THE POLITICAL TEACHINGS OF THE *FALĀSIFA*

The importance of political philosophy for the *falāsifa* is now generally appreciated. Leo Strauss was the first modern scholar to state that al-Fārābī "presented the whole of philosophy proper within a political framework."[23] Muhsin Mahdi, the leading scholar today of medieval Islamic political philosophy in general and al-Fārābī in particular, has in various studies explicated the nature of the Islamic tradition of Platonic political philosophy founded by al-Fārābī. According to Mahdi, al-Fārābī "brought to the fore the theme of the relationship between philosophy and politics in a context where the overriding question was the relationship between philosophy and religion."[24] The political philosophy of the *falāsifa* focuses on subjects such as the true happiness and perfection of man and how one ought to live one's life in order to achieve these goals. Accordingly, this philosophy is concerned with the various roles of religion and of philosophy in the well-being of the city and in the attainment of individual human happiness. The Islamic *falāsifa* wrote as Muslims living in an Islamic community and, in particular, sought to adapt Plato's political teachings to their own religious communities. To what extent did their political teachings on the relationship between religion and philosophy influence medieval Jewish thought?

The influence of the political teachings of the Islamic *falāsifa* upon Jewish thought is best seen in Maimonides.[25] This influence is reflected in his discussions of such topics as the purpose of law, the differences between divine law and human law, the nature of human perfection, the nature of prophecy, the relation between the prophet and the philosopher, the role of the prophet in the city, and the extent to which man is a political animal.

In his discussion of these topics it is possible that Maimonides was influenced directly by Plato or by Galenic or Neoplatonic summaries of Plato's dialogues. It is certain, however, that the predominant influence upon his political teachings was that of al-Fārābī and to a lesser extent Avicenna and Ibn Bājja. After Maimonides, when the primary language of philosophy for Jews in the West became Hebrew, Jews who did not have access to Arabic or Latin translations no longer had direct access to Plato or any Greek summaries of the dialogues. The only version of a Platonic text translated into Hebrew was Samuel ben Judah of Marseilles' version of Averroes' *Commentary on Plato's Republic*, completed in 1320 and thus one of the last of Averroes' commentaries to be translated into Hebrew. Samuel wrote that until his translation "no part of this science [i.e., political science] was translated or came into our possession, neither from the pen of the Philosopher (i.e., Aristotle) nor from anyone else, except what is to be found in the *Book of the Principles of Existing Things* [that is, the *Political Regime*] of al-Fārābī."[26] While Samuel's statement is not completely accurate,[27] it does reflect his own knowledge, that of a learned Provençal student of philosophy in the early fourteenth century. Accordingly, not only did the Hebrew reader not have access to the political teachings of Plato, he barely had access to the political teachings of the *falāsifa*. To the extent that this was true, the *falāsifa* exerted their influence upon Hebrew thinkers in the area of political philosophy directly through a few texts of al-Fārābī and mostly indirectly through Maimonides' *Guide*.

Thus, for example, Nissim of Marseilles, writing in the first quarter of the fourteenth century, is influenced by al-Fārābī's *Political Regime* in his discussion of the need for a ruler and the account of the perfect ruler, by al-Fārābī's *Enumeration of the Sciences* in his approach to religion and philosophy, by Averroes' *Epitome of the "Parva Naturalia"* in his discussion of prophecy, but most of all by Maimonides' *Guide*.[28] Within decades of Samuel's translation, new translations of political works by al-Fārābī, Avicenna, Ibn Bājja, Ibn Ṭufayl, and Averroes appeared and Hebrew commentaries were written on many of them, but the prime conduit for propagating the political teachings of the *falāsifa* remained Maimonides' *Guide*. The situation was quite different in the areas of logic, physics, psychology, and metaphysics, where major writings and commentaries of the *falāsifa* were translated into Hebrew, were well known, and their influence more direct.

THE ART OF WRITING OF THE *FALĀSIFA* AND THEIR JEWISH FOLLOWERS

The influence of the *falāsifa* upon Maimonides' political teachings in particular as well as upon later Jewish political thought in general extended beyond the treatment of particular subjects to the art of writing about them. Avicenna had written that "it is not proper for any man to reveal that he possesses knowledge he is hiding from the vulgar [*al-'āmma*] . . . Rather, he should let them know of God's majesty and greatness through symbols and similitudes."[29] Maimonides in a similar vein speaks of the "secrets and mysteries of the Torah" and the need to conceal them from the vulgar. He explains in the introduction to the *Guide* that his "purpose is that the truths be glimpsed and then again be concealed, so as not to oppose that divine purpose which one cannot possibly oppose and which has concealed from the vulgar among the people those truths especially requisite for his apprehension."[30] Maimonides relates that the sages, who possessed knowledge of God, spoke in parables and riddles when they wished to teach something of this subject matter.[31] In his introduction, he discusses his own esoteric method of writing the *Guide* and gives pointers to his qualified readers on how to understand his meaning. Later in part I, he explains that the true opinions concerning the secrets and mysteries of the Torah were not hidden, enclosed in riddles and treated by all men of knowledge with all sorts of artifice through which they could teach them without expounding them explicitly, because of something bad being hidden in them, or because they undermine the foundations of Law . . . Rather have they been hidden because at the outset the intellect is incapable of receiving them . . . This is the cause of the fact that the "Torah speaketh in the language of the sons of man" [BT Yevamot 71a, BT Bava Meṣi'a 31b] . . . This is so because it is presented in such a manner as to make it possible for the young, the women, and all the people to begin with it and to learn it. Now it is not within their power to understand these matters as they truly are. Hence they are confined to accepting tradition with regard to all sound opinions that are of such a sort that it is preferable that they should be pronounced as true and with regard to all representations of this kind – and this in such a manner that the mind is led toward the existence of the objects of these opinions and representations but not toward grasping their essence as it truly is.[32]

In other words, Maimonides wishes to assure his vulgar reader that although the Torah, the sages, and he himself engage in concealment, this is not because the teachings that are so hidden undermine the faith. Rather it is a consequence of the different intellects of man. Some are able to understand the secrets of the Torah as they truly are, while most others must understand these truths through tradition and through representations of them. The truths are basically the same, but they are known in different ways. As for knowing these secrets as they truly are, Maimonides had assured the reader in the introduction that "these great secrets are [not] fully and completely known to anyone among us."[33]

Maimonides' distinction between his intended readers and the vulgar readers or between the few and the many reflects the approach of the *falāsifa*. Al-Fārābī, for example, had written in his *Attainment of Happiness*:

[N]ations and the citizens of cities are composed of some who are the elect [*al-khāṣṣa*] and others who are the vulgar [*al-'āmma*]. The vulgar confine themselves, or should be confined, to theoretical cognitions that are in conformity with unexamined common opinion. The elect do not . . . but reach their conviction and knowledge on the basis of premises subjected to thorough scrutiny.[34]

This distinction between the elite and the multitude was understood by all the *falāsifa* and is the underlying reason for their esotericism.

This does not mean that they agreed either on the limitations of human knowledge or on the intellectual capabilities of the multitude. In fact, there was no standard position. The issue of the limitations of human knowledge for Maimonides and the Islamic *falāsifa* has been discussed in recent decades in several important studies.[35] As for the intellectual capabilities of the multitude, it is, as we have seen, agreed by the *falāsifa* that they cannot know things by demonstration or as they really are. The disagreement concerns what precisely they are capable of grasping. Thus, for example, Maimonides insisted that they be taught to believe that God is incorporeal; while Averroes maintained that this was not a suitable belief for the multitude.[36]

Maimonides' explanation for the need for esotericism, cited above, is itself inevitably esoteric. Is it true that the sages and the philosophers do not conceal their teachings "because of something bad being hidden in them, or because they undermine the foundations of law"? A century after Maimonides, Isaac Albalag wrote in his book, *Tiqqun ha-De'ot*, that Maimonides taught creation in place of eternity. But was this Maimonides' true position or simply his exoteric one? Scholars today disagree, but Albalag suggested that "it is possible that, in his discretion, the Master did not think it useful to reveal what the Torah has concealed from the vulgar."[37] Albalag explained that at the time of Maimonides "the theory of the eternity of the world was altogether alien to the minds of the common people, so much so that the simple believers imagined that if anyone accepted it he so to speak denied the whole Torah."[38] In other words, for Albalag, Maimonides exoterically put forward the philosophically indefensible opinion of creation because the multitude in his day could not bear the truth of eternity, which view would have undermined the foundations of law for them. In a similar vein, Gersonides argued that certain of Maimonides' teachings were forced by theological considerations. Thus, for example, he writes:

> It seems to us that Maimonides' position on this question of divine cognition is not implied by any philosophical principles; indeed reason denies his view, as I will show. It seems rather that theological considerations have forced him to this view.[39]

Gersonides related to Maimonides exoteric teachings which he claimed could not stand up to philosophic argument. For Gersonides,

Maimonides was compelled to hold these views because he believed the philosophic teachings undermined the faith. In other words, both Albalag and Gersonides among others held that Maimonides put forward exoteric and philosophically inadequate teachings concerning the secrets of the Torah precisely because he believed the philosophic views undermined the belief of the multitude.[40]

Maimonides could respond to these accusations that the secrets of the Torah need to be concealed not because they undermine the faith, but because, given the intellectual capacities of the vulgar, they could lead them astray. This raises the question of the difference between knowing something as it truly is and accepting it by tradition as true. In other words, what is the difference between the knowledge of the few and the beliefs of the many? These questions are treated most directly by al-Fārābī in his *Attainment of Happiness*, his most important work on the relation between philosophy and religion. There he writes that philosophy is prior to religion in time and that religion is an imitation of philosophy. "In everything of which philosophy gives an account based on intellectual perception, religion gives an account based on imagination."[41] According to al-Fārābī, the function of the philosopher is thus not only to learn the sciences, to know the beings, to attain supreme happiness, but also to exploit his wisdom for the good of the multitude who can only come to know the images. Al-Fārābī writes that the "perfect philosopher is the one who not only possesses the theoretical sciences, but also the faculty for exploiting them for the benefit of all others so that they too can reach happiness or perfection according to their capacity."[42] Only the man who has grasped the truths can represent the images of these truths to others. As Mahdi explains, al-Fārābī assigns to the philosopher a function ordinarily associated with the prophet, the founder of a religion.[43] Al-Fārābī thus describes here the emergence of natural religion whereby the philosopher brings into being and establishes a religion in a natural way by means of his knowledge and imagination, without divine revelation. Now there is some disagreement among scholars as to whether Maimonides saw the relation of Judaism to philosophy in precisely this light, but there is no question that al-Fārābī's statements in the *Attainment of Happiness* influenced his thinking.

Interestingly, the *Attainment of Happiness* and indeed the entire trilogy, *The Philosophy of Plato and Aristotle*, of which it is the first part, were not translated into Hebrew, despite the great respect held for their author and their important subject matter. Shem-Ṭov Falaquera in the mid-thirteenth century wrote an abbreviated paraphrastic Hebrew version of the three books of the trilogy in his *Reshit Ḥokhma*, but did not specify that his paraphrase was based on al-Fārābī. Rather he wrote that his words were those of "Aristotle or of the philosophers of his school."[44] To the extent that Falaquera's paraphrase influenced other authors, it may be seen as an illustration of the way in which Arabic thought at times penetrated directly into Jewish philosophic discourse without the author's awareness of its source. In addition, Falaquera's paraphrase is itself of interest for the way in which a thirteenth-century thinker, very well read and strongly influenced by the *falāsifa*, sought to present their political teachings to his Jewish reader.[45]

Falaquera alone among the Jewish medievals, or moderns for that matter, attached enough value to al-Fārābī's most important writings on the relation between philosophy and religion, the *Philosophy of Plato and Aristotle* as well as chapters from the *Book of Letters*, to translate them into Hebrew. Remarkably, he omits their most interesting and controversial sections, such as the one from the *Attainment of Happiness* cited above. Al-Fārābī suggests in these sections that philosophy alone is necessary for human happiness and perfection. Religion is an imitation of philosophy that is useful for teaching and governing the multitude, but does not contribute to the perfection of the philosopher's intellect. Falaquera was not prepared to go that far. He was not prepared to say that true religion is an imitation of philosophy and comes after it. Philosophy, for him, may be necessary for human happiness, but it is not sufficient.

THE GENRE OF SUPERCOMMENTARY: GERSONIDES AND HIS SCHOOL

As we have seen, in the areas of logic, physics, psychology, and metaphysics, where major writings and commentaries of the *falāsifa* were translated into Hebrew and well known, their influence is manifest and direct. Aristotle was the Philosopher, but Jews learned Aristotelian science primarily through the commentaries of Averroes. Shortly after Qalonimus ben Qalonimus completed the project of the translation of Averroes' epitomes and middle commentaries on natural science and thus made possible the thorough study of Aristotelian science and philosophy in Hebrew, a new genre of literature emerged with Gersonides' commentaries (written between the years 1321 and 1324) on Averroes' commentaries. Gersonides' supercommentaries were the most popular of the genre, but similar commentaries on Averroes were written by Gersonides' students and colleagues in subsequent years.[46] These supercommentaries explicated the commentaries of Averroes in a way similar to that in which Averroes had explicated the texts of Aristotle. One significant difference is that while Averroes' commentaries could be read independently of the book of Aristotle upon which they commented, this was usually not the case for the supercommentaries.[47] Rather, like the medieval Hebrew Biblical or Talmudic commentaries, they were intended to be read along with the text upon which they commented.

Gersonides states explicitly that his purpose in these supercommentaries on the epitomes is "to explain concisely the epitomes of Averroes on the physical writings of Aristotle, for even though most of what Averroes says is very clear, there remain some profound things that he does not sufficiently explain."[48] His stated aim is more ambitious in his introduction to the middle commentaries on the physical writings:

> In the places where our opinion does not agree with that of Aristotle, we will mention our opinions and refute those of Aristotle . . . This is in addition to the benefit that follows from such a commentary for the students in helping them understand some difficult things.[49]

But these different statements of purpose should not be interpreted to mean that Gersonides is acquiescent in his commentaries on the epitomes. Jesse Mashbaum, for example, has shown how in his commentary on Averroes' *Epitome of the "De Anima"* he rejects positions of both Aristotle and Averroes on human intellection as formulated in Averroes' *Epitome* and *Middle Commentary*.[50] Similarly, Ruth Glasner, who has contributed more than any other scholar to our appreciation of Gersonides as a boldly original interpreter of Aristotle and Averroes, has time and again cited Gersonides' commentaries on the epitomes of the books on natural science as well as those on the middle commentaries to illustrate his rejections of fundamental Aristotelian teachings presented therein, such as the Aristotelian accounts of natural motion and violent motion.[51] But these studies and others that illustrate Gersonides' role in the supercommentaries as a critic of teachings of both Aristotle and Averroes should not cloud the simple fact that Gersonides was himself an Aristotelian who very much valued the commentaries of Averroes. Thus Charles Manekin, who has studied Gersonides' supercommentaries on the books of the *Organon* and has investigated his role as an informed and competent critic of aspects of Aristotle's logic, has noted that Gersonides "thanks Averroes for performing zealously the task of a commentator, which, he says, is to determine the true intentions of the author and not to distort them for the sake of criticism."[52]

The fact is that medieval Jewish Aristotelians studied Aristotelian science through the commentaries of Averroes and respected him as *the* Commentator. While Averroes himself repeatedly praised Aristotle in the highest of terms for having originated and completed the sciences and thus saw his own task simply to explain the truths that he taught (and if absolutely necessary to correct mistaken teachings subtly), supercommentators like Gersonides, despite their high estimations of Aristotle and his Commentator, were less dogmatic and less hesitant to criticize them.[53]

THE WANING OF THE INFLUENCE OF THE *FALĀSIFA* ON JEWISH THOUGHT

The influence of the *falāsifa* on post-Maimonidean Jewish thought is evidenced in several areas: (1) the study of science and philosophy according to the proper order, which entails first mastering logic, then studying natural science according to the order of the books of the Aristotelian corpus, and only then studying metaphysics; (2) the study of logic, natural science, and metaphysics through the books of Aristotle as interpreted by Averroes; (3) the impact of Plato in matters of political philosophy as his thought was adapted to religious communities by al-Fārābī and later *falāsifa*; (4) a subtle writing style that considers the different intellectual capacities and shortcomings of potential readers; and (5) theological-philosophic discussions such as those related to the existence of God, his attributes, his knowledge of particulars, creation, prophecy, providence, free will, ethics, immortality of the soul, and the happiness and perfection of man.

It would be a mistake to imagine that Jewish thinkers learned science and philosophy from the *falāsifa*, but were uninfluenced by their theological discussions. Indeed those Jews who, following the recommendation of Maimonides, learned science from Averroes' commentaries inevitably had to confront his theological teachings that could be found embedded in the commentaries. It is only reasonable that if they respected his philosophy and science, they would consider carefully his theological philosophy. It thus is not surprising that when Rabbi Ḥasdai Crescas wrote his *Light of the Lord*, as part of his efforts to strengthen the faith of the Jewish communities of Spain after the devastating massacres and mass conversions of 1391, he began with a pioneering critique of fundamental teachings of Aristotelian/Averroist natural science. After all, it was this science that led some of its followers to believe in an impersonal God and an eternal world without the possibility of miracles, a world that held little hope for the immortal existence and happiness of the individual soul. For Crescas, it was not reason that was to blame, but the "weak premises" of Aristotelian/Averroist science and "the fallaciousness of its proofs and the fraudulence of its arguments."[54] In his defense of Judaism against this science, Crescas, like al-Ghazālī before him, employed his extensive knowledge of Aristotle and the *falāsifa*. Crescas was determined to play by their rules and refute the teachings of the philosophers on the basis of Aristotelian logic and proof. Here again one may see a striking similarity with al-Ghazālī. Al-Ghazālī was the only Islamic student of philosophy who prefaced his critique of that philosophy with a separate, clear, and even, at times, improved account of that philosophy. Crescas was the only Jewish student of philosophy who prefaced his critique of Aristotelian philosophy and science with a separate, clear, and even, at times, improved account of that philosophy. Crescas carefully presented the arguments of Aristotelian/Averroist science in order to refute those that were not valid. Yet his critique of that science – with his revolutionary ideas of infinity, space, vacuum, motion, time, and matter and form – was not immediately successful, even among opponents of Averroist philosophy. Jews continued to study Averroes' Aristotelian commentaries in the fifteenth century, but perhaps thanks to Crescas, al-Ghazālī's Avicennian science as presented in the *Intentions of the Philosophers* suddenly became a respected alternative.[55] Moreover, Jewish scholars were becoming more and more influenced by the new approaches of the Latin scholastics. At the same time the *falāsifa*-inspired radical theological teachings and concomitant esotericism that were to some extent a hallmark of thirteenth- and fourteenth-century Jewish Aristotelianism were slowly fading into oblivion. The *falāsifa* were still read, but by the mid-fifteenth century, it was no longer possible to speak of their predominant influence.

NOTES

1 H. A. Wolfson, *Philo: Foundations of Religious Philosophy in Judaism, Christianity, and Islam*, 2 vols. (Cambridge, MA: 1947), vol. II, 459.

2 Consider Wolfson's description of the "synthetic mediaeval philosopher, made up of all the common elements of the Christian, the Moslem, and the Jewish philosopher," in *Philo*, vol. II, 446–55.

3 There are no philosophic discussions in the ancient Rabbinic literature. See S. Lieberman, "How Much Greek in Jewish Palestine," in A. Altmann (ed.), *Biblical and Other Studies* (Cambridge, MA: 1962), 130, who states categorically that "Greek philosophic terms are absent from the entire ancient Rabbinic literature." See also Wolfson, *Philo*, vol. I, 91–2, and W. Z. Harvey, "Rabbinic Attitudes toward Philosophy," in H. J. Blumberg and B. Braude (eds.), *"Open Thou Mine Eyes": Essays on Aggadah and Judaica Presented to Rabbi William G. Braude on his Eightieth Birthday* (Hoboken, NJ: 1992), 83–101. Harvey concludes (101): "The Rabbis considered philosophy to be foreign to their concerns. They did not use technical philosophic terms, and did not write down systematic answers to philosophic questions." Cf. D. Novak, "The Talmud as a Source for Philosophical Reflection," in Frank and Leaman [234], 62–80. To be sure, theological and cosmological speculations may be found in early Hebrew cryptic texts, such as *Sefer Yeṣira* (*Book of Creation*).

4 On al-Kindī's influence on Israeli, see A. Altmann and S. M. Stern, *Isaac Israeli: A Neoplatonic Philosopher of the Early Tenth Century* (Oxford: 1958), esp. 27–31, 37–9, 42–5, 68–70, 143–5, 186, 210.

5 S. Pines, "Jewish Philosophy," in P. Edwards (ed.), *The Encyclopedia of Philosophy* (New York: 1967), vol. IV, 262–3.

6 See, for example, Endress [67], and chapter 2 above.

7 For example, al-Ghazālī [111], 4, singles out al-Fārābī and Avicenna; Ibn Ṭufayl omits mention of al-Kindī in his introduction to *Ḥayy ibn Yaqẓān*; Maimonides does not recommend him in his letter to Ibn Tibbon (see below); and Ibn Khaldūn excludes him in his list of the greatest Islamic philosophers (see Ibn Khaldūn, *The Muqaddimah*, trans. F. Rosenthal [Princeton: 1967], vol. III, 116).

8 See Mahdi [190], esp. 1–3. For a very different characterization, see M. Fakhry, *Al-Fārābī: Founder of Islamic Neoplatonism* (Oxford: 2002).

9 For this sketch, I will not consider al-Muqammaṣ, whom as we have indicated parts little from the path of the Islamic theologians.

10 Husik [238], 14.

11 Saadia Gaon, *The Book of Beliefs and Opinions*, trans. S. Rosenblatt (New Haven, CT: 1948), 27–8.

12 Judah Halevi, *Kuzari*, trans. H. Hirschfeld (New York: 1964), I.67.54; cf. I.89.62.

13 I use the technical Arabic term *falāsifa* (lit.: philosophers) to refer to those philosophers who followed in the tradition of Islamic philosophy inaugurated by al-Fārābī.

14 See S. Pines, "Shī'ite Terms and Conceptions in Judah Halevi's *Kuzari*," *Jerusalem Studies in Arabic and Islam* 2 (1980), 210–19. Pines argues that the philosophic doctrine presented in *Kuzari* I.1 is patterned after Ibn Bājja, while that presented in the critique of philosophy in book V is that of Avicenna. He suggests that "in the course of the longish interval of time which possibly separates the composition of book I from that of book V, Judah Halevi was exposed to the influence of Avicenna's writings" (216). Pines adds that Halevi "was greatly impressed" by Avicenna, and may have tried, despite his critique of Avicenna's doctrines, to adapt his own ideas to "this newly discovered framework" (219). See further D. Lobel, *Between Mysticism and Philosophy: Sufi Language of Religious Experience in Judah ha-Levi's "Kuzari"* (Albany, NY: 2000), 170–1.

15 Husik [238], 198–9.

16 See T. A. M. Fontaine, *In Defence of Judaism: Abraham Ibn Daud* (Assen: 1990), and A. Eran, *Me-Emuna Tamma le-Emuna Rama* (Tel-Aviv: 1998).

17 Gersonides, *Wars of the Lord*, trans. S. Feldman, 3 vols. (Philadelphia: 1984–99), introduction, vol. I, 93.

18 III.3, vol. II, 107.

19 Ḥasdai Crescas, *Or Hashem* (*Light of the Lord*), introduction, trans. in W. Harvey, "Ḥasdai Crescas's Critique of the Theory of the Acquired Intellect" (Ph.D. diss., Columbia University, 1973), 363.

20 For an account of such Neoplatonic trends, see D. Schwartz, *Yashan be-Qanqan Ḥadash* (Jerusalem: 1996).

21 See Harvey [235]; for editions of the letter, see 51 n. 1.

22 On the medieval Arabic-to-Hebrew translations of philosophic texts and on the influence of Averroes' commentaries, see my article in Frank and Leaman [234].

23 See, for example, L. Strauss, *Persecution and the Art of Writing* (Glencoe, IL: 1952), 9.

24 Mahdi [190], 3.

25 The influence of the political writings of the *falāsifa* on Maimonides has been the subject of numerous studies over the past fifty years.

26 Translated by L. V. Berman in his "Greek into Hebrew: Samuel ben Judah of Marseilles, Fourteenth-Century Philosopher and Translator," in A. Altmann (ed.), *Jewish Medieval and Renaissance Studies* (Cambridge, MA: 1967), 309–10. The following year Samuel made Aristotle's *Nicomachean Ethics* available to the Hebrew reader through a translation of Averroes' *Middle Commentary on the "Ethics."* Samuel's biographer, Lawrence Berman, has written that through the translation of these two fundamental works of political philosophy, Samuel "introduced into the curriculum of Hebrew philosophical studies a new discipline" (ibid., 302).

27 For example, Qalonimus ben Qalonimus had translated al-Fārābī's *Enumeration of the Sciences* in 1314. In the thirteenth century, Shem-Tov Falaquera had translated various passages from the political writings of the *falāsifa*.

28 See Nissim of Marseilles, *Ma'ase Nissim*, ed. H. Kreisel (Jerusalem: 2000), author's introduction, 8–30, and ch. 4, 70–1.

29 Avicenna [88], X.2, trans. M. E. Marmura, in Lerner and Mahdi [189], 100–1. Virtually the same formulation is found in *al-Najāt* (Cairo: 1938), 305.

30 Maimonides, *Guide of the Perplexed*, trans. S. Pines (Chicago: 1963), I, introduction, 6–7. Hereafter *Guide*.

31 *Guide*, I, introduction, 8.

32 *Guide* I.33, 71. Similarly in I.17, 43, he explains that "it is incumbent upon us . . . not to state explicitly a matter that is either remote from the understanding of the multitude or the truth of which as it appears to the imagination of these people is different from what is intended by us."

33 *Guide* I, introduction, 7.

34 Al-Fārābī, *Attainment of Happiness*, trans. M. Mahdi, in *Alfarabi's Philosophy of Plato and Aristotle* (rev. edn., Ithaca, NY: 1969), sec. 50, 41.

35 The landmark such study to which others respond is S. Pines, "The Limitations of Human Knowledge according to Al-Farabi, ibn Bajja, and Maimonides," in I. Twersky (ed.), *Studies in Medieval Jewish History and Literature* (Cambridge, MA: 1979), 82–109.

36 Cf. the selections in I. Twersky, *A Maimonides Reader* (New York: 1972), 44–5, 246–8, 251, 265, 286, 418, with Averroes, *Kitāb al-kashf 'an*

manāhij al-adilla, trans. I. Najjar, *Faith and Reason in Islam: Averroes' Exposition of Religious Arguments* (Oxford: 2001), 51–2, 56–62, 75–7.

37 Cited in Sirat [239], 241.

38 Sirat [239], 242.

39 Gersonides, *Wars of the Lord*, III.3, vol. II, 107.

40 Gersonides himself, whose own explicit theological-philosophic teachings were no less radical than those attributed to Maimonides' esoteric positions, promised to write in a clear straightforward fashion without "rhetorical flourishes or obscure language" as the profundity of the subject was sufficient to ward off the unqualified reader (*Wars of the Lord*, introduction, vol. I, 101). In contrast, Ḥasdai Crescas held: "There is nothing in these things, i.e., the science of physics and metaphysics, which requires secrecy and concealment if, by God, that in them which is heretical and destructive of theistic religion is not called secrets of the Torah" (cited in S. Pines, "Scholasticism after Thomas Aquinas and the Teachings of Hasdai Crescas and his Predecessors," *Proceedings of the Israel Academy of Sciences and Humanities* 1, no. 10 [1967], 51 n. 99).

41 Al-Fārābī, *Attainment of Happiness*, sec. 55, 44–5.

42 Ibid., sec. 54, 43.

43 Mahdi, *Philosophy of Plato and Aristotle*, introduction, 7.

44 *Reshit Ḥokhma* (Berlin: 1902), 61.

45 See my "Falaquera's Alfarabi: An Example of the Judaization of the Islamic *Falāsifah*," *Trumah* 12 (2002), 97–112.

46 See R. Glasner, "Levi ben Gershom and the Study of Ibn Rushd in the Fourteenth Century," *Jewish Quarterly Review* 86 (1995), 51–90. Glasner has shown that Gersonides not only composed the first supercommentary on Averroes, but that most other known supercommentaries from the fourteenth century, not written by him, were composed by his students, who studied Averroes' commentaries under his direction.

47 On this point, see J. Mashbaum, "Chapters 9–12 of Gersonides' Supercommentary on Averroes' *Epitome of the 'De Anima'*: The Internal Senses" (Ph.D. diss., Brandeis University, 1981), lxv–lxvi.

48 Gersonides, *Commentary on Averroes' Epitome of the "Physics,"* London, Jew's College MS. Bet Hamidrash 43, fol. 126r.

49 Gersonides, *Commentary on Averroes' Middle Commentary on the "Physics,"* Paris MS. Bibliothèque nationale héb. 964, fol. 1v. The extent of Gersonides' critique of Aristotelian science in his supercommentaries is just now coming to light. For a clear illustration, see R. Glasner, "Gersonides' Theory of Natural Motion," *Early Science and Medicine* 1 (1996), 151–203, and "Gersonides on Simple and Composite Movements," *Studies in History and Philosophy of Science* 28 (1997),

545–84. See, in general, Glasner's "On the Writings of Gersonides' Philosophical Commentaries," in *Les méthodes de travail de Gersonide et le maniement du savoir chez les Scolastiques*, ed. C. Sirat (Paris: 2003), 90–103, esp. 98–101.

50 Mashbaum, "Gersonides' Supercommentary," xxxviiiff. In contrast, Mashbaum remarks that "in his treatment of the internal senses other than intellect, Gersonides follows Averroes with little demurral. His comments are limited for the most part to mere explication of the text" (liii).

51 See the articles referred to in n. 49, above.

52 C. Manekin, "Preliminary Observations on Gersonides' Logical Writings," *Proceedings of the American Academy for Jewish Research* 52 (1985), 94.

53 Although see Glasner, "Theory of Natural Motion," 151, who observes that Gersonides "does not introduce his new ideas [on natural motion] systematically, and does not argue openly with either Aristotle or Averroes. His ideas are conveyed through a subtle and sophisticated work of exegesis."

54 Crescas, *Light of the Lord*, introduction, 363–6.

55 See W. Z. Harvey and S. Harvey, "Rabbi Ḥasdai Crescas's Attitude toward al-Ghazālī" [Hebrew], in N. Ilan (ed.), *The Intertwined Worlds of Islam: Essays in Memory of Hava Lazarus-Yafeh* (Jerusalem: 2002), 191–210.

CHARLES BURNETT

18 Arabic into Latin: the reception of Arabic philosophy into Western Europe

In the history of Western philosophy the role played by texts written in Arabic is crucial. This can be seen from the sheer volume of works that were translated (see the table that follows this chapter). We have hints of Arabic-speaking teachers of philosophy. Adelard of Bath (fl. 1116–50) speaks of his *studia Arabica/Arabum studia* (in reference to natural philosophy) and *magistri,*[1] which he probably encountered in southern Italy and Sicily. Stephen of Pisa (fl. 1127), who wrote on cosmology in Antioch, expresses his debt to "a certain Arab."[2] Kamāl al-Dīn ibn Yūnus of Mosul (d. 1242), the greatest Muslim teacher of his time, in turn, boasted of Christians among his pupils; one of Ibn Yūnus' pupils, Sirāj al-Dīn Urmawī, became a member of Frederick II Hohenstaufen's household and wrote a book on logic for him.[3] Andrea Alpago (d. before 1546) acquired knowledge of Avicenna's psychology from the Shī'ite scholar Muḥammad ibn Makkī Shams al-Dīn al-Dimashqī (d. 1531) in Damascus.[4] But it is through the surviving Arabic texts and their translations that we can best gauge the extent of the impact of Arabic philosophy. The works translated reflect the various genres current in Arabic.

(1) Arabic translations of Greek philosophical works, of which the great majority are those of Aristotle or commentaries on them. The *Republic* of Plato, though translated into Arabic, was not subsequently translated into Latin. Certain opinions of philosophers other than Aristotle survive in doxographies: see (5) below.

(2) The summary or *questio*: e.g., among al-Kindī's *rasā'il* ("letters" or "treatises"), *On Sleep* deals with questions arising from Aristotle's *De Somno et Vigiliis*; his *On the Five*

Essences, those from the *Physics*; and his *On Moistures and Rain* (part of the Latin *De Mutatione Temporum*), those from the *Meteora*. Al-Kindī's model was the *questiones* of Alexander of Aphrodisias (2nd cent. C.E.), three of which were also translated from Arabic into Latin. Also to be mentioned in this context is the Pseudo-Avicennian *Book on the Heavens and the World* which brings together sixteen questions arising from Aristotle's *De Caelo*.[5]

(3) The systematic treatise on *falsafa* (Peripatetic philosophy). The most important text of this kind is Avicenna's *al-Shifā'* (*The Healing*, namely from ignorance). The title was wrongly (but aptly) translated into Latin as *Sufficientia*, as if Avicenna's single comprehensive work was a sufficient replacement for the several books of Aristotle.[6] Al-Ghazālī's *Aims of the Philosophers* provided a compendious and easily digestible summary of Avicenna's philosophy.

(4) The commentary. The Arabic tradition of commentaries on Aristotle, deriving from that of the Greek, develops from al-Fārābī, through Ibn Bājja (Avempace) to Averroes. Ibn Bājja was known in the medieval West only through the works of Averroes.

(5) The doxography. The Greek model for the arrangement of opinions of diverse philosophers under topics was a text by Aëtios of Rhodes, translated by Qusṭā ibn Lūqā in the ninth century. This was followed by a number of Arabic works, among which Ḥunayn ibn Isḥāq, *Ādāb al-falāsifa* (*Witty Sayings of the Philosophers*) was translated into Castilian. A faint echo of a Greek doxography survives in the alchemical *Turba Philosophorum* (whose Arabic text is lost), which preserves some opinions of Presocratic philosophers among a welter of spurious attributions.

These Arabic works became known in the West from the late eleventh century onward. The beginnings can be discerned amongst the interest in medicine and natural philosophy among scholars in southern Italy, where a medical school in Salerno had long been established, and where Alfanus, archbishop of Salerno (d. 1085), translated from Greek Nemesius' *On the Nature of Man*, under the title *The Trunk of Physics* (*Premnon Physicon*). It was at Salerno that

Constantine the African arrived from Tunisia with a collection of books in Arabic whose contents he went on to translate in the ideal academic environment of the abbey of Montecassino, the mother house of the Benedictine Order. The Arabic texts were products of the thriving school of medicine in Qayrawān, represented especially by the work of Isaac Israeli and his pupil Ibn al-Jazzār. Constantine or his colleagues also translated texts belonging to the realm of physics: Isaac Israeli's text *On the Elements*, the chapter on the elements from the Arabic version of Nemesius' *On the Nature of Man*, a short text on mineralogy, and Qusṭā ibn Lūqā's *On Physical Ligatures*.[7] Moreover, the medical translations, especially that of the *Royal Book* of 'Alī ibn al-'Abbās al-Majūsī (a work known in Latin as the *Pantegni*), were used by scholars of the first half of the twelfth century, such as William of Conches and Bernardus Silvestris, as sources for their own philosophy of nature.[8] It was perhaps in this environment that Adelard of Bath picked up the Arabic learning that he purports to provide in his *Questions on Natural Science*, though specific Arabic texts from which he could have drawn this learning have not been identified.

ARABIC *FALSAFA* AS THE CONDUIT OF ARISTOTELIAN PHILOSOPHY

The burgeoning interest in natural philosophy in the early twelfth century presages the establishment of a completely new field of learning in the Latin Middle Ages, which was to supplement the traditional education in the seven liberal arts, divided into the arts of speaking (grammar, logic, and rhetoric) and the mathematical arts (arithmetic, geometry, music, and astronomy). It led to the recovery of Aristotle's works on natural philosophy (*libri naturales*), from both Greek and Arabic sources. Most of the Greek texts evidently came from Constantinople, where the principal translators, James of Venice and Burgundio of Pisa (d. 1193) could be found together in 1136 involved in the negotiations between the Eastern and Western Churches, though *Magna Graecia* (southern Italy and Sicily) and Antioch were also places where Greek manuscripts and scholars could be found. The majority of the *libri naturales* were translated from Greek in the twelfth century, but the presence of two translations of the same work, and the omissions of parts of the corpus, suggest that the process was rather haphazard.[9] In the case of translations from Arabic, on the other hand, a more systematic program can be discerned, and this was centered in Toledo.

There are several reasons for the preeminence of Toledo as the main place for translation from Arabic into Latin from the mid-twelfth century onward. As the metropolitan city of the Iberian peninsula it was the cultural capital, and the home of well-educated Latin clergy from outside the peninsula. The predominant language of the inhabitants, however, was Arabic, and libraries of Arabic manuscripts could be found in the city. Moreover, Toledo was the closest place of refuge for Jewish scholars escaping from the intolerant regime of the Almohads who had taken over Islamic Spain in 1147. Also, perhaps not without significance is that the last of the line of the kings of Saragossa, Ja'far Aḥmad III Sayf al-Dawla, was given a residence in Toledo in 1140 and was treated as an honorable resident of the city. His library had been accessible to Michael, bishop of Tarazona, the patron of the translator Hugo of Santalla, before Ja'far moved to Toledo. We know only of texts on mathematics, the science of the stars, and divination that are likely to have come from his library, but it is worth noting that Ibn Gabirol (or Avicebron, d. 1058 or 1070) and Ibn Bājja (d. 1139) had resided in the kingdom of Saragossa, and their books may have enriched the royal library.

The translation of Arabic philosophical works in Toledo follows a double trajectory, which can be associated respectively with the near contemporary scholars, Gerard of Cremona (1114–87), a canon of the cathedral, and Dominicus Gundisalvi (fl. 1162–90), an archdeacon of Segovia resident at the cathedral. The path followed by Gundisalvi is the subject of the next section of this chapter. A list of the translations made by Gerard was drawn up by his pupils (*socii*) after his death.[10] It is arranged according to subject matter, starting with his contribution to the traditional seven liberal arts (logic, geometry, and astronomy are represented); then turning to the new arts of *philosophia* and medicine. Whereas in earlier Latin works, *philosophia* was the subject of the seven liberal arts, here it is equivalent to Arabic *falsafa* and is applied to natural philosophy, and metaphysics.

Gerard would have known the program of *falsafa* from al-Fārābī's *On the Classification of the Sciences*, which he translated. For here, each of the main divisions of learning are described, from grammar and logic, through mathematics, natural philosophy, and metaphysics, to politics, jurisprudence, and theology. Moreover, the relevant books by Aristotle are mentioned. Evidently as a preparation for the study of natural philosophy, Gerard translated the *Posterior Analytics* under the title *The Book of Demonstration* (the work's descriptive title, commonly used in the Arabic tradition); for in it is explained how a philosophical argument should be conducted. Judging from the order of the works in the list of the *socii*, metaphysics – the investigation of the ultimate causes of things – was regarded as preceding physics.[11] Gerard chose to translate not the *Metaphysics* of Aristotle (mentioned by al-Fārābī), but rather an Arabic text based on the *Elements of Theology* of Proclus, whose title is literally translated as "the exposition of pure goodness," but which became known in the West more commonly simply as *On Causes* (*De Causis*).[12]

In natural philosophy itself Gerard appears to have followed al-Fārābī's template faithfully. For al-Fārābī divides the faculty into eight parts or "inquiries" (*fuḥūṣ*), and translations of the texts relevant to the first three of these are listed in the same order by the *socii*: the *Physics*, the *De Caelo*, and the *De Generatione et Corruptione*. There then follows *On the Causes of the Properties of the Four Elements*, a Pseudo-Aristotelian work on the different parts of the earth and their elemental constituents, that naturally falls between the *De Generatione et Corruptione*, and the text mentioned in the fourth "inquiry" of al-Fārābī: the first three books of the *Meteora*. These three books were translated by Gerard, and this, apparently, is as far as he got. But his enterprise was continued by his successors. For Alfred of Shareshill, deliberately evoking the authority of al-Fārābī, added the fourth book of the *Meteora* (the subject of al-Fārābī's fifth inquiry), in the Greek–Latin translation of Henricus Aristippus, and translated two chapters of Avicenna's *Shifā'* to supply the topic of al-Fārābī's sixth inquiry: namely, minerals.[13] Alfred went on to translate Nicholas of Damascus' *De Plantis*, which was attributed to Aristotle and corresponded to al-Fārābī's seventh inquiry, and, finally, Michael Scot completed (before 1220) the series in natural philosophy by translating the Arabic collection of Aristotle's nineteen books on animals (al-Fārābī's eighth inquiry).[14]

The main advantage of the Arabic Aristotle over the Greek was that it was part of a lively tradition of commentary and teaching up to the time of the translators themselves. Hence Gerard was able to translate along with Aristotle's texts those of his commentators, both the Greeks, Alexander of Aphrodisias and Themistius, and their Arabic successors, al-Kindī and al-Fārābī. It is likely that the seeds of writing Latin commentaries were also sown in Toledo (the evidence of glossed translations of works on medicine and the science of the stars from the city suggests this), but the first extant examples are the glosses of Alfred of Shareshill to the *Meteora, On Stones and Minerals* and *On Plants*.[15] These were soon supplemented by translations of the commentaries of Averroes (who had been writing in Córdoba at the same time as Gerard was active in Toledo), in which the lead seems to have been taken by Michael Scot in the early thirteenth century. The Long Commentaries of Averroes included the entire commented text as *lemmata*. Thus the *lemmata* provided new translations of Aristotle's *Physics*, *De Caelo*, *De Anima*, and *Metaphysics* in the early thirteenth century, and scholastic philosophers could compare alternative interpretations to the Greek–Latin translations of the same works.[16] Finally, now that the translation of the works of physics and metaphysics had been completed, attention was turned to other areas of the Aristotelian corpus: the *Rhetoric*, the *Poetics*, and the *Ethics*. To this task Hermann the German, working in Toledo, applied himself between 1240 and 1256, translating a summary of the *Nicomachean Ethics* (the *Summa Alexandrinorum*), the *Rhetoric* (together with excerpts from Arabic commentators), and Averroes' Middle Commentary on the *Poetics*, which substituted for Aristotle's own work on the subject.

Arabic texts, therefore, contributed massively to the building up of a coherent curriculum of Aristotelian philosophy, represented by the numerous manuscripts of the *Corpus Vetustius* and *Corpus Recentius*, which was to remain at the center of university training for many centuries to come. The fact that they were *Arabic*, and issued from Muslim lands, did not cause a problem. They were simply the best texts available, and Averroes provided the most dependable and comprehensive commentaries on Aristotle's works. If there were errors, they were errors of philosophers in general, and not of Arabic philosophers in distinction to Latin philosophers. For scholastic philosophers Latin was the sole medium of their scholarship, and different translations of the same text were welcomed as providing different ways of getting to the "truth" of Aristotle.[17] The translators, from Gerard of Cremona, through Alfred of Shareshill, to Michael Scot and Hermann the German, had filled in the gaps in knowledge among the Latins and, through their translation and interpretation, had recovered the ancient and perennial wisdom.

But from our perspective we can see that the Arabic origins of this restitution of Aristotle had a decisive effect on the *nature* of the medieval curriculum in philosophy. Greek manuscripts provided the raw texts of Aristotle's works. But the Arabic tradition supplied not the "pure" Aristotle of the fourth century B.C.E., but rather, as Cristina D'Ancona has shown in this volume, the late Neoplatonic curriculum, in which Aristotle's metaphysics was crowned with a rational theology issuing from the Platonic tradition. Hence the *De Causis* could naturally be incorporated into a corpus of Aristotle's works. These Neoplatonic elements can be seen even more clearly in other texts of Arabic philosophy which were never integrated into the Aristotelian corpus.

ARABIC TRADITIONS INDEPENDENT OF THE ARISTOTELIAN CORPUS

The second trajectory stemming from Toledo follows a parallel course to the first. Its beginnings might be seen in the translation of a short treatise "on the difference between the spirit and the soul" by Qusṭā ibn Lūqā, made by John of Seville for Raymond, archbishop of Toledo (1125–52). Here a medical account of the corporeal spirit is juxtaposed with a commentary on the definitions of the soul by Plato and Aristotle respectively. Noteworthy is the fact that Aristotle is not privileged, but given as an authority in the company of Plato (whose *Phaedo* and *Timaeus* are mentioned), Theophrastus, Empedocles, and Galen. The choice of text may have been made because of the relevance of psychology to theology, in which the nature of the individual human soul was much discussed. But Qusṭā's work was not only picked up immediately in the work of scholars operating in Spain, from Petrus Alfonsi, through Hermann of Carinthia, to Gundisalvi; it also set in motion the translation of a whole series of texts on the soul and the human intellect. First, Avicenna's *On the Soul*, and texts on the intellect by Alexander of Aphrodisias, al-Kindī, and al-Fārābī, all apparently translated in the circle of Gundisalvi; then two texts on the conjunction of the intellect within man with the active intellect by Averroes and one by his son, Abū Muḥammad 'Abdallāh, translated in the early thirteenth century; and finally the Long Commentary on Aristotle's *De Anima* by Averroes. The intellect was a subject which Aristotle was thought to have failed to discuss,[18] and the controversy aroused in the West by Averroes' supposed opinion that the potential and the active intellect are both single entities outside man is well known.[19]

Avicenna's *On the Soul* is part of his *Kitāb al-shifā'*, which provided an up-to-date and easily accessible account of logic, mathematics, physics, and metaphysics. It took into account the opinions of the doctors of medicine (Avicenna, after all, had also written the medical encyclopedia, the *Canon of Medicine*). As well as describing the function of each of the five "outer senses" of sight, hearing, smell, taste, and touch, Avicenna also set up a system of five "inner senses," common sense, imagination, the cogitative faculty, estimation, and memory; these held different positions within the brain. This orderly arrangement of faculties, in which physiology and psychology were brought together, had no equivalent in Aristotle, but owed more to Galen, and was to have a great appeal among Western scholars.[20]

Another item that achieved prominence was metaphysics, or the concern with the first causes of things. The direct knowledge of Aristotle's *Metaphysics* in the Latin scholarship in the twelfth century is meager. The first translation was probably made in the middle of the twelfth century by James of Venice, possibly in Constantinople. But only the first four books of James of Venice's translation survive (in two twelfth-century manuscripts and some later ones).[21] Only in the thirteenth century is there evidence of a proliferation of versions and copies of the *Metaphysics*, with the appearance of the lemmatized text translated with Averroes' Long Commentary, the *Translatio Composita* (or *Metaphysica Vetus*), and finally the version of William of Moerbeke.

Latin scholars had always known of the existence of Aristotle's work. This was largely through Boethius, who, at various points in his two commentaries on Aristotle's *De Interpretatione* and his commentary on the *Categories*, refers to "further discussion" in *libri quos* [*Aristoteles*] *meta ta phisica inscripsit*. Already in manuscripts of Boethius' works the three Greek words *meta ta physica* were combined into one *metaphisica*, and twelfth-century scholars, such as Abelard and the author of the *Liber Sex Principiorum*, quoting Boethius, refer simply to the *Metaphysica*.[22] But Latin philosophers of the twelfth century drew their metaphysics from other sources.

It has already been mentioned that, for this subject, Gerard of Cremona translated an Arabic text based on the *Elements of Theology* of Proclus, namely, the *De Causis*. This work was copied and diffused more quickly than any other translation by Gerard,[23] and survives in numerous manuscripts (ca. 250). The popularity of the *De Causis* represents a general interest in metaphysics which dates at least from the early years of the twelfth century, when Adelard of Bath promises to discuss "*nous* [intellect], *hule* [matter], the simple forms and pure elements" and "the beginning or beginnings (of things)."[24] In the last phrase Adelard is probably deliberately recalling the words of Plato's *Timaeus*, the principal text on natural philosophy before the rediscovery of Aristotle's *Libri Naturales*, in which the fictional "Timaeus" refuses to talk "de universitatis vel initio vel initiis" (Plato, *Timaeus*, 48C). But, whether or not Adelard fulfilled his promise (we have no evidence that he did), other scholars did rise to the challenge.

Honorius Augustodunensis (first half of the twelfth century) revived the ninth-century Neoplatonic metaphysics of Scotus Eriugena by paraphrasing his *Periphyseon*. But Hermann of Carinthia turned to Arabic sources. In 1143 he wrote a cosmology which he called the *De Essentiis* (*On the Essences*).[25] The whole of the first section of this work is devoted to exploring the nature of the First Cause. It is a concise essay on metaphysics. Hermann starts by defining what things "are"; these "essences" are comprised under five genera: cause, movement, place, time, and *habitudo*. There are three principles: the efficient cause, that "from which" (the formal cause), and that "in which" (the material cause). The efficient cause in turn is divided into a "first or primordial cause" and a "secondary cause." The primordial cause is the same as Aristotle's Prime Mover, the Demiurge of Plato's *Timaeus*, and the Christian God. There follow the proofs of his existence: by revelation, and by deduction from composite and moving things. The essay ends with a definition of the two movements of the primordial cause: creation, which is of *principles*, created from nothing and occurring at the beginning of time, and generation, which is of *things*, generated from the principles, and being continuous up to the present day. In generation

God uses an instrument, which is the "secondary cause," and which turns out to be the created universe itself. Hermann derives much of his terminology and some of his arguments from the first chapter of Boethius' *Arithmetic* (the definition of "essences"), and the *Vetus Logica*. His argument that the primordial cause must be the *causa et ratio* for everything else, on the other hand, recalls a well-known phrase in Plato's *Timaeus*, the dialogue on which the *On the Essences* is modeled.[26] But what is most striking is how he uses Arabic sources for developing his argument. The very idea of five essences recalls similar lists of five basic principles in al-Rāzī, Pseudo-Apollonius, and al-Kindī.[27] But other sources are explicitly named. The most significant of these is the *Great Introduction to Astrology* of Abū Ma'shar (787–886), which Hermann had translated in 1140, three years before writing the *On the Essences*. Abū Ma'shar's use of Aristotelian philosophy was recognized and described in detail by Richard Lemay.[28] The Arabic astrologer does not mention any work of Aristotle by name, and none of his several citations of the "Philosopher" follows a text in Aristotle verbatim. Nevertheless, most of the first part of his eight-part book, on the validity of astrology, on the way the stars act on this world, and on forms, elements, composition, and the results of composition, is imbued with Aristotelian philosophy. In his discussion of the First Cause, Hermann quotes Abū Ma'shar's words that "the generating cause is prior to everything that is generated."[29] Another phrase in the same discussion quotes one of Abū Ma'shar's authorities: "For this, according to Hermes the Persian, form is the adornment of matter, but matter is the necessity of form."[30]

The section on metaphysics in the *On the Essences* was, in turn, a major source for Dominicus Gundisalvi's *On the Procession of the World*.[31] This work is concerned with how one can come to an understanding of God's existence, and the different ways in which things are caused by God and his creatures. While in Hermann we have seen how Arabic sources are brought in to corroborate and supplement Latin ones, in the *On the Procession of the World* we see a continuation of this process: Gundisalvi exploits translations made on his own initiative, and those of his fellow Toledans, of works by al-Fārābī, Avicenna, al-Ghazālī, and Ibn Gabirol. In addition, his arguments appear to be influenced by another work of which a Latin translation was not made: namely, *Kitāb al-'aqīda al-rafī'a* (*Book of the Exalted Faith*) of Abraham ibn Da'ud.[32]

Abraham ibn Da'ud was a Jewish scholar who fled from Córdoba to Toledo because of the persecution of the Almohads shortly before 1160, and there wrote several texts on philosophy, astronomy, and history, in Arabic and Hebrew. It is very likely that he is the "Avendeuch Israhelita" who wrote a letter, addressed to a prospective (but unnamed) patron, advertising the fact that he intended to translate Avicenna's *al-Shifā'*, and including translations of two sample passages. It seems as if he was successful in securing the patronage of the archbishop of Toledo, for we next encounter him as collaborating with archdeacon Gundisalvi on the translation of Avicenna's *On the Soul*. The other texts that Gundisalvi translated may also reflect the scholarship of Jewish philosophers in Spain. The substantial work *Fons Vitae* was written by the Jewish mystic and poet, Solomon ibn Gabirol, while Avicenna and al-Ghazālī were the main philosophical authorities of Ibn Da'ud.[33]

Thus, in Toledo, we can see, running parallel, first, a program of translating Aristotle with his Arabic commentators, inaugurated by Gerard of Cremona. This program reflects the interest of Muslim philosophers in al-Andalus, among which al-Fārābī's literal interpretation and commentary on Aristotle was possibly already introduced in the late ninth century, and followed by Ibn Bājja in eleventh-century Saragossa and Averroes in late twelfth-century Córdoba.[34] Second, there is a program of translating works of the Avicennian tradition, favored by Jewish scholars in Islamic Spain, directed by Dominicus Gundisalvi.[35] There was some overlap between these two programs, since Gundisalvi and Gerard sometimes translated the same works, such as al-Fārābī's *On the Classification of the Sciences*, Isaac Israeli's *On Definitions*, and al-Kindī's *On the Intellect*. Moreover, both were inspired by al-Fārābī's *Classification*: Gerard to translate the Aristotelian texts listed by al-Fārābī, Gundisalvi to write his *On the Division of Philosophy*, of which al-Fārābī's text is the main source.[36] But the very fact that there are two separate translations of some texts indicates that the two programs were separate. Michael Scot brought together the two traditions by translating both Aristotle's *On Animals* from Arabic, and by translating the equivalent section on zoology in the *Shifā'*. Hermann the German used both the Arabic commentators, al-Fārābī and Averroes, and the *Shifā'* to complement his translation of Aristotle's *Rhetoric*, and this combination of the results of the two Toledan traditions is characteristic of scholastic philosophers of the thirteenth century and afterward.

THE THIRTEENTH CENTURY

In the thirteenth century in general the barrier between Arabic and Latin scholarship was more porous than it had ever been. We see not so much tributaries from the Tigris and Euphrates, but rivers running directly into Latin channels, and spreading out into an alluvial plain. There were several reasons for this. First, in Spain Arabic had become the language of the intellectual classes of Toledo and of the nobility, thanks to the ascendancy of the Mozarabic community and their influence over the settlers from northern Spain and further afield. Second, in Sicily and southern Italy, Arabic-speaking scholars were encouraged to collaborate with Jews and Christians, thanks to the support of Frederick II and the intellectual vibrancy of his court. Third, the popes for the first time showed an active interest in promoting scholarship of the highest kind, whether in Rome or in Viterbo. Finally, throughout the Mediterranean as a whole there was a greater exchange of ideas than there had ever been before.

Some results of this situation were that, instead of simply making a literal translation of a single text from Arabic, Latin scholars used a whole range of Arabic texts (which they read in Arabic) to compose their Latin works. We have already seen how Hermann supplemented his version of Aristotle's *Rhetoric* with Arabic commentaries of which there are no independent Latin translations. At the same time Pedro Gallego, bishop of Cartagena (1250–67), compiled a text on zoology, in which, aside from using Aristotle's and Avicenna's *On Animals*, he gives passages from the Middle Commentary of Averroes and a lost work on the *On Animals* by Abū al-Faraj ibn al-Ṭayyib (d. 1043). Gonzalo Pérez "Gudiel" (d. 1299), of Mozarabic stock and an Arabic speaker, in his positions as bishop of Burgos, archbishop of Toledo, and cardinal at Rome, and finally as the founder of the university of Alcalá de Henares (1294), not only commissioned translations of parts of the *Shifā'*, but also collected Arabic manuscripts and Latin and vernacular translations of Arabic texts. He was accompanied by Alvaro of Toledo, who translated an Arabic astrological text, and wrote commentaries and glosses on other Latin translations of Arabic cosmological and astrological texts which show that he was reading Arabic texts directly (including, probably, al-Ghazālī's *Tahāfut al-falāsifa*). Meanwhile, in Barcelona, Ramón Martí (ca. 1220–ca. 1285) was drawing on a wide range of Arabic philosophical texts: in his *Pugio Fidei* he cites (aside from those works already well known in the Latin) al-Fārābī's commentary on the *Physics*, Avicenna's *Kitāb al-ishārāt wa al-tanbīhāt* and *Kitāb al-najāt*, al-Rāzī's *Shukūk 'alā Jālīnūs* (*Doubts about Galen*), al-Ghazālī's *Tahāfut*, *al-Munqidh min al-ḍalāl*, *Mīzān al-'amal*, *al-Mishkāt al-anwār*, *Iḥya' 'ulūm al-dīn*, *Kitāb al-tawba* and *al-maqṣad al-asnā fī asmā' Allāh al-ḥusnā*, as well as Averroes' *Tahāfut al-tahāfut* and *al-damīma*.[37] His pupil, Arnald of Villanova, could also read Arabic, and as well as translating Avicenna's *On Medicines for the Heart* and Galen's *On Palpitation* (*De Crepitatione*), appears to have used Arabic texts directly in his original writings.[38] The supreme example of this process occurs in the case of Alfonso X (*el Sabio* "the Wise") who, even before he became king of León and Castile in 1252, was sponsoring translations of texts from Arabic, and compilations on individual subjects based on a wide range of Arabic texts. His principal interests, however, were in astronomy, astrology, magic, and Islamic law codes, and the resultant texts, in Castilian, have only incidental relevance to philosophy, such as the statement at the beginning of a text on the properties of stones and gems attributed to Aristotle, "who was the most perfect of all the philosophers." The *Secret of Secrets*, purportedly Aristotle's advice on political philosophy to his pupil Alexander the Great, was also translated into Castilian before the end of the thirteenth century. Many of the Arabic texts used by Alfonso X may have come into his possession after the fall of Córdoba (1236) and Seville (1248); in the latter city he attempted to set up a school of "Arabic and Latin."

The translations of the commentaries of Averroes show a particularly clear example of "internationalism." The works of Averroes arose within the context of Andalusian Aristotelianism, which we have already sketched in respect to the translation program of Gerard of Cremona; from the same context comes al-Biṭrūjī's rejection of Ptolemaic astronomy in favor of an explanation of the movements of the heavenly bodies which is compatible with Aristotle's physics. Within a surprisingly short period after Averroes' death his works were being translated by both Christian and Jewish scholars, sponsored especially by Frederick II. Michael Scot, who is said to have known Hebrew as well as Arabic, translated, as a sequence of texts on cosmology, al-Biṭrūjī's work and Averroes' Long Commentary on Aristotle's *De Caelo*.

The writings of Albertus Magnus in particular show a knowledge of several Arabic philosophical texts of which we do not have evidence of full translations into Latin, such as al-Fārābī's commentaries on Aristotle's logic and physics, which may have reached him through this process of seepage through a porous wall, and a similar situation can be observed in the case of his fellow Dominican, Arnold of Saxony.[39]

The spread of Arabic philosophical works in the thirteenth century, as evidenced by their existence in libraries, has been comprehensively documented by Harald Kischlat.[40] The preeminence of Arabic sources for Western philosophy can be seen in the fact that, when Giles of Rome criticizes the errors of the philosophers,[41] all the philosophers named are Arabic or wrote their philosophy in Arabic (Maimonides), with the exception of Aristotle himself. Even in the case of Aristotle, Giles uses the Arabic–Latin translations of the *Physics*, *Metaphysics*, and the *De Anima*, since he takes them from the lemmatized texts in the Long Commentaries of Averroes (the Greek–Latin *Physics* is also used). He also uses Alfred of Shareshill's translation of the Pseudo-Aristotelian *De Plantis*.

PARA-PHILOSOPHICAL WORKS

One might be surprised to find, as one of the books from which Giles of Rome takes philosophers' errors, a work with the title *On the Theory of the Magic Arts* (*De Theorica Artium Magicarum*). What has magic to do with philosophy? The work was, in fact, attributed to the well-known "philosopher of the Arabs" al-Kindī, although neither was al-Kindī known as the "philosopher of the Arabs" to Latin scholars, nor has *On the Theory of the Magic Arts* been found in Arabic. The presence of its doctrines[42] among the "errors of the philosophers," however, does alert us to strands of philosophical thought which were conveyed neither through the main-line Peripatetic tradition, nor through Avicenna.

We must be aware that our own conception of philosophy is different from *philosophia* in the Middle Ages, which in turn is not a stable term. It migrates, for example, from being applied by Latin scholars to the seven liberal arts, to being split into the "three philosophies" (moral, natural, and "first" philosophy or metaphysics) of the scholastic period. Gundisalvi in two works (including the translation *On the Rise of the Sciences*) describes the "particular divisions of natural philosophy" as "astrological judgements, medicine, natural necromancy, talismans, agriculture, navigation, alchemy, and perspective," most of which we would hardly consider philosophical. Nevertheless, we have to bear in mind that Arabic philosophical ideas were transmitted via texts on these subjects as well, even though they were not incorporated in the teaching curriculum of *philosophia* at the universities. The indebtedness of Abū Ma'shar's *Great Introduction to Astrology* not only to Aristotle's works on natural philosophy, but also to his logical works, has become increasingly obvious to scholars, and the first seven chapters also of Māshā'allāh's *On the Elements and Orbs* are an exposition of celestial physics. Medicine, notoriously described by Isidore as a "second philosophy," was also a conveyor of philosophical ideas, especially in regard to the elements of bodies and to ethics. "Natural necromancy," by which Gundisalvi would have meant the art of harnessing the occult forces in nature, especially through the use of talismans (which is his next division), appealed to the authority of Aristotle and Plato, and adapted Aristotle's words on the relation of soul to body to that of the spiritual force within the talisman.[43] In agriculture and navigation the impact of Arabic learning did not occur until a later period. But alchemy provides a rich and largely unexploited hunting ground for Arabic philosophical ideas. This includes the *On the Soul* of Pseudo-Avicenna and the underpinning Hermetic philosophy of bonds between all parts of the universe, and, in general, of a "biological" view of generation, involving at every level the mixture between male and female principles, which can be found in Hugo of Santalla's translation of Pseudo-Apollonius' *On the Secrets of Creation*. Finally, the science of perspective, or "how one sees things," described for the first time in the West in the Latin versions of al-Fārābī's *On the Classification of the Sciences*, combined mathematics with physics and medicine, and, through the anonymous translation of Ibn al-Haytham's magisterial *Optics*, engendered a tradition of writing on perspective that engaged some of the West's greatest scholars, Witelo, John Peckham, and Roger Bacon.

LATE MEDIEVAL AND RENAISSANCE TRANSLATIONS OF ARABIC PHILOSOPHICAL WORKS

Direct Latin translations from Arabic texts continued to be made in the fourteenth century. Among these are those of Ibn al-Haytham's *On the Configuration of the World*, surviving in a single Toledan manuscript (Madrid, Biblioteca nacional, MS. 10059), and Averroes' *Incoherence of the Incoherence*, translated by a scholar variously called "Calo the Jew" and "Calonymos ha-Nasi" for Robert of Anjou, king of Naples, in 1328. At the same time, however, that Calo the Jew was translating an Arabic text into Latin, Calonymos ben Calonymos (who may or may not be the same scholar) was translating a large number of scientific and philosophical texts from Arabic into Hebrew, and after this time there was a shift from translating directly from Arabic into translating the Hebrew versions of Arabic texts.

From the earliest period Jewish scholars had always played an important role in introducing and interpreting Arabic texts for Christian scholars writing in Latin. We have already seen the significance of Avendauth and the Andalusian Jewish philosophical tradition for Gundisalvi. Alfred of Shareshill expressed his debt to the Jew Solomon, and Michael Scot was criticized by Roger Bacon for not knowing his source language sufficiently but relying on a converted Jew called "Andrew" (we know that he used the services of a Jew called "Abuteus" in translating al-Biṭrūjī).

As part of the humanist movement in Italy from the late fifteenth century onwards, scholars returned to Greek and Arabic sources, both to discover texts that had never been translated into Latin before, and to improve the quality of extant medieval Latin translations (which they regarded as being written in barbarous Latin). Thus, at the turn of the sixteenth century, Andrea Alpago revised Gerard of Cremona's translation of Avicenna's *Canon of Medicine* by consulting manuscripts in Damascus, and, at the same time, translated some short philosophical texts by Avicenna which had never been translated before. Particular interest was shown in the works of Averroes, but in this case scholars turned to Hebrew versions. At least thirty-eight of Averroes' commentaries were translated into Hebrew from the early thirteenth century onwards, and Jewish scholars such as Levi ben Gerson (Gersonides) wrote "super"-commentaries on some of these commentaries. The reasons for translating Hebrew versions included the facts that first, Christian scholars of the Renaissance were more likely to know Hebrew than Arabic because of their interest in both Biblical studies and the mystical Kabbalah; second, that Jewish scholars were available to help them, especially after the expulsion of the Jews from Spain in 1492; and third, that Hebrew was regarded as being so close to Arabic that it did not really matter whether an Arabic work was translated from Hebrew rather than directly from Arabic.[44]

Most of the translations from Hebrew into Latin were made by Jewish scholars, the most prolific of whom was Jacob Mantino (d. 1549). The ambitious editors of the complete works of Aristotle with all the commentaries of Averroes, published in eleven volumes from 1550 to 1552 by the Giunta brothers in Venice, commissioned Mantino to revise earlier translations of Averroes and provide new translations. The Giuntine edition added further philosophical works by Arabic authors, including some short letters on logic which have not yet been identified. But it was published just at the time when two interrelated developments in European intellectual culture were getting under way. The first of these was the study and publication of texts in their original languages, which led, in 1584, to the setting up of an Arabic press in Rome by Giovan Battista Raimondi. The second was the separation of the study of Arabic texts from the mainstream of European academic education. From the mid-thirteenth to the mid-sixteenth century at least, students of philosophy in Western Europe, following the Peripatetic tradition, used the works of Avicenna, al-Ghazālī, and Averroes as an integral part of their syllabus. In the course of the sixteenth century chairs in Arabic began to be set up in European universities, and the foundations for the modern discipline of Oriental Studies were laid. But this professionalism in the study of Arabic marked the end of the period in which Arabic philosophy was part of the fabric of the European intellectual tradition.

NOTES

1 Adelard of Bath, *Questions on Natural Science*, in Adelard of Bath, *Conversations with his Nephew*, ed. and trans. C. Burnett (Cambridge: 1998), 82–3 and 90–1 for references to Arabic studies. An "old man" (*senex*) in Tarsus gave a practical demonstration to Adelard that the human body is made of a web of nerves and blood vessels (ibid., 122–3).

2 Preface to the fourth book of the *Liber Mamonis*, ed. in C. Burnett, "Antioch as a Link between Arabic and Latin Culture in the Twelfth and Thirteenth Centuries," in A. Tihon, I. Draelants, and B. van den Abeele (eds.), *Occident et Proche-Orient: contacts scientifiques au temps des croisades* (Louvain-la-Neuve: 2000), 1–78 (see 56).

3 H. Suter, *Beiträge zur Geschichte der Mathematik bei den Griechen und Arabern* (Erlangen: 1922), 7–8. Frederick's personal contact with Arabic teachers is discussed in C. Burnett, "The 'Sons of Averroes with the Emperor Frederick' and the Transmission of the Philosophical Works by Ibn Rushd," in Aertsen and Endress [134], 259–99.

4 M.-T. d'Alverny, "Avicenne et les médecins de Venise," *Medioevo e Rinascimento: studi in onore di Bruno Nardi* (Florence, 1955), 177–98 (see 185).

5 See O. Gutman, "On the Fringes of the *Corpus Aristotelicum*: The Pseudo-Avicenna *Liber Celi et Mundi*," *Early Science and Medicine* 2 (1997), 109–28.

6 Scholars of Western philosophy often mistakenly call Avicenna's *Shifā'* a "commentary" on Aristotle. This is not so, and Avicenna never implies this, but rather refers to his work as "a comprehensive work arranged in the order which will occur to me." The relation of the work to that of Aristotle is mentioned only in the introduction to the Latin translation of the section on the soul: "the author . . . has collected together what Aristotle said in his books *On the Soul, On Sense and What is Sensed*, and *On Intellect and What is Intellected*." See Hasse [251], 1 and 6.

7 See C. Burnett, "Physics before the *Physics*: Early Translations from Arabic of Texts Concerning Nature in MSS British Library, Additional 22719 and Cotton Galba E IV," *Medioevo* 27 (2002), 53–109. The last work examines the nature of the supposedly occult effects of talismans.

8 See D. Elford, "William of Conches," in *A History of Twelfth-Century Western Philosophy*, ed. P. Dronke (Cambridge: 1988), 308–27. The discussion of the elements at the beginning of the *Pantegni* was especially important in this respect.

9 The richest discussions of this process remain those in the articles of Lorenzo Minio Paluello, collected in his *Opuscula: The Latin Aristotle* (Amsterdam: 1972).

10 The list is edited and discussed in detail in Burnett [245].

11 In the following paragraph the order of texts is that given by the *socii*, and is not necessarily the chronological order followed by Gerard himself, none of whose translations is dated.

12 For a recent conjecture concerning the origin of the *De Causis*, see M. Zonta, "L'autore del *De Causis* pseudo-aristotelico: una nuova ipotesi," in R. B. Finazzi and A. Valvo (eds.), *La diffusione dell'eredità classica*

nell'età tardoantica e medievale: il "Romanzo di Alessandro" e altri scritti (Alessandria: 1998), 323–30.

13 The four books of the *Meteora* were combined with these two (in Latin, three) chapters, and the whole was supplied with a commentary by Alfred: this implies that Alfred was responsible for the combination.

14 The Arabic collection included the *Generation of Animals*, the *Parts of Animals*, and the *History of Animals*, but not the two short works that completed the Greek corpus.

15 For these glosses see J. K. Otte, *Alfred of Sareshel: Commentary on the Metheora of Aristotle* (Leiden: 1988); G. Freibergs (ed.), *Aspectus et Effectus: Festschrift for Richard Dales* (New York: 1993), 105–11; and R. French, "Teaching Meteorology in Thirteenth-Century Oxford: The Arabic Paraphrase," *Physis* 36 (1999), 99–129.

16 Quite frequently these Arabic–Latin versions appear in the margins of the Greek–Latin translations of Aristotle's *Libri Naturales*.

17 It is noticeable that a scholar such as Albert the Great would refer to a *vetus translatio* and a *nova translatio*, but not to *Graeca interpretatio* and a *Saracenica interpretatio*.

18 Cf. Abū Muḥammad 'Abdallāh ibn Rushd (the son of Averroes), *On the Conjunction*, (2): "This is that question which the Philosopher promised to explain in his *De Anima* [i.e., *De Anima*, III.7, 431b17–19], but that explanation has not come down to us": C. Burnett, "The 'Sons of Averroes,'" 287. See also chapter 9 above.

19 See Davidson [208].

20 Hasse [251], 127–53.

21 At about the same time, another translator made an independent translation from Greek, known as the *Translatio Anonyma* or *Metaphysica Media*, which I have suggested elsewhere may have been made in the context of a group of translators associated with Antioch, whose work had little impact: see C. Burnett, "A Note on the Origins of the *Physica Vaticana* and the *Metaphysica Media*," in R. Beyers et al. (eds.), *Tradition et traduction: les textes philosophiques et scientifiques grecs au moyen âge latin. Hommage à Fernand Bossier* (Leuven: 1999), 59–69.

22 G. Vuillemin-Diem, *Metaphysica lib. I–XIV, Recensio et Translatio Guillelmi de Moerbeka*, 2 vols. (Leiden: 1995).

23 It was copied into an English manuscript before 1200 (MS. Oxford, Selden supra 24) and known to Alexander Nequam at about the same date.

24 Adelard, *Questiones Naturales*, 226: *de NOY, de hyle, de simplicibus formis, de puris elementis . . . de initio vel initiis*.

25 Hermann sets forth the principles of his metaphysics in *De Essentiis*, 58vB–60rE (ed. C. Burnett [Leiden: 1982], 76–88), but develops specific themes throughout the work.

26 *Omne autem quod gignitur ex causa aliqua necessario gignitur; nihil enim fit cuius ortum non legitima causa et ratio praecedat* (Plato, *Timaeus*, 28A).

27 Al-Kindī's text *De Quinque Essentiis* was translated by Gerard of Cremona, but substitutes "matter" for *habitudo*.

28 R. Lemay, *Abu Ma'shar and Latin Aristotelianism in the Twelfth Century* (Beirut: 1962). For a recent analysis of Abū Ma'shar's philosophical position see P. Adamson, "Abū Ma'shar, al-Kindī and the Philosophical Defense of Astrology," *Recherches de philosophie et théologie médiévales* 69 (2002), 245–70.

29 *Omni quoque genito causa genitrix antiquior* (Hermann of Carinthia, *De Essentiis*, 80). This phrase is attributed to "the Philosopher" in bk. 1, ch. 4 of Abū Ma'shar's *Great Introduction*, ed. R. Lemay, 9 vols. (Naples: 1995–6), vol. II, 39 (Arabic) and vol. VIII, 12 (Hermann's translation).

30 *Sic enim apud Hermetem Persam: forma quidem ornatus est materie; materia vero forme necessitas*: cf. bk. V, ch. 4 of Abū Ma'shar, *Great Introduction*, vol. I, 313, and vol. VIII, 76.

31 Dominicus Gundissalinus, *The Procession of the World (De Processione Mundi)*, trans. J. A. Laumakis (Milwaukee: 2002).

32 M. Alonso, "Las fuentes literarias de Domingo Gundisalvo," *Al-Andalus* 11 (1946), 159–73; Laumakis (see previous note), 14–15.

33 The *Liber de Causis* was also attributed to "Avendauth" in its earliest manuscript (Oxford, Selden supra 24), and, in its Arabic form, is cited mainly by Jewish philosophers in Spain (including Ibn Gabirol): see R. Taylor, "The *Kalām fī Maḥḍ al-Khair* (*Liber de Causis*) in the Islamic Philosophical Milieu," in Kraye, Ryan, and Schmitt [60], 37–52, at 41.

34 See D. Gutas, "Aspects of Literary Form in Arabic Logical Works," in Burnett [50], 54–5.

35 M. Zonta, "Avicenna in Medieval Jewish Philosophy," in Janssens and de Smet [97], 267–79, at 267–9, points out the dependence of Andalusian Jewish scholars, from the first half of the twelfth century onward, on works by Avicenna and al-Ghazālī (Judah Halevi, Joseph ibn Saddiq, and above all, Abraham ibn Da'ud).

36 Gundisalvi was also probably responsible for translating al-Fārābī's *Directing Attention to the Way to Happiness*, which is an exhortation to the study of philosophy, whose message is repeated at the beginning of his *On the Division of Philosophy*: "to wisdom pertain all those [sciences] which either illuminate the soul of man for the recognition of truth, or which ignite it toward the love of goodness, and all these

are the sciences of philosophy" (ed. L. Baur, *Beiträge zur Geschichte der Philosophie des Mittelalters*, vol. IV, parts 2–3 [Münster: 1903], 5). For Gundisalvi's significance in general see A. Fidora, *Die Wissenschaftstheorie des Dominicus Gundissalinus* (Berlin: 2003).

37 A. Cortabarria, "La connaissance de textes arabes chez Raymond Martin O.P. et sa position en face de l'Islam," *Cahiers de Fanjeaux* 18 (1983), 279–300.

38 J. Paniagua, *Studia Arnaldiana* (Barcelona: 1994), 319–34.

39 I. Draelents, "Arnold de Saxe," *Bulletin de philosophie médiévale* 34 (1992), 164–80, and 35 (1993), 130–49.

40 Kischlat [252].

41 Giles of Rome, *Errores Philosophorum: Critical Text with Notes and Introduction*, ed. J. Koch, trans. J. O. Riedl (Milwaukee: 1944); written ca. 1270, according to Koch.

42 These include: "the future depends simply and without qualification upon the state of the supercelestial bodies"; "all things happen of necessity"; "heavenly harmony alone brings all things to pass"; "the form imaged in the mind exercises causality over things outside the mind"; "prayers addressed to God and to spiritual creatures have a natural efficacy for conserving what is good and excluding what is evil."

43 See *Picatrix*, ed. D. Pingree (London: 1986), I.v.36.

44 These points are illustrated in C. Burnett, "The Second Revelation of Arabic Philosophy and Science: 1492–1562," in C. Burnett and A. Contadini (eds.), *Islam and the Italian Renaissance* (London: 1999), 185–98.

Arabic philosophical works translated into Latin before ca. 1600

In the following table, the translations are arranged according to the chronological order of the author in the Arabic original. In the second column the Latin translator is named, and a date and place for the translation is given when it is known. Works that have not survived in Arabic, or in the Latin translation, or which have not been identified, are marked with an asterisk. Translations made via the intermediary of a Hebrew text are marked with an obelisk.[1] The order of works in the list of translations drawn up by Gerard of Cremona's students after his death (1187) is given in bold.[2] The most recent editions of the Latin texts have been given; AL = Aristoteles Latinus; ASL = Aristoteles Semitico-Latinus; AvL = Avicenna Latinus. For Averroes/Ibn Rushd's works, the serial number in Gerhard Endress, "Averrois Opera," in Aertsen and Endress [134], 339–81, is given in bold. For Renaissance editions, the dates of first publication are given. Certain works which primarily belong to other genres, such as mathematics and medicine, have been added because they include substantial discussions of topics germane to falsafa: e.g., Ptolemy's *Almagest*, whose first book deals with questions also present in *De Caelo*, Abū Ma'shar's *Great Introduction to Astrology*, which deals with several issues of physics and logic, and Pseudo-Apollonius' *On the Secrets of Nature*, which treats of the animal, vegetable, and mineral kingdoms.

Text	Translator
Aristotle, *Posterior Analytics*	Gerard of Cremona (1; AL IV, 3)
Aristotle, *Rhetoric*	Hermann the German (Toledo, between 1240 and 1250)
Aristotle, *Physics*	Gerard of Cremona (**34**; AL VII, 1.2)
Aristotle, *De Caelo*	Gerard of Cremona (**35**)
Aristotle, *De Generatione et Corruptione*	Gerard of Cremona (**37**)[3]
Aristotle, *Meteora*, bks. I–III (paraphrase of Yaḥyā ibn al-Biṭrīq)	Gerard of Cremona (**38**; ASL 12)
Aristotle, *Metaphysics*, a fragment of the beginning of Alpha Meizôn	Perhaps the same translator as that of al-Kindī's *De Radiis*.[4]
Aristotle, *On Animals* (19 bk. version)	Michael Scot (before 1220; ASL 5)

(*cont.*)

(*cont.*)

Text	Translator
Summa Alexandrinorum (a compendium from the *Nicomachean Ethics*)	Hermann the German (Toledo [?], 1243–4)
Pseudo-Aristotle, *On the Pure Good* = Proclus, *Elements of Theology*	Gerard of Cremona (**33**; *De Causis*)[5]
*Pseudo-Aristotle, *On the Causes of the Properties of the Four Elements*	Gerard of Cremona (**36**; bk.1 only)[6]
Pseudo-Aristotle (Nicholas of Damascus), *On Plants*	Alfred of Shareshill (ca. 1200; ASL 4)
Pseudo-Aristotle, *Theologia* = Plotinus, *Enneads* (selection)	Moses Arovas and Pier Nicolas Castellani (1519)
Pseudo-Aristotle, *Secret of Secrets*	(a) John of Seville (ca. 1120; partial)[7] (b) Philip of Tripoli (ca. 1220; complete)[8]
On the Apple (*The Death of Aristotle*)	†Manfred (ca. 1260; *De Pomo*)[9]
Ptolemy, *Almagest*	(a) Abdelmessie Wittoniensis (ca. 1130)[10] (b) Gerard of Cremona (**22**)
Alexander of Aphrodisias, *On the Intellect*	Gundisalvi (?)[11]
Alexander of Aphrodisias, *On Time*, *On the Senses*, and *That Augment and Increase Occur in Form, not in Matter*	Gerard of Cremona (**39**)[12]
*Themistius, Commentary on *Posterior Analytics*	Gerard of Cremona (**2**)[13]
*Themistius, Paraphrase of *De Caelo*	†Mosè Alatino (1574)[14]
Nemesius, *On the Elements* (= *On the Nature of Man*, ch. 6)	Anonymous (Constantine the African?)[15]
Pseudo-Apollonius (Bālīnūs), *On the Secrets of Nature*	Hugo of Santalla (ca. 1150)[16]
Kalīla wa Dimna, translated from Middle Persian by Ibn al-Muqaffaʿ	(a) †John of Capua, *Directorium Humanae Vitae* (1263–78) (b) Raymond of Béziers (1315)

(*cont.*)

Text	Translator
*Māshā'allāh (Messehalla, d. ca. 815), *On the Elements and Orbs* (*On the Knowledge of the Movement of the Orb*)	Gerard of Cremona (**25**)[17]
Ḥunayn ibn Isḥāq (d. ca. 873), *Witty Sayings of the Philosophers*	*Libro de los buenos proverbios* (no Latin translation known)
**Turba Philosophorum*	Anonymous[18]
Qusṭā ibn Lūqā (fl. 9th c., Costaben Luce), *On the Difference between the Spirit and the Soul*	John of Seville (between 1125 and 1152)[19]
Qusṭā ibn Lūqā, *On Physical Ligatures*	Constantine the African (before 1198)[20]
Abū Ma'shar (d. 886, Albumasar), *Great Introduction to Astrology*	(a) John of Seville and Limia (1133) (b) Hermann of Carinthia (1140)[21]
*al-Kindī (d. after 870, Alkindi), *On the Five Essences*	Gerard of Cremona (**41**)[22]
al-Kindī, *On Sleep and Vision*	Gerard of Cremona (**43**)
al-Kindī, *On the Intellect*	(a) Gundisalvi (?) (*De intellectu*) (b) Gerard of Cremona (*De ratione*)
*al-Kindī, *Two Letters on Weather Forecasting*	Anonymous (*De mutatione temporum*)[23]
*al-Kindī, *On Rays* (*The Theory of the Magic Arts*)	Anonymous (perhaps the same translator as that of fragment of Aristotle, *Metaph.* Alpha Meizôn)[24]
al-Kindī, Commentary on *Almagest*, bk. 1	*Hugo of Santalla
al-Fārābī (d. ca. 950, Alfarabi), *On the Classification of the Sciences*	(a) Gundisalvi (b) Gerard of Cremona (**42**)[25]
al-Fārābī, *On the Intellect*	(a) Gundisalvi (?)[26] (b) †Abraham de Balmes (Vat. lat. 12055)
al-Fārābī, *Directing Attention to the Way to Happiness* (*K. al-tanbīh 'alā sabīl al-sa'āda*)	Gundisalvi (?), *Liber exercitationis ad viam felicitatis*[27]
al-Fārābī, *The Sources of the Questions* (*'Uyūn al-masā'il*)[28]	Anonymous fragmentary translation (*Fontes questionum/ Flos Alpharabii secundum sententiam Aristotelis*)[29]

(*cont.*)

(*cont.*)

Text	Translator
al-Fārābī, *On "De Interpretatione"*	Abbreviated excerpts[30]
*al-Fārābī, *On the Syllogism*	*Gerard of Cremona (**3**), unidentified in Latin
al-Fārābī, *On "Posterior Analytics"*	Cited by Albert the Great
*al-Fārābī, *Introduction to the Book of Rhetoric* (*Ṣadr kitāb al-Khiṭāba*)	Hermann the German (*Didascalia in Rhetoricam Aristotelis ex Glosa Alpharabii*)[31]
*al-Fārābī, *On "Physics"*	*Gerard of Cremona (*Distinctio super Librum Aristotilis de Naturali Auditu*; **40**)[32]
al-Fārābī, *Explanation of the Problems in the Postulates of the Fifth Book of Euclid*	Gundisalvi (?)[33]
al-Fārābī, *On the Perfect State* (beginning only)	†Afonso Dinis of Lisbon and magister Alfonsus conversus (Abner of Burgos)?: *De Perfectione Naturali Intellectus*, chs. 5–6[34]
*Pseudo-Fārābī, *On the Rise of the Sciences*	Unknown 12th-century translator (Gundisalvi?)
Ikhwān al-Ṣafā', *Letter on Proof*	Anonymous[35]
Ikhwān al-Ṣafā', *Letter on Geography*	Anonymous (*Epistola Fratrum Sincerorum in Cosmographia*)[36]
Ikhwān al-Ṣafā' *Final Letter*	*Liber de Quattuor Confectionibus*[37]
*Isaac Israeli (ca. 855–907), *On the Elements*	Gerard of Cremona (**54**)[38]
*Isaac Israeli, *On the Description and Definition of Things*	(a) Dominicus Gundisalvi (?) (b) Gerard of Cremona (**55**)[39]
Avicenna (d. 1037, Ibn Sīnā), *The Healing* (*al-Shifā'*), prologue of Juzjānī	Avendauth (with the aid of an unknown Latinist)[40]
j1 (Logic), f1 (*Isagoge*), bk. 1, chs. 1 and 12	Avendauth (with the aid of an unknown Latinist)
j1, f1, bk. 1, chs. 2–11, 13–14, bk. 2, chs. 1–4	Unknown 12th-century Toledan (?) translator(s) (not Gundisalvi)
j1, f5 (*Posterior Analytics*), bk. 2, ch. 7	Gundisalvi (*De Convenientia et Differentia Scientiarum*, within his *De Divisione Philosophiae*)[41]

(*cont.*)

Text	Translator
j1, f8 (*Rhetoric*) (excerpts)	Within Hermann the German's translation of Aristotle's *Rhetoric*
j2 (Natural Science), f1 (*Physics*), bks. 1–3 (beginning only)	Unknown 12th-century Toledan (?) translator(s) (AvL)
j2, f1, bks. 3–4 (continuation of previous translation)[42]	Juan Gonzalves de Burgos and Salomon (Burgos, 1275–80; AvL)
j2, f2 (*On the Heavens*)	Juan Gonzalves de Burgos and Salomon (AvL)[43]
j2, f3 (*On Generation and Corruption*)	Juan Gonzalves de Burgos and Salomon (AvL)
j2, f4 (*On Actions and Passions*)	Juan Gonzalves de Burgos and Salomon (AvL)
j2, f5, bk. 1, chs. 1 and 5 (*On Stones and Minerals*)	Alfred of Shareshill (ca. 1200; *De Congelatione et Conglutinatione Lapidum*)[44]
j2, f5, bk. 2, 1–6 (*Meteora*)	Juan Gonzalves de Burgos and Salomon (Burgos, 1275–80)
j2, f5, bk. 2, 6 (*On Floods*)	Alfred of Shareshill (?) (ca. 1200)
j2, f6 (*On the Soul*)	Avendauth and Gundisalvi (AvL)
j2, f7 (*On Plants*)	**Liber eiusdem (Avicenne) de Vegetabilibus*[45]
j2, f8 (*On Animals*)	Michael Scot
j4 (*Metaphysics*)	Gundisalvi and an unknown collaborator (AvL)
Ibn Sīnā, *Letter on Medicines for the Heart*	(a) chs. 2–7 by Avendauth and Gundisalvi, inserted into Avicenna's *De Anima*[46] (b) Arnold of Villanova (ca. 1300) (c) Andrea Alpago (1527; a revision of a)
Ibn Sīnā, *Compendium on the Soul (Maqala fī al-nafs)*	Andrea Alpago (1546; *Compendium de Anima*)[47]
Ibn Sīnā, *Treatise on the Destination (of the Soul)* (*Risāla aḍḥawīya fī al-ma'ād*)	Andrea Alpago (1546; *Liber Mahad*)
Ibn Sīnā, Extracts from *The Marginal Notes (on the Soul)* (*Ta'liqāt*)	Andrea Alpago (1546; *Aphorismi de Anima*)

(*cont.*)

(*cont.*)

Text	Translator
Ibn Sīnā, *Letter on Definitions* (*Risāla fī al-ḥudūd*)	Andrea Alpago (1546; *De Diffinitionibus et Quaesitis*)
Ibn Sīnā, *Divisions of the Intellectual Sciences* (*Aqsām al-ḥikma*)	Andrea Alpago (1546; *De Divisione Scientiarum*)
*Pseudo-Ibn Sīnā, *Book on the Heavens and the World*	Gundisalvi (*Liber Caeli et Mundi*; ASL 14)
Abū Wafā' al-Mubashshir ibn Fātik, *Choicest Maxims and Best Sayings* (1048–9)	(a) Gerard of Cremona (the sayings of Ptolemy, in the preface to the *Almagest*) (b) John of Procida (?) (*Liber Philosophorum Moralium Antiquorum*)[48]
Al-Ghazālī (d. 1111, Algazel), *Prologue to the Aims and the Destruction of the Philosophers*	Anonymous[49]
Al-Ghazālī, *The Aims of the Philosophers*	Magister Johannes and Gundisalvi (*Summa Theorice Philosophie*)[50]
Al-Ghazālī, *The Destruction of the Philosophers*	Included within Ibn Rushd, *The Destruction of the Destruction* q.v.
*Ramon Llull's Arabic logical compendium, dependent on the logic of *The Aims*	Ramon Llull (*Compendium Logicae Algazelis*; Montpellier, 1275–6 or 1288)[51]
Ibn al-Haytham (965–ca. 1040, Alhazen) *On the Configuration of the World*	(a) *Liber Mamonis* (Stephen the Philosopher, mid-12th c.; adds commentary) (b) In Oxford, Canon. misc. 45 (late 13th c.)[52] (c) In Madrid, BN, 10059 (before early 14th c.)[53] (d) †Abraham de Balmes (MS Vat. lat. 4566)
Ibn al-Haytham, *Optics*	Two unknown translators before the late 13th century[54]
*Ibn Gabirol (1021–58 or 1070, Avicebron), *Fount of Life*	Johannes Hispanus and Gundisalvi (*Fons Vitae*)

(*cont.*)

Text	Translator
Ibn Bājja (d. 1139, Avempace), *Letter of Farewell (Risālat al-wadā')*	†Abraham de Balmes (*Epistola Expeditionis*; MS Vat. 3897)
Ibn Ṭufayl (ca. 1100–85), *Ḥayy ibn Yaqẓān*	†Unknown translator (before 1493; MS Genoa, Bibl. Univ. A.IX.29)
Ibn Rushd (1126–98, Averroes), *Epitomes on Logic* (1–9)	(a) †Abraham de Balmes (1523) (b) †Giovanni Francesco Burana (1524; *Prior Analytics* only)
Ibn Rushd, Middle Commentary on **Isagoge* (10)	(a) William of Luna (b) †Jacob Mantino (1550/2)
Ibn Rushd, Middle Commentary on *Categories* (11)	(a) William of Luna (b) †Jacob Mantino (1550/2)
Ibn Rushd, Middle Commentary on *De Interpretatione* (12)	(a) William of Luna (?)[55] (b) †Jacob Mantino (1550/2)
Ibn Rushd, Middle Commentary on *Prior Analytics* (13)	(a) William of Luna (?) (b) †Giovanni Francesco Burana (1524)
Ibn Rushd, Middle Commentary on *Posterior Analytics* (14)	(a) William of Luna (?) (b) †Giovanni Francesco Burana (1550/2)
Ibn Rushd, Long Commentary on *Posterior Analytics* (19)	(a) †Abraham de Balmes (1523) (b) †Giovanni Francesco Burana (1550/2) (c) †Jacob Mantino (1562; fragment)
Ibn Rushd, Middle Commentary on *Topics* (15)	(a) †Abraham de Balmes (1523) (b) †Jacob Mantino (1550/2; bks. 1–4)
Ibn Rushd, Middle Commentary on *Sophistici Elenchi* (16)	†Abraham de Balmes (1523)
Ibn Rushd, Middle Commentary on *Rhetoric* (17)	(a) Excerpt in Hermann the German's translation of Aristotle's *Rhetoric* (b) †Abraham de Balmes (1523)
Ibn Rushd, Middle Commentary on *Poetics* (18)	(a) Hermann the German (Toledo, 1256, AL 33) (b) †Abraham de Balmes (1523) (c) †Jacob Mantino (1550/2)

(*cont.*)

(cont.)

Text	Translator
Ibn Rushd, Middle Commentary on *Physics* (21)	(a) †Abraham de Balmes (MS Vat. lat. 4548) (b) †Jacob Mantino (1550/2), bks. 1–3
*Ibn Rushd, Long Commentary on *Physics* (22)	(a) Michael Scot (?) (1501)[56] (b) Hermann the German (?) bk. 7 and bk. 8, comm. 80–6 only[57] (c) Theodore of Antioch (1501; Proemium) (d) †Jacob Mantino (1550/2; Proemium)
Ibn Rushd, Middle Commentary on *De Caelo* (24)	†Paolo Ricci (1511)
Ibn Rushd, Long Commentary on *De Caelo* (25)	Michael Scot (?) (1501)[58]
Ibn Rushd, Epitome of *De Generatione et Corruptione* (26)	(a) †Vitale Nisso (1550/2) (b) †Abraham de Balmes (1552)
Ibn Rushd, Middle Commentary on *De Generatione et Corruptione* (27)	Michael Scot (?) (1501)
Ibn Rushd, Epitome of *Meteora* (28)	†Elias del Medigo (1488)
Ibn Rushd, Middle Commentary on *Meteora* (29)	(a) Michael Scot (?) (1501; bk. 4 only) (b) †Elias del Medigo (1488; fragment)
*Ibn Rushd, Middle Commentary on nine books of *De Animalibus* (30)	(a) Michael Scot (?) (b) †Elias del Mendigo (MS Vat. lat. 4549; bks. 12-beginning of 14) (c) †Jacob Mantino (1521)
Ibn Rushd, Epitome of *De Anima* (31)	(a) †Elias del Medigo (MS Vat. lat. 4549; part of bk. 3) (b) †Abraham de Balmes (1552)
*Ibn Rushd, Long Commentary on *De Anima* (33)	(a) Michael Scot (?)[59] (b) †Jacob Mantino (1550/2; bk.3, chs.5 and 36)
Ibn Rushd, Epitomes of *Parva Naturalia* (34)	(a) Michael Scot (?)[60] (b) †Abraham de Balmes (1552)

(*cont.*)

Text	Translator
Ibn Rushd, Epitome of *Metaphysics* (35)	†Jacob Mantino (1523)
*Ibn Rushd, Middle Commentary on *Metaphysics*, I–VII (36)	†Elias del Medigo (1560)
Ibn Rushd, Long Commentary on *Metaphysics* (37)	(a) Michael Scot (?) (1472)[61] (b) †Elias del Medigo (1488; preface to bk. Lambda) (c) †Paolo Ricci (1511; preface to bk. Lambda) (d) †Jacob Mantino (1550/2; preface to bk. Lambda)
*Ibn Rushd, Middle Commentary on *Nicomachean Ethics* (38)	Hermann the German (Toledo, 1240; 1501)
*Ibn Rushd, Epitome of Plato's *Republic* (39)	(a) †Elias del Medigo[62] (b) †Jacob Mantino (1550/2)
Ibn Rushd, Questions on Logic (40)	(a) †Elias del Medigo (1497) (b) †Abraham de Balmes (1523)
Ibn Rushd, Questions on Natural Science (41)	†Abraham de Balmes (MS Vat. Ottob. 2060)
Ibn Rushd, *Letter on the Primacy of Predicates in Demonstrations*	†Abraham de Balmes (*Epistola de Primitate Praedicatorum in Demonstrationibus*; 1550/2)
Ibn Rushd, *On the Substance of the Orb* (42)	(a) Michael Scot (?) (b) †Abraham de Balmes (chs.6–7; 1550/2)
*Ibn Rushd, *On the Separation of the First Principle* (41)	†Afonso Dinis of Lisbon and magister Alfonsus conversus (Abner of Burgos), Valladolid, mid-14th c.[63]
Ibn Rushd, *On the Possibility of Conjunction with the Active Intellect*, treatises 1 and 2 (43)	(a) †Afonso Dinis of Lisbon and magister Alfonsus conversus (Abner of Burgos)?: *De Perfectione Naturali Intellectus*, chs. 2–4 = tr. 1 and 2 (b) †Calo Calonymos ben David (1550/2; tr. 1)

(*cont.*)

(*cont.*)

Text	Translator
Abū Muḥammad ʿAbdallāh Ibn Rushd (the son of Ibn Rushd), *On the Possibility of Conjunction*	Anonymous (*De intellectu*; early 13th c.)[64]
Ibn Rushd, *al-Damīma* (55)	Ramón Martí (*Epistola ad amicum*)[65]
Ibn Rushd, *The Incoherence of the Incoherence (Tahāfut al-Tahāfut)*	(a) Calo Calonymos (1328) (b) Calonymos ben David (1527)[66]
*al-Bitruji (d. 1204, Alpetragius) *On the Movements of the Heavens*	(a) Michael Scot and Abuteus Levita (Toledo, 1217) (b) †Calo Calonymos ben David (1531)
Maimonides (1135 or 1138–1204), *Guide to the Perplexed*[67]	(a) †John of Palermo (*Dux Neutrorum*) (b) †J. Buxtorf (*Dux Perplexorum*, 1629)
Maimonides, *Liber de uno Deo Benedicto* (= *Guide*, bk. 2, chs.1–2)	Anonymous (13th c.)
Maimonides, *Liber de Parabola* (= *Guide*, bk. 3, chs. 29–30 and 32–49)	Anonymous (early 13th c.)
*Ibn Ṭumlūs, *Question*	†Abraham de Balmes (1523)
*Abū al-Qāsim ibn Idrīs, *Questions concerning the Knowledge of Genus and Species*	†Abraham de Balmes (1523; *Quaesita de Notificatione Generis et Speciei*)
*Abū al-Qāsim Muḥammad/Maḥmūd ibn Qasim, *Question*	†Abraham de Balmes (1523)
*Abū ʿAbd al-Raḥmān (?) ibn Jawhar (Abuhabad Ahadrahman ben Iohar), *Letters*[68]	†Abraham de Balmes (1523)

Notes

[1]Details are given in G. Tamani, "Traduzioni ebraico-latine di opere filosofiche et scientifiche," *L'Hébreu au temps de la renaissance*, ed. I. Zinguer (Leiden: 1992), 105–14. I am very grateful to Dag Nikolaus Hasse for providing further information from a chapter of his *Habilitationsschrift*: "Arabic Sciences and Philosophy in the Renaissance."

[2] See Burnett [245], 276–81.

[3] Parallel texts are included in G. Serra, "La traduzione araba del *De generatione et corruptione* di Aristotele citata nel *Kitāb al-Taṣrīf* attribuito a Jābir," *Medioevo* 23 (1997), 191–288.

[4] In MS. Vat. Ott. Lat. 2048, see C. Martini, "The Arabic Version of the Book *Alpha Meizon* of Aristotle's *Metaphysics* and the Testimony of the MS. Bibl. Apostolica Vaticana, Ott. Lat. 2048," in J. Hamesse (ed.), *Les traducteurs au travail: leurs manuscrits et leurs méthodes* (Turnhout: 2001), 173–206.

[5] Ed. A. Pattin, in *Tijdschrift voor filosofie* 18 (1966), 90–203. New edition in preparation by Richard Taylor; cf. R. C. Taylor, "Remarks on the Latin Text and the Translator of the *Kalām fī maḥḍ al-khair/Liber de Causis*," *Bulletin de philosophie médiévale* 31 (1989), 75–102. For Pseudo-Aristotelian works in Arabic and Latin, see Kraye, Ryan, and Schmitt [60].

[6] Ed. S. L. Vodraska, Ph.D. diss., London University, 1969.

[7] H. Suchier, *Denkmäler Provenzalischer Literatur und Sprache* (Halle: 1883), 473–80.

[8] Ed. with Roger Bacon's commentary by R. Steele, *Rogeri Baconi Opera Hactenus Inedita*, vol. V (Oxford: 1920), 2–172.

[9] Ed. M. Plezia (Warsaw: 1960).

[10] C. Burnett, "'Abd al-Masīḥ of Winchester," in L. Nauta and A. Vanderjagt (eds.), *Between Demonstration and Imagination: Essays on the History of Science and Philosophy Presented to John D. North* (Leiden: 1999), 159–69.

[11] Ed. G. Théry, "Autour du décret de 1210: II. Alexandre d'Aphrodise," *Bibliothèque thomiste* 7 (Kain: 1926), 74–82; see also C. Burnett, "Sons of Averroes," 282. The translations of Gundisalvi (Dominicus Gundissalinus) fall between ca. 1160 and ca. 1190.

[12] Ed. Théry, "Autour du décret," 92–7, 86–91, and 99–100.

[13] Ed. J. R. O'Donnell, *Medieval Studies* 20 (1958), 239–315.

[14] Ed. S. Landauer (Berlin: 1902).

[15] Ed. C. Burnett in "Physics before the *Physics*," *Medioevo* 27 (2002), 53–109 (86–105).

[16] Ed. F. Hudry in *Chrysopoeia* 6 (1997–9), 1–154.

[17] Ed. J. Heller (Nuremberg: 1549).

(*cont.*)

Notes (*cont.*)

[18] Ed. J. Ruska, *Quellen und Studien zur Geschichte der Naturwissenschaften und der Medizin* 1 (Berlin: 1931).

[19] Ed. J. Wilcox, "The Transmission and Influence of Qusṭā ibn Lūqā's *On the Difference between Spirit and the Soul*," Ph.D. diss., City University of New York, 1985.

[20] Ed. in J. Wilcox and J. M. Riddle, "Qusṭā ibn Lūqā's *Physical Ligatures* and the Recognition of the Placebo Effect," *Medieval Encounters* 1 (1995), 1–50.

[21] Both translations ed. in R. Lemay, Abū Ma'shar al-Balkhī, *Liber Introductorii Maioris ad Scientiam Judiciorum Astrorum*, 9 vols. (Naples, 1995–6; see vols. V and VIII).

[22] This and the following two items are ed. in A. Nagy, *Beiträge zur Geschichte der Philosophie des Mittelalters*, vol. II, pt. 5 (Münster: 1897).

[23] Ed. C. Burnett in G. Bos and C. Burnett, *Scientific Weather Forecasting in the Middle Ages: The Writings of al-Kindi* (London: 2000), 263–310.

[24] Ed. M.-T. d'Alverny and F. Hudry, *Archives d'histoire doctrinale et littéraire du moyen âge* 41 (1974), 139–259.

[25] Ed. González Palencia, 2nd edn. (Madrid: 1953) (new edn. in preparation by H. Hugonnard-Roche).

[26] Ed. E. Gilson, "Les sources gréco-arabes de l'augustinisme avicennisant," *Archives d'histoire doctrinale et littéraire du moyen âge* 4 (1929), 4–149 (115–26).

[27] Ed. D. Salman, *Recherches de théologie ancienne et médievale* 12 (1940), 33–48.

[28] This is a collection of comments on Aristotle's logic. Al-Fārābī's summaries of at least the *Categories* and the *De Interpretatione*, as well as his commentaries on the *Prior* and *Posterior Analytics*, were known to Albertus Magnus: see M. Grignaschi, "Les traductions latines des ouvrages de la logique arabe et l'abrégé d'Alfarabi," *Archives d'histoire doctrinale et littéraire du moyen âge* 39 (1972), 41–107.

[29] See I. Bignami-Odier, "Le manuscrit Vatican latin 2186," *Archives d'histoire doctrinale et littéraire du moyen âge* 11 (1938), 133–66, at 137, 154–5.

[30] Ed. M. Grignaschi, "Les traductions latines."

[31] Ed. M. Grignaschi and J. Langhade, *Deux ouvrages inédits sur la réthorique* [sic] (Beirut: 1971).

[32] Cf. a text ascribed to al-Fārābī in L. Thorndike and P. Kibre, *A Catalogue of Incipits of Mediaeval Scientific Writings in Latin* (London: 1963), col. 1253: "Liber de natura loci ex latitudine et longitudine: Quod naturam loci scire oportet in scientia naturali . . ."

[33] Incorporated into a Latin commentary on Euclid's *Elements* in Vatican, Reg. Lat. 1268, fols. 72r–73r, ed. C. Burnett, "Euclid and al-Fārābī in MS

Vatican, Reg. Lat. 1268" in *Festschrift Gerhard Endress* (Leuven: 2004), 411–36.

[34]The *De Perfectione* was rewritten with reference to the Hebrew by Alessandro Achillini (1501); both texts are edited in M. Geoffroy and C. Steel, *Averroès, La béatitude de l'âme* (Paris: 2001).

[35] The text is ascribed to "Mahometh discipulus Alquindi" (Muḥammad, a disciple of al-Kindī), and entitled *Liber Introductorius in Artem Logicae Demonstrationis*. Ed. Nagy, *Beiträge*, vol. II, pt. 5, 51–64. See further C. Baffioni, "Il *Liber Introductorius in artem logicae demonstrationis*: problemi storici e filologici," *Studi filosofici* 17 (1994), 69–90.

[36] Ed. P. Gauthier-Dalché, *Revue d'histoire des textes* 18 (1988), 137–67.

[37] Ed. A. Sannino, "Ermete mago e alchimista nelle biblioteche di Guglielmo d'Alvernia e Ruggero Bacone," *Studi Medievali* 41 (2000), 151–89; see C. Baffioni, "Un esemplare arabo del Liber de quattuor confectionibus," in P. Lucentini et al. (ed.), *Hermetism from Late Antiquity to Humanism* (Turnhout: 2003), 295–313.

[38] Printed in *Opera Omnia Isaac* (Lyons: 1515).

[39] Both versions ed. J. T. Muckle, *Archives d'histoire doctrinale et littéraire du moyen âge* 11 (1938), 300–40.

[40] Ed. A. Birkenmajer, "Avicennas Vorrede zum 'Liber Sufficientiae' und Roger Bacon," in A. Birkenmajer, *Etudes d'histoire des sciences et de la philosophie du moyen âge* (Wroclaw: 1970), 89–101. The information on *The Cure* comes from M.-T. d'Alverny, "Notes sur les traductions médiévales d'Avicenne," article IV in d'Alverny [248]. The *Shifā'* is divided into *jumul* (sing. *jumla*), which are progressively subdivided into *funūn* (sing. *fann*), *maqālāt* or "books," and *fuṣūl* (sing. *faṣl*) or "chapters." The first two chapters of the logic (j1, f1, bk. 1, chs. 1 and 2) are respectively entitled *Capitulum Primum et Prohemiale ad Ostendendum quid Contineat Liber Asschyphe* and *Capitulum de Excitando ad Scientias*.

[41] Ed. L. Baur, *Beiträge zur Geschichte der Philosophie des Mittelalters*, vol. IV, pts. 2–3 (Münster: 1903), 124–33 (see also 304–8).

[42] Corresponding to bk. 3, chs. 1–10 in the Arabic. Arabic bk. 3, chs. 11–15 and bk. 4 do not appear to have been translated into Latin.

[43] Ed. M. Renaud, *Bulletin de philosophie médiévale* 15 (1973), 92–130.

[44] Ed. E. J. Holmyard and D. C. Mandeville (Paris: 1927).

[45] Only as an item in the 1338 catalogue of the library of the Sorbonne.

[46] Ed. Van Riet, *De Anima*, vol. II, AvL, 187–210.

[47] This and the following translations by Alpago were made in Damascus in ca. 1500; see M.-T. d'Alverny, "Andrea Alpago, interprète et commentateur d'Avicenne," article XIV in d'Alverny [248].

(*cont.*)

Notes (*cont.*)

[48] Ed. E. Franceschini in *Atti del Reale istituto veneto di scienze, lettere ed arti* 91 (1931–2), 393–597 (the Latin is translated from the Spanish *Bocados de oro*). For this sort of wisdom literature in Arabic see Gutas [22].

[49] D. Salman, "Algazel et les latins," *Archives d'histoire doctrinale et littéraire du moyen âge* 10 (1936), 103–27 (125–7).

[50] Part on logic ed. C. Lohr, *Traditio* 21 (1965), 223–90 (239–88); metaphysics and physics ed. J. T. Muckle (Toronto: 1933).

[51] Ed. C. Lohr, Diss. Freiburg/Br., 1967, 94–123 (this compendium was also put into Catalan verse by Llull).

[52] A Latin translation of a lost Castilian version made by "Abraham Hebreus" for Alfonso X of Castile; ed. J. L. Mancha in M. Comes et al. (eds.), *"Ochava espera" y "Astrofísica"* (Barcelona: 1990), 133–207 (141–97).

[53] Ed. J. M. Millás Vallicrosa, *Las traducciones orientales en los manuscritos de la Biblioteca catedral de Toledo* (Madrid: 1942), 285–312.

[54] Ed. M. Smith, *Transactions of the American Philosophical Society* 91.45 (2001).

[55] Ed. R. Hissette (Leuven: 1996).

[56] An *editio minor* is being prepared by G. Guldentops.

[57] See H. Schmieja, "Secundum aliam Translationem: Ein Beitrag zur arabisch-lateinischen Übersetzung des grossen Physikkommentars von Ibn Rushd," in Aertsen and Endress [134], 316–36.

[58] Ed. F. J. Carmody and R. Arnzen (Leuven: 2003).

[59] Ed. F. S. Crawford (Cambridge, MA: 1953).

[60] Ed. E. L. Shields (Cambridge, MA: 1949).

[61] An *editio minor* is being prepared by D. N. Hasse.

[62] Ed. A. Coviello and P. E. Fornaciari (Florence: 1992).

[63] Ed. in C. Steel and G. Guldentops, "An Unknown Treatise of Averroes," *Recherches de théologie et philosophie médiévales* 64 (1997), 86–135 (94–135).

[64] Arabic, Hebrew and Latin versions ed. C. Burnett and M. Zonta, *Archives d'histoire doctrinale et littéraire du moyen âge* 67 (2000), 295–335.

[65] Ed. M. Alonso, *Teología de Averroes: estudios documentos* (Madrid: 1947), 357–65.

[66] Ed. B. H. Zedler (Milwaukee, WI: 1961).

[67] For the medieval Latin translations of Maimonides, see W. Kluxen, "Literargeschichtliches zum lateinischen Moses Maimonides," *Recherches de théologie ancienne et médiévale* 21 (1954), 23–50.

[68] The last four items are included in *Epistolae seu Quesita Logica Diversorum Doctorum Arabum precipue Averroys*. The original Arabic texts are not known, and the last three authors have not been identified.

HOSSEIN ZIAI

19 Recent trends in Arabic and Persian philosophy

In this chapter I will discuss Arabic and Persian philosophical trends as presented in texts mainly from the sixteenth and seventeenth centuries and their more recent continuation. Philosophical activity continued especially in the lands marked by the geopolitical boundaries of Persianate influence, centered in the land of Iran as marked since the Safavid period beginning in 1501.[1] Of the philosophers in the earlier, formative period of Arabic philosophy, it was Avicenna whose works made the most direct and lasting impact on all subsequent philosophical trends and schools. The structure, techniques, and language of Avicenna's philosophy – best exemplified in his two main works, *al-Ishārāt wa al-tanbīhāt* and *al-Shifā'* – define a holistic system against which all subsequent philosophical writings, in both Arabic and Persian, are measured. Avicenna's philosophical texts give Arabic and Persian Peripatetic philosophy its technical language and methodology, as well as setting out a range of philosophical problems in semantics, logic, ontology, epistemology, and so on. Later trends must be regarded as refinements and developments from within philosophical texts already established by the twelfth century C.E.

Some Orientalist and apologetic historians have chosen imprecise, general descriptions such as "theosophy," "Oriental wisdom," "transcendent theosophy," "perennial wisdom," "mystical experience," and the like, to describe an entire corpus of texts after Avicenna.[2] I will avoid such imprecise descriptions and focus on the philosophical intention and value of the texts themselves, rather than the supposed "spiritual," "Ṣūfī," or "esoteric" dimension of a wide and ill-defined range of Arabic and Persian texts. As Fazlur Rahman has written, we interpret post-Avicennian texts in terms of an ill-defined mysticism only "at the cost . . . of its purely intellectual and philosophical hard core, which is of immense value and interest to the modern student of philosophy."[3]

The most significant philosophical trends after Avicenna attempt to reconstruct consistent, holistic systems that *refine*, rather than *refute*, a range of philosophical propositions and problems, thus rescuing philosophy from the charges brought against it by al-Ghazālī. Increasing significance is also placed on constructing philosophical systems more compatible with religion. The philosophical system with the deepest impact on later trends, second only to that of Avicenna, is the "philosophy of Illumination" of Suhrawardī.[4] The system defines a new method, the "Science of Lights" (*'ilm al-anwār*), which holds that we obtain the principles of science immediately, via "knowledge by presence" (*al-'ilm al-ḥuḍūrī*). About half a century after the execution of Suhrawardī in Aleppo in 1191, the philosophy of Illumination was heralded as a "more complete system" (*al-niẓām al-atamm*) by Illuminationist commentators starting with Shams al-Dīn al-Shahrazūrī.[5] The aim to build such "complete" or holistic systems is distinctive of later philosophical trends, especially in the seventeenth century. Such systems aim to expand the structure of Aristotelian philosophy to include carefully selected religious topics, defending the harmony between philosophy and religion.

In what follows I will therefore examine, first, the relation of these holistic systems to the older Peripatetic and newer Illuminationist traditions; second, the question of a "harmonization" between philosophy and religion, focusing on the work of the Persian philosopher Ibn Torkeh Iṣfahānī; and finally, specific philosophical problems of interest in the later tradition. It should be emphasized that though many thinkers in the later tradition, from Suhrawardī onward, do discuss "mystical" phenomena, and especially the epistemology of experiential and inspirational knowledge, they do so from the perspective of philosophy. The representative figures of later trends are rationalist thinkers and scientists (*'ūlama'*); none were members of Ṣūfī brotherhoods, and almost all – especially from the seventeenth century on – belonged to the *'ulamā'*, that is, the Shī'ite clerical classes.[6]

SYSTEMATIC PHILOSOPHY

Intense philosophical activity took place from the mid-sixteenth century, first in Shīrāz and subsequently in Isfahān, lasting for about a century and a half. This has been described as a "revival of philosophy," which led to what has been called "the school of Iṣfahān." The most important figure of this period is Ṣadr al-Dīn Shīrāzī, Mullā Ṣadrā, who was the student of the school's "founder," Mīr Dāmād, and whose greatest philosophical achievement is his *magnum opus*, *al-Ḥikma al-muta'āliya fī al-asfār al-arba'a al-'aqliyya* (usually referred to simply as *Asfār*). His system and "school" are also called *al-ḥikma al-muta'āliya*, or metaphysical philosophy.[7] Mullā Ṣadrā's many philosophical works, as well as his commentaries and independent works on juridical and other religious subjects, fall within the school's rational and "scientific" (*'ilmī*) intention. Ensuing scholastic activity of the Shī'ite centers based on this system continues today. A significant development, which probably owes more to philosophers such as Ṣadrā than some would admit, is the theoretical Shī'ite syllabus of the intellectual sciences (*'ulūm-e 'aqlī*), the higher levels of which include the study of the *Asfār* preceded by the study of philosophical textbooks, notably Athīr al-Dīn al-Abharī's *Hidāya al-ḥikma* (*Guide to Philosophy*), on which numerous commentaries, glosses, and super-glosses have been written including one by Ṣadrā himself. In short, the system *al-ḥikma al-muta'āliya* and its repercussions still define intellectual Shī'ism at present.

Unlike Avicenna's *al-Shifā'*, the *Asfār* has no separate section on logic or physics; it thus departs from the Peripatetic division of philosophy into logic, physics, and metaphysics, seen not only in Avicenna but also in such textbooks as the aforementioned *Hidāya al-ḥikma*. Instead the emphasis is on the study of being, the subject of the first of the *Asfār*'s four books. The work also differs structurally from Suhrawardī's *Philosophy of Illumination*, and Ṣadrā rejects Illuminationist views regarding many philosophical problems. Still he follows Illuminationist methodology, despite refining Suhrawardī's positions in light of Ṣadrā's understanding of Peripatetic philosophy. His overall Illuminationist outlook is evident in several domains.

(A) THE PRINCIPLES OF SCIENCE AND EPISTEMOLOGY. In the *Asfār* "primary intuition" takes the place of Aristotelian definition (*horos, horismos*, Avicenna's *al-ḥadd al-tāmm*) as the foundation of science and syllogistic reasoning. This non-Peripatetic position, which is claimed to be Stoic in its original formulation, posits a primary intuition of time-space, and holds that "visions" and "personal revelations" (including religious revelation) are epistemically valid. Ṣadrā here follows the Illuminationists in holding that knowledge by presence (*al-'ilm al-ḥuḍūrī*) is prior to predicative knowledge (*al-'ilm al-ḥuṣūlī*). He also dispenses, as Suhrawardī had, with the central role of the Active Intellect as the tenth intellect of a numbered, discrete (that is, discontinuous) cosmology, in obtaining first principles. He praises the Illuminationist notion of a multiplicity of intellects (*kathra 'uqūl*), which are distinguished only by equivocation in terms of degrees of "more" and "less," as an "improvement" on the Peripatetic model. This gives rise to Ṣadrā's theory of the "unity" or "sameness" of the knower and the known, perhaps the most discussed theory in all recent philosophical writings in Arabic and Persian. The influence of Ṣadrā's epistemology continues today, as in the work of the eminent Shī'ite philosopher, Seyyed Jalāl al-Dīn Āshtiyānī.[8]

(B) ONTOLOGY. The "primacy of quiddity" (*aṣāla al-māhiyya*) is a central tenet of Illuminationism, but is rejected by Ṣadrā in favor of the "primacy of being" (*aṣāla al-wujūd*). Illuminationists also divided metaphysics into two parts: *metaphysica generalis* and *metaphysica specialis*, that is, the study of pure being as opposed to the study of qualified being. This division, upheld and refined by Ṣadrā, is incorporated into every philosophical work in the later tradition, up to the present.

(C) SCIENCE AND RELIGION. Aristotle's views on the foundation of philosophy are refined and expanded by Ṣadrā. His theory of knowledge is more along the lines of Illuminationist principles, according to which knowledge is not founded primarily on the input of sensation and abstraction of universals, but rather on the knowing subject (*al-mawḍū' al-mudrik*) itself. This subject knows its "I" – *al-'ana'iyya al-muta'āliya* – by means of the principle of self-consciousness. The "I" intuitively recovers primary notions of time-space, accepts the validity of such things as the primary intelligibles, and confirms the existence of primary truths and of God. The system is thus seen later as providing a philosophical foundation more congenial to religious doctrine. This paves the way for the triumph of *al-ḥikma al-muta'āliya* in the scholastic Shī'ite centers of Iran. If we ponder the impact of Ṣadrā's system on Shī'ite political doctrine, we may fathom how intellectual Shī'ism, as the dominant recent trend in philosophy, has embraced the primacy of practical reason over theoretical science, especially in the last century. Theoretical philosophy is subject to the Illuminationist critique that it is impossible to reach universal propositions that are always true – the Peripatetic "laws of science." Instead "living" sages in every era are thought to determine what "scientific" attitude the society must have, upholding and renewing the foundations using their own individual, experiential, subjective knowledge.

Let me explain further. An Avicennian universal proposition must be both necessary and always true. But, because of the unavoidable contingency or possibility of the future (*al-imkān al-mustaqbal*), the validity of a "law" deduced now may be overturned at some future time by the discovery of exceptions. Furthermore, the most foundational, necessary knowledge that is true at all times must, it is argued, satisfy the Platonic dictum that all knowledge is based on further knowledge. It cannot then be predicative, that is, have the form "S is P" – otherwise we would have an infinite regress. Rather, it is through knowledge by presence at a *given* time that the knowing subject "sees" (*yushāhid*, a technical term meaning both external sight and intellectual grasp of "internal" realities) the object, and obtains knowledge of this object in a durationless instant. There is thus an atemporal relation of knowledge between the subject and object, which occurs when the subject is "sound" (i.e., has a heightened intuition and visionary experience, or a functioning organ of sight in the case of external vision), when there exists an appropriate "medium," which may be "intellect," "sense," "inspiration," "dream," etc.; and when there are no barriers between subject and object. This primary, intuitive, and immediate knowledge serves as the foundation for the syllogistic construction of scientific laws. But the foundations will have to be renewed by other subjects in all future time, or in all other possible worlds, based on the "observations" of those subjects. In recent Shī'ite political philosophy this is the role given to the most learned Shī'ite scholastic of the time.[9]

(D) HISTORY OF PHILOSOPHY. This is an area first touched upon by the classical historians and biographers of scientists (including physicians, philosophers, and other specialists) such as Ibn Abī Uṣaybi'a, al-Qifṭī, Abū Ya'qūb al-Sijistānī, Ibn Juljul al-Andalūsī, and others. Ṣadrā goes further in giving a systematic analysis of the history of philosophical ideas and schools. He divides those philosophers he deems significant into four groups: first, the Pythagoreans, Plato, and the Platonists, who agree to some extent with the Illuminationists; second, the "earlier" Peripatetics; third, the "later" Peripatetics – distinguished at times from a "pure" Aristotelian position, where Proclus and Porphyry are usually included; and fourth, the Illuminationists, whom he calls "followers of the Stoics." The division between "earlier" and "later" (*al-mutaqaddimūn, al-muta'akhkhirūn*) Peripatetics is also found in previous authors like al-Baghdādī, Suhrawardī, al-Shahrazūrī, and Quṭb al-Dīn al-Shīrāzī.

One discussion of this history is to be found in *Asfār* III.iii.4. Here Ṣadrā takes up, among other issues, the question of God's knowledge and the epistemology of knowledge by presence as a description of God's knowledge. He distinguishes seven schools of thought, the four philosophical ones just mentioned, as well as two "theological" schools and a "mystical" school.[10] This classification of the history of philosophy reflects Shahrazūrī's *al-Shajara al-Ilāhiyya*, composed three centuries before the *Asfār*.[11] Among the "school of the followers of the Peripatetics" (*madhhab tawābi' al-mashshā'īn*) Ṣadrā includes al-Fārābī and Avicenna, their followers, such as Bahmanyār (Avicenna's famous student and author of *al-Taḥṣīl*), Abū al-Abbās al-Lawkarī, and "many later Peripatetics" (*kathīr min al-muta'akhkhirīn*).[12] The "later Peripatetics" include only Muslim philosophers. Al-Kindī is not mentioned, and in fact his name appears rarely in the *Asfār* in general. (Notice also the exclusion of Fakhr al-Dīn al-Rāzī, who is considered a *mutakallim* by the Illuminationist philosophers, notably by Shahrazūrī in his history of philosophy, *Nuzha al-arwāḥ*, and in his philosophical encyclopedia, *al-Shajara al-Ilāhiyya*.[13] Ṣadrā, too, dismisses al-Rāzī's *kalām* methodology.)[14] This group is said to uphold "primacy of being" (*aṣāla al-wujūd*) and the eternity of the world (*qidam*), while rejecting bodily resurrection. They posit that the soul is separated from the body but their position on the question of the immortality of the individual soul is unclear. Of their views Ṣadrā accepts only the ontological view of the "later Peripatetics."

Next is "the school of the Master Shihāb al-Dīn [Suhrawardī] al-Maqtūl, follower of the Stoics, and those who follow him, such as al-Muḥaqqiq al-Ṭūsī, Ibn Kammūna, al-'Allāma [Quṭb al-Dīn] al-Shīrāzī, and Muḥammad al-Shahrazūrī, author of *al-Shajara al-Ilāhiyya*."[15] The attribution of "Stoic" to the Illuminationist school appears in many places in the *Asfār*. But concerning certain "novel" philosophical issues, such as the distinction between the idea of "intellectual form" (*al-ṣūra al-'aqliyya*) and the idea of "archetypal form" (*al-ṣūra al-mithāliyya*), Ṣadrā is careful to use the term "Illuminationist" (*al-ishrāqiyyūn*). The Stoic epithet is added only in conjunction with questions that relate to logic and physics, while in matters that pertain to epistemology, cosmology, and eschatology, "Illuminationist" is used alone.[16] Among the central doctrines of this "school" is said to be that of the real existence of the forms of things outside the mind (*al-qawl bi-kawn wujūd ṣuwar al-ashyā' fī al-khārij*), be the things corporeal or not (*mujarradāt aw māddiyyāt*), or simple or not (*murrakabāt aw basā'it*). This "naive realism" is indeed a cornerstone of the recent trends and does continue certain Illuminationist views.[17]

Next is "the school attributed (*al-mansūb*) to Porphyry, the first of the Peripatetics (*muqaddam al-mashshā'īn*), one of the greatest followers of the first teacher," in other words the earlier Peripatetics. The reference to Aristotle ("the first teacher") alludes to the *Theology of Aristotle*, that is, the Arabic Plotinus. Among the views associated with this "school" is their view that the intelligible forms (*al-ṣuwar al-ma'qūla*) share "unity" (*ittiḥād*) with God, and through the Active Intellect with a "select" number of humans. Aristotle himself is not always associated with a "school," but is deemed an exemplum against whom every philosophical position is to be judged.

Finally there is "the school of the divine Plato." It is possible that Ṣadrā here means Plato himself rather than a continuing "school of thought." If so then Ṣadrā is distinguishing the philosophical position of Plato himself as distinct from later syncretic, so-called

"Platonic" texts. Ṣadrā clearly attempts to refer to Plato himself by using the phrase "*qāla Aflāṭūn al-sharīf* (the noble Plato said)" rather than, as elsewhere, "*fī madhhab al-aflāṭūniyya* (in the school of the Platonists)."[18] The central philosophical doctrine here is said to be the "objectified" reality of the Separate Forms (*al-ṣuwar al-mufāraqa*) and the intelligible Platonic Forms (*al-muthul al-'aqliyya al-aflāṭuniyya*), a position upheld strongly by Ṣadrā. On this basis, he adds, God's knowledge of all existents (*'ilm Allāh bi-al-mawjūdāt kulluhā*) is proven. Thus al-Ghazālī's anti-rationalist polemic that the philosophers do not uphold God's knowledge, and that deductive reasoning cannot prove it, is rejected. The ensuing scholastic Shī'ite intellectual tradition regards this as a triumph of Ṣadrā's.

Of interest for us in this chapter is that what properly characterizes recent philosophical trends is the above-mentioned "second school," namely the Illuminationists. Recent and contemporary trends are dominated by this school, taken together with the new emphasis placed on religious philosophy by Ṣadrā. For example, in relation to the issue of immortality and resurrection, Ṣadrā seemingly attempts to "prove" the resurrection of a kind of *imaginalis* or "formal" body (*badan mithālī*, a notion later found in the nineteenth-century philosopher Sabziwarī). In doing so he departs from the Illuminationist doctrine of the immortality of a separate, disembodied soul. In many areas of detailed philosophical arguments Ṣadrā states both the Avicennian and the Illuminationist views and adjudicates between them, sometimes providing a third, more refined position. This new expression of philosophy would be accepted by the leading Shī'ite thinkers, and gradually even by the majority of Shī'ite clergy at present. This is how Ṣadrā's legacy lives, not perhaps as unbound, analytic philosophy but as an accepted religious system of thinking, with the claim that it promotes reason as the main tool of upholding the tenets of revealed religion, as well as the specifically Shī'ite doctrine of inspirational authority in the domain of political theory.

In sum, the main philosophical position of the new holistic system, metaphysical philosophy, which defines the dominant recent trends of philosophy in the Iranian Shī'ite domain, may be outlined as follows. First, philosophical construction is founded on a primary intuition of time-space, and visions and personal revelations are valid epistemological processes. Knowledge by presence is considered to be prior to predicative knowledge, and the separate intellects are considered to be multiple, even uncountable (*bi-lā nihāya*), and to form a continuum. This is in stark contrast to the Peripatetic model of discrete, numbered, separate intellects. The ontological position of the later school is not very clear, but in my view it is more along the lines of "primacy of being" (*aṣāla al-wujūd*), though it is set out in the terms of the Illuminationist view of being as continuum. In any case, this position is central to the tradition; it is discussed in great detail in Ṣadrā's *Ta'līqāt* (*Glosses*) on *Ḥikma al-ishrāq*.[19] The Platonic Forms are objectified, and the *mundus imaginalis* of Illuminationist cosmology is considered to be a separate realm whose existence is attested by the intuitive mode of "experience." Finally, metaphysics is divided into two parts: *metaphysica generalis* and *metaphysica specialis*. This marks an Illuminationist departure from Avicennian pure ontology, the study of being qua being (*wujūd bi-mā huwa wujūd*). It includes discussion of such subjects as mystical states and stations, love, secrets of dreams, prophecy, sorcery, and the arts of magic.

ṢĀ'IN AL-DĪN AND THE HARMONY OF RELIGION AND PHILOSOPHY

The use of epistemology to ground Islamic religious belief goes back at least as far as al-Fārābī's *Book of the Opinions of the Inhabitants of The Virtuous City*, in which the ideal ruler is the legitimate lawgiver because of his connection with the divine; this is based on the theory of union with the Active Intellect. The attempt to construct an Islamic religious philosophy continues beyond the formative period of the tenth century, and later thinkers express religious philosophy in terms more "Islamic" than Hellenic. The unbound reason of Greek philosophy, which would grant primacy to reason over revelation, was attacked by al-Ghazālī and then by a host of lesser figures, leading to the hard blow dealt by Ibn Taymiyya in his *Refutation of the Rationalists* (*al-Radd 'alā al-manṭiqiyyīn*).[20] An influential figure who did much to recover the idea of the harmony between religion and philosophy, as well as mysticism (*'irfān*), was Ibn Torkeh 'Alī b. Moḥammad Khojandī Iṣfahānī (d. ca. 1432), known often by his title, Ṣā'in al-Dīn, in Shī'ite scholarly circles.[21] Since Ṣā'in al-Dīn was identified with the emerging clerical classes, his use of philosophy to uphold religion was deemed acceptable, which paved the way for later, more creative thinkers like Ṣadrā. Thanks to figures like Ṣā'in al-Dīn, the Shī'ite clergy came to accept the notion of the "intellectual sciences" (*al-'ulūm al-'aqliyya*), which use philosophy as philosophy, without reducing it to the role of a "handmaiden," and which treat Greek philosophers with reverence instead of the hostility evinced by anti-rationalists like Ibn Taymiyya. Ṣā'in al-Dīn was an example of those educated, scholastic thinkers who also held position at courts of temporal rule (in his case the Gūrkānid Ilkhans). The manifestly political philosophical core of this trend was allied to a real political agenda.

Ṣā'in al-Dīn's works are now accepted to have been among the first to harmonize philosophical method, religious doctrine, and "mystical" (*'irfān-e naẓarī*) knowledge. In recent studies that discuss philosophical trends in intellectual Shī'ism, Ṣā'in al-Dīn is hailed as one of the scholars in Iran who began to construct systematic rationalist religious philosophy with a distinct "Shī'ite" emphasis on *'ilm* (knowledge). He affirmed divinely inspired, but rationally upheld, principles of religion that would insure the continuance of just rule. The idea that each age has its own personification of knowledge (*a'lam*), and especially the popularization of this idea, are in part a result of Ṣā'in al-Dīn's work. As Sadughi has shown, significant twentieth-century Shī'ite scholars of the "intellectual sciences" (*'ulūm-e 'aqlī* is incidentally a term perhaps first popularized by Ṣā'in al-Dīn) such as Ziyā' al-Dīn Dorrī (d. 1336 A.H.), Āqā Mīrzā Moḥammad Qomshe'ī (d. 1306 A.H.) and his mentor Mīrzā Moḥammad 'Alī Moẓaffar, Āqā Mīrzā Maḥmūd al-Modarres al-Kahakī al-Qommī (d. 1346 A.H.), and Āqā Seyyed Moḥammad Kāẓem al-Lavāsāni al-Tehrānī (d. 1302 A.H.) all studied Ṣā'in al-Dīn's most significant text, *Tamḥīd al-qawā'id*.[22] This work is best described in contemporary technical language as a text on phenemenology and philosophy of religion, in which the fundamental political doctrine of the legitimacy of divinely inspired rule by select members of the *'ulamā'* class is upheld.

Of interest for the understanding of how philosophical theory influences Shī'ite political thinking is the little-noticed fact that Ṣā'in al-Dīn is among the first to draw on the Illuminationist epistemology of knowledge by presence and use it to give priority to intuitive and inspired knowledge, especially in the case of primary principles. The development of Shī'ite religious philosophy does, of course, incorporate ideas from traditions other than *falsafa*. For example, it employs non-polemical, "scientific" *kalām* to attack anti-rationalist, Ash'arite political and theological dogma. Equally, Qur'ānic exegesis is used to support rationalist jurisprudence. Here Ṣā'in al-Dīn presented easily accessible rational analyses of the five Pillars of Islam and similar subjects. As Āshtiyānī shows, Ṣā'in al-Dīn's "political" intention, as a scholar serving Gūrkānid, universalist Islamic ambitions, was to compose most of his texts in a language and style comprehensible by the multitude.[23] All of this led to wider acceptance of the doctrine that the *'ulamā'* should be entrusted with upholding just rule. Ṣā'in al-Dīn's innovative ideas, still extant in more than sixty works, played a central role in shaping the intellectual tradition of Iranian Shī'ism, especially the popularization of the core of the new Shī'ite political philosophy: the idea of rationally proven, divinely inspired knowledge in the service of just rule. Increasingly the "citizens" are not given an active role, but are led to believe in the doctrine of obedience and "imitation" (*taqlīd*) in all matters, including the political. This paves the way for the central institution of the religious leader as the "source of imitation" (*marja'-e taqlīd*).

PHILOSOPHICAL PROBLEMS IN RECENT ARABIC AND PERSIAN TEXTS

The history of the philosophical tradition beginning a century or so prior to the School of Iṣfahān, and continuing down to the present, has yet to be written. The few texts published in critical editions do provide us with a basis from which we can select certain problems and themes of philosophical interest, but we have to proceed cautiously. There are very few philosophical treatises in Arabic or Persian prior to the sixteenth century devoted to a specific, singular topic – what we would today call a "monograph." There are exceptions, notably *al-Sīra al-falsafiyya* (*The Philosophical Way of Life*) by the brilliant ninth-century Persian scientist Abū Bakr al-Rāzī, and a few others that fall within the general domain of political philosophy. But philosophical compositions are predominantly inclusive, and treat comprehensive sets of problems. This is true of all of Avicenna's major works, and of non-Peripatetic works as well.

For example, in the technical works of Suhrawardī and others, even when the main structure of philosophical texts is changed, the philosophical problems are still discussed in a comprehensive way.[24] This tendency toward comprehensive works seems to continue up to the fifteenth or even the sixteenth century; even authors who wanted to deal with specific problems were constrained to make their innovative contributions within the context of commentaries, glosses, and super-glosses on existing comprehensive texts.

I cannot say exactly when the practice of composing separate philosophical treatises finally became widespread. This is because of the paucity of published philosophical texts, especially those from the mid-fourteenth century (the end of the scientific revival in northwest Iran, promoted by the Mongols and the first of the Ilkhāns, and directed by the Persian philosopher and scientist, Khājeh Naṣīr al-Dīn al-Ṭūsī) to the sixteenth century. But I have examined the few anthologies of Arabic and Persian texts, as well as the few critical editions of texts by authors from the sixteenth to the nineteenth centuries.[25] This allows me to indicate a fair number of monographs on specific subjects. Many of these treatises deal with specific ontological problems; notably, something like literary genres spring up devoted to the topics of the "proof of the Necessary" (*ithbāt al-wājib*), the "unity of being" (*waḥda al-wujūd*), the "relation between quiddity and being" (*ittiṣāf al-māhiyya bi-al-wujūd*), and other related ontological topics. Others deal with problems of cosmology and creation, and especially the "temporal creation" or "becoming of the world" (*ḥudūth al-ʿālam)*, and also "eternal creation" (*ḥudūth dahrī*). Still others deal with epistemological problems. Foremost among these are treatises on Mullā Ṣadrā's famous "unity of knower and the known" (*ittiḥād al-ʿāqil wa al-maʿqūl*) and related issues. Finally, a fairly large number of treatises reply to questions or objections, or take the form of dialogues or disputations between scholastic figures.

It is noteworthy that there are very few, if any, monographs (among those known to me) on topics in formal and material logic. The only such monographs are usually in the form of dialogue and disputation and deal with the philosophy of language. Prominent are the problem of the "liar paradox" and other logical paradoxes with ontological implications.[26] Those few works on logic of the seventeenth century in particular that have been published are simplified textbooks, in the style and manner of standard Peripatetic textbooks, which follow the structure of Aristotle's *Organon*, usually excluding the *Poetics*. This is perhaps best exemplified in Ṣadrā's own textbook on logic, *On the Refinement of Logic* (*al-Tanqīḥ fī al-manṭiq*).[27] Still, we can isolate a few problems of interest in logical works of this period.

(A) LOGICAL PARADOXES AND PHILOSOPHY OF LANGUAGE. The well-known liar paradox of antiquity, that the statement "I am lying" can be neither true nor false, becomes the subject of a heated debate in the sixteenth century in the southern Iranian city of Shīrāz.[28] This debate may have continued in the later tradition, along with others on topics in theoretical logic (not counting semantics and semiotics),[29] but we have little evidence for it. Indeed this may be an indication of the recent lack of interest in theoretical philosophy as an independent intellectual pursuit. The debate on the liar paradox was between two of sixteenth-century Iran's leading scholastic philosophers, Ṣadr al-Dīn Dashtakī and Jalāl al-Dīn Dawwānī. The name of the paradox is *shubha kull kalāmī kādhib*, which combines the term *shubha*, literally meaning "doubt" or "ambiguity," with the short form of the proposition *kull kalāmī kādhib*, which literally means "all of my statements are false." In expanded expressions of the proposition, and by way of analysis, temporal modifiers are added, such as "now," "tomorrow," "forever," etc.[30]

The story of the unfolding debate is both historically and philosophically interesting. Later scholars join the debate and themselves write monographs trying to "resolve" the paradox, by upholding one of the two positions, that of Dawwānī or that of Dashtakī. Dashtakī first sparks the controvery in his "glosses" (*ḥawāshī*) to a commentary on an earlier scholastic work by Qūshjī, which mentioned the paradox.[31] Dawwānī then writes at least two "responses" to the position expressed by Dashtakī, later composing a fairly lengthy monograph on it himself.[32] This shows serious involvement in a theoretical issue, going well beyond what is usually assumed to have been a lifeless scholastic tradition of glosses and super-glosses on standard texts. Here we have important representatives of the sixteenth- and early seventeenth-century intellectual endeavor in Iran devoting a great deal of time to analysis and discussion of a long-standing logical paradox. This is an indication of the continuity of innovative thinking, and serves as an important historical lesson regarding later philosophical trends in general. Philosophically, while it is not possible to go into the details of the debate here, it is worth summarizing Dashtakī's analysis. Not unlike today's logicians, he distinguishes between the first- and second-order truth and falsity of the proposition, and thus insists on the need to distinguish ordinary or natural language on the one hand, and meta-language on the other. This original insight was both deep and novel for its time: an example of how such monographs could be an instrument for genuinely analytical approaches to solving philosophical problems.

(B) ONTOLOGY. Monographs on ontological topics and problems dominate the philosophical discourse in recent Arabic and Persian philosophy. The subject also occupies the major portion in almost all books on philosophy in general. Recent philosophical discourse has refined the earlier distinction between general and special metaphysics, and focused on the study of being as being, but has also taken a phenomenological approach to the topic. However, Avicennian ideas (the essence–existence distinction, the modalities of being, and the proof of the "Necessary Being") continue to define this discipline. Suhrawardī's ideas that being is a continuum and is equivocal also exert influence. As we have seen, both live on in the systematic presentation of Ṣadrā. The disagreement between the primacy of being and primacy of essence is still debated and often used to distinguish differing camps of philosophy. Related areas of study include the question of whether the number of categories can be reduced (*ḥaṣr al-maqūlāt*), as first proposed by Suhrawardī, perhaps under Stoic influence. This involves removing the study of categories from the logical corpus of the *Organon*, and situating it instead in the study of principles of physics. Thus, for example, the category of substance is reduced to the category of motion: a dynamic conception referred to as "substantial motion" (*ḥaraka jawhariyya*), a central idea of Mullā Ṣadrā's.[33]

(C) THEORIES OF CAUSALITY. I will conclude by examining Mulla Ṣadrā's discussion of an important problem of causality. My choice of both problem and philosopher serves, I hope, to demonstrate in a final way the basic objectives of this chapter. The text in question is *Ta'līqāt 'alā Sharḥ ḥikma al-ishrāq* (*Glosses on the Commentary on the Philosophy of Illumination*), a highly refined philosophical discourse in a precise technical language, which shows the amazing breadth of Ṣadrā's knowledge of philosophy up to his time, extending from the Greek masters to the great Persian figures, as well as a high level of penetrating analysis, well beyond that of the scholastic tradition of commentaries, glosses and textbooks. It is a set of glosses on a commentary by the thirteenth-century philosopher Quṭb al-Dīn Shīrāzī, which is in turn a commentary on a work of Suhrawardī's.[34] But the scholastic nature of this exercise belies the innovation of the ideas Ṣadrā presents here; ideas that he would not have presented in a more "public" discourse.

Ṣadrā presents his theory of causality by first examining the types of priority.[35] He is responding to Suhrawardī's statement that "the priority of cause over effect is a mental one, and not a temporal one." Ṣadrā explains that "priority" is when two things exist such that one may exist without necessitating the other, but the other is necessitated only when the first is necessitated. Ṣadrā now announces that, in addition to the "five famous types" of priority,[36] there are other types he will discuss. For the first significant additional type of priority, Ṣadrā has coined the phrase "priority in terms of Truth" (*taqaddum bi-al-ḥaqq*). This is the priority of the ranks of being generated from "the First" down to the lowest level of existence. In a way this is the same type of priority Suhrawardī called "priority in terms of nobility" (*taqaddum bi-al-sharaf*), yet Ṣadrā wants to distinguish his "priority in terms of Truth" from all other types. His intention is to provide an exposition of his own view of emanation, and the view of his teacher Mīr Dāmād that creation is "eternal generation" (*hudūth dahrī*). This allows him to harmonize a philosophical understanding of "causality" with religious commitment to "creation."

He does this by arguing that mere ranking of nobility does not imply the inclusion of what is lower "in" the higher, as the ranks of being are in God. Nor is priority in terms of causality adequate, according to the standard view of such priority. Priority of position, place, rank, or time also fails to capture the priority of the rank of created beings. He finally states that this type of priority by Truth (*taqaddum bi-al-ḥaqq*) is something "apparent" (*ẓāhir*), known by those who are resolute in the experiential cognitive mode. What, then, is *taqaddum bi-al-ḥaqq*? If it cannot be captured by any notion of causality, whether essential, natural, or mathematical, then it can be known only by the subject's own understanding of "truth," *ḥaqq*. It is grounded, then, in immediate and subjective knowledge by presence. Here Ṣadrā is anticipating Hume's rejection of the rationalist concept of causality, by arguing that there is neither a logical nor a metaphysical relationship between cause and effect. Only the subject's *own* understanding determines "causality," and hence defines priority in being. However, Ṣadrā's position is distinct from Hume's in that Ṣadrā does accept "real priority" (*taqaddum bi-al-ḥaqīqa*), which he states to be priority of a thing over that which is existent because of it. So Ṣadrā's view is more realist than Hume's, where mere "perception" is the only observed "relation" between two things.

It seems to me, though, that *taqaddum bi-al-ḥaqq* is compatible with the Illuminationist position that being is equivocal, and the ensuing doctrine that beings are ranked in a priority of nobility. Ṣadrā's position on "true priority" does favor the "religious" view of creation, evoking as it does a unique relation between God and what he creates; and he insists that we must know the truth (*ḥaqq*) immediately in order to understand the "causal" connection between two things related "in terms of truth." Still he does not reject the traditional understanding of other types of causation, but only claims that it does not capture "priority in terms of truth." This places his thinking within philosophy rather than religion as such.

From the sixteenth century to the present, Islamic philosophy has been dominated by a scholastic tradition that continues in its interpretation of the ideals of classical Arabic philosophy, and leads to the final acceptance of philosophy by religion. In Ṣadrā's unified system, the select religious scholars, possessing knowledge and inspiration, were confirmed as the legitimate "guardians" of just rule. This system also became the basis for the continuity of philosophy. Although higher philosophy is today still mostly studied only "extracurricularly" (*dorūs-e khārej*), the scholastic tradition has incorporated certain aspects of philosophy into its core curricula. For instance, semantics is included in the study of the principles of jurisprudence, and a standard, simplified formal logic is included in "primers" studied by all beginning seminary students. Representative members of the Shī'ite clergy propose also the doctrine of independent reason (*ijtihād*) in principles of jurisprudence, which marks the final harmonization of philosophy with religion.[37] The dominant philosophical themes in the past centuries have been ontology, creation and cosmology, theories of knowledge (especially unified theories deemed capable of describing extraordinary types of knowing such as inspiration and intuition), psychology (though this has been reduced in the main to eschatology), philosophical hermeneutics, and a few other similar topics. Much more work remains to be done in Western scholarship on this recent philosophical tradition, and this work needs to begin from the realization that there is much here that is genuinely philosophical.

NOTES

1 The wide-ranging intellectual impact of Iranian influences has led some, notably the late French Orientalist Henry Corbin, to give the name "Iranian Islam" to many domains of inquiry and expression including the philosophical. See Corbin [161].

2 Phrases like "Oriental wisdom" (as in Corbin's translation of *ḥikma al-ishrāq* as "sagesse orientale") and "transcendent theosophy" misrepresent the analytical value of the philosophy of Illumination, presenting it as mystical or visionary, rather than presenting Islamic philosophy as philosophy.

3 Rahman [167], vii.

4 See H. Ziai, "Shihāb al-Dīn Suhrawardī: founder of the Illuminationist school," in Nasr and Leaman [34], vol.1, and chapter 10 above.

5 See Shams al-Dīn Shahrazūrī, *Sharḥ ḥikma al-Ishrāq*, ed. H. Ziai (Tehran: 2001), 7.

6 See the recent work by Sadughi [258], which shows that all of the hundreds of philosophers from the seventeenth century to the present were from the *'ulamā'*, with the notable exception of Muḥammad Ḥasan Qashqai and Jahāngīr Qashqai (see pp. 30, 84, 105, 167), who were noble tribal Qashqai khans.

7 Given Ṣadrā's explicitly philosophical aims, this term is to be preferred to the prevalent "transcendent philosophy." In almost every contemporary Persian book on intellectual subjects Ṣadrā is rightly hailed for his success in describing a *rational* (*'aqlī*) system, which is thought to lend philosophical legitimacy to Shī'ism as a whole. See Sadughi (258) for lists of Shī'ite scholastics who have taught Ṣadrā.

8 Āshtiyānī is perhaps the leading creative thinker in the scholastic Shī'ite world. He is one of the few Shī'ite scholastics who, because of his scholarly collaboration with Henry Corbin, is known to Western scholarship at least in name, and a few of his text editions of philosophical work are also known. For a simple overview of the epistemological stance see Sohravardī, *Partow Nāmeh* (*The Book of Radiance*), ed. and trans. with an introduction by H. Ziai (Costa Mesa, CA: 1998), xvi–xx. See also Yazdi [157].

9 See further Ziai [262].

10 Ṣadr al-Dīn al-Shīrāzī, *al-Asfār al-arba'a* (Tehran: n.d.), vol. VI, 180ff.

11 See Hossein Ziai, "The Manuscript of *al-Shajara al-Ilāhiyya*, a Philosophical Encyclopedia by Shams al-Dīn Muḥammad Shahrazūrī," *Irān Shināsī* 2 (1990), 89–108.

12 *Asfār*, vol. VI, 187.

13 See Ziai, "The Manuscript of *al-Shajara al-Ilāhiyya*."

14 Al-Rāzī's *al-Mabāḥith al-mashriqiyya* ought not to be considered an Illuminationist work as some have suggested: see 'Alī Aṣghar Ḥalabī, *Tārikh-e Falāsefe-ye Īrānī* (Tehran: n.d.), 123.

15 *Asfār*, vol. VI, 187.

16 See Ziai [158], ch. 1.

17 See Ziai [158], 34–9.

18 See for instance *Asfār*, vol. III, 509ff.

19 I have prepared a critical edition of part I of this work, which is now in press (Tehran: forthcoming). Āshtiyānī makes ample use of this text; see his *Sharḥ-e ḥāl va ārā-ye falsafī-ye Mullā Ṣadrā* (*The Life and Philosophical Doctrine of Mullā Ṣadrā*) (Qom: 1998), 228–31.

20 See Ibn Taymiyya, *Against the Greek Logicians*, trans. W. B. Hallaq (Oxford: 1993).

21 Given Ibn Torkeh's obscurity in Western scholarship I will provide the reader with a fairly detailed list of references: J. Na'ini's introduction to his Persian translation of Sharastānī's *al-Milal wa al-niḥal*, titled *Tanqīḥ al-adilla* (Tehran: 1335 A.H.); M.-T. Danesh-Pajouh, *Fehrest-e Ketāb-Khāne-ye Ehdā'ī-ye Seyyed Mohamad-e Meshkāt* (Tehran: 1332 A.H.), vol. III, 425ff.; H. Corbin [161], vol. III (Paris: 1972); S. A. M. Behbahani, "Aḥvāl va Āsār-e Ṣā'in al-Dīn Torkeh-ye Iṣfahānī," in Mohaghegh and Landolt [255], 87–145; Sadughi [258]. Ṣā'in al-Dīn's work *Tamḥīd al-qawā'id* has been edited by S. J. D. Āshtiyānī with a 200-page analytical introduction, and glosses on the work. There have been previous lithograph editions, not free of error.

22 Sadughi [258], 25, 45, 47, 61.

23 See Ṣā'in al-Dīn, *Tamḥīd al-qawā'id*, 3–8. Āshtiyānī's seminal study documents Ṣā'in al-Dīn's impact on Mullā Moḥsen Fayḍ-e Kāshī,

'Abd al-Razzāq Lāhījī, and other Shī'ite *'ulamā'*, and shows why Mīr Fendereskī, Bahā' al-Dīn 'Āmelī, Mīr Dāmād, and Mullā Ṣadrā acknowledged Ṣā'in al-Dīn's thought. See further A. M. Behbahani, "Aḥvāl va Āsār-e Ṣā'in al-Dīn Torkeh-ye Iṣfahānī," in Mohaghegh and Landolt [255], xvi–xxii.

24 For a discussion of the new structure see, for example, Suhrawardī [152], xxiii–xxviii.

25 Perhaps the best anthology is Corbin and Āshtiyānī [254]. Twelve treatises have been published as *Majmū'eh-ye rasā'il-e falsafī-ye Ṣadr al-muta'allihīn*, edited by H. N. Iṣfahānī (Tehran: 1966). Works of the significant nineteenth-century scholastic, Hādī Sabziwārī, have been edited as *Rasā'el-e ḥakīm Sabzevārī*, ed. S. J. D. Āshtiyānī (Tehran: 1991). Also useful for the study of Arabic and Persian philosophy, especially concerning scholastic figures, is the journal *Kherad-nāmeh-ye Mullā Ṣadrā*.

26 For example, numerous short monographs responded to Ibn Kammūna's paradox on whether the Necessary Being is unique.

27 See *Majmū'eh-ye rasā'il-e falsafī-ye Ṣadr al-muta'allihīn*, 193–236.

28 This was at the time an important center of learning, which produced several scholars that would influence the development of the "school of Iṣfahān." For a discussion of the main scholastic philosophers of Shīrāz see Q. Kākā'ī, "Mīr Ṣadr al-Dīn Dashtakī," *Kherad-nāmeh* 1, 3.3 (1996), 83–9. Ṣadr al-Dīn Dashtakī and his son, Ghiyāth al-Dīn Dashtakī, are two outstanding figures of sixteenth-century trends in philosophy; the father wrote a monograph on *Ithbāt al-Wājib* (*Proof of the Necessary Being*), which as mentioned above is a representative work of the philosophical genres of this period. Another of his monographs on ontology is titled *Risāla fī wujūd al-dhihnī* (*Treatise on the Ideal* or *Mental Being*). Both these works were extensively read later, notably by Ṣadrā, who mentions them in his *Asfār*. The son, Ghiyāth al-Dīn Dashtakī, wrote a commentary on one of Suhrawardī's less technical Illuminationist texts, *Hayākil al-nūr*.

29 Semantic theory in general, called *'ilm dalāla al-alfāẓ*, continues as an initial chapter (*bāb*, or *faṣl*) of textbooks on the "principles of jurisprudence" (*uṣūl al-fiqh*), but is totally removed from the philosophical discourse as such in the later tradition.

30 See, e.g., *Risāleh-ye 'ibra al-fuḍalā' fī ḥall shubha jadhr al-aṣamm*, by yet another of the sixteenth–seventeenth-century scholastic figures, Shams al-Dīn Muḥammad Khafrī, ed. A. F. Qaramaleki, *Kherad-nāmeh* 1, 4.4 (1996), 86–9. Here the paradoxical proposition is "all of my statements now are false." Note that here, in the title of the paradox, the phrase "all my statements are false" is replaced by *jadhr al-aṣamm*,

"the square root of an imaginary number" (the term *aṣamm* stands for the square root of −1; literally it means "the most dumb," i.e., "devoid of sense"). The implication here, anticipating the analysis of the paradox in the sixteenth and seventeenth centuries, is that the proposition is itself devoid of sense, like asking "what is the square root of −1?" according to the mathematics of the day.

31 See A. F. Qaramelaki, "Mo'ammā-ye jadhr-e aṣamm dar ḥowzeh-ye falsafī-ye Shīrāz (The Liar Paradox in the Philosophical Circle of Shīrāz)," *Kherad-nāmeh* 1, 4.4 (1996), 80–5. The author lists (82 nn. 12–17) some of the earlier known presentations of the liar paradox in Arabic and Persian, the oldest by al-Fārābī, the most important by Ibn Kammūna.

32 Jalāl al-Dīn Dawwānī, *Nahāya al-kalām fī ḥall shubha kull kalāmī kādhib*, ed. A. F. Qaramelaki, *Nāmeh-ye mofīd* 5 (1996).

33 On notions of being in the Ṣadrian tradition, there is as yet no fully adequate treatment, but a good place to start is Rahman [167]. Excellent, though a bit outdated in style, is M. Hörten, *Philosophische von Shirazi* (Halle: 1912). The best accounts in Persian are those by Āshtiyānī: not only his *Sharḥ-e ḥāl va ārā-ye falsafī-ye Mullā Ṣadrā* (*On Mullā Ṣadrā's Life and his Philosophical Ideas*) (Qom: 1999), but also an independent work called *Hastī* (*Being*) (Tehran, several reprints), which may be recommended as a representative and engaging work from the recent scholastic tradition.

34 I have prepared an edition of the *Ta'līqāt*, which is now in press; unfortunately only a lithograph has so far been available (Tehran: 1313 A.H.), and this is nigh impossible to use.

35 He does so against the background of his distinct Illuminationist epistemology. Ṣadrā holds that knowledge by presence is prior to knowledge acquired through syllogistic reasoning, especially in the case of first principles and knowledge of the Necessary Being. And he further holds that knowledge of a thing is primarily knowledge of its cause. The Peripatetics are said to be unable to demonstrate the Necessary Being, since everything is known by its cause, and the Necessary Existent has no cause. Now, knowledge by presence takes place when the knowing subject (*al-mudrik*) has an atemporal "relation" (*al-iḍāfa*) to the object (*al-mudrak*), as we saw above. When such knowledge is obtained, the "cause" is known in a durationless "instant" (*ān*). But, following the Illuminationists, there is no order of priority between knower and known; this is the position discussed in what follows. The view solves not only the problem of how we know God, but also rejects temporal priority as the basis for distinguishing cause and effect, as will become clear below.

36 In other words the four discussed by Aristotle at *Categories*, 14a26–b15, plus causation.

37 This is exemplified by many twentieth-century jurists also known and revered for their philosophical teachings, such as Abū al-Ḥasan Qazvīnī, Allāmeh Ḥusayn Ṭabāṭabā'ī, Mehdī Āshtiyānī, Jalāl Āshtiyānī, and Mehdī Ha'irī Yazdī.

SELECT BIBLIOGRAPHY AND FURTHER READING

This bibliography is intended to supply the reader with references to basic works for further reading on the subject. After some general works, several suggestions have been supplied for each chapter. The bibliography is not intended to be comprehensive, but merely to provide an initial resource. For a comprehensive bibliography of secondary literature on Arabic philosophy up to the year 1999 see:

Daiber, H. [1] *Bibliography of Islamic Philosophy*, 2 vols. (Leiden: 1999).

There is also a bibliography that has been published in installments:

Druart, T.-A. and Marmura, M. [2] "Medieval Islamic Philosophy and Theology: Bibliographical Guide," in the *Bulletin de philosophie médiévale* 32 (1990), 35 (1993), 37 (1995), and 39 (1997), and most recently in *MIDEO* 24 (2000), 381–414. An updated version appears at http://philosophy.cua.edu/tad/biblio.cfm.

There are several journals that routinely publish articles on Arabic philosophy. *Arabic Sciences and Philosophy* and *Zeitschrift für Geschichte der arabisch-islamischen Wissenschaften* are particularly focused on this area. Relevant articles also appear frequently in journals devoted to medieval philosophy, such as *Documenti e studi sulla tradizione filosofica medievale, Medieval Philosophy and Theology*, and *Recherches de philosophie et théologie médiévales*, and also in journals devoted to Middle Eastern studies, such as *Der Islam, Islamic Studies, Mélanges de l'Institut dominicain des études orientales (MIDEO)*, and *Journal of the American Oriental Society* (*JAOS*).

General works and collections of articles

Baffioni, C. [3] *I grandi pensatori dell'Islam* (Rome: 1996).

Booth, E. [4] *Aristotelian Aporetic Ontology in Islamic and Christian Thinkers* (Cambridge: 1983).

Burrell, D. [5] *Knowing the Unknowable God: Ibn Sina, Maimonides, Aquinas* (Notre Dame, IN: 1986).

[6] *Freedom and Creation in Three Traditions* (Notre Dame, IN: 1993).

Corbin, H. [7] *History of Islamic Philosophy*, trans. L. Sherrard (London: 1993).

Craig, E. (ed.) [8] *Routledge Encyclopedia of Philosophy* (London: 1998), has entries on numerous Arabic philosophers.

Cruz Hernández, M. [24] *Historia del pensamiento en el mundo islámico*, 2 vols. (Madrid: 1981).

D'Ancona Costa, C. [9] *La casa della sapienza: la trasmissione della metafisica greca e la formazione della filosofia araba* (Milan: 1996).

D'Ancona, C. (ed.) [10] *Medioevo* 23 (1997), a special issue devoted to Arabic philosophy and sciences.

Davidson, H. A. [11] *Proofs for Eternity, Creation, and the Existence of God in Medieval Islamic and Jewish Philosophy* (Oxford: 1987).

Druart, T.-A. (ed.) [12] *American Catholic Philosophical Quarterly* 73 (1999), a special issue devoted to Islamic philosophy.

[13] "Philosophy in Islam," in A. S. McGrade (ed.), *The Cambridge Companion to Medieval Philosophy* (Cambridge: 2003), 97–120.

Elamrani-Jamal, A. [14] *Logique aristotélicienne et grammaire arabe* (Paris: 1983).

Endress, G. [15] "The Defense of Reason: The Plea for Philosophy in the Religious Community," *Zeitschrift für Geschichte der arabisch-islamische Wissenschaften* 6 (1990), 1–49.

Encyclopedia of Islam [16] 2nd edn., 11 vols. (Leiden: 1960–2002).

Fakhry, M. [17] *A History of Islamic Philosophy*, 2nd edn. (New York: 1983).

[18] *Philosophy, Dogma and the Impact of Greek Thought in Islam* (Aldershot: 1994).

Genequand, C. [19] "La philosophie arabe," in *Les Arabes et l'occident* (Geneva: 1982), 51–63.

Goulet, R. (ed.) [20] *Dictionnaire des philosophes antiques* (Paris: 1989–).

Gutas, D. [21] "Ethische Schriften im Islam," in W. Heinrichs (ed.), *Orientalisches Mittelalter: neues Handbuch der Literatur Wissenschaft*, vol. V (Wiesbaden: 1990), 346–65.

[22] "Classical Arabic Wisdom Literature: Nature and Scope," *JAOS* 101 (1981), 49–86.

Hasnawi, A., Elamrani-Jamal, A., and Aouad, M. (eds.) [23] *Perspectives arabes et médiévales sur la tradition scientifique et philosophique grecque* (Louvain: 1997).

Hourani, G. (ed.) [25] *Essays on Islamic Philosophy and Science* (Albany, NY: 1978).

Hyman, A. and Walsh, J. J. [26] *Philosophy in the Middle Ages* (Indianapolis: 1973), includes translations of several Arabic philosophical texts.

Kraemer, J. L. [27] "The Islamic Context of Medieval Jewish Philosophy," in Frank and Leaman [234], 38–68.

Leaman, O. [28] *An Introduction to Classical Islamic Philosophy* (Cambridge: 2002).

Marmura, M. E. (ed.) [29] *Islamic Theology and Philosophy* (Albany, NY: 1984).

Maróth, M. (ed.) [30] *Problems in Arabic Philosophy* (Piliscsaba, Hungary: 2003).

Morewedge, P. (ed.) [31] *Islamic Philosophical Theology* (Albany, NY: 1979).

(ed.) [32] *Islamic Philosophy and Mysticism* (Delmar, NY: 1981).

(ed.) [33] *Neoplatonism and Islamic Thought* (Albany, NY: 1992).

Nasr, S. H. and Leaman, O. (eds.) [34] *History of Islamic Philosophy*, 2 vols. (London: 1996).

Netton, I. R. [35] *Allāh Transcendent: Studies in the Structure and Semiotics of Islamic Philosophy, Theology and Cosmology* (London: 1989).

Pines, S. [36] *Studies in Arabic Versions of Greek Texts and in Mediaeval Science* (Jerusalem: 1986). This is vol. II of *The Collected Works of Shlomo Pines.*

[37] *Studies in the History of Arabic Philosophy*, ed. S. Stroumsa (Jerusalem: 1996). This is vol. III of *The Collected Works of Shlomo Pines.*

Qadir, C. A. [38] *Philosophy and Science in the Islamic World* (London: 1990).

Rosenthal, F. [39] *The Classical Heritage in Islam*, trans. E. Marmorstein and J. Marmorstein (London: 1975). Translation of *Das Fortleben der Antike im Islam* (Zürich: 1965). Contains numerous brief primary sources in translation.

[40] *Greek Philosophy in the Arab World* (Aldershot: 1990).

Sharif, M. M. [41] *A History of Muslim Philosophy*, 2 vols. (Wiesbaden: 1963–6).

Stern, S. M., Hourani, H., and Brown, V. (eds.) [42] *Islamic Philosophy and the Classical Tradition* (Oxford: 1972).

Stern, S. M. [43] *Medieval Arabic and Hebrew Thought*, ed. F. Zimmermann (London: 1983).

van Ess, J. [44] *Theologie und Gesellschaft im 2. und 3. Jahrhundert Hidschra*, 6 vols. (Berlin: 1991–5).

Walzer, R. [45] *Greek into Arabic: Essays on Islamic Philosophy* (Oxford: 1962).

Watt, M. W. [46] *Islamic Philosophy and Theology* (Edinburgh: 1962, rev. edn. 1985).
Wolfson, H. A. [47] *Studies in the History of Philosophy and Religion*, ed. I. Twersky and G. H. Williams, 2 vols. (Cambridge, MA: 1973, 1977).
[48] *The Philosophy of the Kalam* (Cambridge, MA: 1976).
Ziai, H. [49] "Islamic Philosophy," in T. Honderich (ed.), *The Oxford Companion to Philosophy* (Oxford: 1995), 419–21.

From Greek into Arabic: Neoplatonism in translation

Burnett, C. (ed.) [50] *Glosses and Commentaries on Aristotelian Logical Texts: The Syriac, Arabic and Medieval Latin Traditions* (London: 1993).
D'Ancona, C. [51] *Recherches sur le "Liber de Causis"* (Paris: 1995).
[52] "Commenting on Aristotle: from Late Antiquity to Arab Aristotelianism," in W. Geerlings and C. Schulze (eds.), *Der Kommentar in Antike und Mittelalter: Beiträge zu seiner Erforschung* (Leiden: 2002), 201–51.
Endress, G. [53] *Proclus Arabus: Zwanzig Abschnitte aus der Institutio Theologica in arabischer Übersetzung* (Wiesbaden: 1973).
[54] "Die wissenschaftliche Literatur," in H. Gätje (ed.), *Grundriss der arabischen Philologie*, vol. II (Wiesbaden: 1987), 24–61.
Endress, G. and Kruk, R. (eds.) [55] *The Ancient Tradition in Christian and Islamic Hellenism* (Leiden: 1997).
Gutas, D. [56] "Paul the Persian on the Classification of the Parts of Aristotle's Philosophy: A Milestone between Alexandria and Baghdād," *Der Islam* 60 (1983), 231–67.
[57] "The 'Alexandria to Baghdad' Complex of Narratives: A Contribution to the Study of Philosophical and Medical Historiography among the Arabs," *Documenti e studi sulla tradizione filosofica medievale* 10 (1999): 155–93.
[58] *Greek Thought, Arabic Culture: The Graeco-Arabic Translation Movement in Baghdad and Early Society (2nd–4th / 8th–10th centuries)* (London: 1998).
[59] *Greek Philosophers in the Arabic Tradition* (Aldershot: 2000).
Kraye, J., Ryan, W. F., and Schmitt, C. B. (eds.) [60] *Pseudo-Aristotle in the Middle Ages: The "Theology" and other Texts* (London: 1986).
Peters, F. E. [61] *Aristoteles Arabus* (Leiden: 1968).

Al-Kindī and the reception of Greek philosophy

Adamson, P. [62] "Al-Kindī and the Mu'tazila: Divine Attributes, Creation and Freedom," *Arabic Sciences and Philosophy* 13 (2003), 45–77.

[63] "Before Essence and Existence: Al-Kindī's Conception of Being," *Journal of the History of Philosophy* 40 (2002), 297–312.
Atiyeh, G. N. [64] *Al-Kindī: The Philosopher of the Arabs* (Rawalpindi: 1966).
D'Ancona, C. [65] "Aristotelian and Neoplatonic Elements in Kindī's Doctrine of Knowledge," in Druart [12], 9–35.
Druart, T.-A. [66] "Al-Kindī's Ethics," *Review of Metaphysics* 47 (1993), 329–57.
Endress, G. [67] "The Circle of al-Kindī: Early Arabic Translations from the Greek and the Rise of Islamic Philosophy", in Endress and Kruk [55].
Ivry, A. [68] *Al-Kindi's Metaphysics* (Albany, NY: 1974).
Jolivet, J. [69] *L'intellect selon Kindī* (Leiden: 1971).
Al-Kindī [70] *Rasā'il al-Kindī al-falsafiyya*, ed. M. Abū Rīda (Cairo: 1950–3).
[71] *Œuvres philosophiques et scientifiques d'al-Kindī*, ed. and trans. R. Rashed and J. Jolivet, 2 vols. so far (Leiden: 1997–).

Al-Fārābī and the philosophical curriculum

Alon, I. [72] *Al-Fārābī's Philosophical Lexicon*, 2 vols. (Warminster: 2002).
Druart, T.-A. [73] "Al-Fārābī's Causation of the Heavenly Bodies," in Morewedge [32], 35–45.
[74] "Al-Farabi and Emanationism," in J. F. Wippel (ed.), *Studies in Medieval Philosophy* (Washington, DC: 1987), 23–43.
[75] "Al-Fārābī, Emanation and Metaphysics," in Morewedge [33], 127–48.
Gutas, D. [76] "The Starting Point of Philosophical Studies in Alexandrian and Arabic Aristotelianism," in *Theophrastus of Eresus: On his Life and Work*, ed. W.W. Fortenbaugh (New Brunswick, NJ: 1985), 115–23.
Walzer, R. [77] *Al-Farabi on the Perfect State* (Oxford: 1985).
Yarshater, E. (ed.) [78] "Al-Fārābī," in *Encyclopaedia Iranica* (New York: 1999), vol. IX, fasc. 2, 208–29.
Zimmermann, F. W. [79] *Al-Fārābī's Commentary and Short Treatise on Aristotle's "De Interpretatione"* (London: 1981).

The Ismā'īlīs

Daftary, F. [80] *The Ismā'īlīs: Their History and Doctrines* (London: 1990).
De Smet, D. [81] *La quiétude de l'intellect: néoplatonisme et gnose ismaélienne dans l'œuvre de Ḥamīd al-Dīn al-Kirmānī (Xe/XIe s.)* (Leuven: 1995).
Netton, I. R. [82] *Muslim Neoplatonists: An Introduction to the Thought of the Brethren of Purity*, 2nd edn. (London: 2002).
Stern, S. M. [83] *Studies in Early Ismā'īlism* (Jerusalem: 1983).

Walker, P. E. [84] *Early Philosophical Shiism: The Ismaili Neoplatonism of Abū Ya'qūb al-Sijistānī* (Cambridge: 1993).
[85] *The Wellsprings of Wisdom: A Study of Abū Ya'qūb al-Sijistānī's Kitāb al-yanābī'* (Salt Lake City, UT: 1994).
[86] *Abu Ya'qub al-Sijistani: Intellectual Missionary* (London: 1996).
[87] *Ḥamīd al-Dīn al-Kirmānī: Ismaili Thought in the Age of al-Ḥākim* (London: 1999).

Avicenna and the Avicennian tradition

Avicenna [88] *Al-Shifā': al-Ilāhiyyāt*, ed. G. Anawati et al., 2 vols. (Cairo: 1960). French trans. Avicenna, *La métaphysique du Shifā'*, trans. G. Anawati, 2 vols. (Paris: 1978). An English translation by M. E. Marmura is forthcoming from Brigham Young University Press.
Druart, T.-A. [89] "The Soul and Body Problem: Avicenna and Descartes," in T.-A. Druart (ed.), *Arabic Philosophy and the West: Continuity and Interaction* (Washington, DC: 1988), 27–49.
Gilson, E. [90] "Avicenne et la notion de cause efficiente," *Atti del XII congresso internazionale di filosofia* (Florence: 1960), 121–30.
Gohlman, W. E. [91] *The Life of Ibn Sina: A Critical Edition and Annotated Translation* (Albany, NY: 1974).
Goodman, L. E. [92] *Avicenna* (London: 1992).
Gutas, D. [93] *Avicenna and the Aristotelian Tradition* (Leiden: 1988).
[94] "The Heritage of Avicenna: The Golden Age of Arabic Philosophy, 1000–ca. 1350," in Janssens and De Smet [97], 81–97.
Janssens, J. [95] *An Annotated Bibliography on Ibn Sīnā (1970–1989)* (Leuven: 1991); *First Supplement (1990–1994)* (Louvain-la-Neuve: 1999).
[96] "Creation and Emanation in Avicenna," *Documenti e studi sulla tradizione filosofica medievale* 8 (1997), 455–77.
Janssens, J. and De Smet, D. (eds.) [97] *Avicenna and his Heritage* (Leuven: 2002).
Jolivet, J. [98] "Aux origines de l'ontologie d'Ibn Sīnā," in J. Jolivet and R. Rashed (eds.), *Études sur Avicenne* (Paris: 1984), 19–28.
Marmura, M. E. [99] "Some Aspects of Avicenna's Theory of God's Knowledge of Particulars," *JAOS* 82 (1962), 299–312.
[100] "Avicenna's Proof from Contingency for God's Existence in the *Metaphysics* of the *Shifā'*," *Medieval Studies* 42 (1980), 337–52.
[101] "Avicenna and the Kalam," *Zeitschrift für Geschichte der arabisch-islamischen Wissenschaften* 7 (1991–2), 172–206.

Rahman, F. [102] "Essence and Existence in Avicenna," *Mediaeval and Renaissance Studies* 4 (1958), 1–16, continued in "Essence and Existence in Ibn Sīnā: the Myth and the Reality," *Hamdard Islamicus* 4.1 (1981), 3–14.

Reisman, D. (ed.) [103] *Before and After Avicenna* (Leiden: 2003).

Wisnovsky, R. (ed.) [104] *Aspects of Avicenna* (Princeton, NJ: 2001).

[105] *Avicenna's Metaphysics in Context* (London: 2003).

Yarshater, E. (ed.) [106] "Avicenna," in *Encyclopaedia Iranica* (New York: 1999), vol. III, 66–110.

Al-Ghazālī

Fakhry, M. [107] *Islamic Occasionalism* (London: 1958).

Frank, R. M. [108] *Creation and the Cosmic System: Al-Ghazālī and Avicenna* (Heidelberg: 1992).

[109] *Al-Ghazālī and the Ash'arite School* (Durham, NC: 1994).

Al-Ghazālī [110] *al-Munqidh min al-ḍalāl* (*The Deliverer from Error*), ed. J. Saliba and K. Ayyad (Beirut: 1967).

[111] *The Incoherence of the Philosophers* (*Tahāfut al-falāsifa*), trans. M. E. Marmura, 2nd edn. (Provo, UT: 2000).

Gianotti, T. [112] *Al-Ghazālī's Unspeakable Doctrine of the Soul* (Leiden: 2001).

Griffel, F. [113] *Apostasie und Toleranz in Islam: die Entwicklung zu al-Gazalis Urteil gegen die Philosophie und die Reaktionen der Philosophen* (Leiden: 2000).

Hourani, G. F. [114] "Ghazālī on the Ethics of Action," *JAOS* 96 (1976), 69–88; repr. in Hourani, *Reason and Tradition in Islamic Ethics* (Cambridge: 1985), 135–66.

Kukkonen, T. [115] "Possible Worlds in the *Tahāfut Al-Falāsifa*: Al-Ghazālī on Creation and Contingency," *Journal of the History of Philosophy* 38 (2000), 479–502.

Marmura, M. E. [116] "Ghazali and Demonstrative Science," *Journal of the History of Philosophy* 3.2 (1965), 183–209.

[117] "Al-Ghazālī's Chapter on Divine Power in the *Iqtiṣād*," *Arabic Sciences and Philosophy* 4 (1994), 279–315.

[118] "Ghazalian Causes and Intermediaries," *JAOS* 115 (1995), 89–100.

[119] "Ghazali and Ash'arism Revisited," *Arabic Sciences and Philosophy* 12 (2002), 91–110.

Shehadi, F. [120] *Ghazali's Unique Unknowable God* (Leiden: 1964).

Watt, M. W. [121] *Muslim Intellectual: A Study of al-Ghazālī* (Edinburgh: 1963).

Philosophy in Andalusia: Ibn Bājja and Ibn Ṭufayl

Altmann, A. [122] "Ibn Bajja on Man's Ultimate Felicity," in *Harry Austryn Wolfson Jubilee Volume*, vol. I (Jerusalem: 1965), 47–87.

Conrad, L. I. (ed.) [123] *The World of Ibn Ṭufayl: Interdisciplinary Perspectives on Ḥayy Ibn Yaqẓān* (Leiden: 1996).

Cruz Hernández, M. [125] *Historia del pensamiento en el-Andalus*, 2 vols. (Madrid: 1985).

Dunlop, D. M. [124] "Remarks on the Life and Works of Ibn Bājja, Avempace" in *Proceedings of the Twenty-Second Congress of Orientalists* (Leiden: 1957), 188–96.

Harvey, S. [126] "The Place of the Philosopher in the City according to Ibn Bājja," in Butterworth [187], 199–234.

Hourani, G. [127] "The Principal Subject of Ibn Ṭufayl's *Ḥayy Ibn Yaqẓān*," *Journal of Near Eastern Studies* 15 (1956), 40–6.

Ibn Bājja [128] *Rasā'il Ibn Bājja al-Ilāhiyya*, ed. M. Fakhry (Beirut: 1968).

Ibn Ṭufayl [129] *Ḥayy ibn Yaqẓān*, ed. L. Gauthier (Beirut: 1936).

Gauthier, L. [130] *Ibn Thofayl, sa vie, ses œuvres* (Paris: 1909; repr. 1983).

Goodman, L. E. [131] *Ibn Tufayl's Hayy ibn Yaqzān* (New York: 1972).

Lettinck, P. [132] "The Transformation of Aristotle's 'Physical Philosophy' in Ibn Bājja's Commentaries," in F. J. Ragep and S. P. Ragep (eds.), *Tradition, Transmission, Transformation* (Leiden: 1996), 65–70.

[133] *Aristotle's Meteorology and its Reception in the Arab World: With an Edition and Translation of Ibn Suwār's "Treatise on Meteorological Phenomena" and Ibn Bājja's "Commentary on the Meteorology"* (Leiden: 1999). See also Lettinck [197].

Averroes

Aertsen, J. A. and Endress, G. (eds.) [134] *Averroes and the Aristotelian Tradition* (Leiden: 1999).

Averroes [135] *Averrois Cordubensis Commentarium Magnum in Aristotelis "De Anima" Libros*, ed. F. S. Crawford (Cambridge: 1953).

[136] *Faith and Reason in Islam: Averroes' Exposition of Religious Arguments*, trans. I. Y. Najjar (Oxford: 2001).

[137] *Ibn Rushd's Metaphysics: A Translation with Introduction of Ibn Rushd's Commentary on Aristotle's "Metaphysics," Book Lām*, trans. C. Genequand (Leiden: 1984).

[138] *Middle Commentary on Aristotle's "De Anima,"* trans. A. L. Ivry (Provo, UT: 2002).

[139] *On the Harmony of Religion and Philosophy: A Translation, with Introduction and Notes, of Ibn Rushd's "Kitāb faṣl al-maqāl" with its*

Appendix (Ḍamīma) and an Extract from "Kitāb al-kashf fī al-manāhij al-adilla," trans. G. F. Hourani (London: 1967).

[140] *Tahāfut al-tahāfut (The Incoherence of the Incoherence)*, trans. S. Van Den Bergh (London: 1969).

Druart, T.-A. [141] "Averroes: The Commentator and the Commentators," in L. P. Schrenk (ed.), *Aristotle in Late Antiquity* (Washington, DC: 1994), 184–202.

Endress, G. [142] "Averroes' *De Caelo*: Ibn Rushd's Cosmology in his Commentaries on Aristotle's *On the Heavens*," *Arabic Sciences and Philosophy* 6 (1985), 9–49.

Hyman, A. [143] "Aristotle's Theory of the Intellect and its Interpretation by Averroes," in Dominic J. O'Meara (ed.), *Studies in Aristotle* (Washington, DC: 1981), 161–91.

Kogan, B. [144] *Averroes and the Metaphysics of Causation* (Albany, NY: 1985).

Taylor, R. C. [145] "Averroes on Psychology and the Principles of Metaphysics," *Journal of the History of Philosophy* 36 (1998), 507–23.

[146] "Improving on Nature's Exemplar: Averroes' Completion of Aristotle's Psychology of Intellect," in P. Adamson, H. Baltussen, and M. W. F. Stone (eds.), *Philosophy, Science and Exegesis in Greek, Arabic and Latin Commentaries* (London: 2004).

[147] "*Cogitatio, Cogitativus* and *Cogitare*: Remarks on the Cogitative Power in Averroes," in J. Hamesse and C. Steel (eds.), *L'élaboration du vocabulaire philosophique au Moyen Age* (Louvain-la-Neuve: 2000), 111–46.

[148] "'Truth Does Not Contradict Truth': Averroes and the Unity of Truth," *Topoi* 19 (2000), 3–16.

Suhrawardī and Illuminationism

Aminrazavi, M. [149] *Suhrawardi and the School of Illumination* (Richmond, Surrey: 1996).

Corbin, H. [150] *Sohrawardī et les platoniciens de Perse* (Paris: 1971–2); this is vol. II of Corbin [161].

Nasr, S. H. [151] *Three Muslim Sages* (Cambridge: 1964).

Suhrawardī [152] *The Philosophy of Illumination*, ed. and trans. J. Walbridge and H. Ziai (Provo, UT: 1999).

[153] *The Philosophical Allegories and Mystical Treatises*, trans. W. M. Thackston, Jr. (Costa Mesa, CA: 1999).

Walbridge, J. [154] *The Science of Mystic Lights: Qutb al-Din Shirazi and the Illuminationist Tradition in Islamic Philosophy* (Cambridge: 1992).

[155] *The Leaven of the Ancients: Suhrawardi and the Heritage of the Greeks* (Albany, NY: 2000).

[156] *The Wisdom of the Mystic East: Suhrawardī and Platonic Orientalism* (Albany, NY: 2001).

Yazdi, M. H. [157] *The Principles of Epistemology in Islamic Philosophy: Knowledge by Presence* (Albany, NY: 1992).

Ziai, H. [158] *Knowledge and Illumination: A Study of Suhrawardī's "Ḥikmat al-Ishrāq"* (Atlanta, GA: 1990).

[159] "The Source and Nature of Authority: A Study of al-Suhrawardī's Illuminationist Political Doctrine," in Butterworth [187], 304–44.

Mysticism and philosophy: Ibn 'Arabī and Mullā Ṣadrā

Chittick, W. C. [160] *The Sufi Path of Knowledge: Ibn 'Arabi's Metaphysics of Imagination* (Albany, NY: 1989).

Corbin, H. [161] *En Islam Iranien*, 4 vols. (Paris: 1971–2).

Hadot, P. [162] *Philosophy as a Way of Life: Spiritual Exercises from Socrates to Foucault*, ed. A. Davidson, trans. M. Chase (Oxford: 1995).

Ibn 'Arabī [163] *Fuṣūṣ al-ḥikam*, ed. 'A. 'Afīfī (Cairo: 1946).

[164] *al-Futūḥāt al-Makkiyya*, 4 vols. (Cairo: n.d.; repr. Beirut: n.d.).

Morris, J. W. [165] "Ibn 'Arabī and his Interpreters," *JAOS* 106 (1986), 733–56.

Mullā Ṣadrā [Ṣadr al-Dīn Shīrāzī] [166] *Al-Ḥikma al-muta'āliya fī al-asfār al-'aqliyya al-arba'a*, ed. R. Luṭfī, I. Amīnī, and F. Ummīd, 3rd edn., 9 vols. (Beirut: 1981); new edn. with scholia of Ḥasanzāda Āmulī, 2 vols. so far (Tehran: 1995–).

Rahman, F. [167] *The Philosophy of Mullā Ṣadrā* (Albany, NY: 1975).

Rizvi, S. H. [168] *Mullā Ṣadrā Shīrāzī: Philosopher of the Mystics* (Cambridge: forthcoming).

Rosenthal, F. [169] "Ibn 'Arabī between Philosophy and Mysticism," *Oriens* 31 (1988), 1–35.

Logic

Black, D. L. [170] *Logic and Aristotle's "Rhetoric" and "Poetics" in Medieval Arabic Philosophy* (Leiden: 1990).

Elamrani-Jamal, A. [171] "Ibn Rushd et les *Premiers analytiques* d'Aristote," *Arabic Sciences and Philosophy* 5 (1995), 75–92.

Endress, G. [172] "Grammatik und Logik: arabische Philologie und griechische Philosophie im Widerstreit," in B. Mojsisch (ed.), *Sprachphilosophie in Antike und Mittelalter* (Amsterdam: 1986), 163–299.

Gutas, D. [173] "Aspects of Literary Form and Genre in Arabic Logical Works," in Burnett [50], 29–76.

Jabre, F., Al-'Ajam, R., Dgheim, S., and Gihamy, G. [174] *Encyclopaedia of Arabic Terminology of Logic* (Beirut: 1996).

Lameer, J. [175] *Al-Fārābī and Aristotelian Syllogistics: Greek Theory and Islamic Practice* (Leiden: 1994).

Madkour, I. [176] *L'"Organon" d'Aristote dans le monde arabe*, 2nd edn. (Paris: 1969).

Maróth, M. [177] *Ibn Sīnā und die peripatetische Aussagenlogik* (Leiden: 1989).

Rescher, N. [178] *Temporal Modalities in Arabic Logic* (Dordrecht: 1967).

[179] *The Development of Arabic Logic* (Pittsburgh: 1964).

Rescher, N. and vander Nat, A. [180] "The Theory of Modal Syllogistic in Medieval Arabic Philosophy," in N. Rescher et al. (eds.), *Studies in Modality* (Oxford: 1974), 17–56.

Sabra, A. I. [181] "Avicenna on the Subject Matter of Logic," *Journal of Philosophy* 77 (1980), 746–64.

Street, T. [182] "Arabic Logic," in J. Woods and D. Gabbay (eds.), *Handbook of the History and Philosophy of Logic*, vol. I: *Greek, Arabic and Indian Logic* (Amsterdam: 2004), 523–96.

Thom, P. [183] *Medieval Modal Systems: Problems and Concepts* (Aldershot: 2003).

von Grunebaum, G. E. (ed.) [184] *Logic in Classical Islamic Culture* (Wiesbaden: 1970).

Ethics and politics

Alfarabi [185] *The Political Writings: Selected Aphorisms and Other Texts*, trans. C. E. Butterworth (Ithaca, NY: 2001).

Averroes [186] *Averroes on Plato's Republic*, trans. R. Lerner (Ithaca, NY: 1974).

Butterworth, C. E. [187] *The Political Aspects of Islamic Philosophy* (Cambridge, MA: 1992).

Galston, M. [188] *Politics and Excellence* (Princeton, NJ: 1990).

Lerner, R. and Mahdi, M. (eds.) [189] *Medieval Political Philosophy: A Source Book* (Toronto: 1963).

Mahdi, M. S. [190] *Alfarabi and the Foundation of Islamic Political Philosophy: Essays in Interpretation* (Chicago: 2001).

Parens, J. [191] *Metaphysics as Rhetoric: Alfarabi's Summary of Plato's Laws* (Albany, NY: 1995).

Strauss, L. [192] "Farabi's Plato," in S. Lieberman (ed.), *Louis Ginzberg Jubilee Volume* (New York: 1945), 357–93.

Natural philosophy

Dhanani, A. [193] *The Physical Theory of Kalām: Atoms, Space and Void in Basrian Mu'tazilī Cosmology* (Leiden: 1994).

Hasnawi, A. [194] "La dynamique d'Ibn Sīnā: la notion d' 'inclination' (*mayl*)," in J. Jolivet and R. Rashed (eds.), *Études sur Avicenne* (Paris: 1984), 103–23.

[195] "La définition du mouvement dans la *Physique* du *Shifā'* d'Avicenne," *Arabic Sciences and Philosophy* 11 (2001), 219–55.

Hogendijk, J. P. and Sabra, A. I. (eds.) [196] *The Enterprise of Science in Islam* (Cambridge, MA: 2003).

Lettinck, P. [197] *Aristotle's "Physics" and its Reception in the Arabic World: With an Edition of the Unpublished Parts of Ibn Bājja's "Commentary on the Physics"* (Leiden: 1994).

Pines, S. [198] *Studies in Islamic Atomism*, ed. T. Langermann, trans. M. Schwartz (Jerusalem: 1995). Translation of *Beiträge zur islamischen Atomenlehre* (Berlin: 1936).

Rashed, M. [199] "*Kalām* e filosofia naturale," in *Storia della scienza*, vol. III: *La civiltà islamica* (2002), 49–72.

Rashed, R. and Morelon, R. [200] *Encyclopedia of the History of Arabic Science*, 3 vols. (London: 1996).

Rashed, R. [201] "Al-Qūhī vs. Aristotle: On Motion," *Arabic Sciences and Philosophy* 9 (1999), 7–24.

Rosenthal, F. [202] *Science and Medicine in Islam* (Aldershot: 1990).

Sabra, I. A. [203] *Optics, Astronomy and Logic: Studies in Arabic Science and Philosophy* (Aldershot: 1994).

Psychology: Soul and Intellect

Averroes [204] *The Epistle on the Possibility of Conjunction with the Active Intellect*, trans. K. Bland (New York: 1982).

Avicenna [205] *Avicenna's Psychology*, trans. F. Rahman (Oxford: 1952).

Black, D. L. [206] "Conjunction and the Identity of Knower and Known in Averroes," in Druart [12], 159–84.

[207] "Estimation (*Wahm*) in Avicenna: The Logical and Psychological Dimensions," *Dialogue* 32 (1993), 219–58.

Davidson, H. A. [208] *Alfarabi, Avicenna, and Averroes on Intellect* (Oxford: 1992).

Druart, T.-A. [209] "Al-Rāzī's Conception of the Soul: Psychological Background to his Ethics," *Medieval Philosophy and Theology* 5 (1996), 245–54.

[210] "The Human Soul's Individuation and its Survival after the Body's Death: Avicenna on the Causal Relation between Body and Soul," *Arabic Sciences and Philosophy* 10 (2000), 259–74.

Al-Fārābī [211] *Risāla fī al-ʿaql* (*Treatise on the Intellect*), ed. Maurice Bouyges (Beirut: 1948). Partial English translation in Hyman and Walsh [26], 215–21.

Goodman, L. E. [212] "A Note on Avicenna's Theory of the Substantiality of the Soul," *Philosophical Forum* n.s. 1 (1968), 547–63.

Ivry, A. [213] "Averroes on Intellection and Conjunction," *JAOS* 86 (1966), 76–85.

Marmura, M. E. [214] "Avicenna's 'Flying Man' in Context," *Monist* 69 (1986), 383–95.

[215] "Al-Ghazālī on Bodily Resurrection and Causality in the *Tahāfut* and the *Iqtiṣād*," *Aligarh Journal of Islamic Thought* 2 (1989), 46–75.

Taylor, R. C. [216] "Personal Immortality in Averroes' Mature Philosophical Psychology," *Documenti e studi sulla tradizione filosofica medievale* 9 (1998), 87–110.

Wolfson, H. A. [217] "The Internal Senses in Latin, Arabic, and Hebrew Philosophic Texts," *Harvard Theological Review* 28 (1935), 69–133. Repr. in Wolfson [47], vol. I, 250–370.

Metaphysics

Bauloye, L. [218] "A propos du 'fondamental' et de 'l'essentiel' dans le commentaire d'Averroès sur la *Métaphysique* d'Aristote," *Revue de philosophie ancienne* 13 (1995), 225–38.

[219] "Le genre des substances dans la métaphysique d'Averroès," *Documenti e studi sulla tradizione filosofica medievale* 12 (2001), 143–53.

Black, D. [220] "Mental Existence in Thomas Aquinas and Avicenna," *Mediaeval Studies* 61 (1999), 45–79.

Bertolacci, A. [221] "The Doctrine of Material and Formal Causality in the *Ilāhiyyāt* of Avicenna's *Kitāb al-Shifāʾ*," *Quaestio* 2 (2002), 125–54.

[222] "From al-Kindī to al-Fārābī: Avicenna's Progressive Knowledge of Aristotle's *Metaphysics* according to his Autobiography," *Arabic Sciences and Philosophy* 11 (2001), 257–95.

[223] "The Structure of Metaphysical Science in the *Ilāhiyyāt* (*Divine Science*) of Avicenna's *Kitab al-Shifāʾ* (*Book of the Cure*)," *Documenti e studi sulla tradizione filosofica medievale* 13 (2002), 1–69.

Druart, T.-A. [224] "*Shay'* or *Res* as Concomitant of 'Being' in Avicenna," *Documenti e studi sulla tradizione filosofica medievale* 12 (2001), 125–42.

Janssens, J. [225] "Al-Ghazzālī's *Tahāfut*: Is it Really a Rejection of Ibn Sīnā's Philosophy?" *Journal of Islamic Studies* 12 (2001), 1–17.

Marmura, M. E. [226] "Avicenna on Causal Priority," in Morewedge [32], 65–83.

[227] "Avicenna on Primary Concepts in the *Metaphysics* of his *al-Shifā'*," in R. M. Savory and D. A. Agius (eds.), *Logos Islamikos: Studia Islamica in Honorem Georgii Michaelis Wickens* (Toronto: 1984), 219–39.

[228] "The Metaphysics of Efficient Causality in Avicenna (Ibn Sina)," in Marmura [29], 172–87.

[229] "Quiddity and Universality in Avicenna," in Morewedge [32], 77–87.

Shehadi, F. [230] *Metaphysics in Islamic Philosophy* (Delmar, NY: 1982).

Wisnovsky, R. [231] "Notes on Avicenna's Concept of Thingness (*Shay'iyya*)," *Arabic Sciences and Philosophy* 10 (2000), 181–221.

[232] "Towards a History of Avicenna's Distinction between Immanent and Transcendent Causes," in Reisman [103], 49–68.

[233] "Final and Efficient Causality in Avicenna's Cosmology and Theology," *Quaestio* 2 (2002), 97–123.

Islamic thought and Jewish philosophy

Frank, D. H. and Leaman, O. (eds.) [234] *The Cambridge Companion to Medieval Jewish Philosophy* (Cambridge: 2003).

Harvey, S. [235] "Did Maimonides' Letter to Samuel ibn Tibbon Determine which Philosophers would be Studied by Later Jewish Thinkers?" *Jewish Quarterly Review* 83 (1992), 51–70.

(ed.) [236] *The Medieval Hebrew Encyclopedias of Science and Philosophy* (Dordrecht: 2000).

Harvey, W. Z. [237] *Physics and Metaphysics in Hasdai Crescas* (Amsterdam: 1998).

Husik, I. [238] *A History of Mediaeval Jewish Philosophy* (1941; repr. Mineola, NY: 2002).

Sirat, C. [239] *A History of Jewish Philosophy in the Middle Ages* (Cambridge: 1985).

Steinschneider, M. [240] *Die hebraeischen Übersetzungen des Mittelalters* (Berlin, 1893).

Tamani, G. and Zonta, M. [241] *Aristoteles Hebraicus* (Venice: 1997).

Wolfson, H. A. [242] *Crescas' Critique of Aristotle* (Cambridge, MA: 1929).

[243] *Repercussions of the Kalam in Jewish Philosophy* (Cambridge, MA: 1979).

Zonta, M. [244] *La filosofia antica nel medioevo ebraico* (Brescia: 1996).

Arabic into Latin: the reception of Arabic philosophy into Western Europe

Burnett, C. [245] "The Coherence of the Arabic–Latin Translation Program in Toledo in the Twelfth Century," *Science in Context* 14 (2001), 249–88.

Butterworth, C. E. and B. A. Kessel (eds.) [246] *The Introduction of Arabic Philosophy into Europe* (Leiden: 1994).

Cranz, F. E. [247] "Editions of the Latin Aristotle Accompanied by the Commentaries of Averroes," in E. P. Mahoney (ed.), *Philosophy and Humanism: Renaissance Essays in Honor of Paul Oskar Kristeller* (Leiden: 1976), 116–28.

d'Alverny, M.-T. [248] *Avicenne en Occident* (Paris: 1993).

Daiber, H. [249] "Lateinische Übersetzungen arabischer Texte zur Philosophie und ihr Bedeutung für die Scholastik des Mittelalters," in J. Hamesse and M. Fattori (eds.), *Rencontres de cultures dans la philosophie: traductions et traducteurs de l'antiquité tardive au XVIe siècle* (Louvain-la-Neuve: 1990), 203–50.

Jolivet, J. [250] "The Arabic Inheritance," in P. Dronke (ed.), *A History of Twelfth-Century Western Philosophy* (Cambridge: 1988), 113–47.

Hasse, D. [251] *Avicenna's "De Anima" in the Latin West* (London: 2000).

Kischlat, H. [252] *Studien zur Verbreitung von Übersetzungen arabischer philosophischer Werke in Westeuropa 1150–1400* (Münster: 2000).

Wolfson, H. A. [253] "The Twice-Revealed Averroes," *Speculum* 36 (1961), 373–92, with revised version in Wolfson [47] vol. I, 371–401.

Recent trends in Islamic philosophy

Corbin, H. and Āshtiyānī, S. J. D. (eds.) [254] *Anthologie des philosophes iraniens depuis le XVIIe siècle jusqu'à nos jours*, 4 vols. (Tehran: 1972–).

Mohaghegh, M. and Landolt, L. (eds.) [255] *Collected Papers on Islamic Philosophy and Mysticism* (Tehran: 1971).

Rahman, F. [256] "The Post-Formative Developments in Islam," *Islamic Studies* 1 (1962), 1–23, and 2 (1963), 297–316.

Sadra Islamic Philosophy Research Institute [257] *Islam–West Philosophical Dialogue: The Papers Presented at the World Congress on Mulla Sadra*, vol. I. *Mulla Sadra and Transcendent Philosophy* (Tehran: 2001).

Sadughi, M. [258] *Post-Sadr-ul-Muti'allihin Mystics and Philosophers* [*sic*] (Tehran: 1980).

Schmidtke, S. [259] *The Theology of al-'Allāma al-Ḥillī* (Berlin: 1991).
[260] *Theologie, Philosophie und Mystik im zwölferschiitischen Islam des 9./15. Jahrhunderts* (Leiden: 2000).

Wisnovsky, R. [261] "Some Remarks on the Nature and Scope of Arabic Philosophical Commentary in Post-Classical (ca. 1100–1900 CE) Islamic Intellectual History: Some Preliminary Observations," in P. Adamson, H. Baltussen, and M. W. F. Stone (eds.), *Philosophy, Science and Exegesis in Greek, Arabic and Latin Commentaries* (London: 2004), vol. II, 149–91.

Ziai, H. [262] "Knowledge and Authority in Shī'ī Philosophy," in L. Clarke (ed.), *Shiite Heritage: Essays on Classical and Modern Traditions* (Binghamton, NY: 2001), 359–73. Recent trends are also covered extensively in Nasr and Leaman [34].

INDEX

Note: the definite article al- is disregarded for the purposes of alphabetization.

Dates for all authors from the Arabic philosophical tradition are given at the front of this volume. Modern scholars are indexed only when their names appear in the body of a chapter, or when their views are discussed in detail in a footnote.